75

110·0/14↯

Will as Commitment and Resolve

Will as Commitment and Resolve

*An Existential Account of
Creativity, Love, Virtue, and Happiness*

JOHN DAVENPORT

FORDHAM UNIVERSITY PRESS
New York ■ *2007*

Copyright © 2007 Fordham University Press

All rights reserved. No part of this publication may be reproduced, stored in a retrieval system, or transmitted in any form or by any means—electronic, mechanical, photocopy, recording, or any other—except for brief quotations in printed reviews, without the prior permission of the publisher.

Library of Congress Cataloging-in-Publication Data

Davenport, John J., 1966–
 Will as commitment and resolve : an existential critique of virtue, love, and happiness / John J. Davenport.—1st ed.
  p. cm.
 Includes bibliographical references and index.
 ISBN-13: 978-0-8232-2575-0 (cloth : alk. paper)
 ISBN-10: 0-8232-2575-5 (cloth : alk. paper)
 1. Will. 2. Ethics. 3. Conduct of life. I. Title.
BJ1461.D27 2007
128'.3—dc22
                                                                        2007018583

Printed in the United States of America
09 08 07   5 4 3 2 1
First edition

TO ROBIN

And to the memory of my grandparents:
Gladys Sperry, Pierce Sperry,
Daisy Davenport, and Louis Davenport II

Contents

Acknowledgments   xv

Preface   xvii
    The Project of an Existential Theory of Personhood

Part I: The Idea of Willing as Projective Motivation

1   Introduction   3
     1. The Heroic Will   3
     2. The Existential Theory of Striving Will as Projective
        Motivation   8
     3. An Outline of the Main Argument   10
        3.1. The Defense of Thesis One by Articulation of
            the Existential Conception of Willing   12
        3.2. The Negative Defense of Thesis Two by the
            Critique of Psychological Eudaimonism   14
        3.3. The Positive Defense of Thesis Two: Case
            Studies in Projective Motivation   16
     4. The Limits of This Analysis   20
        4.1. Autonomy and Motivation Theory   21
        4.2. Action Theory and Psychology   21
        4.3. Emotion and Volition   22
        4.4. Value Theory   23
        4.5. The Historical Examples   23
     5. A Reader's Guide: Ways through the Text   24

2   The Heroic Will in Eastern and Western Perspectives   28
     1. The Paradigmatically "Eastern" Attitude toward Will
        and Willfulness   29

	1.1. Hindu, Buddhist, and Daoist Examples	29
	1.2. Greek Examples	32
	1.3. Augustine and Luther	35
	2. The Paradigmatically "Western" Attitude	37
	2.1. Baconian Hope	37
	2.2. Will to Power as a Corrupt Species of Striving Will	39
	3. The Continental Inversion	42
	4. Contemporary Moral Psychology as Corrective	44
3	From Action Theory to Projective Motivation	47
	1. The Decline of the Will	47
	1.1. Freud and Hobbes	48
	1.2. Locke, Hume, and the Cambridge Platonists	49
	1.3. William James	52
	1.4. Gilbert Ryle and Ludwig Wittgenstein	54
	2. Kane's Three Senses of "Will"	56
	3. Four Basic Concepts of the Will	60
	3.1. The Minimalist Concept	60
	3.2. The Volitionalist Concept	62
	3.3. The Decision-as-Agency Concept	69
	3.4. The Existential Concept of Striving Will	79
4	The Erosiac Structure of Desire in Plato and Aristotle	86
	1. Toward an Existential Theory of Motivation	86
	1.1. The Transmission Principle: A Problem in the Theory of Motivation	86
	1.2. The Existential Core Argument	90
	2. Plato's Erosiac Model of Motivation	92
	2.1. Introduction to *Orexis*	92
	2.2. Three Types of Desire in the *Republic*	97
	2.3. The Lack Model in the *Symposium*	101
	2.4. Diotima and Aquinas: Formal Egoism, Intended Goods, and By-Products	106
	3. From Plato's Middle Soul to Aristotle's Intellectual Appetite	111
	3.1. *Thumos* as Indeterminate Motive-Power	112
	3.2. Williams on Homer's Moral Psychology	116
	3.3. Aristotle's Generalization of the Middle Soul	118
5	Aristotelian Desires and the Problems of Egoism	122
	1. Aristotle and the Typology of Erosiac Desire	122
	1.1. Aristotle's Psychology of Animal Motivation in the *De anima*	122

1.2. The Distinction between D2 and D3 Desires　126
　　1.3. D2 and D3 Desiderative States in Aristotle　135
　　1.4. D2 and D3 States in MacIntyre's Moral
　　　　 Psychology　140
　2. Formal and Material Egoism　142
　　2.1. Formal Egoism and Satisfaction　143
　　2.2. Material Egoism: Feinberg's Analysis Expanded　149
　　2.3. The Paradox of Hedonism and the Paradox of
　　　　 Material Egoism　159
　　2.4. Targetable and Nontargetable By-Product Goods:
　　　　 Elster's Analysis　163

Part II: The Existential Critique of Eudaimonism

6　Psychological Eudaimonism: A Reading of Aristotle　171
　1. The Highest or Complete Good in Aristotle's
　　　Eudaimonism　172
　　1.1. Toward a Uniquely Ultimate End: Three Criteria
　　　　 for the Highest Good　172
　　1.2. "Most Complete" as a Nonholistically Inclusive
　　　　 Relation　177
　　1.3. Self-Sufficiency as a Maximally Comprehensive
　　　　 or Holistically Inclusive Relation　180
　2. Excursus: Maximal Inclusivism, Virtue Inclusivism, and
　　　Dominant-End Models　187
　3. The A-Eudaimonist System: An Idealized Aristotelian
　　　Model　195

7　The Paradox of Eudaimonism: An Existential Critique　201
　1. Elements of the Pure Motive of Virtue　202
　2. Annas and Kraut on the Motive of Virtue in
　　　Friendship　206
　3. The Paradox of Eudaimonism: Desiring Eudaimonia as
　　　a By-Product of Virtue　211
　4. Why the Paradox Cannot Be Solved by Denying that
　　　Eudaimonia Motivates Virtue　214
　5. Magnanimity as Aristotle's Answer to the Paradox　218
　6. Why the Paradox Cannot Be Solved by Second-Order
　　　Desire Subsuming First-Order Desire　222
　7. The Existential Solution: Pure Motives as Projects of
　　　the Striving Will　227

	8. The Paradox as One of Several Related Objections to Eudaimonism	231
8	Contemporary Solutions to the Paradox and Their Problems	235
	1. Cooper's Solution: Virtuous Motivation as a Constitutive Means to Eudaimonia	236
	2. Gottlieb's Solution: Pushing Desire for Eudaimonia into the "Background"	240
	3. Indirect Eudaimonism: a Possible Parfitian Solution?	244
	4. Sherman on Friendship	248
	5. Practices, Virtue, and External Eudaimonism	251
	5.1. Four Kinds of Practice	251
	5.2. MacIntyre on the Structure of Practices	255
	5.3. Marx on Unalienated Labor	259
	5.4. Rawls on Practices	261
	5.5. Hursthouse's Habituation Version of External Eudaimonism	263
	6. Watson's Pure Aretaic Naturalism	269
	7. Social Holist Eudaimonism as a Radical Solution?	273
	7.1. MacIntyre's Joint Goods	274
	7.2. Brink and Spinoza	279
	8. Conclusion: Toward a Rejection of the Transmission Principle	282

Part III: Case Studies for the Existential Will as Projective Motivation

9	Divine and Human Creativity: From Plato to Levinas	287
	1. Thick and Thin Concepts of Motivation	287
	2. The Neoplatonic Projective Model of Divine Agapē	289
	2.1. The Erosiac Thesis and Perfection in *Republic* II	289
	2.2. Plato's Late Alternative: Overflowing Superabundance as Projective Motivation	292
	2.3. Divine Agape and the Open View of God in Christian Theology	296
	2.4. The Judeo-Christian Heritage of Projective Motivation	300
	3. Arendt on Creative Work	303
	4. Levinas on Superabundant Will and Volitional Generosity	307
	4.1. The Agapic Revelation of Alterity	308

	4.2. The Projective Structure of Metaphysical Desire	309
	4.3. Levinas on the Will	315
5.	The General Structure of Projective Motivation	318

10 Radical Evil and Projective Strength of Will 326
   1. Why Eudaimonism Misses Virtue and Vice in Their Most Radical Forms 326
      1.1. Aristotle's Apollonian View of Virtue as a "Mean" 326
      1.2. From Vice as Ignorance and *Akrasia* to Radical Evil 330
   2. Toward an Existential Theory of Radical Evil: Six Forms of Volitional Hatred 332
      2.1. Sadistic Cruelty 337
      2.2. Fanatical Cruelty and Motive Switches 339
      2.3. Malicious Anger 346
      2.4. Envy, Superiority, and Spite 350
      2.5. Malevolence, Torture, and the Will to Misappropriation 357
      2.6. Demonic Autonomy 362
   3. Aquinas and Kierkegaard on Evil: A Response to MacIntyre 363
   4. Projective Strength of Will versus *Enkrateia* 366
      4.1. Kierkegaard and Kupperman on Character 366
      4.2. Roberts's Analysis 368

11 Scotus and Kant: The Moral Will and Its Limits 371
   1. The Medieval Shift away from Eudaimonism: Scotus and the Moral Will 371
      1.1. From Aquinas to Scotus: Kent on Virtues of the Will 372
      1.2. Scotus on the Will to Justice 376
   2. Kant and the Projective Motive of Duty 384
      2.1. From Scotus to Kant 384
      2.2. Kant and the Will's Highest Function 386
      2.3. The Limits of Deontic Projection: Kant's False Dichotomy and Practical Identities 400
   3. Projective Willing and Libertarian Freedom 406
      3.1. Projective Motivation Is Not Necessarily Libertarian 406
      3.2. Allison and Ameriks on Freedom in Kant's Practical Philosophy 409

12 Existential Psychology and Intrinsic Motivation: Deci,
   Maslow, and Frankl   418
   1. Twentieth-Century Psychological Theories of
      Motivation   418
   2. From Drive Theories to Intrinsic Motivation   422
   3. An Existential Reinterpretation of Intrinsic Motivation   428
   4. Maslow's Eudaimonism   432
   5. Frankl's Existential Will to Meaning   436
      5.1. Meaning as a By-Product of Self-Transcending
           Devotion   436
      5.2. The Alterity of Values to Which the Will
           Responds   440
   6. How Caring Benefits the Agent: Frankfurt on Means
      and Ends   443
   7. Self-Esteem as By-Product   449
   8. Willed Carelessness: Emily Fox Gordon's Case   452
   9. Willed Inferiority: Sartre   455

13 Caring, Aretaic Commitment, and Existential Resolve   458
   1. Frankfurtian Care as Projective Motivation   459
      1.1. Care and Self-Unification over Time   460
      1.2. Caring Involves Reflexive Volitional Attitudes   462
      1.3. Caring Is Based on Volitional Commitment   464
      1.4. Volitional Love as Nonappetitive Motivation   468
   2. Aretaic Commitment and Backward-Looking
      Considerations   472
      2.1. The Concept of Commitment   472
      2.2. MacIntyre and Aretaic Commitment   474
      2.3. Williams against Consequentialism   475
      2.4. Anderson, Frankfurt, and the Priority of the
           Object   478
      2.5. Blustein on Commitment   482

14 An Existential Objectivist Account of What Is Worth Caring
   About   487
   1. Existential Objectivism   488
   2. Caring and the Good in Recent Political Philosophy   490
   3. Three Initial Reasons for Objectivism   494
      3.1. Caring about the Worth of Our Cares   495
      3.2. The Intersubjective Intelligibility and
           Criticizability of Cares   497
      3.3. Goods Internal to Practices are Worth Caring
           About   498

4. Frankfurtian Arguments for Subjectivism and
   Objectivist Rebuttals   500
   4.1. Two Kinds of Importance   500
   4.2. The Nygrenian Fallacy   503
   4.3. The Rejection of Strict Proportionalism: Wolf's
        Analysis   505
   4.4. Does Optionality Entail Subjectivity?   509
   4.5. Does Essential Particularity Entail Subjectivity?
        Raz's Analysis   513
   4.6. Do Objectivist Values Lack Noncircular
        Grounds?   519
5. The Reciprocal Relation between Value Insight and
   Volitional Resolve   523
6. Toward a Taxonomy of Significant Grounds for Caring   527

Conclusion   539
The Danger of Willfulness Revisited

Notes   547

Glossary of Definitions, Technical Terms, and Abbreviations   657

Bibliography   665

Index   691

Acknowledgments

The main ideas for this project grew out of the first half of my 1998 dissertation, which was titled *Self and Will* and directed by Karl Ameriks at the University of Notre Dame. However, less than a third of this book has any parallel in my Ph.D. thesis, so Karl is certainly not to blame for any problems. Although my argument is closely related to Kant's critique of the eudaimonist view that happiness is the proper function of human reason (and thus of human nature generally), the historical analyses and my theory of projective motivation go beyond anything found in Kant, and so the great German deontologist is the subject of only one episode in this story. Still, Karl's criticisms and advice were an indispensable help in formulating some of the initial ideas for this theory.

Among so many others who provided encouragement and questions, I want to single out for special thanks David Solomon, Fred Dallmayr, and Stephen Watson. The discussions of Kant, virtue ethics, and Levinas owe a great deal to their insights—and indeed, my conception of the will can be regarded as a development and expansion of Levinas's notion of metaphysical desire. In addition, my intellectual debts to Alasdair MacIntyre are too enormous and obvious to need stating. Though he must disagree with much of this work, I hope to have added in some small way to the new dialogue among traditions that he started. The other great debt in this work, as in much of what I have published, is to Harry Frankfurt. Here I can only repeat MacIntyre's refrain that constructive criticism of a philosopher's work is the greatest compliment one can pay.

Although this book does not discuss Kierkegaard at any length, the inspiration of countless Kierkegaard scholars stands behind it. In particular, I would like to express special appreciation to Edward Mooney, who has helped through the years in too many ways to name, including many valuable suggestions on how to make this work more readable. MacIntyre was right when he wrote that giving can never be equally reciprocal and we can only hope to pass on to others in the future the great benefits of generosity that we have received. It is also a pleasure to thank my colleague Merold

Westphal, who has provided advice on this work and helpful comments and support throughout my years at Fordham University. In this respect, he is like virtually all my colleagues at Fordham, who have seen strengths rather than weaknesses in my own philosophical pluralism. It is a high honor to serve with such a faculty.

I would also like to thank Helen Tartar and Nicholas Frankovich of Fordham University Press for their encouragement and patience. Copyediting this work was a two-year process involving enormous labor by Gill Kent, to whom I am enormously appreciative. This book also could not have been finished without the help of my research assistant, Scott O'Leary. Thanks also to Kyle Hubbard for his work on the index.

Now to my institutional debts. The main work on the manuscript of this book began during the summer of 2001 with the aid of a Fordham Faculty summer fellowship and continued with the help of one course reduction from our standard 3/3 load during the fall of 2002. The project also benefited from the opportunity to teach seminars on moral psychology at both the graduate and undergraduate level. Finally, chapters 13 and 14, which were initially conceived as part of a new book project on autonomy, were completed during the first weeks of an NEH Summer Fellowship in June of 2004.

In truth, however, the ultimate source of this book lies much earlier in my biography. Although its terminology reveals a Heideggerian pedigree, the idea expressed by the term "projective motivation" was with me long before I read any philosophy. I have hung onto it, perhaps out of a spirit of resistance, through twenty years of studying and teaching a philosophical canon in which few of the greatest authors recognize self-motivational phenomena. In short, I acquired my idea of the will from the literary masterpieces of Tolkien and Donaldson, which I read in high school. This book is a testament to their view of the great powers and dangers of the human spirit. I also saw the striving will at work in my parents and grandparents, who in their own ways each exhibited great volitional strength.

But my greatest debt of all—one that transcends all these others—is to my wife Robin, without whom there would be not only no book but probably no author either. In addition to all her love and support, she has also read most of the manuscript for grammar and typos. In her career, Robin gives new meaning to the biblical phrase, "Wonderful Counselor." In mothering our two wonderful children, she reveals the true meaning of commitment. I was drawn to Princeton University Press after college by interests in Kierkegaard, Jung, and the Bollingen Series, but I found Robin there instead. Thank goodness I learned enough from Kierkegaard not to make his mistake! We are the choices we make, and not all of mine have been good, but something gave me the grace to get the most important one right.

PREFACE
The Project of an Existential Theory of Personhood

The Issue

Although it remains popular among educated readers of the general public, enthusiasm for the existentialist approach to personhood has been declining in academic philosophical literature since the late 1970s. In analytic philosophy, metaphysical writings on personal identity over time have dismissed existentialist contributions on the complex temporality of selfhood as obfuscation. Likewise, mainstream metaphysical authors have a new semantics for possibility, necessity, and essential properties; as a result, they have difficulty in making sense of the existentialist claim that for persons, "existence precedes essence," unless this is read just as a rather confusing way of saying that we enjoy some sort of libertarian freedom. Few grasp that the existentialist objection to "personal essences" is a rejection of theories such as Molinism, Leibnizian monads, Kantian noumenal character, and Aristotelian teleology, all of which the existentialist views as inaccurate forms of determinism about human choice and motivation.

Moreover, since the development of contemporary modal logic, debates about the metaphysics of free will have been rewritten in a language relative to which older existentialist writings on freedom may seem outdated. Debates on whether moral responsibility for particular actions and omissions requires any sort of libertarian freedom, as existentialists commonly held, have also become much more complex since Harry Frankfurt's 1969 presentation of putative counterexamples to the Principle of Alternate Possibilities. Yet these debates hardly ever touch on the crucial question for existentialists: namely, what kind of freedom is required for responsibility for our own personality, character, and overall direction in life? This crucial question is addressed today only indirectly, as part of the theory of autonomy. Among neo-Kantians, compatibilist theories of autonomy have gained popularity, while their neo-Aristotelian critics often regard existentialism as the last gasp of enlightenment individuality. Iris Murdoch accuses existentialism of reducing the person to a bare point of freedom; Alasdair MacIntyre describes the existential self as an isolated, solipsistic, ghostly, and arbitrary free will. And this critique is fair against Sartre's model of the "for-itself" of consciousness, which ignores both social and natural constraints on the development of our identities and becomes what Michael Sandel calls a totally unencumbered self "dispossessed" of its ends.[1]

Developments in feminist ethics and recent Continental philosophy have reinforced this criticism, arguing that persons are essentially social beings who can understand themselves or even develop a "self" only in terms of their relations to others, including shared values, norms, and relationships of "care" that define the sphere of activities in which they conduct their lives. In pragmatism and some forms of radical hermeneutics, the notion of personhood itself is treated simply as a social convention or device we require as an underpinning for our moral and legal language games or as a convenient metaphysical fiction needed to maintain our shared "public conception" of justice.[2] In other deconstructive accounts, subjectivity remains, but not as a property of "the self" and only as an ineffable "freedom" that relates to the world but not to itself.[3]

Thus, in analytic and Continental moral psychology, existentialism has become passé. It is also widely regarded as having little relevance for contemporary philosophy of mind, which in recent decades has focused on whether the intentionality of mental states is something more than the tendency to produce various kinds of behavior and whether the sentience that computers would have to enjoy to count as conscious beings is irreducible to physical properties of brain states. This debate is today largely about whether any form of nonreductive physicalism will work, giving us mental states that are conceptually distinct from brain states but without having to tolerate any nonphysical level of reality (other than sets). The few writers on mind (such as Daniel Dennett and Owen Flanagan) who extend their analysis of consciousness to a conception of will and freedom generally advocate a naturalistic account of these phenomena, ignoring classical existentialist objections against such reductionism.

But here, as elsewhere, the existential tradition is ignored only at one's peril. Sartre's most central point about human consciousness, deriving from ideas going back through Husserl and Fichte to Kant, is that it involves prereflective awareness of itself as subject of intentional states rather than as an object. Yet this insight and its implications for models of self-awareness seem to be virtually unknown in contemporary Anglo-American philosophy of mind. Leading authors in this tradition, from Paul Churchland to William Lycan to David Armstrong, defend an introspective or reflective theory of awareness without even realizing that they need to rebut Sartre's rather devastating criticism of such theories. Their approach is thus an anachronism that can be respected in the analytic world only because its practitioners are ignorant of a whole tradition of thought that refuted this approach over fifty years ago. Whether we accept the phenomenological tradition's entire understanding of consciousness or not, relative to its insights today's leading introspective theories of sentience must seem obviously or even trivially mistaken. This should be something of an embarrassment to contemporary analytic philosophy of mind.

Likewise, psychological theory ought not to dismiss existentialism out of hand as having too voluntaristic a conception of human motivational powers. For theories of motivation in empirical psychology are influenced by the history of moral philosophy, in which the dominant debate today is between a range of neo-Humean positions according to which all motivation terminates in desires we simply acquire naturally or accidentally, and neo-Kantian views according to which some motivation ultimately stems from a choice to follow impartial rational judgments. These extremes leave no room for the rich picture of self-motivational capacities that existentialist writers explored (even if it was never systematically explained). Part of the goal of this book is to begin this systematic explanation, filling a large gap in the existential tradition.

Bringing Existentialism Back into Contemporary Debates

Evidently then, a philosopher who hopes to demonstrate the contemporary relevance of existentialism has his work cut out for him. He needs to develop a conception of personhood that is recognizably existentialist—or similar in key ways to the self as described by writers such as Kierkegaard, Heidegger, Jaspers, and Sartre—but which takes into account the last fifty years of developments in the many different areas of philosophy that directly affect our understanding of what it is to be a person. Pursuing this goal requires work on several different fronts in order to bring ideas from the existentialist tradition back into contemporary debates. Thus my larger agenda is to develop a revised existential account of personhood covering at least the following ten areas:

1. the lived experience of freedom and the development of morally significant character;
2. an account of individuality and freedom compatible with the narrative structure of our identity and our social nature as agents who hold one another morally responsible and who use language in ways involving implicit validity claims of several kinds;

3. the role of the will in shaping the ethos of a person, and the capacities of human motivation;
4. the concepts of autonomy and authenticity, and related intrapersonal or reflexive aspects of the will;
5. the freedom-conditions on moral responsibility for actions, decisions, and character;
6. the notion of essence, objectionable forms of "essentialism" about individual persons, and in what sense there could be an "essence" of personhood;
7. the relationship between self-consciousness and willing in the structure of the self;
8. the arrow of time, our knowledge of modality, and their relation to libertarian freedom;
9. a deliberative conception of democracy that is appropriate to the existential self;
10. the function of faith in God, or personal relationship with the divine in the development of a self, and the related existential problem of evil.

Of course, this is an ambitious program. But a unified, consistent account that could speak to both contemporary analytic and Continental literature in these ten areas could restore existentialism to the prominence that it deserves by addressing the main metaphysical and moral questions of philosophical anthropology. The result will be a more sophisticated existentialism that can be presented in today's terms as a serious challenge to current dogmas in metaphysics and moral psychology and be defended against the ascendant naturalistic, Humean, rationalistic, compatibilist, or pragmatist alternatives. This conception of personhood will in turn provide new and better bases for ethics, the foundations of political philosophy, and perhaps even theology.

With the invaluable help of Anthony Rudd as coeditor, I have made a start on this agenda in *Kierkegaard After MacIntyre*. Essays by several scholars in this collection address areas 1 and 2 in the foregoing list by clarifying Kierkegaard's existentialist conception of personhood in relation to themes in contemporary moral philosophy. My own essay, "Towards an Existential Virtue Ethics," sketches out an existentialist account of our experience of freedom and defends the deep connection between ethical obligation and authentic willing. This essay also goes some way toward explaining the idea that the social and individual sides of human experience are *equiprimordial*: Although human persons are essentially social beings with nonvoluntary relations to others, it is also essential to their personhood that they develop a volitional relation *to themselves*, which is manifested in their "work" on their own motivational character. This intrapersonal dimension of personhood is not simply derivative from or reducible to the interpersonal dimensions. Thus the existentialist emphasis on the *individuality* of human personhood is defended. Human persons are essentially social, but each person also essentially transcends her sociality and can change her acquired character. This does not conflict with the promising idea that a basis for ethics can be found in our social constitution.

This Book and Subsequent Steps

Will as Commitment and Resolve represents the next and most complex step in renewing the existentialist tradition. Focusing on the most influential historical accounts of motivation, along with some attention to closely related questions in moral theory and religion, this book lays the groundwork for all the subsequent steps. In particular, without an adequate conception of willing, one cannot get to the root of long-standing dilemmas concerning freedom of the will or understand the freedom required for the full range of moral responsibility. The idea of willing as a self-motivating process is also required to make sense of personal autonomy, authenticity, and various forms of inauthenticity or "bad faith" that have concerned classical existentialists. The content of normative ethics also depends in crucial ways on starting from the right conception of the will.

Of course, the nature of the will and its relationship to human motivation is an enormous topic, and I focus only on those aspects of a theory of will and motivation that will be most important for these later steps. Tasks 4 and 5 require focusing directly on autonomy and especially on Frankfurt's claim that persons are distinguished by their capacity to be concerned about and "identify with" or "alienate" their own first-order motives for acting. A full understanding of autonomy and authenticity depends on making sense of this great Frankfurtian insight; but Frankfurt's own approaches to explaining it all fail, because they never adequately distinguish volitional states with agent-authority from ordinary desires, which do not come with agent-authority built in. Frankfurt's phenomenological investigation of how we adopt and pursue reflexive goals concerning our own motivational character sheds light on the existentialist picture of selfhood, but only the existential tradition has the resources to make sense of Frankfurt's notion of volitional "identification," and his closely related notion of volitional "caring." I will argue that when we take a stand for or against particular dispositions, desires, and emotions as possible motives for acting, this can best be explained in terms of the notion of projective motivation developed in the present book. So *Will as Commitment and Resolve* is, among other things, a prolegomena to my next book on volitional identification and autonomy.

The analyses of caring and commitment come first, in the final chapters of *Will as Commitment and Resolve*, because they are conceptually more basic.

As later books will, I hope, show, an existential phenomenology of the will and autonomy also has interesting implications in many other areas. In the philosophy of mind, I will argue that the forms of self-consciousness unique to human beings cannot be understood without reference to our volitional self-relations. In normative ethics, I will argue that an agapē ethics cannot adequately be formulated without an existential account of willing. When it is rightly conceived, such an ethics will prove superior to other leading utilitarian, deontological, and neo-Aristotelian approaches. In political philosophy, I will argue that the deliberative account of legitimate democracy, which we find both in the republican tradition in America and in Continental discourse ethics, requires that individual citizens be much more than Hobbesian agents. In fact, it requires that they have the kind of motivational capacities described in this work, that they be existential agents as well as rational beings. These arguments will provide further support for the overall coherence of the new existentialist picture.

The Analytic-Phenomenological Method

Finally, since I blend ideas from different philosophical traditions and historical periods, a brief explanation of my method may be in order. Although I employ many of the same analytical and historical tools as do others writing on my topics, my method is also broadly speaking *phenomenological*. Although this is not generally in the foreground of my discussion, it becomes important at some crucial junctures in the argument.

In general, by a phenomenological approach I mean one that distinguishes between the primary phenomena to be explained in some area of philosophy and the rival theoretical explanations that construe these phenomena in different ways. The phenomenological approach presumes that we usually can discern, however imperfectly, some important phenomena that serve as paradigm cases or fixed points of reference for analyzing a particular problem or concept. This evidence or experience functions as an initial clue or proleptic outline of the concept at issue.[4] The task of theoretical explanation is then to provide as convincing an account of these phenomena and their grounds of possibility as can be given, where what counts as "convincing" is *itself guided by the shape of the phenomena that present themselves* more or less clearly in common human experience. Thus the first aim of theoretical explanation is to follow where the phenomena lead rather than to make them fit the mold of a metaphysics to which one is antecedently committed. This principle, which corresponds both to Husserlian eidetic science and to the Habermasian communicative ideal of reaching conclusions based solely on *the force of the better argument* alone, is important in my case for deciphering how we can even begin to analyze concepts such as the will, volitional identification, and freedom.

Of course I am aware that objections have been raised against this principle and the phenomenological method in general. Let me mention and briefly respond to three such objections.

A. The Hermeneutic Objection

The "phenomena themselves" are never pure givens; our reception of them is mediated by a host of unexamined presuppositions (some of them theoretical and even metaphysical), which vary both culturally and historically—and it could not be otherwise for beings like us.

B. The Linguistic Objection

Our evaluation of whether an explanation meets, satisfactorily accounts for, or (in older lingo) adequately saves the phenomena is always mediated by linguistic structures whose implications exceed our capacity to make them certain beforehand in reflection and which also vary over time.

C. The Underdetermination Objection

Two theories may save all the phenomena equally well, leaving us to decide between them on other criteria.

In my view, the caveats expressed by A and B show only that judging an explanation's convincingness according to the pure phenomenological approach (or philosophical "strict science" in Husserl's sense) is always a counterfactual *ideal*, not that we should not try to approximate this ideal as best we can, nor that we have no ways to tell when we have done a better or worse job at approximating it. We cannot spell out a method that could be rationally agreed on in advance to resolve disputes about the content, relevance, and reliability of our phenomena between parties in different traditions and cultures; but the process of spelling out rival descriptions usually reveals differences in quality of interpretation that would be apparent to neutral observers—were there any—which are therefore usually also apparent to honest and self-critical although situated observers like ourselves and our interlocutors. And the problem that we cannot ever be entirely neutral observers is *itself* revealing for several issues in philosophical anthropology and epistemology. In other words, objections A and B themselves reveal some transcendental conditions of our experience that provide useful information for philosophical anthropology in their own right (for example, that we are not *so* situated that we cannot even realize that we are situated, and so on).

Objection C poses different problems, but for the most part, the difficulty to which it refers becomes serious only in the philosophy of science and the philosophy of physics in particular; in moral philosophy and philosophical anthropology we never get theories that clearly save all the most relevant and reliable phenomena and so we never get ones that do so *equally* well. The problem is more one of a *phronetic* judgment between incomplete accounts with different and still-imperfect virtues. There is no solution for this other than continuing the debate for indefinitely many further rounds. Thus qualified, the method I follow can still bear valuable fruit if it is done well.

I

The Idea of Willing as Projective Motivation

I

Introduction

How far from both muscular heroism and from the soulfully tragic spirit of unselfishness that unctuously adds its little offering to the sponge cake at a kaffee klatsch is the plain, simple fact that a man has given himself completely to something he finds worth living for.[1]

I. The Heroic Will

Like many of key terms in philosophy, the word "will" is used in many different ways, and it has a complex etymology (connected to *willa* in Old English and *voluntas* in Latin). In his attempt to bring this term back into psychotherapy, the psychologist Irwin Yalom lists several prominent senses of "willing":

> It is the mental agency that transforms awareness and knowledge into action, it is the bridge between desire and act. It is the mental state that precedes action (Aristotle). It is the mental "organ of the future"—just as memory is the organ of the past (Arendt). It is the power of *spontaneously* beginning a series of successive things (Kant). It is the seat of volition, the "responsible mover" within (Farber). It is the "decisive factor in translating equilibrium into a process of change . . . an act occurring between insight and action which is experienced as effort or determination" (Wheelis). . . . It is a force composed of both power and desire. . . . To this psychological construct, we assign the label, "will," and to its function, "willing."[2]

It is clear that the different theorists Yalom cites here are *not* offering explanations of the same item in our experience, and this is why any philosophical analysis of willing must first fix the basic sense(s) or concept(s) that it hopes to explain. Otherwise we will be trying to combine or decide between apparently conflicting explanations that are really shooting at different explananda, or targets of analysis.

This book is about the will in what can loosely be called its "heroic" sense, as committed striving or passionate resolve. "Willing" in this ordinary language or prephilosophical sense is commonly associated with perseverance and even inflexibility. My younger daughter once opened a fortune cookie containing the message: "You have an iron will, which helps you succeed in everything." However, the kind of willing that existentialism considers central to personhood is certainly not limited to contexts of battle or world-historic struggles or grappling with great adversaries. Volitional heroism is not primarily exemplified by the warrior-kings of archaic societies (or their poetically enlarged literary representations). Instead, my existential account regards strength of will as the backbone of every distinctively human life, however outwardly humble. In its most primordial sense, volition is personal *resolve*, or choice that is motivated by the agent's self-assertive commitment to final goals and ends.[3] The will admired in our heroes is a kind of *striving* toward ends that involves committing the agent's whole self to the task. Although it is really an ongoing activity, we sometimes also call this striving will a *state* of firm resolve.

There are two other closely related ways of glossing the basic concept of willing that is the target of my analysis or the phenomenon that my existential theory purports to explain better than rival accounts. The striving will is that in us through which we, rather than the forces which surround us on every side, play an active role in forming our own character and thus in shaping our own destiny. It is also, as Kant saw, the capacity to pursue ends for something beyond the satisfactions that they promise to bring us when reached. The person who exercises her will in discovering and pursuing a meaningful life need not hold, with Beowulf, that "renown" or recognition from one's compatriots is the highest end of life. But her will is appropriately called "heroic" if it recognizes and responds to values that make goals worth pursuing, even when these transcend the product-value of the goal once achieved or realized—for such devotion to an end or goal is not conditioned simply by the value and chances of success.[4] In this sense, heroic willing is what Kierkegaard called "infinite passion."[5] The common notion of "strength of will" is directly related to this original sense of the word: our will is our capacity to face adversity and struggle to overcome obstacles in pursuit of a worthwhile goal—even when there is little real hope of success and probably no poet to eulogize it.

These notions of determination or sustained effort remain the primary sense of "willing" for most people working or writing outside of legal, psychoanalytic, and philosophical contexts. They are widespread in modern novels by many authors who seem to be genealogically unrelated to existential philosophy. J. R. R. Tolkien, for example, was much concerned with striving will. In his discussion of the tenth-century fragmentary poem *The Battle of Maldon*, Tolkien notes that as the English lost the battle to the Vikings, the English commander's retainer gave voice to the deepest value in his tradition:

> as he prepares to die in the last desperate stand, [he] utters the famous words, a summing up of the heroic code. . . . "Will shall be sterner, heart the bolder, spirit the greater, as our strength lessens." It is here implied, as is indeed probable, that these words were not "original," but an ancient and honoured expression of the heroic will.[6]

Likewise, in his famous *Beowulf* essay, Tolkien emphasizes W. P. Ker's idea that in Norse mythology, the forces of Chaos and the profane represented by the monsters must win in the end, "but the gods, who are defeated, think that defeat no refutation."[7] The Norse solution to the problem of evil and chaos is what Kierkegaard called "infinite resignation": perseverance despite the certainty that "all men, and all their works shall die."[8] In the face of defeat without salvation from the God beyond time, the Norse honor code finds "a potent but terrible solution in naked will and courage."[9] The same idea makes its way into the professor's own epic narrative. In *The Lord of the Rings*, as Frodo and Sam near Mount Doom but seem certain to perish before reaching their goal, Tolkien tells us: "But even as hope died in Sam, or seemed to die, it was turned to a new strength. Sam's plain hobbit-face grew stern, almost grim, as the will hardened in him."[10]

Even today, almost every reader of this passage is likely to understand what Tolkien meant, for this sense of "willing" as dedicated striving toward a crucial goal (which moves us in a way quite unlike all bodily inclinations and natural yearnings) is both individually recognizable in some of our own experiences and collectively recognized in our mixed cultural heritage(s) as essential for a person to have "character" and to be capable of virtue. It is also closely related to the idea of *commitment:* as W. H. Auden notes in his essay on Tolkien's trilogy, "Once he had chosen, Frodo is absolutely committed."[11] As Stanley Hauerwas argues, "the idea of character in its most paradigmatic [i.e., moral] usage indicates what a man can decide to be as opposed to what a man is naturally."[12] "Character" in this autonomous or volitional sense suggests a certain strength of will and continuity in identity-defining commitments, whatever the agent's less voluntary personality traits may be: "when we speak of a man as 'having character,' we are more apt to be thinking of something like integrity, incorruptibility, or consistency."[13] To have volitional character is what I have called a *proto-virtue*: it is a constitutive prerequisite both of virtuous character and at least of great vices.[14]

Yet in the history of Western philosophy, this most crucial sense of the "will" as the source of autonomous or identity-forming motivation has never been fully understood. Rather, it has for the most part been systematically excluded or truncated within theories of motivation deriving mainly from ancient Greek conceptions of the desire for happiness. In contemporary theories of action, if it is recognized at all, volition is usually construed simply as a kind of mental act or decision by which we form intentions. This interpretation usefully distinguishes volition from the prior motives that do not themselves constitute intentional purposes, but it has obscured the older tradition according to which will plays a motivational role, striving to carry out decisions about specific actions. Will in the striving sense also concerns how we acquire our most important or governing ends in life—that is, those final goals whose personal and collective significance has the deepest importance for us, defining who we are or what we stand for in the most uncompromising way. Whether or not it involves libertarian freedom, this process of setting our ultimate ends or defining our ultimate concerns cannot plausibly be pictured as a discrete act of choice among clearly predefined options nor as a simple act of decision in which we form an intention to pursue some final end. Rather, "decision" in this customary sense presupposes prior motives that it does not change, including some ultimate ends. The development, setting, or definition of these ends is a distinct process of agency that has no widely recognized label in contemporary action theory.

Striving in the executive sense (trying to act on intentions) is recognized as corresponding to a distinct sense of "will" even by antimetaphysical positivists like Gilbert Ryle, who rejects the concept of "will" as a myth of the Cartesian soul. Ryle has to acknowledge that in addition to ordinary distinctions between "voluntary" and "involuntary," we have the experience of "nerving or bracing ourselves to do something,"[15] or making an "effort of will." Given his determination to eliminate "will" as a form of agency or operation distinct from other mental or bodily acts, Ryle tries to explain such efforts as merely patterns of attention, such as being focused on the mission at hand. He insists that:

> it is no part of the definition of resoluteness or of irresoluteness that a resolution should actually have been formed. A resolute man may firmly resist temptations to abandon or postpone his task, though he never went through a prefatory ritual-process of making up his mind to complete it. But naturally such a man will be disposed to perform any vows which he has made to others or to himself.[16]

Of course a strong-willed person need not literally make vows to himself or perform other ritual speech-acts to cajole himself into action. But, *pace* Ryle, this hardly means that resoluteness is a state that just happens to a person rather than an active undertaking of her agency. Nor does the fact that one may backslide on a resolve entail that it involves no distinctively volitional element: efforts of striving will do not by definition succeed in the way that deciding entails an intention.[17]

In existential literature, this crucial form of "willing" was extended to end-setting and conceived as a kind of resolve or determination of the whole self. Fichte described it as "'self-positing activity,' a subject's 'taking itself' to be in relation to, or directed towards [an] . . . object or goal,"[18] and even claimed that this "practical striving of the I" was the basis of human consciousness of the world.[19] Beyond sensibly determined inclinations, this "pure will has an original (moral) determinancy of its own."[20] As the existential psychologist Yalom writes, the word "will" has rich connotations precisely because "it conveys determination and commitment," most paradigmatically in the form of promises.[21] In the work of Yalom's predecessor, Viktor Frankl, willing is conceived as a process by which we take up tasks and purposes whose pursuit is intrinsically valuable or meaningful to beings like us. In so doing, we find that our lives acquire meaning for us or personal significance that is essential for healthy and mature agency.

Following Frankl, I argue that the kind of will that distinguishes *persons* is not simply the capacity to form an intention or to make a choice between different possible actions but rather a capability for commitment or resolve in which the agent sets for himself some significant and often difficult or challenging project, plan, or goal. This view draws support from Harry Frankfurt's insight that persons are distinguished from other animals by their unique motivational abilities.[22] As I interpret it, the volitional resolve that constitutes devotion to some ultimate end is itself a kind of motivation unlike other sorts, distinct in particular from the various appetites typically named "desires" and from emotions involving such desires. There are several different sorts of desire, but they share in common the feature that the person is moved by *the attractiveness of an object* to desire it (or moved by its repulsiveness to flee it). The eudaimonist tradition favors the idea that all motivation has this magnetic form. For example, George Wilson defines a goal as "something attractive. We attend to it and organize our resources around it because we want it."[23]

By contrast, existential commitment involves what I call *projective motivation*, in which we give ourselves ends to which we may not have been previously attracted at all, although we recognize some kind of value in them. Through projective resolve, we set new goals for ourselves or take up new projects and concerns, *making it our business* to care about something or someone; or we renew and strengthen our devotion to a standing end. This kind of motive innovation carries us creatively beyond our prior desires and inclinations. It may also help us carry out our intention when prior desires for our intended act are too weak. In later chapters, I review different types of desire, because the general structure of projective motivation can be explained only by contrast with the "erosiac" form of human desire described by Plato and Aristotle as the basis of their eudaimonism, which is the focus of Part II of this book. Part I focuses on clarifying the concept of heroic or striving will that is to be explained in terms of projective motivation and distinguishing it from other senses of "willing" found in contemporary action theory.

2. The Existential Theory of Striving Will as Projective Motivation

Thus the overall goal of this book is to draw attention to the importance of willing in the heroic or striving sense and to argue that it is best understood in terms of the theory of projective motivation. The broader account that interprets core character, life-meaning, and the formation of a "self" in terms of striving will, and then explains this phenomenon in all its manifestations in terms of projective motivation, I call "the new existential theory of the will."

The new existential description of heroic or striving will points toward the idea of *self-motivation* as underlying the specific virtues in which heroic will is most noticeable. In particular, this ordinary language concept seems to refer to two closely related capacities: (1) the ability to generate *new* motivation in positing goals for oneself and committing oneself to them; and (2) the ability to *supplement* or add to the motivation found in preexisting desires by an "effort of will," renewed determination, or devotion of more energy and resources toward pursuit of an existing goal. Since the latter is most apparent in overcoming obstacles, it is closely associated with courage, making it the more familiar of the two aspects of self-motivation suggested here. But I call both forms "projective motivation" on the belief that they share a common psychic structure.

I use the term "projection" in the Heideggerian sense to indicate that the agent *sets* herself a goal, or gives herself an end, or motivates herself to pursue it. In such cases, the agent does not experience her motivation as a passive effect of perceptions or judgments that reveal desirable objects but rather experiences the motivation as *actively formed*. But because the term "projection" has other, established meanings, my use of it could easily be misunderstood. In moral theory, philosophers in the Humean tradition have held that values are "projected" by human attitudes, desires, and emotions onto a world that in itself is value-neutral, meaning that their objective reality is illusory. Similarly, in personality theory, psychologists have held that persons "project" onto other people (including their therapist) or onto superhuman beings what are really aspects of their own psyche. For instance, I see my child as insolent because I am angry at my boss, or I imagine God as having all the qualities of a loving father that I wish I could be.

What I mean by "projection" is something absolutely distinct from these metaethical, psychoanalytic, and anthropological senses of the term. In the *existential* sense, we "project" ends for ourselves rather than simply discovering them as appealing to preexisting appetites within us, and we "project" ourselves toward the goals we set rather than simply finding ourselves drawn to them. This does not mean that we project desirable characteristics onto the object or goal to make ourselves want it. That we participate actively in the genesis of some motivation rather than being merely its passive recipient does not mean that we create a fictional picture of our end or produce some externalized image of our own thought. Nor does it mean that we arbitrarily hurl ourselves toward some end for no reason. Rather, there are always putative grounds for volitional projections: there is always a story to be told about *why* an agent projected some goal or set of activities for herself. Chapter 14 defends an objectivist account of the practical reasons that agents can have for projecting different kinds of ends. Although the metaphysical status of these reasons is not my topic in this book, my objectivism about practical reasons commits me at least to some form of moderate realism about values that can justify setting new ends or strengthening resolve in pursuit of them.

Given the potentially misleading Humean or Feuerbachian connotations of "projection," I could have called these self-motivational processes something else, like "transformative motivation" or "self-composing" motivation; but all the alternatives seemed either more awkward or to presuppose something about the role of such motivation in autonomy that remains to be demonstrated. In cognitive psychology today, the closest analog to what I call projective motivation is labeled "intrinsic motivation" to mark the idea that the agent values the relevant ends for their own sake.[24] For my purposes, however, this distinction is not precise enough, since an agent can (and surely does) value her own happiness as a final end. It is not the finality of ends but rather their transcendence of the agent's own good that most clearly reveals the kind of self-motivational activity that this new body of psychological work recognizes—the kind that is distinctive of *willing* in the existential sense.[25] Moreover, if I used the term "intrinsic motivation" instead of "projective motivation" throughout, I would be giving the misleading impression that I am contributing to this genre of work in cognitive psychology. Hence I have stuck with "projective" with the hope of reviving its Heideggerian usage.

The idea that motivation can be directly initiated or evoked by some kind of inner activity or mental effort is bound to prompt the question of what $motivates_2$ this $activity_1$ or effort. On pain of infinite regress, the answer cannot be that some further $activity_2$ generates this $motivation_2$ to form some $motive_1$. To stop the regress, the answer must be that *nothing* $motivates_2$ the projection of ends or $motivation_1$-composing activity itself. Yet this activity, which is "willing" in its existential sense, is a response to perceived *reasons* for the relevant ends and/or for the process of pursuing these ends— reasons that do not already constitute *motives* when we consider them. Projective motivation thus amounts to the idea that persons can respond to reasons for action that remain external to their present "motivational set" by *internalizing* them, or giving them motivational force. This is clearest when the objective grounds to which projection of some end E responds are ones that do not already draw us toward E "erotically," in the most general sense of this term. Since this contrast between *erosiac* and *projective* motivation is fundamental for my existential theory of the will, a large part of the book is devoted to exploring and defending it. This requires distinguishing between the thin or merely formal notion of a "motive" prevalent in contemporary theories of action and practical rationality and the thick or substantive notion of motivation as a kind of psychological state with its own phenomenology, which is distinguished from other states by the way it is experienced as bringing the agent to form plans or intentions.

Contemporary theories of motivation generally focus on the formal role of beliefs and desires as reasons for action and on what kind of rationality these may involve. This has taken the focus away from the character of different kinds of motivation as conative experiences. A phenomenology of motives means more than simply considering "what it is like" to be motivated in a given way; it also involves looking at the *intentional structure* of motivational attitudes, or the comportment of the agent toward the object, as evidenced in our experiences of these attitudes. This book returns the focus to the experienced structure of various kinds of human motives, beginning with a review of the erosiac structure of "desire" (*orexis*) in Platonic and Aristotelian thought.

3. An Outline of the Main Argument

Given the many topics covered in this book and the complexity of my approach in some sections, readers may find it helpful to have a map of the main line of argument—that is, a brief overview of the central themes of the individual chapters and an explanation of how they fit into the overall argument. This section explains the seventeen steps of the main argument and their division in the three parts of the book.

The book includes several other features to help readers follow the main thread of the argument through its many turns. At the end of this chapter is a Reader's Guide which suggests ways to move from one part of the text to other parts, depending on one's interests and levels of prior preparation. Each subsequent chapter also begins with a summary of the chapter's topics and their relation to neighboring chapters. Following the summary, some chapters also include brief introductions or reviews of progress. The detailed Glossary at the end of the book allows one to keep track of named terms and principles. Extensive cross-references throughout indicate related discussions in other parts of the text.

The book as a whole has two main theses: (1) that the existential conception of the striving will is a coherent and distinctive alternative to rival conceptions in Eastern thought, Western eudaimonism, and contemporary action theory; and (2) that this existential conception is correct in predicting that projective motivation plays a central role in moral motivation and other self-defining commitments that shape the ethos of a person. The book is subdivided into three parts because the defense of Thesis Two is divided into negative components (critiquing competing models) and positive components (directly defending the existential model). Most of the arguments for Thesis One are given in Part I of the book; most of the negative arguments for Thesis Two are developed through the critique of eudaimonism in Part II; and most of the positive arguments for Thesis Two are presented in the case studies that comprise Part III.

However, there are a few complications within this otherwise linear development. First, the idea of projective motivation is further explained and refined in the first chapter of Part III (chap. 9) because the definition developed there depends on a *contrast* with the erosiac model and psychological eudaimonism, which are explained in Part II. Chapter 9 also provides several case studies illustrating this refined conception of projective motivation. Second, the analyses of friendship and practices in chapter 8 are developed as part of the critique of eudaimonism, but they also provide some positive illustrations of projective motivation, like the case studies in Part III. Third, the analysis of radical evil in chapter 10 includes the other, darker side of the existential critique of eudaimonist accounts of virtue developed in Part II. However, the emphasis in chapter 10 is again on positive evidence for the existence of projective motivation. Fourth, the existential theory of willing sketched in Part I is incomplete without the account of reasons or grounds for willing developed in the defense of existential objectivism in Part III. But the list of objective grounds depends on the case studies. Thus, for reasons of narrative continuity, points relevant to the defense of each main thesis are found in all three parts of the work. But, these complications aside, the first main thesis is the focus in Part I, and the second main thesis is the focus in Parts II and III.

3.1. The Defense of Thesis One by Articulation of the Existential Conception of Willing

The defense of the first main thesis has several parts, three of which are meant to provide framing background for the main arguments. Together they provide a preliminary account of what willing in the existential sense means and why it is a distinct concept from free choice.

1. Chapter 2 begins with an account of the ordinary language or prephilosophical concept of heroic willing, which is explained in the existential conception of striving will.

2. This chapter then offers a preemptive response to the objection that this concept of willing is uniquely Western. I argue that the same idea is present in paradigmatically "Eastern" thought, but it is construed negatively as willfulness or the will to self-aggrandizement. Comparison and contrast of "Eastern" and "Western" views on heroic willing reveals the possibility of a moderate concept of volitional determination or resolve that is distinct from its corrupt forms as the *conatus ascendi* or *libido dominandi.*

3. Chapter 3 argues that willing in this sense of resolve or self-motivating determination is not adequately described or explained in contemporary action theory. I consider four different pictures of willing that emerge in the recent history of philosophical theories of action. However, even the best of these accounts, which equates the will with the power of decision through which we form the intentions and purposes that distinguish human action from mere behavior, misses the phenomena of projective motivation. Thus it leaves out much of what gives willing its existential significance. This discussion also shows why projective motivation, if it exists, plays a deeper role than decision or choice in establishing the character or ethos of a person.

This historical analysis gives just enough content to the existential conception of willing that we can see what has to be shown to justify it: we have to prove that human persons are capable of *projective motivation.* But it is not immediately obvious how to go about this, first, because the concept itself needs much more clarification, and second, because the most likely examples that might be cited to illustrate it will be explained without projective motivation by the eudaimonist tradition that dominates contemporary virtue ethics. To solve these problems, one might engage recent analytic work on motivation and try to make conceptual arguments for projective motivation. But, as already noted, such theories often begin from a thin concept of "motive" without full attention to the phenomenology of motivational experience. Moreover, recent work on motivation by Davidson, Williams, Mele, Dancy, and others may be influenced in subtle and not readily perceived ways by assumptions derived from the eudaimonist tradition that tend to obscure projective phenomena.

Therefore it seems better first to engage the eudaimonist tradition in detail, both because it provides a substantive conception of motivation that serves as a foil for the existential account and because a critique of this model suggests that we need to hypothesize projective willing to explain virtuous motivation itself. As explained in the opening section of chapter 4, the core of the larger argument for main Thesis Two requires the idea that motive-states that we can experience without necessarily intending to act on them generally have what I call the erosiac structure. So this structure must be explained before subsequent arguments for the existence of projective motivation can proceed.

4. Chapter 4 clarifies the idea of projective motivation by contrast with the erosiac model of motivation first systematically set out by Plato, focusing in particular on the account of desire-as-lack in the *Symposium*. Drawing on work in contemporary moral psychology, I distinguish three different types of desire in Plato's broad sense and distinguish targetable from nontargetable goals.

5. Chapter 5 argues that Aristotle's psychology largely follows the core claims of Plato's model, except that the quasi-volitional role played by Plato's *thumos* or middle soul is taken over by "intellectual appetite." I defend and develop the distinction between the three main types of erosiac desire recognized in this account. But the intellectual appetite account does not recognize striving will as having any independent motivational power distinct from rational desires for the good that informs choice, and thus all human motivation is explained in broadly erosiac terms.

6. Chapter 5 also argues that there is a legitimate sense in which the erosiac model constructed from Plato and Aristotle is formally *egoistic*. I distinguish formal egoism from other more familiar kinds of egoism (as a doctrine about human motivation) and consider one highly important kind of argument against motivational egoism, namely the argument that it is self-defeating. I then ask whether a version of this paradox of self-defeat applies to formal egoism.

It is important to note that the burden of this argument does not fall primarily on the historical accuracy of my readings of Plato and Aristotle. Although I think these interpretations are fair and, I hope, provide interesting insights into these much-studied authors, what is crucial for my main argument is that the erosiac model *as I reconstruct it* is as coherent and strong a rival to the existential account as possible. If there are ideas in Plato, Aristotle, or their successors that would strengthen this account of motivation, then they should be added to it. Slightly different versions of the erosiac model are to be found in Aquinas and other medieval philosophers, and it would be interesting to consider whether any of their insights allow us to improve this model. Relative to the sketch I have given, though, we can understand projective motivation negatively as *non-erosiac*.

3.2. *The Negative Defense of Thesis Two by the Critique of Psychological Eudaimonism*

Any psychological theory according to which all motivational experiences are explainable in erosiac terms dispenses with willing in the existential sense and needs to be refuted to defend my second main thesis. The paradigm case of such a theory is what I call *psychological eudaimonism* (PE), which consists of the erosiac model plus two further motivational and normative theses:

(a) that all desire is unified (in an appropriate sense) in the desire for eudaimonia, flourishing, or well-being of the agent—his individual good and components of it that are joint goods essentially shared with others; and

(b) that an enlightened understanding of our eudaimonia extends this fundamental desire for it to ethical goods, including the species of "nobility" that are intended for their own sake by virtuous agents.

This position is to be distinguished from what we might call *rational eudaimonism* (REu), which is the thesis that an agent's practical reasons for action are all unified (in the justificatory sense) in considerations concerning the agent's flourishing and its necessary conditions (including joint goods necessarily shared with the others). According to REu, then, all practical reasons to pursue or avoid any X ultimately derive their normative force from X's capacity to promote or hinder the agent's eudaimonia. Each version of REu must provide some account of what the agent's true good includes, as must each version of PE. The distinction between REu and PE is very important, because someone could apparently endorse the former in her normative account of reasons without necessarily endorsing the latter in her moral psychology.[26]

Such a position would face difficult questions about how or whether certain key reasons arising from requirements of human eudaimonia could play any action-guiding role (without which they cease to be *practical* reasons). We might also consider whether rational eudaimonism could be combined with an existential conception of willing that allows for projective motivation. I briefly address these issues in chapter 7, section 4, and chapter 8, sections 3 and 5.5. While I believe that an adequate existential account of willing requires a conception of practical reasons that extends beyond those recognized by REu—and I sketch out such a conception in chapter 14—critiquing REu is not my main purpose in this book. The defense of main Thesis Two requires only that PE be refuted.

As in my analysis of the classical erosiac model, this part of the argument begins by consulting historical examples (especially Aristotle) in order to reconstruct in systematic form the most fair and representative version of PE I can conceive, which I label *A-eudaimonism*.[27] Its name is chosen to suggest this model's plausible attribution to Aristotle and Aquinas; but again, the success of my main line of argument does not depend on it reflecting Aristotle's or Aquinas's view with complete accuracy. It would be affected only if some misinterpretation of their texts has caused me to miss some way of strengthening PE against the existential critique I offer. The critique itself is a version of the paradox of egoism described in chapter 5, extended to the formal egoism involved in A-eudaimonism. Here are the main steps in this part of the argument:

7. Chapter 6 focuses on Aristotle's eudaimonism as a case study and argues that when eudaimonia in the *Nicomachean Ethics* is understood as holistically including all other human goods, we can construct a theory (A-eudaimonism) in which there is a unique highest good, the desire for which embraces and underlies all other desires. The question is whether such a conception of motivation is compatible with the virtue ethics that it is supposed to support.

8. Chapter 7 argues that Aristotle's conception of virtuous motivation as aimed at the noble for its own sake is incompatible with A-eudaimonism. The paradox of A-eudaimonism is that the agent's flourishing requires the by-product benefits of caring about goods that are materially unconnected to the agent's own good. But such by-products are not directly targetable without self-defeat. Given Aristotle's account of the role that happiness plays in motivation and moral virtue, there is an internal conflict that cannot be solved in his own terms. I consider Aristotle's own attempt to resolve this problem and other worthy attempts by Kraut and Annas, and argue that they all fail. A-eudaimonism generates a paradox that is structurally similar to familiar paradoxes of egoism unless it is supplemented by projective motivation.

9. Chapter 8 has three tasks. First, it evaluates several different contemporary neo-Aristotelian efforts to resolve the paradox of eudaimonism, including ideas proposed by John Cooper, Paula Gottlieb, Alasdair

MacIntyre, and Gary Watson, and argues that none avoids the need to postulate projective motivation. This helps explain why the revival of virtue ethics has been unable to show how the goals we ought to pursue and the virtues required to sustain pursuit of them are fully traceable to (or explainable from) the telos of human psychology or the nature of human agency. Second, this chapter addresses versions of external eudaimonism and indirect eudaimonism that accept the paradox but construct other ways for knowledge of the psychological requirements of human flourishing to guide communities of human agents toward those motive-states that will promote eudaimonia. Third, this chapter argues that the same paradox arises in neo-Aristotelian accounts of friendship and MacIntyre's account of practices; for projective motivation plays a key role in both these phenomena.

3.3. The Positive Defense of Thesis Two: Case Studies in Projective Motivation

With psychological eudaimonism and the erosiac model as a foil, Part III begins by developing a more rigorous account of projective motivation and striving will. This restatement is driven by the analysis of the main historical case study, which explains the beginning of a countertradition opposed to psychological eudaimonism that runs from the late Plato through Scotus and Kant to the existentialists and alterity theorists such as Levinas. Thus what Part III presents is not a random series of case studies but a historically related set of ideas moving from the counter-eudaimonist tradition in medieval and early-modern philosophy into existential psychoanalysis and contemporary Continental and analytic moral psychology. Seen this way, it is clear that these ideas constitute a *tradition* in MacIntyre's sense—a vital but underappreciated and often suppressed tradition in which the existential conception of striving will is the keystone. The task of Part III is to do for this existential tradition what MacIntyre did for eudaimonism, reconstructing its central ideas in more rigorous and defensible form.

The case studies providing positive evidence for Thesis Two follow a roughly historical progression, beginning with the emergence of the projective idea in theological conceptions of divine creativity and its extension to human creativity. The discussion of themes in Arendt and Levinas is inserted at this point, out of historical sequence, because their themes build directly on the idea of divine agapē. I then return to problems with eudaimonistic accounts of weakness and strength of will, which lead to Scotus's decisive break with Aquinas's conception of moral motivation. This paves the way for Kant's account, which fails only in restricting striving will to deontic contexts. In this light, it makes sense that existential psychoanalysis and contemporary analytic work in moral psychology discover a much broader range of possible commitments that can be formed by projective willing. Here is a fuller summary of the steps in Part III:

10. Chapter 9 begins with the example of divine creativity as an ideal counterexample to the erosiac model. For Plato himself appears to have recognized that his erosiac conception of motivation generates a theological problem concerning why God would want there to be a physical universe. This problem led to an alternative concept of divine creative motivation that serves as the first historical paradigm of projective motivation.

11. This revolutionary idea is taken up in a long tradition that understands agapic regard and (more broadly) pure creative initiative in projective terms. This idea develops in Christian theology up to Kierkegaard, who inspired Anders Nygren's analysis of agapic versus erosiac love. We find the same basic idea in Continental philosophers from Martin Buber and Dietrich von Hildebrand to Hannah Arendt and Emmanuel Levinas. Generalizing from these examples, we may say that the antieudaimonist tradition in Christian and Jewish theology seems to be united precisely by its recognition that a crucial element is missing in Aristotelian and Thomistic moral psychologies. Without this element, we cannot understand love and hatred in their pure volitional forms; nor, therefore, can we understand the essence of good or evil. However, a problem originates with Nygren that is inherited by Levinas and Harry Frankfurt: namely, the idea that agapic love can have no reasons or basis at all in the nature of the beloved. This error is corrected in the refined model of projective willing presented at the end of chapter 9, which distinguishes projective from erosiac motives by their content-to-agent directions of fit rather than by the absence or presence of any reasons for the goal. According to this model, the projection of ends always has grounds either in the product-value(s) of the ends or in the process-value(s) of pursuing these ends. Thus the existential model of the will is saved from the arbitrariness that results from Nygren's version.

12. This refined model is illustrated and defended by the study of "radical evil" in chapter 10. The chapter begins with a critique of the Aristotelian account of vice as weakness or ignorance. There are two problems here: psychological eudaimonism reduces evil to weakness of will, and it reduces strength of will to mere *self-control*, that is, resistance to appetitive or emotional temptations. Both these diagnoses can be refuted by a clear look at the phenomena. First, some kinds of evil motivation, which I label "radical," reveal volitional strength rather than weakness. Noting important differences among several kinds or levels of ill will, I argue that the projective model helps explain these differences and make sense of the fact that evil projects can be pursued with the utmost commitment or resolve of the whole self. I then consider in each case what reasons may ground the projection of different kinds of harm to others for their own sake. I also defend

this Kierkegaardian idea of radical evil against MacIntyre's critique. Second, the same kind of willpower at work in cases of self-control is also observable in strong-willed agents who encounter no little internal emotional or appetitive resistance. Existential accounts of volitional strength are therefore more convincing than eudaimonist accounts.

13. Chapter 11 traces this idea that virtues and vices are primarily volitional dispositions into Duns Scotus's innovative conception of the will to justice or righteousness as the true form of moral motivation. I argue that as Scotus conceives it, this motive is clearly projective in structure and is closely related to the projective conception of divine and human agapé that Scotus develops from the Christian idea of divine creativity described in chapter 9. Scotus is the bridge between the ancient and modern portions of this tradition, since his picture directly anticipates Kant's model of the good will.

14. Chapter 11 also defends three theses with respect to Kant. First, the moral will in Kant's *Groundwork* is a species of projective motivation; hence if the Kantian motive of duty is possible, then my main Thesis Two is true. But second, much of the discontent with Kant's model in contemporary moral psychology results from the fact that Kant, like Scotus, thought that a pure moral will was the *only* kind of projective motivation, the only sort that did not simply convert instinctual drives and acquired appetites into maxims by choosing the principle of subjective preference satisfaction. The best neo-Kantian authors, such as Korsgaard, now acknowledge that Kant's own account of self-motivation is much too narrow precisely because it leaves out several kinds of personal commitments made for reasons *other* than universal justice or fairness to all agents capable of autonomy. Thus Thesis Two is broadened into the claim that persons can projectively commit themselves to almost any end that can be found in intelligible thick conceptions of good or worthwhile lives. Kant is correct, in my view, that we can move ourselves to act for the sake of deontic moral considerations (assuming these can be spelled out adequately); but Kant *does not go far enough* in recognizing a wide variety of volitional devotions that are autonomous in the same sense as motivation by the moral law in his account, in opposition to preexisting desires he describes as contingent impulses and inclinations of the pathological psyche.

Third, I argue that Kant, like Scotus, sees libertarian freedom as essential to the will that generates its own motivation to love justice, obey the moral law, or respect persons as inviolable ends. However, the essential structure of projective motivation does not *by itself* entail libertarian freedom. An argument for libertarian freedom has to come either from the conditions of responsibility for acting and willing or possibly from the conditions of modal awareness, that is, having the concept of nonactual possibilities, and other modal concepts founded on this. But these parts of the existential system are beyond the scope of this book.

15. Thus in models of divine creativity, agapé, and moral motivation in Scotus, Kant, and Nygren, we find both precedent and evidence for the existential model of the will. Chapter 12 looks at the emergence of this idea in twentieth-century psychology, especially in the new study of "intrinsic motivation" and in Viktor Frankl's mid-century theory of life-meaning. Frankl's studies concern how human beings shape life plans and help endow their lives with personal meaning (i.e., meaning that is subjectively experienced by the agent). In the psychoanalytic tradition, Frankl's existential critique of Maslow's eudaimonism turns out to be a less rigorous version of the critique of psychological eudaimonism that I give in chapter 7. Frankl's success with logotherapy thus provides strong evidence for the importance of objective values as grounds for projective motivation in the existential model. I support this position with a case study on the self-defeating nature of self-absorption and a critical discussion of Harry Frankfurt's argument that caring is justified by its by-product benefit to caring agents.

16. Chapter 13 takes up Frankfurt's innovative analysis of "caring" as a distinctively volitional phenomenon and argues that we can make sense of this claim and Frankfurt's evidence for it only by understanding such caring as a form of projective motivation with a reflexive component concerning the agent's first-order motives. Starting from work by Elizabeth Anderson, Bernard Williams, Jeffrey Blustein, and others, I then argue that the kind of "commitment" that is an essential component of Frankfurtian caring is not only projective but also distinguished by consequence-transcending grounds. The reasons for an "aretaic" commitment exceed the product-value of the ends to which the agent devotes himself. This feature explains the *unconditionality* found in certain volitional loves, ground projects, or self-defining commitments without fanatically insulating them from critical reason.

17. Chapter 14 defends against Frankfurt's various criticisms a moderate objectivism about broadly ethical criteria (and other "nonmoral" grounds) for worthwhile objects of caring. I argue that (a) there must be nonarbitrary discernible grounds for caring and commitment with objective significance for all agents (against some forms of liberal neutralism); and (b) among these we find many "ethical" considerations in the broad classical sense, including truth, beauty, and aspects of human welfare. In this respect, my account will resemble some "new natural law" list theories of the good. However, my account differs from them by emphasizing, with Ross and Moore, that many ends with intrinsic value worthy of our attention are not themselves components of human well-being or flourishing

(although our volitional relation to them may be part of our good). Since the importance of such ends is not derived from the requirements of justice to persons as ends-in-themselves, their axiological basis requires some other explanation that we still lack.

Following Kierkegaard and Joseph Raz, my analysis retains a sense in which human persons do *create* their own meaning through the volitional appropriation of possible ends; but they could not do this if there were not a variety of forms of intrinsic value that exist (in some way) *prior to the existential will*, to which the will can projectively respond. The chapter concludes with a list, derived from the case studies throughout the book, of both product- and process-values that can potentially ground or rationalize setting long-term goals and purposes that can give meaning to a human life.

This striking result provides starting points for a subsequent existential theory of personal autonomy and authenticity. In particular, it suggests that *human autonomy is founded on the alterity of values*, without which the will that generates autonomous motivation could not operate. This is a generalized and more plausible version of Levinas's result that personal autonomy depends on our being infinitely responsible for the other person, or our experiencing non-erosiac "desire" for their alterity or "Face." Although he was on the right track, Levinas repeated Kant's error and limited his attention to the intrinsic value of persons. In fact, it is not only the highest or inviolable value of persons as ends-in-themselves but the entire range of values comprised in the beautiful, the true, the good, and the meaningful on which our autonomy is based. This is what remains in the existential model of Aquinas's thesis that the human will is constituted with a fixed telos outside itself. Our will is innately oriented to a diverse range of values that extend beyond our *eudaimonia*, and no specific set of them functions as our telos in the classical sense or as defined in A-eudaimonism. However, without being-in-a-world of values worth caring about, we would be able to will nothing at all. This point also distinguishes my moderate account of our volitional powers from the pretensions of Nietzschean will to power. The book concludes with a few reflections on *balancing* the value of volitional commitment to relationships, projects, and goals with the value of authentic response to others whose freedom transcends our agendas.

4. The Limits of This Analysis

Given the range of topics and historical figures taken up in the seventeen steps summarized above, it is important to emphasize several ways in which the tasks of this book are limited, in some cases awaiting further work.

4.1. Autonomy and Motivation Theory

There is no way to construct a decisive demonstration of the existential model of striving will, but together, I believe that the critique of eudaimonism in Part II and the case studies in Part III provide a compelling case for taking this model seriously. This case could be further strengthened by showing that the theory of projective motivation provides solutions to unsolved problems in the theory of personal autonomy. If personal autonomy and authenticity cannot be adequately understood without the existential model of distinctively volitional motives developed in this book, this would be a powerful confirmation of the existential theory. Now, the accounts of caring and commitment that are the focus of chapters 13 and 14 are closely related to the most important work on autonomy and authenticity in the twentieth century, but this topic requires a separate book for adequate treatment. Thus in this book I avoid any in-depth discussion of Frankfurt's notion of volitional identification and its familiar problems, postponing this rich topic for a subsequent volume. Similarly, in this book I avoid any in-depth discussion of contemporary analytic theories of motivation. But in the subsequent volume, the theory of projective motivation must obviously be related to this important body of recent work.

4.2. Action Theory and Psychology

My analyses of both contemporary action theory and psychological theories of human motivation are also limited in obvious ways. I have been able to address only the few ideas from theories of agency that are crucial for my argument, and this book makes no attempt to develop an account of practical reason that could serve as the basis for a normative ethics. However, the ideas developed here provide a foundation for a critique of contemporary analytic theories of action and practical reason.

There is also a lot of important new work in empirical psychology that is relevant to my main theses, which could not be reviewed here for simple reasons of space. The discussions in chapter 11 merely touch on some of the relevant topics, such as the theory of intrinsic motivation. However, psychological analyses of empirical data on motivation are often much more dependent than they realize on basic philosophical assumptions about motivation that inform their interpretation of the evidence. This is especially true, I think, in the development of highly influential recent theories of personality types and trait theory, which are relevant for conceptions of character and virtue. An existentialist must reject several of these accounts, such as the Myers-Briggs–type theory, both as ignoring the will and as too essentialist. For this reason, it is helpful to approach psychological research on motivation and character with an adequate philosophical framework already in place.

4.3. Emotion and Volition

There is a also a rich and growing literature on emotions, in both philosophy and psychology, which is relevant to my theses. Philosophical theories of emotions have undergone radical transformations in the past century, and many of the newer theories concerning the role of rational judgment in emotions are clearly related to my account of willing. Moreover, this significant progress in the philosophy of emotions has led some moral philosophers to assume that it must be in this domain (if anywhere) that we can locate a psychological home for those ground projects, cares, and commitments that we need to understand in order to make progress in finding new foundations for ethics in the broadest sense. But in fact, even the newer cognitive theories of emotion cannot fully explain (or, in some cases, even accommodate) these crucial motivational states. That is because, as the existential tradition has long known, these cares and commitments have volitional features that distinguish them from the sorts of motivation involved in most of the many different kinds of states that we call emotions (for in fact, "emotion" is at best a family term covering several different genuses of psychological states). It may be that various species of emotion—for example, anxiety, interest in a worthy challenge, pride in accomplishment, romantic love, or even spiteful hatred—are closely related to states of caring and commitment. But if so, this is not because aretaic commitment reduces to a kind of emotion, but rather because some "emotions" are really derivative from or dependent on more fundamental volitional states that are not essential to many other species of emotion.

A full review of recent work on motivation would allow a defense of this claim that volitional resolve is not an intrinsically "emotional" process, in the most familiar connotations of that term. These two categories have a more complex relationship than this: (1) When we have clarified the distinctive characteristics of volitional states in their existential sense, we may well see that some motivational states currently described as "emotions" are better understood as states of will. (2) When the moral psychology of volitional motivation is explained (at least in outline), then in this light we may be able to see how distinct emotional states that are not themselves volitional may nevertheless help explain or ground acts of projective motivation or agent resolve. (3) Once the account of will as projective motivation is developed into a full understanding of autonomy or self-determination, we may be able to see how the cultivation and/or suppression of various emotional states may be involved in volitional caring and commitment. In short, several important kinds of willing in the projective sense may *identify* the agent with various related emotions, even though the volitional states are not simply reducible to these emotions.

Because emotional states can stand in these necessary relations with projective motivational states, the two can easily be confused, and this makes it imperative to understand willing in the projective sense *before* exploring its relations with emotion in greater detail. However, for my phenomenological method, this is also a problem, because illustrations of projective motivation will almost always be closely tied to related emotional states, and hence descriptive analysis must work hard to avoid conflating the two. Thus the work in this book needs to be supplemented with a full existential analysis of emotions as part of the broader project of an existential anthropology and existential virtue ethic.

4.4. Value Theory

Although the final chapters of this book make a small contribution to debates about practical normativity and value theory, I have not tried to engage recent work on the range and status of values in any detail. Although I favor moderate realism about values, my task in this book is not to defend any particular thesis about the metaphysical status of intrinsic values. I am only concerned to argue that we seem to find values that extend beyond our own well-being, and that they can serve as a ground for caring and commitment of the self to significant ends without themselves *causing* the motivation that arises from the volitional process of projecting goals based on them. This "middle way" seems to me to capture what is right in both (1) accounts according to which persons actively generate their own projects and interests by endowing with meaning objects and goals that are not in themselves significant; and (2) accounts according to which persons only passively respond to value and significance that is already "there" in the world. A full defense of this middle view does require undertaking the burdens of metaphysical argument, especially since it is part of my larger project to reject both eliminativism and naturalistic reductions of values: values can be correlated with but not reduced to value-neutral properties, just as consciousness can be correlated with but not reduced to physical properties. But these parts of my larger project are beyond the scope of this book.

4.5. The Historical Examples

Finally, it would obviously require an entire book longer than this one to do justice to all the literature on Aristotle's theory of virtue and eudaimonia

24   Will as Commitment and Resolve

that is relevant to my argument. In this flourishing area in contemporary philosophy, there is so much to learn from and respond to that my brief critique of a handful of prominent defenses of Aristotle will necessarily seem inadequate to experts in this field. The same holds for my evaluation of Kant. The literature on Kant's theory of the moral will is too large even to survey adequately here, and so I have chosen my examples carefully, considering and replying to only a few representative accounts. Here again, an expert specializing in Kant's practical philosophy will doubtless find my argument insufficient. To such concerns, I can only repeat the caveat that my main theses are not primarily historical, and so the historical interpretations are primarily illustrative in function.

This book belongs to a special genre of philosophy that we might call *wide-angle syntheses*. It aims to bring together ideas from a broad spectrum of historical periods and from both analytic and Continental thought in the twentieth century. Such a synthesis aims to develop new ideas while also demonstrating their historical precedents through a discussion of a wide array of thinkers, themes, and cases. Such works also generally aim to reach beyond academic philosophers to the broader world of the humanities and the interested public. The downside is that one cannot go into as much detail in any one part of the argument as would be desired in a monograph focused only on that topic. But there must be a place for such wide-angle works in philosophy today if we are to achieve paradigm shifts in our understanding rather than only to elaborate on topics already placed within dominant interpretative framework(s).

5. A Reader's Guide: Ways through the Text

One great advantage of this book's synthetic approach is that it offers something for almost any reader, from the undergraduate interested in philosophy to specialists in particular areas. Readers with more background in Continental philosophy will find the discussion of analysts such as Harry Frankfurt accessible, and likewise, analytic philosophers with little or no exposure to contemporary Continental thought should find Levinas discussed in terms they can easily grasp. (For example, between Frankfurt and Levinas stands Nygren, and the book is designed to make such genre-crossing connections apparent.)

This section is intended to give some suggestions, beyond what can be gleaned from the Analytical Contents, for readers who may first be interested in parts of the book but not the whole. It will also indicate which sections are less technical and thus more generally accessible and which are more technical and thus may require more specialized background. The introduction to each chapter gives more detailed guidance. In general, I use named principles and abbreviations as a simple way to save space and keep track of key ideas, and readers can find a list of these in the Glossary at the end. I also occasionally introduce natural deductions with numbered steps to help clarify the structure of my arguments for readers who appreciate this sort of aid. But readers who do not can generally skim over these deductions without losing the thread of the analysis. In my view, philosophy is not necessarily better when done with p's and q's, but there is also no reason to *avoid* symbolic or schematic representations of complex arguments where these may help clarify or make the ideas more comprehensible. Either way, the goal is to make the ideas more accessible and the arguments more well-reasoned.

Historical Topics

Readers primarily interested in specific historical figures or periods will probably find adequate guidance in the Analytical Contents. Sections focused on Plato, Aristotle, Scotus, and Kant are clearly marked. There is no one section devoted entirely to Aquinas, unfortunately, but his thought figures at points in chapters 4, 5, and 10. Likewise, readers with some background in virtue ethics or neo-Aristotelian thought will find plenty of interest in chapters 7, 8, and chapter 13, section 2.

Religion

Anyone whose interests are primarily in religion or philosophy of religion or in religious ethics might want to start with chapter 9. However, agapic love is also an important theme in chapter 11, section 1.2, and chapter 10 defends the idea that hatred can parallel agapic love in purity (see esp. sect. 2.6). As these suggestions indicate, this is certainly the kind of book that different readers can profitably begin at different points, working their way back to the main argument from more specific subarguments and using the Glossary to understand any piece of terminology defined in earlier chapters.

General Readers

Readers without advanced training in philosophy but interested in existentialism and the will may want to steer clear of more technical sections on analytic philosophy. Such readers can start with the contrast between "Eastern" and "Western" paradigms in chapter 2, the exploration of radical evil in chapter 10, and the discussion of Frankl and Emily Gordon's case in chapter 12. The discussions of MacIntyre on practices in chapter 8 and the discussion of egoism in the second half of chapter 5 have also proven accessible, although both include a couple of slightly more technical pages, which one could easily skim through. Although it contains items that will mean more to readers familiar with Aristotelian ethics, chapter 6, section I could also provide an introduction to the argument of the *Nicomachean Ethics* I for college students or the interested general reader. I like to think that the explanations of Kant's motive of duty, Levinas's "metaphysical desire," and Plato's *Symposium* might play equally useful pedagogical functions.

Continental Thought

Readers primarily interested in twentieth-century Continental philosophy might want to start with chapter 2, since the contrasts developed there have lots of resonances in contemporary Continental ethics, and the brief discussions of Nietzsche and Nancy will be familiar territory. One could jump directly from the end of chapter 2 to chapter 9, including the sections on Arendt and Levinas, which contain this book's main contributions to ongoing Continental debates. However, the discussion of Arendt may make slightly more sense in light of the analysis of themes in Marx's 1844 manuscripts in chapter 8, section 5.3. None of these sections is very technical, and among them, only the Levinas section presupposes any prior background. Continental readers will easily recognize my contrast between projective and erosiac motivation as a development of Levinas's narrower version of a similar contrast. Anyone primarily interested in this theme could read chapter 4 for a more rigorous development of the erosiac model and skip the discussions of Aristotle and eudaimonism by moving straight to chapter 9 on the agapic model. Taken together, these two chapters obviously describe each side of the main contrast around which the whole book is structured.

Analytic Philosophy

Readers who are more interested in the book's contributions to *analytic action theory and moral psychology* but less interested in the historical content might wish to begin with the review of conceptions of the will in chapter 3. This chapter concludes with the first definition of projective motivation, and one could in principle move straight from that point to chapter 9, section 5, where projective motivation is defined more precisely in terms of directions of fit. However, the intervening five chapters are not simply a detour through eudaimonism back to the elaboration of the projective concept. It will help to read the first sections of chapter 4 to understand how the contrast with the erosiac model works, and to attend to the distinction among the three types of erosiac desire and the discussion of egoism in connection with Elster's work in chapter 5. Finally, all of chapters 13 and 14 are devoted to issues in contemporary moral psychology, especially Harry Frankfurt's work on caring.

Technical Sections

The book contains a few more technical sections, including the discussion of the core argument for the existential theory of willing in chapter 4, section 1.2, and the last section of chapter 6 on the A-eudaimonist core argument. Both these sections are helpful for comprehending the overall argument of the book.

Less vital technical discussions are found in chapter 7, section 3.6, on first- and second-order desires; chapter 9, section 2.1 on divine perfection and section 5 on the structure of projective motivation; and chapter 11, section 2.2 on Kant's argument that the motive of duty cannot consist in a desire for any particular set of consequences. In chapter 6, the excursus on the interpretation of the highest good in Aristotle is more complex, but not because of any challenging deductions. Any of these technical sections can be skipped without losing the overall thread.

The distinction between three types of erosiac desire in chapter 5, section 1, can look technical because of the labels, but it is fairly straightforward and intuitive and is constantly referred to throughout the rest of the book. The same is true of the explanation of egoism and the analysis of Aristotle's conception of the highest good in chapter 6: it is aided by diagrams and named principles, but it is not logically that complex. The later chapters on psychology, caring, and commitment involve some fairly sophisticated conceptual distinctions but little complex deductive apparatus.

Chapter 2 introduces my main themes more concretely by considering the familiar sense of "willing" as heroic striving that seems to have been largely forgotten in contemporary accounts of action, autonomy, and freedom. It argues that this heroic sense of "willing" was given a bad name by major schools of Eastern philosophy and by several Western thinkers who also saw it as the will to domination. A countertradition in Western philosophy has defended the heroic will, but often only in its corrupt forms as a will to ascendance. Between these "knockers" and "boosters," there is a more basic existential conception of the striving will, which it is the task of this book to clarify and defend.

2

The Heroic Will in Eastern and Western Perspectives

Overview. This chapter relates the concept of "heroic" or "striving" will introduced in chapter 1 to a positive attitude toward self-assertion prominent in certain Western thinkers and defends it against criticisms found in opposing Eastern traditions. By locating the volitional phenomena at stake within this long-running debate, this chapter distinguishes the existential conception from the extremes in both traditions and defends a moderate view of the will's positive potential. Topics covered run from Hindu and Buddhist teachings through Augustine to Luther, Nietzsche, and contemporary Continental thought. The analysis is accessible to the general reader but also provides a historical frame that should be novel even to readers with advanced training.

The first chapter began by introducing the concept of "heroic" willing as a self-motivated effort to set goals and strive to pursue them; it distinguished this concept from other, thinner notions of the will. This distinction will be developed in more detail in chapter 3. But first, it will be useful to address a fundamental objection to pursuing this concept of willing: namely, that the heroic striving will is biased toward dubious Western values, and so any existential conception developed from it risks valorizing precisely the kind of ambition and self-assertion that prevents peace, enlightenment, and salvation from suffering. The objection is not simply that the existential view is culturally parochial or fails to capture universal features of personhood; more deeply, it is that the existential model encourages one to see life as a conquest or quest for mastery over others or over the world. To examine this concern and to set the stage for the subsequent analyses, I start by acknowledging two opposing attitudes toward the striving will in the history of philosophy and indicating how my account hopes to move between them.

I. The Paradigmatically "Eastern" Attitude toward Will and Willfulness

Underlying many disputes between different philosophical interpretations of the will in Western philosophy is a basic difference in attitude toward willing as such. Since this contrast concerns many thinkers over long periods involving significant cultural changes, I can do no more than paint it in broad strokes, omitting the detailed references that a full history of this subject would involve. The goal here is merely to present the contrast in basic outline, rather than to give a complete account or evaluation for any of the traditions in Eastern philosophy touched on here.

1.1. Hindu, Buddhist, and Daoist Examples

There is a long tradition of Hindu and Buddhist thinkers who have, sometimes explicitly but more often implicitly, doubted the value of willing per se. This tradition, going back at least to the ancient Indian Upanishads, looked negatively on individual self-assertion as a source of conflict and held that true peace could be attained only by a kind of giving up of individuality in favor of group consciousness or even the loss of self in a primordial oneness with the whole of Being. Thus in the Taittireeya Upanishad, we are told to imagine a man with all his worldly desires satisfied and to multiply this by a hundred million times; compared to this, we are told, "A man full of revelation, but without desire, has equal joy."[1] The sages who originated this view thought that willing could only mean self-assertion in a violent or misappropriative sense: in their view, "will" stands for the arrogance that not only imposes form on nature but also desecrates the sacred, forces itself on others, and in general seeks to dominate everything its agent sees as alien. "The impure, self-willed, unsteady man misses the goal and is born again and again."[2] In other words, his willfulness prevents his enlightenment and escape from the cycle of reincarnation.

We are familiar with this view in its more recent guise as the suspicion that active pursuit of demanding worldly goals reflects a deeper desire for self-aggrandizement, an assertion of one's own priorities over everything else, a determination to impose one's will by force, mastering and controlling anything that resists. In fact, this idea is so deeply embedded in the sources of all human culture that the archetypal concept of the profane is expressed partly in terms of that which is mastered, bound down, and destined by the sacred,[3] with the implication that only the Divine has the right to willful appropriation of anything in this world. The willful, proud man will introduce chaos and disrupt this order by trying to possess and dominate, to seize what can never rightfully be his. This negative attitude toward willing thus went hand in hand with the soteriological conception of salvation as self-transcendence via total renunciation of all appropriation and ambition. "The person of superior integrity takes no action, nor has he any purpose for acting."[4] Similarly, a much later text reads: "A noble heart never forces itself forward," since that would be proud self-assertion, and the monk is unconcerned with glory or shame.[5]

In this view, enlightenment leads not to a galvanizing of the will but rather to its dispersal. As Aldous Huxley put it in his laudatory summary of "Mortification and Non-Attachment" in philosophy, "Enlightenment comes when we give up our self-will and make ourselves docile to the workings of Tao in the world around us and in our own bodies, minds, and spirits."[6] Indeed, on this view, ultimate harmony implies a state transcending *all* motivation, a peace in which one is free from the disquieting disturbance of cares and thus beyond the trials of the *samsara*, this world of self-imposed suffering: "As the sun, the eye of the world, is not touched by the impurity it looks upon, so the Self, though one, animating all things, is not moved by human misery but stands outside."[7] The problem is how to tell this supreme state above all motivation from the state below it, that is, the mere inertia of a stone, or the lifelessness of a corpse (Plato, *Gorgias* 492e), though Zen Buddhism might deny that the distinction matters.

In part, this understanding of willing as essentially violent and egoistic seems to trace to the assumption that will serves the ends of pleasure or that will is a kind of strategic practical rationality aimed at desire gratification. In Hindu, Buddhist, and also Daoist religious texts, we find this picture of willing closely associated with a famous critique of hedonism. As Joel Kupperman explains, we owe to Buddhist teachers the arguments (1) "that pleasure typically involves attachment, in that one comes to crave more of (or a repetition of) what is pleasant," so that, given the misfortunes of human existence, "a life oriented towards pleasure will, in effect, alternate fever . . . with boredom"; (2) that since pleasure requires prior frustration, "a realm of constantly guaranteed instant gratification points towards entire boredom"; and (3) that a life devoted to chasing ever-elusive total pleasure, which recedes the closer we get to it, is degrading, self-deceiving, and ultimately humiliating.[8] A will that simply serves the desire for pleasure, then, cannot bring happiness and dignity to human life.

Moreover, all worldly attachments to goods subject to luck are a sign of inferior comprehension on this view. Lao Tze teaches that "Many loves entail great cost; many riches entail heavy losses."[9] This seems to imply that it is better not to love, since emotional attachment leads to violence—a frequent theme in the Eastern tradition. This extends to all forms of commitment to worldly ends: "One should remain ever free of involvements."[10] For engagement in any worldly project not only makes us subject to fortune but also leads to the temptation to hate and dominate whatever stands in our way. As that latter-day Daoist Master Yoda says: "Fear leads to hate, and hate leads to suffering."[11]

Quite similarly, the third-century-B.C. Buddhist aphorisms of the *Dhammapada* teach inner peace through detachment: "Good men, at all times, surrender in truth all attachments," all worldly ambitions.[12] "Eudaimonia," or happiness in its most holistic sense, consists in freedom from dependence on the insecure (temporal, material) objects of desire pursued by average persons in family and social life:

> Let the wise man leave his home life and go into a life of freedom. In solitude that few enjoy, let him find his joy supreme: free from possessions, free from desires, and free from whatever may darken his mind.
> For he whose mind is well-trained in the ways that lead to light, who surrenders the bondage of attachments and finds joy in his freedom from bondage, who free from the darkness of passions shines in pure radiance of light, even in this mortal life he enjoys the immortal Nirvana.[13]

Yet this work is insightful enough to recognize that the spiritual discipline of the sage is also one kind of heroic effort: "Those who have high thoughts are ever striving," although their "passion is peace."[14] So the striving will of the sage to reject all worldly desires and bodily lusts must involve a form of motivation distinct from all such appetites, and it can be described in timocratic metaphors (as Plato also saw): "the greatest of victories is the victory over oneself," and thus the sage's life is "lived with courage and powerful striving."[15]

This striving for wisdom is essentially different from the quests of "those who shamelessly are bold and self-assertive, crafty and cunning" in pursuit of temporal goods. Rather, the sage exhibits the inner strength of "those who peacefully strive for perfection, who free from self-seeking are not self-assertive, whose life is pure, who see the light."[16] It seems that the Buddhist authors of this work clearly recognize a virtuous form of motivation initiated by the self, but they reserve it for the will to detachment and deny it to any form of worldly ambition. In that sense, as Chris Gowans points out, "Kant's insistence that the will is the locus of moral value is reflected in the Buddha's belief that the moral quality of our intentions is what is primarily important in determining the morality of our actions."[17] But they disagree about what the ultimate motive of moral actions is.

It is interesting in this light that the *Bhagavad Gita* also opens with the metaphor of war, although its hero, Arjuna, refuses to fight his kinsmen and, like Socrates, would rather suffer than do evil.[18] His teacher, Krishna, advises him to fight anyway, without concern for earthly pain and pleasure, since the soul is immortal and cannot be killed.[19] On this view, it is possible to fight in the outer, visible world without any real inner care for this world's pleasures or powers. But to achieve this inner detachment itself requires a kind of volitional focus or effort; by contrast, "endless are the thoughts of the man who lacks determination."[20] Indeed, Krishna recommends a kind of pure discipline that does not even directly target enlightenment: "Set thy heart upon thy work, but never on its reward; Work not for reward, but never cease to do thy work."[21] Thus although the sage transcends all desires and passions and rejects all quest for possession of earthly goods, he does so by cultivating "an unwavering mind."[22]

Jeffrey Blustein describes this as a form of negative "caring about caring," that is, an effort directed at "the elimination of cares, towards disengagement from life." He also notes that in the Buddhist ideal, even this higher-order will to detachment is supposed ultimately to undo itself: "Eventually, when we have severed our attachments to the world and freed ourselves of all first-order cares, caring about [not] caring will also fall away."[23] There is clearly a difficult question here about how willing can eliminate itself; this seems on its face to be a pragmatic contradiction, although I will not argue here that it is metaphysically impossible. What remains clear is that the Hindu, Buddhist, and Daoist traditions regard first-order devotions to goals external to the self as attachments that prevent one from attaining Nirvana, or blessed peace.

For convenience, I label this as the paradigmatically "Eastern" attitude toward willing. But I do not mean that there were no philosophers from Eastern cultures who dissented from it.[24] There is not only a good deal of diversity among different traditions in Eastern philosophy and religion but also diversity of interpretation of central doctrines among different authors and subtraditions within a broad context such as Buddhism. So my summary of "the" Eastern view is to some extent a simplifying caricature, although it will be heuristically sufficient for my purposes.

1.2. Greek Examples

To this crucial caveat I add another: I do not mean that only philosophers born and educated in Eastern cultures subscribed to this view, which is labeled "Eastern" only for convenience. The classical Greek thinkers I discuss in subsequent chapters were heavily influenced by this broadly "Eastern" tradition, as were the Roman Stoics and other Hellenistic philosophers. This debt owed to earlier Eastern religion is the reason why Huxley was able to interpret Greek philosophers and Eastern sages as part of the same universal tradition or "perennial philosophy." Except for the Sophists, not only do all the major Greek schools repeat and refine the Hindu/Buddhist critique of hedonism, reshaping it in novel ways; they also agree with the Buddha's argument that it is a mistake to "seek enduring happiness by trying to attach ourselves to things that are in constant change."[25] In addition, the whole later tradition of eudaimonist moral philosophy from its beginning implicitly assumed that individual self-assertion is likely to be a sign of unbridled passion or uncontrolled *thumos*, which is self-destructive. The problem is not that self-will or assertiveness must necessarily be materially egoistic (i.e., acquisitive or ambitious for power), for its aims may not always be self-interested in this sense. More fundamentally, the problem is that self-will is perceived as inherently *chaotic*, unpredictable and disorderly, and insubordinate in its presumptuousness. The rule of right reason, by contrast, imposes a kind of calm control that is unmoved in itself. Or if it is moved by the beauty of the Good, rational appetite is eventually dispersed at the attainment of true happiness, which, lacking nothing desirable, must be completely unmotivated to change. This is correlated with the classical idea of perfection as a stasis without any reason for change, personified as an unmoved mover. The Divine is unperturbed by any kind of will to development, because that would signal imperfection.[26] For example, as Nussbaum notes, Epicurus held that "The gods are complete: that is what it is to be divine, without limit or need."[27]

Of course, the different classical schools reflect differing degrees of influence by the Eastern ideal on classical philosophy. In their emphasis on *ataraxia* or "tranquillity," the Epicureans and Stoics valorized dispassion in a way that Aristotle did not. As Nussbaum writes, "These philosophers do not simply analyze the emotions, they also urge, for the most part, their removal from human life. They depict the flourishing human life as one that has achieved freedom from disturbance and upheaval, above all by *reducing the agent's commitments to unstable items in the world*."[28] Just as for the Hindu sages, the erosiac conception of motivation as a lack or disturbance in our psychic homeostasis, coupled with the instability of fortune, implies that strong emotions regarding luck-affected goods will be destructive to our happiness. If these emotions are contingent or avoidable rather than natural and necessary, then we should excise them to avoid unsatisfiable desires. Plato likewise argued that virtue would be sufficient for eudaimonia, and hence the guardians of his ideal republic would have "no room for the emotions of pity, fear, and grief. For nothing that is not a lapse in virtue is worth taking very seriously."[29] This attitude is explicitly opposed to caring deeply about particular loved ones, as Nussbaum notes. And she admits that "There seems to be something cold and even brutal in the wise man's self-sufficiency, in this hardness with which he denies his need of others and limits his investment in their lives."[30] Yet this is the result of the Eastern sage-ideal and its rejection of all active engagements in temporal affairs as veiled forms of self-will.

Aristotle does not go this far, since on his account, human eudaimonia must involve noble activities, especially philosophical contemplation and high-minded engagement in the affairs of one's state moved by civic concern for the common good, and the noble sentiments or emotions that go along with such activities. As Nussbaum says, for Aristotle, "there are things in the world that it is right to care about."[31] But seen against the larger background of a philosophical culture steeped in the Eastern paradigm, this must be recognized as Aristotle's way of *incorporating* into the eudaimonistic model an ideal that is essentially out of tune with its Eastern origins, that is, an ideal of self-assertion and courageous challenge-seeking that comes instead from archaic Greek poetry, from the old Homeric honor code. In other words, Aristotle is compromising between the Hindu ethic inherited through Plato and a diametrically opposed Homeric ethic that it was Plato's chief goal to overthrow. Indeed, it is the primary purpose of all philosophy in the Socratic tradition to resist and overcome this feudal concept of nobility based on the charismatic rule of the warrior-king, along with the powers of fate that help or hinder his cause without moral principle.[32] So Aristotle's ideal of the active life of virtue may not at first glance seem particularly close in spirit to the ideal of the Hindu sages; but that is only because within their basic framework, Aristotle tames and domesticates precisely that kind of timocratic, glory-seeking self-assertion that led the Hindu sages to regard all willing as *conatus ascendi*, or as violent self-imposition upon the world. For this purpose, Aristotle finds that recognizing the extent to which our happiness remains subject to fortune can be important because it makes pity possible and saves us from the hubris of the pitiless tyrant.[33]

Arguably, the Stoics still valued active effort toward positive results (when "appropriate") more than the Epicureans did, since they rejected the idea that negative equanimity as mere freedom from desire or pain was an intrinsic good. Thus Cicero criticizes Epicurus for holding that the mere absence of pain is a real (kinetic) pleasure: "This is not the sort of thing than can arouse appetitive desire. The static condition of freedom from pain produces no motive force to impel the mind to act."[34] By contrast, he understands virtue as involving "a steadfast seriousness of purpose";[35] it is a form of heroic resolve aimed at positive moral ends and not only at detachment. For example, it includes above all the courage to die without hesitation for one's country in battle—something the less timocratic Epicureans rarely praised, though they preached against fear of death. It could also include the courage to commit suicide when honor demanded it.[36] Virtue is thus both cognitive and volitional, or noetic and spirited, for the Stoics: "Virtue requires a vast amount of study and experience, which the other arts do not. Moreover virtue demands life-long steadiness, firmness of purpose, and consistency."[37] This emphasis on heroic striving distances Cicero somewhat from the Hindu sages.

1.3. Augustine and Luther

Nevertheless, the enormous influence of this Eastern heritage extends far beyond those thinkers who are explicitly conscious of any "Oriental" debt. For instance, it is clearly seen in the attitudes of St. Augustine, who feared that the human will is inherently prone to reject any external authority or objective standards above it: "It turns towards its own private good when it wants to be under its own control."[38] Like the Hindu and Buddhist teachers and the Stoic thinkers they influenced, Augustine believes that what appears on the outside as lust for pleasures or inordinate desire for any worldly good begins inwardly as rebellious self-assertion against God: "For it is pride that turns one away from wisdom . . . someone whose good is God wants to be his own good, as if he were his own God."[39] Thus all sin begins with insubordination of the will; the devil originally turns from God toward himself, because he "wills to enjoy his own power in perverse imitation of God."[40] This is precisely the "willfulness" so masterfully expressed in Milton's portrait of Satan in *Paradise Lost*: "Better to reign in Hell than serve in Heaven."[41] To strive for any achievement made up of temporal goods is to be part of "the city of this world, a city which aims at dominion, which holds nations in enslavement, but is itself dominated by that very lust of domination."[42]

Indeed, Augustine sees this *libido dominandi*, the "lust for power" exhibited by the Roman people,[43] as the basic tendency of the unrepentant and unsaved human will. Although God made human beings equal in his image, and did not intend any human beings to have dominion over others,[44] "Pride hates a fellowship of equality under God, and seeks to impose its own dominion on fellow men."[45] Thus the will to dominate is the basic form of corruption in Augustine's analysis, although he does allow that all natural human powers, including the powers of our will, are good in themselves; they are simply subordinate to eternal goods, such as justice.[46]

Extending Augustine's thought, Luther and Calvin arguably took the further step of regarding all human self-assertion as willfulness or a stubborn will to misappropriation of powers and rights not given to us by God; in other words, whatever our will initiates is an expression of pride or a rejection of our natural place. In that case, the humility and repentance necessary for salvation cannot themselves be volitional undertakings but must consist in a diminishment of the will. The humbled person will give up dogged pursuit of her own projects and let herself be guided by God. Salvation, thus understood as total capitulation to God which breaks the self-aggrandizing drive and pride in all one's pursuits and practices, is itself not earned or voluntarily chosen but received solely as grace. And if such grace could even be voluntarily refused or accepted by our own power, then either stance would still be at least partially a self-determined act of the will. So, given that willing is proud, we must say that the very acceptance of grace is also caused solely by God.[47] Thus it is the interpretation of willing as essentially profane that motivates the doctrine of salvation *sola fide*.

Luther provides perhaps the clearest illustration of this profanization of the will. In his vitriolic response to Erasmus's argument that total divine determination of the will would render pointless any effort for moral self-reform, Luther wrote: "You say: Who will endeavor to reform his life? I answer: Nobody! No man can! God has no time for your self-reformers, for they are hypocrites. The elect who fear God will be reformed by the Holy Spirit. The rest will perish unreformed."[48]

Erasmus had already posed the insightful objection that *publishing* the doctrine of total divine predestination as an edifying religious teaching is pragmatically self-contradictory, since this doctrine implies that the act of teaching it cannot change any reader's soul. To this, Luther responds:

> These truths are published for the sake of the elect, that they may be humbled and *brought down to nothing* and so saved. The rest resist this humiliation. They condemn the teaching of self-desperation [or spiritual helplessness]. They wish to have left a little something that they may do themselves. Secretly they continue proud, and enemies of the grace of God.[49]

It is abundantly clear in these passages that Luther regards *any* human initiative whatsoever—any movement of the will not solely caused by God and attributable only to Him—as a misappropriation of divine right, an arrogation of power, or nothing more than a willful refusal to submit. Salvation requires complete "humiliation," a state in which the independent human will is totally *eliminated*, brought down to "nothing." Yet in spite of himself, Luther here inadvertently implies something strictly inconsistent with his total predestinarian doctrine, namely that human beings do retain a single power: the higher-order will to refuse saving humiliation, to keep their will alive against the order to surrender unconditionally to the Sovereign who demands a total monopoly on all volitional power. In other words, the one and only thing we can truly will on our own initiative is to rebel; or, at least when God allows us to act on our own, this is the only thing we can do. Since no effort of ours can contribute even in the smallest way to our salvation, "does it not evidently follow that when God is not present to work in us, everything we do is evil?"[50] For Luther, then, rebellion would almost seem to be our natural function, our very telos! Our nature, then, must be completely destroyed for us to be saved.

2. The Paradigmatically "Western" Attitude

2.1. Baconian Hope

The view bequeathed to us by Augustine and brought into modern pietist faith by Luther has ever been in tension with another view in Western philosophy, which is especially prevalent in the history of Western political thought. It dates back at least to the heroic conception of courage in the honor codes of the Attic tribes in Homeric times and of the Germanic shield-kings in the Dark Ages of northern Europe. At the core of this view is the idea that *taking initiative can be good*, that motivating oneself to creative endeavors or undertaking challenging quests for noble ends is a key part of what makes life meaningful. In this countertradition, self-assertion is viewed in a positive light and need not constitute rebellion nor pride in the sense of a will to misappropriation. The self-assertive individual may distinguish herself from her peers, but this can be a side effect of dogged pursuit of noble goals for their own sake. The agent's motive in taking initiative or departing from the status quo need not be hatred of rivals, nor a resolve to reject tradition out of hand, nor a determination to self-aggrandizement by any means necessary. These arrogant attitudes are certainly possible for the human will in its heroic or striving sense, but they are hardly its only possible expressions. Even the desire to conquer and rule can be positive when directed against forces that should be overcome, such as the recalcitrance of a nature that prefers not to yield its fruits and the natural evils of human misfortune and suffering.

Centuries later, this is precisely the spirit we find in Francis Bacon's great hopes for a positive science with technological results that will improve human well-being and in John Stuart Mill's strident calls for social reforms, such as universal education, that will relieve ignorance and misery for the masses. As Charles Taylor argues (contra Heidegger and some Frankfurt School thinkers), although technology and instrumental reason may have become "an iron cage" for us, their rise has *not* been rooted solely in a will to domination that flatters our "self-determining freedom" nor in "an overdeveloped *libido dominandi*" that seeks mastery of nature for its own sake.[51] Rather, we have developed technology and complex means-ends reasoning in part to advance the causes of "ordinary life":

> The sense that the life of production and reproduction, of work and the family, is what is important for us, has also made a crucial contribution, for it has made us give unprecedented importance to the production of the conditions of life in ever-greater abundance and the relief of suffering on an ever-wider scale. . . . We are heirs of Bacon, in that today, for instance, we mount great international campaigns for famine relief or to help the victims of floods. We have come to accept a universal solidarity today, at least in theory, however imperfect in practice, and we accept this under the premiss of an active interventionism in nature. . . . This practical and universal benevolence also gives a crucial place to instrumental reason.[52]

Taylor's insight is that the quest for scientific knowledge as a source of technological solutions to everyday problems has often exemplified all the undaunted determination and perseverance of which the heroic will is capable; this quest has not been simply an arrogant *conatus ascendi* or will to conquer the resistant and glorify the self. Likewise in religious, moral, and political affairs, many of our greatest teachers and reformers—ironically even those who espouse paradigmatically "Eastern" attitudes toward willing, like Luther—have been persons who took great risks, initiated creative breaks from the past, and struck out in a new direction. In short, they have been strong-willed persons of character. Certainly the leaders of fascism, with their intense will to domination, also illustrated the negative possibilities of striving will as an essential human capacity; but the self-aggrandizing purposes they pursued are hardly the *only* ones to which human persons can devote their whole being.

Thus, as our heroes demonstrate, passionate assertion of one's willpower in dogged pursuit of worthwhile goals is *not* equivalent to or necessarily connected with "self-assertion" in any sense that connotes competitive desires, egoism, status-seeking, or vicious pride. Recognition of this fact I will call "the Western attitude." For "industry," in the old sense of applying oneself to beneficial tasks, became a key virtue in the attitude Weber rather misleadingly labeled the "Protestant work ethic." This involves more than just a willingness to work hard for a stable place in the world and social status with one's peers. It also involves valuing creativity, invention, and originality and conceiving these as goods to be achieved only through risking a quest for the new—and so understood, this attitude was hardly limited to Protestants in the modern period. The passion for innovation is not necessarily a treachery against established authority; rather, to live and grow spiritually, we have to find challenges and continually enhance the old with the new. Human beings intrinsically tend to find fulfillment not just in variety per se, but in variation of tasks, obstacles, and tests of excellence. We look for opportunities to apply our ingenuity to persisting problems and even to find new problems to solve if we do not have enough already. This attitude also says that ambition can be good when properly focused and constrained. Not only can it function as the engine of progress for society; proper ambition within moral limits is also essential to a person's sense of his or her self-worth. As John Rawls has rightly said, our society holds that the freedom to pursue one's just conception of the good is itself a great good, essential to self-esteem.[53]

This "Western" attitude is also likely to see quietude or lack of initiative as a sign of complacency, weakness, or despair rather than as a sign of spiritual purity. Elements of this view have achieved a prominent place in the frontier tradition and Emersonian ideals of "self-reliance" that so strongly influence current American ideology. For example, think of our typical praise for the "self-made man" (or woman), the "go-getter" attitude in business, or the person who "pursues his dream." We also tend to respect someone who values his or her work for its own sake. Consider W. Howard Ulrich of Lancaster, Pennsylvania, who continued working at Morgan Stanley until he was *ninety* years old, served on his high school alumnae board and his church's building committee, and helped run the local Optimist Club.[54] It seems most unlikely that Mr. Ulrich was motivated primarily by the lure of money, status, pleasure, or any other external incentive; rather, it is more likely that he was kept going so long by his dedication to these tasks—a motivation sustained by his own will.

2.2. Will to Power as a Corrupt Species of Striving Will

Unfortunately, in the history of Western philosophy, this positive attitude toward willpower was first theoretically framed and interpreted only in reaction to the Eastern negation of the heroic will. And as a negation of the original negation, like all negative reactions, this willpower ideology accepted too many of the presuppositions of the position that it dialectically inverted. In particular, its most vehement spokesmen in early-modern Western political philosophy tended to accept far too readily the leading Eastern idea that all willing is willfulness, or that self-assertion in all its forms is veiled conceit or concealed self-aggrandizement. Thus, at least in *philosophical* defenses of the paradigmatically Western view (as opposed to its literary representations and its actual embodiment in many persons' lives), this Eastern judgment was usually not denied; rather, the most extreme philosophical exponents of the Western attitude simply insisted that such willfulness is glorious, courageous, manly, or great. Harking back to the (defeated) amoral Homeric conception of nobility and virtue (the *kalon* and *arête* in their charismatic sense), every expositor of this view, from Greek Sophists such as Thrasymachus and Callicles to early-modern writers like Machiavelli and Hobbes, proclaimed that willing *is indeed* all that the Hindu sages and their manifold followers condemned it for being. They only insisted that instead of condemning the will for this, we should revel in its vitality and celebrate its haughty self-validation. In effect, they said that this flame of will may consume itself, as the sages predicted, but in the meantime it will burn twice as bright for living half as long![55]

This position is, of course, most fully developed and defended by Nietzsche, whose theory implausibly regards all human motives as expressions (conscious or unconscious) of the "will to power" or *libido dominandi*—the drive for hierarchical triumph or ascendance over others—which he regards as the essence of all "life." Nietzsche is innovative in his theory of motivation since, unlike so many others, he rejects the idea that we can explain all human action in terms of the desire for overall happiness or the drive to satisfy various instinctual and learned desires. This is sometimes understood as a simple inversion of rational control over desires and passions. Thus, as Robert Solomon puts it, Nietzsche's "vigorous and spine-chilling notion of the 'Will to Power' . . . emphasizes not aesthetics but something else, 'energy,' 'enthusiasm,' 'strength,' as well as 'self-mastery,' which does not mean the conquest of the passions but rather their cultivation."[56] This cultivation, however, involves the determination to self-expression that Nietzsche sees as underlying all consumptive organic desires and emotional yearnings. But in the name of this mystical life-force, which is the impulse to domination or absolute ascendance, Nietzsche rejects every moral ideal that could make social life or cooperation for a better world possible. With the Hindu sages and their descendants in mind (including his father, a Lutheran minister), he dismisses these "slave moralities" as attempts to subvert our noblest destiny or to drain the life-force from our will. Thus the will as simple creative projection of goals or plain engagement with long-term ends and projects because of their intrinsic value is entirely obscured in Nietzsche's jeremiad against moral obligations to others.

Thus Nietzsche celebrates the heroic will *only in its corrupt forms*; he defends the heroic will against the Eastern critique only by equating it precisely with the deficient mode of striving will against which this critique had a good deal of validity. He portrays the heroic will as an agonistic struggle for superiority, a beautiful but tortured assertion of self against everything else, a pure *conatus ascendi* in Spinoza's sense.[57] While Nietzsche took himself to be reviving the ideal of heroic character in Norse/Germanic mythology, in fact he promoted only a distorted amoral version of it.[58] All that is valuable in the heroic will, including its existential importance for the formation of the self, must now be retrieved from behind the shadow that Nietzsche cast over it.

This problem is not unique to Nietzsche, of course. It also infects Emerson's exaggerated conception of individual independence and private conscience as the measure of "manliness" and authentic life.[59] Earlier, it sometimes appears in Hobbes's celebration of human inventiveness and Bacon's enthusiasm for new inquiry, the creation of new scientific methods, and "the art itself of invention and discovery."[60] Bacon praises thinkers with the "spirit" of empirical inquiry that is "not enslaved to their own or to other people's dogmas but favoured freedom."[61] Yet he constantly protests that his rejection of Greek metaphysics and traditional logic is not for the sake of personal ambition, but rather for "human progress and empowerment."[62] Thus in modern Western authors in whom the idea of striving will is salient, the distinction between its pure form and its corrupt expression as the "will to will" (a phrase that first occurs in Nietzsche's *Nachlass*) or the ambition to make one's mark on the world is often obscured.

This explains how, in his otherwise insightful history of the will in modern philosophy, as great an intellectual historian as Yirmiyahu Yovel could mix features generic to the striving will in all its forms with other features peculiar to its arrogant and self-aggrandizing species. In broad brush strokes, Yovel writes that:

> The modern will is typically self-assertive, expansive, and individualistically shaped; in most of its varieties it strives to self-realization and self-enhancement, to personality and autonomy; it stresses initiative and the attribution of responsibility.... The modern will openly questions tradition, values novelty and innovation, unsettles rigidly received rules.... In all that the will is typically restless, stretching beyond itself and its present situation in constant search of the new, the distant, the different.[63]

This description captures part of the paradigmatically Western recognition of the positive potential in striving will, in particular the idea of transcending one's existing desires and seeking new challenges. As Yovel says, "the human will tends to posit for itself the goals it pursues."[64] But his description also makes the will formally self-interested, and he still interprets it as an expression of the "mind's fundamental Eros," now oriented toward material and worldly goals.[65]

The almost Marinettian futurism of Yovel's characterization derives from confusing the *way* that projective volition generates new motivation with particular goals typically pursued through willed striving in the modern period, such as the displacement of traditional orders, or self-aggrandizement through risk and conquest: "The modern will refuses to conform to the constraints of the world as given. It strives to change the world in its own image and interests: to reshape and control outer nature (through technology, planning, resource exploitation, etc.)."[66] Although this surely describes Bacon, it seems to be a short step from this to the will as "enframing" or possessing the world. Thus Yovel cites colonialism as the attitude that "the new geographic and ethnic horizons were to be filled and dominated by an expansive human (i.e., European) will."[67] Beyond simple monetary greed, he surmises that the Spanish conquistadors were driven by "a will that wills its own infinite use and exertion."[68]

This is a plausible explanation of Cortez, but the will to domination of the world, or to the pure enjoyment of one's willpower in facing any challenge, is not the only possible (or even the paradigm) form of projective motivation. Self-motivation as creative initiative does not necessarily aim at overturning traditional orders, at rebellious self-assertion, or at the conquest of other wills independent of our own. Projective motivation is a *way* of setting and pursuing ends; it has no essential relation to positing self-aggrandizing or militaristic ends. It is also possible to will the beautiful, the true, or the good, to restrain one's ambitions within right limits, or to attune oneself to values that require putting aside one's interest in molding the world's material or making a mark on reality. As Ogion tells his apprentice Sparrowhawk in Ursula Le Guin's *Wizard of Earthsea*, "Manhood is patience. Mastery is nine times patience," and the world does not exist merely for our use or delight in power.[69] In devotion to an order higher than his own will, Ogion's will is stronger than Cortez's. Thus, to defend the paradigmatically Western conception of striving will as potentially good or to recognize the proper value of what John Casey calls the "active virtues (so admired by Hume and Gibbon), which make a man formidable" does not require endorsing the "assertive, proud ethical tradition" of Homer.[70] Nor does it necessarily require denying the Kantian position that moral worth cannot depend on fortune but only on factors that the agent can control:[71] that is an independent normative question.

3. The Continental Inversion

Not surprisingly, many thinkers in recent Continental philosophy have reacted to the Nietzschean version of the modern will with one more dialectical inversion, taking them back to something like the original Eastern attitude that he so vehemently despised. This third negation is perhaps clearest in the philosophy of Emmanuel Levinas, who appears to condemn not only willing as active initiation or goal-seeking planning but even ordinary intentional states of perception and judgment as "violent," grasping, and essentially other-subordinating. In short, the violence of willfulness now infects *all* human intentionality, turning our minds into consuming centers bent on appropriating or absorbing the world into ourselves, or making it fit into our preconceptions and the terms of our own consciousness. Haunted by Nietzsche and Sartre, and determined to restore the possibility of agapē—the non-egoistic neighbor-love that Nietzsche diagnosed as *ressentiment* and Sartre rejected as impossible—Levinas becomes almost Augustinian in his fear that anything short of total submission to the Other to whom we are always-already responsible is a symptom of pride and willfulness. All the requirements of reciprocity and mutual recognition in universalist ethics become suspect as likely covers for the acquisitive self or for possessive, totalizing, violent, and domineering self-assertion, reckless of our relations to others and inimical to caring attentiveness to individual needs. And this Levinasian view, which would have sickened Nietzsche and confirmed his worst fears, has influenced a whole generation of later French and American thinkers.

To take just one example, in an innovative book, Jean-Luc Nancy argues that the freedom that is "the essential fact of existence"[72] cannot be understood as the correlate of any kind of *necessity* known to philosophy nor explained in terms of any modal concept of possibility or causality,[73] for this always turns freedom into the "free *will*" that makes the subject into the master of its representations.[74] Like the existentialists preceding him, Nancy is opposed to the idea that freedom is just a *property* that persons possess or something that entities simply exhibit or instantiate if they are individual subjects.[75] So he follows Heidegger in rejecting what he understands as the "voluntaristic will"[76] and all theoretical explanations of freedom, which only block our experience of freedom as a practical openness or "free space" for existence.[77] Like Heidegger, he avoids interpreting freedom in terms of will, for the latter is tainted as Fichtean "will to will," or arrogant self-assertion for its own sake. Thus the concept of will has once again become suspect in Continental thought, just as it has been for very different reasons in twentieth-century analytic philosophy.

Despite being strongly influenced in his break with Freud by "Nietzsche's Dionysian will—an exuberant, creative affirmation of life,"[78] Otto Rank understood better. Against both extremes, he writes that "The will in itself is not as 'evil' as the Jew-hating Schopenhauer believes along with the Old Testament, nor as good as the sick Nietzsche would like to see it in his glorification."[79] Rather, it is the capacity by which the ego defines itself through "end-setting," which Rank encouraged in therapy. As such, the will is not reducible to will to power or to "willfulness, obstinacy, protest, insistence, and aggression."[80] Without exercising his or her will to set life goals that are not forced on her by an "alien will" (nor by reaction against such coercion), a person cannot achieve an authentic identity, or "develop himself into that which he is."[81] Even if this suggests an overly individualistic conception of goal-setting, it is a valuable corrective to the antivolitional bias of much recent Continental thought.

4. Contemporary Moral Psychology as Corrective

I agree with Rank that the extreme positions in both the Eastern and Western attitudes toward the will are wrong. The resources to correct these errors and establish a clearer picture of willing are found in diverse work on ethics and moral psychology in both recent analytic and Continental philosophy. Within philosophical research on closely related topics such as autonomy, caring, integrity, character, virtue, and self-understanding, as well as in work on moral theory, we find the clues needed to see what was right in the Western attitude toward willing without merely inverting or simply ignoring the Eastern critique. In this literature, we find a convergence from many directions on the conclusion that willing *understood as commitment* to lasting causes and life projects is central not only to becoming a self or individual unified by resolute cares but also to having a meaningful and fulfilling life.[82] "Will" is not primarily a matter of subduing some material for the sheer joy of conquering, or mastering some recalcitrant force, or dominating whatever is alterior to our will or independent of us. This will-to-will interpretation confuses existential willing with its *perversions*, or deficient modes.

Reconstructing the alternative *moderate* idea of willing and justifying the positive attitude toward it in Western thought are the main aims of this book. This is partly a normative task, although my goal is not to develop a specific system for making moral judgments or to present a specific normative ethics. However, my task is closely related to "ethics" in the broad sense of an inquiry into how best to live one's own life (including what kinds of communities are required for the best sort of human life). For, as I construe it, the will's most important function is precisely to set life goals, define personal ambitions, and provide the motivational staying-power necessary to pursue worthwhile ends in the face of adversity.

Interestingly, many of the best authors in recent moral theory, such as Joel Feinberg, Peter Railton, Michael Stocker, and Derek Parfit, have argued that such primary projects or goals of an agent's life may not be *egoistic* in any substantive sense, since her own pleasures, power, or material resources may form no part of the intended end. But they have not explained why agents *devote themselves* to such ends nor even what it really means to devote oneself to something. Likewise, authors such as Harry Frankfurt and Bernard Williams also recognize the fundamental importance of non-egoistic "ground projects," or selfless ends that can be as important to us as life itself, or with which we can *identify* wholeheartedly, in defining the practical identity of our self.[83] But since they are interested primarily in using such examples against a certain style of moral theory—in particular, construing such projects and pursuits as "personal" or private imperatives that can conflict with the impartiality of neo-Kantian moral standards—they have not said enough about *how we form* such ground projects or wholehearted commitments or what kind of motivation they involve. So although the notion of commitment has come to play a crucial role in recent moral psychology and in metaethical debates, its relationship to classical accounts of human motivation remains unanalyzed, and thus its radical implications are not yet perceived.

Some philosophers who rely explicitly or at least implicitly on this concept of commitment even seem to think that figuring out what it involves is a task we should simply leave to empirical psychology—as if the answer could not make any fundamental difference to ethics. They forget that contemporary psychological theories are still crucially conditioned and influenced by precisely the dominant philosophical theories of motivation of the past—that is, the eudaimonist, Hobbesian, Humean, and Kantian ones—that we may need to reevaluate. Whether any of these doctrines can adequately explain the phenomena of caring and commitment—and if not, what revisions we might have to make to accommodate these phenomena—is exactly what we need to know. While empirical psychology may help in this analysis, it cannot be a theoretically unbiased or neutral source of information. Only a philosophical analysis that places this question in its required historical context and that provides a critical phenomenology of these experiences can address this matter adequately.[84]

At the same time, unfortunately and ironically, writers focusing on philosophical accounts of human motivation have largely ignored these phenomena of caring and commitment that are central to recent attempts to revive ethics in its broadest sense. In analytic moral psychology, recent scholarship intended explicitly to address the nature of human motivation has focused largely on the relation between different species of "desire" and various kinds of belief, especially moral judgments in the neo-Kantian sense. But the resolution of recent debates about "internalism" and "externalism" depends on questions about the will as a motivational faculty.

In Chapter 13, I will argue that to play the roles they do in our lives, ground projects and long-term commitments require that the agent actively sustain a certain kind of *resolve* to continue pursuing the end despite changes in external circumstance and a reflexive determination to continue caring about one's goal, whatever other desires may conflict with it. These states involve an ongoing effort not just to pursue the goal but to keep it *as* a central goal of one's life; the agent exercises a determination to stay on target. I will speak of these distinctive motivational states involving such self-motivation as states of *the will*. In this sense, "the will" is, then, a *motivational faculty*, a psychological capacity for the special kind of self-motivation we see in forming commitment and maintaining resolve. Without understanding the will in this way, we cannot make sense of concepts that are indispensable for a moral theory that goes beyond questions of basic social justice to the broad ethical issues about how to live, what to strive for, or how we can shape our own character.

As I will argue in Chapter 14, if we are persons defined by willing in the sense explained in this book, then Frankfurt's question concerning what is *worth* caring about must be both important to us[85] and at least partially answerable on rational grounds as well. Differently put, there must be some objective criteria, at least partially accessible to reflective human reason, through which we can recognize the value of different goals and objects of pursuit—as well as the value of these pursuits themselves. It is on the basis of such recognition that we can commit ourselves to life projects. We want the purposes to which we devote our time and energy to be *worth* attention in their own right. Even if some part of their value is imposed by our caring itself, this movement must still be based on some other discernible value that we did not simply invent or posit. Thus it undermines the possibility of authentic caring to assume that our cares can have no articulable basis or that they cannot even be subject to philosophical critique. The values that are the basis of our caring may not play much role in determining our political judgments about the basic structure of society, but we could not be persons, let alone citizens, without them.

However, Frankfurt was reluctant to reach this conclusion, and thus, despite his intended departure from Kant, his account of what we care about has remained too formal.[86] A substantive analysis of our grounds for caring includes attention to the classical triad of the True, the Beautiful, and the Good but also attention to other less familiar criteria. My account of these criteria for caring, as cursory as it is, is thus an essential part of my existential theory of the will. For, as I argue, we can make reference to such criteria without having to trace their importance for us to a traditional eudaimonist version of teleology.

To lay the ground for these later analyses, chapter 3 further develops the distinction between my moderate conception of striving will and typical usages of "will" and "volition" in recent analytic philosophy. Conceptions of willing in contemporary action theory arise from developments in the modern period that thinned out the motivationally thick concept of willing at issue between the "Eastern" and "Western" paradigms.

3

From Action Theory to Projective Motivation

Overview. The first half of this chapter looks at the rejection of "the will" as a psychological faculty in modern thought, and the second half considers the revival of volitional concepts in action theory since the mid-twentieth century. It serves as an introduction for readers with no advanced background in this field, but also challenges prevailing dogmas in contemporary action theory. The final section shows how the heroic conception of striving will adds the motivational function missing from recent analytic interpretations of willing as a stage in the genesis of intentions or free actions.

I. The Decline of the Will

It would be an understatement to say that "the will" was out of fashion in twentieth-century thought, especially in academic psychology and philosophy. The very term suggested to many leading theorists the idea of some scholastic faculty, a metaphysical fiction as outmoded as aether in physics. During the heyday of behaviorism in psychology, Gilbert Ryle taught a whole generation of philosophers that "the language of 'volitions' is the language of a para-mechanical theory of the mind" with no basis in ordinary language.[1] Such was Ryle's influence that in the 1960 *Encyclopedia of Philosophy* there was no entry on "Will," and the entry on "volition" was devoted entirely to theories concerning what makes something a voluntary or intentional action.

Ryle's dogma is still common in fields as diverse as analytic philosophy of mind, some genres of Continental philosophy, clinical psychotherapy, and even personality psychology. For example, on tests and inventories widely used today to give people career advice, to make employment decisions, and for other important purposes, "personality types" are defined in terms of behavioral traits, interests, interaction styles, and emotional dispositions, without any reference to the person's ultimate priorities, values, or willed direction in life.[2] In all these fields, the idea that "the will" is a special capacity distinguishing human persons from other animals remains out of fashion. Although the will is making a comeback, a majority of scholars in these disparate domains still refuse to recognize a role or place for volitional phenomena in any sense *irreducible* to other folk concepts, such as belief, desire, intention, disposition, behavioral pattern, interpersonal style, rationalization, mood, and so on.

This tendency to reduce "willing" to something else had a long history before twentieth-century developments. Before looking at contemporary theories of action and motivation, it will help to have some background in the history of philosophy and psychology in the modern period.

1.1. Freud and Hobbes

In psychology, the decline of the will is due most directly to the influence of Sigmund Freud. As the prominent existential psychotherapist Irwin Yalom writes:

> Freud's model of the mind . . . was based on Helmholtzian principles—that is, was an antivitalistic, deterministic model where the human being is activated and controlled by "chemical-physical forces reducible to the force of attraction and repulsion." Freud was unrelenting on this issue. . . . Behavior is a vector, a resultant of the interplay of internal forces.[3]

In other words, Freud's conception of motivation was fundamentally Hobbesian: the motive on which we act is simply the upshot of a contest between inclinations that themselves ultimately trace to pain and pleasure stimuli. In *Leviathan*, after having defined "deliberation" as the "alternate Sucession of Appetites, Aversions, Hopes, and Fears . . . no lesse in other living Creatures than in Man,"[4] Hobbes says:

> In *Deliberation*, the last Appetite, or Aversion, immediately adhering to the action, or to the omission thereof, is that we call the Will; the Act, (not the faculty) of *Willing*. And Beasts that have *Deliberation*, must necessarily also have *Will*. The Definition of *Will*, given commonly by the Schooles, that it is a *Rationall Appetite*, is not good. For if it were, then could there be no Voluntary Act against Reason. For a *Voluntary Act* is that, which proceedeth from the will, and no other. . . . *Will therefore is the last Appetite in Deliberating.* And though we say in common

Discourse, a man had a Will once to do a thing, that neverthelesse he forbore to do; yet that is properly but an Inclination, or Appetite.[5]

On this view, the will is not a form of agency standing *above* our appetites and aversions; it is simply whatever desire emerges as strongest in the economy of our attractions and repulsions. As a result, there is no sense in which we can act voluntarily out of appetite but *against* our real will, since there is nothing more to our will than the last appetite on which we act. Since Hobbes equates our will with our strongest desire, or perhaps the final intention embodying this desire, his theory is also minimalist: we enjoy no volitional powers beyond those included in our powers of appetite and instrumental reasoning.

Hobbes's definition of will is important in the history of modern philosophy because it launches the "post-Cartesian" period, eliminating the Platonism that remained in Descartes's account of the will in the *Meditations*.[6] As Hans Oberdiek comments in his history of the will, Hobbes's doctrine that deliberation "amounts to nothing more than a tiny war of desires and aversions . . . would seem to eliminate the will altogether," at least in the sense of an independent executive *or* motivational faculty.[7] Hobbes insists that freedom is simply the ability to do what one desires without external constraint, and that our psychology involves no "second-order agency of the will" that could stand above states like desires and inclinations in order to shape from them persisting purposes and intended plans of actions that carry us into the future. As Thomas Pink argues, this denial of second-order agency

> has proved enormously influential since. In particular, it has marked Anglo-Saxon theory, from Hume through to Ramsey, the pioneer of modern rational choice theory, and Ryle. . . . And this Anglo-Saxon tradition of disbelief or at least doubt in second-order agency still has plenty of supporters. Daniel Dennett, for example, has wondered whether there really is an agency of decision-making which explains our actions. . . . And in his moral psychology . . . Bernard Williams denies that action arises out of second-order agency of the will.[8]

However, before we consider this legacy in contemporary action theory, we should consider three other episodes in modern philosophy that set the stage for twentieth-century debates.

1.2. *Locke, Hume, and the Cambridge Platonists*

Following Hobbes, Locke attacked the notion that the mind contains distinct "faculties" as implying that each is a "distinct agent" within us, and defined the will as an unanalyzable power of bringing about change;[9] Hume followed him by defining the will as "the internal impression we feel and are conscious of, when we knowingly give rise to any new motion of our body, or new perception of our mind."[10] Thus what we call "willing" is merely an epiphenomenon of the kinesthetic internal sense, an impression *caused by* the initiation of some first-order action, whether bodily or mental.

Hume follows this by arguing that the "different stations in life," or natural classes, and the "uniformity of human actions" within nations and individuals show that psychology is run by the same kind of regular laws as physical mechanics.[11] Since in ordinary life we constantly rely others' actions being predictable and rooted in stable dispositions, "whoever reasons after this manner, does *ipso facto* believe the actions of the will to arise from necessity."[12] And even more influentially, Hume argued, against the classical view that reason should rule the passions, "that reason alone can never be a motive of any action of the will" and "can never oppose passion in the direction of the will."[13] Thus the will was not only generally reduced to an impression involved in first-order action but more specifically conceived as the economy of desires and aversions arising from expectations of pleasure and pain.[14] Hume offered a more nuanced account of our natural passions than Hobbes and Locke (including "calm desires and tendencies," such as social dispositions).[15] But he set the stage for later utilitarian models of the will[16] and for the subsequent view (found in Adam Smith and many romantic authors) that human motives decompose without remainder into simple egoistic desires for self-related goods and sympathetic desires for the good of others with whom one feels an emotional bond (of family, community, or common species).

In the same period, the Cambridge Platonists and their followers, such as Jonathan Edwards, agreed with Locke in rejecting faculty psychology and freedom as simple alternative-possibilities liberty but held to a more rationalist theory of the will as cognitively motivated by judgments about the value of ends. In his *Freedom of the Will*, as John Smith explains, Edwards defends the idea of "moral necessity," a psychological determinism in which "the will always follows the last dictate of the understanding."[17] Our will is determined by the strongest motive, which is equivalent to "the mind's apprehension of the greatest apparent good," although the particular way our apprehension works develops like a habit over time (and is influenced by grace).[18] Thus while the will is cognitive, it is teleologically determined; as Oberdiek says, for Edwards "the apparent good draws us towards it like a powerful magnet draws iron filings."[19]

In his manuscript on free will, Ralph Cudworth similarly argued against the voluntarist idea of a "blind will" that "still remaineth as free, and indifferent to do or not this or that, as if the understanding had given no judgment at all in the case, and doth at last fortuitously determine itself without respect to the same either way."[20] Like Edwards after him, Cudworth stressed that will and understanding are not separate faculties, since it is the "man or soul"—meaning the single agent or self—who does both.[21] Following the eudaimonist tradition, Cudworth conceives such agent causation as rooted in the essential propensity of our psychological nature, that is, the "constant, restless, uninterrupted desire or love of the good as such, or happiness." This means that we always will our apparent good.[22] But unlike Edwards, Cudworth also objects to the simple rationalist position that "the blind faculty of will always necessarily follows the last practical judgment of the understanding" about the greatest good,[23] since (as Aquinas held) the "good" we essentially desire is so general and hidden that our desire can be "diversely dispensed out, and placed upon different objects, more or less."[24] Yet Cudworth denies that this means the will can just choose indifferently between apparent goods and, again like Edwards, he holds that the "hegemonic, or ruling principle in a man" is *dispositional*, and its understanding or judgment of the apparent good is shaped by prior choices.[25] But unlike Edwards, for Cudworth this means that "this hegemonicon" is a "self-forming and self-framing power" *itself* activating man's innate natural desire for the good, which, through its own "purposes and resolutions, ... designs and active endeavours," alters its own dispositional tendency to judge or apprehend the good more in one way than in others.[26] This seems to imply a conception of the will as executive agency, contrary to Locke.

But these more subtle views about the will's influence on motivation did not win out against the doctrine of Hobbes and Hume that "every human act may be explained as the causal outcome of one's desires and beliefs at the time of action."[27] Nor is Edwards's or Cudworth's Platonic conception of motivation as grounded in the desire for the good necessarily incompatible with Hume's position that it is not "contrary to *reason* to prefer even my own acknowledg'd lesser good to my greater."[28] For Edwards and Cudworth must say that such a *desire* is unnatural, that it is desire rather than reason that is malfunctioning in Hume's example. They agree with Hume that motivation terminates in beliefs about our apparent good and in consequent desires, but they give final control to the "general appetite to good, and aversion to evil," which Hume treats as just one motive among others in his list of "calm desires."[29]

In Britain, the idea of will as second-order agency standing above all prepurposive desires in the agent was developed by Butler and Reid. Butler writes that "there is a superior principle of reflection or conscience in every man which distinguishes between internal principles of the heart [i.e., natural motives] as well as his external actions," and "It is by this faculty ... that he is a moral agent, that he is a law to himself."[30] As Korsgaard explains, Butler's distinction between motive-power and authority requires that "When you deliberate, it is as if there were something over and above all of your desires, something which is you, and which chooses which desire to act on."[31] Similarly, Reid distinguishes "the determination of the mind to do, or not to do something which we conceive to be in our power" from "every motive and incitement" on which the will acts.[32] Reid also insists that choices based on practical deliberation are fully imputed to the agent and are "always accompanied with authority."[33] This view anticipates Kant's account of decision as giving normative status to the motives on which we intend to act. But Butler and Reid do not clearly defend Kant's idea of practical reason as self-motivating (see chap. 11); and outside the rationalist tradition, few philosophers thought of the will as having any control over the formation of motives themselves.

To take one example, in his prize essay, Schopenhauer distinguishes between "freedom of action," which is the ability to behave in accordance with an already given volition, and "freedom of *willing*."[34] But for him, even the latter only concerns whether the will is free to form or not to form an intention based on motivating objects presented by cognition. Thus his question is the same as Leibniz's: "does the entrance of a motive into the consciousness necessarily bring about the volition, or does the will retain complete freedom either to will or not to will?"[35] Note that this question has nothing to do with the original formation of motives themselves. As his translator comments, for Schopenhauer, "the free will reveals itself in its tendency to respond to motives. . . . the extent of its freedom will be proportionate to the scope of the motives to which it may respond." Thus freedom is ultimately traceable to the enlargement of the intellect's cognitive powers.[36] In this sense, Schopenhauer anticipated James's approach.

1.3. William James

In the late nineteenth century, William James gave a new account of the will that built on the legacy of the empiricist tradition and anticipated several developments in contemporary action theory.[37] From the Aristotelian premise that will concerns actions that are in our power, James first concludes that "the only *direct* outward effects of the will are bodily movements."[38] Voluntary control of movements is attained only after we have learned of these movements by experiencing them as involuntary behavior: "Reflex, instinctive, and emotional movements are all primary performances"[39] that build up the "kinaesthetic impressions" necessary for us to control our limbs through an internal body image.[40] In cases where the body image is disrupted, such "volitional" control over our movements is impaired.[41] James then argues at length, in response to Bain, Wundt, and

Helmholtz, that no "feeling of innervation" or "outgoing discharge" is necessary as an antecedent to action in voluntary bodily movements.[42] Like Hobbes, James defends the view that "all our thoughts of movement [are] of sensational constitution"; but he argues that this still leaves room for spontaneity or "scope for our inward initiative to be shown" in focusing on some sensations rather than others.[43] This link to sensation, which supplies our understanding of different movements and their ends, is needed to explain

> what that "idea of a movement" is which must precede it in order that it be voluntary. It is not the thought of the innervation which the movement requires. It is the anticipation of the movement's sensible effects, resident and remote, and sometimes very remote indeed. Such anticipations, to say the least, determine *what* our movements shall be.[44]

James's entire account of the will, then, amounts to spelling out in much more detail than Hobbes could (with the benefit of experimental results in nineteenth-century psychology) the mechanisms by which states of "desire" are represented and can account for bodily movements. No notion of *constituting* motives by decisions or sustaining motivation by committing oneself to care about some person, issue, or thing ever enters into James's analysis.

The nearest James comes to giving "decision," or executive volitional agency, any role is in cases where tie-breaking is needed between various sensual representations pulling on the agent. Sometimes "the bare idea of a movement's sensible effects [is] its sufficient mental cue" and sometimes an "additional mental antecedent, in the shape of a fiat, decision, consent, [or] volitional mandate" is required.[45] The former is a voluntary "ideo-motor action," which makes up the "habitual goings and comings and rearrangements of ourselves which fill every hour of the day,"[46] while the latter is a special case. James believes that "every representation of a movement awakens in some degree the actual movement which is its object," or produces a *tendency* (however weak) to move in this way, and only "an antagonistic representation" can keep it from automatically producing ideo-motor action. This is so because "consciousness is *in its very nature impulsive*," or movement-generating.[47] Only in such cases, where there are competing tendencies, is "the express fiat, or act of mental consent to the movement" needed. What such fiat does is to "neutraliz[e] . . . the antagonistic and inhibitory idea," letting the other representation take effect. Thus fiat does not *evaluate* motivating representations of sensible effects in any way distinct from that in which such representations themselves motivate us; it simply adds one more representation to the pile, thus releasing the "inner spring" that translates into "motor discharge."[48] Hence, just as Hobbes said, the process of deliberation is simply a vector-summing of thoughts about action that are in tension, or of mental representations of opposed objects of action. As James said:

> The result is that peculiar feeling of inward unrest known as *indecision*. ... As long as it lasts, with the various objects before the attention, we are said to *deliberate*; and when finally the original suggestion either prevails and makes the movement take place, or gets definitively quenched by its antagonists, we are said to *decide*, or to *utter our voluntary fiat*, in favor of one or the other course.[49]

The act of fiat or consent turns out to be the "last appetite" again.[50] Thus Oberdiek gives too much credit to James in suggesting that his notion of fiat shows that "will is not simply the last appetite or aversion adhering to action," but rather a way in which "We organize and systematize our diverse perceptions, aspirations, emotions, and beliefs through deliberation into a choice."[51] For the deliberation preceding the fiat is just a more complex version of Hobbesian deliberation: "The process of deliberation contains an endless degree of complication. At every moment of it our consciousness is of an extremely complex object, namely the existence of the whole set of motives and their conflict."[52] The outcome is a matter of "the oscillations of our attention" and the "associative flow of our ideas,"[53] and *not* of any agency standing above these. So Oberdiek is right that James identifies as voluntary those actions "which must be performed attentively and which, in doing, we experience a feeling of resolve, effort, or fiat."[54] But this self-resolving conflict is not "resolved" in the *existential* sense. James's introspective feeling of fiat is simply another version of the "feeling" of initiative that Hume said we experience as an after-effect "when we knowingly give rise to any new motion of our body."[55]

1.4. Gilbert Ryle and Ludwig Wittgenstein

This Jamesian model set the tone for subsequent treatments of volition in both psychology and philosophy in the twentieth century. Gilbert Ryle assumes that "the prime function of volitions, the task for the performance of which they were postulated, is to originate bodily movement."[56] Likewise, Ludwig Wittgenstein says that since James, "the prototype of the act of volition is the experience of muscular effort."[57] Though there are apparently more "active" cases, such as when "I deliberate whether to lift a certain heavyish weight, decide to do it, ... then apply my force to it,"[58] they are not "voluntary" in any special sense that does not apply to less reflective acts like casually scratching an itch or spontaneously getting out of bed; the voluntary or "volitional" is merely a family-resemblance concept.[59] Wittgenstein does critique and reject James's ideo-motor theory of action as caused by the kinesthetic sense of the bodily act, just as he rejects Wundt and Helmholtz's "innervation" theory of action as distinguished by a sense of trying to move muscles.[60] In general, however, he thinks that "willing" just refers to acting voluntarily or to performing intentional actions, such as particular bodily movements or mental acts like imagining.[61]

As Michael Scott says, concluding his review of Wittgenstein's late writings on action, "the will, if it is conceived as a special type of mechanism or originator of action, plays no role. The voluntariness of an action is shown by the agent's mental states, dispositions, forms of behavior, feelings etc.," that establish the action's context.[62] Thus Wittgenstein denies that willing is a separate executive *action* of deciding or motivating our actions, distinct from such first-order intentional acts themselves:

> In the sense in which I can ever bring anything about (such as a stomach-ache through over-eating) I can also bring about an act of willing. In this sense I bring about the act of willing to swim by jumping into the water. Doubtless I was trying to say: I can't will willing; that is, it makes no sense to speak of willing willing. "Willing" is not the name of an action; and so not the name of any voluntary action either.[63]

As I read this, Wittgenstein means to give a *reductio* of volitionalism: if willing were itself a kind of action, then it would in turn be something we could *will* to do. But since willing is identical with intending, and there is no will to intend prior to the intention itself, willing is not itself an act.[64]

This is Wittgenstein's famous regress argument against volition as a distinct form of agency. If willing were an action, Wittgenstein thinks, it would be like *trying* to perform a first-order intentional act. But an act such as raising my arm does not feel like trying to manipulate an instrument; there is no sense of effort *other* than that involved in actually tightening the muscles that move the arm.[65] Thus "the sensation of innervation which is supposed to constitute the consciousness of the act of will"[66] is merely that involved in intending any mental cognition or physical movement under our control. The subjective experience we call "volition" cannot be anything more than the kind of tension we feel in straining to lift a heavy weight, since there is no prior, distinct sense of *trying to make* such an effort: our behavior and its correlated kinesthetic sensation are all we find when we introspect such supposed paradigm cases of "willing."[67] Wittgenstein's denial that we can "will willing" is thus symptomatic of the attitude that volition is merely the subjective experience of attempting to do something *already intended*; on this assumption, willing as a distinct action of volition-formation could be experienced only as a *trying to try*, which is either redundant or merely a case of instrumental self-manipulation. Will is not, as we imagine (due to deceiving linguistic analogies), a pure unmoved moving power or "motor which has no inertia in itself to overcome"; since willing is not an act that we can try to perform, the frustratable-versus-unfrustratable distinction does not apply to it at all.[68]

A similar regress argument is given by Ryle as a *reductio* of the thesis that volitions are what "makes actions voluntary, resolute, meritorious and wicked." The problem is that "predicates of these sorts are ascribed not only to bodily movements" but also to inner thought processes such as studying or trying to write something, which can be subject to praise or blame:

> Some mental processes then can, according to the theory, issue from volitions. So what of volitions themselves? Are they voluntary or involuntary acts of mind? Clearly either answer leads to absurdities. . . . If my volition to pull the trigger is voluntary, in the sense assumed by the theory, then it must issue from a prior volition and that from another, *ad infinitum*.[69]

This argument obviously depends on the dubious assumption that there is only *one sense* of "voluntary," namely, "being caused by a volition." For only given this premise can it follow that if a volition is voluntary, then it is caused by another volition, etc. Thus, like Wittgenstein, Ryle attacks a straw man. Neither of their critiques applies to theories according to which non-volitional bodily or mental actions are made *contingently* voluntary by intentions, while intentions themselves (or the decisions in which they are formed) are *essentially* voluntary expressions of primary agency.

Yet it was primarily on the basis of such flawed regress arguments that Anscombe and Davidson rejected the idea of will as a special kind of internal agency and proposed instead what Pink calls the "Pro-Attitude" interpretation of voluntary action. In the following two sections we will see how these developments in modern philosophy influenced twentieth-century action theory and examine three different concepts of the will that it produced. Within this large literature, I have selected only some representative examples of the different views, since the goal is to arrive at a new concept of the will that goes beyond the conceptions developed in action theory.

2. Kane's Three Senses of "Will"

The best single book about the will in twentieth-century philosophy is Robert Kane's masterpiece, *The Significance of Free Will*. The main goal of

Kane's tour de force is to defend a sophisticated version of leeway-libertarian incompatibilism in the debates about the sort of freedom required by moral responsibility. This question is not my present topic, but, as Kane rightly says, it was a mistake in mid-twentieth-century philosophy to think that we could eliminate the notion of "will" from the analysis of moral freedom. Despite the revival of this notion in more recent theories of action and moral psychology, Kane writes: "the deeper connections between the will and longstanding questions about freedom are still not well understood, to my mind, even by those who are familiar with current debates."[70] I agree: part of the reason there still remain deep and seemingly unresolvable disagreements about the conditions of moral freedom, despite the advances and efforts of so many talented philosophers in the last forty years, is that our background notion of the will itself remains inarticulate in certain key respects. As I hope to show, our efforts to comprehend human freedom are hampered by some fundamental mistakes in our understanding of the relationship between "will" and motivation, mistakes that trace to the classical roots of Western philosophy. Overcoming these barriers should open the way to a more profound interpretation of moral freedom than has hitherto been possible. In short, we cannot solve the main riddles about "freedom of the will" without better understanding the nature of the will that is supposed to be the locus of freedom.

This chapter considers four different senses of "will," moving from the most minimal concept of "willing" employed in the literature of action theory to what I consider to be the most substantive and important sense of the term. In the process, I argue that recent developments away from the minimalist concept point toward the need for a much better understanding of "willing" in the most substantive sense, but contemporary theory has not reached this point. This four-step division of will-concepts is different in content and function from the taxonomy that Kane gives in the beginning of his book, but looking at his distinctions will help clarify and support my own taxonomy.

Kane distinguishes between "three traditional senses" of the word "will" (and its cognates in other languages). The first is "*desiderative* or *appetitive will*," which refers to the state of wanting, or desiring, or being inclined to some result or end.[71] The second sense is *rational will*, or "a set of powers defined in terms of a family of concepts whose focal member is practical reasoning." Will in this sense, which is the primary one for Kane, concerns the making of two kinds of action-related judgments: "practical (or normative) judgments . . . about what ought to be done (or about what the best thing is to do), and choices or decisions" through which the agent forms an intention to act now or in the future.[72] Kane describes these senses of will as two sides of a single process:

Wants, desires, preferences, and other expressions of desiderative will are among the *inputs* to practical reasoning—they function as reasons or motives for choice or action. By contrast, choices, decisions, and intentions, the expressions of rational will, are the outputs of practical reasoning, its products. If there is indeterminancy in free will, on my view, it must come somewhere in between the input and output—between the desiderative and rational will.[73]

We should pause to notice that this process as Kane envisions it is very much like the process described by Thomas Aquinas in the *Summa Theologica*. In brief, Aquinas takes up Aristotle's notion of practical deliberation and *boulēsis* or rational wish, adds to it the notion of an intention to act as the proper output of the will or "rational appetite," and includes a limited form of libertarian freedom between the two.[74] As Kane points out, this medieval notion of rational appetite sounds like a disposition but, unlike "sensuous appetite," it presupposes "powers to form and act upon rational desires"; in other words, it involves "rational willing," or will in Kane's second sense.[75]

Third in Kane's list is will in the sense of an "endeavor," making "an effort," or "trying" to do something. For this, Kane adopts Brian O'Shaughnessy's term, *striving will*.[76] Although O'Shaughnessy developed this as part of what I will call a "volitionalist" theory of action, according to which all intentional actions involve "volitions" in the sense of efforts or tryings, Kane is not concerned to defend or refute this theory of action. Rather, for him, we experience ourselves as trying or making an effort when we face some kind of resistance, as, for example, in a case where our prior motives clash (or our desiderative will is divided); in such cases, the effort we make to resolve the conflict plays a central role in some kinds of "self-forming willings."[77] For example, in prudential and moral choices, we may experience a strong temptation to some act A, while we are also "committed to moral beliefs and long-term plans" that conflict with A.[78] It turns out to be vital for Kane's account that such efforts are themselves explained by agents' already existing character and motives, as triggered by their present circumstances: "It is because their efforts are thus a response to inner conflicts embedded in the agent's prior character and motives that their prior character and motives can explain the conflicts and why the efforts are being made, without also explaining the outcomes of the conflicts and the efforts."[79] For Kane, we can have leeway-libertarian freedom because in cases where the motivational "inputs" of the will are conflicted and thus do not by themselves determine the intention-forming decision "outputs," there is room for *efforts to decide* to mediate between these poles of the process, bringing about different possible results from the same inputs.[80]

But there are problems with this picture—not as an explanation of libertarian freedom (which is not my present concern) but rather in its background moral psychology. First, Kane's account is supposed to explain how you can be "the ultimate creator (prime mover, so to speak) of your own purposes,"[81] but it appears from his model that you can form purposes only out of the various objects of your *preexisting* desires or appetites. Second, although Kane recognizes that "efforts" of will can also be "directed at sustaining or carrying out intentions or purposes already formed in the face of obstacles,"[82] Kane conceives this kind of striving as a species of "self-forming willing" only when it resolves conflict again (in this case, conflict between standing intentions and contrary desires). Apparently he does not imagine such efforts to sustain a purpose P as adding any *new motivation* to P beyond that which is derived from prior incentives and the will's tie-breaking supplement. This seems to imply that if the appetites contrary to P now clearly outweigh the motivation involved in setting P, and so there is not an indeterminate mix of motives, the will cannot decide to sustain P. On this picture, even a person's efforts to control his first-order motives by focusing his attention in certain ways derive their power entirely from a prior desire "to control and modify his behavior" and they constitute self-forming willings only if this desire and those he is attempting to control are in indeterminate balance.

Third, when we consider the nature of the intentions that result from rational willing, as Kane emphasizes, we see that future-directed intentions are very often nested within layers of longer-range intentions relating to "broader purposes." Citing groundbreaking work by Michael Bratman, Gilbert Harman, Carlos Moya, and others, Kane points out that in coordinating our activities and deliberations in accordance with "larger plans," an agent's intentions can "also embody an agent's 'commitments' to future goals."[83] But what are such commitments, and how are they formed (do they also flow entirely from preexisting motives and prior decisions flowing from earlier motivational sets, etc.)? And third, how do we distinguish these motives that we experience as "commitments" from those that we experiences as "temptations," as in Kane's examples?

In explaining this distinction, it cannot be simply that the commitments envision longer-term goals that take more time to realize and involve a more complex set of plans and coordination of tasks. For not all temptations are toward short-term gratifications; some can incline toward more remote possible ends and can even require elaborate planning to achieve. For example, imagine someone who gets an urge to abandon his family and live in luxury on an offshore island resort. He seriously considers going for it and begins planning his bank robbery, his escape route, how to make the authorities believe he is dead, and so on. Yet in the end, this whole scheme is really just a complex temptation at odds with what he himself would earnestly describe as his most fundamental commitments in life. Presumably to experience a serious temptation is both to experience one's intentions being somewhat unfixed or changeable—so following the temptation is a real volitional possibility—and to find this course at odds with the values and ongoing projects with which one already identifies. So understanding this phenomenon requires some interpretation of identification and autonomy. To get at the root of this problem, it will be helpful to reconstruct some of Kane's categories of willing in a different ordering reflecting essential disagreements about the will and agency in twentieth-century philosophy.

3. Four Basic Concepts of the Will

3.1. *The Minimalist Concept*

My ordering begins with those theories that either dispense altogether with "the will" as a set of powers in Kane's sense or at least reject the will in both his second sense as an executive function that deliberates and decides and his third sense as a type of effort or trying to form an intention. Ironically, philosophers sometimes arrive at a minimalist view by simply *equating* the idea that we have wills with the idea that we enjoy libertarian freedom. In some versions of libertarianism, an act of will becomes a simple act of *consent* to some motivating reason or desire rather than an act of decision flowing from or even helping to constitute these motives. This separation, which Kane's picture of the will-process is meant to avoid, has led to a host of interrelated objections that the will is only an "arbitrary" or "decisionistic" power whose election of one option among many cannot itself be rationally explained or substantively motivated. It is unfortunate that such a pure voluntarist equation of will with a liberty for alternate actions is now widely thought of as representing "the existentialist" position.[84] Peter van Inwagen provides a better example:

> I use the term "free will" out of respect for tradition. My use of the term is not meant to imply that I think there is such a "faculty" as "the will." When I say of a man that he "has free will" I mean [only] that very often, if not always, when he has to choose between two or more mutually incompatible courses of action . . . each of these courses of action is such that he can, or is able to, or has it within his power to carry it out.[85]

Since van Inwagen does not even say that the alternative "courses of action" each require something like an intention, it seems that "will" in his minimalist sense could exist in any system that without varying its current properties could behave in different ways in a single circumstance—perhaps even if it lacked mental life or consciousness entirely. So by itself this definition is compatible with a "libertarian behaviorism."[86] Notice that if we remove libertarian freedom from this minimalist concept of willing, then we are left with the eliminativist view that there is no such "thing" as the will at all, that the notion is a mere disease of our language that fools us into to reifying certain feelings we have when acting.

Within contemporary action theory, this view that we can dispense with the very idea of "volition" is based on the claim that the conceptual vocabulary of intentional action can explain everything we need to account for. The two most developed versions of this theory that I treat here are those of Daniel Dennett and Donald Davidson. Both are indebted to the work of Wittgenstein and his student, G. E. M. Anscombe. In one of his first statements of this view, Dennett writes:

> The account of intention that has been given includes no talk about volitions or willing. That is because, as Anscombe argues, the verb "to will" is a hoax. There are no such things as acts of will or volition.[87] . . . The idea that willing is some sort of radiation generated by gritting the teeth and saying, "move, move, move," is hopeless. It arises, no doubt, from such experiences as lying in bed and saying to oneself "I must get up, I must get up, it's late. On the count of three: one, two, three," until one finally gets up. . . . The fact of the matter—that sometimes the thoughts seem to help and sometimes not—suggests that thinking to oneself is merely an accompaniment or by-product of the actual business of determining action.[88]

Instead, Dennett argues, the brain makes the decision one way or another unconsciously according to whether the right "balance is tipped" in one's neural activity (which need not be recognized verbally) so that one seems to "will" to get up.[89] In this case, giving verbal stimulation to one's own neural activity is exactly analogous to some third party giving such stimulation: "the success in both cases, of course, would depend on the relevance and abundance of the information produced," which need not be conscious.[90] Most of all, "The notion that must be avoided is that awareness is in any way a centre *from* which efficacious signals, volitions, or any sort of psychic radiation emanates."[91]

So Dennett denies that the psychic states that cause intentional movements or bodily actions are essentially conscious and that they have any special role or distinct status in the mind's processes. This might seem to make it difficult for Dennett to distinguish more "habitual" or routine actions done with little agonizing forethought from actions fraught with experiences of choice, but he would simply say that the latter involve more activity in the higher linguistic neural pathways than the former.[92]

Donald Davidson's causal theory of intentional action, which developed over the course of several essays, is more subtle than Dennett's and closer to certain aspects of the Aristotelian tradition as well. As Carlos Moya summarizes in his excellent book on action theory, Davidson's fundamental aim throughout his work on action was to show, against the Hempelian nomological models of causation, that "rationalizations," which explain acts in terms of the agent's prior beliefs and desires, "are a species of causal explanation."[93] He hoped to show this by arguing that when a certain set of beliefs and desires (or other pro-attitudes) are the reasons for which an action was done, they must not only justify the act (or make psychological sense of it) but also cause it. Thus in his early paper on "Actions, Reasons, and Causes," Moya says, Davidson initially conceived intentional action as both the causal result of a pro-attitude plus some belief, *and* as the deductive result of a practical syllogism starting from propositions expressing a belief and a desire.[94] The act is "caused" by its rationalization (the practical deduction), even though the proposition expressing this causal relation will be true only as a singular claim in each case, not deducible from a lawlike connection between kinds of reason and kinds of action.[95]

Like Dennett, then, Davidson hoped to show that intentional actions can be caused without the intervention of any mysterious "volitional" agency. As with Aristotle, his moral psychology requires nothing more than rational belief-forming capacities and various desires (which can perhaps be trained through habituation). Davidson changed this in later papers only by introducing "intentions" as a distinct element in the account and by reformulating his initial practical syllogism explanation of how practical reasons come to justify intentional action. It is doubtful that this move really avoids the problem of actions resulting from wayward causal chains unrelated to the reasons that the agent would cite in explaining her behavior; but deciding this issue is not vital here. This is enough to classify Davidson's view as a quasi-Aristotelian minimalist theory of willing.

It was in response to this sort of view defended by Ryle, Wittgenstein, Anscombe, Dennett, and Davidson that the theorists in my second group defended the ineliminability of "volitions" in what turns out to be a rather novel sense of the term.

3.2. The Volitionalist Concept

At the second level, we find various interpretations of "willing" as a kind of effort or trying that either constitutes or is the immediate cause of so-called "basic actions" (out of which more complex actions are supposedly composed). As Kane puts it, this is the view of "theorists who identify efforts or tryings with volitions, and argue that volitions, so understood, are involved in all intentional action."[96] The most extensive defense of such a view is given by Brian O'Shaughnessy in his two-volume study.[97] O'Shaughnessy meticulously works through different possible accounts of the mental antecedents to physical or bodily action. But this also reveals the limits of his approach: for him, the question of whether we "will" anything depends on how we bring about intentional first-order acts—something that many nonhuman animals can also do. "Willing" in his sense is not a distinct activity in the transition from motives to articulate intentions nor does it determine the autonomy of one's motivations. This applies generally to a whole family of views in contemporary action theory that Robert Audi dubs "volitionalism."

In his helpful summary of this literature, Audi surveys several "varieties of volitionalism," which he describes as "a theory of the nature of action which gives a central place to one or another kind of willing."[98] Several of these theories, such as Hugh McCann's, portray volitions as mental "actions" that prompt outward performances or, as in Lawrence Davis's theory, as "attempts or tryings," which are a special class of actions.[99] Like O'Shaughnessy, D. M. Armstrong and Raimo Tuomela "conceive volition as roughly equivalent to trying," a mental effort that can causally explain action.[100] Others, such as Michael Zimmerman, have equated volition with a "kind of decision," while philosophers in the Millian tradition, including Wilfred Sellars and Myles Brand, have described volition as one type of intention which is the "proximate cause of action."[101]

All these conceptions start with a thin concept of will as a mental state that is necessary or even sufficient to cause intentional bodily movements (or outward acts). They save "willing" in this thin sense from the minimalists by conceiving it as a distinct element in the structure of first-order actions. Usually, except when it includes libertarian freedom, this structure is meant to apply not just to persons but potentially to other animals as well. So the notion that willing itself (quite apart from its freedom) is something essential to and distinctive of persons is lost. Moreover, although will in this twentieth-century "volitionalist" sense is a kind of mental "striving," as Kane said, it is only an effort to act *as intended* or an attempt to initiate basic motions of body or thought (e.g., trying to redirect one's attention when suddenly distracted from a crucial task at hand). Volition *implements* or *enacts* intentions already formed. It has nothing especially to do with shaping one's underlying motives for acting, or forming fundamental commitments, or integrating them with one's existing values and priorities.

Perhaps "volition" in the mental-trying sense could be said to include the process of mustering resolve to sustain our commitments against adversity. But if so, volitionalist accounts do not adequately distinguish the kind of volitional effort that deeply affects the ethos of a person from other types of mental "striving," for example, psychomotor efforts such as trying hard to control a largely numbed arm when waking from a deep sleep, or trying to focus one's eyes where the optometrist instructs, or trying to pour just the right amount of milk into our coffee. Thus this approach does not isolate and explain the heroic kind of "striving will" that plays a unique role in shaping our character and life goals and keeping us committed to them despite adversity.

As Audi explains, some "volitionalist" accounts recognize volitions as having a special kind of self-referential content. For example, Carl Ginet holds that in exerting bodily movement, I do not simply will the exertion: rather, I will "my exerting . . . I will that my willing—this very willing of whose content we speak—cause the exertion."[102] This is insightful, since it brings out the essential reference to the agent's individual identity and authorship of her actions that we find in all intentions, including those aiming at immediate bodily movement. But it does not recognize willing in Kane's second and central sense. What unites all these "volitionalist" accounts, as Audi points out, is just the conviction that volition is a class of mental events that "are, or are crucial in, producing action—if not its immediate causes, then its closest psychological causes."[103] Such theories start from "the picture of actions as caused by such elements as the agent's desires, beliefs, and decisions" and try to provide a "causal factor which *genetically unifies* actions in terms of a common kind of origin, even if not necessarily an ultimate origin, in the psychology of the agent."[104] In this popular contemporary outlook, willing is interpreted relative to a set of problems in action theory that already assume, for the most part, that motivation is defined by the limits of interaction between beliefs and desires (and possibly emotions, if these are not reducible to belief-desire compounds).

Although these "volitionalist" action theories are not limited to human acts, they do have a relationship to moral theory. An essential part of their goal is to show that "volitions" in their sense must be posited if we are to explain the conditions that make actions voluntary and thus morally imputable to their agents. This is an effective argument against minimalism, because Hobbes and his empiricist followers agreed that "volition" is equivalent to whatever conditions make human actions *voluntary*, which is a condition of responsibility. Following Aristotle, for an action to be voluntary, it must both be done intentionally (arising from "internal" sources) and uncoerced. Within this schema, the volitionalists hold that to do an act A intentionally is to cause A (or its components) by a volition in the sense of an effort or endeavor to A.[105]

The volitionalist theories thus build on an older tradition in which the concept of will is defined by its practical function: "willing" is whatever psychic state plays the role of making the action that follows from it intentional and thus potentially voluntary. In his history of the will, Hans Oberdiek stresses this idea that volition is used "to distinguish between intentional and unintentional action, a grave matter in many criminal law cases."[106] For example:

> Self-controlled action, as Aristotle explains it, serves as an important forerunner to our own notion of "voluntariness." For in Aristotle's account, self-controlled (or voluntary) actions are those where an agent, acting with the appropriate degree of knowledge and without compulsion, seeks an end because of some kind of desire (*orexis*) originating within him.[107]

Oberdiek sees the contributions subsequent to Aristotle primarily as giving us more adequate criteria for making this distinction, for example, by adding the idea that the will is "a phenomenon of subjective, introspective consciousness, a mental event preceding action" (Descartes),[108] and by adding the notion of *intention* to distinguish human actions from mere behaviors (Aquinas).[109] The function of the will as a philosophical concept on Oberdiek's reading thus agrees with today's volitionalists: "A theory involving 'volitions' promises not only to distinguish involuntary from voluntary behavior, but to explain how voluntary actions occur and what counts as an action."[110]

Similarly, in his own interesting account, Oberdiek argues (following Davidson, Donagan, and others) that act-descriptions and predications of "is voluntary" must be treated intentionally: "an agent acts voluntarily only when the act-description is one which the agent is aware describes his act."[111] Departing from traditional usage, Oberdiek distinguishes between "free" and "voluntary" actions, so that coerced actions may be voluntary yet unfree;[112] in this attenuated sense of "voluntary," the set of voluntary acts is equivalent to the set of acts caused by a volition; for example, a wink is willed, a blink is not. Though, like other volitionalist theories, his account convincingly responds to minimalists like Ryle, it still treats the will only in terms of what Thomas Pink calls "first-order agency," or the capacity to perform first-order actions—doings with a purpose explained by attitudes "such as desires and intentions" that are not themselves aimed at forming desires, intentions, or any other such action-explaining attitudes.[113]

This kind of volitionalism is also found in some contemporary theories of autonomy as voluntary action under certain conditions of practical rationality. For example, Gert and Duggan distinguish three senses of voluntariness:

> In ordinary discourse the term "voluntary" as applied to actions has a number of senses which though related are, nonetheless, distinct. Of these, three are central: (1) a voluntary act is simply an intentional (as opposed to accidental) act; (2) a voluntary act is a free (as opposed to constrained) act; (3) a voluntary act is an intentional act done by an agent who has what we have described as the ability to will (volitional ability) to do that kind of action.[114]

The first two conditions are roughly equivalent to voluntariness in Oberdiek's sense; the third adds to this a complex condition requiring that the agent can *recognize* "coercive" and "noncoercive incentives" for doing a particular act X and would usually *respond* to them in appropriate fashion, for example, by not doing X when coercive incentives for not doing it are present, by sometimes doing it when noncoercive incentives for doing it are present, and so on.[115] There are many kinds of incentive: "moral, prudential, patriotic," monetary, and so on, and in order to act freely, an agent need only be able to have beliefs that there are incentives of the many kinds normal people recognize and respond to them such that he "almost always" acts in accordance with coercive incentives, and sometimes acts in accordance with noncoercive incentives.[116] By contrast, a son who obsessively visits his mother's grave due to guilt feelings either cannot "believe that he should not visit her grave, or if he can come to believe this it does not affect his actions."[117] Gert and Duggan suggest that those who cannot recognize common incentives or interests "are in that respect like delusional psychotics," while those who recognize but do not rationally respond to incentives "are in that respect like compulsive or phobic neurotics."[118]

Like John Fischer's explanation of agent control, this analysis assumes that the idea of autonomy is meant primarily to embody standards of normal reason-responsiveness, and so Gert and Duggan build into their conditions an *objective* (if rather unspecified) range of reasons or "incentives" that autonomous agents must be able to recognize and respond to appropriately. They gloss over the problem that what such reasons or incentives are will be in part socially determined. More important for my purposes, they entirely ignore the question of whether autonomy requires any ability to *control one's incentives* oneself or any *distinctive kind* of motivation (which may hardly be "incentival" in form). Thus they still conceive volition entirely in terms of first-order agency: "we define 'willing' as doing intentionally or trying to do."[119] Autonomous willing is merely attempting or performing intentional action that is sufficiently reasons-responsive.

One of the best arguments against this volitionalist tradition is given by Carlos Moya. In developing his case, he retrieves insights from some of the minimalists that are lost in volitionalist models (even though Moya does not in the end agree with the minimalists either). According to Moya, the volitionalist approach is motivated by the problematic minimalism of older accounts of action. For example, in the British empiricism of Hobbes and Locke, "Willing to move our bodies is, properly speaking, a mental *happening* caused by some motive or desire."[120] If we reject this assimilation of actions to events, then we have to explain how actions that essentially involve events or happenings (or what McCann calls "results") are constituted. But if each result becomes a result by being caused by a more basic action, and each such action also involves a result, we have an infinite regress. The solution to this problem, according to "new volitional theory" (Moya's term for Audi's "volitionalism") is to posit *absolutely basic actions* that involve no results or events distinct from these acts. These maximally basic actions are, as we have seen, "volitions" in the sense of (intentional) mental efforts to "execute intentions" and are thus experienced as states of trying to do whatever the agent already intended or striving to execute an existing plan to realize the agent's purpose.[121]

Moya seems to reject the idea that such trying volitions can be what execute intentions because of the following dilemma: "volitions can only solve the result problem if they do not involve physical happenings; but if they do not involve physical happenings they cannot be executive"—not, at least, without positing a mysterious interaction between mental and physical substances.[122] I am not sure that this objection is decisive, since Brian O'Shaughnessy's dual-aspect theory is designed precisely to avoid it. As Moya says, for O'Shaughnessy, "Being mental, and having physical effects, trying is the point where mind reaches the body, a mental 'pineal gland.'"[123] Moya raises technical objections designed to show that "trying" in O'Shaughnessy's sense could only be trying to move one's body in some way, not trying to do any nonbasic action like start a car or go into town.[124]

I do not think these arguments are decisive in showing that all "efforts" involved in executing intentions are physical efforts of some kind: one could, for example, "try" in O'Shaughnessy's sense to remember someone's name or to execute some other intention aimed at a purely mental result. In any case, Moya concludes that "Between intention and overt physical action we do not need an intermediate trying, for trying is just starting the action"; and in the case of "spontaneous bodily movements" like raising one's arm, this is something we just know how to do by "natural, unlearnt ability."[125] Again, I am not sure that this is right, for it seems to me that the volitionalist project begins from the fact that we often *can* introspectively detect an act—or at least a distinct mental moment—of trying to initiate the bodily sequence involved in an outward action: this moment involves a thought that we might articulate as "now I will do what I planned to!" or "now let's begin!"—even though, of course, we rarely articulate this thought in such a reflective propositional form. In fact, we often begin implementation of ordinary short-term intentions (like picking up a fork) with so little reflective awareness that this moment of mental trying approaches the vanishing point.

But even if this is right, it does not save volitionalism as a complete theory of intentional action. For although there is *something* to the idea that the execution of many kinds of intention involves basic mental acts of effort or tryings, Moya argues convincingly that such "volitions" cannot be the essence of agency, or what *constitutes* our movements as intentional action. As he explains, the regress problem that motivated volitionalist theories depends on the assumption that all actions other than basic ones (or trying volitions) "have results, that is, non-actional or act-neutral events that are necessary, but not sufficient, for the corresponding action to take place."[126] But this assumption is false, as Moya shows by the key example of "meaningful action," or *communicative action* (using Jürgen Habermas's familiar term for the same thing). Actions with symbolic meaning are not just basic actions done in the context of some convention governing the meaning of signs; rather, their ability to draw on conventionally established meanings derives from the "commitment" they involve to related future actions.[127] Although some meaningful or communicative acts, "such as greeting someone or making a move in chess," do not involve commitments to *specific* future actions (such as letting the visitor in or moving one's pawn to K4), they do involve following the rules or implicit norms of the communicative practice presupposed by such acts. And as Wittgenstein showed, "following a rule in the present commits the agent to certain other actions in the future."[128] Thus all communicative action presupposes the capacity to form future-directed intentions. It is worth adding that Habermas arrived at very similar conclusions in his highly nuanced work on communicative action.[129]

This account reveals the basic inadequacy of the volitionalist approach: by centering agency in basic actions, it misses what is most essential to the intentionality of human actions, namely, its "holistic" nature. "Intentional states are necessarily a network, a whole system. They are not discrete separate items."[130] It is their place in a network of narrative significance, which gets its holism from the norms to which intentions implicitly commit us, that gives our actions their intentional quality. This quality does *not* derive, then, from the character of mental states (like reasons or trying volitions) that various causal theories have held to cause actions. This insight also finds strong support in Alasdair MacIntyre's narrative theory of action and intention[131] and in similar accounts in the hermeneutic tradition.

3.3. The Decision-as-Agency Concept

As we have seen, in contemporary philosophical theories of action, it is now usual to distinguish between (1) bodily movements or cognitive achievements such as directing one's attention; (2) the intentions to act a certain way that guide such movements and make them *actions* (performances under a subjective description); and (3) the *motives* from which intentions derive, which typically fall into two classes: desires and emotions, and reasons (judgments and beliefs). Depending on the theorist, practical judgments and beliefs may or may not be able to motivate by themselves, absent any prior desire for the end for which we intend to act. Within this scheme, volition could be identified with either the *executive* or the *motivational* side of the structure of an action: it is either (A) the effort to enact an intention to perform bodily movements or thought processes, which makes these performances into *actions* by connecting them with the intention; or (B) the desires that the agent believes the act will help satisfy or his all-things-considered judgment that this act is the thing to do in the circumstance. In neither case is the origin of the intention *itself an action* distinct in character from the "first-order" mental and physical acts that it intends.

Yet in nonphilosophical discourse or ordinary language, the notion of "will" retains much richer connotations. As Thomas Pink has argued, in "ordinary psychology," the decision-making by which we form intentions to act and apply reasons to plan future actions itself counts as a special type of intentional action. For Pink, volition thus has the more substantive sense of *second-order agency*. By this, it should be noted, Pink is not referring to Frankfurt's notion of "second-order volitions," which are part of his theory of autonomy. Rather, Pink's thesis is that the "willing" that is essential to the structure of ordinary first-order intentional action must itself be understood as a special activity in its own right:

> First we have our everyday actions and attempts at action—our first-order agency. Then we have, among the psychological states which explain and rationalise our first-order agency, some such as intentions whose formation constitutes agency too. That agency, of which the most intuitive case is decision-making, is our second-order agency. By tying our action control to prior decision control, a Psychologising conception of freedom ties the freedom of our first-order agency to a capacity for second-order agency.[132]

This concept of decision as a special kind of action can be traced, as Pink suggests, back through Aquinas to the Stoics, who both conceived the will in terms of second-order agency. The Stoics distinguished human from animal agency by "the human capacity for *sunkatathesis*, or making assent to propositions about how one should act."[133] The Stoics conceived such intention-forming acts of "consent" as "an agency of practical judgment,"[134] which is an integral part of our species essence as "rational animal." Augustine adds to this Stoic agency the concept of *liberum arbitrium* or libertarian freedom. However, as Kahn argues, "Augustine's concept of the will does not get a fully philosophical development until it is integrated within a theoretical model of the psyche, namely Aristotle's."[135] The concepts of deliberate action and choice had to be brought together in a more adequate account of second-order agency. Still, in Augustine, as with his predecessors, "there is no *one* concept that ties together the voluntary, *boulēsis* or desire for the end, and *prohairesis*, or deliberate desire for the means. But it is precisely the role of *voluntas* in Aquinas to perform this work of conceptual unification."[136]

Kahn describes in detail the development of this idea of *voluntas* and its superiority as an analysis of will over Aristotle's divided model. Since "Aquinas partially identifies *liberum arbitrium* with *voluntas* or 'the will' as the power to makes decisions. . . . [h]e thus establishes a close connection between the will and the concept of freedom that is unparalleled in Aristotle or any Hellenistic Greek discussion of *boulēsis*."[137] Aquinas thus introduces what Pink would call a psychologizing account of *voluntas* as an executive agency.

Pink's psychologizing notion of freedom thus involves a concept of volition as a capacity or power that goes beyond anything found in "volitionalist" models of first-order intentional action.[138] Unlike "volitional or conational theories of action," which equate volitions with states "whereby we try to move our bodies," a decision to act in Pink's sense *forms* intentions, while tryings *follow from* or execute intentions once they are formed:

> To take a decision to act is not, like trying, to initiate bodily movement, but rather to form a persisting psychological state—a state of intention in which we are left motivated to act as decided. Decisions are forms of agency which explain intentions; whereas tryings, like bodily actions, are quite distinct forms of agency which intentions explain.[139]

Pink argues that our "ordinary conception of freedom" or control, which does not derive merely from the notion of moral responsibility,[140] implies such a capacity for second-order agency: "Not only do we suppose ourselves to have a freedom to act otherwise; we suppose ourselves to have the freedom to decide and intend otherwise as well."[141] But decisions are not arbitrary gestures; Pink argues that the formation of intentions itself counts as agency because it shares the same kind of *practical rationality* as first-order acts.[142] Reasons for an act A are also reasons to form an intention to A.[143] Thus, with respect to first-order acts, a decision has a *motivational* function: "our actions are not just explained by beliefs and desires. Our actions are often explained by what appear to be further actions [e.g., 'decisions']— actions that are performed in the head, and which somehow generate the motivation for the actions which they explain."[144]

On this account, there is thus an important asymmetry between acts of will or decision and the first-order actions whose guiding intentions are formed by these decisions.[145] The intentions constitutive of first-order actions (whether mental or physical) are not sufficiently explained by the beliefs and desires that motivate them; they also require a decision to form this intention rather than other intentions that would have different motives.[146] Decisions, however, *are* sufficiently explained by their motives or follow immediately from them without needing a further decision to form a decision to act on these motives. We might fear a regress objection to this claim: since all actions are intentional, and Pink construes decision as a kind of action, then decisions must involve intentions, which would then have to be formed by further decisions, and so on.

This objection is just another version of the argument we noted earlier from Wittgenstein that any conception of willing as a distinct or special act of the mind would imply the absurd possibility of willing to will. Brian O'Shaughnessy makes a very similar argument against decisions as actions: citing the Wittgenstein passage we discuss above, he says that Φ is "the willing of some φ" if Φ is "the act of bringing about φ," where φ is, for example, a "limb movement" like "the event of an arm rise."[147] When Φ (a "volition") is thus construed as the carrying out of a preexisting intention, a further act θ that wills or brings about Φ would make no sense. For θ-ing here, O'Shaughnessy considers nerving or "getting myself" to shoot some fellow; but if this does not refer to some kind of imaginative self-manipulation (like promising myself rewards for doing it), then it cannot be distinct from the act of shooting him (Φ), which is "the making happen of a finger movement" on the trigger (φ).[148]

The problem with both Wittgenstein's and O'Shaughnessy's arguments is their assumption that acts of will are only *executive* in relation to existing intentions, initiating the process of carrying them out. Only on this interpretation does an act of decision become the carrying out of *an intention* to form intentions to act. So interpreted, decisions seem unnecessary; moreover, as Pink says, the "Pro-Attitude model" is underwritten by the notion that nothing that was not a reason or justification for *doing A* could still be a reason for deciding to do A, and so the latter is superfluous.[149] Yet as he argues, our control over our decisions or intention formation is "direct" rather than merely instrumental: "The agency which gives us decision and intention control is agency which *constitutes* the taking of a particular decision to act, rather than agency which *causes* that decision to be taken."[150]

In other words, we do not control our decisions by performing some further "decision-causing action," since our control over decision is *direct*.[151] Thus normally the "intention to decide to A" is formed *with the very decision* that forms the intention to A; decisions are in this sense immediately self-executing. Within first-order action, an intention to act in such-and-such a way may not be carried out (either because the agent changes her mind before the time arrives or because its implementation is blocked by external impediments). But at the second-order level, there is no such distance between forming the intention to decide and actually deciding.[152]

Some accounts of autonomy also conceive the will as second-order agency in Pink's sense. For example, Stampe and Gibson define "the will" as "the intention-forming powers of the mind, or traditionally, 'the power of choice,'"[153] and define "'decision' or 'choice' to mean just a mental event or act of mind in which an agent came to have the intention to do something A, where that event or act is one of such a kind that the agent's reasons for doing A *might* have been the cause of that intention."[154] This is a weaker condition than Pink's reason-applying conception of decision, but it still rules out intentions directly installed by neurologists or brought about by hypnotic suggestion, for example. Stampe and Gibson argue convincingly that "internal barriers" may prevent a person from freely deciding or forming an intention to act and thus prevent her from acting autonomously; for example, an agoraphobic woman does not freely remain in her room.[155] But they explain this by saying that her decision to remain in the room is unfree because it lacks "the condition of the will that makes it possible for an agent to make the rational decision about what to do," where *rational* is defined internally or subjectively:

> the rational action being what would be best "relative to" the desires of some agent and the evidence he or she actually possesses. (Thus, to be able to make "the rational decision" is, on one standard view, to be able to make that decision the implementation of which would tend to maximize the satisfaction of one's desires, if the relevant beliefs were true.[156]

Stampe and Gibson anticipate the objection that in this sense, the agoraphobic woman *does* decide rationally, since she satisfies her strongest desire (i.e., to avoid open spaces), though at the cost of frustrating other desires, like the urge to see her friend.[157] But they suggest that what makes her will unfree is rather that counterfactually, even if, "in her own estimation," going out were worth the risk of a panic attack, she still would not decide to do what would then be the subjectively rational thing for her to do; her will cannot track rationality in alternate possible variations of her circumstance. Similarly, what makes us unfree in a holdup is that even though we act rationally in handing over our wallet to the gunman, *were* we to believe that the rational thing was to defy him, we would be too scared to do it.[158] Stampe and Gibson compare this notion of free will to a "free-working mechanism: like a weathervane, which is not stuck in one position, but rather can point in the direction of the wind, whatever direction the wind may blow." Although a stuck weather vane may point in the right direction if by accident the wind is flowing in that direction today, it is not free, since it does not track the wind.[159]

In response, we might doubt that a robot that perfectly decided the best action in the circumstances relative to the goal of fulfilling its programming could have anything like "a will."[160] But aside from this intuitive problem, Stampe and Gibson's conception of autonomy offers an implausibly indirect account of the feeling of coercion in such situations. Even if I thought I could defy the gunman had I reason enough to do so (e.g., if my wallet contained the only copy of a formula for a cure to AIDS) the fear on which I act in the *actual sequence* where it is not outweighed is not a motive with which I *identify*, in Frankfurt's sense.[161] If volitional identification involves a form of commitment or resolve that is distinct from ordinary preferences and desires for our well-being, such a self-motivating capacity might allow for a more direct explanation of the agoraphobic's unfreedom as well: she may resolve to leave her home with the plan of meeting a cherished friend downtown, even though she thinks she is unlikely to follow through on this, given her condition (the resolve thus expresses a kind of defiance or alienation of the emotion on which she still reluctantly grants that she is likely to act). In fact, she is not able to form a real intention to open the door, because the intentions guiding her first-order acts are governed by a strong desire for enclosure that overrides the alternate motivational force of her resolve. Unlike Stampe's and Gibson's account, this more direct explanation does not equate volition with intention control or decision motivated solely by preexisting desires and beliefs. Like Pink, then, Stampe and Gibson do not recognize in will as second-order agency any *motivational* capacity distinct from desires or practical reasoning about the good.

Kane appears to endorse a similar decision-as-agency concept in his account of the "rational will." He finds the roots of this concept in Augustine and Bramhall, who both held that decisions are a special kind of *action*, which in turn "normally bring about intentions to act—intentions are their results." And since intentions have purposes or goals as part of their content, he concludes that "a choice or decision can be described as both the formation of intention and the creation of a purpose that subsequently guides action."[162]

The key point here, as in Pink's argument, is that prior desires or internal reasons to act cannot by themselves, or in combination with beliefs, just become purposes that explain actions as intentional. Rather, something else has to happen in the agent first: some of the ends pointed out by our preexisting desires have to be *taken up* into intentions. This is the crucial point overlooked by minimalist theories, such as Donald Davidson's, which "held that explanations of action could be given in terms of beliefs and desires (or wants) alone, with the intermediary notion of intention playing no indispensable role."[163] On the contrary, Kane rightly endorses recent arguments, such as Alfred Mele's, that intentions are formed at the termination of practical reasoning, and that it is only once an intention is formed that the agent really has a purpose or goal of action, since merely having a pro-attitude toward some outcome is not the same as its being one's purpose: "what is desired or wanted is not always selected as a goal."[164]

Similar criticisms of Davidson's initial belief-desire model are made by Carlos Moya. Like Anscombe and Davidson, Moya holds that agency is closely related to intentional action: "a certain piece of behavior is an action if, and only if, it is intentional (or intentionally performed) under some description. . . . There are non-intentional actions, or non-intentional true descriptions of actions, only because there are intentional actions, or intentional true descriptions of actions."[165]

In other words, something counts as a kind of action only because it can be done intentionally; either it is what Moya calls a "pure action" that can only be done intentionally (like marrying or making a chess move or lying), or it is what he calls a "neutral" action type that can be done intentionally or unintentionally (like offending or kicking).[166] But, building on his model of meaningful actions (discussed above), Moya argues that aside from simple actions aimed only at an outcome in the immediate moment (e.g., routine or habitual intentional acts like scratching an itch), most human intentions involve a kind of *commitment* to act on the reasons (beliefs, desires, and other considerations) that explain them or "rationalize" them in Davidson's sense. For example, while driving home, "My intention to get home or my intention to turn involve a certain kind of rational commitment: if I have those intentions I ought to engage in certain appropriate actions on pain of incoherence. We could call these intentions 'future intentions.'"[167] Thus intentions add something essential to action over and above desired aims, plans, and rules for acting, something irreducible to other elements of action:

Only when one commits oneself to act so as to match an ideal has one formed an intention. Intentions, I contend, are not mere desires, aims, plans, or rules: they are commitments to act so as to match their content (the desired, aimed at, or planned action). Aims, plans, and rules can remain inert. Only by constituting (part of) the content of an intention do they become efficacious as guides to action.[168]

On this view, fully intentional actions involve pragmatic commitment, and so forming such intentions seems to require an *act of* pragmatic commitment. Moya's account thus implies that "decision" in Pink's and Kane's sense amounts to a reflexive act in which the agent commits herself to future goals and standards that form requirements of narrative coherence for her continued agency. Such commitment is "the core of agency," according to Moya.[169]

Given this normative character, it is clear that intentions transcend "mere dispositions or tendencies to act."[170] Like Pink and Kane, Moya urges that desires, beliefs, and internal reasons for action in general become part of the explanation of action only *through* the formation of intentions:

Reasons are not, by themselves, causes of actions. Our reasons do not give rise to our actions as heat gives rise to the boiling of water. Only when we intend or decide to act on these reasons do these reasons become efficacious. . . . Agency is what makes [internal] reasons efficacious, and not conversely. It belongs to the human condition that we have to commit ourselves to act and to engage in acting in a concrete and definite way because desires, beliefs and drives are never decisive for us, rational and reflective beings, as, on the contrary, they are for most animals.[171]

For only normal human beings, who have the concept (as opposed to the mere intuition) of time, have the capacity for the future-oriented commitments involved in fully intentional action; other animals are capable of "minimally intentional actions" aimed at the immediate present or done from routine and instinct but not of planning intentionality with its normative dimension.[172] Thus, if "the will" refers to our capacity to form intentions involving such pragmatic commitments, only human beings have a "will." In the decision-as-agency concept, then, we have finally located a sense of "willing" that, even without a full account of moral freedom, is distinctively human.

This concept is lacking in Davidson. Beginning with problems in accounting for weakness of will, Davidson modified his original quasi-Aristotelian theory of action to include intentions to perform an action as something over and above the beliefs and pro-attitudes that rationalize the action. The intention to A, now identified with the all-out summary judgment that A-ing would be better than any other available actions, does not necessarily follow from the beliefs and pro-attitudes that explain or rationalize A-ing. Nor is intending to A identical with A-ing. Moya diagnoses this shift as a result of Davidson implicitly recognizing the distinct status of future intentions.[173] But despite these modifications, Davidson's late model of intention does not recognize that intentions are the result of decision as second-order or reflexive agency. He still equates an intention with an unconditionally positive disposition to an action or practical judgment about it.[174]

Following Bratman, Moya shows that several problems arise for this conception of intentions, because "all-out judgments are at least implicitly comparative," whereas intentions are not.[175] I can, for example, simultaneously have two intentions to do two different things (either together or separately) while judging all-out that one is preferable to the other.[176] Moreover, the commitment model of intention allows for conditional intentions (intending to do A provided that a given condition is satisfied) whereas the all-out judgment model cannot. These difficulties, together with the problem of wayward causal chains, show that we cannot understand intentions as simply *caused* by the reasons that rationalize them.[177] Summarizing these criticisms, Moya says: "In viewing intentions as all-out pro-attitudes Davidson conceives them as too similar to desires not to face problems before cases of intending which are not cases of judging the object of the intention as the most desirable alternative."[178]

Although Moya does not describe his own alternative to Davidson's causal account as a theory of "willing," it should be clear by now how similar his alternative is to Pink's theory of decision and Kane's concept of rational willing. Moreover, all of these accounts are indebted to Kant's understanding of willing as an activity in which we create intentions on the basis of considerations that we (at least implicitly) take to be practical reasons that could also apply in similar circumstances in the future or that function as practical rules for us. As Christine Korsgaard explains in her thorough account of this idea, the normative problem arises for human beings, unlike all other known animals, because our natural inclinations and impulses do not "dominate" us; hence we can raise the question: "Is this desire really a *reason* to act? The reflective mind cannot settle for perception and desire, not just as such. It needs a reason. Otherwise . . . it cannot commit itself or go forward."[179]

The key idea in this conception of action does not follow, however, simply from the premise that we are not dominated by prepurposive desires and impulses because we can reflect on them. By itself, this premise is compatible with the claim that we sometimes simply fail to reflect and act straightaway on prepurposive motives arising in our consciousness, without any maxim. The Kantian theory requires the stronger premise that whenever we act on intentions formed voluntarily through decision (or whenever we perform what Aquinas would call a "human action"), we are implicitly endorsing the motives incorporated into our purposes *as reasons* for future action in similar circumstances. Korsgaard clarifies this in her response to Nagel: we "are committed to making the same decision on *some* range of possible occasions."[180] This means that in deciding, we endorse some reason for action that is more than a singular prescription. Call this the Kantian Principle of Action (KPA): voluntary action entails "commitment" to a practical reason.

Note that the sense of "commitment" involved here is a fairly thin one: it is normative because it implies a prima facie reason for future action, a consideration that is in principle repeatable. This is weaker than the kind of identity-conferring "commitment" that is essential to what Korsgaard calls[181] "practical identity" (see chapter 11, section 2.3), which is also the commitment involved in volitional caring (see chapter 13). "Commitment" in this stronger sense is not implied by every voluntary action. Some evidence for the Kantian principle can be found by introspective investigation of voluntary action, for we find that in the intention-forming decision, "the ego sides spontaneously" with motivating inclinations or emotions.[182] Korsgaard argues that KPA is implicit in the practical point of view: "It is from within the deliberative perspective that we see our desires as providing suggestions which we may take or leave."[183] This can be strengthened into the claim that we have to see ourselves as *agent causes* of our decisions,[184] but KPA in itself does not include this metaphysical postulate.

Together, Pink, Kane, Moya, and Korsgaard provide formidable evidence for the decision-as-agency concept of willing. However, they still fail to address a remaining fundamental question about the way that acts of "will" in this sense can be *motivated*. Their approach shows that the purposes for which we act, as embodied in the network of intentions that guide our acts (or the narrative descriptions under which our acts are intentional and thus potentially voluntary as well)[185] can be thought of as *created by us* out of our prior motives or reasons for acting. Pink speaks of this creation of purpose as adding motivating force to the prior motives, and this seems plausible. Moya adds, again convincingly, that the prior reasons that inform the creation of new purposes will have to include, in addition to new facts, our whole network of past intentions and the pragmatic commitments to particular actions and norms bound up with them. But beyond these formal observations, these theories tell us virtually nothing about the *actual content or structure* of the original motives (aside from past intentions) that we have at our disposal and what sorts of purposes we can make out of them. On their view, this is simply a question of empirical psychology beyond the boundaries of philosophical theories of agency.

Kane, for example, explains that practical reasons in the "internalist" sense of "psychological attitudes" that can "play a role in the etiology of choice or action" mean pretty much the same thing as a "motive" that can be cited in explaining that action or in explaining the formation of the intention that the action executes.[186] But such remarks on the formal role of reasons and motives constitute an account of "rational willing" only because willing in this sense concerns merely the formation of intended purposes out of prior motives, not the nature or generation of these motives native to human psychology or deriving from individual life experience. So although decision-as-agency accounts give us a fairly robust concept of willing in comparison to the volitionalist and minimalist concepts, they remain focused on a *motivationally thin* function; "willing" in the sense of decision-making as a kind of second-order agency still plays no direct role in shaping what we might call *primary motivations* (those that do not come from standing intentions but that inform and help explain the act of forming a particular intention or creating a given purpose). While the will plays a robust role in the structure and generation of intentional action, it remains almost entirely dependent on those primary motive "inputs" (to use Kane's term) that make acts of decision possible. In Aquinas, too, while *voluntas* is clearly a kind of second-order agency, the motives between whose influences it moves in forming intentions remain entirely determined by sense appetites, imagination, habit, and practical reason. Although the will may be an executive agent, it works from a fixed background of motives that only alter over time as a result of the will's actions, the experiences these produce, and changes in external circumstances. This assumption Kane, Pink, Stampe, Gibson, and Moya seem to share with their volitionalist and minimalist foes: the concept of the will is defined in terms of action and intention alone. It can be extended in a general theory of agency including "autonomous" action, but the theory of motivation is a separate question. If there is any sense of "will" beyond what follows from the structure of agency, this could only be "will" as an expression for libertarian freedom. A theory of the will is complete, then, once we have the right theories of action, autonomy, and moral freedom. It does not require any further phenomenology of human motivation itself. That task, it is assumed, can simply be left to psychology.

This is the basic assumption that unites what I call (from this point on) *motivationally thin theories* of the will. Despite large differences between these theories, they all treat willing as an operation that can be fully described in formal metaphysical terms without looking in detail at the psychological contents of willing, the experienced structures of motives, or their roles in what I call *the ethos of a person*. This phrase is a convenient shorthand for the whole way a person experiences life; how it is (or is not) meaningful to him; how his own character and sense of value grow and change over time; and (in the broadest sense) what kind of "personality" he has. Thin theories of the will abstract from the question of whether willing in their sense—or any other—plays any special role in expressing or shaping the ethos of a person. In other words, they take for granted that the will is (if anything at all) simply an operation of mind that is to be identified by its unique formal role in the general structure of intentional action: *"willing" is a concept native to action theory, not the theory of motivation.* This is true whether the will is conceived in "volitionalist" fashion as the formation of a trying, or in the second-order agency fashion as the formation of an intention to act, or in a libertarian variant of either of these models as election between different possible tryings, intentions, or decisions as agent-causing intentions, and so on.

On such thin views, the experience of preexisting motives that serve as inputs for practical deliberation and decision can be called "appetitive willing," as Kane puts it; but here the term "will" has a totally different sense, because such prior appetites are regarded as generated by a set of psychological processes that are quite distinct from practical willing. Willing in any thin sense, such as practical reason and intention formation, is represented as having at best only an indirect effect on appetitive willing. The thin concept of willing as the practical process of forming intentions and purposes can be interpreted in more minimalist or more robust ways, with those conceptions that involve decision-making as second-order agency being the most robust today. But none of them sees practical willing as directly involved in controlling, shaping, or forming our motives themselves. If willing is itself motivational, as I argue in the rest of this book, then even the decision-as-agency model of willing still gives us an incomplete picture, despite its superiority over volitionalist and minimalist models.

3.4. *The Existential Concept of Striving Will*

Existentially thick theories of the will, by contrast, hold that willing in its primary and most important sense is a phenomenon unique to the psychology of persons that is picked out or identified by its special roles in shaping the ethos of a person, or (for short) its *existential functions*. "Willing" is not, then, simply a formal concept of action theory, that is, a concept determined primarily by its metaphysical role. Its metaphysical senses are secondary relative to its primary practical meaning as a special psychological process with a complex phenomenology and anthropological significance. In particular, existentially thick theories regard the will as a *motivational process involved in intention formation* and thus as a psychological and ethical concept (in the broadest sense of this term).

As I argue in the introduction, this rich sense of "will" is still alive in nonphilosophical or ordinary discourse. For example, in familiar usages, "will" is associated with "determination," "diligent purposiveness,"[187] and making difficult decisions; it signifies a way of focusing one's energies on doing something, or inward *resolve* to pursue a certain course, which is often especially apparent in the face of adversity. Kane would apparently explain these as instances of "striving will," involving an *effort to execute* an intention formed by decision on the basis of preexisting motives. But this thin interpretation of striving will in contemporary action theory is inadequate because it implies that all the motivation involved in such an executive effort is inherited from the preexisting motives in the etiology of the intention. Instead, the familiar phenomena of "heroic willing" actually suggest the *creation of new motivation* and also *the reinvigoration and consolidation* of existing motives in the agent. In contrast to Kane's characterization, the existential conception of "striving will" emphasizes these twin motive-shaping functions.

This idea is also found throughout the genre of existential psychology. For example, Rank's complaint against Freud is not simply that he excludes will in the sense of free decision. Rather, Rank focuses on the idea that volitional strength exhibited in creative initiative is characteristic of the "normal man."[188] Thus he defines the will as a motivational faculty: it is "a positive guiding organization and integration of self" that transcends "instinctual drives."[189] This familiar motivational sense of "volition" is not to be restricted, as Iris Murdoch suggests, "to cases where there is an immediate straining, for instance occasioned by a perceived duty or principle, against a large part of preformed consciousness."[190] The motivational quality named by "will" does not always *require* an experience of inner tension, or a phenomenal quality we might describe as an inner "gritting of mental teeth," as for example, when Whoopie Goldberg struggles to hand over her check for $4 million to the Salvation Army nuns in the film *Ghost*. The striving will as a source of self-motivation is just as much in evidence when someone commits himself, without reservation, to doing something he already had other reasons for wanting to do (perhaps joining a team whose other members already like him) when these predecisional motives were not by themselves sufficient to motivate his decision. In such cases, the will adds something new and has reasons independent of prior desires for doing so. Or so I argue.

As we see in chapter 9, this existential version of striving will has theological roots. For the moment, however, I am only concerned to ask how such an idea could be framed within the terms of contemporary action theory at all. We can outline in a provisional way what it would mean for there to be *essentially volitional* motivation that can neither exist outside willed purposes nor derive from other prior motives that can move the agent without her intending to act on them. "Motives" as action theorists now describe them include such states as desires, emotions, or other pro-attitudes and internal reasons for acting that are *prior or external to the intentions they motivate*; as we have seen, to inform actions, such motives have to be taken up by decisions and made into purposes for the sake of which we intend to act. "Volitional" motives, if they exist, would have to have a different, internal relation to decision and intention: they could motivate only *in becoming* our purposes. In other words, they would involve a special way of being motivated to action that always involves taking them up or actively intending to act on them. In this sense, incorporation by decision (or some analogous process), or expression in the agent's intention, is already *built into this distinctive way of being motivated*. By this, I do not mean simply that a volitional motive has the property of being "a motive that has become a purpose through being taken up into an intention by the decision which formed it." Of course, it follows necessarily that any motive with *that* property also operates as a purpose in action attempted or planned. Rather, I mean that there is a kind of motivation distinguished by its experiential structure *and* that this motivational structure cannot occur without the ends or goals envisioned becoming intended purposes of their agent. These motives are themselves volitional states, because we bring them about in the higher-order *resolve* to pursue certain goals or to embody these ends as purposes in our intentions. The resolve involved here, as we shall see, may arise through a process that is distinct from decision in its ordinary senses of intention formation or election among options.

This hypothesis can also be framed the other way around, starting from intentions. The entire decision-as-agency tradition (from Aquinas, through Scotus and Kant, to the present) has emphasized that intentions are not simply *caused* by motives, like one force causing another in an event-causal mechanism. Thus Hauerwas defends Richard Taylor's view that an accurate description of an act must include "an essential reference to an agent,"[191] because the description requires an intention that exists within "the agent's perspective."[192] Like our intentions, our motives have being only within the whole gestalt of our agency; as Hauerwas puts it, "in moving ourselves as agents we embody the motives that give our action and ourselves their peculiar unity and form—in a word, their character."[193] This explains why the intentions that we form in response to our motives also shape to some extent what future motives we will experience.[194] It is only an extension of this idea that *present* motives are also always partially determined in their specific content and strength by being "embodied" in intention. If this is right, then the power of forming intentions includes the capacity to modify, mold, or perhaps crystallize prior motives that are always somewhat malleable, or partially indeterminate in some cases. This explains why, as Hauerwas observes in raising a problem for Aristotle's action theory, "The end is seldom determined apart from the consideration of the means necessary to achieve it," which itself may only be fixed in *prohairetic* choice.[195] Yet if both the ends at which our motives aim and the specific manner in which they are directed toward these ends can be fixed or specified in the process of forming plans of action with particular purposes, perhaps the intention-forming capacity's power to shape its own motive-inputs can extend even further in some cases. Perhaps it can form new motivation that need not depend on prior appetition or emotion at all—motivation that can arise entirely *within* intention-forming agency.

If such essentially volitional motivation exists, then "striving will" plays a direct role in determining both the substantial direction and the strength of some of the motives on which we act. This contrasts directly with all the others models of willing we examined, in which we can derive the ends or purposes of our intentions only from our preexisting motivational set. On these views, we can perhaps indirectly alter our motivational set through our actions but we cannot directly generate new motivation in the process of forming intentions to act for some purpose. For reasons explained in the introduction, I call these volitional states in which the motivation is directly generated by the striving will "projective motives," or "states of projective motivation." I hope not only to show that projective motivation exists but also to make clear why it plays certain crucial existential roles that explain its significance in our lives.

Thomas Pink comes closest to this idea of projective motivation when he suggests that we do build up our own motives in one sense by *reinforcing* or adding to the motivating power of the prior motives on which we decide to act. Pink sees this especially in the phenomena of resolve or determination to stick to future intentions, in which we experience a strengthening of our initial motivation. As he says, decisions control future actions in a direct or "essentially non-manipulative" fashion[196] by "perpetuating the force of the considerations that have already motivated it."[197] But Pink does not see that for this to be possible, the will must be more than the faculty of decision or the intention-forming module of the mind. For the abstract function of forming intentions does not by its mere form determine anything about *how strongly or in what different ways* we may be motivated to pursue our intended goals. As we'll see below, in most traditional theories of motivation, it was held that both the mode and the strength of our motivation to pursue our intended purposes are always a direct function of the kinds and degrees of "motive pull" present in the preexisting motives out of which our purposes were formed. If projective motivation is possible, then this is false.

So the existentialist should agree with Pink that in "ordinary psychology," the decision-making by which we form intentions to act and apply reasons to plan future actions itself counts as a special type of intentional action. But for Pink, this action of the will is motivated simply by practical judgments about the desirability of ends; willing derives from prior "desiderative" or "rational" motives, or some combination of the two, as in familiar classical and medieval accounts. Though decisions form purposes that may not be completely determined by preexisting motives, decisions still do not directly affect the prior motives on which they depend. Though Pink allows that "one can form intentions that are not accompanied by any conviction that what is intended is desirable" or that are not explained by practical judgment about reasons to act, in his view this happens only in deviant cases: "the core function of intention formation is to apply or execute our practical judgments about how we should act."[198] This is where the new existentialist dissents. For her, the "will" can do more than form a reason-considering decision to act in some definite way or other; in addition, it includes the capacity to generate its own native form of *motivation* that is different from all the prior motives that we know as generated by instinct, inclination, and evaluative judgment about our good, which also influence our decisions.

It is important to emphasize that what I am calling here the "existential concept" of striving will does not necessarily include or depend on a libertarian, agent-causal, or otherwise incompatibilist theory of the freedom required for moral responsibility. Any complete existential conception of moral freedom must include such incompatibilist conditions and a non-Molinist account of libertarian freedom and autonomy. But as I make clear in chapter 11, section 3, the question of libertarian freedom can usefully be bracketed and postponed for future work, since the idea of projective motivation is not *in itself* a libertarian concept. If the will is free in the libertarian sense, this will doubtless be part of any full explanation of why it can play such a central role in shaping our life-narrative. And it is easy to see in this light how the striving will (in our existential sense) could so often be conflated with libertarian freedom and thus eventually with the act of decision in which freedom seems to rest in the process of forming intentions and acting. But to understand the will's existential functions in human life, we have to know about its psychological character, including the structure of motivation unique to it, and not *only* about its freedom. Thus when the will is reduced simply to a faculty of free decision or free intention formation, we lose sight of much of its existential significance for the ethos of personal agents.

The Next Steps

Of course, I have not yet shown that projective motivation as outlined here *is* possible or that there is any evidence in favor of thickening the decision-as-agency concept of willing to include motivation-generating powers as well. We have only located the crucial point where the existential concept of the heroic or striving will departs from contemporary accounts in analytic action theory. The evidence in favor of the existential concept is the theme of the next chapters, in the following way.

First, in chapter 4, I argue that Plato's concept of desire as eros sets the basic paradigm for most later Western philosophical models of motivation in general, including Aristotle's notion of "rational appetite." In chapter 5, I refer to Aristotle in distinguishing three types of desire conforming to Plato's general schema and distinguish the "formal egoism" of Aristotle's psychology from traditional forms of material egoism, whose paradoxes Aristotle's eudaimonism avoids. However, as I argue in chapters 6 and 7, a rigorous reconstruction of Aristotle's eudaimonist account of human motivation reveals similar paradoxes in the relation between virtue and happiness. I argue that if something like Aristotle's virtue ethics is true, then not all motivation can have the form of "desire" as described in classical Greek accounts and in Aristotle's own psychology. In chapter 8, I canvas several possible responses to this existential critique of eudaimonism and argue that they all fail to resolve the fundamental problem; thus virtue still requires projective motivation.

In chapter 9, I explain what projective motivation means in more detail, starting from the paradigm case of divine creativity as it was conceived in the Neoplatonic tradition leading to existential theology. I then lay out the formal structure of projective motivation seen in this paradigm case and offer several plausible illustrations of this phenomenon in human experience (in addition to the virtuous motives and practices already discussed in chapters 7 and 8). Chapter 10 then argues that we also see evidence of projective motivation in the phenomena of radical evil as opposed to the eudaimonist model of vice as ignorance or *akrasia*. The better understanding of "strength of will" afforded by the existential model leads into chapter 11, which argues that Duns Scotus rejects the eudaimonist approach for what is the first clearly projective account of moral motivation. Likewise, Kant's ethics and moral psychology require a limited form of projective motivation. Although I think the "will to justice" as understood by Scotus and Kant provides strong evidence for the existential model against eudaimonism, I still argue that Kant conceives our volitional capacities far too narrowly—a problem that can be solved only by articulating other possible non-deontic grounds for projecting ends. This thesis is defended again in chapter 13, which argues that we need to accept the projective model of the striving will to make sense of the crucial phenomenon of *existential commitment*, and in chapter 14, where I develop an account of the main grounds for commitment to ends.

4

The Erosiac Structure of Desire in Plato and Aristotle

Overview. This chapter begins by explaining how an investigation of the Greek "erosiac" model of motivation supports the main argument for the existential conception of the striving will. The sketch of projective motivation given at the end of chapter 3 can be filled out by contrast with the conception of desire developed in Plato's moral psychology, which is then incorporated into Aristotle's eudaimonism. The focus in sections 2 and 3 of this chapter is on themes from Plato's *Lysis, Meno, Republic,* and *Symposium* that should be accessible to general readers. Readers interested only in the concepts extracted from these texts that are used in the book's main argument for the existential view can focus on sections 2.4 and 3.2.

I. Toward an Existential Theory of Motivation

1.1. The Transmission Principle: A Problem in the Theory of Motivation

The previous chapter concluded with the suggestion that the existential concept of the will as a form of second-order agency in Pink's sense involves not only deliberation and decision-making but also a distinct kind of striving that generates new motivation either in setting new purposes or in executing a standing intention or plan. As I argued, this is distinct from striving in the sense of "trying" to carry out a formed intention, where the motivation for such an effort is entirely derivative of the motivation for forming the intention in the first place. Now, this existential concept of willing challenges not only the motivationally thin concept of the will that underlies all the conceptions of volition in contemporary action theory, but also the various models of human motivation that underlie this thin concept of willing. In fact, it is reasonable to regard the thin concept, which conceives volition in terms of "practical willing" in Kane's sense, as a natural outcome of the main models of motivation in the history of Western philosophy. This is explained by the following historical hypothesis: in their earliest forms, the main models of motivation that have influenced Western moral psychology all predate and condition the development of executive-agency accounts of the will in late antiquity and early medieval philosophy, and the more sophisticated conceptions of decision and practical deliberation developed in contemporary action theory and theories of practical reason, respectively.[1] If this is right, then there is an important sense in which our conceptions of the "volitional" processes of intention formation and practical reasoning are controlled by deep prior assumptions about human motivation—assumptions that often do not surface in action theory. Some theory of motivation is genealogically prior to any theory of the will as an element in human agency, even if the latter theory does not discuss motivation directly at all.

For example, as we saw in chapter 2, the main alternative models in contemporary action theory all presuppose what I will call the *Transmission principle* (TP): when we have formed intentions to act, our motivation to pursue our intended purposes inherits both (1) *all* its strength and (2) *all* its intentional direction and content immediately from prior psychological states that are either (a) already motivating in their own right (such as desires) or (b) motivating when combined with these (such as beliefs). The difference between such prior states and the motivation involved in intending to act for a given purpose is simply that the former can be experienced as motives (or as parts of motives) without actually intending to act on them. To mark this, let us call these psychological attitudes that incline us to form intentions "prepurposive motives" (or PPMs). For example, on the basis of a desire for revenge or an emotion of resentment, we might form an intention to harm someone in such a way that he (and others) will know the harm comes intentionally from us. Our motive to act on this intention draws its content and strength from these prior motives: the intended result will satisfy our desire or perhaps express our emotion. Now TP can be restated as follows: volition (including decision and its other forms) does not generate any new motivation; it only *transmits* motivation from PPMs into the intended purposes and into efforts to enact those intentions. Or, equivalently, our intended purposes derive all their motivational power and direction from prior motives in our "internal set," as Bernard Williams famously called our standing psychic repertoire of PPMs.[2] In such models, which find their clearest modern precedent in David Hume's moral psychology, we cannot generate new motivation directly in the process of forming intentions and setting their goals or in trying to carry them out. At most, we extend existing desires to new cases or clarify what we already have internal reason to do by acquiring new descriptive beliefs or learning that some of our former beliefs were false.[3]

Although theories of motivation vary widely in contemporary moral psychology, TP is a central element in virtually all of them. For example, it underlies the common view that we act on our strongest desires—a view that Alfred Mele has restated in more rigorous form as the theory that we act on our strongest "buffer-free" desire for an action seen as within our power.[4] Mele's account presupposes the crucial distinction between *motives* and *intentions*. As we saw in chapter 3, *intention* in contemporary action theories refers to the first-personal understanding of what we are doing or planning to do that makes our bodily movements into an *action* as opposed to mere behavior—and on some accounts, intentions are formed by decisions. We always act under a certain description or with a certain *aspect* of our behavior as our intentional object: for example, "walking into the store to get a soda" rather than "trying to avoid someone on the sidewalk coming toward me." As this example illustrates, intentions must include at least the proximate *end* toward which the action is consciously directed in order to pick out the right aspect or description of the behavior which is essential to the act.

Motives, by contrast, are all assumed to be prepurposive: they are not in themselves formed intentions that explain actual or planned movements of the mind or body, causing these to count as actions; rather, they typically lie behind the possible formation of many different intentions and explain why the agent fixes on the ends involved in his specific intentions to act this or that way. As Steven Sverdlik argues in a helpful article, motives correspond to the beginning or major premise in a practical-syllogism reconstruction of our action, which is why we think "that motives are usually more general in content than the resulting intention," and that "a given intention (or action) could be the result of a number of different motives."[5]

Sverdlik observes that the question about what "motives" are has rarely been addressed in "English-language philosophy" because "Action theory now largely concentrates on intention, desire, belief, and the (usually undefined) concept of motivation." He begins with six "relatively uncontroversial" propositions about motives:

1. They are "actual psychological states or events."
2. They are "at least part of the cause of an action or the decision to act."
3. While they precede an action, motives "typically continue to be present or operative as the act takes place" [this is Sverdlik's weaker version of TP].

4. They are mentioned typically to "explain why the agent acted as she did."

5. From the agent's viewpoint, her motives specify "what is of value about her action" (or what valuable end it realizes).

6. "The two main types of motive seem to be emotion and desire."[6]

Sverdlik then argues that if we consider them from within the Davidsonian belief-desire model of action, "It seems clear that motives belong to the conative, desiring side of the story," since beliefs do not seem to be "even a part of the motive for an action." Factual beliefs "concerning means, consequences, or specifications of general desires" acquire motivating force only when they are connected to some desire. Of course, "internalists" have defended the idea that some evaluative beliefs *do* constitute motives to act, but Sverdlik replies that externalists about moral motivation can hold that the motive is "some separate state of desire which is entailed by the belief" about one's obligations.[7] This is roughly to say that the externalists do not need anything more than a desire that follows from the evaluative judgment it involves.[8] Similarly, "the emotions we regard as motives characteristically give rise to desires to act in ways related to the content of the emotions";[9] for example, fear gives rise to the desire to flee from the relevant danger.

If this is right, then beliefs and emotions become motivating only by way of desires, and the best hypothesis is that the motive is the "ultimate desire" from which the end in our intention is derived.[10] And since "the identity of an action rests partly on what intention it incorporates," on all the leading views about act individuation, "all intentional actions (or all actions under the descriptions in which they are intentional) have a motive."[11] In sum, on Sverdlik's view, which is fairly representative of the current literature, certain beliefs and emotions may cause desires, and these in turn motivate the formation of intentions, which get their ends from *at least* one (though possibly more than one) ultimate desire(s): "intentions are formed as a way of pursuing the agent's goals or desires."[12] Intentions thus derive their motivational direction and strength from prior terminal desires and emotions, as TP says. And "motive" and "desire" are practically synonymous in Sverdlik's account, since both mean whatever plays the relevant functional role in the identity of the intention and action.

This brief look into contemporary motivation theory shows why the debate between neo-Humean and neo-Kantian views on moral motivation may shed light on whether TP should be taken for granted. More generally, the correctness of TP is really central, though often unrecognized, in current debates between externalist and internalist positions on motivation.

But a discussion of this literature is beyond the scope of this book. I postpone it in part because it will be easier to evaluate this debate once the existential conception of striving will is clear.

1.2. The Existential Core Argument

It is now evident why the existential account of striving will sketched in chapters 2 and 3 cannot be defended without refuting TP. This in turn requires showing that the dominant models of motivation in our philosophical tradition are incomplete, since they leave out forms of motivation experienced in our intended purposes that do not trace in any direct way to prior motivating states. The most likely way to show this would be to find purposes or intentions (on which some agent acts or tries to act) whose motivational structure is recognizably *different* from all prepurposive motivational states and which never originates outside of purposes (i.e., never in a PPM). In other words, if volitional motivation generated in the striving will is possible, its intentional structure should be different from those of PPM states—even though all motives share a conative "direction of fit" (in which the world conforms to the end envisioned) that contrasts with the cognitive direction of fit characteristic of beliefs (in which the content believed conforms to the world).

But traditional philosophical accounts of human motivation do not recognize or distinguish any motives other than PPM states in the explanation of human intentions. This is why I said at the end of chapter 3 that if experience reveals the existence of such essentially purposive motives, which arise within decisions and decision-like processes, then we will need radically to rethink our traditional models. This suggests a way to proceed in justifying the existential model. If we can find any distinguishing features of recognized prepurposive motives *other than* the world-content direction of fit that is shared by all motive-states, then we could look for any motivational experiences contrasting with these features as possible cases of projective motivation.

Ideally, this approach calls for a complete survey of prepurposive motives as a preliminary task: we (1) start from as complete as possible a conception of PPM states; (2) explain what it would be for some state of motivation to differ in intentional structure from all these PPMs despite sharing the same world-content fit; and (3) provide evidence that various motive-states with this different intentional structure exist or need to be postulated to explain other evident psychological phenomena. But the first task as written—namely, developing a complete account of prepurposive states that are both experienced as intrinsically motivating and can inform our decisions, purposes, or specific intentions to act—is unmanageably large. It has proven difficult enough in recent work in moral psychology to counsel a more limited approach.

Hence, rather than simply surveying all the different sorts of states that can counts as PPMs on different theories of motivation and trying to evaluate what is common to them all, I will start instead with the particular theory of prepurposive motivation that is both the richest in content and historically the most influential: that is, the one I call (borrowing from Alan Soble) the "erosiac" model of Plato and Aristotle.[13] This theory focuses on what Wayne Davis calls "appetitive desire," which connotes "cravings, yearning, longing and urge."[14] This gives us a distinguishing feature of PPM states apart from their world-to-content direction of fit:

The Weak Erosiac Thesis (WET): all *prepurposive* motive-states have the general "erosiac" structure of an appetitive lack-seeking-completeness.

By itself, WET leaves open the possibility that some of our motives for intentional action might not be "erosiac" in experienced form because they might not be PPMs. But since TP eliminates the possibility that the process of decision or conscious formation of intentional purposes can add anything new to the content or strength of the agent's existing PPMs, such purposive motives must inherit the erosiac structure of their prepurposive sources. Hence TP together with WET entails

The Strong Erosiac Thesis (SET): all motives operative in intentional action have the general "erosiac" structure of lack-seeking-completeness.

Starting with WET as a working hypothesis thus gives us a way to distinguish projective motives from PPMs and to refute TP. If we can show that some of our purposive motives operative in intentional action are not erosiac in form, then we falsify SET and thus also refute TP. Here is the argument as a natural deduction:

1. Weak erosiac thesis (WET) & transmission principle (TP) $\Rightarrow$ strong erosiac thesis (SET) [by def. of WET, TP, SET]
2. There are some actual cases of non-erosiac purposive motivation $\Rightarrow \neg$SET [by def. of SET]
3. $\neg$SET $\Rightarrow \neg$(WET & TP) [from 1 by *modus tollens*]
4. There are some actual cases of non-erosiac purposive motivation [premise supported by phenomenological analysis of examples and thought experiments]
5. $\neg$SET [from 2 and 4 by *modus ponens*]
6. $\neg$(WET & TP) [from 3 and 5 by *modus ponens*]
7. WET [premise supported inductively by familiar prepurposive motives, e.g., D1–D3 desires]
8. $\neg$TP [from 6 and 7 by elimination]

The erosiac hypothesis concerning PPMs makes it conceptually possible to define projective motivation in a way that contrasts with PPMs and gives us premise 7.

Thus, in my three-step sequence, the modified first task is to explain the erosiac theory of prepurposive motives, which is introduced in this chapter and developed in chapters 5 and 6. Chapter 9 completes the second task by explaining how projective motivation can have an intentional structure distinct from the erosiac structure of PPMs. All the other chapters contribute to the third task, which is to give evidence for premise 4 in this core argument. Chapters 7 and 8 really develop an indirect argument for premise 4 through a critique of psychological eudaimonism. The later chapters support premise 4 directly by examples.

An objection to this whole strategy of argument would arise if there were any richer accounts of prepurposive motivation than those in the eudaimonist tradition. For then non-erosiac motive-states might still be prepurposive rather than essentially purposive. But it is fairly clear that, aside from Kant, most philosophers in the modern period offer sparse accounts of motivation that are more impoverished than the Greek erosiac model. Hence evidence that the richer Greek account is incomplete is automatically evidence of the even greater incompleteness of these sparser modern models. On the other hand, while Kant begins to see the lacuna in the Greek erosiac model, his own alternative does not recognize everything the Greek model leaves out. Thus an existential moral psychology recognizes a range of possible human motives extending beyond the conjunction of erosiac PPMs and moral motives in the deontic sense. It stands on the opposite end of the spectrum from the most reductive material egoist accounts of human motivation.[15]

2. Plato's Erosiac Model of Motivation

2.1. Introduction to Orexis

As this outline of my strategy indicates, one of the central tasks of this book is to critique a certain view of human motivation that originates in classical Greek philosophy and dominates scholastic thought up to the late Middle Ages, when it begins to give way alternately to the more reductive theories of Hobbes and the empiricists and to the richer conceptions of Scotus and Kant. This classical view emphasizes that in every psychological state that can motivate action, the agent experiences what we might call a *teleological pull*: the agent is "moved" toward the desired end as if drawn by a magnetic force within it. The notion of pull or attraction is more basic than the notion that the state of perfection according to our nature is the "prime mover" in all our motives: this eudaimonist idea is built on the more basic concept of psychological magnetism. Eudaimonism applies this magnetic metaphor to all motive-states, even in brute impulses or drives arising directly from animal instinct. On this view, as Ben Vedder summarizes, "desire is experienced as a propensity or inclination which is directed towards something which is still absent" or lacking.[16]

This notion of a teleological pull seems to be contained in the Latin words from which we get our primary senses of "desire" in English. For example, Latin lexicons commonly define *desidero* as "to long for, to wish for greatly, to miss"[17] or, even more clearly, as "to long for what is absent or lost, to wish for; to miss, find a lack of."[18] The related word, *desiderium*, often has the more specific sense of "grief for the absence or loss of" some person or thing.[19] This connotation of missing something, or being in a state in which the *absence of lack* of some good is salient, seems to go back to the common senses of the ancient Greek word transliterated as *orexis*, which standard lexicons such as Liddell-Scott-Jones define as "a *longing* or *yearning after* a thing."[20] In Greek philosophy, a state of *orexis* implies an intentional attitude toward what is wanted. As Nussbaum explains, "*orexis*" is "a 'reaching out for' an object; and all forms of *orexis* see their object in a certain way, supplying the animal with a 'premise of the good.'"[21] In fact, Nussbaum argues that Aristotle largely coined the word "*orexis*" to help show that every kind of motive that explains "goal-directed animal movement" shares a property that distinguishes it from "a purely mechanical response."[22] This is the property of responding to a perceived "lack of self-sufficiency or incompleteness."[23] Nussbaum is correct that this makes animal movement more "active" than movement by the influx of physical force.[24] However, as an essentially psychic cause irreducible to physiological processes, *orexis* is still passive in a different but crucial sense: we are *drawn* toward the goal by its prospect of completing us when we attain it.[25]

The psychic passivity of such teleological magnetism is seen in the relation between *orexis* and *pathos*, whose species were typically interpreted by the Greeks as a kind of force of appeal flowing from the desired object, present or absent, either to the eyes or to the mind (nous).[26] Plato's discussion of motivational terms in the *Cratylus* is significant here, even if it is more philosophical than etymological:

> Nor is there any difficulty about *epithumia* (desire), for this name was evidently given to the power that goes (*iousa*) into the soul (*thumos*). And *thumos* has its name from the raging (*thusis*) and boiling of the soul. The name *himeros* (longing) was given to the stream (*rhous*) which most draws the soul; [420a] for because it flows with a rush (*hiemenos*) and with a desire for things and thus draws the soul on through the

impulse of its flowing, all this power gives it the name of *himeros*. And the word *pothos* (yearning) signifies that it pertains not to that which is present, but to that which is elsewhere (*allothi pou*) or absent, and therefore the same feeling which is called *himeros* when its object is present, is called *pothos* when it is absent. And *erôs* (love) is so called because it flows in (*esrei*) from without, and this flowing is *not inherent in him who has it*, [420b] but is introduced through the eyes.[27]

I am not concerned with the accuracy of Plato's etymologies but rather with their implication that to be moved is passively to *undergo* attraction, to be affected by something external, though not in the way that physical forces buffet our bodies. Motivation occurs in us, but it is not something the agent actively undertakes or makes. It flows from the external good through the agent and back to its source, drawing the agent with it like a boat on a stream. And when this kind of motivation aims at an object not immediately possessed, it is *pothos*, that is, a state of *pathos* or yearning for what the agent lacks.

As Thomas Gould notes in his discussion of *pathos*, "We no longer think of strong emotions as outside agents, but the Greeks had always done so."[28] This is true not only of rage and raw sexual lust but also of calmer experiences of attraction, according to Gould: "*Eros*, also poetic inspiration, are things that happen to us, not things we do." Plato and his followers see most experiences of pathos as *negative* rather than romantic or inspiring, since they involve reason surrendering to lower parts of the soul.[29] This explains why Lucretius, like other Epicureans, would judge that sexual eros is like a disease. Nussbaum summarizes his argument as follows:

> Lovers inflict pain on one another (IV.1079–83). They do so because they perceive their desire for the other person as a source of pain—a wound or ulcerous sore in the self (IV.1068, 1069, 1070). Their condition of neediness is experienced as an open hole, a lack of self-sufficiency, accompanied by weakness . . . in sexual intimacy, they seek to heal these wounds—or, as Lucretius also puts it, to extinguish the fire that burns them (1086–87), thus achieving a state of self-sufficiency.[30]

Thus the lack model implies that experiences of sexual eros and other *pathē* will never be pleasant in themselves. Yet, as I will argue, Plato retains the general passive form of magnetic attraction even for motive-states involving practical reason and discernment of the Good. As Iris Murdoch— one of Plato's greatest students—puts it, "Good is the magnetic center towards which love naturally moves. . . . Love is the tension between the imperfect soul and the magnetic perfection which is conceived as lying beyond it."[31] Although Plato did not make *orexis* into a term of art, his general sense of eros is clearly its forerunner.[32] To avoid confusion, such being-drawn-toward or teleological pull as a general feature in the experience of motivation obviously needs to be distinguished from specifically sexual attraction. To mark this distinction, Alan Soble helpfully invents the adjective "erosiac" for the former, while reserving "erotic" for the latter.[33] But in distinguishing eros and agapē, Soble's characterization of erosiac love emphasizes its being object-focused and property-based: "The central claim of the first view [the eros tradition] is that something about y is central in accounting for x's love for y."[34] In my view, this is not what distinguishes erosiac motivation; rather, its distinctive character lies in being caused by the agent's perception of properties in the object that are *attractive* in any sense implying an absence that the agent is drawn to fill by appropriation of that object. On this approach, all erosiac motivation will be property-based, but it need not follow that all property-based love is erosiac. For the latter to follow, we would need the additional premise that the only properties that can ground love are ones that "attract" in the relevant sense.

For example, in Plato's aporetic discussion of friendship in the *Lysis*—an early dialogue that clearly influenced Aristotle—Socrates puzzles over how one good person can be friends with another, since similar or "like" individuals apparently have nothing to offer their partner that he lacks or needs. This is the origin of a long dispute about whether friends should be similar in qualities and interests or different yet complementary, since "opposites attract."[35] The value of complementarity derives from conceiving goodness itself in a proto-*eudaimonistic* sense as whatever is required to be complete beyond all need:

> But, you will say, the like man is not a friend to the like man, but the good will be a friend to the good, in so far as he is good, not in so far as he is like....
>
> And I should rejoin, Will not the good man, in so far as he is good, be found to be sufficient for himself?...
>
> And if he does not want anything he won't feel regard for anything either....
>
> And what he does not feel regard for, he cannot love.[36]

It is interesting that Aristotle tried to resolve this classical puzzle about why a good person needs or even enjoys friends *without* rejecting its central claim about human motivation: he proposes that friends are external goods that even the virtuous person requires for happiness—not for the pleasure or advantage that they may supply but rather to provide occasions for active expression of virtuous desires—which is central to the individual's completeness.[37] It would be a mistake, then, to say that Aristotle's account of noble love for friend is simply the diametric opposite of friendship in the *Lysis* as mere egoistic concern for the friend as "useful."[38]

In the *Lysis*, Socrates is explicit in holding that any form of desire requires some kind of incompleteness: he states that body or soul "is friendly with good [*agathon*, the helpful] on account of the presence of evil [*kakon*, the harmful]."[39] In other words, desire requires an absence in our well-being that is harmful to us, and our desire will be for the good that can fill this absence and eliminate the harm it represents. Of course, it follows from this that sheer harm to our well-being, or the opening of some new lack or want in us, can never be an end we intend for its own sake: thus "For nothing, I'm sure, can be friendly with evil."[40] This thesis, which I call the *Platonic principle* of motivation, is also central to the opening argument in the *Meno*: nobody "wishes to be miserable and wretched," and so nobody desires things they know will be bad for them.[41] The one serious challenge to this principle in Plato's corpus—namely, Callicles' argument that a noble person will let his appetites "become as large as possible," since "those who have no need of anything are virtually dead"—is rejected on the basis of the leaky sieve analogy.[42]

Socrates appears to qualify his analysis later in the *Lysis*: since desires themselves are intermediate between good and evil (as the *Symposium* will explain in more detail later), they could not exist in a world where evil (i.e., harm or loss of well-being) was extinct, so there must be "some other cause of loving and being loved." Yet he still holds the erosiac thesis: "that . . . which feels desire, feels desire for that of which it is in want."[43] He simply recognizes that a good can be perceived as lacking in an agent in another way besides resulting from some contingent harm (like sickness or robbery). What *naturally belongs* to a person she will tend to want or perceive as lacking when she does not actually possess it, just as if something she owns had been stolen: "that which by nature belongs to us, it has been found necessary for us to love."[44] Although the dialogue then ends without a final explanation of how friendship is possible, Socrates hints at a solution implied by the foregoing analysis: "if there is a difference between that which belongs to us and that which is like us," we may be able to say "what is meant by a friend."[45] In other words, in order to give an erosiac account of friendship, we first need a full account of our nature, which will show what our *eudaimonia* requires. We might then be able to see why friends are an essential part of our good, that is, why they naturally belong to us, why we feel incomplete without them, as if something were missing or lost—even if they are also "similar" to us in key respects. This again suggests that the account of desire in the *Lysis* is not meant to be materially egoistic; Socrates is not endorsing the Sophist conception of all motivation as aiming at one's own pleasure, power, wealth, and honor.

In his insightful analysis of Socratic ethics, Terence Irwin explains these ideas concerning human motivation in terms of Socrates' "eudaemonism." In the *Euthydemus*, as at the end of the *Charmides*, Socrates endorses "rational eudaemonism," that is, the thesis that all rationally justified actions pursue only the agent's happiness for its own sake and everything else for the sake of this happiness.[46] But, as we see in the *Lysis*, he also endorses the psychological thesis that there must be "primary objects of love" for any motivation to begin, and the *Euthydemus* suggests that only happiness "meets the conditions laid down in the *Lysis* for being a primary object of love."[47] Thus Socrates also endorses "psychological eudaemonism," which implies that virtue is also chosen because it is best for the agent.[48] This is also required, Irwin suggests, for Socrates' arguments in the *Laches* and *Charmides* that "wisdom is sufficient for happiness": this conclusion will follow only if "intentional choice of the lesser apparent good is impossible," which in turn holds only if psychological eudaimonism is true.[49]

This is my rephrasing of Irwin's analysis: what he actually says is that psychological eudaimonism (PE) entails that *akrasia* is impossible;[50] and if this is true, then "Socrates is right to ignore the non-cognitive aspects of each virtue," that is, to equate virtue with wisdom.[51] But I think Irwin gives too strong a definition of PE. On his definition, the doctrine is that people's desires are always *rational* in the sense that they desire whatever it seems to them will maximize their own eudaimonia. This may be the doctrine that Socrates' arguments in several early dialogues require. But a weaker version of PE holds only that a person's motives all ultimately aim at something he apprehends as a good for himself—though perhaps not as his greatest possible good. This weaker version of PE is compatible with *akrasia*, but it still includes "the psychological eudaemonist view that all desires are focused on the good" of the agent, which Irwin rightly finds in *Gorgias* 467–68.[52] Thus weak PE may better represent Plato's view in the middle dialogues, which arguably allow for some kind of *akrasia* yet still maintain the fundamental erosiac thesis that an agent's desires are for something he perceives as fulfilling a need or potentially supplying something he lacks. On this view, any desired object, even if its value appears to be comparatively lesser, must in itself seem to bring the agent closer to completion or to that state of self-sufficiency (*autarkeia*) in which we have everything we could want.[53]

2.2. Three Types of Desire in the Republic

In contemporary literature, this feature of desire is so familiar that it is often assumed without question to be the form of motivation *as such*, and so it hardly ever becomes a theme for reflection. But in ancient moral psychology it was a frequent topic. Following the analysis in the *Lysis*, Plato developed this idea in two well-known discussions of desires as experiences of "lack" that anticipate objects that would supply what is lacking in the desiring subject and thus restore her natural equilibrium. The first occurs near the beginning of Socrates' argument for a tripartite division of the soul in the *Republic*:

> What then, said I, of thirst and hunger and the appetites generally, and again, consenting and willing . . . ? Will you not say, for example, that the soul of one who desires either strives for that which he desires or draws towards its embrace what it wishes to accrue to it, or again, insofar as it wills that anything be presented to it, nods assent to itself thereon as if someone put the question, striving towards its attainment?[54]

Socrates classifies "will" (wish and choice, *boulēsis* and *prohairesis*) with desire here, but for the moment I am concerned only with the *intentional structure* of desire that he identifies. Each desire has an intentional correlate that is essential to its meaning: "Each desire in itself is of that thing only of which it is its nature to be."[55] From this it follows that "mere thirst" has "mere drink" as its object, whereas only a qualified version of this basic desire, such as "hot thirst," specifically desires "cold drink" as its object.[56]

Although this distinction between pure and qualified desires and their pure and qualified correlates has seemed contentious to some commentators concerned about its role in Socrates' argument for the division of reason and desire, it actually points toward an important phenomenological distinction between two kinds of desiderative states, which I will label D1 and D2. Briefly, D1 includes any unqualified urge that has an intentional object, when this object is generic and without any cognitive specification, whereas "preference desires" (D2) are qualified versions of such urges, directed onto an object with a more concrete specification for the agent. Socrates also insists that a desire for "good drink" rather than for drink as such is a qualified desire, distinct from the raw impulse.[57] But, as Plato argues, the qualification "good" seems to introduce something new here, because such an evaluation of the object has a kind of objective force lacking in D2 preferences, in which the qualification of the object as desirable may be wholly agent-relative. When instead the judgment that X is good is made in some agent-neutral sense, it makes a claim on others that they should also see X as good and so possibly desire it. Desires correlated with an object thought to be good in any such objective sense I will call "evaluative desires" (labeled D3). By contrast, "thirst that is just thirst is neither of much nor little nor good nor bad, *nor in a word of any kind.*"[58] So qualifications of the desired object by kind concepts take us into states beyond the

D1 level, either by introducing subjective preferences or by introducing objective validity claims about goods we should all desire.

Desires of all three types are experienced as a disturbance in or difference from a state of total satisfaction or bliss; the sense of lacking or falling short of this state *is* the desire, which aims at an end that seems to promise restoration of this state of *natural equilibrium*. This is clearest with respect to bodily inclinations in the *Philebus*, where, as Cynthia Hampton explains, "In general, wherever the natural union of the indefinite with the definite is destroyed within a creature, the result is pain, and when the union is restored, pleasure is produced (32A–B)."[59] Similarly, W. H. Auden writes, "Animals . . . do not go on quests. They hunt for food or drink or a mate, but the object of their search is determined by what they already are and its purpose is to restore a disturbed equilibrium."[60] On the Platonic view, human beings do go on quests because they can conceive more remote and abstract goals that have to be defined in the search for them, since our common conception of the ideal state is so much more indeterminate. As Alasdair MacIntyre puts it in his famous reconstruction of Plato's eudaimonist model, the unity of an individual human life is like that of a quest story. Personal identity requires

> . . . the unity of a narrative embodied in a single human life. To ask "What is the good for me?" is to ask how best I might live out that unity and bring it to completion. To ask "What is the good for man?" is to ask what all answers to the former question must have in common.[61]

Here the telos of our highest D3 desire is still conceived as a form of completeness in which the quest terminates, an equilibrium in which our complete good is achieved. The basic structure of the end thus remains the same in all three forms of desire.

Of course, in the *Meno*, Plato famously had Socrates argue that people can desire only what appears "good" to them (in the sense that it brings advantage or contributes to their happiness), which seems to imply that some rational evaluation, whether right or faulty, is implicit in *every* motivational state.[62] Relative to this simplistic analysis, the moral psychology of the *Republic* seems to be a clear advance, since it distinguishes the rational evaluation involved in some desire-states from appetitive states lacking this element, which intend their objects without a *judgment* that they are "good" in any objective sense. Thus, as Gary Watson argues in a famous paper on autonomy, there is a real "distinction between wanting and valuing," which is central to Plato's ethics.[63] While "On Hume's account, Reason is not a source of motivation," for Plato, "the rational part of the soul is not some kind of inference mechanism. It is itself a source of motivation. In general form, the desires of Reason are desires for 'the Good.'"[64]

Rational or evaluative desires, in other words, have the D3 structure briefly sketched above. On Watson's reading, for Plato there is a necessary connection between the evaluation and the motivation: "to think a thing good is at the same time to desire it (or its promotion)," and thus the values it confers provide "*reasons* for action." By contrast, lower kinds of desire have objects that "may not be thought good."[65] Although this way of putting the contrast tends to suggest that there is no state in between raw sensitive impulses (D1) and *boulēsis*, or evaluative desire (D3), the advance on the *Meno* account is still clear. As Irwin explains, Plato answers Socrates' arguments (in the early dialogues) against the possibility of incontinence by explaining "how action on appetite is intelligible if it is independent of beliefs about the good."[66] Such actions are intelligible because human beings, like lower animals, are naturally prone to some pure desires for rationally unqualified objects: these desires are as self-explanatory as the rational desire for happiness. As we see in lower animals, action on such appetitive desires can be intentional without being coordinated by "the agent's conception of an overall good."[67]

In another way, however, the *Republic* analysis preserves a central part of the intuition at work in the *Meno* and *Protagoras*, namely the idea that desires of any sort—purely appetitive or rationally qualified—are "attractions" toward something that, insofar as it "attracts," functions *like* a "good" recognizable by intellect. In a nonjudgmental sense, then, mere food or nourishment is the "good" for which mere hunger is the desire. The *Republic* recasts the *Meno* principle that every desire is for what is evaluated or represented as good for us into the more basic principle that every desire is for its correlate "good" and is *moved by* the thought that this good will satisfy it. This principle is more inclusive in application since it covers D1 and D2 states as well as D3 evaluative desires. Thus, although Plato emphasizes the contrast that Watson highlights between "valuing" and "desiring"—or, more accurately, between rational desires and lower appetites—Plato also recognizes that they have something in common: every desire has the motivational structure of yearning for an object that promises to satisfy a salient lack. Thus "the soul of the thirsty, in so far as it thirsts, wishes nothing else than to drink, and yearns for this and its impulse is towards this."[68] In general, "affections," like "diseases," produce impulses that "draw and drag" the agent toward their end, just as do positive evaluations of some possible end made by the rational part of the soul.[69]

One might be tempted to object that Plato meant this analysis to apply only to lower, instinctive appetites such as hunger and thirst, since he immediately goes on in *Republic IV* to analyze "high spirit" and reason in different terms, and D3 desires require at least some involvement of evaluative cognition or practical judgment. However, as we see in the *Symposium*, in Socrates' and Diotima's speeches, the "lack structure" of desire is explicitly reformulated in order to extend it to motivation by the good as the object of judgment, or to what I have called D3 states involving objective evaluation of the conditions of our well-being.

2.3. *The Lack Model in the* Symposium

The second set of passages presenting the strong erosiac thesis occur in the last four speeches of Plato's *Symposium*. The lack structure of eros is most obvious in Aristophanes' myth of sexual desire as unconscious longing for a state of "primeval wholeness" or primordial bodily oneness with one's heterosexual or homosexual correlate.[70] Following Agathon, Socrates clarifies this point about the *intentionality* of love: "it is the nature of Love to be the love of somebody...."[71] Moreover, its attitude toward its object is one of *longing*: "Then isn't it probable, said Socrates, or rather isn't it certain that everything longs for what it lacks, and that nothing longs for what it doesn't lack?" (*Symposium* 200 a-b).

This implies, contra Agathon's speech, that love lacks the divine beauty and happiness that it loves or that it seeks. Yet Socrates' premise seems to ignore that we sometimes continue to long for good things such as health and riches when we already have them. Against these potential counterexamples, Socrates notes that in such cases, "what you want is to go on having them, for at the moment you've got them whether you want them or not." And since the contingency of fortune and mortal fate deprives us of the certainty of enjoying such things *permanently*, "desiring to secure something to oneself forever may be described as loving something which is not yet to hand."[72] This interpretation of the potential counterexamples has the crucial implication, made explicit in Diotima's speech, that our true end is a *transcendent* one: "we are bound to long for immortality as well as for the good—which is to say that Love is a longing for immortality."[73] For only in a state of union with divine nature will our longing be fully satisfied. Thus Plato conceives eudaimonia as an otherworldly end that transcends human nature.[74]

We may add a further point here to defend Plato's analysis. If someone objects that we must have a desire to possess good things *in the present moment* in order to explain our pleasure or happiness in having them right now, then the premise that we can desire only what we lack can be made counterfactual: to desire X entails that if one lacked X, one would long for it and be dissatisfied without it. Thus our satisfaction with X in the present moment of possessing it can be explained by our sense that we have *avoided* the desire and sense of "lack" that we would experience in the nearest possible worlds in which we did not possess X. Although we often speak loosely of our *continuing to desire* something simultaneously with having it, Plato can regard this as an inaccuracy of ordinary language: our happiness is really due to the (temporary) *termination* of the desire in the possession or presence of X, together with the *disposition* to desire X again should we ever lose it. This is why Aquinas, following Plato's logic, conceives "delight" as "simply the resting of the appetite in a good,"[75] and holds that the most complete fulfillment of desire must involve certainty of being unable to lose its object. The upshot of this analysis is Plato's most general formula for desire: "And therefore, whoever feels a want is wanting something which is not yet to hand, and the object of his love and of his desire is whatever he isn't, or whatever he hasn't got—that is to say, whatever he is lacking in."[76] And from this it easily follows that love itself cannot be or have the beauty that it desires.

I am not concerned here with the familiar arguments that Socrates' inference is invalid, because we should distinguish between lacking/possessing an attribute or property like "beauty" and lacking/possessing a beautiful object.[77] For suppose that sexual attraction to another person's bodily beauty in fact aims at something like a certain complex set of intimate experiences with that bodily form and at the release of physiological tensions which involve pleasurable stimulation and psychological satisfaction. If this (or some similar complex) is what sexual "possession" of another person's bodily beauty means, then it is clearly an experience we can lack in the relevant sense despite ourselves having physical attributes that might inspire such a desire in others. What the sexually desiring person lacks is this tactile experience of *another's* beauty;[78] having the desire really does imply lacking the experience it envisions. That this agent-relative property is (part of) the usual target of sexual love does not, of course, imply that every kind of desire for beauty must be agent-relative, so the question of whether we can desire beauty that we possess can still be raised for nonsexual loves. A complete refutation of Agathon would really require showing that in every case, the good sought in the love is one that the lover lacks.

Whether Socrates' refutation of Agathon can be defended this way or not, it is crucial to see that Socrates' lack formula is meant to apply to *all* recognized forms of human motivation and not just the *epithumia*, such as hunger and sexual attraction. Andrew Payne is quite right that in the *Symposium*, Plato treats *eros* as a species of *epithumia* and does not (contra Halperin) treat it as a kind of rationally evaluative wish (or *boulēsis*).[79] However, the lack structure found in *eros* is not regarded by Plato as peculiar to the *epithumia*: rather, it is also true of *boulēsis* and, in general, every form of *orexis*, and this is precisely why Plato can speak *metaphorically* of orektic states like the philosopher's desire for wisdom as if it were a kind of *eros*. Thus Diotima insists that *eros*, or love in the more general sense, "includes every kind of longing for happiness and the good,"[80] including states that are clearly not *epithumia* as defined in the *Republic*.[81] Commenting on this, Payne writes:

> Over the course of Diotima's speech the focus of eros expands greatly, but it never loses certain epithumetic qualities. Eros is a self-interested longing for an object which it lacks, a desire which places the lover in an asymmetrical relation with the beloved. These epithumetic qualities stand behind the claim that Diotima does not simply change the subject away from the common meaning of eros to the rational desire for happiness and the good.[82]

I agree with the claim that Diotima is not simply equivocating; however, her main point is precisely that these features of sexual desire, which Payne calls "epithumetic qualities," are *not* limited to distinctively epithumetic appetites after all: rather, they are the formal features of all motivational states, all forms of *orexis*. Thus we can talk about the formally "erosiac" structure of desires without limiting ourselves to lower appetites shared by human beings and other animals. Still, Socrates' general formula for desire does need refinement, because as it stands it would imply that we desire *anything* we happen to lack, when in fact only some of these "absences" are salient and thus only some of them become intentional objects. Diotima's speech accomplishes this refinement.

Diotima begins by fending off an objection to the conclusion of the argument against Agathon: namely that it would entail that Love is "bad and ugly." Instead, she says that the "lack" implied by desire does not entail the opposite quality, but is rather an *intermediate* state: to desire beauty is to be "on the way" to it, rather than simply to lack it, like someone who is ugly. Similarly, she portrays love as "halfway between mortal and immortal," a "powerful spirit" that acts as medium or hermeneut between impoverished human beings and the gods who enjoy perfect beauty and goodness.[83] In her invented fable, Love is the son of Need and Resource, begotten on the same day as Aphrodite's birth.[84] The implication is that Love has enough resources at least to see or imagine what it lacks and thus to start on the way toward it or to pursue it[85]—just as in the theory of "recollection," or *anamnesis*, some trace of the knowledge lacked is requisite in order to make its absence salient and to provide a proleptic preconception of what we are looking for, which makes its recovery possible (as in Heidegger's hermeneutic notion of "forehaving"). Thus Diotima adds that, just as the gods do not seek for wisdom and truth, since they have it,

> Nor, for that matter, do the [totally] ignorant seek the truth or crave to be made wise. And indeed, what makes their case so hopeless is that, having neither beauty, nor goodness, nor intelligence, *they are satisfied with what they are, and do not long for the virtues they have never missed.*[86]

This is almost identical to an argument in the *Lysis* that those who desire wisdom must at least understand that they are not yet wise or recognize the good they lack (which is obviously a major Socratic theme).[87]

The "lack" that is essential to desire therefore cannot be a complete separation from the good lacked, as happens with a good that is irrelevant to beings of our kind, which is an "absence" to which we are naturally indifferent. Rather, it is one that is *felt* as a void precisely because we have some partial sense of the end, some anticipatory trace or hint of its importance for well-being, which allows it to become our intentional object or to "hook onto" us, drawing us into the intermediate state of "becoming" or moving toward it.[88] Being able to desire higher goods is thus itself an advantage over creatures that cannot even experience this lack in the requisite way. This explains the route from Plato's erosiac model in the *Symposium* to Aristotle's ethics: the goods we can desire are a reflection of our nature, so our erosiac capacities will provide some indication of our telos.

Diotima argues that objects gain their relevance to us—and hence become salient enough to motivate—by their apparent *goodness*. This argument commences after the dialectical turning point when Socrates asks what value Love can have for us if it is not itself the good or beautiful.[89] Diotima responds indirectly, beginning with the suggestion that desire for the beautiful is really only one part or aspect of Love: "You see, what we've been doing is to give the name of Love to what is only one single aspect of it,"[90] that is, sexual attraction. In fact, she insists that love properly includes only desire for what is evaluated as beneficial:

> I know it has been suggested, she continued, that lovers are people who are looking for their other halves. But as I see it, Socrates, Love never longs for either the half or the whole of anything except the good. For men will even have their hands and feet cut off if they are once convinced that those members are bad for them.[91]

The desire to lose a limb evaluated as fatally diseased is clearly an evaluative or D3 desire, just like the rejection of bad water. In the *Republic*, of course, the thirsty man's aversion to drink that he evaluates as poisoned is attributed to reason, and "desire" in the narrower sense of *epithumia*, or appetites shared with animals, is restricted to D1 urges (and possibly their D2 applications). But Diotima's point is precisely that D3 motivational states share the same general lack structure: indeed, they display it more clearly and definitely. Love, in the most general sense of a movement drawn by the absence of something "good" as intentional object, is thus found at all three "levels" of the tripartite soul, from the instinctual desire of beautiful bodies, to the "spirited" desire for honor and for noble "laws and institutions,"[92] to the intellectual loves of scientific knowledge, philosophical wisdom, and finally the Form of Beauty itself.[93]

In the *Symposium*, then, the meaning of *eros* is broadened from sexual desire to love for every significant good that we can recognize as lacking or needed to complete us. This is presented as the model of all human motivation: *we are drawn toward completion.* This certainly does not mean that all motivation is a brute *conatus* in some direction, because the general "erosiac structure" is also found in cases where reason has to evaluate the different goods pursuable in our situation. As Gadamer writes in his informative commentary on the *Philebus*:

> The blindness of the life-urge, which prevails in everything, exists completely apart from any choice. The other "choice" or option balancing the blind life-urge is choosing itself—for which one has already decided as soon as one begins weighing these two against each other. And this choice presupposes knowledge [of some good]. What makes human beings human is the fact that they must ask about the good and must give preference to one thing over another (*prohairein*) in conscious, deliberate decision.[94]

Because for Plato all motivation is *teleological*, pulled by final ends that seem to be naturally part of our well-being or holistic good, only wisdom or right understanding of our good enables us to make such decisions well. As Giovanni Ferrari writes, the second group of speeches (by Aristophanes, Agathon, Socrates, and Diotima) are united by their view of love, "not as sundered into good and bad, but as a single aspiration, common to all, and directed (despite differences of sexual orientation) at the same generic object—wholeness."[95] Although Socrates disagrees with Agathon's inference that Eros is beautiful and good "because he is love of the beautiful and good," Socrates agrees with Agathon that the generic object of love is the "*kallos*—one word in Greek, but with a semantic range requiring many in English: the beautiful, the fine, the noble, the good (197b3–9)."[96] And as Ferrari perceives, Diotima's argument that love remains praiseworthy even though it does not itself have the good it seeks "reinstate[s] the message of Aristophanes' tale: that love is above all a search for what has been lost. Aristophanes only misidentified the loss: It is not the other half, but our good,"[97] which Diotima understands in its most holistic possible sense as an immortality in which we possess the good always and with absolute security.[98]

2.4. Diotima and Aquinas: Formal Egoism, Intended Goods, and By-Products

However, Ferrari, like many commentators, does not seem to recognize the depth of the problems raised by Diotima's main point against Socrates. Unlike Socrates, she holds that "Love is not exactly a longing for the beautiful," but rather for "the conception and generation that the beautiful effects."[99] This suggests that Eros is properly desire for the product that results from the pursuit of beauty (and, in some cases, from union with it); hence it only indirectly wants the beautiful object itself. Sexual desire, for example, is not simply desire to be united with bodily beauty; at bottom it is an existential desire for the good of immortality, which we can achieve only deficiently through organic procreation.[100] The same divine end would seem to be the real "good" for the sake of which the Form of Beauty itself is desired, since genuine immortality of the soul is said to be the product of this Form's revelation: "if ever it is given to mortal man to put on immortality, it shall be given to him who sees the Form."[101] In other words, whereas Socrates agreed with Agathon that Eros is desire to find and possess the *kalos* as an end-in-itself, Diotima's analysis in fact returns us to Aristophanes' view that what Eros really wants is the wholeness that *results* from finding the *kalos*.

By claiming that the *ergon* or proper function of Eros is "giving birth in the beautiful,"[102] then, Diotima is really modifying Socrates' account to fit the framework of *eudaimonism*, which requires that the apprehended goods that can attract desire must be related to the *agent's own well-being* in some way. As I will explain in more detail in chapter 5, this "formal egoism" must be distinguished from various versions of material egoism (asserted, for example, by the Sophists and Thomas Hobbes); it means only that the prospect of the agent's own happiness, however materially conceived, is what ultimately moves him: "Plato was as certain as Socrates had been that what all human beings always want most is their own true well-being. Happiness, *eudaimonia*, the state of being God-blessed, is defined as that which all men desire (*Symposium* 205a)."[103]

So understood, the formal egoism essential to eudaimonism is simply a clarification or corollary of the *strong erosiac thesis*, pointing out that to be felt as lacking, the good that moves desire must be apprehended as lost by the agent or missing from the agent—as if a piece of himself had gone astray. As Aquinas puts it, "each thing desires its own fulfillment and therefore desires for its ultimate end a good that perfects and completes it."[104] This means that the agent desires its highest object *for* the completion it will apparently provide to her. Otherwise stated, the thesis of formal egoism simply makes clear that all motivation according to the erosiac model is *appropriative*, aimed at incorporating something into the agent or possessing it for him. This is what Anders Nygren meant by calling Platonic Eros "acquisitive love."[105] If we distinguish between (a) an object or state that attracts or moves us to desire it and (b) the attainment or possession of that object or state that ends our desire by providing the missing component of our well-being, then the strong erosiac thesis implies that desirable objects only become goals for us in form (b). This is equivalent to the thesis of formal egoism.

This point has often been confused in the critical literature. For example, Vlastos protests against Nygren's analysis, which I have largely endorsed, saying that love as explained by Diotima is not rightly understood as "egocentric" or "acquisitive":

> it is only too patently Ideocentric and creative. But while it gives no more quarter to self-indulgence than would Pauline agape or Kantian good will, neither does it repudiate the spiritualized egocentricism of Socratic *philia*. That first description of the aim of eros in Diotima's speech—"that one should possess beauty for ever"—is never amended in the sequel in any way that would make egocentric eros a contradiction. . . . It is not said or implied . . . that "birth in beauty" should be motivated by love of persons. . . . What we are to love in persons is the image of the Idea in them.[106]

Vlastos's claim is that Platonic love falsely appears egocentric to Nygren only because it is love of an abstract ideal, not love of individual persons as particulars, with all the "kindness, tenderness, compassion, concern for the freedom, [and] respect for the integrity of the beloved" that such interpersonal love requires.[107] But while Vlastos is surely right that Plato is not trying to explain or understand this kind of interpersonal love, and that his alternative "Ideocentric" Eros is not *materially* egoistic, he clearly admits the sense in which it is *formally* egoistic. To love the Idea of Beauty "for its own sake," according to Plato, *is* to be drawn toward its value because of the completeness that would come from possessing it eternally.

Two similar examples should suffice to illustrate this idea. To Diotima, what we want is not that the Form of Beauty should simply *exist* for its own sake. Rather, our ultimate goal is the vision of it which somehow unites us with it, bringing us (since this is the perfect object) the total completeness that is the telos of all erosiac desire. Likewise, Aquinas explains that "Happiness is said to be the supreme good of man because it is the attainment or enjoyment of the supreme good."[108] And since, for Aquinas, this attainment is the Beatific Vision—an idea partly inspired by Diotima's vision of the Form of Beauty—this good must by its nature be unlosable once attained: "Since happiness is the complete and sufficient good, the desire of man must be brought to rest and all evil excluded. Now man naturally desires to hold on to the good which he has, and to have the assurance of keeping it."[109] Aquinas relies on this conclusion that the complete good must be perfectly secure in arguing that the complete good is not attainable in this life but transcends our natural state.[110] Like Diotima, Aquinas recognizes that in D3 states, desire is a response to *rational grounds* for wanting the object or a response to an apprehension of the end as valuable for life (in different possible ways). As a response, it is *moved by* these perceptions and judgments, which is what Aquinas means by the dependence of appetite on evaluative intellect. For example, in discussing God and the Holy Spirit, Aquinas argues that every "intellectual nature" must have a will, because understanding must incline it to its proper end (in a fashion analogous to natural or non-volitional appetites):

> every inclination of the will arises from this: by an intelligible form a thing is apprehended as suitable or affective. To be affected toward something—so far as it is of this kind—is to love that thing. Therefore, every inclination of the will and even of the sensible appetite has its origin from love. For from the fact that we love something, we desire that thing if it be absent.[111]

This is a clear statement of the idea that all motivation (including intellectual motivation, or volition) is desiderative in the general sense of Platonic Eros.

However, Diotima's proposal that Eros longs for the begetting that the beautiful effects can also be read as implying that our desire is not simply (a) to *attain* some good (or attractive or beautiful) end E; or (equivalently) (b) to gain the contribution that attaining E makes to our well-being; but rather (c) to realize a distinct good P, which is the *product* of pursuing or attaining E. This is problematic, because such a product-good can arise from pursuing or attaining E without the agent expecting it, or at least without her intending it.[112] In such cases, Socrates seems right that attaining E (as a contribution to his completeness) is the good toward which the agent is erosiacally motivated; the desired good is not actually P, as Diotima's proposal would imply on this reading. So why would Plato introduce this alternative analysis as superior to Socrates'? One possibility is that as a eudaimonist he needs to explain the fact that there apparently are possible ends of action E whose attainment seem in themselves to have little directly to do with the agent's well-being; therefore, if these can be final ends for us, formal egoism (and hence the strong erosiac thesis) would be false. For such ends, the eudaimonist might adopt Diotima's explanation and say that it is the fulfillment produced by gaining these ends (or begat in them) that really motivates us. But if that is his reasoning, then the eudaimonist is in trouble. For, as Aquinas recognizes, it is wrong to say that the activity in which our highest good consists "is desired because of the delight it gives."[113] Rather, delight is the unintended (even if expected) *by-product* of pursuing and possessing (or resting in) the transcendent good of God for its own sake:

> It must be noted, then, that delight is a proper accident which follows upon happiness or some part of happiness, for a man is delighted when he possesses some good suitable to him [or naturally completing him]. . . . Clearly, then, even the delight which follows upon the perfect good is not the essence of happiness, but something resulting from it as its proper accident.[114]

In other words, the good that motivates by attracting is that which will *end our desire* by making us whole, not the psychological satisfaction that is experienced in such repose. We may understand this as distinguishing between goods of forms (b) and (c) above.[115] Additionally, Aquinas draws on this distinction in arguing that the will's movement or motivation depends on an attractive good outside its own states or operations: "Nor does the will seek good for the sake of repose, for if this were the case, the very act of will would be the end. . . . Rather it seeks to be at rest in the activity because that activity is its good."[116]

However, as Ferrari's analysis shows, Plato is aware of the problem that intended ends may be distinct from their by-products, and he even has Diotima make use of this distinction to show how lower forms of specific love can lead to higher forms. A certain kind of lover is "prone to become more deeply fascinated by the beauty that issues from his love than by the beauty that first attracted it. This displacement of attention is what motivates his climb to each new level on the upward path."[117] For example, motivated by *eros* for a particular body's beauty, he produces a poetry lauding this bodily beauty. But then he reflects on this product: "His 'beautiful' words have beauty as their topic—not the beauty of this body alone, but also bodily beauty in general, because to praise something is to insert it in a comparison class."[118] Recognizing this more general good, he starts desiring it instead: he is drawn to "thoughts and expressions of beauty," which in turn produce a better, more noetic soul. Seeing this beauty produced in his own soul, he desires to produce it in others, such as friends or apprentices: the product of this new desire is "edifying speeches intended to bring out the beauty of the soul (that is, decency of character, 210b) entrusted to his care."[119] Then he turns to the beautiful topic of this discourse, and in desire for the education of good character in general, he works to produce good laws and institutions. His attention shifts now to these products: his desire switches to the beauty of the knowledge that produced them and finally to the beauty of the Good itself which is the final object of such knowledge. So understood, the Ascent can be summarized as shown below (pairing its stages with doxastic levels of insight in the Divided Line in *Republic* VI):

At every stage of this Ascent, "the initiate's concern is transferred from the beauty that enticed him to the beauty that he has generated."[120] The final product is the true virtue and immortality that comes from fulfilling the highest form of *eros* in the vision of Beauty itself. And this is the final stage because, as Ferrari says, this final product (immortality, perfect wholeness) is not itself qualified as beautiful or as a good that could in turn attract our desire for it, so our attention does not switch from the Form to our enjoyment of it.[121] This seems to agree precisely with Aquinas's point that noetic delight before God cannot itself be our desired end, because it is the kind of good that can *only* be a by-product. To pursue it directly as our end would be self-defeating.

This analysis will prove extremely helpful throughout our investigations. What it shows is that some valuable states that can result from pursuit and attainment of other goods are only *contingently* by-products of such processes: they can also be directly wanted (e.g., in D3 desire) and pursued for their own sake without self-defeat. Let us call such objects *targetable* goods.[122] Diotima's Ascent works because some types of goods targetable by D3 desires can *also* be produced as by-products of lower desires. Thus the lower desires can be *converted into* new desires for their own by-products. And the

	Diotima's Ascent of Eros	Result Begotten	Maieutic Transition	Level of Insight
1st	Love of physical beauty in one specific attractive body	Beautiful speech, rhetoric (to woo the beloved)	Sees "that the beauty in one body is akin to the beauty in another body"	(none)
2nd	Love of beautiful speeches and poetry	*Imitative* art and aesthetic sensitivity	Learns to love beauty in the soul	(*ekasia*)
3rd	Love of beautiful souls and concern to educate particular youth	*Inventive* crafts, edifying discourses	Learns to see all beauty in souls as the same and to love learning	(*pistis*) Practical know-how; right opinion
4th	Love of learning, knowledge, and wisdom; "great ocean of beauty"	Philosophical dialectic, "the abundance of philosophy"	Learns the beauty of *scientific* knowledge; beauty in all different kinds of learning	(*diánoia*) Knowledge based on demonstrable principles
	Love of Beauty and the Good itself	Vision of Beauty; Immortal virtue	[nothing]	(*noesis*) Beatific insight beyond all words

Ascent stops at the point where the agent desires to attain a good the appropriation of which produces only a *nontargetable* by-product good, that is, one that is not directly willable (and so no further conversion can occur). In fact, since this good is simply *eudaimonia* itself (understood as including immortality), it would be more accurate to say that the vision of the Form of the Beautiful produces *no* by-product good (c) that is really distinct from (b) attaining or enjoying that Form.

So Diotima's model proves to be as coherent as Aquinas's, as long as we recognize that in the *last* stage of the Ascent, it becomes misleading to say that what Eros really desires is something begotten in the good attained. Rather, at this stage the object is the Universal Good, which is the agent's comprehensive good; thus erosiac motivation can aim no higher than at attaining this perfect good. In other words, erosiac motivation can aim at begetting a product-good *P* as a result of attaining some distinct end *E* only if attaining *E is an imperfect good* for the agent. The perfect good, by contrast, is understood as having no valuable by-products that it does not already include. Thus, once the end is the perfect good, Socrates' formula for love, rather than Diotima's, must apply.

Plato and Aquinas also seem to affirm the converse: namely, that an imperfect good cannot really be desired just for its own sake (taking its attainment as a final end) by an agent who understands its incompleteness. Since we really desire such an end *E* only because it *resembles or imperfectly participates* in the transcendent good whose attainment constitutes completion for us—or equivalently, because of the perfect good that we beget in ourselves by pursuing *E*—an agent who knows this must desire *E for* its relationship to this transcendent good or for what it contributes to attaining the transcendent good. We may call this thesis that the true finality of an end entails its comprehensiveness the *Transcendent principle* (Trans). Since it implies that only imperfect goods help produce targetable by-products, this principle helps explain Diotima's proposal in response to Socrates. Her notion of "begetting in the beautiful" expresses the idea that our desire for non-comprehensive goods really aims at more than we know: its true goal transcends mere attainment of finite goods precisely because they are imperfect. We really aim not just at these partial goods but at the whole Good *through* them. As we will see, this point becomes crucial in evaluating Aristotle, whose conception of *eudaimonia* is not as transcendent as Plato's or Aquinas's.

3. From Plato's Middle Soul to Aristotle's Intellectual Appetite

Before going further, it may be helpful to clarify how I am approaching ancient philosophy in this analysis. There is an important methodological distinction between at least three "levels" of scholarship on ancient philosophers such as Plato and Aristotle. First, we have studies by classicists, trained experts in Greek language and literature, some of whom focus on the corpus of authors like Plato and Aristotle as their specialization. For someone who regularly teaches these philosophers at an introductory level to undergraduates, it can be quite disturbing to read such works: consider, for example, John Rist's impressive study arguing that *Nicomachean Ethics* Books 2 to 4 reflect Aristotle's new conception of the "productive intellect" in the *De anima* and are later than Books 1, 8, 9, and 10, which Aristotle at the time of his death still planned to rewrite to reflect his new conception of *nous* as a separate substance.[123]

Second, we have studies by philosophical specialists in ancient philosophy who are concerned primarily to establish the right interpretation of these canonical texts and to draw important philosophical conclusions from them. For example, in this category we have works like Julia Anna's definitive study of the contrasts between major schools of ancient moral philosophy,[124] which is primarily a historical study but secondarily a positive contribution to ongoing debates in ethics. Third, we have authors whose primary expertise and focus is on contemporary debates in moral psychology and normative theory but who wish to bring into these debates what they regard as crucial insights or errors in ancient moral philosophy. For example, in this broad genre, we have Gary Watson's analysis of the difference between perfectionist or virtue accounts and consequentialist normative theories,[125] Harry Frankfurt's critique of Aristotle's conception of character,[126] and Alfred Mele's interpretations of *akrasia*, self-control, and autonomy.[127]

Of course, these are only rough genre distinctions, and there are many authors who write in more than one of these genres.[128] But they are sufficient to clarify my use of Plato and Aristotle, which obviously belong in this third genre: my primary intention is to draw on these ancient philosophers in order to contribute to contemporary debates in moral psychology. In the next chapter, I use themes in Aristotle to develop and extend the typology of motives within the genus of "erosiac desire" already sketched in my discussion of Plato. In the remainder of this chapter, I argue that the heroic notion of striving will was largely suppressed or covered over in the Western tradition at the point when Plato's conception of the "middle part of the soul" as the seat of spirited courage became Aristotle's faculty of rational desire or "intellectual appetite."[129]

3.1. Thumos *as Indeterminate Motive-Power*

Although Plato is without doubt the main classical source of the erosiac structure of desire that dominates later analyses in Western philosophy and psychology, as we will see, he also contributed in two ways to the development of the existential conception of striving will. In chapter 9, I consider the radical implications of the Neoplatonic model of divine creativity as a primary historical source for the projective conception of striving will. In another, more modest way, Plato contributed to the idea of "the will" as a motivational capacity rather than simply as the locus of decision-making. While Plato does not seem to anticipate the important concept of decision as second-order agency—which has to wait until the Stoics—his theory of the tripartite soul does provide a distinct place for those forms of motivation that, when properly trained and directed, were thought by Greeks to be the basis of courage.[130] Since the virtue of courage is closely associated with our "heroic" capacity to pursue our ends despite difficulty or adversity, it provides one natural sense of "strength of will."

If we identify *thumos*, or the "high-spirited temper" that Plato defines as the middle part of the soul, simply with some form of sudden "anger" that is likely to provoke ill-considered reactions or with a desire for vengeance, then it will seem to be just an "irascible" species of the same motivational genus in which we find the various "concupiscent" appetites for sensual pleasures (to use Aquinas's terms).[131] Although Plato also certainly thought of this middle soul as responsible for the cycles of revenge promoted by the archaic Greek honor code (which he critiques in the *Crito*), he did not reduce the *thumos* to either an angry temper or vengeful spirit. Rather, he saw something else in this middle soul, something that was largely obscured by later philosophical reinterpretations of *thumos* within new divisions of the soul: namely, a motivational "energy" that lies latent in us (though in some more than others) without being intrinsically directed toward particular goals, which can therefore be channeled by reason to provide a *boost or reinforcement* for the motivation provided directly by our D3 desires for goods discerned by reason. This was the positive potential that Plato thought could be harnessed by our rational mind, or *nous*, the charioteer of the soul. As Oberdiek comments, for Plato, "the spirited element, or will, involves anger and other emotions, but necessarily involves reason and reasoning as well, for spirit only motivates those open to certain kinds of reasoning."[132]

This hypothesis makes sense of several things Plato says regarding the middle soul and its role. Plato clearly wants to distinguish this part from the lower desires, and thus Socrates rejects the proposal that *thumos* is in "the appetitive" part.[133] For Leontius, both experiences are a D2-type desire to see a macabre spectacle, and yet he disowns, rejects, or condemns this desire (and hence is angry with himself for giving into it).[134] If this is to make any sense as an argument that *thumos* is a distinct "part" or motivational genus, Plato cannot simply mean that Leontius has another D2 desire *not* to view something macabre (perhaps out of fear that it will give him nightmares, for example). For we often experience desires of the same genus that pull in conflicting directions, as when I would like a Coke and a sandwich but have only enough money for one, or when I would like to see a movie tonight and to go to the theater but can do only one. What Plato means to show us is not an agent performing what Charles Taylor has famously called the "simple weighing" of contingently incompatible desire consummations, but rather an agent "strongly evaluating" his desires themselves.[135] Leontius's negative evaluation of his perverse preferential desire has a *higher authority* than the preferential desire itself, because it depends on a rational judgment about "the noble" which, in its implicit validity claim, is intersubjectively binding. This judgment does not come from the *thumos* itself, in Plato's view (since even an irrational child displays *thumos*); rather, the role of *thumos* is to add its motivational *surplus* to the D3 desire deriving from the judgment itself. In this example, the two together still fail to control the appetite, but that is irrelevant to Plato's main point: as Vander Waerdt explains, the point is that "the θυμοειδές [spirited part] as the natural allay or the λογιστικόν [rational part], with its own ἐπιθυμίαι [appetitive power] provide[s] a source of motivation independent of the other two parts," and thus this spirited part is not just a division of the irrational faculty, as Aristotle makes it.[136]

Now, Plato does not conceive this motivational supplement of *thumos* as directed by or generated in the agent's determined effort to commit to the pursuit of some final end. In other words, he certainly does not envision it as created in an existential decision. But he clearly does think that it can serve reason (nous) as a motivational engine to help control the lower appetites and to keep the agent on course toward rationally desired goods. This seems to be the main point of the famous analogy that Socrates draws between reason as the shepherd who controls wayward sheeplike appetites, and *thumos* as the dog who helps the shepherd perform this function.[137] It also helps explain the importance of a well-trained *thumos* for *karteria*, the capacity to endure ill fortune, which is crucial to virtue in the *Republic*.[138] *Thumos* admittedly has nothing to do with "will" as the faculty of "decision" in Kane's sense; but in classical moral psychology, the idea of a middle soul provided a locus for what we have later come to call *strength of will*. Thus failure of this part helps make *akrasia* possible for Plato,[139] and its proper development helps avoid *akrasia*. As David Carr explains:

> on this model rather more is required for good conduct than just knowledge of the good; wisdom requires the assistance of spirit or will, for example, to secure the obedience of appetite to the principles

of right conduct that it formulates. Roughly speaking, then, temperance may be defined as the condition in which the appetites are subjected to discipline by the will; courage consists in the exercise of the will for the discipline of passion and appetite in accordance with principles of right reason; and wisdom is a matter of the right instruction or direction of the will for the reasonable control of passion and appetite.[140]

In accord with the erosiac model, however, it is axiomatic for Plato that *thumos* as a genus of motivation must be moved by the felt lack of one kind of *generic good* that the agent desires to possess because he is incomplete without it. Plato follows the Homeric tradition in holding that the good which it is *thumos*'s special role to desire is *honor*, merit, rank, or status as "noble" (*kalon*) in the evaluations of one's relevant circle of peers. For him, this naturally includes a demand to be treated justly and righteous indignation at undeserved harms.[141] And as Plato well knows, in the archaic worldview of pre-Homeric Greece, centering as it did on the timocratic ideal of the warrior-king, nobility was synonymous with worldly power, charisma as a leader, and external success in prosecuting one's conquests. Since on this conception, any failure to succeed in realizing one's determined purpose would count as shameful (the opposite of noble), we can see why the *thumos* would have a general tendency to supplement any other desire that has motivated some challenging plan of action. This helps explain Plato's much-discussed remark that even a young human child displays *thumos*.[142]

This passage has concerned commentators, since it could be taken to suggest that *thumos* really is nothing but "anger" as an irascible emotion also found in higher animals. But Plato should be understood as imagining that the child is angry not simply because it fails to satisfy a given desire but because it has an *additional* passion to get "its way" in whatever it desires and pursues. This additional motive is for mastery *as such* (thus it looks like the innate "willfulness" that the Hindu sages condemned and that Augustine saw as the mark of original sin). It makes perfect sense for Plato, coming out of the Homeric tradition, to see this anger in the child as the early expression of the same motivational force that will later add its impetus to the agent's pursuit of whatever purposes he has formed, because not to see them through or to succeed is shameful. We might say that for Plato, even the young child is already sensitive to the shame implied in not being able to realize the goal of its action.[143]

Instead of seeing this willful spirit purely as fury at any opposition to its desires or as a dangerous desire for worldly ascendance, Plato saw that it has a positive function under the ethical reinterpretation of "the noble" which was the central aspiration of his moral philosophy. Once the noble was identified with a life of unconditional commitment to rationally discerned and impartial ideals of justice for all, the desire for honor would become the desire for what is intrinsically beautiful or dignified in morally meritorious acts and characters. Hence in his ideal city-state, the warriors would be assistants of the guardians, whose middle soul was trained to desire the *beauty* of the goods discerned by rational judgment. Their sense of patriotic honor would demand absolute loyalty not to a warrior-king but rather to the laws and institutions of their state whose rational beauty they could appreciate, even without being able to give the *logos* or philosophical justification of these institutions. In this sublimation of the Homeric *thumos*, we see Plato's view that the passion for honor, like other emotions, has a malleable nature that can be trained to respond to practical reason.

3.2. Williams on Homer's Moral Psychology

On this interpretation, Plato's version of *thumos* as the middle soul provides a partial basis for later ideas of the existential will as a motivational faculty. Plato is not concerned to explain the process of making choices but is, rather, concerned to incorporate the heroic will of epic poetry within his framework. In this light, it seems especially ironic that some contemporary writers have referred to the moral psychology implicit in this tradition as a basis for rejecting the concept of decision as a form of second-order agency, which emerged in later theories of action. For example, in *Shame and Necessity*, Bernard Williams admits that practical willing as a faculty of making decisions and associated senses of individuality are not found in Homeric literature; but he insists that these ideas "are not so much the benefits of moral maturity as the accretions of misleading philosophy."[144] And despite his own criticisms of utilitarianism for obscuring the separateness of persons as moral agents, Williams argues that the only "unity" needed to "have thoughts and experiences" and to explain our sense of ourselves as agents is the unity of the "living person" as an animated bodily whole which we find in Homer's characters.[145] They make "decisions" in the same sense in which we ordinarily do, Williams claims: simply by acting "for reasons."[146]

As Williams convincingly argues, in most Homeric cases, intervention by the gods in human decisions simply represents the fact that "why one reason should prevail rather than another, or take over someone's attention, can remain hidden."[147] Thus: "The interventions of the gods, then, operate within a system that ascribes action to human beings; and deliberations, as result of which they act; and therefore, reasons on which they act. In ascribing reasons to people, it also ascribes to them desires, beliefs, and purposes."[148]

What more is needed? If there is any notion of "will" still absent here, Williams says, it could only be a metaphysical illusion introduced by later philosophical corruption of ordinary language and intuitions, for "the complex net of concepts in terms of which particular actions are explained" was otherwise "the same for Homer as it is for us."[149] In particular:

> Homer has no word that means, simply, to decide. But he does have the notion. For he has the idea of wondering what to do, coming to a conclusion, and doing a particular thing because one has come to that conclusion, and *that is what a decision is*. . . . All that Homer seems to have left out is the idea of another mental action that is supposed necessarily to lie between coming to a conclusion and acting on it; and he did well in leaving it out, since there is no such action, and the idea of it is the invention of bad philosophy.[150]

My analysis in chapter 3 shows that Williams's bare assertion that our philosophically unencumbered understanding of action supports this Homeric baseline is little more than Rylean dogma. As Pink argues instead, "everyday beliefs about decision-making," intention, and freedom point strongly in the direction of the idea that intention formation is itself an action. This concept of the will as second-order or executive agency is "the common-sense psychology," and it is only because "Enlightenment psychologies" that radically revise ordinary intuitions have been dominant for centuries now in academic philosophy that the thin concept of volition for which Williams finds Homer's resources sufficient appears at all adequate.[151]

Second, and even more important, if Homeric literature does not develop the concept of decision, surely this is because it is focused instead on the way heroic willing generates new motivation in the process of defining its purposes. Williams himself concedes that "what is ordinarily called will" includes the notion of "efforts of will."[152] He insists that Homeric characters can make such efforts, both outwardly and "within the mind," as when a man "dialogues with his own *thumos*," or consults his heart, in order to discover with which course of action "he is more identified."[153] Odysseus demonstrates a capacity for "endurance" of suffering and frustration of immediate impulses to realize long-term goals, a "capacity to hold out against feeling or desire."[154] This shows that the idea of heroic willing as an effort to build up one's own motivation by commitment to the task or determination to persevere on the course one has set is present in Homer. Williams fails to appreciate this because, following Nietzsche's critique of Kant, he assumes that the reason "progressivists" find the will lacking in Homer is that his notion of action "did *not* revolve round a distinction between moral and nonmoral motivations."[155] But whether this is true or not, the will as a motivational power is not simply identical to *moral* motivation in any allegedly "abstract modern sense."[156] In short, the Homeric epics may provide insights lacking in contemporary action theory, but nothing in the classical idea of heroic *thumos* is actually inconsistent with the modern idea of practical willing as decision-making agency, nor does it provide any evidence for a minimalist conception of the will.

3.3. Aristotle's Generalization of the Middle Soul

Hence nothing in Williams's argument undermines my suggestion that Plato's conception of *thumos* retains elements of the Homeric conception of heroic willing, out of which subsequent philosophical reflection could have developed the existential conception of striving will as a self-motivating power. The reason this did not happen is crucial for understanding how in scholastic philosophy "the will" came to be interpreted as a faculty of decision-making that derives its motives from a form of desire (sharing the general erosiac structure) aimed at intelligible goods. Following the logic of his own erosiac model, Plato's philosophical descendants generalized his idea of the middle soul from an indignant desire for honor into the general power of desiring rationally discernible goods or components of human well-being and choosing among means to them or specifications of them. Thus the middle soul became *composite*: not an irreducible third genus of motivation but simply the appetitive engine of evaluative or practical reason, the point of contact between the rational (*logon*) and the irrational (*alogon*) in a fundamentally bipartite moral psychology.[157] This is Aristotle's portrayal of the "intellectual appetite" in Book I of his *Nicomachean Ethics*. Here are key parts of the passage in which this idea is introduced:

> Of the irrational element one division seems to be widely distributed, and vegetative in its nature. . . . There seems also to be another irrational element in the soul—one which in a sense, however, shares in a rational principle. . . . No doubt, however, we must none the less suppose that in the soul too there is something beside reason, resisting and opposing it. In what sense it is distinct from the other elements does not concern us. Now even this seems to have a share in reason, as we said; at any rate in the continent man it obeys reason—and presumably in the temperate and brave man it is still more obedient; for in them it speaks, on all matters, with the same voice as reason.[158]

Aristotle's phrasing here clearly echoes Plato's discussion of the tripartite soul in the *Republic IV* at several points, and it is no accident that his examples of temperate and brave men are exactly those whose appetite and spirit were in harmony with reason on Plato's view. But we can see a key difference: his model is fundamentally bipartite, and it is one *subdivision* of the irrational part that is responsive to practical reason, at least if well trained.[159] Aristotle adds "That [the higher part of] the irrational element is in some sense persuaded by reason is indicated also by the giving of advice and by all reproof and exhortation."[160] This recalls Leontius reproving his own desires in Plato's famous example of *thumos*;[161] but the part that is thus amenable to reason is no longer narrowly conceived as a passion for honor or distinguished from other desires and passions that rise above instinctive organic drives (which could be considered vegetative): "For the vegetative element in no way shares in reason, but the appetitive and in general the desiring [*orektikon*] element in a sense shares in it."[162]

As Sarah Broadie argues in her penetrating analysis of Aristotle's division of the soul, by saying that the "sensitive, desiderative and emotional part of the human soul is not strictly rational" yet its function is "to 'listen to reason,'" he means to emphasize how it differs from "the human soul's nutritive part, and also from the desiderative part of nonrational animals."[163] She also emphasizes that for Aristotle, the appetite amenable to reason can be influenced by the *external* authority of other persons (as with warriors following the guardians in the *Republic*), and that this is Aristotle's analogy for its internal relation to the agent's own practical reason.[164] In this persuasive relationship, the reason-oriented desiring part can follow practical reason *willingly*—at least out of respect and love for the authority figure rather than sheer fear of threat—and at the limit it can "always be immediately at the ready to fall in with and lend its energy to any project prescribed by the internal analogue of authority."[165] Note how this notion of "lending its energy" agrees with Plato's conception of the *thumos* as potentially a motivational supplement to reason.

Yet this resemblance is misleading, since, as we see in the next chapter, the various types of motive-states now classed together within Aristotle's rationally oriented desiring part are all fundamentally erosiac in structure—whereas the "energy" that Platonic *thumos* could lend almost appeared to be projective. Instead, Aristotle's rationally oriented desiring part functions as a *generic faculty* of erosiac attraction to appropriable good or value, which is open-ended enough to be directed to virtually anything by practical reason and flexible enough to acquire dispositions to desire anything that can be apprehended or interpreted as a good (differing in this essential plasticity from the instinctually fixed desires of nonrational animals).[166] As Oberdiek says, "in Aristotle's account, self-controlled or voluntary actions are those where an agent, acting with the appropriate degree of knowledge and without compulsion, seeks an end because of some kind of desire (*orexis*) originating within him."[167] *Prohairesis* thus channels orektic motivation into particular voluntary actions without generating any new motivation in the process.

So if we define the "middle" position in our psychic hierarchy narrowly as the position of the *reason-aiding* faculty—the position that was occupied by the striving spiritual energy of *thumos* in Plato—then Aristotle *replaces* the middle soul with the maximally generalized faculty of erosiac motivation, whose highest potential is found in dispositions of erosiac attraction to rationally endorsed ends that no lower animal can desire.[168] Alternatively, if we define the "middle" position widely as *whatever* comes between our highest cognitive powers (which can conceive universals) and our absolutely irrational inclinations and appetites (shared by all sentient animal life), then we have a broad territory that could potentially include several different kinds of psychic states. In this territory occupied by the *thumos* in Plato, Aristotle puts the rationally oriented or rationally trainable desires *together* with the lower "practical" part of reason.[169]

This crucial development in Aristotle also helps explain how in philosophy the concept of will came to be understood as a faculty of decision-making. Later thinkers in the Judeo-Christian tradition began to regard the human capacity for resolve and striving for purity in the soul as crucial for the life of faith; and in order to give it a classical precedent, they associated "will" in this original existential sense with Plato's middle soul as the "heart" of human beings. "To take heart," "to have heart," "to be hearty or great-spirited"—these phrases are still associated for us with courageous commitment, with giving one's full effort, and with the strength of will to strive for difficult goals. But Aristotle and his followers in scholastic theology reconceived the middle soul or "heart" as the general faculty of deliberative desire, or the entire aspect of the psyche in which motives can arise from (or at least be shaped by) practical deliberation about achievable goods and thereby determine "decision" as the choice of a particular act. *Prohairesis*, or "choice," is therefore defined by Aristotle as a "deliberate desire of things in our power,"[170] and the proper function of the middle soul is precisely to produce such "choices." Choosing thus became this final upshot of will as intellectual appetite, which as an executive power of decision inherits its motivation entirely from the preexisting desires for apparent goods as presented by practical reason (which together make up intellectual appetite). And though they are influenced by reason, all these desires share the erosiac form (as we will see below). *Prohairesis* taking place in the rational appetite produces no new motivation but only *transmits* the erosiac motivation of a prior desire. Hence the Transmission principle becomes intrinsic to eudaimonist moral psychology without being explicitly recognized and defended, and willing is reduced to a transitional moment between intellectual appetite and action.

Arguably, *prohairesis* for Aristotle is still a more limited faculty than "the will" in Aquinas, who believes it can form intentions on the basis of virtually any kind of prepurposive desire (whether it is a rational wish for some articulable good or some other lower emotion or appetite). Like other commentators, John Cooper argues that Aristotle understands nonrational desires as "active psychological movement[s] toward getting in an appropriate way, or experiencing or doing, whatever it is that the desire is for," so that desires in this sense will cause voluntary movement if they are unchecked.[171] If this is right, then for Aristotle many voluntary actions can begin without going through *prohairesis* at all. It will be only those actions that are motivated by *boulēsis*, or rational wish, that count as "chosen" in a deliberate act of forming an intention to pursue one's desired end in a certain particular way. Or, as Broadie urges, perhaps prohairetic acts can also be an "unhesitant expression of our moral nature" that are the same as we would decide in deliberation, since they are guided by dispositions formed through acting on rational wishes in the past.[172] By contrast, the Stoics hold that epithumetic appetites like sensual cravings and anger can be acted on intentionally only if we decide to act on them, and this requires "reasoned thought that the actions they are moving the agent to do are to be done."[173]

However, my quarrel is not with Aristotle's conception of deliberative choice nor with the executive agency view of the will that derives from this conception together with his analysis of the voluntary: despite their manifold problems, these theories represented clear advances in Aristotle's time, which were further refined in Aquinas's theory of action and intention.[174] My concern is rather with the embedded assumption that all the motivation that can go into deciding on action and pursuing one's intentions is both predecisional motivation and erosiac in form. I believe this assumption determines basic features of Aristotle's eudaimonist approach to ethics and leads to certain paradoxes internal to psychological eudaimonism. My critique of Aristotle's eudaimonism as a basis for an ethic of virtue will single out the underlying reliance on erosiac motivation as the source of several problems that remain unresolved in the eudaimonist tradition. But before these problems can be explained, we must better understand Aristotle's division of human motives and his version of the strong erosiac thesis, which are considered in the next chapter.

5

Aristotelian Desires and the Problems of Egoism

Overview. The first half of this chapter focuses on the distinction between three kinds of desire, starting from Aristotle's analysis of the human psyche and bringing in conceptual distinctions from contemporary neo-Aristotelian work on motivation by Watson, Taylor, MacIntyre, Murphy, and others. The second half of the chapter, which distinguishes among various types of egoism and their paradoxes, is slightly more technical; but in addition to major figures in the modern period, it engages Feinberg's critique of egoism, which is widely taught to undergraduates.

I. Aristotle and the Typology of Erosiac Desire

1.1. Aristotle's Psychology of Animal Motivation in the De anima

The previous chapter concludes that by replacing Plato's middle soul with his "intellectual appetite," Aristotle embeds the Transmission principle into his moral psychology: all voluntary actions, including those emerging from *prohairesis* or practically rational choice, derive the content and strength of their motives from preexisting desire-states of one sort or another. In this chapter, I argue that Aristotle's psychology commits him to the weak erosiac thesis: all the prepurposive motives that can move us to voluntary action have the erosiac structure first described by Plato.

In its broad outlines, Aristotle's psychology also recognizes a hierarchical order of different motivational states, among which three kinds of erosiac desire like those we find in Plato figure most prominently. As John Cooper argues, Aristotle uses *"orexis"* as a general term for occurrent desires, and Aristotle follows Plato's view that practical reason itself can motivate in a way quite distinct from other nonrational desires:

In many places (in *Eudemian Ethics*, *Magna Moralia*, in *de Anima*, in *de Motu Animalium*, and in the *Rhetoric* and *Politics*, but, curiously, none in the *Nicomachean Ethics*), Aristotle explicitly divides *orexis* (that seems to be his established word for movements of the soul towards or away from action) into three kinds: *epithumia* or appetite, *thumos* or spirited, competitive impulses, and *boulēsis*. And he repeatedly makes it clear that *epithumia* and *thumos* are the two genera of nonrational desire, while *boulēsis* is his preferred name for the movement towards action produced by the use of reason itself, on its own.[1]

Stanley Hauerwas understands the division slightly differently: "A desire (*orexis*) for Aristotle is simply that aspect of a creature's action by which it is moved to an end by which it expects to gain pleasure. Aristotle recognizes three different species of desire: wish (*boulēsis*), passion (*thumos*), and appetite (*epithumia*)."[2] By "pleasure" here, Hauerwas could mean generic satisfaction that takes different forms depending on which species of *orexis* we have in mind. But Hauerwas argues that Aristotle erred not only in failing to distinguish intention as an element of action but also in limiting desire to ends "that give us pleasure. For although *boulēsis* is desire modified by reason, it is still limited to desire for ends which give pleasure."[3] However, since bouletic states do not anticipate the same kind of satisfaction as appetitive ones, Hauerwas's complaint must be that Aristotle limits desire to ends seen as likely to *benefit the agent* in some way. If so,[4] then this chapter will be a development of Hauerwas's point.

To make sense of these concepts, it helps to start by reviewing some basic themes from Aristotle's *De anima*, which distinguishes different kinds of psyche by the motive-states and kinds of movement they are capable of causing. There Aristotle's hierarchy begins with the "vegetative" (or nutritive) and "locomotive" souls. What Aristotle calls vegetative movement, as in plant growth and the operation of our digestive system, are completely unconscious operations that we would now regard as complex regulated feedback mechanisms (let us label these "D0" causes). Such mechanisms are not moved by conscious desires of even the most basic instinctive sort ("D1"). Aristotle does not attribute any movement of a whole animal within its environment to such nutritive mechanisms, because he assumes such local movement always requires sensation[5] and that sensation is always conscious.[6] Hence Aristotle thinks that local movement requires at least the sensation of touch and thus a sentient awareness of pleasure and pain that could cause an appetite at least of the D1 sort, since some kind of (conscious) appetite is needed to cause bodily movement. The "nutritive faculty" cannot be the source of voluntary local movement, because "movement is always for an end and is accompanied by either imagination or appetite [*orexis*]; for no animal moves except by compulsion unless it has an impulse towards or away from an object."[7]

Here "impulse" involves some conscious apprehension of the end to be obtained. Noting that "Appetite is one form of *orexis*, a 'reaching out for' an object," Nussbaum argues that "Even the bodily appetites—hunger, thirst, sexual desire—are seen by Aristotle as forms of intentional awareness, containing a view of their object" that can be altered by rational inspection.[8] Aristotle did not perceive that some animals move without any kind of appetite at all, because he did not know about cases of so-called *tropistic behavior* that are controlled by a simple mechanism or program that can go awry and produces aberrant or repeated behavior if its routine is disturbed.[9] Although it need not be, tropistic behavior is usually interpreted as entirely unconscious in animals—such as insects—in which it predominates.[10] This makes it as much a D0 state as the "hectic activity" and adjustments constantly going on in unconscious, automatic systems such as digestion.[11] Aristotle would probably have to count such behavior as compelled or involuntary, although his paradigm case of compulsion is an external force acting on the body.[12]

In any case, Aristotle holds that all voluntary movement must flow from some kind of *orexis* or desire. As Professor Lear summarizes Aristotle's explanation in the *De anima:*

> Human action is a species of animal movement. All animal movement, Aristotle argues, must flow from desire [*orexis*]. Lesser animals have basic appetites [*epithumia*] as well as sense perception, and imagination based on their sensory awareness. But their movements would be incomprehensible on the basis of sensation and imagination alone.[13]

Aristotle defends his hierarchy of the different kinds of "soul" by noting how they form a cumulative system, with "higher" powers always found with lower ones, but not vice versa. Higher animals with the powers of calculation, thought, and speculative intuition of universals have all the powers of lower animals, including imagination, sensation, and basic appetites, but the converse does not hold.[14] The "basic appetites" that are shared between human beings and the simplest animals capable of conscious desire will therefore include a whole range of conscious impulses that are both instinctive and linked to physiological needs. These are what I called DI desires: "brute urges" or impulses that are either intrinsic to the proper biological functioning of the body, such as hunger, thirst, sexual attraction, and perhaps certain kinds of disgust or aversions (e.g., to what smells or tastes foul), or instinctively driven conscious feelings, such as panic in a flight response. As appetites, of course, they also have intentional content:

they are *for* some sort of object (e.g., food) or for some sort of body-related state (safety from physical threat). But they pull or draw their subject toward these apprehended objects or states without the need for any rational endorsement of these objects or states as being good for all similarly situated animals.[15] As dispositions to behave in characteristic ways, these basic urges and inclinations do have biological functions that *we* can understand (and thus we can discriminate "normal" from "abnormal" or aberrant versions of these appetites); but this understanding is not necessary for the envisioned object or state to attract the animal subject to these appetites.

Otherwise put, D1 desires require no cognitive evaluation. Like basic sense qualia (such as colors and sounds), they are consciously experienceable without any connected linguistic thought or propositional attitudes (though they may often be accompanied by such thoughts in higher animals capable of language). On this hypothesis, there is a discernible level of "feelings" that are purely qualitative states, although they are closely connected with physiological reactions. For example, the newborn infant's first instinctive urge for milk is conscious but probably without any more articulation than the feeling of an undifferentiated need, though it soon learns to associate this with whatever sources of milk are provided. However, what distinguishes D1 impulses proper is not simply the lack of linguistic articulation but their failure to fix any *specific object* as the source of the desired gratification. For example, the infant's urge is not initially toward any one thing *represented as* potentially satisfying it but is a pure feeling of need that is instinctively directed to the right source of satisfaction.

As Plato's analysis suggested, we can distinguish such D1 appetites in this impulsive sense as generic "urges" from another kind of state in which the urge is *specified* as desire for a particular sort of object seen as likely to satisfy the urge. In such a case, the agent's appetite will not be satisfied by just any object that will satisfy the underlying D1 urge; rather, her appetite will be (more) satisfied by some relevant subset of this range, and so we must speak of this as a *different* desire: for example, a desire for a beer, rather than raw thirst. It is different not only in specificity but also in the *kind* of intentional content it involves. For by itself, the D1 urge is a "blind" *conatus*: its subject has virtually no idea *what* it is an appetite for until instinctual responses provide him or her with some experience. At least at this level, we can clearly say, with William Desmond, that "what desire wants, needs, and is committed to, is a fulfilling life."[16] D1 drives aim for the most part at the biological bases of life (although without conscious judgment about those bases). Whether all kinds of desire aim at "life" in any more robust sense remains to be seen.

By contrast, at least some image, sensual memory, or *phantasia* of the satisfying object-type is needed for a D2 "appetite" (the broader category including what Aristotle calls *epithumia*). And in human beings, the desired kind of object or state is also usually named or linguistically recognized and hence communicable to others. When we think of such D2 appetites as growing out of some more generic D1 impulse or drive, we say that the agent has "acquired a taste" for a particular kind of object or state. This "taste" is a new desire, although it would not have arisen were it not for prior behavior motivated by the unsaturated D1 urge or experiences of this urge being satisfied. The fundamental difference, then, is that no D2 appetite forms automatically by "nature"; although nonhuman animals are also capable of such appetites, they develop only as the animal's biologically innate drives interact with the environment. Because of their specific intentional content, such D2 states can also move us directly to form an *intention* that then guides bodily movements, such that the intention and movements together constitute an "action" (e.g., drinking a beer). Furthermore, by connection with instrumental reasoning, such an intention can anchor a *plan of action*, or an encompassing intention that guides a whole series of actions calculated to reach the desired end (e.g., driving to the store to buy some beer).

1.2. *The Distinction between D2 and D3 Desires*

D2 desires thus correspond to what MacIntyre and Anscombe have called "surd not further to be explained wanting [*sic*]."[17] Although Anscombe questions the possibility of such motives and denies that they can figure in practical reasoning, MacIntyre correctly notes that we can reason from an object simply "*as wanted*," rather than as good in some other way. He points out that Hume's alternative system of practical reasoning is based on this point.[18] Thus the category of D2 desires also includes *brute preferences*, which are the only motive-state entertained by most contemporary models in rational decision theory. If agent S has a D2 appetite for object O1 that is (overall) stronger than her D2 appetite for object O2, then we say that she *prefers* O1 to O2, but not for any reason other than the relative strengths of the desires.[19] One way of explaining this might be to refer both appetites to a common root in some D1 state as an *unsaturated* urge toward a range of possible satisfying objects. Thus thirst is an instinctive drive, but I learn to prefer grape juice to lemonade among objects that satisfy the D1 desire. But this kind of causal explanation is not essential to the notion of a D2 preference or brute ranking.[20]

It is part of the nature of brute preference-orderings that an agent acting only on the appetites they represent can (and perhaps even must) pursue not only her most preferred object but also her next most preferred and on down until items lower in the order conflict with some above them.[21] If my strongest desire is to see the opera and my next strongest is to see the movie, then I might go to the opera first and the movie next, unless they are playing at the same time. Since their objects are qualified only *as desired*, the conflict between such D2 appetites can concern only limitations external to the motives themselves, such as physical or perhaps mental constraints that prevent them from being jointly pursuable. Hence my D2 preference for one over another incompossible object of distinct desires involves what Charles Taylor has aptly termed "simple weighing."[22] In weighing which object pleases me more, the objects are only *subjectively placed* on a scale relative to other objects with the potential to satisfy my appetites. As a result, the multiple D2 appetites do not conflict *essentially* because their contents involve no contrastive evaluations making reference to values independent of D2 desires. For example, a D2 desire to swim and a D2 desire to eat some cake can conflict only for contingent reasons of circumstance, such as that eating cake gives me a cramp that prevents me from swimming. As Taylor says, "Not being contrastively described, these two desired consummations are incompatible, where they are, only contingently and circumstantially."[23]

In agreement with MacIntyre, Taylor notes that simple weighing (or D2 appetites) still has sufficient content to ground what he calls "weak evaluation" or strategic analysis to discover contingent incompatibilities between my appetites, along with an instrumental calculation concerning how to maximize one's overall preference-satisfaction. And where there is no incoherence in my preference hierarchy, D2 appetite can sometimes be sufficient for an instrumental plan to guide a whole course of action.

Consider an example in which a D2 appetite results when Matthew's innate sexual impulse (a D1 urge) gets channeled by experience toward a certain "type" of woman as a potential mate (this "type" being a particular constellation of physical, stylistic, and personality features that Matthew might be at least partially able to describe). Now Cheryl, appearing to be a token of this type, becomes the object of Matthew's D2 sexual appetite. Matthew describes this in reassuring terms simply as a desire "to go out with Cheryl and get to know her better." Of course, reasons and motivations of quite a different nature certainly might enter into the formation of an actual intention to ask Cheryl on a first date. But at this point, we are imagining a case in which all the agent's acts toward Cheryl are done with "only one thing in mind" and are motivated solely by their instrumental relation to the likely satisfaction of an appetite for sexual union. Once Matthew has a plan of action, his prepurposive D2 desire to have sex with Cheryl provides the motivation to do particular things that are likely to advance this plan (e.g., he forms the intention to "call Cheryl tonight").

The purposive motivation to carry out such intentions is transmitted from the originally prepurposive D2 appetite and so remains on the same level.

Inclinations or appetites in the D2 sense can also be "final" when they stand at the top of the instrumental chain motivating other more particular desires. Of course, this does not require that the agent has a settled intention or plan explicitly articulated and mapped out for himself; the relation of a final prepurposive D2 appetite to appetites for particular things that will promote the satisfaction of the first appetite may, for the agent, remain tacit or internally unarticulated. Yet in every case, the D2 appetites or inclinations are distinguished by the fact that intended objects (or mental contents) are *purely subjective* in the following important sense: they depend on no *evaluations that make a validity claim on others looking for their agreement*. Just in experiencing a D2 appetite (as distinct from acting on it), the agent is not even implicitly committed to expecting any kind of interpersonal ratification; in some cases, he may not even care if his appetite is *intelligible* to third parties.

If past enjoyment has caused me to want to listen to Mozart's *Eine kleine Nachtmusik*, my wanting this does not imply that others should want the same thing or enjoy hearing the same piece. But if my desire is motivated by *reasons* about the music's qualities of the sort that others should be able to recognize (for them to count as "reasons" at all), then my desire is not a D2 appetite, by definition. Such an evaluative desire (or D3 state) thus *automatically* includes at least some motivation to communicate faithfully to other competent evaluators within one's linguistic community the existence of the desire and the evaluation of the desired object upon which it is based. To "want" something in *this* distinctive sense is *eo ipso* to want our desire for it to be justified by the facts about the object—something that in principle should be recognizable by others, at least if they are sufficiently similar in competencies and experience. Like any concern for projects on which one could base an intelligible sense of one's practical identity, D3 desire involves an implicit validity claim and the related reference to an intersubjectively recognizable "horizon of significance" that does not itself arise from or depend on the agent's desires.[24]

Contrast this with Matthew's case, in which he may want Cheryl to understand his desire to go out with her so that she agrees to the date, but his reasons for communicating his D2 appetite to her are purely strategic; he is not rationally committed to her agreeing that he should choose her on some objective criteria of merit. Nor, for his purposes, need he want her to think that *she* has good reasons to go out with him or that he is in some objective sense worthy of being desired: he only needs her to share the same brute preference for a date. Hence, in most cases at least, the content of D2 desires is communicable; but if the D2 desire itself motivates the agent to communicate its existence to others, it can motivate this only *strategically* as a means to its own satisfaction. And thus, unsurprisingly, D2 appetites may often motivate the agent subject to them to hide their existence or misrepresent them to others instead. In these respects, all D2 appetites function exactly like "brute preferences" in standard rational decision theory;[25] one person's preference for chocolate ice cream involves no claim whatsoever about what flavor of ice cream another person should prefer. My telling the soda-shop waiter that I would like chocolate is (considered by itself) just strategic action—though I might do it in a polite way for moral reasons. Similarly, as Cooper points out, for Aristotle nonrational desires may involve propositional content, but their apprehension of the apparent good does not rest on any chain of reasoning showing it to be good.[26]

So even though they are routinely communicated, and this is basic to the coordination of much human interaction, D2 appetites involve no "validity claim," or implicit reference to normative standards of warrant, nor any implicit acceptance of the burden to provide reasons for the desire to others in a critical exchange. It is not even essential to the experience of a D2 desire that others be able to understand what a D2 appetite *means* to its subject—though this may often be required by a derivative instrumental need that the subject has for others to help him in satisfying his desire. For example, I need the chef to understand my preference for a "medium-well-done" steak so that he knows how to cook it the "way I like it." But if the chef is presumptuous enough to ask me *why* I want my steak this way, when everyone of cultured taste knows that it is best medium-rare (since this allows the full flavor to emerge, etc.), there is no answer I could give. My preference, though it is cognitively specific rather than an unsaturated instinctual urge, is not motivated by any reasons with normative force, so it is not on the same level as the type of aesthetic evaluation with which the chef is challenging it. A being who was capable only of D2 appetites would be as deaf to the chef's appeal as my cat is to my frustrated plea that his pill is *good for him* in an objective biological sense.

Of course, since a normal human being is not like the cat in this respect, in practice D2 appetites may often be psychologically associated with other states that involve more objective evaluation. Even Cheryl's belief that Matthew is "cute" might qualify, since this involves a judgment that others could share if it is warranted, and this in turn motivates certain reactive dispositions in her, such as disagreement, anger, surprise, or even resentment toward her friends when they most firmly deny that Matthew is "cute." Of course, "cute" is a vague term, and it may often be used to indicate a brute preference; but I am imagining that in Cheryl's case it does not express a sheer subjective preference for Matthew, however intimately connected it might be to other merely D2 appetites in her psyche. There are many polysemic evaluative terms, such as "cute," which have no particular ethical significance, but whose application often seems to involve an evaluative attitude with more robust reason-giving significance than brute preferences.

One might object to this analysis on the grounds that all desires give us *some* sort of reason to act, namely a reason to *satisfy* the desire. Against this objection, I note Gary Watson's insight that

> any desire may provide the basis for a reason in so far as the non-satisfaction of the desire causes suffering and hinders the pursuit of ends of the agent. But it is important to notice that the reason generated in this way is a reason for *getting rid* of the desire, and one may get rid of a desire either by satisfying it or by eliminating it in some other manner (by tranquilizers, or cold showers). Hence this kind of reason differs importantly from the reasons based upon the evaluation of the activities or states of affairs in question. For in the former case, attaining the object of desire is simply a means of eliminating discomfort or agitation, whereas in the latter, that attainment is the end itself.[27]

This gives us another way of explaining the distinction between D1-D2 states and D3 evaluative desires. Watson's point is that a D1 or D2 desire for an object whose "goodness" is apprehended only in its brute power to draw our practical attention toward it can be said to generate a minimal disjunctive "reason" either to satisfy the desire or get rid of it, whereas D3 states or "valuations" generate non-disjunctive reasons to pursue the desired object or goal.

Mark Murphy makes essentially the same point in his critique of contemporary desire-fulfillment models of welfare: whereas something (*x*)'s being an aspect of one's well-being "always provides a reason for one to act to secure *x*," merely having a "desire for *x*" gives the agent "only a reason to secure *x* or to rid him- or herself of the desire for *x*." As Murphy argues, even idealized versions of the desire-fulfillment model (e.g., with full information conditions) will be subject to this criticism:

> For since all genuine strong subjectivist theories do not discriminate among desires on the basis of content, it will be possible for bizarre and pointless desires, like a fundamental desire to avoid touching brown boxes, to persist or even to be made present for the first time in one's preferred hypothetical desire situation. But these are desires that one has no reason to try to satisfy, no matter how well-informed the agent that has them; the most one might have reason to do is

either to [try to] satisfy them or to rid oneself of those desires. This would be enough to show that strong subjectivism is a false view.[28]

This critique works because strong subjectivist theories about well-being define it entirely in terms of the satisfaction of what I have called D1- and D2-type desires—although the idealizing conditions in modified versions of this approach are (unsuccessful) *ad hoc* attempts to force the rational desiderata of D3 desires into D2 preferences. Likewise, an objective list conception of well-being tries to specify the goods that we have objective reason to desire in the D3 sense. Taylor's point that such desires involve "strong evaluations" can then be rephrased as the point that D3 desires involve and express the agent's defeasible judgments about what constitutes his objective well-being. That is why, in D3 desires, a non-disjunctive reason to attain the end motivates the desire for the object; as Watson says, "We aim to satisfy, not just eliminate, [rational] desire."[29]

It also explains why D3 desires have to be learned through experience and/or teaching: unlike innate drives, the relevant reasons for regarding the object as *desirable* or the ability to apply language involving strong evaluative contrasts must be acquired. Hence MacIntyre can say that "This type of educated desire is what Aristotle calls *boulēsis* as contrasted with nonrational emotion, *thumos* and appetite, *epithumia*."[30]

These points clarify the distinction sketched in chapter 4 between subjective D2 appetites and D3 desires that involve evaluative attitudes or judgments concerning the objective value of the desired object that imply the existence of in-principle intersubjectively shareable reasons for the judgment. We can sum up the differences we have identified as follows:

1. As we saw in the analysis of Plato's *Republic*, drawing on Gary Watson's distinction between valuing and mere wanting, D3 desires give their subject reasons to pursue their objects and to maintain the desire itself (since they qualify their object as objectively desirable), whereas D2 appetites give their subject only *disjunctive* reasons to satisfy them *or* to eliminate them.

2. Drawing on Charles Taylor's related distinction, D3 desires involve contrastive or *strong evaluations* that not simply rank good objects of desire higher than bad ones on the scale of cardinal comparisons. D2 appetites constitute brute preferences, in which there is a *simple weighing* of the preferred object over other options.

3. Drawing on Jürgen Habermas's idea that normative judgments are distinguished by their *illocutionary force* as implicit validity claims on the free rational agreement of other competent evaluators, we saw that D3 desires involve what the agent takes to be reasons for a categorical positive evaluation of the desired object that should be

rationally endorsable by others irrespective of their particular D2 preferences.

By describing the positive evaluation of the desired object as "categorical," I mean here that it need not depend on the object having any instrumental value toward the satisfaction of desires that the agent has and others might not share. The agent moved by a D3 desire is rationally committed to a willingness *in principle* to explain the reasons for his desire to others who, irrespective of individuating psychological differences, should be able to understand *why* the agent is moved by these reasons and endorse these as reasons for desiring the object.[31] However, for D3 desires, this still requires all the agent's relevant interlocutors to share the fundamental desire for well-being or for the good in the generic sense of "flourishing." This is why Plato's *Meno* describes such "good" things as beneficial and "bad" things as harmful or injurious (*Meno* 77A–E). Thus, following a medieval schema, we may add as a fourth condition that:

  4. D3 desires are for some object or state of affairs (X), where X is apprehended in its aspect *as valuable to us* (or *as good for us*) in some respect for reasons (Y) related to human well-being. In short, X contributes in some way to human flourishing.

The phenomenal quality of being motivated to gain or realize X may be conscious without explicit reflection on reasons Y, but such reasons are implicit in the D3 desire and should be discursively articulable on reflection (by a competent interpreter)[32] in such a way as to draw forth an agent's agreement that this is indeed "why she wanted X." Some D3 desires may depend on more explicitly made comparative judgments (e.g., that V is *better* than W in some respect). But what is common to them all is that the evaluative attitude—the apprehension of X as good or valuable—usually straightaway involves motivation to form the intention to act so as to realize X, unless other motivational states interrupt, override, or counteract it. This is not a claim that reasons for X external to the agent's existing motives immediately motivate her, since I assume that the general desire for well-being is in place. Given this orientation, the agent's desire for X flows smoothly out of her evaluation of X, although the latter may involve lengthy deliberation and even discussion of its merits with others. In theories that recognize only states up to and including D3 states, decision or choice is usually construed as deliberation about which D3-desired objects to pursue now, and it works by clarifying and comparing our evaluations so that one option in our available range emerges as better (either intrinsically, or as a means to our prior ends, or both), which makes it more "desirable" as a result.

Thus we may think of D3 desires as syntheses of a value judgment and the attraction toward the apprehended object that this value tends to stir up in the agent. This is quite different from the kind of internal connection between evaluative conviction and motivation to act accordingly that Humean noncognitivists recognize, however, for, strictly speaking, Humean moral psychology does not allow for D3 desires at all. Humean accounts of motivation as rooted in noncognitive sources usually characterize all desires in the D2 fashion: for example, David Lewis says that desires are not blind urges, since they can connect with beliefs about the means that will bring us what we want, but the wanting itself expresses only subjective expected value, not objective "choiceworthiness."[33] As Lewis summarizes the Humean claim, "our actions serve our subjective expected value according to our subjective degrees of belief."[34] On this model, "belief serves desire" only by generating an expected value for a less specific proposition A out of the values for the more specific cases that A covers or includes.[35] Other than these additive connections in the desire calculus, there are no necessary connections between beliefs (such as objective value-beliefs) and desires:

> If there are universal correlations between certain beliefs and certain desires, that too is a contingent matter. Someone might have no desire at all for joy, knowledge, or love. Someone might believe just what you and I believe, and still have no desire at all for joy, knowledge, or love. Indeed, someone might believe just what G. E. Moore believed about the simple, non-natural properties of these things and still have no desire for them.[36]

The familiar anti-Humean who maintains the possibility of D3 desires in which the desire necessarily follows from a given evaluative belief can grant that what Lewis says is true for D2 inclinations or preferences. But in Lewis's subsequent arguments against various anti-Humean alternatives, he seems to think that Humeanism could be false only if the *role* of "desire" as a folk-psychological concept itself required that something standing in necessary connection to beliefs should count as a "desire."[37] For example, the simplest anti-Humean theory that Lewis critiques just *equates* desires with certain credences or beliefs that they require—a theory that he maintains generates contradictions whenever the credences involved are less than certain.[38]

However, in contrast, my schema for D3 desires does not build in a *necessary* connection between the evaluative beliefs and the motivational state, although some conceptions of desires in the D3 sense would add this feature. For our D3 desire to be distinct from a D2 preference or inclination, it need only be a state in which the agent is motivated to pursue some end *because* of her evaluation (E) of its objective value or choiceworthiness. This implies the counterfactual that if she lacked E, then she would not have the relevant D3 desire, but *not* the counterfactual that if she lacked the desire, she would lack E. So the evaluation is possible in principle without the desire, but when present, the desire embodies the evaluation. This model also leaves open the possibility that without E, the agent might have a quite different D2 desire for her object, which gives her object a high expected utility or preference-satisfaction value from her perspective. When she has E, she might well have D3 and D2 simultaneously, and she might also have D3 without D2. So the presence or absence of D2 varies independently of E, and any connection they have would be contingent, since E is not what *motivates* a subjective preference or mere inclination like D2. By contrast, the evaluative desire D3 requires E as its counterfactually necessary condition.

Aristotelian anti-Humeans sometimes write as if D3 desires *automatically* follow from objective value judgments; when coupled with the prudential capacity to make reliable judgments about what contributes to flourishing, the disposition to such desires is sometimes offered as an analysis of virtue. But there is evidence to show that the connection between "pure" evaluative attitudes and D3 desires is not this tight. If it is possible to evaluate some object or end X as valuable or good in some respect (as healthy, beautiful, noble, etc.) without any accompanying desire for it (or aversion to it), then evaluative attitudes can be distinguished from D3 desires or action-oriented motives that evaluations often accompany.[39] Some forms of "internalism" are construed so as to deny this possibility when the D3 desire is grounded in moral considerations. But, as Alfred Mele argues in a recent article, the phenomenon of "listlessness," which "consists in the total absence of motivation to engage in activities that formerly were matters of deep personal concern,"[40] is possible despite the persistence of moral beliefs or convictions. In such conditions—for example, perhaps in a serious depression—an agent may have the evaluative attitude which is normally embodied straightaway in a D3 desire, but now she does not experience this motivation. Aristotle also implies the possibility of such states in one of his arguments that "mind" [*nous*] cannot be the cause of forward "local movement":

> Further, neither can the calculative faculty or what is called "mind" [*nous*] be the cause of such movement; for mind as speculative never thinks what is practicable, it never says anything about an object to be avoided or pursued, while this movement is always in something which is avoiding or pursuing an object. No, not even when it is aware of such an object does it at once enjoin pursuit or avoidance

of it; e.g., the mind often thinks of something terrifying or pleasant without enjoining the emotion of fear. It is the heart that is moved (or in the case of a pleasant object some other part).[41]

Thus Aristotle also seems to recognize pure speculative evaluations that, although they are about actionable values, may not be motivating in themselves without our general desire for happiness standing behind them. Instead, Aristotle says, "mind practical" is "capable of originating local movement," but only by calculating means to ends given by desire (in the general sense of *orexis*), "for that which is the object of appetite [*orexis*] is the stimulant of mind practical."[42] This suggests that without the underlying desire for happiness, the evaluations that figure in *boulēses* would not be motivating. In support of this point, Cooper also recognizes that in the *De anima*, Aristotle holds that nous and *dianoia* by themselves do not produce motivation except when coupled with some form of *orexis*, which may be boulēsis, that is, rational desire.[43] Following McDowell, we may construe this orektic state as an embracing "conception of how to live" that is inseparable from uncodifiable evaluative judgments about the good, but the cognitive and conative sides of this gestalt remain formally distinct.[44]

1.3. D2 and D3 Desiderative States in Aristotle

Given this conviction that all types of desire-states share the formal erosiac structure, it is easier to understand why Aristotle insists on the unity of "appetite" (*orexis*) as one general power of the soul with diverse manifestations. As we have already seen, Aristotle repeatedly links lower "desires" (*epithumia*) to sensation and immediate physical gratification; if an animal has "sensation, then necessarily also imagination and appetition, for where there is sensation, there is also pleasure and pain, and where these, necessarily also desire."[45] Hunger and thirst are typical instances of such epithumetic desire,[46] and since epithumetic desires arise in response to "feelings of pleasure and pain,"[47] they are not influenced by long-run considerations but only by "what is just at hand: a pleasant object which is just at hand presents itself as pleasant and good, without condition in either case, because of want of foresight."[48] Desire in this epithumetic sense seems to be ambiguous between what we have described as raw biological urges without representation (D1) and inclinations that are directed to preferred objects (D2).

To link Aristotle's conception of desire to the foregoing analysis, it will help to subdivide further the D2 category into those desires that arise directly from the *specification of* instinctive impulses by intending particular objects represented as satisfying these impulses, and other "preferences" that have specific intentional content without objective evaluation claims but are not simple specifications of generalized urges. In both cases, instinct alone is insufficient to *explain* the D2 desire, since there are other objects that might satisfy our instinctive urges besides the objects we actually desire. But a D2 desire for chocolate ice cream represents something as pleasant in a way more closely linked to satisfaction of a biological urge than, say, a desire to read biographies (as opposed to romance novels). Yet the latter stands on the D2 level if it involves no evaluation that makes a claim on others or invokes no principle with interpersonal significance. Let us call the former "biologically grounded inclinations" and the latter "culturally grounded inclinations."[49]

In his attempt to distinguish desires from "valuations," Watson makes a point relevant to this subdivision of the D2 category. He notes that desires *other* than "appetitive or passionate desires" (e.g., those for a particular kind of food or sexual partner) may exhibit "independence of evaluation,"[50] meaning that we can experience them "against our will" or "unfreely." For example:

> One may be disinclined to move away from one's family, the thought of doing so being accompanied with compunction; yet this disinclination may rest solely upon acculturation rather than upon a current judgment of what one is to do. . . . Or, taking another example, one may have been habituated to think that divorce is to be avoided in all cases, even though one sees no justification for maintaining one's marriage. In both of these cases, the attitude has its basis solely in acculturation and exists independently of the agent's judgment.[51]

These aversions as Watson construes them are culturally grounded inclinations rather than D3 desires; even though they seem "more akin to evaluation than to appetite" since they may be expressed in evaluative language,[52] they are only habitual preferences lacking the strong evaluation involved in D3 desires. There are presumably many similar preferences and inclinations that have cognitive content without objective evaluative significance and yet remain only distantly related to innate biological instincts and the impulses they generate.

On this analysis, Aristotle's sense of "desire" as *epithumia* lines up with biologically grounded inclinations, while his notion of "passions" seems closer to culturally grounded preferences and the feelings that go with them. His conception of *epithumia* emphasizes what such D2 inclinations have in common with raw D1 states: namely, an intimate connection to bodily needs, biological instincts, and physiological alterations produced by physical stimuli. Now, D2 inclinations on my analysis need not be motivated ultimately by the pursuit of physical pleasure or avoidance of physical pain;

as Elliott Sober and David Wilson note, "hunger sometimes accompanies the desire to eat," but not always: "Desires need not be accompanied by disagreeable sensations that disappear once the desire is satisfied."[53] It is important to understand that the erosiac model does not conceive all appetitive pull as a *physical* feeling of attraction. In D3 desires, the sense of lack need not be felt as "painful" at all, although it remains a disturbance seeking requital. Some D2 states may be brute preferences without any immediate link to visceral sensations. Yet in the epithumetic subcategory of D2 states, this physiological connection will hold.[54]

However, as we have seen, desire in this sense as *epithumia* is only one of three species of *orexis* for Aristotle:

> If any order of living things has the sensory, it must also have the appetitive [*orektikon*]; for appetite is the genus of which desire [*epithumia*], passion [*pathos*], and wish [*boulēsis*] are the species; now all animals have one sense at least, viz. touch, and whatever has a sense has a capacity for pleasure and pain, and therefore has pleasant and painful objects present to it, and wherever these are present, there is desire, for desire is just appetition of what is pleasant.[55]

Orexis (here translated as "appetite"), Aristotle's general term for any state of motivation, thus emphasizes the connection between these different types of desire. In his critique of thinkers who divide the soul into only the "calculative, the passionate, and the desiderative [or *epithumetic*]," Aristotle takes it as a *reductio* of their position that they cannot treat *orexis* in general as one of the basic faculties:

> It is absurd to break up the last-mentioned faculty, as these thinkers do, for wish is to be found in the calculative part and desire and passion in the irrational, and if the soul is tripartite appetite [*orexis*] will be found in all three parts.[56]

The point is just that each of Plato's "parts" has its own form of longing, or *orexis*: "wish" is motivation produced by the rational part of the soul, while "passion" is the motivation produced by the spirited part, and *epithumetic* desire is the motivation produced by the lowest part of the tripartite soul (bodily drives and sensory inclinations). Aristotle holds that it is more relevant to treat *orexis* as a unified faculty (the *orektikon*) because otherwise it would cut across the tripartite soul, leaving each of Plato's three parts with both motivational *and* nonmotivational aspects, which would be peculiar. On the tripartite account, mind would then engage in speculative thinking but also in wishing, and the lowest part would engage in sensation but also in *epithumesis*. To Aristotle, it makes more sense to treat mind, sensation, and appetite in general [*orexis*] as the basic types of soul, thus allowing *all* forms of motivation to be rooted in a single faculty:

That which moves therefore is a single faculty and [is] the faculty of appetite [*orexis*]. . . . As it is, mind is never found producing movement without appetite (for wish is a form of appetite; and when movement is produced according to calculation it is also according to wish), but appetite can originate movement contrary to calculation, for desire [*epithumia*] is a form of appetite. Now mind is always right, but appetite and imagination may be either right or wrong. That is why, though in any case it is the object of appetite which originates movement, this object may be either the real or the apparent good.[57]

The tripartist could respond that "appetite," or *orexis*, divides into *three* forms corresponding to his three parts, but the result would be messy, for it would leave us with six parts of the soul. Commenting on this passage, Lear says:

> we find wishes in the part of the soul which reasons about how to act, and we find desires in the "irrational" part of the soul: for example, the basic appetites for food and sex. . . . It seems that either Aristotle must give up the idea that the soul has parts, or he must find a way of conceiving the source of movement to be a single part of the soul. He chooses the latter option. There appear, he says, to be two sources of movement, practical mind and appetite. Practical mind differs from theoretical mind in that it is concerned with how a desire can be satisfied. . . . Aristotle located both practical mind and appetite within a single faculty of the soul responsible for movement: the desiring part [*to orektikon*].[58]

Thus Lear, like most Aristotle scholars, portrays Aristotle as holding a fundamentally bipartite model of the human soul (ignoring the vegetative part), within one of which there are two basic types of motivation, one irrational and the other amenable to reason (with passions in between):

The Appetitive Soul [*orektikon*]		The Rational Soul [*nous*]		
appetite (*epithumia*)	passion (*pathos*)	practical mind (*boulēsis*)	deliberate choice (*prohairesis*)	speculative mind (*nous*)
		(Rational	Appetite)	

However, the previous passage from the *De anima* clearly suggests that wish can be for an object that appears to be but is not actually good, implying that "wish" is not, strictly speaking, part of reason or *nous*. This may not mean that "practical mind" is simply part of *orexis* but rather that wish is the *aspect* of *orexis* that connects mind to motivation, which *combined* make rational appetite. Thus in his *Nicomachean Ethics*, Aristotle says that the "irrational element" of the soul includes both nutritive and appetitive divisions, and the latter (or at least part of it) "shares in a rational principle"[59] since in continent, temperate, and brave men it obeys or "is in some sense persuaded by reason."[60] If this is right, then "practical mind" or "intellectual appetite" does seem to form a kind of "middle soul" between the strictly rational and strictly irrational in Aristotle's conception, although it is a *compound* middle soul (as I argued in the earlier discussion of *prohairesis*).

Aristotle's division of the soul is contested among interpreters, but for my purposes, the crucial point is that Aristotle attempts to find one universal structure for all motivation on the model initially furnished in Plato's *Lysis* and *Meno*: namely, the teleological schema in which movement or action is the result of the agent's being *drawn* by an object apprehended as "good" in some way—real or apparent. His understanding of "wish" (*boulēsis*) or the motivation produced in "practical mind" is obviously similar to the four-part schema for D3 desires given above.[61] But "desires," or biological inclinations in the form of D1 or D2 states, are supposed to have a similar structure: the object appears as pleasant *first*, and the agent is drawn toward it like a beacon *second* (in logical though not necessarily temporal order). Thus while "wishes" have real evaluative contents (as in my D3 schema), and epithumetic "desires" are mere D2 states with representational content but no evaluative interpersonal significance, Aristotle says they are linked by the fact that in both cases, "the object of appetite [*orexis*] starts a movement and as a result of that thought gives rise to movement, the object of appetite being to it a *source of stimulation*."[62]

Aristotle's insight is that what both D2 and D3 states have in common is their *magnetic* form or, in Platonic terms, their basic erosiac sense of a lack, or incompleteness, in the presence of an object that seems to promise completion or satisfaction of the lack. The agent is thus stimulated by and drawn toward this object. As Lear says (using the term "desire" widely for *orexis* in general):

> There must be something which moves animals to move, and this motive force is desire. Desire and animal movement have a similar structure: desire is desire for an object *which the animal is lacking*, an animal movement is directed toward the object of desire.... Humans distinguish themselves from other animals by their ability to think and by the fact that in addition to appetites [*epithumia*] they have more sophisticated desires—for example, the desire to understand. Human action cannot be understood merely as an attempt to satisfy basic appetites.[63]

Yet the lack structure shared by all the different species of appetite is the reason why, as Lear emphasizes, awareness of an appetite is an essential part of the motivational state itself.[64]

Hence, like Plato's dialogues, Aristotle's treatises support the idea that, although they differ in the status of their cognitive content, preferential inclinations and evaluative desires share two important features: (1) the attraction of the object as represented or intended is primary, while the subjective feeling of the agent is secondary in response to the object; and (2) the object is desired *because* realizing it not only contributes to well-being but does so in the particular sense of fulfilling a want or tending to restore the agent to a kind of equilibrium of which the desire itself is a *disturbance* (or "affection" in the archaic sense). These two features make up what I call the fundamental structure of "desire-as-lack."

1.4. D2 and D3 States in MacIntyre's Moral Psychology

Interesting support for this reading of Aristotle may be found in the fact that Alasdair MacIntyre's model of human motivation takes Aristotle's theory of motivation as I describe it to be sufficient to account for the phenomena. In his Carus Lectures, MacIntyre describes the process by which human beings achieve their natural telos, becoming "independent practical reasoners" (his alternative to Kantian autonomy), as one in which human agents learn to "stand back" from their given desires and evaluate them.[65] This means that human beings can have *reasons* for their actions with a kind of normative significance unavailable to other acting animals—the kind of significance that Korsgaard roots in practical reflection (see chap. 3, sec. 3.3). Like Korsgaard, MacIntyre says that to have a reason justifying one's actions, it is never sufficient simply to have a desire that the act seems likely to satisfy:

> Why not? Because it is always relevant to ask why I should at this particular time in these particular circumstances choose to act on this particular desire rather than on some other. At any particular time I have some range of projects, of goals, and of desires. So when I propose to myself to act on this particular desire, I have to ask "Is it at this time and in these particular circumstances best to act so as to satisfy this particular desire."[66]

The difference, for MacIntyre, consists in the fact that practical reflection can recognize goods as objective components of well-being in a way that D2 appetites cannot. This makes possible a kind of practical comparison other than brute preference-ordering. Goods internal to practices and social roles are one kind of intrinsic good,[67] but the most comprehensive standpoint of practical reflection seeks to order these goods, along with the satisfaction of D2 desires, with human flourishing as its ultimate end and standard:

We therefore need to distinguish between what it is that makes certain goods goods and goods to be valued for their own sake from what it is that makes it good for this particular individual or this particular society in this particular situation to make them the object of his or her or their effective practical regard. And our judgments about how it is best for an individual or a community to order the goods in their lives exemplify this third type of ascription, one whereby we judge unconditionally about what it is best for individuals or groups to be or do or have.[68]

Unlike Korsgaard and other neo-Kantians, then, MacIntyre insists that rational evaluation of D2 desires is itself ultimately motivated by the embracing D3 desire for our flourishing. The categorical or unconditional imperatives that serve as standards for evaluating given appetites are imperatives of flourishing, and the kind of reflection that characterizes independent practical reasoners is motivated by and serves the purpose of attaining eudaimonia. Thus MacIntyre explicitly rejects the Kantian idea that autonomous practical reflection might transcend erosaic motivation entirely:

> It is not of course that the child becomes able to act without desire. The notion of acting without desire is itself a phantasy and a dangerous one. It is rather that the child becomes open to considerations regarding its good. It develops a desire for doing, being, and having what it is good for it to do, be, and have.[69]

In other words, it develops D3 desire and the ability to distinguish this from mere D2 appetite.

Learning this distinction depends in part on recognizing that what is best for my well-being is partly a matter of expert knowledge about which I lack the kind of automatic authority that I enjoy concerning the experience of my D2 appetites: "I am not similarly authoritative in respect of judgments about what it is good or best for me to do or be or have."[70] The "transformation of the child's desires and passions" through habituation involves modifying "infantile" forms of her or his desires,[71] which depends on involving her or him in "a set of social relationships which are not at all of her or his own making" at the beginning.[72] In part, this transformation works by developing the child's ability to imagine "different or alternative futures" involving "different and alternative sets of goods to be achieved, with different possible modes of flourishing."[73] This is because "learning how to detach oneself from one's immediate desires" depends on evaluating their causal relationship to a "range of goods . . . presented by alternative futures,"[74] which will be the objects of D3 desires.

It is significant that nothing in MacIntyre's account requires us to move beyond Aristotle's model of human motivation (although we have to add the concept of intention to his theory of action, as well as libertarian freedom based on comparative judgment). A form of practical wisdom based on D3 desire is the highest element in the tale he tells concerning how we become independent practical reasoners. Thus his theory remains *formally* (though obviously not materially) egoistic in structure:

> What I become able to do, if I acquire an adequate sense of self, is to put in question the relationship between my present set of desires and motives and my good. What constitutes a good reason for my doing this rather than that, for my acting from this particular desire rather than that, is that my doing this rather than that *serves my good*, will contribute to my flourishing *qua* human being.[75]

This reference to the agent's own good confirms that MacIntyre's theory of practical reasoning stays within the limits of eudaimonism, and this is why the kinds of objective reasons for acting on a desire that he allows are only those that figure in D3 desires, not projective motives. A "desire for x" is "a desire for what it is good and best for me to desire"[76] only if so desiring is consistent with my happiness or flourishing (holistically understood); this must be the final measure in any formally egoistic theory.

2. Formal and Material Egoism

We have seen that a more robust model of D1, D2, and D3 desires seems to account for all the motives in the moral psychology of the *De anima* (as well as in MacIntyre's model). As a result, Aristotle seems to be committed to the weak erosiac thesis and, given his analysis of *prohairesis*, also to the Transmission principle. If the argument so far is correct, then Aristotle's moral psychology involves much the same *formal egoism* that we found in Plato's *Symposium*. However, this has to be carefully distinguished from the kind of psychological and moral egoism that the Sophist school defended. As Bernard Williams writes:

> neither Plato nor Aristotle thought of the ethical life as a device that increased selfish satisfactions. Their outlook is formally egoistic, in the sense that they suppose that they have to show each person that he has good reason to live ethically, and the reason has to appeal to that person in terms of something about himself, how and what he will be if he is a person with that sort of character. But their outlook is not egoistic in the sense that they try to show that the ethical life serves some set of individual satisfactions which is well defined before ethical considerations appear.[77]

This distinction between formal and material egoism is crucial but needs to be clearer than Williams makes it here. In the following sections I will suggest a way of understanding this distinction, consider a famous paradox that undermines material egoism, and explain how formal egoism purports to avoid it. This will prepare us for the critique of eudaimonism in chapter 7.

2.1. Formal Egoism and Satisfaction

As with Plato, Aristotle's own version of the erosiac thesis commits him to a type of formal egoism. For in both subjective D1-D2 desires and objectively evaluative D3 desires, the agent aims at a pleasure or a good that can in some way be appropriated into his own being; this is the basic teleological structure or formal direction essential to *orektic* desire. It is part of the *noematic structure or formal meaning* of an end desired in any of these senses that achieving it implies restoring a kind of motivational equilibrium or harmony which is experienced as lacking in the salience of that end. This is not to say that this "equilibrium" or "requiting of a felt incompleteness" is a *separate* end to which the object of desire is an instrumental *means*, but rather to say that an essential *aspect* of any orektically desired end is its relation to the agent's completion. The character of the motivation experienced in these diverse states is always such that its intentional correlate appears under the aspect of an "object that fulfills a lack," *however else* this content and the kind of "lack" it involves may differ. For example, I have a D2 inclination for "a beer-as-quenching-thirst" or I have a D3 desire for "education as a means to knowledge-that-I-lack." A desire for X in any orektic mode involves a sense on the part of its agent, however vague and perhaps unarticulated, that accomplishing or gaining X will requite an incompleteness or restore him to a state of psychic balance or holistic equilibrium.

The type of "satisfaction" this involves differs quite substantially between D1, D2, and D3 states: in the case of both brute urge gratifications and the fulfillment of more fine-grained or discriminating inclinations, the satisfying object or state simply attracts without being qualified by any objective judgment about its agent-neutral properties (the sort of qualification found in evaluative desire). Thus the agent's reflective judgment that the goal of a D1 or D2 desire will be satisfying to her is subjective or *desire-dependent* in a way that the judgments involved in D3 desires are not; for in D3 desires, the goal attracts only *because* it is first judged to be the kind of thing that would satisfy our nature and needs, whether we had any appetite for it or not. Nevertheless, in all these cases, the agent's original "upsurge" toward the goal, or first-personal experience of motivation to act, involves a sense of some kind of deficiency in her well-being; it is an anticipation of *filling in an absence*. D1, D2, and D3 states share this structure of a "pull" on the agent: the agent is initially passive and is moved from her stasis by something that attracts or pulls her toward it; so, speaking loosely, we could say that her motivation is a being-pulled-along. In dynamic terms, "end-pull" rather than "agent-push" is primary in all forms of *orexis*.

As a result, there is an important sense in which the satisfaction that the end appears likely (or is judged) to cause for the agent is an essential part of *what* is desired in D1-D3 states. I will refer to this as "satisfaction *internal* to the object of desire." Given their erosiac structure, it would be misleading to say that in these states, (a) the agent is simply motivated to pursue some end E, and (b) *as a result*, obtaining or realizing E will produce satisfaction as an external consequence distinct from E. Perhaps there is a sense in which (a) and (b) hold for any possible kind of human motivation, if only because human beings naturally enjoy effectiveness in pursuit of their goals. I will call this satisfaction related to competence, which is an *external* effect of getting whatever we want or intend just because we want it or have formed the intention to pursue it, the *by-product satisfaction of practical effectiveness*. It is one kind of by-product satisfaction that may pertain to success in action on the basis of virtually any type of first-order motive. Perhaps we also gain some by-product satisfaction from receiving by luck what we desire, but generally this is much less satisfying, especially if the desired end is one that can be realized by processes other than luck.

Now, to internalize either of these by-product satisfactions into the object of our desire would obviously signal confusion, since they are positive feelings that can be achieved only by desiring and effectively pursuing something else for its own sake. This was Francis Hutcheson's insight in his version of an argument against hedonistic egoism, which is also found in Bishop Butler:

> According to Hutcheson, the pleasures of satisfying our desires presuppose the existence of the very desires which are directed upon some object or event other than pleasure, . . . if desires could be aroused with the view to obtaining the joys of their own gratification, then the most fantastic desires could be aroused . . . just by the thought of the pleasures which would be gained if I were to have and gratify these desires. . . . Similarly, it is logically impossible for a desire to have as its object its own gratification.[78]

This is surely correct, for if gratification were the original motive, then a rational agent would want above all else to cultivate whatever set of first-order desires provide the most intense combination of gratifications when satisfied, relative to the opportunity to satisfy them in his circumstances. So if the desire to eat mud produces significant gratification in those who have the desire and satisfy it, and the agent lives near loamy fields, then he would desire to eat mud for an easy high; similarly for the masochistic desire to be beaten, if he lives around many sadists. Since this is absurd, by *reductio*, the gratification attendant on satisfying desires cannot be the true object of desires.

The stronger claim that this is metaphysically impossible holds only if gratification is *defined* as by-product satisfaction. In that case, we might still imagine a new second-order desire D_2 for the by-product satisfaction that will be caused by reaching O, the object of a first-order desire D_1. But we would have no direct way to pursue satisfaction of D_2, because it depends on being attracted to O in itself, and regarding O as a means to the second-order goal of D_2 tends to undermine O's attractiveness. Thus this second-order goal could only be pursued indirectly, which is why desiring$_2$ this unusual goal (that D_1 be satisfied) does not translate directly into desiring$_1$ O. Moreover, upon getting O, and experiencing by-product satisfaction of D_1 as a result, and thus also gratifying our explicitly entertained D_2, we might experience an additional by-product satisfaction (however faint) at having attained what we wanted in D_2 as well. Thus the possibility of a satisfaction external to the formal object of any desire always remains: there is no way to get *all* possible by-product satisfaction within the intentional content of our desired ends. A possible surplus always escapes our end in view; some satisfaction can always come as a *surprise*.

But although this Hutchesonian argument refutes psychological hedonism, it cannot refute the erosiac model because it does not apply to the type of satisfaction that is *internal* to the object of a D1, D2, or D3 desire. Hutcheson apparently thought that his argument would disprove Locke's erosiac conception of desire as a disturbance seeking equilibrium through gaining "some absent good,"[79] and he does reasonably distinguish "desire proper" from painful "organic sensations" that may accompany a desire.[80] But no contradiction is involved in the idea that the object of a desire includes its role in requiting a lack or completing the agent. For the erosiac model does not reduce all desires to unpleasant physiological states, nor does it say that desires are for the *by-product* satisfaction that the agent derives from realizing the desired good; rather it says that they are for some object, activity, or state *qua* providing something saliently lacking, negating a felt negation-of-completion, or metaphorically plugging a hole in the self, restoring the agent's psychic equilibrium. As Paul Tillich put it with reference to types of love, "The *appetitus* of every being to fulfill itself through union with other beings is universal and underlies the *erōs* as well as the *philia* quality of love."[81] Indeed, Tillich seems to endorse Plato's version of formal egoism when he says:

> In the loving joy about the "other one" the joy about one's own self-fulfillment by the other is also present. That which is absolutely strange to me cannot add to my self-fulfillment. . . . Therefore love cannot be described as the union of the strange, but as the reunion of the estranged.[82]

His version of the lack principle is that "Unperverted life strives for that of which it is in want."[83]

In other words, the goal desired in any kind of erosiac desire is *agent-relative* in a crucial sense, even if it is based on an agent-neutral evaluation of the end's value for human well-being (and hence the desire involves a validity claim for others similarly situated); for the goal is seen as part of the agent's own *completeness*. As we said in discussing Plato, the intentional content of the agent's desire is the possession (or enactment) of some object, activity, or state without which he cannot feel whole; the desire is for something *qua* partly or wholly completing the agent and thus *as* appropriated by him, or united to him, or done by him. To take a simple example from common sexual interests, what is desired is not simply the hair, breast, or foot in itself, but rather *my touching or stroking* the hair, breast, or foot.[84] To achieve this goal may also cause by-product satisfaction (e.g., a feeling of success), but internal to the goal itself is a kind of "satisfaction" of the agent—in this case, in a partly sensual erotic pleasure.

This analysis of formal egoism (FE), based on the erosiac model, provides a deeper *explanation of* a simpler and more familiar concept of FE as the doctrine that "every end that an agent pursues is apprehended as part of her *self-realization* or *perfection*." Something like this thin concept of formal egoism is proposed by Henry Sidgwick when trying to explain why he wishes to exclude any quasi-eudaimonistic formulation of "self-love" in defining "egoism":

> I conclude that the notion of Self-realisation is to be avoided in a treatise on ethical method, on account of its indefiniteness: and for a similar reason we must discard a common account of Egoism which describes its ultimate end as the "good" of the individual; for the term "good" may cover all possible views of the ultimate end of rational conduct. Indeed it may be said that Egoism in this sense was assumed in the whole ethical controversy of ancient Greece; that is, it was assumed on all sides that a rational individual would make the pursuit of his own good his supreme aim: the controverted question was whether this Good was rightly conceived as Pleasure or Virtue or any *tertium quid*.[85]

But the egoism that Sidgwick describes here as the doctrine of "Self-realisation" and that he regards as "a form into which any ethical system may be thrown, without modifying its essential elements"[86] actually has more content than his description makes clear. In Platonic and Aristotelian traditions, FE holds that every motive on which we act aims at some end apprehended as part of our self-realization because it is something the lack of which has become salient to us, either because of brute attraction to it or because of the judgment that it is an objective constituent of our well-being. And when FE is understood in this thicker or more robust way, it is much less clear that every normative theory of moral requirements will be consistent with FE, as Sidgwick assumes and has influenced many others in assuming.

For example, Julia Annas reminds us that the type of "happiness" that every school in ancient Greek ethics took to be our supreme desire is not "a determinate and specific state, [or] a state of feeling good about something."[87] Rather, it refers to a general and indeterminate sort of "good" for the agent that can go beyond satisfaction in any narrow sense to include her living a well-integrated, complete life, a "concern for her life being as it should."[88] But like Sidgwick, Annas mistakenly thinks this means that "desire" in the ancient Greek sense is just a placeholder for *any* kind of motivation: "For the ancients, desire, *orexis*, is the most general kind of motivation to do something that we can have. It covers wanting of various kinds, and also covers motivation generated by reasons, including ethical reasons."[89]

This would reduce the strong erosiac thesis, which claims that all motivation is *orektic*, to an empty tautology. If this thesis is to have any content, then desire or *orexis* cannot be used simply as a shorthand for "being motivated to pursue some end." And as we saw, in the *De anima* at least, Aristotle follows Plato in giving a substantive analysis of *orexis* as being drawn toward an end that is qualified as apparently fulfilling some lack in the agent. Of course ethical dispositions and moderate attitudes that are essential to living a fully human life may be precisely what are perceived as lacking or not fully realized and thus desired in D3 fashion. But the underlying sense that the good is a kind of equilibrium and that I am drawn toward my end because it will help restore that equilibrium is necessary to understanding *what it means*, as Annas puts it, that "I do all these things [whatever I do], simple and complex, because I see them as contributing to my *telos*, my final end which is my final good."[90]

In other words, in ancient ethics, the lack analysis provides the sense in which desiderative motivation refers to *the agent's* good. As Nussbaum says, Aristotle's *orexis* is appropriative: it is a "grasping after some object in order to take it to oneself."[91] What the agent can desire as "*her* good" is not simply as an unbound variable whose value can be filled in by any sort of end whatsoever. For some things cannot be perceived as absent for me or lacking in me *prior* to my motivation to pursue them. If this were not the case, then the thesis that happiness or flourishing is our ultimate end would be an empty tautology that could do no work in moral philosophy.

For this reason, I cannot agree with Annas's claim that, given the generality of *orexis*, the doctrine of a final good that is the end of all our motivations "does not imply that there is any special kind of motivation that we have to our ends."[92] Formal egoism has more content than this implies. It adds something crucial to the ancient psychological thesis that "all action is aimed at some good"[93] and to the logically independent thesis that, as a famous Thomist put it, "no one can really deny that he seeks well-being" for himself.[94] This thesis asserting the ubiquity of self-interest (the ubiquity thesis, or UT) is much weaker than FE; the desire for happiness may indeed be present in all rational agents, as Kant also held, but this does not entail that it is our *chief* desire or that it somehow subsumes all other motives, either as the whole of which they are parts or as the normative condition of any normative authority they may have for us.[95] Formal egoism synthesizes these two weaker theses in the claim that the desire for happiness is "fundamental in the sense that no human being can avoid acting in terms of attaining complete well-being so far as possible."[96] Although this leaves open many different possible conceptions of the happiness to be pursued, it does relate all pursuable goods formally to "the self" of the agent. In *orexis*, we desire goods that we can somehow "attain or appropriate," or unite to our being, in order to make our being more complete.[97]

This formulation of FE also makes clear (as Sidgwick's does not) that this is a doctrine not just about how it is rational to behave or how we ought to act, but about how we *are always* motivated. In this respect, it is about the same question as other forms of "psychological egoism," as opposed to "moral egoism"—since the latter may acknowledge the possibility of non-egoistic motivation but still tell us that we ought (or that it is most rational) not to act on such motives or that we should do whatever will maximize our own well-being (conceived either in terms of subjective D2 desire-satisfactions or in terms of an objective list of D3-desirable objects and states).[98] So understood, FE has enough content to raise puzzles, for example, about how anyone could be motivated to sacrifice his life for another's (for how could this constitute *his* good in any plausible sense?).[99] However, formal psychological egoism remains quite distinct from every version of *material* psychological egoism in not further specifying the kinds of goals that human agents can be motivated to seek for their own sake. For example, Rawls distinguishes material egoism from the "sense of justice" as a motive by saying:

> An egoist is someone committed to the point of view of his own interests. His final ends are *related to himself*: his wealth and position,

his pleasures and social prestige, and so on. Such a man may act justly, that is, do things that a just man would do; but so long as he remains an egoist, he cannot do them for the just man's reasons.[100]

This clearly implies that material egoists have only certain kinds of ends, which are not just formally related to the agent's possession or experience (as in FE) but materially related to his resources, status, and avoidance of pain. The person acting from a sense of justice has a non-egoistic end in this sense even if, as Rawls goes on to argue, giving this motive priority in one's life may contribute to one's own good. This analysis takes us in the right direction but it needs refinement to clarify the notion of goods materially benefiting the agent.

2.2. Material Egoism: Feinberg's Analysis Expanded

A definition of material psychological egoism (MPE) adequate for my purposes can be extracted from a famous paper by Joel Feinberg in which he argues that every type of psychological egoism that could present a challenge to traditional morality has to involve substantive claims about the self-interested nature of the ends that agents can be moved to pursue.[101] Thus psychological egoism cannot be defended with such abstract arguments as: "Every action of mine is prompted by motives or desires or impulses which are my motives and not somebody else's," or "Whenever I act, I am always pursuing my own ends or trying to satisfy my own desires."[102] For no synthetic thesis about the content of humanly pursuable ends can follow from this truism of action theory, which is analytic as long as we grant that the concept of voluntary action requires that an agent do some act for her own reasons or on her motives. Says Feinberg:

> It is not the genesis of an action [in the self] or the *origin* of its motives which makes it a "selfish" one, but rather the "purpose" of the act or the objective of its motives: not where the motive comes from (in voluntary action it always comes from the agent) but what it aims at determines whether or not it is selfish.[103]

This is even clearer in the case of moral egoism, which cannot be simply a recommendation to do whatever we really want to. As Korsgaard says, "the egoistic principle is concerned with the *content* of the will, not with the very act of willing."[104] A straightforward way to make this plausible is to supply an illustrative list of different types of ends, distinguishing intuitively between those that directly contribute to the agent's material or psychological well-being (possibly even without being desired) and those that do not. But, as Korsgaard also argues, the distinguishing factor cannot be (as Williams suggests) simply that "I" or "my own" is mentioned in the end desired or aimed at. For this factor picks out not egoism but rather *narcissism*:

> For instance, someone in the grip of a pathological case of remorse or masochism might want that they should suffer. Or someone might want to be the author of some good thing of which he himself may never get the benefit, like someone who wants to be the one who discovers a cure for cancer . . . [or] the godfather's desire that his own family should remain in power. . . . Are these desires egoistic? They contain a self-reference, but they certainly do not all concern things that you want *for* yourself, in any intuitive sense.[105]

As these examples show, the intended end's being *about* us or *involving* us (as an individual or as a member of a group) is not enough to make it materially *self-interested*—although it might be enough to make it narcissistic or "self-centered," especially if the role we must play in the envisioned outcome or end is more prominent than impartial reason warrants.[106] Rather, a self-interested desire must be for our own *possession or enjoyment* of some good that seems to add something to our material well-being or pleasure—either individually (in purely egoistic desires), or jointly with others (in desires of a mixed nature). We do not need to limit this set to a single kind of "incentive, say those associated with appetite or pleasure," as Korsgaard suggests.[107] Rather, as Moore argues, rational egoism is much broader than hedonism because "The Egoist is the man who holds that a tendency to promote his own interest is the sole possible, and sufficient, justification of all his actions," where his interests include not only pleasure but also "advancement," "reputation," a "better income," and related goods of status.[108] As the nature of such goods implies, to count as self-interested, the goal must involve beneficial objects or states coming to or being *appropriated by* the self in suitable senses. When this is understood, it becomes clearer that not all the ends we aim at are materially self-interested.

The following definitions will allow us to state Feinberg's point more perspicuously:

> **First-order intrinsic good:** any good object, goal, or end that we can intelligibly pursue for its own sake. For example:
> - to be nourished by food would be a physiological first-order good;
> - to be educated would be a mental first-order good;
> - the prevention of pollution might be an environmental first-order good.

Note that this definition does not assume that these ends are good just because we desire them; rather, it could be that they are on an objective list of ends we ought to desire because of their goodness. Nor does this definition necessarily include all first-order ends that agents can pursue, for I leave open the possibility that an agent might perversely pursue for its own sake something that he takes to be good for no one or no thing in the world.

Self-interested first-order intrinsic good: first-order goods that contribute directly to the agent's material well-being, mental health, contentment, or enjoyment. For example, here is a roughly Hobbesian list of things that we pursue *as assets, opportunities, or types of hedonic experience*:

- first-order pleasure: gratification of physical appetites, pleasures of bodily sensation, pleasures in being entertained or amused, and so on;
- power, influence, control over others;
- honor, fame, glory;
- shelter, security, protection from misfortune, basic liberties, and a stable political environment;
- health, including adequate sustenance, activity, and chances for mental development;
- wealth and income, which enable us to provide for needs and satisfy other desires;
- peace of mind (no disturbing thoughts or anticipation of suffering, and so on).

Note that self-interested first-order desires for such goods are not necessarily *immoral*; the desire to quench my thirst is the desire for a certain sensory state of my own body, and so it is "selfish" in the natural sense but not necessarily in the moral sense of being wrong. Since it involves no inherent injustice or violation of nature, this goal could only be wrong because of other factors in the circumstances, for example, because the supply is limited and others presently need to drink more than I do. Similarly with desires for possessions I will enjoy, money to buy possessions that will amuse or delight me, and simple sensual pleasures like taking a walk on a warm spring morning. Agents commonly consider such goods as directly adding to their well-being or as constituting additional positive value in their set of possessions and experiences, even when they are not desired. By contrast, there are other goods that add to our well-being only if we already care about them:

Non-self-interested first-order intrinsic good: a good end that transcends the agent's simple being—i.e., does not directly constitute any part of the agent's material welfare or psychological contentment. For example:

- knowledge of the world (scientific discovery, insight in the humanities);
- the well-being of a friend or family member;
- creative achievements (the goods aimed at by arts and crafts);
- scientific achievement, for example, finding the cure for cancer;
- bringing progress and justice to third-world nations.

This category of intelligible ends that are not by themselves materially connected to any aspect of the agent's simple well-being (even if they might cause some agent-relative good to come about) includes goods that will be experienced by or belong only to some other person or persons, ends that are strictly part of nonhuman welfare (such as the survival of some endangered species), and abstract ends disconnected from the agent (such as the truth about some mystery or the beauty of some work of art yet to be). I regard these as typical species of the genus we could call "non-self-related" or "self-transcending" ends. I will ignore here important controversies about exactly what ends should be listed in this category, but I hope the intuitive idea is clear enough: what unites this category is the *alterity* or *alienness to the agent's simple being*. X's "simple being" encompasses material resources that X owns, psychic characteristics (such as talents and mental capacities) that belong to X, and hedonic states that do not depend on X already having a given contingent desire or concern. In terms of these definitions, material psychological egoism (MPE) would be the thesis that

> **MPE:** All our actions are ultimately motivated by (D1, D2, or D3) desires for self-interested first-order intrinsic goods. We never pursue other goals except as means to these ends.

As these lists suggest, paradigm species of MPE would be the theories of human motivation traditionally found in Machiavelli's *The Prince* and Hobbes's *Leviathan*, according to which, desires for self-preservation, pleasures, power, glory, and security drive all human actions and relationships.[109] Notice, however, that my definition of MPE does not say that all motives are embraced or conditioned by the desire to *maximize* our first-order goods. Although maximization would be found in any standard version of material *moral* egoism (MME) as a requirement of practical reason,[110] we should not saddle the psychological egoist with the assumption that the egoism he finds in human nature always includes an *overriding* desire to maximize one's self-interested first-order goods; a person still could be egoistic without being that rational.[111] In this respect, however, MPE will differ from FE, since the idea of seeking completeness or a state lacking nothing already includes implicit within it a kind of threshold or qualitative maximum at which we always necessarily aim, according to FE (however bad our aim might be).

Even to assert an MPE doctrine, then, we must first define that category of nonselfish final ends that we wish to *rule out* as impossible for human persons to seek for their own sake; otherwise our MPE thesis will be empty or vacuous. But this means that we must start by acknowledging or recognizing a category of ends that we could intelligibly imagine human beings, or at least some other kind of rational agent, pursuing—and then deny that we can in fact take ends in this category as final. This perhaps explains why MPE becomes more implausible the more substantively its claim is specified. For, as I formulated it, MPE can easily be defeated by plausible cases of what I call *pure* motives, that is, those in which the agent acts for some agent-transcending final end. As Feinberg points out, this can include cases in which the final end is a non-self-interested first-order good (such as cases of *benevolence*) and also cases of pure *malevolence* in which the agent pursues for its own sake some non-self-interested first-order harm to another person or to the world.[112] The MPE defender can question whether there are such cases, for example, on grounds that we deceive ourselves and ignore ulterior self-interested motives behind apparently non-self-interested acts, but such arguments carry a very heavy burden of proof if they hope to show that such ulterior motives operate in every case, or that non-egoistic motives are psychologically *impossible* for human beings.[113] It may be hard to establish the agent's motive in any given case, but it is very implausible to believe that we never aim at agent-transcending goods as final.

Notice that Feinberg's example of the fallacious argument from all my motives being mine to MPE would be *valid* if it were the quite distinct argument from all my motives being *orektic* desires to FE. But then the argument, although valid, would be trivial, since formal egoism is defined in terms of the erosiac structure of all desires of the sort that ancient Greek philosophers call *orexis*. However, the superficial resemblance between the two arguments may explain the historical origin and popularity of the fallacious argument for MPE that Feinberg refutes.

Here is an example that suggests this link. In the midst of explaining one of Derrida's basic theses about human interests and desires, John Caputo makes the assertion (apparently inspired by Nietzsche) that there is no motivation not originally driven by the agent's concern for his own satisfaction; rather, there are only more or less "selfish" forms of it:

> We are all more or less narcissistic, for that is what the agent/subject *is*. The agent, Aristotle and the medievals said, acts for its own good. If the agent expends all its energies on the other without return, that is after all what the agent *wants*, and that is how the agent gets her kicks.[114]

Now, Caputo's statement involves a simple but instructive equivocation on "wanting." It would be true *a priori* that *anything* that an agent works for is "what the agent wants" only if "wanting X" is emptily defined just as "seeking to realize X" or "being motivated to pursue X." But such a definition of desire is so abstract that it entirely fails to support the Derridean view that Caputo here means to defend (which is a version of material egoism). For under Caputo's empty definition of desire, an agent could "want" an end that is entirely non-egoistic in content. What Aristotle and Aquinas defend is, rather, formal egoism, and they do *not* base this on such an empty equation of "desire" with "any motive whatsoever"; rather, they base their view squarely on the structural conception of desire in the erosiac model. To expand Feinberg's point, when we abstract the concept of "wanting" from this erosiac model, then from the fact that I act on my "desires," nothing at all follows about the content desired *or about the formal relation* of one's ends to the one's own eudaimonia. One can get neither MPE *nor* FE from the premises of Caputo's argument by themselves.

Following this non sequitur, in the same passage Caputo manages to commit the related fallacy of inferring that apparently altruistic actions are really egoistic in intent simply because the agent enjoys them. With cases of benevolence in mind, Feinberg (following Garvin) nicely explains this common mistake:

> Not only is the presence of pleasure (satisfaction) as a by-product of an action no proof that the action was selfish; in some special cases, it rather provides conclusive proof that the action was unselfish. For in those special cases the fact that we get pleasure from a particular action *presupposes that we desired something else*—something other than our own pleasure—as an end in itself and not merely as a means to our own pleasant state of mind.[115]

This point can be made clearer if we distinguish between what Feinberg calls pleasure$_1$ and pleasure$_2$,[116] or better:

First-order pleasure as a category of self-related goods, including:

- pleasant stimulation of the five senses; and
- pleasant stimulation of our aesthetic sensibilities; and
- amusement and other pleasurable states of mind produced by entertainment, thrill, and so on,

and

Second-order satisfaction as the mental fulfillment that results from (a) *motivation toward* some first-order good G for its own sake, when we add to it either (b) the active *pursuit of* G, or (c) this pursuit along with successful *achievement of* G through our efforts. For example:

- the pleasure of raising prizewinning horses or in general excelling at horse breeding;
- the pleasure of writing a great novel or painting an inspiring painting;
- the pleasure of giving a superb performance of a difficult part in a play;
- the pleasure of managing to climb the Matterhorn despite its challenges;
- the pleasure of helping one's child grow up confident and well-adjusted;
- the pleasure of helping a friend succeed at solving some difficult problem;
- even the spiteful pleasure of bringing about a political opponent's downfall (just for its own sake and irrespective of whether it helps us get into office).

As Feinberg says, all of these pleasures require that we *already* care about the relevant first-order goods intrinsically, or desire them for their own sake, quite independent of the second-order pleasure we may get from pursuing and possibly attaining these ends. If I had no intrinsic interest in writing a beautiful poem but did it just to get a good grade, then producing the poem *by itself* would not give me the relevant second-order satisfaction—though getting the grade might satisfy other desires. In some cases, perhaps I can even get this kind of second-order satisfaction as a by-product simply of *pursuing* worthwhile ends, whether or not I achieve them. Therefore the fact that I may derive second-order satisfaction from pursuit and/or realization of my first-order ends gives no support to MPE whatsoever. A similar argument has been made by James Rachels in his textbooks, and indeed, as Carolyn Morillo has noted, the basic point of this "by-product theory" has become familiar enough to count as a staple ingredient in introductory ethics classes.[117] All I have done here is to reconstruct the point more clearly with the help of more precise definitions of different kinds of goods.

As I suggested, it is possible that *some* type of by-product satisfaction derives from achieving *any* first-order purpose that I have intentionally undertaken as a final end. If so, then even realizing a self-destructive goal will bring some second-order satisfaction, but again, this cannot be the motive or aim of the self-destructive action. Possibly, even when our act is aimed only at some first-order pleasure for its own sake (say, in going out to a movie to relax), there is also a weak by-product satisfaction from achieving that sort of goal, *in addition* to the first-order pleasure itself. For human beings inherently seem to enjoy feeling effective in the pursuit of any significant goal and often to enjoy (though in a lesser way) getting what they are pursuing by sheer luck. But, as Sober and Wilson note, nothing about the material or content of first-order motive-states follows from this thesis: "From the premise that people want their desires to be satisfied, nothing follows concerning whether their ultimate desires are egoistic or altruistic."[118]

Formal egoism makes this question more complex because it holds that the desired end is *conceived as* gratifying the agent's subjective preferences or restoring some absent or missing part of his overall well-being. We must distinguish this satisfaction that is part of the end desired and pursued both from first-order (material) pleasure and from the "external-to-intention" *consequent* satisfaction that usually results from achieving our intended goal (perhaps because of a standing desire$_2$ to get whatever we desire$_1$). Formal egoism therefore implies that no intelligible end is pursued *only or simply* as agent-transcending: non-self-interested ends are really apprehended as having an agent-relative qualification. Appropriation or enjoyment of the good enters into the intentional content of any desire$_1$ on this model, not as a distinct goal for which the object is merely instrumental, but as an aspect of that object or material end.

A Complex Material Egoism?

As I define it, MPE includes several different varieties of psychological egoism, but of course I make no claim that my formulation covers every material egoist conception of the springs of human action, and arguably its classical sources already suggest that my model is too simple. For in the *Leviathan*, Hobbes's explanation of why the state of nature descends into a chaotic mutually self-defeating war gives a crucial role to a few glory-seeking warlords who will attack others even when they have sufficient material resources and these are sufficiently secure against attacks by other simple material egoists. We could conceive such a warlord's motive as involving desire for a *second-order egoistic end*: namely, the relative superiority of his first-order self-related material goods to others' holdings of the same (or comparable) goods. I call this a second-order end because its definition mentions first-order human goods and/or harms in its interpersonal comparison. In general, I treat a second-order end as any goal that consists in a certain relationship among first-order goods or harms, either within the agent or across persons. Thus seeking to balance certain first-order goods within one's life would count as a second-order end, and so would any goal concerning the *relative* holdings of various goods between persons or other significant bearers of natural value (e.g., animals, plants, ecosystems).

So a more complete definition of material egoism would expand its conditions beyond first-order MPE (or *simple egoism*, as I call it) and include the pursuit of such egoistic or self-regarding second-order ends. A paradigm example would be Rousseau's status-seeking bourgeois, who is more concerned about his social rank and privileges *relative to others* than about his own holdings of important external goods and liberties as measured absolutely.[119] In fact, according to Rousseau, citizens can become so concerned about their superiority to others, including their power over them, that they may accept tyranny as the price: "citizens allow themselves to be oppressed only insofar as they are driven by blind ambition; and looking more below than above them, they consent to wear chains in order to be able to give them in their turn to others."[120]

This kind of motive arises in human community, according to Rousseau, because of a natural human tendency to turn our attention from merit as an absolute first-order good to the *relative difference* between the merits of different persons: "Each one began to look at the others and wanted to be looked at himself, and public esteem had a value." The emotions of vanity, contempt, shame, and envy emerge from this shift in focus.[121] Egoistic motivation becomes more complex with such interpersonal comparisons; for instance, a person X who desires another person Y to envy him is moved by a third-order desire for an apparent good consisting in Y's second-order desire for some first-order good G because X has it—i.e., not in itself but rather G *qua possessed-by-X*. Complex desires like envy-enjoyment remain egoistic to the extent that the final end is pursued *as* supposedly adding to the agent's own well-being. The problem is that in such cases, the satisfaction sought seems to depend on the agent and others to whom he is comparing himself already having more basic desires. But I will not attempt a more rigorous definition of complex material egoism here because its complications will not be necessary for my main argument. However, they will be relevant again in the discussion of radical evil in chapter 10.

A New Hedonism?

Finally, according to another view that might be dubbed "affect-arousal hedonism"—to distinguish it from classical Epicurean and modern Benthamite hedonism—my model of material egoism would instead be too complex, because there is really only *one* experience that is the causal basis of all human motivation, namely the kind of euphoric bliss experienced when parts of the limbic system (e.g., the hypothalamus) are stimulated naturally by dopamine releases or artificially by electrical currents.[122]

Morillo sketches such a view, which she calls the "reward event theory (RET)," and argues that it is empirically plausible enough to challenge the Feinberg-Rachels pluralistic model of multiple non-egoistic final ends with contingent by-product satisfaction. Her claim that RET might be able to reduce our apparent "focus" on a wide range of seemingly final ends to a single type of experience hinges on the hypothesis that the pursuit and realization of these ends become *associated* in learning these desires with "the reward" experience (in lesser strength than in cases where its strong stimulation by electrical or chemical means can overwhelm all other motives): "Thus, the operation of the reward event in more mixed phenomena may be buffered in such a way that focus [of attention] shifts; but the reward event would still be the aspect of these more complex experiences which is what we are motivated to obtain." While the conscious focus of our motive may vary, the reward event remains "the anchor of motivation."[123] In other words, our focus on outward objects beyond the self (for which "there are good evolutionary reasons")[124] deceives us. What we *really* want, though we do not recognize it, is the hedonic reward that we experience when, for example, we help our friend or listen to Mozart's music,[125] or start a political reform movement that might bear fruit only after our death; for even then, when imagining the goal achieved, "such envisagement, particularly when vivid, can link directly to the reward event. (Is that not what fantasy is about?)."[126]

If RET is right, then, what I called by-product satisfaction is not really a side effect after all; in fact, it is a weaker version of the *same* reward we experience in orgasm, a cocaine high, or direct electrical stimulation of the pleasure centers, and *it* is our real aim—that single positive feeling that alone we are programmed to seek.

Although it poses an intriguing challenge, the main difficulty for this kind of naturalistic hedonism is in making plausible the extreme hypothesis that somehow *every* other familiar kind of goal that we are inclined to interpret as final for the agent when providing an intentional explanation of various kinds of action could have become so strongly associated with this single type of rewarding brain event (or perhaps a small range of such types of reward). Call this the monistic thesis.[127] Neither (1) the promising hypothesis that such a reward underlies physical appetites for food, water, and procreation, nor (2) the insightful point that when "mainlined" in ways that evolution never intended, such basic euphoria can stimulate our instinctual craving to a point that it overwhelms all other interests or concerns, seems by itself to provide *any* evidence for the monistic model of all motivation, let alone conclusive evidence for it. The growing empirical evidence for (1) and (2) cannot count as evidence for the monistic thesis while higher goals do not seem to provide the same kind of visceral payoff.

It might seem that some evidence is provided for RET by the observation that severe clinical depression can rob our familiar concerns and interests of their motivating force. Morillo asks, "Might a massive failure of connections with reward events account for such a massive failure of motivation?"[128] But clearly, to interpret depression this way, we already have to think that such "connections" with hedonic reward normally do the motivating—and that is precisely what is at issue. We might speculate instead that neurochemical problems interfere with the normal cognitive pathways involved in caring about or being interested in agent-transcending goods—and the lack of these motives makes everything seem pointless as well as robbing the depressed agent of all second-order or by-product satisfaction.

Against Morillo's monistic thesis, there is the simple introspective point that the joy I experience in seeing some complex other-regarding good transpire—for example, the overthrow of some terrible foreign tyrant, even though he posed no real threat to our national security—simply does not *feel at all* like the relief of getting a splinter out, beyond the utterly vacuous sense in which both are "positive" experiences. Even while under physical discomfort or withdrawal from a chemical high, one can still feel a quite different kind of satisfaction in accomplishing some worthwhile goal (e.g., being one step closer to kicking the habit). Indeed, RET makes it hard to explain the common intuition that there are incommensurabilities between different kinds of goods. Finally, experience reveals plenty of cases in which an activity that is initially motivated by desire for a visceral reward starts to be carried out for its own sake.[129] But why would anyone trade a stronger reward experience for a weaker one—which is how RET must describe such changes?

In sum, the RET or affective hedonism model shows that it is not *conceptually* impossible for a kind of "satisfaction" to be the single (unconscious) goal of all human motivation. But nothing like sufficient evidence for such a radically revisionary theory of human motivation is on the horizon. Simple material egoism remains more empirically plausible and thus a more significant target for existential critique.

2.3. *The Paradox of Hedonism and the Paradox of Material Egoism*

Our account of simple material egoism is sufficient to explain a crucial objection to this psychological doctrine that is closely related to Feinberg's objection against what he calls "the psychological egoistic hedonist" who focuses exclusively on obtaining a kind of "pleasure." It turns out that Feinberg has in mind here what I call second-order or by-product satisfaction—perhaps because he follows Bentham and Mill in calling the satisfaction derived from a wide range of different activities "pleasure."[130] The problem is that this kind of hedonist has mistaken his goal:

This is the famous "paradox of hedonism": the single-minded pursuit of happiness is necessarily self-defeating, for the surest way to get happiness is to forget it; then perhaps it will come to you. If you aim exclusively at pleasure itself, with no concern for the things that bring pleasure, then pleasure will never come.[131]

Feinberg illustrates this point with the splendid example of Jones, who does not care about religion, or knowledge, or scientific discovery, or fine arts, or nature, or sports, or literature, or civic activities, or political causes, or friendships with others, or "any kind of handicraft, industry, or commerce."[132] The *only* thing he cares about for its own sake is happiness itself. But it is obvious, says Feinberg, that Jones cannot be happy, for "pleasure and happiness presuppose desires for something other than pleasure and happiness." Thus if there are truly happy people, egoistic hedonism must be false: we must be capable of caring about first-order goals aside from our happiness as ends in themselves.[133]

Again, Feinberg's argument needs some fleshing out. He presents it simply as an evident empirical truth that human happiness requires sincerely pursuing as final ends the sorts of things Jones either ignores or regards only as means to happiness. There is wide support for this idea. It echoes Mill's claim that an "exciting" life is one engaged with challenging work, noble causes, and rich relationships, whereas one of the main sources of misery is egoistic self-absorption.[134] Similarly, Derek Parfit asserts that "If my strongest desire is that I be happy, I may be less happy than I would be if I had other desires that were stronger"; and he offers examples in which it is better on the whole for an agent to be disposed to act on motives that would, in some circumstances, make her *self-denying* or lead her to reject options that would increase her well-being.[135] Parfit makes a similar point about consequentialism: since "most of our happiness comes from having, and acting upon, certain strong desires . . . [which] include the desires that are involved in loving certain other people, the desire to work well, and many other[s]," if everyone became a "pure do-gooder" who only cared about maximizing happiness, there would be much less of it as a result.[136]

This is a development of Williams's famous critique of act-consequentialism, in which he argued that a pure utilitarian agent who cared only about the second-order goal of maximizing *collective* happiness might not herself be as happy as other agents who form commitments to other first-order ends (especially including ends that are agent-transcending).[137] As Williams says, "It may even be that . . . many of those with commitments, who have really identified themselves with objects outside themselves, who are thoroughly involved with other persons, institutions, or activities or causes, are actually happier than those whose projects and wants are not like that."[138] In lacking such specific first-order projects, causes, and involvements, a *single* pure utilitarian or "do-gooder" may not be indirectly self-defeating, because she is not an egoist aiming to maximize her own happiness. But if happiness usually does depend on having more specific first-order goals, then Parfit is right that the utilitarian agent could not rationally will that everyone become a pure utilitarian agent like her. Similarly, following Rawls, Harry Frankfurt suggests that a pure utilitarian agent is one without a genuine self, who cannot be sustainably committed to any particular ideals or personal values except to the extent that he is certain he will never encounter circumstances in which abandoning these cares and commitments would increase collective well-being.[139] All of these arguments involve much the same empirical claim about human psychology and the bases of happiness that we find in Feinberg.

But in fact there are several different problems with egoism (as a description of human motivation or as a recommendation about how to act and live) that can be distinguished using our analysis of simple material egoism.

(1) The *paradox of material egoism* arises when an agent pursues only self-related first-order goods for their own sake and takes no agent-transcending goals as ends in themselves. This would be the case, for instance, with the Hobbesian simple egoist as traditionally understood. If in fact much of the fulfillment that makes life worthwhile derives as by-product satisfaction from the pursuit of *non-self-interested goods* for their own sake—as virtually every moralist indebted to the eudaimonist tradition has argued down the ages—then the simple material egoist will necessarily miss all of this and thus be self-defeating. This point seems implicit in what Williams says, and it is at least closely related to Parfit's point too.[140] In the extreme case in which this egoist seeks only first-order *pleasure*, he could in principle maximize his desire-satisfaction by remaining forever hooked up to a machine that constantly stimulated the pleasure centers of his brain while taking care of his other bodily needs.[141] Yet it seems obvious that such a banal existence could not be the most fulfilling life possible for us, since it is does not draw on any of our higher capacities or potential for more complex activities and relationships. This will also be true to a lesser extent in the less hedonistic versions of MPE. But since human persons sometimes do attain kinds of fulfillment that transcend such banality, MPE must be false.

(2) Strictly speaking, Feinberg's "paradox of hedonism" describes the quite different case in which an agent tries to make *second-order satisfaction* itself his sole final end, or ultimate goal. This is self-defeating because such satisfaction cannot be directly pursued, and making the pursuit of other first-order goods instrumental to second-order satisfaction robs them of their power to cause or create second-order satisfaction in the agent. In this paradox, the agent defeats herself by omitting the required material base

for by-product happiness—much like the pure utilitarian do-gooder according to Williams, Parfit, and Frankfurt. Feinberg's "Jones" does not even pursue self-interested first-order goods for their own sake, let alone *non*-self-interested first-order goods; he pursues only a self-related second-order goal. This would also be the case for a person whose primary goal in life was to have a higher social status than, say, his twin brother, but who therefore did not care about any of the goods that he would have to care about and excel in pursuing in order to achieve such status. When we say that such a person is destined to failure in his fundamental project, this conclusion does not depend simply on evident empirical judgments about the greater significance or fulfillment that human beings tend to gain as by-products of complex activities involving self-transcending goals rather than by direct pursuit of self-related first-order goods (as in the paradox of material egoism). Instead, failure follows necessarily from the concepts, assuming that they apply to human life: turning a derivative second-order good into our sole ultimate end, and thus turning all the pursuits and activities on which it depends into *means* to this good, is *necessarily self-defeating*.

If this is right, then (2) is the stronger paradox. However, it now seems slightly misleading to call it the "paradox of hedonism," since that term typically connotes a person who aims only at various first-order psychic states, such as sensual pleasures, entertainment, and psychological tranquility (lack of worry, etc.). Feinberg's "Jones" is really an odd kind of second-order hedonist, and so we might call his problem the *paradox of abstract egoism*. As Korsgaard notes, this paradox goes back at least to Joseph Butler. A person who prefers second-order or "subjective" satisfaction (as Korsgaard calls it) over the objective realization of the relevant first-order goal is irrational, since this would imply that he does not care about this goal in itself. Yet "[h]e must care about it, or he could not get the subjective satisfaction: that was Butler's point."[142] Interestingly, this point also finds empirical support in psychological studies refuting the hypothesis that altruistic actions are motivated by the agent's desire for the satisfaction of being recognized by others (or even by himself) as the one who helped the person in need.[143] This is unsurprising, since it is conceptually implausible that altruistic acts are motivated by desire for this kind of psychological reward, which is essentially a by-product of selfless concern.

However, neither (1) nor (2) are straightforwardly paradoxes of *formal* egoism, since that doctrine is meant to be compatible with agents pursuing non-self-interested or agent-transcending first-order goods for their own sake (though also as part of happiness). Formal egoism also does not constrain the agent, like Jones, to second-order satisfaction as her single final end. If there is a similar "paradox of formal egoism," then, it is less obvious and it will take more work to show it.

2.4. Targetable and Nontargetable By-Product Goods: Elster's Analysis

In approaching the question of whether there is a related paradox of formal egoism, it will help to inquire further whether we really are sure that (2) is right: that is, are the motives of Jones (the abstract egoist) necessarily self-defeating? For this kind of paradox is less well understood than (1), the paradox of material egoism. Moreover, in discussing the *Symposium*, we saw the Ascent explained in terms of the *redirection* of the agent's focus from an end E that produces some by-product good G, to G itself as his final end. We can illustrate this as follows, with single-line arrows for intention and double-line arrows for efficient causation:

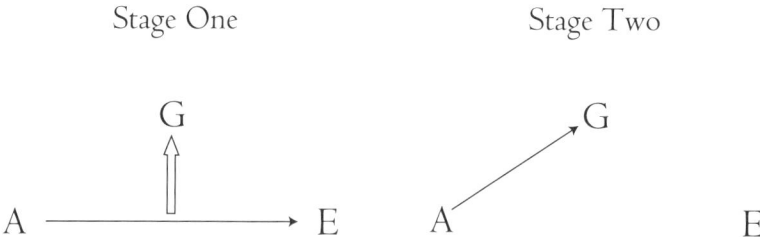

This is possible because the side effect G in Stage One is what we called a *targetable good*, which can then be directly pursued in Stage Two; hence it is only *contingently* a by-product in Stage One. But if there are nontargetable goods, which can result *only* as side effects of targeting other ends for their own sake, then the agent's motivation could not be redirected toward these without becoming self-defeating. And this is most likely to be a problem if such a nontargetable by-product is itself attractive to the agent, as adding materially or psychologically to her well-being, and therefore likely to be *desired* in some kind of orektic mode. Can we justify the paradox of abstract egoism by showing that this is what happens if all of someone's motives trace to desire for second-order satisfaction?

In some of his earliest pathbreaking work in rational choice theory, Jon Elster argues at length that there is a recognizable class of states that are "essentially by-products" and therefore remain "inaccessible" in the sense that they cannot *rationally* be directly willed or directly commanded.[144] Among Elster's many brilliant examples,[145] some clear members of this class are:

1. total spontaneity of response to events (the paradox of flow);
2. acting in a way that others will judge as "natural," unforced, or indifferent to how one is judged (Stendhal's paradox);
3. going to sleep (the paradox of insomnia);

    4. not thinking about some undesirable subject matter, or ignoring some distraction, irritant, or nuisance (the paradox of inattention);

    5. deceiving oneself—a case that Elster draws from Sartre's paradox of "bad faith";

    6. having no critics—a case from Zinoviev's dialectics of persecution;

    7. humility understood as the absence of pride (the paradox of humility);

    8. being freely recognized by another as completely independent of him (Hegel's paradox of the master's dependence on the slave).

None of these states is logically contradictory in itself, but it is pragmatically self-defeating to will them.[146] Many of the most obvious instances of this class are negative or privative states, and privative mental states are especially prominent here. This raises the question of whether the only reason any negative state ¬X can be volitionally inaccessible or essentially nontargetable is because trying to avoid ¬X tends to cause ¬X. For instance, "the absence of consciousness of something cannot be brought about by an activity of consciousness."[147]

Elster argues that there are also positive states that are essentially by-products, but some of these cases I do not find as plausible: for example, sexual lust, romantic love (and related emotions), certain kinds of confidence and effectiveness in war and politics, virtues such as courage, and even "autonomy" (as characterized in his account of broad rationality). These, as well as many other positive states such as concentration on a problem, can *often be hindered* by reflection on them or self-consciousness about them, and thus overly eager efforts to achieve them are often self-defeating because they necessarily involve fixing too much (or the wrong kind of) attention on them. Remaining calm while taking a test is a familiar example; trying to become sexually aroused or to feel romantic love toward someone may be other examples. Yet these are not essentially by-product states, because there are often fairly direct techniques to cause (or at least facilitate) these psychic states. The right kind of reflexive attitude toward one's own psychic states, which aims to alter them slowly through fixing attention on justifying reasons for the preferred states, may inspire the confidence necessary to relax in taking the test or the appreciation of the other's qualities necessary for romantic interest, and so on. Similarly, an effectiveness in competitive games that may derive as a by-product from being unconcerned about one's fate or unworried about critics can often be achieved (albeit with more difficulty) by direct methods, such as building up one's strength or defenses against attack.

Nor is it clear that autonomy and authenticity are essentially by-products or are *always* defeated by direct efforts toward them; rather, we must distinguish between different kinds of reflexive intention or higher-order motive. Elster is right that trying to be "original" by simply avoiding anything preferred by one's peers or parents cannot make us authentic; so this approach to authenticity will be self-defeating. But authenticity should not be reduced to originality alone (and especially not to originality in this adolescent sense). Critical reflection on whether we have sufficient objective reasons for valuing some goal or endorsing our desires for it or emotions toward it need not be so simplistic in its assessment of what constitutes a "good practical reason" for our second-order attitudes.

Clearly any existential account of autonomy and authenticity as stages in the ideal of mature human agency cannot agree that these states are completely beyond the reach of intentional cultivation or that working toward these second-order goals through reflexive efforts to manage one's own first-order psychic states must *always* involve "one thought too many." I believe there is a vital psychic space *between* self-defeating forms of self-involvement or excessively reflective obsession with oneself, on the one hand, and totally unplanned action aimed at first-order goals external to our own psyche with no reflective self-awareness, on the other. Non-self-defeating forms of "care of the self" must occupy this important middle ground. Overextension of the "one thought too many" critique leads to the impression that only completely wanton agency could be authentic (and that is a *reductio*). This complex question, however, must await a full analysis of autonomy and authenticity.[148]

There are other, better examples of positive states that are essentially by-products, or untargetable. *Belief* that P, or *being convinced* about something, cannot generally be produced by willing or directly pursuing it.[149] There are indirect approaches to belief or conviction—for example, by reading or informing oneself about the relevant issue—but the results of such dialectical means to one's end are necessarily unpredictable. If genuine *conviction on the merits* is the intended result, then the rational evaluation required could in principle lead one to a conclusion incompatible with the one initially desired. If inquiry "with an open mind" is the only available method, we cannot ensure our initially preferred outcome. Becoming convinced by way of sheer self-manipulation offers only a simulacrum of rational conviction.

This case is instructive, because it suggests a sufficient condition for positive states that are essentially by-products. S will be such a state if:

1. S can be produced only by a certain kind of causal or psychological process P; *and*

2. The intentional initiation of P, together with all other factors F that we can directly control, is insufficient to guarantee S and can lead to results incompatible with S.

In such cases, we can go only some of the way toward bringing about S; factors beyond our control must take us the rest of the way. This means that *luck*, in its broadest sense, must be involved in causing S, but it does not require that S is a kind of thing that can only result from a fluke (like coincidences), or some deviant causal chain. Condition (2) requires only that we cannot in principle know in advance what the outcome of initiating P will be. Rationally justified assent to a particular proposition does seem to be an instance of S in this paradigm, and there are probably many others.

Another example might be *requited* romantic love. To some extent, my love for R might inspire her to love me in return but it could not *guarantee* that R would return my love; yet there might be no other way to encourage R to reciprocate in the way desired other than by expressing my love for her. Perhaps another factor I could control in wooing R would be how *possessive or controlling* I appeared (since it is well known that trying to coerce romantic affection from another is self-defeating). I could avoid being overly possessive by, for example, intentionally refraining from objecting too strongly if R wanted to date someone else on a trial basis before deciding between us. While this might be a necessary condition for R to return my affection, it certainly could not guarantee it. Yet it remains better than my other alternative, which would be to act like the stalker in *Fatal Attraction*—behavior that is certain to drive R into the arms of my competitor more quickly than just about anything else I could do. This example takes us into the realm of states that are essentially by-products relative to *interpersonal* action, in the sense that they cannot be brought about by direct coercion or command.[150] The reciprocation of romantic love is certainly one of these states, and anyone who does not learn this will probably fail in efforts to cultivate such a love relationship. The freely given recognition desired by Hegel's master is similar.

This analysis leaves open many questions, such as whether, or within, what limits states that are essentially by-products can be brought about *indirectly* by technical strategies that work to produce those first-order psychic states that will in turn produce the initially desired outcome as their by-product.[151] But this abbreviated analysis will be sufficient for our purposes in assessing the paradoxes of egoism. Given that second-order satisfaction is *by definition* a side effect of pursuing other first-order goods for their own sake, it follows that it is essentially a by-product in Elster's sense. Moreover, second-order satisfaction results only from processes that can also lead to frustration rather than satisfaction. The only approach to it involves risking its opposite. Thus such satisfaction cannot be directly targeted even after it is first experienced—unlike the higher goods "begotten" in the pursuit of lower forms of beauty in the *Symposium*. There might be artificial simulacra of such second-order satisfactions that we could intentionally produce—such as the vain self-admiration of someone who counts up exactly how many good deeds he has done each week—but the true object slips through the fingers of anyone who tries to grasp it directly or treat it as a possession subject to control by his will.

Feinberg's paradox of hedonism, which I renamed the paradox of abstract egoism, is thus a genuine practical antinomy: the direct pursuit of the abstract egoist's goal is necessarily self-defeating. And to the extent that the richest or most rewarding life, or happiness in the fullest sense possible for beings with human capacities (eudaimonia), necessarily involves second-order satisfaction as an essential component, eudaimonia must also be in part essentially a by-product, as Feinberg suggests. Given the further empirical premise that such eudaimonia includes second-order satisfaction that results only as a by-product of pursuing *non-self-related* first-order goods for their own sake, then the paradox of material egoism will also follow.

In the next chapter, we will see that this further premise is central to the eudaimonist project's justification of the life of virtue over a life of material egoism. However, we already have some reason to suspect that trying to avoid material and abstract egoism by basing ethical norms on a moral psychology that affirms formal egoism as its bedrock psychological axiom will not entirely allow us to escape these paradoxes of self-defeat. For the two fatal problems we have found with material and abstract egoism, respectively, both seem to be rooted not just in the nature of the goods that each type of agent takes as her ultimate aim but also in the one feature that these aims have in common: namely, that they are *about oneself*, or directly connected to what I call the agent's simple being. The wealth, sensual pleasures, power, and glory that the Hobbesian egoist pursues are quite different from the second-order satisfaction that the abstract egoist takes as her ultimate end, but both are *agent-related* goods that are meant (when realized) to be appropriated into the being of the agent. These goals are sought for the agent's psyche (in the case of second-order satisfaction), or in order to extend the agent's bodily powers (in the case of technical artifacts), or to add to his "social body," that is, his property, effects, position, and so on.

We might summarize this point by saying that all egoistic paradoxes of self-defeat are rooted in the *possessiveness* of egoism. In pursuing objects or goods in order to appropriate them into his "self," the agent remains fundamentally *self*-interested and hence unable to break out of the mirror world in which all lines of significance or value return ultimately to his own simple being. It is this grasping or appropriating aspect of his nature—his perception of all pursuable goods in terms of their ripeness for control or possession or consumption, his measuring of all kinds of importance by their effects on or for himself—that defeats him. Egoism and its tendency to self-defeat are rooted in this fundamental narcissism—that is, this refusal to value *alterity*, states of the world or other beings that are not possessed or first apprehended as pleasures.

But if so, then formal egoism will also be self-defeating, although in a more subtle way than material or abstract egoism. For, as I argue, to see every worthwhile end in terms of what either the end itself or the activity of pursuing it might contribute to my "self-realization" is not a neutral attitude. It colors the object of every kind of *orexis*, every type of desire in the erosiac sense, with a formal *agent-relativity*: this object and/or the pursuit of it must enlarge, complete, or fulfill the self. For otherwise it could not be *desired* (in the ancient Greek sense) at all; it could only be *projected* by an agent as a goal that he does not already want, or of which he has no prior need. Since it excludes such projective motivation, formal egoism seems to cut us off from the agent-relative benefits of agent-transcending concerns and commitments just as much as material and abstract egoism do. The full defense of this claim is the subject of chapter 7.

II

The Existential Critique of Eudaimonism

6

Psychological Eudaimonism: A Reading of Aristotle

Overview. This chapter is an interpretative reconstruction of several key ideas in Aristotle's *Nicomachean Ethics*, with some reference to Aquinas's *Treatise on Happiness* along the way. It will be intelligible to anyone who has read Aristotle; undergraduates may find the analysis of Aristotle's theory in section 1 useful quite apart from its role in my larger argument. section 2 concerns more advanced questions in the interpretation of Aristotle; section 3 presents in propositional form the model of human motivation to be critiqued in later chapters. Hence readers interested in following the main argument of the book without revisiting the *Nicomachean Ethics* in detail could simply read section 3, which provides the basis for discussion in the next two chapters.

Introduction

In this chapter, I prepare the way for an existential critique of a eudaimonist view of human motivation, taking Aristotle as my focus. I begin by framing what I consider to be the most defensible version of eudaimonism consistent with the erosiac conception of human motivation. I show that this is a plausible reading of Aristotle, although I am primarily concerned about the implications of the most defensible form of psychological eudaimonism itself, whether it is properly attributed to Aristotle or not. Since my goal is to describe the best version of eudaimonist moral psychology and then critique it, I sidestep some questions of textual exegesis by making charitable assumptions about Aristotle's meaning that would require "at least a book" (to use Derek Parfit's apt phrase) for a full defense. However, the resulting model of "A-eudaimonism" will clearly be Aristotelian in spirit.

This will be a sufficient basis for constructing the main existential objection to the eudaimonist project.

I. The Highest or Complete Good in Aristotle's Eudaimonism

The belief that human motivation is exhausted by the three states of orektic desire described in the previous chapter—instinctive impulses (D1), subjective preferences and inclinations (D2), and evaluative desires (D3)—provides the basis for Aristotle's analysis of happiness as the embracing human goal. Despite the wealth of commentaries on this ideal, I think it is fairest to begin by summarizing Aristotle's approach to the highest or complete good as I see it, with reference to the central controversy regarding the "inclusiveness" of the human good as our ultimate end.

1.1. Toward a Uniquely Ultimate End: Three Criteria for the Highest Good

In his *Nicomachean Ethics I* (*NE*), Aristotle follows Plato's *Gorgias* in critiquing two kinds of material egoism: the life aimed at pleasure and the life aimed at honor, power, and ascendance in political status over others. He generally follows Plato's notion that virtue is the key both to true nobility (the *kalon*) and to happiness in its most *holistic* sense (involving a sense of overall well-being, the joy of excelling at all one is capable of doing, of having arrived in life, or having found one's proper role). His ground for a normative analysis of the virtues is meant to be a better understanding of this ideal than Plato provided in his notoriously abstract and perplexing Form of the Good (*eidos ta agathon*), which is decisively rejected in *NE* I.6. Yet Aristotle's approach is still to begin with what he considers to be the most general things we can say about human motivation and related branches of knowledge in order to move from these to more specific accounts of our natural goal. At the most general level, he begins a multipronged analysis that requires some reconstruction, since a particular branch of it will begin in one section of *NE* I, then pause while other topics are addressed, and then recommence later in other sections (which is unsurprising if the text we possess is the result of incomplete lecture notes, perhaps even redacted from more than one of Aristotle's courses at the Lyceum).

The analysis begins, famously, with Plato's distinction between what I simply call "final" ends pursued for their own sake and things done at least partly as a means to such final ends (*Rep*. II 357b–58a). Final ends are then subdivided into activities done for their own sake and desirable products that are not themselves human activities (*NE* I.1 1094a5). Next we have the suggestion that the ends-means relation is *relative*: if X is a means to Y,

Y may still be a means to Z, and so on. This "chain" of means-ends relationships, as I call it, suggests a kind of natural hierarchy of practical significance: whatever is further to the right in such a chain has higher or more general practical importance for human life than whatever is further to the left. Aristotle takes directly from Plato (without questioning it) the assumption that this natural hierarchy is *virtually identical* to the hierarchy of arts and sciences that has arisen spontaneously in a self-organizing human society using expert knowledge to manage its affairs for the common good. Thus "crafts" (the term I use for *technē*—arts or sciences that require and employ some kind of expert theoretical knowledge)[1] are directly associated with their defining ends from the start of Aristotle's text: as in Socrates' argument against Thrasymachus in *Republic I* (341d–42e), Aristotle's analysis assumes that each of the defining ends for the sake of which a distinct craft exists must be *some objective good* that is ostensibly part of human well-being (and thus a natural object of what I have called D3 desire). It is this direct relationship of crafts with final ends that allows him to say: "In all such cases, then, the ends of the ruling sciences are more choiceworthy than all the ends subordinate to them, since the lower ends are also pursued for the sake of the higher" (*NE* I.1 1094a15–16). Just as ends are arranged in a natural hierarchy, so are their associated crafts.

Aristotle next argues that the natural hierarchy we find in ends is no accident but a necessary result of the structure of human motivation. This is the famous argument that the chain of relative means-ends relationships cannot extend infinitely, so there must be *some* final end(s) (*NE* I.2 1094a19–23). (The text here is not clear about the possible plurality of the regress-stopping ends, but since Aristotle recognizes that later, we can add it for him here.) This argument has been subject to much dispute down the ages. I pause to note only that the argument can be made valid if we are allowed two extra assumptions to fill out what the existing text actually says: (1) we have to assume that there *is* some act A that we are now motivated to do (and this Aristotle surely would have taken for granted); (2) we must take Plato's erosiac model of motivation as given. I believe this is always operating as a background assumption in Aristotle—one that is so fundamental that it is rarely thematized. Then it is easy to see how the anti-regress argument goes. For by (2), if I am motivated at all, there must be some final end I desire that would help complete me. If there were no such end, then orektic desire could never begin, and this is what Aristotle means in saying that "we do not choose everything because of something else—for if we do, it will go on without limit, so that *desire will prove empty and futile*" (*NE* I.2 1094a21, emphasis added). Although this may be a general truth, we can see it clearly only if we start from some substantive conception of desire, such as the erosiac model. And since by (1) I am motivated to A, it follows that: (3) either A is itself what I desire (my requiting terminus) or it is only a means to such a satiating final end; (4) either way there is some final end involved in my being motivated, and so, by dilemma; (5) there is some final end. If the argument so described seems nearly circular, it is only because we are recognizing how much has been packed into the underlying notion of "desire."

This argument is immediately followed by Aristotle's very important remark that knowledge of the highest good should have great practical value:

> Then surely knowledge of this good also carries great weight for [our] way of life; if we know it, we are more likely, like archers who have a target to aim at, to hit the right mark. If so, we should try to grasp, in outline at any rate, what the [highest] good is, and which is its proper science or capacity. (*NE* I.2 1094a23–27)

Notice, if this is right, that it would be natural for there to be already a science, art, or "craft" aimed at producing this highest good, and identifying this would be helpful as a clue to the nature of this good. Aristotle's intuitive picture seems to be something like the following table (with vertical arrows indicating means-to-ends relations):

Chain of Ends	Chain of Crafts
Highest end(s) (not means to anything else)	Ruling art(s) or science(s)
↑	↑
subordinate ends	subordinate crafts
↑	↑
lowest means, basic acts	lowest techniques and skills

On the left side of this diagram, we have reached the conclusion only that there must be some final end(s) and that if there turned out to be only one truly final end among these, it would be our highest good. But on the right side, Aristotle sees a more definitive answer among our relevant starting data: "political science" seems to be the highest ruling craft, since it orders the study and activities of all the other crafts, and thus "its end will include the ends of the other sciences, and so will be the human good" (*NE* 1094a38–b8).[2] As Stephen White says, "the most 'authoritative' . . . pursuit in any system has the overall good of the system as its end," and "politics is the most authoritative pursuit in any community."[3]

Here Aristotle seems to suggest for the first time that a *unique* highest end (for which I reserve the term "ultimate end") will be that which in some sense "includes" all other ends that can intelligibly be pursued as final ends. As Susanne Hill argues, the idea that "the ends for which a thing acts are hierarchically ordered, some being ends for the sake of further ends, culminating in a single, ultimate end," is also found in Aristotle's *Physics* and *De anima*.[4] Here the sense of "inclusion" still seems to be understood in terms of the means-ends relation, however; it seems to be that all other crafts are *partly* for the sake of the goal of political science, although also partly for their own sake too, whereas the ultimate good that politicians should seek is sought *only* for its own sake and never for the sake of anything else.[5] I define this relation of "nonholistic inclusion" as follows:

> A is *included* nonholistically in B if either A is just a means to B (A is not pursued for its own sake), or A is an end-in-itself and also always pursued as a means to B (never exclusively for its own sake).

Irwin's reading of the passage on the hierarchy of crafts brings up quite a different sense of "inclusion":

> The sciences concerned with *praxis* (action in the strictest sense) are concerned with activities that are worth pursuing for their own sakes. The supreme science does not make these activities purely instrumental; it includes them in the activities that it prescribes as the highest good. This passage introduces the important idea that the highest good is an ordered compound of noninstrumental goods, explained further in 7 § 1–5.[6]

Irwin refers here to the section where we meet the notion of the "most complete end." His gloss makes it sound as if Aristotle said that a given (specific) final end can be seen as *part* of a larger, "compound" final end, which could be conceived as a certain non-mereological relationship among its parts. But the text in I.2 does not by itself support this "holistic" notion of inclusion, which comes up only later. The emphasis is instead on the *superiority of noninstrumentality:* that is, the thesis that being pursued solely for its own sake (never also as a means to anything else) makes an end higher in *intrinsic value* than ends that are typically pursued both for their own sake and also as a means to something else.

Now, this thesis is not self-evidently true, though Aristotle and most of his expositors assume that it is. (A) Listening to a favorite piece of classical music is something I may do solely for its own sake, not as a means to anything else; while (B) reading a philosophical work on moral psychology is something I may do both for the intrinsic value of its insights and as a means to teaching a course on the topic next semester. Yet despite the fact that the activity in (B) is also a means, I may nevertheless judge it to be higher in the sense of more intrinsically valuable than the activity in (A). (C) Likewise, I might have children both for their own sake and for the pleasure of their company, while (D) I pursue some casual entertainment purely as a final end; yet I rank (C) far above (D). So the "superiority of noninstrumentality" thesis is false.⁷ However, looking for noninstrumentality may nevertheless be a way of trying to narrow down intrinsic goods to a single good that could count as highest; hence I will ignore this important objection, while we are tracing Aristotle's effort to find criteria sufficient to assure a uniquely highest good in the structure of human motivation.

In the text of the *Nicomachean Ethics* that has come down to us, Aristotle next digresses into a metadiscussion of the kind of inexact practical knowledge involved in political science and ethics and the dependence of philosophical reflection on acquired virtue in this domain (*NE* I.3–I.4). When he returns to the "point from which we digressed" (*NE* I.5 1095b13)—by which he apparently means the prior discussion of the different "fine and just things, which political science examines" (*NE* I.3 1094b15)—he begins discussing three leading conceptions of happiness (eudaimonia). But oddly, this discussion starts before he has finished his analysis of the criteria defining the highest good or shown that eudaimonia generally fits these criteria.⁸ Still, another crucial criterion for the highest good emerges in the critique of the life devoted to honor (the "political" life in the traditional/familiar sense but not in Aristotle's own ideal sense of politics). Aristotle says that honor or glory in the eyes of others "seems to be too superficial to be what we are seeking; for it seems to depend more on those who honor than on the one honored, whereas we intuitively believe that the good is something of our own and hard to take from us" (*NE* I.5 1095b25–27).

This idea that the highest good should be resilient against chance and fortune—such as the fickle turns of people's opinions—is one we have already met in Plato's *Symposium*, where this criterion is taken to its logical limit in the ideal of an *absolutely unlosable good* possessed with maximum security—something that Diotima thinks is achieved only by the gods. For Plato, the "security" or "stability against fortune" criterion, as we may call it, becomes "total independence of fortune," and interestingly, Aquinas also defends the criterion in this absolute form: "Happiness is the most stable good" and "happiness has stability of itself and always."⁹ For this criterion in its absolute Platonic form is crucial to Aquinas's argument that our ultimate end is world-transcendent or supernatural—not just in the sense of being attainable only in another life but also in the sense of being the experience of the Good that informs the goodness of all particular or noncomprehensive goods: "Now the object of the will, or human appetite, is the universal good. . . . Hence it is evident that nothing can bring the will of man to rest except the universal good. This is not found in any created thing but only in God, for all creatures have goodness [only] by participation."¹⁰

Aristotle is not quite so demanding, since he famously concedes (to popular opinion in his society, and to the poets) that some minimum of "external goods" subject to fortune—such as money, good looks, and successful children—may be necessary for complete happiness or "blessedness" (*NE* I.8 1099a30–99b6). Yet he still insists that happiness is something that can be pursued by design, with the right education (like the goals of the various crafts), and "it would be seriously inappropriate to entrust what is greatest and finest to fortune" (*NE* I.9 1099b15–24). The stability criterion is also clearly at work in Aristotle's argument that we cannot call a person wholly happy during his lifetime (when the overall character of his life is not yet fixed) and in his related argument that activities in accord with virtue are the most important or primary constituents of happiness:

> for we suppose happiness is enduring, and definitely not prone to fluctuate, but the same person's fortunes often turn to and fro. . . . But surely it is quite wrong to take our cue from someone's fortunes. For his doing well or badly does not rest on them. . . . Indeed the present puzzle is further evidence for our account. For no human achievement has the stability of activities in accord with virtue, since these seem to be more enduring even than our knowledge of the sciences. (*NE* I.10 1100b2–15)

So a person with the inner strength of virtue does not worry about minor mishaps and bears even major misfortunes well, playing as best as possible whatever "hand of cards" life deals her. The point is that dispositions of character that constitute virtues are *resilient against outward misfortune* and thus shield us at least partly from the effects of disaster, preventing us from becoming wholly miserable in their wake. As Aristotle says of the good person in difficult circumstances, "even here what is fine shines through, whenever someone bears many severe misfortunes with good temper, not because he feels no distress, but because he is noble and magnanimous" (*NE* I.10 1100b30–33). I am emphasizing this point for two reasons: first, because Aristotle is often misportrayed in contemporary ethical theory as *totally* opposed to the ideal of justice "independent of fortune" that plays such a large role in the moral theories of Kant and Rawls;[11] and second because this particular passage suggests that the central role played by "magnanimity" or "great-souledness" or "proper pride" (*meglapsychia*) in Aristotle's normative theory of the virtues is due to the underlying idea that the eudaimonistic value of the virtues depends crucially on their providing stability against misfortune to their agent—an idea to which I return in section 3 below.

1.2. *"Most Complete" as a Nonholistically Inclusive Relation*

So far, we have identified three criteria of the highest good: it is a final end; it is the goal of the ruling craft; and it involves the greatest security against misfortune possible for human beings. These criteria, however, are still not enough to show that there must be *one* final end that we can regard as the *ultimate* goal in more than name only, that is, that there is some *intelligible unity* to "the" highest good. This idea is developed in the passages immediately preceding the famous argument that the human function (*ergon*) is "activity and actions of the soul that involve reason" (*NE* I.7 1098a14). Leading up to this key argument, we find Aristotle picking up his earlier reasoning concerning the chain of means-to-ends just at the point where the argument against an infinite regress leaves off. He restates its conclusion: "And so, if there is some end of everything achievable in action, the good achievable in action will be this end; if there are more ends than one, [it] will be these ends" (*NE* I.7 1097a23–34). The anti-regress argument is clearly compatible with either of these solutions; yet at this point, the latter solution would make our ultimate end little more than a simple logical conjunction of all the various final ends we might pursue ("pursue A & B & C . . ."), with no way of assuring us that conflicts among them could be resolved. This is clearly an inadequate conception of the ultimate end, so Aristotle offers the following:

> Since there are apparently many ends, and we choose some of them (for instance, wealth, flutes, and in general instruments) because of something else [i.e., as a means to other ends] it is clear that not all ends are complete. But the best good is apparently something complete. And so, if only one end is complete, the good we are seeking will be this end; if more ends than one are complete, it will be the most complete [τελειος] end of these. (*NE* I.7 1097a26–30)

Despite the continuing dispute over the meaning of "most complete" in this and other passages in *NE* I (some of which I consider in the next section), the *simplest* explanation seems to be that Aristotle still understood "completeness" (or literally "end-ness") just as what I have called finality (i.e., being an end-in-itself), and understood "most complete" (or "most end-like") just as he did nonholistic "inclusiveness" in the analysis of the chain of crafts. As Bostock suggests, an end is "unconditionally complete" if and only if it is "pursued always for its own sake, and never for the sake of something else." Yet as he rightly points out, this is not enough "to ensure that there can be only one end which is . . . 'unconditionally complete.'"[12]

We might move closer to isolating such an ultimate end if we define the *most* nonholistically inclusive end as one that satisfied the following two conditions:

(a) it is always chosen *only* as a final end, never as a means to any other final end; and
(b) every other final end is *also* pursued as a means to it.

Bostock also reads "most complete" in this way as a maximality condition specifying a uniquely all-inclusive end.[13] Admittedly, the next paragraph in Aristotle's text suggests only the first of these two conditions (a) for an end that is "complete without qualification." But in the subsequent paragraph, when Aristotle for the first time explicitly asserts that eudaimonia fits his definition of the highest good, both of my conditions for maximal nonholistic inclusiveness are implied. Aristotle says of happiness that "we always choose it because of itself, never because of something else" and that four other final ends (as paradigm examples) are also chosen because happiness is among their *results*: "Honor, pleasure, understanding, and every virtue we certainly choose because of themselves, since we would choose each of them even if it had no further result; but we also choose them for the sake of happiness, *supposing that through them we shall be happy*" (NE I.7 1097b1–7; emphasis added).

Read as a nonholistic relation, this means, as Irwin suggests, that "Every good that is chosen both for itself and for the sake of the highest good is separate from (not a part of), and strictly instrumental to, the highest good, even though it is also chosen for its own sake."[14] This is not the conclusion of Aristotle's analysis, however, because he probably recognized that it still may not solve the problem of multiple complete ends left by the argument against an infinite regress in the chain of motivation. For why should we think that there can be only *one* "most nonholistically complete end" as defined above, that is, an end that is fully (or unconditionally) complete *and* nonholistically includes all the other ends (which are therefore not fully complete by themselves)? Although Aristotle lists four final ends as also pursued for the sake of happiness, perhaps other final ends are pursued for the sake of some other unconditionally complete final end. Unless there is a good that nonholistically includes *all* other final ends (so that all activities or states pursued for their own sake are also sought as instrumental means to this fully complete good), then our most important goal could *still* end up as just one among a short list of fully complete (or unconditionally final) ends that we never pursue as a means to anything else.[15] In addition to these models with multiple fully complete ends, we also have possible models in which *no* end is fully complete, because every end that is pursued at least partly for its own sake is *also* pursued for the sake of some other such end, forming a "web" of motivation with no absolutely terminal endpoints. We can illustrate these two models as follows, putting ends pursued at least partially for their own sake at the top of the chart (unconditionally final ends thus appear *only* on the top row).

More than one unconditionally final end   *No unconditionally final end*

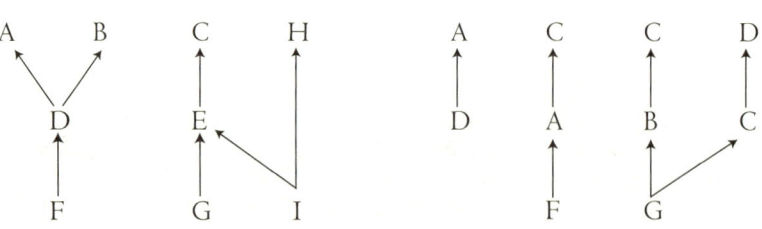

Both these diagrams are compatible with the anti-regress argument, which requires only that there are some final ends, not that there are any fully complete ends. But in each diagram, there fails to be *any* end that nonholistically includes *all* other final ends. Of course, Aristotle's strategy could be (as it is sometimes thought) simply to argue that *in fact* we find only one fully complete end (happiness) which therefore includes all other final ends: on this reading, he is arguing that an empirical inspection of human psychology and sociology reveals exactly one fully final end that nonholistically includes all others.[16] But it would be much more theoretically satisfying if Aristotle could show that in principle there must be a single highest good. If unconditional completeness alone will not get us this result, then perhaps there is some *other* sense in which there must be an ultimate good that includes all other final ends.

A cautionary note: since Aristotle was the first philosopher to try working out this difficult question about human motivation in detail, it would hardly be surprising if he did not think of every such nuance or develop a rigorous response to every such objection. Rather, it is remarkable that his groundbreaking analysis reaches the level of rigor we find in it. However, if Aristotle did realize that his nonholistically inclusive good had not ensured uniqueness for the sort of reasons I describe, then it would make perfect sense for him to move toward comprehensiveness as an essential condition of the highest good.[17]

1.3. *Self-Sufficiency as a Maximally Comprehensive or Holistically Inclusive Relation*

To guarantee a uniquely ultimate end, Aristotle seems to require both a further criterion for completeness and a holistic sense in which the ultimate end "includes" all other final ends. The new criterion comes precisely in the next section, where Aristotle discusses "self-sufficiency," which may be the most important passage in Book I:

The same conclusion [that happiness is complete] also appears to follow from self-sufficiency. For the complete good seems to be self-sufficient. ... we regard something as self-sufficient when all by itself it makes a life choiceworthy and lacking in nothing; and that is what we think happiness does. Moreover, we think happiness is most choiceworthy of all goods; it is not counted as one good among many. [If it were] counted as one good among many, then, clearly, we think it would be more choiceworthy if the smallest of goods were added. ... Happiness, then, is apparently something complete and self-sufficient, since it is the end of the things achievable in action. (*NE* I.7 1097b7–21)

In the middle of this passage (elided in my quote) we also find Aristotle's claim that our happiness must include the happiness of our family and fellow citizens, since we are political creatures. Aristotle apparently sees this as confirmation of the self-sufficiency of eudaimonia: since we are *zoon politikon*, our happiness would "lack something" significant to us if it did not include the well-being of our community, and so would not be self-sufficient; therefore (by *modus tollens*) our highest good must include this social dimension.[18] It must also cover our complete life, since otherwise we could have the highest good yet lack desirable activities or states in other times or aspects of our lives (which violates self-sufficiency). Notably, completeness is also defined this way in *Metaphysics* Δ: things are called complete if they lack nothing proper to their excellence.[19]

So understood, it is clear that the self-sufficiency criterion comes directly from the erosiac model of human motivation: to be the highest good is to satisfy all natural desire, so that the agent possessing the highest good *lacks nothing*. The idea that eudaimonia cannot be just the best in a list of distinct goods but must in some sense *include all naturally significant goods* also follows from the ideal of the highest good implied by the erosiac model: if any good added to X can make X better in the sense of more thoroughly satisfying natural erosiac desire, then X by itself is not self-sufficient, since the agent possessing X *still lacks* some significant good needed for her life to be perfect.[20]

In trying to spell out why there can only be one highest good, then, Aristotle looks to the very heart of the erosiac model of motivation stemming from Socrates and articulates its deepest implications. If all human motivation is desire aiming at a state in which we lack nothing and desire itself is suspended in total fulfillment, then that state is the ultimate end of all action. So if there seem to be distinct final ends at which we aim, then there must be some relationship between them if that ultimate end is to be unified in a practical sense that could provide guidance for life. This explains how the erosiac model entails self-sufficiency in the highest good, which in turn points toward the idea that the highest good must *embrace within itself or comprehend* all other ends that are naturally final for us.

Irwin suggests that it is also possible to read the passage detailing honor, pleasure, and virtue as pursued both for their own sake *and* for the sake of happiness as suggesting that eudaimonia is a "comprehensive" or holistic good that *directly* includes other final ends within it:

> The highest good, chosen for its own sake, is composed of non-instrumental goods that are chosen both for their own sake and for the sake of the highest good. . . . To choose them for the sake of happiness is not to choose them purely as instrumental means, since the "for the sake of" relation, as Aristotle understands it, includes the relation of part to whole.[21]

If this is right, it helps to distinguish Aristotle's view from Plato's, since Irwin has argued that Plato's Socrates holds that "virtues are purely instrumental to happiness and not to be valued for their own sakes"[22] (although as unified in wisdom they are always the only effective means to this universal end).[23] By contrast, Aristotle employs his distinction between action (*praxis*) and crafts aiming at producible goods (*poiēsis*) (whose skills can be misused) to deny that virtue is the craft of happiness: "Part of the point of Aristotle's distinctions is to show how virtue is not purely instrumental . . . the virtuous action is itself the end, and is therefore a part of—not simply instrumental to—the final good that is happiness."[24]

This holistic conception of the highest good is superior because it allows for noninstrumental parts of eudaimonia.[25] To Irwin's description I add two points: for the sort of "comprehensiveness" that he has in mind, (a) the relationship of the other final ends within the highest good could not be a simple logical conjunction or mereological sum but would have to be some kind of *harmonious ordering*; and (b) the highest good would have to include an ordered relation between *all* of the other truly final goods we can pursue for their own sake. For, as Lear points out, given Aristotle's starting assumption that "all human action is grounded in desire [*orexis*]," if there were no such unity in our highest good, then:

> There would be various ends which we pursued for their own sakes which were not themselves subordinate to any other ends. Life would potentially be ultimately neurotic. For if the various ends-in-themselves called for conflicting actions in a given situation, we would be pulled this way and that. There would be no way of acting that satisfied our conflicting desires. . . . But the hope is that the world is such and man's nature is such that there is at least a possibility of leading a non-neurotic life. The hope is that it is at least possible for a man's motivational structure to form *a harmonious whole*.[26]

In other words, the harmonious ordering of ends in the ultimate end must make possible a strong type of narrative unity in a life devoted to such ends. Can we have more than "hope" that this is possible? Clearly, the availability of this sort of practical harmony, or *existential coherence*, as I have called it,[27] will not be guaranteed by a highest good that only *nonholistically* includes all other final ends. For on that model, if one final end E1 conflicts with another end E2 in some situation so that pursuing E1 to its logical extreme rules out happiness (by ensuring that desire for E2 will be unsatisfied), we could *still* decide to pursue E1 without reserve; for, although we desire E1 for its own sake *and* as a means to happiness, the former can still trump the latter. To avoid this, clearly the required harmony among ends must imply that we pursue a given final end only *in the ways and to the extent* that it is compatible with measured pursuit of other significant final ends as parts of the same whole. It is, then, the erosiac conception of human motivation that guarantees the possibility for which Lear hopes, by pointing to what I called the *holistically* inclusive notion of the highest good.

This conclusion agrees with Bostock's view (following Ackrill) that Aristotle has "an 'inclusive' conception of man's ultimate end, for this is taken to include activities in accordance with each of the many human excellences, each pursued for its own sake (as well as for the sake of the whole to which they contribute."[28] It also agrees with Irwin's favored interpretation of "the most complete end" as "the one that includes the other ends; we are not to pursue an unordered collection of ends, but [rather] the complete single end that is the whole formed by them."[29] If this is taken seriously, in light of the erosiac model, it implies that in some way we experience desire for all discrete final ends *as expressions or instantiations* of the ultimate desire for the highest good. As I put it in my (much too brief) treatment of this topic in *Kierkegaard After MacIntyre*:

> the desire for the highest good flows through and is present in (ordinate and inordinate) desires for all particular intrinsic goods. This transcendent desire is then the well-spring of the more particular desires not in the instrumental sense, but in the constitutive sense that we desire happiness itself only by desiring all these particular things. ... In Heideggerian terms, the desire for eudaimonia is the "jointure" of all desires.[30]

Probably the clearest statement that there must be such a unified urdesire underlying all our other desires is given by Aquinas in his argument that our will cannot be "simultaneously related to diverse things as ultimate ends." His first argument for this is as follows:

> each thing desires its own fulfillment and therefore desires for its ultimate end a good that perfects and completes it. . . . The ultimate

end, then, must so entirely satisfy man's desire that there is nothing left for him to desire. It cannot be his ultimate end if something additional is required for his fulfillment. Hence it is not possible for desire to tend to two things as though each were its perfect good.[31]

In this crucial passage, we see Aquinas's erosiac model of the will, its consequent formal egoism, and the idea of self-sufficiency interpreted as a whole *embracing* all truly desirable goods.

This idea is obviously closely related to the transcendent principle (Trans) that we found in the *Symposium*, which holds that no end can naturally be desired for its own sake unless it is comprehensive in the holistic sense (see chap. 4, sec. 2.4). But Trans is a very strong thesis, for it implies that what appear to be particular final ends in everyday life are not really final after all. This thesis is perhaps developed most fully in the Thomistic mystical tradition: for example, C. S. Lewis interpreted the "desire for heaven" this way, as underlying our desire for other goods, such as natural beauty:

> The books or the music in which we thought the beauty was located will betray us if we trust to them; it was not in them, it only came through them, and what came through them was longing. These things—the beauty, the memory of our past—are good images of what we really desire; but if they are mistaken for the thing itself, they turn into dumb idols, breaking the hearts of their worshippers. For they are not the thing itself.[32]

However, since Aristotle cannot agree that "we remain conscious of a desire that no natural happiness will satisfy,"[33] he must not define the highest good in a way that would make it supernaturally transcendent. He can hold only the *weak transcendent principle*: no activity, state, or product can be unconditionally complete or *fully* final (or desirable *solely* for its own sake) unless it is the whole union of goods that is comprehensively good, so that one who possesses it lacks nothing naturally desirable. This allows us to desire familiar things like natural beauty or a good game for their own sake, as long we are *also at the same time desire them as part of our eudaimonia.*

This weaker version of the transcendent principle is still enough to ensure that there is only *one* fully complete (or unqualifiedly final) end, *and* that it is sufficient for us or comprehensively satisfying. It is also enough to entail the principle of formal egoism: all intrinsic goods desirable for their own sake must be sought, at least in part, *as* components of the agent's good, or as appropriable by the agent. As Bostock puts it, "Aristotle clearly means that each person seeks (or should seek) *his own eudaimonia.*"[34] We can now use this principle to define the idea of an "all-embracing" good:

G is the *all-embracing good* if, for every other final end E, E is desired not only for its own sake but also *as part* of the ordered whole of intrinsic goods that is G.

We can think of Weak Trans as equivalent to the thesis that there must be such an all-embracing good.[35] Using all the concepts explored in this interpretation of Aristotle, let us now sum up the criteria of the highest human good or supreme end as he seems to have envisioned them.

Criteria Defining the Ultimate End of All Human Motivation

1. It is *the goal of the highest art/science*, or ruling craft (which nonholistically includes all others), i.e., "political science" (in its classical sense).
2. It is *unconditionally complete* or fully final, which means:

    (a) It is a final good, that is, a terminal end desirable for its own sake, *and*

    (b) It is not desired for the sake of (i.e., as a means to, or as a constitutive part of) any other complete or final good [stronger version: it *cannot* be desired as a means to anything else].

3. It is *comprehensive* in the sense of holistically including *all* other naturally desirable final ends as constitutive parts of itself. This means:

    (a) It is more than a mereological sum or logical conjunction of first-order final ends. It is an *ordered harmony* of all other final ends, or a *way of organizing* the various intrinsic goods so that their pursuit forms a balanced whole in human life.

    (b) As a result, the highest good is the ground of possibility of existential coherence or practical narrative unity of purpose in a human life and hence of inner psychological harmony of the self.

    (c) Thus it also *embraces* all the other naturally desirable intrinsic goods; for the agent to desire these ends for their own sake is *eo ipso* to desire them as part of her own comprehensive good. In other words, it is only by being embraced in this sense within the highest good that any other final end acquires its finality. All final ends rightly understood are seen as parts of this embracing end, so no final end is completely final by itself alone, except the comprehensive good (the *weak transcendent principle*).

4. It is *sufficient for us*, that is, the agent who possesses it lacks nothing, and hence all her motivation is requited, satisfied, or finished; she would never have any reason to desire anything else not included in this highest good or to abandon it once she possesses it:

   (a) Given our nature, this means the highest good must have a social dimension: it will include the good of other persons we care about for their own sake. It will also be temporally inclusive: the highest good must also be the good of our complete life rather than only part of our life.
   (b) The highest good must also be as resistant as possible to arbitrary changes of fortunes and depend as much as possible on features of inner character over which we have voluntary control and that secure us against the vicissitudes of society and chance.

This seems to be the most perspicuous way to state the various criteria that the highest good must satisfy to count as the ultimate end of all our motivation, although, of course, other ways of grouping (and naming) these components are possible. There are also some key logical relations between these elements: (3) and (4) entail (2),[36] but not vice versa. And (3) entails (4), but I do not treat self-sufficiency as part of the *definition* of comprehensiveness, since only the former explicitly requires the erosaic thesis. But either (3) or (4) is enough to entail uniqueness, that is, that there must be exactly one highest good. It is also important to note that these *purely formal* criteria of the ultimate end do not by themselves tell us which desires are "natural" to us and hence which ends will figure in the content of *eudaimonia* as our highest good (4a is not strictly formal but it is added only by way of illustration). To determine which of our desires express our true nature, we need the further analysis that begins with the function argument. Yet, as we already saw, for Aristotle it will be our rational D3 desires that express our nature. As Jonathan Lear puts it:

> Happiness is not based on the satisfaction of desires which a person just happens to possess [e.g., D2 preferences]. According to Aristotle, man has a nature: there is something definite and worthwhile that it is to be a human being. Happiness consists in living this noble life: in satisfying the desires that are necessary for man to have in order to live a full, rich life [given his nature].[37]

And this agrees with our analysis of the ultimate end. In terms of the moral psychology of the *De anima,* our unified desire for our highest good (whatever it is) must be our embracing, most comprehensive D3 desire.

2. Excursus: Maximal Inclusivism, Virtue Inclusivism, and Dominant-End Models

My reading clearly advocates a strong version of what commentators now call an "inclusive end," as opposed to a "dominant end," reading of the highest good in *NE* I. Whether or not the description of the highest good as "the most complete end" *by itself* implied holistic inclusiveness for Aristotle, I believe that the criterion of self-sufficiency can be understood only this way.[38] However, I recognize that there has been a wide range of scholarly opinion about Aristotle's conception of the highest good, eudaimonia, and the human function. I will enter only marginally into these debates, since what matters for my overall argument is not whether Aristotle really held precisely the theory I describe, but whether this is the *most defensible* form of eudaimonism, as I maintain.

If Aristotle actually held a dominant-end model, according to which the highest good is just the most intrinsically valuable item in a list of final ends, a contemporary eudaimonist could simply part company with Aristotle on this score and favor the maximally inclusive conception instead. Later I ask whether certain promising variations on the ideal eudaimonism I describe can avoid any of the objections explained in the next chapter against this maximally inclusive form of eudaimonism. Since my critique of eudaimonism depends primarily on the relationship of holistic happiness or flourishing to virtue, I will concentrate on that issue and largely leave aside the difficult question of how to relate practical virtues and ethical achievement to intellectual virtue (*sophia*) and contemplation (*theoria*). It will be enough for my purposes if one plausible version of eudaimonism holds that contemplation (and pure scientific and philosophical inquiry generally) should be conceived as simply the best first-order good in an inclusive harmony of such goods that constitutes eudaimonia rather than as a dominant end that constitutes eudaimonia all by itself.

Whether or not Aristotle should be read as a maximal inclusivist, however, it is important for my purposes to show that some alternatives that have been suggested would not work as well, especially if we hope to maintain the strong erosiac thesis. Hence in this section I briefly examine two sophisticated rivals to maximal inclusivism, beginning with Richard Kraut's attempt to harmonize Books I and X of the *Nicomachean Ethics.*

Kraut holds that Aristotle proposes *two* distinct ideals of happiness, corresponding to two goods, each of which may have "primacy" in a life lived "according" to this good—that is, when it is the "ultimate end" of a life—in the following sense:

> the ultimate end of a life is one that has three features: (a) all other ends in that life are desired for its sake; (b) it is desired for itself; and (c) it is not desired for the sake of any other good in that life. On my reading, contemplation is the ultimate end of the philosophical life, and activity in accordance with ethical virtue is the ultimate end of the political life. The philosopher will engage in ethical activity, but will do so only for the sake of contemplation. . . . By contrast, the political life is one that omits contemplation.[39]

Kraut is led to this view by the need to recognize the primacy given to contemplation in the philosophical life, according to NE X 7–8, along with the need to avoid implying that the philosopher can simply dispense with the practical virtues that have been the focus of the previous eight books.

It is clear that Kraut uses "for the sake of" here as an instrumental or *nonholistic* relation, since he holds that external intrinsic goods (like honor and friendship) can be pursued "for the sake" of the ultimate end in either of these ideals, without eudaimonia *consisting* in (a holistic combination of) these external goods with other intrinsic goods. Rather, in *both* these reasonable answers to the question, "What is happiness?" or eudaimonia, "our ultimate aim, consists *solely* in excellent reasoning activity," or the human virtues.[40] In particular:

> According to the best of these two answers, happiness consists in just one good: this is the virtuous exercise of the theoretical part of reason. . . . Every other good (including the ethical virtues) is desirable for the sake of this one activity. According to the second-best answer, happiness consists in virtuous practical activity.[41]

Putting these pieces together, we see that in Kraut's terms, a given conception determines the content of eudaimonia by specifying what it takes to be the ultimate end in the system of ends dictated by our nature: eudaimonia *consists in* whatever our "ultimate end" really is. Specifying our ultimate end, then, amounts to what I call a conception of our *material telos*, or a *material conception* of eudaimonia (see sec. 3 below).

Given that his "for-the-sake-of" relation is nonholistic,[42] Kraut's highest good can (at most) include other final ends as means to it. As a result, the two conceptions of eudaimonia Kraut describes are logically incompatible. If what really creates eudaimonia for human lives is only excellent contemplation (or the harmonious union of contemplative activities), along with whatever this requires as preconditions, then the ethical virtues (or their harmonious union) are by definition *not* ultimate, since they can also rightly be pursued as a means to contemplation as well as for their own sake. Likewise, if the excellent practical activities (taken jointly) are ultimate, then contemplation must be pursued as a means to practical virtue as well as for its own sake. At most one of these material conceptions of eudaimonia can be correct in its evaluative judgments, or right about our true nature or material telos. Hence it is difficult to understand in exactly what sense the philosophical conception could be "best" and the political "second-best." This comparison seems to require some standard that is neutral between them, that is a *formal concept* of eudaimonia that is dialectically prior to and theoretically distinct from either of these material conceptions. It is this formal concept that I define in section I.3 above as a maximally inclusive holistic or comprehensive good.

Thus Kraut's nonholistic concept of the ultimate end does not by itself determine which of these material conceptions is correct nor guarantee that we have a unified material telos to be described by any conception.[43] For, as we saw, if we define the ultimate end as that which nonholistically includes all others, then only one end can be ultimate by definition, but we have no *a priori* reason for believing that there should be any ultimate good in this sense. Rather, there are three possibilities: (a) there could be just one unconditionally complete or fully final end; or (b) there could be no ultimate end if either (b1) two or more ends are fully final, or (b2) no end is fully final (because each final end can also be pursued a means to another). In both the conceptions Kraut describes, there is an ultimate end, but his concept of ultimacy leaves open the possibility that both are wrong because there is no end that counts as ultimate.[44]

Of course, *if* the formal standard Kraut describes is right, then the contemplative ideal would count as more inclusive than the political ideal and hence *more eudaimon* (as Aristotle seems to claim). But it will be an empirical question whether or not contemplation is really for its own sake and never a means to other ends (such as practically noble goals). The "politician" can respond that just because someone *says* that the ethical virtues are for him a means to contemplation (as well as being valued for their own sake) or that he tries to live a life with contemplation as his material telos, this does not prove that he really will be *more eudaimon* or that his material conception of his highest good really is the ultimate end of human life. Although Aristotle's function argument regards speculative reason as our highest faculty, modern thinkers have found plenty of reasons to doubt this judgment (witness the entire Romantic movement).

This in itself is no decisive objection, since all plausible moral theories will have empirical elements. But the alternative reading seems formidable; as Kraut recognizes, the holistic approach to the formal concept of the highest good seems to point instead to some way of *harmonizing* contemplative / theoretical activities with ethical / practical activities, recognizing both as pursuits valuable in themselves as parts of a whole that is eudaimonia. This reading implies that *neither* of the material conceptions between which Kraut's Aristotle says we must choose is adequate. It is less important for this issue whether a concept of the ultimate end includes external intrinsic goods as constitutive parts or only as necessary means. Kraut focuses on this when he rejects what I have called maximal inclusivism:

> the fundamental thesis of Book I, as I understand it, is that happiness consists in a long stretch of perfectly virtuous activity of the rational soul. That one good can be analyzed into several subdivisions, since Aristotle distinguishes several kinds of perfect virtues of the rational soul. But happiness is not a composite of all compossible intrinsic goods: for example, it does not include physical pleasures, or honor, or friends.[45]

Kraut's main argument against including the external intrinsic goods is that Aristotle's function argument in *NE* I.7 shows our *ergon* to be virtuous activity of the rational soul, *not* all the products of such activities (or such activities plus luck) that we might desire. Although I cannot address the function argument in detail here, I simply suggest that Aristotle does not mean to identify (materially or formally) our "function" and our "highest good." Rather, our natural function is to perform excellently (or virtuously) those activities that either lead to or constitute *that part* of our highest good that is the most authentic expression of our nature, that is the development of our nature's highest potential. On this reading, performing our function well is not the whole of eudaimonia for Aristotle; this is where he departs from Plato and the Stoics. Since it is the most important part of our eudaimonia, understanding the activities comprised by this function is crucial for grasping most of what in fact constitutes our highest good, given our nature. Many views do err in failing to see this and thus misconstrue our material telos by overvaluing bodily and external goods. But the rejection of false material conceptions of eudaimonia (which identify our ultimate goal with health, honor, sensual pleasure, wealth, etc.) does *not* show that the highest good is not formally comprehensive. On the contrary, as I suggested, Aristotle appeals to its comprehensiveness in arguing that these are false material conceptions, since they provide none of the security against misfortune that a comprehensive good must maximize within the limits of our nature.

However, more important than Kraut's exclusion of external intrinsic goods is his further claim that Aristotle does not recognize a material telos consisting of a comprehensive harmony of all forms of human excellence (in their active expression). By contrast, based on a reading of the function argument similar to Kraut's own, Jeffrey Purinton arrives at a non-maximally inclusive concept of the highest good, which he helpfully calls "virtue-inclusivism": for Aristotle, happiness includes (in some holistic combination) *all* virtuous activities, but *only* these, not other external intrinsic goods.[46] This sounds superficially similar to the way Kraut sometimes describes his position; for example, in his recent summary of his book, Kraut writes that Aristotle "consistently adheres to the thesis that happiness consists in just one type of good—virtuous activity."[47] Yet in fact Kraut also rejects both possible versions of virtue-inclusivism, since he denies that for Aristotle, the highest good is materially identical either to (a) a comprehensive holistic harmony of *all* virtues activities (practical/ethical and speculative/intellectual);[48] or to (b) some further good that nonholistically includes or subsumes all these virtues. Rather, Kraut asserts that for Aristotle, the best material conception of eudaimonia is one in which intellectually virtuous contemplative activities nonholistically include all other ethical virtues; in addition to being desired for their own sake, the ethical virtues are desired for the sake of the contemplative virtues, not for the sake of eudaimonia as a separate end embracing them both.

As a result, it is impossible, on Kraut's view, to give a *eudaimonistic* explanation of why someone should sacrifice contemplative activity to other moral demands. Kraut's example is of a son, leading a philosophical life, whose father has taken ill and requires his son's aid. Since this means giving up some time that could have been devoted to contemplation, on the dominant-end interpretation, this means having less eudaimonia: "Aristotle would say that the son must help his father, despite the fact that as a result his life is less desirable than it would otherwise have been."[49] As a result, Kraut concludes that Aristotle is not an egoist in any sense that "enjoins us to give priority to our own well-being by choosing the act that *maximizes* our good"; rather, Aristotle is an egoist only in the weak sense that each agent should always do something that is good for her to some extent.[50] If this is right, however, it is hard to see how the desire for eudaimonia can function as an overall guide to one's life.[51] Should we regard the desire for the father's well-being (one species of the noble) as a desire for a goal entirely distinct from one's own eudaimonia? If so, then it seems that the strong erosiac thesis has been rejected, and thus an agent who felt in every respect complete and wholly satisfied (lacking nothing) could become motivated to pursue such a noble goal for its own sake, as a kind of *surplus* to her own eudaimonia. But this amounts to acknowledging the possibility of projective or non-orektic motivation, which is what the existentialist claims.

By contrast, notice that both the maximally inclusive and virtue-inclusive accounts of the highest good imply that the man in Kraut's example could still be regarded as fulfilling his material telos when he puts off some scientific research to help his aging parent, because his eudaimonia involves a balance of contemplative and ethical virtues, including justice, fidelity, and what the Greeks called "piety." Thus the son who abandoned his father (who had no one else to turn to, whom the son could easily help, etc.)[52] in order to pursue more theoretical research would actually be making himself worse off: by his being unjust, unfaithful, or impious (among other possible characterizations of this action), his character is marred, and he fails to achieve that harmonious balance of activities and states that constitutes his own happiness in the holistic sense. This is the sort of answer that is widely regarded as characteristic of eudaimonism, both as an approach to providing a theoretical foundation for normative ethics and as answer to the question, "Why be moral?" It also clearly seems to be the sort of answer implied by Aristotle's statements that a person who dies for his friend's sake "does indeed choose something great and fine for himself," and that one who sacrifices money for his friend's sake "awards himself the greater good" (*NE* IX.8 1169a26–29). Instead, if Kraut is correct, then Aristotle's view is closer to Scotus's, who held that the "appetites" for happiness and for justice were distinct and irreducible sources of human motivation (see chap. 11).

Let's return, then, to Purinton's virtue-inclusivist alternative. In his carefully reasoned paper, Purinton summarizes and evaluates the debate begun by Hardie[53] and Ackrill,[54] who focused on the passage concluding the function argument, where Aristotle says:

> Now each function is completed well by being completed in accord with the virtue proper [to its kind]. And so the human good proves to be activity of the soul in accord with virtue, and indeed with the best and most complete virtue, if there are more virtues than one. (*NE* I.7 1098a16–18)

Perhaps this is the wrong place to start, since at this point in the text, Aristotle is trying to work *from* his formal criteria for the ultimate good *to* a specific material conception of eudaimonia as the first interpretation of that good. In my view, the meaning of "the best and most complete virtue" should thus be understood as whatever combination of excellences allows us perfectly to fulfill our natural function, which will be equivalent (so Aristotle has argued) to achieving our ultimate good as *already* defined, that is, as the comprehensive good. Still, it would be implausible for Aristotle to think that a single dominant virtue (e.g., theoretical wisdom) could constitute the highest good defined as a holistically inclusive or maximally comprehensive end; if the highest good is comprehensive in my sense, then so must be the unified virtue that realizes or constitutes it. Hence what Aristotle means by "the best and most complete virtue" is obviously closely related to his concept of the uniquely highest or ultimate good.

In his analysis of the debate about *NE* I.7 1098a16–18, Purinton defends a qualified version of Ackrill's reading against Hardie, who maintains that Aristotle's explicit view makes happiness the first-order good of contemplative activity (whose virtue is exclusively *sophia*), and "not an inclusive end, i.e., a '2nd-order' good which includes a plurality of harmoniously balanced 1st-order goods."[55] Purinton's main aim is "to show that Ackrill was right and Hardie wrong about the identity of 'the best and most τέλειος virtue.'"[56] He begins by explaining the dilemma resulting from the fact that Hardie and Ackrill each seem to have convincing criticisms of the other's interpretation. I note only the most telling of these criticisms: (a) when Aristotle says, "if there are more virtues than one" then the best *of these* will be the human good, this seems to exclude some (first-order) virtues; yet (b) only on the inclusivist reading can the conclusion possibly follow from the premises of the function argument or agree with the *Eudemian Ethics*, "where it is quite clear that he means to claim that happiness is activity in accordance with whole virtue."[57]

Two responses to (a) leap to mind. First one might simply say (what nobody seems willing to suggest) that probably here Aristotle is just guilty of a misleading bit of phrasing. Although this is never impossible even in the greatest writer, this suggestion is usually resisted on the grounds that it is more charitable to read Aristotle as cleverly anticipating his argument in Book X that the most *eudaimon* life is one of pure contemplation. Second, one might say that Aristotle leaves open the hypothetical "if there are more virtues than one" not to assert that there *is* a simple multiplicity of virtues without any unity, anymore than he wanted to assert earlier that there is a simple multiplicity of final ends without any unity. Both virtues and ends can be viewed on two levels: their surface multiplicity and their underlying unity. Since Aristotle later defends the idea that virtues form a whole or unity, he ought to think of this whole as transcending in value any single virtue considered in isolation from the whole.

Purinton's response is a good deal more sophisticated. He argues that the second part of Aristotle's definition of the human good, beginning with "if there are more virtues than one," is meant to clarify the first part of this definition by excluding the virtues of the nutritive and sensitive faculties of the irrational part of the soul. Thus "happiness is not an activity in accordance with these lesser virtues, but is rather activity in accordance with 'the best and most perfect virtue,' viz., again, the distinctively human virtue, the virtue of the rational faculty."[58]

Ackrill, then, was fundamentally right, but he erred in accepting his critics' view that in the phrase, "if there are more virtues than one," Aristotle "is raising the possibility that there are more distinctively human virtues—i.e., more virtues of the rational faculty—than one."[59] If instead Purinton is right that this phrase simply accommodates excellences of the nutritive and sensitive parts, then Aristotle is not identifying the good that it is our natural function to realize with one division of distinctively human virtues (the moral or intellectual, and their various components). We can explain what Aristotle is excluding in a way that is consistent with identifying our material telos with the whole formed by the unity of all distinctively human virtues. Moreover, on this reading, Aristotle's conclusion follows from his premises in the function argument.[60] Finally, Purinton argues that at the beginning of NE X.7, "activity in accordance with virtue" refers to human virtue as a whole, which is our telos, according to his reading of the function argument; and Aristotle's statement that "it is reasonable that it be in accordance with the best virtue" is a further conclusion not present in I.7, referring to *sophia* as "the best of the virtues of the rational part of the soul."[61] Although Purinton agrees with Kraut "that in NE 10 Aristotle is distinguishing two distinct species of happiness (rather than describing two elements of a single mixed life)," he rejects Kraut's contention that these two species of eudaimonia are the referents of the two formulations of the human good in NE I.7 1098a16–18.[62]

I find this analysis insightful and would add to it only Ackrill's view that eudaimonia also includes intrinsic goods external to virtuous activity (which, as we saw, Purinton rejects). As I said in reply to Kraut, I think that later in Book I.8, Aristotle clarifies that those activities constituting our natural function comprise only the most vital part of eudaimonia, not the whole of it. So I am not persuaded by Kraut or Purinton that none of the external intrinsic goods are constitutive parts of the ultimate good (as formally defined in Book I). The opposite (maximally inclusive) view seems to me to follow from the erosiac model of desire underlying Aristotle's eudaimonism and from other passages, such as "no one would choose to live without friends, even if he has all the other goods" (NE VIII.1, 1155a2–3)—which clearly implies that the combination of "all the other goods" without friendship would not be self-sufficient.

Certainly Aristotle regards some of the external goods (such as wealth and power) only as instrumentally necessary preconditions for virtuous activity, without constituting any part of happiness by themselves (as Irwin has also argued).[63] But others, such as health, friendship, and perhaps even a challenging career, are better considered parts of eudaimonia as well as instrumental to virtuous activity. If none of the external intrinsic goods were part of eudaimonia, then the main distinction between Aristotle's position and the Stoics, as it was understood in antiquity (e.g., in Cicero's *On Moral Ends* [*De finibus*]) would vanish. Whether I am right on this point or not, however, will make little difference to my critique of eudaimonism, which will apply equally well to Purinton's model, which includes only human virtues, and to maximally inclusivist models.

3. The A-Eudaimonist System: An Idealized Aristotelian Model

Given the difficulties in exegesis and significant disagreements among leading Aristotle scholars about his meaning in key passages, it will be useful to abstract from these historical questions by stating a version of eudaimonist moral psychology that is at least a promising approximation to the foundational claims of the *Nicomachean Ethics*, whose adequacy we can evaluate using contemporary analytic methods. Again, my goal is to lay out what I think to be the *most defensible* version of a recognizably eudaimonist psychology in the mode of Aristotle or Aquinas (rather than, say, the Stoics) and then show that this best possible eudaimonism still fails on the basis of internal problems. I will call this ideal reconstruction "A-eudaimonism."

I begin with the important point that teleological or final causation is not limited to contexts of experienced desire (or *orexis*). A teleological explanation can apply whenever certain kinds of functional analyses are irreducible in explaining why something moves or changes as it does and/or why it is a good or deficient instance of its kind.[64] However, human beings differ from other living things that automatically develop toward fulfillment of their telos unless external interference prevents it. Rather, in human beings, final causation works through a more complex psychic system of desires leading to voluntary action. Therefore, in any system a motivational telos universal to human beings must be an activity or state T, such that:

(a) it is our natural function or "design" to attain T; and
(b) we can acquire motives to act with T as our final goal or end but can also fail to be motivated in the ways necessary to move toward T.

Call this the *common notion* of any motivational telos. Without the notion of some kind of nature, function (*ergon*), or design, the term "telos" can be used only metaphorically. This notion is shared by more than one *formal concept* of the human motivational telos (or "formal telos" for short), each of which defines such a telos in terms of its most fundamental relation to human motives. The A-eudaimonist system begins with the *erosiac* formal concept of the human telos, which has the following features:

I. The subjective psychological experience of desire for our telos. We apprehend our telos as that state the achievement of which would be maximally fulfilling; we anticipate the possibility of feeling complete, lacking nothing desirable at all. Hence the desire to realize our telos, which is built into our nature and essential to us (even if we do not reflectively thematize it as such), is a subjective psychological state that we can discover in ourselves as a desire for holistic satisfaction, or as a desire for perfection.

II. The formal egoism of the desire for our telos. Since we anticipate that this is a *good* of or belonging to the agent herself, we anticipate consuming or appropriating the satisfaction it involves—although this consummation will be ongoing.

III. The relationship between our formal and material telos. These first two features can be used to define our formal telos: it is our final, unconditionally complete, and self-sufficient end. For F to be our formal telos, then, F must embrace all the goods we can rationally pursue, and pursuit of F must underlie all our other motives, such that:

A. Whatever we are motivated to pursue, we pursue either as a means to, as part of, or under the aspect of F. Even if this is only implicit, because the motivation to pursue F is not consciously recognized by the agent as the necessary underlying condition of her motivation to pursue other final ends, it can normally be recognized through due reflection by the agent.

B. We may not always pursue our *true material telos* (M), that is, the good(s) in which our formal telos F actually consists, or that which constitutes or causes F to be realized for us. This is partly because the content of M may not be apparent to us even if we understand our desires as pointing to some embracing good (F) that would be completely fulfilling, and partly because other appetites may overwhelm our rational desires for M even when we gain some understanding of it.

According to A-eudaimonism, then, our material telos M is defined relative to our formal telos F, which is the more fundamental concept. By themselves, however, these conceptual definitions make no existence claims. A-eudaimonism is further committed to the view that something in our experience actually answers to this definition of our formal telos:

The Jointure-of-all-Motives Thesis: There is exactly one unified good F that fits the definition of our formal telos: the motivation to pursue F embraces all our motives, in the sense that they can all be seen as parts of, or expressions or instantiations of, the motivation to pursue F.

While desire for this one good F is necessarily our most fundamental desire, according to A-eudaimonism, we do not automatically know what F actually requires or consists in for beings like us—and this is precisely why proper training of our dispositions and the associated practical wisdom that Aristotle calls *phronesis* are necessary for any pursuit of our telos to stand a decent chance of success. This point helps show why A-eudaimonism is compatible with a kind of libertarian freedom. As Copleston explains, Aquinas holds that anything a human being wills is willed as a real or apparent good, "but he does not necessarily will the actual infinite Good," for he can "allow something other than God to appear to him as the source of happiness."[65]

This is also why there is room for philosophical reflection and debate about what M really is.[66] For example, Aquinas's primary disagreement with Aristotle is about what M is; he thinks it requires union of our speculative intellect with God in a mystical vision of the true divine nature. But he agrees with the jointure thesis that I attribute to Aristotle. For he says that every person "necessarily desires happiness" because the "common notion of happiness is that of a perfect or complete good," and by this he means F as I have defined it: "the perfect good for a man is whatever wholly satisfies his will. Hence to desire happiness is simply to desire that one's will be wholly satisfied, and this everyone desires." This is different from describing "the object in which happiness consists," by which he means our material telos.[67]

As I read them, neither Aquinas nor Aristotle acknowledges that there is really room for intelligent philosophical disagreement about whether the jointure thesis itself is correct.[68] They also seem to take as relatively obvious or uncontroversial a closely related but arguably distinct thesis essential to their ethical systems:

> **The Eudaimonia Thesis:** F is *eudaimonia* (the agent's happiness in its maximally holistic sense), and thus our all-embracing motive is orektic desire for *eudaimonia*.

I distinguish the jointure thesis and the eudaimonia thesis because, interestingly, the latter begins to specify the content of F, albeit only in the most general way. The eudaimonia thesis also clearly involves commitment to the strong erosiac thesis: since our fundamental embracing desire is erosiac in form, all human motivation is ultimately erosiac in form. This is less clear with the jointure thesis, which claims only that there is a unified, all-embracing motive (and correlatively, a uniquely all-embracing goal). In principle, this could be true even if this embracing motive was not erosiac in form, for example, if it were an intrinsic tendency toward some ideal of rationality. However, when the all-embracing good mentioned in the jointure thesis is defined according to the erosiac concept of F, then F must be the comprehensive object of erosiac desire; so the erosiac concept of F along with the jointure thesis implies the strong erosiac thesis.[69]

Thus as I construe it, the eudaimonia thesis does not follow analytically from the definition of our formal telos. I regard the identification of eudaimonia as our formal telos as a *synthetic* claim. I believe Aristotle concurs, for at the point where he says that happiness seems to answer to his prior description of the "most complete" end of human life, he does not seem to take this as following self-evidently from the concept of an ultimate good but only as generally admitted and as the best available first approximation to something fitting the abstract properties of our formal telos, given the available data in our experience.[70] Of course, this presupposes that there is some way to interpret "eudaimonia" in the eudaimonia thesis that does not simply *define* it as "our formal telos." However, on my construal, eudaimonia is intimately related to the erosiac concept of our formal telos, since the latter is defined above as something that *would* perfectly satisfy an all-embracing orektic desire, an erosiac desire underlying all other motives, *if there is one*. Eudaimonia could then be defined as the object of such a desire, since maximally holistic happiness would leave no significant good lacking in the agent. That there is such an all-embracing orektic desire would seem to follow, not from the strong erosiac thesis by itself, but only from this taken together with the jointure thesis. Given these two, then all our motivation traces to orektic desires, and these are joined together in one all-embracing or comprehensive orektic desire, which is by definition the desire for eudaimonia. Then, given the erosiac definition of our formal telos, the eudaimonia thesis will follow. We can summarize this reconstruction of the A-eudaimonist system in the form of the following argument to the eudaimonia thesis:

The A-Eudaimonist Core Argument

1. *The weak erosiac thesis (WET)*: all prepurposive motives (PPMs) are generically erosiac in form.
2. *The transmission principle:* our intended purposes inherit all the content and strength of their motivation from our PPMs.
3. *The strong erosiac thesis (SET)*: all human motives are generically erosiac in form [from 1 & 2].
4. The erosiac concept of our formal telos (F defined in maximally inclusive terms as the comprehensive good sufficient to satisfy all erosiac desire) [conceptual definition based on 3].

5. *The jointure thesis*: there is an embracing good that constitutes our formal telos; our attitude toward this good embraces all human motivation.
6. All human motives are joined in a single, all-embracing erosiac desire for a comprehensively satisfying end, in the realization of which we will lack nothing desirable [from 4 & 5].
7. Eudaimonia: a comprehensively satisfying state, in the realization of which we will lack nothing desirable [conceptual definition].
8. *The eudaimonia thesis*: eudaimonia is the good that constitutes our formal telos [from 6 & 7].

In practice, of course, the Jointure and Eudaimonia theses always go together as essential aspects of A-eudaimonism, but it is heuristically valuable to distinguish them in order to help explain why each of these aspects of A-eudaimonism is subject to distinct criticisms. But whether this identification of our formal telos with eudaimonia is a further synthetic claim in addition to the jointure thesis that human beings have a formal telos recognizable as such in their experience, or whether these are seen as analytically related parts of a single thesis, in neither case is eudaimonia by itself a description of our *material telos* (M). So further claims that specify the content of M beyond identifying it with eudaimonia remain synthetic relative to the eudaimonia thesis.

This brings us to the point that, in addition to these fundamental theses of A-eudaimonism, we have Aristotle's more specific claims concerning the content of M, or the nature of the ideal life that will in fact realize F. This account of M begins with Aristotle's famous function argument in *NE* I.7, is developed in his critique of alternative beliefs about M in popular thought and rival ethical theories, and is completed in his account of the different practical and intellectual virtues and their unity. As Susanne Hill says, Aristotle holds that we will be fulfilled only by the "characteristic activity of human beings," which is "the best and most complete rational activity of which human agents are capable."[71] Although most of what is interesting for normative ethics in Aristotle is found in these parts of his account, it is important to note that someone could differ with Aristotle's detailed characterization of M while still accepting the essential claims of A-eudaimonism, on which I focus.

However, since on my reconstruction, eudaimonia is not just analytically defined as our formal telos, and thus the eudaimonia thesis is a synthetic claim, the A-eudaimonist must certainly regard the eudaimonia thesis as *a start* on filling out the content of M. That our formal telos is identical to eudaimonia, whatever that requires, provides the leading proleptic clue in discerning the content of M: every further claim about M must be referred to this criterion. Since Aristotle goes on to argue that what constitutes eudaimonia for us must be the complete fulfillment of *our nature* as persons, any position that we would call "eudaimonist" in moral theory today has to include some such role for the notion of "nature"—as already indicated above. Thus most A-eudaimonists will at least be committed to the following extension of the above core argument:

9. *The material thesis*: we have a material telos M (as defined above relative to our formal telos F): M is ontologically constitutive of F and epistemically distinct from F.
10. Our material telos M is that which really constitutes or realizes human eudaimonia, whatever people believe the path to happiness involves [from 8 & 9].
11. It is the nature of every organic natural kind to seek the full development and expression of its highest or most distinctive powers and capacities; thus sentient animals of every kind will remain unsatisfied if their distinctive powers are not expressed in activities natural to them [an implicit premise of the function argument].
12. *The naturalistic thesis*: human eudaimonia will be realized by whatever activities and states completely develop, exploit, and express the full potential of our *natural kind* or are required as necessary conditions of this complete development and expression of our full potential [from 10 & 11].

Aristotle certainly continues in the function argument to develop this line of reasoning with the idea that the full development and expression of our potential can be measured by looking at capacities that distinguish human beings as members of one natural kind from all other animals. But I will not include this argument as a fundamental part of A-eudaimonism, since it has been subjected by Bernard Williams to some obvious and still potent objections about "the moral *ambiguity* of distinctive human characteristics."[72] Moreover, it seems that contemporary followers of Aristotle who aspire to build a virtue ethics on eudaimonist grounds can offer other, less objectionable ways of filling out what the full development of our natural potential must involve, as a way of characterizing the contents of eudaimonia.

However, in the next two chapters, I argue that the best attempts to rest accounts of virtuous motivation on eudaimonist foundations all fail because the system of A-eudaimonism sketched in this chapter is subject to a paradox analogous to the paradoxes of material and abstract egoism presented in chapter 5. Virtuous motivation, as described by Aristotle and his contemporary followers, is not embraced in the required way by the agent's desire for her eudaimonia, but rather requires projective motivation.

7

The Paradox of Eudaimonism: An Existential Critique

Overview. This chapter is concerned primarily with eudaimonist conceptions of virtue and friendship and will interest anyone interested in aretaic moral theory. It argues that virtuous motivation is not only materially unselfish but also formally non-egoistic. Starting with two contemporary efforts to make sense of Aristotle's account of friendship, it argues that Aristotle conflates by-product goods and intentional goals. Aiming at our happiness as our highest end is self-defeating, since our happiness is in large part a by-product of motivating ourselves to pursue self-transcending ends or goals. Except for section 6, most of the discussion is not technical and should be accessible to anyone with an undergraduate-level background in Greek virtue ethics.

Introduction

The A-eudaimonist system constructed in chapter 6 provides a clear basis for formulating several important criticisms that have been raised against the eudaimonist project. These include what I believe is the decisive criticism that A-eudaimonism cannot accommodate the kind of moral motivation implied by the very conception of virtues for which it was supposed to provide the objective rational foundation. Together, as we saw, the Transmission principle and the weak erosiac thesis provide the psychological basis for Aristotle's eudaimonism. Yet when he tries to work out a conception of virtue, Aristotle describes forms of ethical motivation that cannot ultimately cohere with his eudaimonist framework. We will see this by exploring what I call the "paradox of eudaimonism," which arises from the formal egoism to which Aristotle's psychology commits him. The point of this critique is to provide a key piece of evidence against the strong erosiac thesis and for projective motivation. The existential conception of the striving will is supported by the argument that unless we enjoy this kind of motivational capacity, the central paradox of eudaimonism could not be avoided in real life, and persons would be trapped in self-defeating motives.

Although I strive to be faithful to Aristotle's texts, my main concern once again in this chapter is not historical but rather conceptual. On some points necessary for my critique, I simply give my own interpretation of Aristotle and postpone consideration of most rival readings until later. Although my primary goal is to lay out the relevant problems, I try to stay with uncontroversial interpretations of Aristotle's main moral and psychological concepts. The existential critique of A-eudaimonism will allow me to relate the existential conception of striving will to important ideas in contemporary neo-Aristotelian ethics and psychology. Thus the critique of A-eudaimonism continues into chapter 8, which considers some important contemporary reconstructions of eudaimonism to see if they can avoid the paradox.

I. Elements of the Pure Motive of Virtue

The central problem raised by the A-eudaimonist system as I have sketched it in the previous chapter is that the formal egoism it involves seems to be deeply incompatible with both our contemporary everyday notions about moral motivation and Aristotle's own account of virtue. For in treating eudaimonism as a system explaining human motivation in terms of D3 desires, I have certainly implied that virtue as classically conceived[1] is formally embedded in the agent's concern for her own well-being, which, however enlightened, is still a formally egoistic orientation. For example, Aquinas embeds virtue in the desire for eudaimonia when he says "the true reward of virtue is happiness, for which the virtuous work is done."[2] Yet I also agree that Aristotle holds—and even goes out of his way to emphasize—that virtuous motivation involves what I call a "pure" concern for "the noble" (*kalon*) for its own sake, as opposed to advantage and pleasure as categories of first-order goods pertaining directly to the agent's material well-being. For he says that we may *do* what, outwardly, the virtuous person would do without doing it from virtuous motives:

> if acts that are done in accordance with the excellences [*aretai*] have themselves a certain character it does not follow that they are done justly or temperately. The agent must also be in a certain condition when he does them; in the first place he must have knowledge,[3] secondly he must choose the acts and choose them for their own sakes,

and thirdly his action must proceed from a firm and unchangeable character.[4]

Thus a virtuous motive is a stable disposition to choose the right act for these circumstances *because* it is (the relevant species of) the noble act in the circumstances (i.e., it is courageous, just, generous, friendly, etc.)—not because it makes us better off. For example, the brave man who encounters terrible dangers "will face them for the sake of what is noble, for this is the end of excellence [virtue]."[5] The virtuous person values a certain end under a description involving the relevant kind of nobility (in this case, courageous action) intrinsically, not instrumentally, and *only* this "pure" motivation contributes to eudaimonia.[6] In general, we may summarize the doctrine of *Nicomachean Ethics* (*NE*) II.4 (with some expansion) as a definition of virtuous motivation with the following three criteria:

Aristotle's Definition of Virtue

A. The agent must have practical knowledge of what is right/noble/appropriate in the case (the practical wisdom called *phronēsis*).

B. The agent must desire to do what is noble for its own sake, form the intention to act on this desire, and so act (unless prevented by coercion or circumstances for which she is not responsible).

C. This desire must be a fully formed motivational state of the agent, following from a firm disposition to desire and choose (different species of) the noble.

So understood, virtue has both motivational and epistemic sides: the disposition to choose actions based on an entrenched desire for the *kalon* (or its species: the generous, the just, the courageous, etc.) along with practical wisdom to distinguish what the noble thing is in the circumstances together produce *prohairetic* "choice" of the particular action.

As we have seen, Aristotle also makes two other claims that can be usefully distinguished from his core definition of virtuous motivation:

D. The rational disposition to desire and choose the noble, along with the practical wisdom to discern the noble (which reciprocally require and support each other), will both be hindered by uncontrolled D1 and D2 appetites and passions; and

E. What the noble (temperate, just, magnificent, friendly, etc.) thing to do is in a given situation cannot be defined by any simple rules, but we can learn it from role models who function as paradigm cases for us and (on the analogy of the arts) we can recognize it by looking for "the mean" between actions that are extreme in one sense or another.

This briefly summarizes how Aristotle arrives at his capsule formula that virtue is a stable disposition to choose moderate or intermediate actions, defined relative to us, as a practically wise person would recognize them (*NE* II.6 1107a1–3).

Now, parts D and E of this doctrine both raise well-known problems about the concept of "the mean" and control of the passions, and part C likewise raises questions about what kind of voluntary control the agent could have over the development of her own entrenched (or even fixed) motivational dispositions.[7] I will put these objections aside until later in order to focus on part B. In interpreting B, however, we must be careful with the level of self-consciousness about virtue that is involved in acting for the sake of the noble.

It is sometimes suggested that a virtuous agent could act virtuously in doing a particular action A without any thought of doing A *as virtuous*. For surely the disposition to choose the noble makes such action spontaneous and unreflective for the thoroughly virtuous agent? But this reading involves a basic confusion: since virtuous action has to involve *choice* in Aristotle's sense, it cannot consist in blind unthinking reactions; it cannot be "habitual" in *that* modern sense. This is what Williams means when he writes that virtue is "an intelligent disposition. It involves the agent's exercise of judgment, that same quality of practical reason, and so it is not simply habit."[8] Similarly, von Wright argues that "the specific virtues do not answer specific act-categories" because they require judgment about the particular act;[9] therefore "To regard the virtues as habits would be to misunderstand the nature of virtues completely."[10]

How we are to characterize virtuous disposition is tricky. Broadie rightly urges that we understand acting "for the sake of the noble" as doing the act in a particular spirit, that is, with "a sense of owing it to oneself to do what is right or best even when this is costly" or otherwise difficult.[11] But she adds:

> It may be that an agent who responds in this spirit will generally respond in this spirit, but on no occasion does this manner of response depend per se on the agent's seeing himself at the time as one who generally responds this way, or on seeing himself as "exercising a virtue." Clearly he must take himself to be doing what is appropriate, and in some sense he knows that he cares about that. . . . Virtue entails general dispositions to act in this way, and with this knowledge [that it would be shameful not to], in particular cases. But to have this disposition, it is not necessary that one think of oneself as having it; and to exercise it, one need not see oneself as having it, or value one's action as the exercise of a virtuous disposition.[12]

This perhaps needs some clarification. The virtuous agent must make use of some kind of thick ethical descriptor in evaluating the act as "noble," and this will correlate with our external description of her motive as virtuous; for example, when the agent thinks, "If I don't rescue him, he will die," or "Because important principles or a person's welfare are at stake, I must stand firm despite the danger," *we* call her first-order motive courageous. But she need not think, "It would be *courageous* to stand firm," since this is really a second-order reflection on the first-order motive just described. This is what Broadie means when she says, "The agent in action must focus on the objects and circumstances of his action, in a manner that cares that his response to them is right. This is different than focusing on his own engagement in virtuous activity."[13] In this sense, the agent avoids having "one thought too many" in acting on virtuous motives. The agent is focused on the world and on judgments concerning the outward-looking properties of his various possible actions, rather than focused on his own moral self-image. As Pincoffs argues, then, the virtuous person is not moved primarily by what John Dewey called "spiritual egotism."[14]

Yet this also must be further qualified. As the two thoughts above suggest, there are different levels of articulation in virtuous intentions. In some cases, discernment of the right action may require more reflection on self, that is, on what we can or should undertake, given our personality, past track record, and so on—and this could involve at least tacit judgments about our own moral worth. In a more general sense, if virtuous action requires choosing the act primarily because of the thick ethical descriptors that the agent applies to it, then he will always-already have a *tacit* (or nonthetic) understanding of the virtuousness of this act—in much the same sense as a person engrossed by the chessboard in front of him may at that moment be entirely devoid of explicit Cartesian second-order judgments about his own consciousness and yet remain tacitly or *nonreflectively* aware of his own concentration on the game.[15] As a result, the agent acting on the motive of virtue in a given case will always be in a position to reflect on the *virtuousness* of this act, should such reflection be occasioned or demanded. As Broadie puts it, "if acting from a *prohairesis* is taking a practical stand, anyway on this occasion, as to the goodness of acting so, then presumably the stand includes recognition, in some sense, of the goodness of the disposition for such action."[16]

I think we can strengthen this point: the agent may not be focused on her own virtue, but she would not be disposed to choose the act for the sake of its thick ethical qualities in the circumstances were she not the kind of person who believes that choosing actions for this sort of ethical quality is *morally more admirable* than acting for first-order pleasure or material advantage. She may not be making this judgment in choosing the particular act, but she must be disposed to this second-order reflective endorsement of her first-order motive if she is really choosing the act primarily for its noble qualities. If this is right, it explains a bit better than Broadie's own analysis how Aristotle's conception of acting on the motive of virtue coheres with the account he gives of magnanimity and its unifying role among the virtues (which I discuss in sec. 3).

2. Annas and Kraut on the Motive of Virtue in Friendship

Given this interpretation of clause B in our definition of virtue, we can examine the central problem it raises: namely, how can virtuous motivation in this sense constitute the agent's performing her natural function and thus attaining (the most important part of) her eudaimonia? For it seems that the motive of virtue defined in B is not a D3 desire: although it involves an objective evaluation of a good to be obtained (and perhaps even a good that is always related to the well-being of some person or group of persons),[17] this good itself is not necessarily apprehended as part of the *agent's own* flourishing or chosen under this agent-relative description. Does this mean that my earlier analysis of Aristotle was unfair in concluding that *orexis* includes only the type of states I have described as D1, D2, and D3 desires? Should we now say that his *Ethics* implies that other *non-erosiac* types of "desire" are possible that, unlike D3 desires, do not even formally involve concern for the agent's own flourishing?

Julia Annas perhaps comes closest to raising this question in trying to make sense of the good person as "self-loving" in Aristotle's account of friendship—a discussion that she rightly sees as having fundamental implications for Aristotle's understanding of all the virtues (not only friendship).[18] She begins by arguing that Aristotle's point in comparing the agent's relations to himself and to his friend (in true friendship of noble character) is not to reduce the latter to the former. Although "self-love is psychologically primary," since Aristotle says that we wish good to ourselves "most of all" (*NE* VIII.7 1159a12–13), we still care about our friends for their own sake as well; thus "Concern for others for their own sake is thus not reduced to a form of self-love."[19] I agree, since Aristotle is clear that in common parlance, "To a friend, . . . it is said, you must wish goods for his own sake" (*NE* VIII.2 1155b31) and in his own view:

> complete friendship is the friendship of good people similar in virtue; for they wish goods in the same way to each other insofar as they are good, and they are good in their own right. . . . Now those who wish goods to their friend for the friend's own sake are friends most of all, for they have this attitude because of the friend himself [i.e., because

of his virtuous character], not coincidentally. Hence these people's friendship lasts as long as they are good; and virtue is enduring *(NE* VIII.3 1156b8–13).

Notice Aristotle's emphasis here on the idea that when friendship arises from such reciprocated goodwill, it fits the security-against-misfortune criterion of the ultimate good. This is precisely because such friendship is a paradigm species of pure love of the noble for its own sake; in this case, we value our friend's well-being and character simply because of his own ethical nobility or moral worth. Aristotle also famously contrasts this pure concern for the good of a deserving friend with any merely instrumental concern for others as a means to one's own pleasure or advantage: "Clearly, however, only good people can be friends to each other because of the other person himself [i.e., for his sake]; for bad people find no enjoyment in one another if they get no benefit [from the other]" (*NE* VIII.4 1157a19–20). The entire analysis of noble friendship in Book VIII draws on the account of virtuous motivation developed in Book II.4–6 and especially on condition B: the pure desire for the noble as a final end. As Aristotle says, "in purpose lies the essential element of virtue and character."[20]

But then, Annas asks, why in Book IX.8 does Aristotle seem to agree that loving oneself "most of all" would imply the sort of blameworthy egoism that always puts one's own interests first in any conflict? Annas suggests that although this does not follow, and hence there is no conflict between "the psychological primacy of self-love" and the importance of "moral and altruistic action" when circumstances call for them, Aristotle allows the connection because many people will assume that if self-love is our strongest motive, "then it seems reasonable to put one's own interests first."[21] So Aristotle allows at least the appearance of conflict here and needs to make sense of the idea that the virtuous person is a *moral* self-lover in a sense quite distinct from vicious types of selfishness or material egoism.

Aristotle diffuses the apparent conflict, according to Annas, by arguing "that true self-love consists in loving, and identifying yourself with, your practical reason, rather than loving bodily or external goods." Since the good of this rational part of ourselves is compatible with the same good in the friend, there is no zero-sum trade-off in the "competition" between virtuous persons for the fine or noble; competing for this "will be just what it is to act because of the noble, in a virtuous and unselfish way. . . . Thus true self-love is compatible with virtuous action aimed at the noble."[22]

Yet when Aristotle tries to explain how the proper self-love involved in virtue is compatible with the good person sacrificing life, money, honors, or other luck-subject goods for his friends, Annas admits that Aristotle's description of altruistic heroism implies an underlying desire for the agent's own moral glory.[23] And she is (rightly, in my opinion) not satisfied with Kraut's resolution of this issue, which says that the virtuous person will not unjustly aim to deprive his rivals of opportunities for noble action. The problem remains that Aristotle seems to make self-love more basic to human motivation than altruistic motives: "The more we stress the point that Aristotle has redefined the content of self-loving behavior, the more striking it remains that self-sacrifice is explained as being, formally, self-love."[24] I think this becomes more understandable if Aristotle is trying to reconcile his own demanding conception of virtuous motivation with the eudaimonist moral psychology he developed as a framework for his normative theory. But this does not mean that he succeeded.

On the contrary, Annas recognizes the seriousness of the problem about how virtuous motivation can count as formally egoistic or self-loving in the ideal eudaimonist sense. How, she asks, can these fit together in the agent's thought or motive process from the first-personal point of view?

> Is the agent supposed to think "I'll sacrifice this money so that my friends can gain more, for that is a generous action, and so noble; and I'm sacrificing mere money and gaining the noble, so I'm assigning myself the greater good, and so come off best after all"? There is clearly something wrong with this thought; the second half undermines the first. The agent cannot give as his end in doing something *both* that he is helping his friends for their sake, *and* that he is assigning himself the greater good of acting virtuously.[25]

Annas is right that something is deeply awry here, but she does not fully capture the problem. So it is easy for Kraut simply to deny that there is any inconsistency between the two parts of the virtuous agent's experienced motive as Annas described it. In his reply, Kraut says, "there is nothing incoherent or morally questionable about mixed motivation: one can be aware of the fact that one is acting both for the sake of others and for one's own sake."[26]

Now, Kraut is entirely correct if he is speaking about cases in which the agent has as her intended goals two (or more) first-order goods, one of which is materially related to her own well-being and another of which is not (say, because it is solely a part of another person's material welfare). Such cases are entirely familiar and unremarkable in human life. For instance, suppose that I lobby my township to replace the crumbling curbs on the block where my house sits. It would be perfectly intelligible if I had multiple motives for doing this: partly for my own aesthetic satisfaction, partly to improve the value of my home, and *also* partly for my neighbors' benefit. A pure egoist, by contrast, would not care about the latter but would lobby for new curbs only for his own material and psychological gain, accepting the benefit to his neighbors as an unintended (albeit probably expected) side effect. But suppose that in my case, the neighbors' good really is one of my final ends. Probably one sufficient condition of this (although perhaps not a necessary one)[27] would be the truth of the following kind of counterfactual: if I lost my self-interested motives for this action, all else being equal, I would still lobby for new curbs, given my intention to do this for my neighbors' benefit. If so, then it seems reasonable to say an altruistic motive was in fact operative in my action alongside self-interested motives.

In addition, I think we can also make sense of cases in which the agent acts to produce some first-order good belonging to another person (or constituting part of his or her welfare) *both* as an end-in-itself *and* as an instrumental means to some further first-order good that might be self-related. Although such double-motive cases are a little less familiar and perhaps occasion more doubt, on reflection I think they prove intelligible. For instance, suppose I decide to take a business associate out to lunch both to thank him for his work on a project that I have been involved in and because I hope that his enjoying a nice meal will encourage him to want to work with me again in the future. Of course, there is no perfect introspective certainty about one's own motives; I might wonder whether I really care about this person as a friend. But suppose, again, that in fact I would still be moved to take him out for a nice meal as a means to bringing him pleasure and communicating my gratitude even if he told me he was retiring and moving to a small island in the South Pacific, never to be heard from again. If so, then in the present case, in which I do expect him to remain in business and nearby, it seems that I aim at his gustatory pleasure and his enjoyment of my gratitude partly for their own sake and partly as a means to my own future opportunities. Although this might not seem as virtuous as acting solely on my other-regarding motives, it also seems clear enough that my action on these asymmetrical mixed motives is quite different from an action motivated solely by opportunistic desire for my own advantage with no concern at all about the business associate's welfare for its own sake.

This shows that Annas has not pinned down the problem, but *not* that there is no problem, as Kraut holds. For if the agent has two entirely independent motives, as Kraut suggests, then how can they be *unified* in the desire for eudaimonia? As we saw in discussing the weak transcendent principle, it would be implausible to postulate that desire for any noncomprehensive end must *also* be desired as an instrumental means to the comprehensive good. And this is clear in the case of virtue: many acts that I might choose just because they are noble will have predictable results that do not add to my material well-being. So it is hard to see how they could also be desired as a means to my eudaimonia quite separately from (or in addition to) their nobility—as if I would still have some incentive to do them quite apart from my virtuous motivation. Rather, it is only plausible that their nobility *itself* will contribute to my eudaimonia. This illustrates again why the weak transcendent principle cannot by itself guarantee unification, and so the idea of an embracing self-sufficient good must do that work. For this to succeed, the pure part of a mixed motive must somehow be brought under the embracing desire for eudaimonia.

To see what this would require, imagine that we try to describe our example differently, as follows: the agent intends to fete her business associate in style in order to bring him enjoyment as a final end and chooses this as her final end *so that* he will appreciate how much she cares about him and hence give her more business. If this worked, it would avoid the problem of unification arising from the *separability or independence* of double motives, for now the agent's motives are not genuinely mixed, in the sense that either would give the agent *some* incentive to action if the other ceased to operate (even if it might not by itself move her all the way to decision or action). This counterfactual condition is not met in our unusual case where we try to produce *motives themselves* as a means to some further end. But, having grasped the unification horn of the dilemma, we now run into the other horn: in our revised description, the case is no longer intelligible because it tries to tell us that the agent intends a certain (other-regarding) end *as final* yet does this *as a means* to another (self-regarding) goal.

Our unintelligible case is one of the unusual class in which motives, or some aspect of them, are used as a means: our agent seems to want the *very finality of* one of her ends to serve as a means to something else. But this makes no sense; I can certainly intend some end G as a final end *and* as a means to some further end H (then I have two independent motives) but I cannot intend *the finality* of G itself as a means to H. In that case, my G-seeking motive is not independent of my H-seeking motive, and thus G cannot be final after all. The attempt to use G's finality as a means to H is a pragmatic contradiction.

We could perhaps render our case intelligible if we imagine that the agent plans to condition her own psyche in some way to produce genuinely altruistic interest in her business associate's good, knowing the benefits that her altruism will bring her. For this to work, she would have to forget the original reason why she began the process calculated to generate her altruism—which means that in unforeseen circumstances, it could lead her to act in ways inimical to the outcome that was her original goal. In such cases of *psychological self-manipulation*, as we may call them, the agent simply acts on one motive at the outset (in this case, a self-interested motive) and as a result, she later acts on an entirely different motive (in this case, an altruistic one). The two relevant motives are temporally separate and causally sequential, not simultaneous mixed motives. But this kind of self-manipulation could hardly be what Aristotle has in mind in his account of formally self-loving yet virtuous action.

3. The Paradox of Eudaimonism: Desiring Eudaimonia as a By-Product of Virtue

This last case points toward the real tension in Aristotle's account of virtuous self-love, which Annas's description of the agent's thought did not quite reveal. The problem is analogous to the paradox of egoism as we analyzed it using Feinberg's and Elster's concept of satisfaction as a derivative *side effect* of willing other ends for their own sake. More specifically, the problem is that in explaining why the virtuous person can be considered a kind of decent self-lover (as the formal egoism of his eudaimonism requires), Aristotle appeals to types of fulfillment that are *essentially by-products* of virtue or that can arise only as effects of pursuing "the noble" for its own sake. For example, when he argues that the virtuous person "more than the other sort, seems to be a self-lover" since "he awards himself what is finest and best of all, and gratifies the most controlling part of himself, obeying it in everything" (*NE* IX.8 1168b29–31), he is manifestly conflating by-product effects with intended goals.[28] The fulfillment that comes from being true to one's natural function, or from ruling oneself in a way consistent with the dignity of one's human status, can only be the result of pursuing *other* goods for their own sake. Similarly, in the passage on which Annas focuses, Aristotle writes, "And so the good person must be a self-lover, since he will both help himself and benefit others by doing fine actions. But the vicious person must not love himself, since he will harm both himself and his neighbors by following his base feelings" (*NE* IX.8 1169a12–14).

Many times in his discussion of friendship, Aristotle emphasizes Socrates' chief idea that evil persons "destroy themselves" (e.g., because they "are at odds with themselves" and *akratic* because enslaved to addictive appetites; *NE* IX.4 1166b7–14). Yet it is clear that Socrates meant that evil persons do this *inadvertently* as a by-product of their motives, not intentionally (for that would contradict the fundamental postulate concerning human motivation in the *Meno* and *Euthydemus*), and Aristotle could not have thought otherwise. But then the parallel sense in which the good person aids himself must also be inadvertent rather than by design—and this explains the rather Socratic air of paradox that critics have found in these passages. For the true difference between the two kinds of "self-love" which Aristotle distinguishes is that the base sort involves intending everything as a means to one's own material well-being, while the noble sort involves desires for the noble in which the agent has no intention to benefit himself at all. Yet Aristotle's way of explaining the distinction seems to obscure rather than clarify this key difference.

In this crucial error, Aristotle is in good company, for he is simply following Plato's statements in the *Republic* IV that because the virtuous person achieves a kind of psychic harmony by ruling his appetites with his reason, he counts as a "friend to himself" (*Republic* IV 443d)—or as bringing himself good much as one brings benefits to one's friend. Although this is meant to conclude Socrates' answer to Glaucon and Adeimantos by showing finally that the just persons will be better off *internally* than vicious persons no matter what their external circumstances may be—and so justice is intrinsically valuable—Plato either does not see or wishes conveniently to ignore that taking this by-product psychological benefit of justice *itself* as our final end would be self-defeating, since this is *not* compatible with choosing just actions simply for their justice as an end-in-itself. Yet, even more than Aristotle, he thinks that clear knowledge of our telos will assure us happiness. As Socrates says to Thrasymachus in the *Republic* I, "Do you believe this is a small thing you try to define? Is it not rather the whole conduct of living, how each one of us may live the most profitable life?" (344E). This sounds very close to Aristotle's metaphor of the archer seeking a clear target to shoot at.

Likewise, Aristotle often speaks as if we could directly pursue such by-product fulfillments or desire them in the D3 sense as parts of our eudaimonia: "if it is more proper to a friend to confer benefits than to receive them, and it is proper to the good person and to virtue to do good . . . the excellent person will need people for him to benefit" (*NE* IX.9 1169b11–13). Strictly speaking, however, if the agent tried to do something for another person as a potential friend because he felt such a "need" or "desire" for something lacking in his life, then the other would rightly feel put off by being treated as a mere means to the agent's eudaimonia. By contrast, if I am truly acting for my friend's good as an end-in-itself, I am *not* doing it because "I need friends to benefit" (in order to be the kind of person I aspire to be or to gain the satisfaction I typically derive from helping my friend do well in some worthwhile endeavor—or however we care to characterize the relevant agent-related by-product goods of friendship). In sum, the right version of Annas's question would be: Is the agent supposed to think, "I'll sacrifice this money so that my friends can gain more, for that is a generous action, and *as a result* I'll gain the fulfillment that naturally comes from such generous action (for people disposed to desire the noble for its own sake), which is the greater good"?

To this version of the question, Kraut's response cannot apply, for the second part of the imagined thought unquestionably *does* undermine the first part. And this is because the agent proposes to pursue directly a self-related good Z that can arise only as a by-product of pursuing an independent other-related good Y as an end-in-itself. But outside of self-manipulation, there is no way the agent can make *pursuit-of-Y* as a whole into a means to anything else. She can pursue Y as a *means* to Z; but Y itself is not a product that brings about Z (since, by hypothesis, only the pursuit of Y for its own sake can bring about Z). Indeed, Aristotle himself sometimes seems to recognize that the pleasure that comes from virtue is a by-product that cannot be directly desired or pursued. Commenting on Aristotle's idea that the pleasure that "completes" virtuous activity is "a sort of consequent end" (*NE* X.4 1174b33), Paula Gottlieb says:

> According to Aristotle, true pleasure is not a directly motivating goal for the good person—it does not provide the reason why the good person enjoys the things she does. Rather, according to Aristotle, pleasure comes about as a result of the good person's having the appropriate attitudes to what is independently good. It is not the cause but the result of the good person's caring about good things; it is a supervenient end (*epigignomenon telos*).[29]

As a point about the pleasure that forms a part of eudaimonia for the lover of virtue (*NE* I.8 1099a6–20), Gottlieb is right that it shows that Aristotle is not advocating any hedonistic form of material egoism, and Alasdair MacIntyre has made a similar point.[30] However, since the paradox of eudaimonism does not charge Aristotle with hedonism, the idea of by-product pleasure would have to be broadened to address that paradox.

This is what Annas does in the answer she gives to her own version of this paradox—an answer that recognizes the nature of the problem better than her explicit formulation did. She says that virtuous motives simply have the unintended effect of being in the agent's own best interests, and hence, from an external (third-person) perspective, we can understand the agent to be "doing" an action that is both noble and self-beneficial:

> The solution is surely that the agent's aim is just acting for the sake of others; in doing this he is in fact getting some good for himself, but this is *not part of his aim.* It is what he is doing in his whole life, which is directed at virtuous actions, and we could say that it explains his actions, but it is not his aim. Self-love of the right kind explains and justifies what the agent does, but it is not what motivates him.[31]

In other words, the virtuous agent's fulfillment is psychologically a *by-product* of her virtuous activities.[32] Strictly speaking, however, an agent only "does" an action under a description in which it is intentional for her, so on this account, it could only be in a *metaphorical* sense that what the virtuous agent is "doing" when she pursues the noble for its own sake is "realizing her own eudaimonia." It is also unclear in what sense we should say that this by-product benefit "explains" the action, since erosiac (or orektic) desire for it played no causal role in the agent's decisions, on Annas's solution. Nor, apparently, could the retrospective justification it provides come to play any motivating role without becoming self-defeating again. Hence although Annas's proposal is an entirely reasonable hypothesis about what actually happens in virtuous action and it accurately reflects Aristotle's demanding conditions on the "motive of virtue," as described above, it does not reconcile these phenomena with the system of A-eudaimonism. Rather, it implicitly rejects formal egoism and implies that an agent's acting for the sake of the noble is projectively rather than erosiacally motivated.

4. Why the Paradox Cannot Be Solved by Denying that Eudaimonia Motivates Virtue

To see that Annas's solution cannot save the A-eudaimonist project, we need to understand in more detail exactly why virtuous motives, as Aristotle himself describes them and as Annas explains them, are incompatible with the notion that all our motives are embraced by an underlying formally erosiac desire for eudaimonia as our all-inclusive end. To begin, let us recall that in chapter 5 we defined a "pure" motive as one that aims at some self-transcending first-order end for its own sake. Now, the pursuit of "the noble" involved in virtuous actions according to Aristotle (and the entire subsequent tradition of virtue ethics in Western philosophy) is clearly a pure motive in this sense, as condition B in the above definition of virtuous motivation implied.

This is Annas's main point in her fullest argument that ancient ethics is not objectionably egoistic, although all the main schools do hold that ethics begins in the agent's reflection on her own life and what is needed to improve it:

> For what I have to develop, in order successfully to achieve my final good, are the *virtues*. . . . Some have a direct connection with the good of others, most prominently justice, which may involve surrendering goods I want to others because they have a just claim on them; but all the virtues are dispositions to do the right thing [for its own sake], where this is established in ways that are independent of my own interests.[33]

Annas's point is *not* that according to ancient eudaimonists, it would be rational from the therapeutic perspective of an agent interested in improving her own life to forget this self-regarding purpose and develop altruistic or other-regarding motives instead—just as it might be rational in cases of deterrence to acquire and display to one's enemies an irrational D2 desire that prefers mutual destruction (even at the price of one's own demise) to submission to certain attacks.[34] Rather, in *The Morality of Happiness*, Annas again tries to resolve the paradox by arguing that a state or activity can form part of my good without my *intending it for this reason*: "There is no reason, *prima facie*, why the good of others cannot matter to me independently of my own interests, just because it is introduced as something required by my final good."[35] Similarly, in response to remaining doubts about egoism, she writes: "But it is no part of the theories we have seen so far that its forming part of my good is *the reason why* I should care about the good of others."[36] Thus the formal egoism involved in eudaimonism as Annas interprets it is entirely consistent with the purity of the motive of virtue:

> The straightforward claim that an ethics of virtue is egoistic, since the agent is concerned about developing her virtues as a way of achieving her final end, is straightforwardly mistaken. . . . An ethics of virtue is therefore at most formally self-centered or egoistic; its *content* can be fully as other-regarding as that of other systems of ethics.[37]

In other words, a pure virtue ethics can rest on a "formally egoistic" moral psychology, but only if we reduce formal egoism to a mere speculative thesis about the effects that the agent's virtuous motives and actions have on her own happiness, although knowledge of these effects plays *no motivational role* in the agent's psyche.

The main problem with this solution is that it means that recognition of the reflexive value of virtuous activity for its agent can *do no practical work* structurally or developmentally in making the agent virtuous. But then, what will be the point *for me* of recognizing, as Annas puts it, that "Achieving my final good, happiness, or whatever that turns out to be, will involve respecting and perhaps furthering the good of others"?[38] On her solution, it would seem that this discovery made while reflecting on my life could only be of *speculative* interest for me, because if it becomes one of my motives for respecting other persons, it will defeat itself by robbing my respect for others of its purity. This respect must be *independent* from any self-regarding motives of mine if it is to improve my own character as a reflexive by-product. So unless we imagine the agent engaging in a strategic game of self-manipulation, the recognition of the eudaimonistic value of pure or non-egoistic motivation is practically impotent from the agent's perspective, on Annas's reading.

At this point, we should recall the distinction between psychological eudaimonism (PE) and rational eudaimonism (REu) introduced in chapter I, section 3.2. Annas's solution seems to be to affirm REu without PE: the eudaimonistic by-product value of virtuous motives justifies these motives, but the agent does not pursue her noble ends for this reason (even if she recognizes it). I will call this combination *external eudaimonism* (EEu), since it holds that the practical reason justifying virtuous motivation (namely, its by-product contribution to the agent's happiness) is external to the agent's own motives for acting virtuously. Any version of EEu faces the thorny problem of explaining how the range of motives on which people act links up with the practical reasons for action that there are according to REu. In particular, it faces the problems of explaining how virtuous motives are generated and whether the agent acting on such motives has to see the ends pursued as justified for their own sake, apart from the by-product benefits that their pursuit might have for him. For example, one way to answer this question would be to concede that virtuous motives involve the projection of goals *qua* noble. This would yield a version of EEu that combines REu with the existential conception of willing. The main problem with this combination is that the projection of ends by the striving will assumes some practical reason for setting these goals, and it seems unlikely that the practical reasons to which the striving will responds in every kind of care or commitment it can form are eudaimonistic reasons.

In any case, Aristotle does not seem to consider such external eudaimonist options. As I emphasized earlier (chap. 6, sec. I.1), Aristotle explicitly asserts that a philosophical reflection on the nature of the highest good will have the highest practical value in helping us shape our lives, just as a clear sight of the target helps the archer shoot in the right direction (*NE* I.2 1097a24–26). And this makes perfect sense if he holds the eudaimonia thesis, according to which the desire for eudaimonia pervades and embraces our desire for every other type of final end, including the noble. For if this is right, an understanding of our material telos will show us what we ought to pursue or what we ought to care about. So Gottlieb is correct when she responds to Annas that "it is implausible to deny that Aristotle thinks that the desire for happiness is a motivating as well as a justifying and explanatory factor in human reasoning."[39] Similarly, Kraut says:

> I am not sure that we can find good textual grounds for attributing to Aristotle's moral agent the kind of self-forgetfulness that Annas' interpretation requires. On her reading, the excellent person does not take into account the point that the heroic action he is about to

perform will be good for him. . . . But as I read Aristotle . . . a moral agent should not be oblivious to comparisons between himself and others, but should instead try to outperform them. If this is correct, then it is perfectly in order for the moral agent who is sacrificing some good for others to reflect that in doing so he is winning something for himself that is better than what others get from him.[40]

I will support this reading with some independent evidence in the next section. But if Aristotle's virtuous agent is more self-conscious about the benefits virtues bring him than Annas's solution allows, then the main problem returns. As Williams says, the problem concerns the agent's attitude toward his own "excellences of character or virtues":

> A center of doubt gathers . . . on the point that when Aristotle seems most removed from modern ethical perceptions, it is often because the admired agent is disquietingly concerned with himself. Aristotle does allow that the good man needs friends, and indeed that friendship is part of the good life; but he finds it necessary to argue for this in order to reconcile friendship with the ideal of self-sufficiency.[41]

So Annas's EEu solution is not open to Aristotle, given his belief that the desire for eudaimonia can somehow motivate persons to a life of virtue. But aside from avoiding the disquieting self-concern implied by formal egoism, Williams has *another* reason for thinking that Aristotle should not have believed that the eudaimonist insight that virtues benefit their agent can do any *dialectical work* in the agent's deliberations. Perhaps the virtuous agent engaging in a philosophical review of his whole life can retrospectively recognize that the "state of well-being" is "constituted in part by the virtuous life":

> But this is not a consideration that one could use to any radical effect in practical reasoning, as he seems to suggest. One becomes virtuous or fails to do so through habituation. One should not study moral philosophy until middle-age . . . [because] only by then is a person good at practical deliberation. But by then it will be a long time since one became, in relation to this deliberation, preemptively good or irrecoverably bad.[42]

In effect, then, Williams thinks Aristotle's own account of moral development ought to move contemporary Aristotelians toward Annas's proposed solution—even if this means modifying some of Aristotle's central claims. But an account of virtues in which the desire for eudaimonia plays no dialectical role in moral development will no longer be eudaimonist in Aristotle's sense since it will reject the idea of an all-embracing desire for a holistically unified comprehensive good.[43]

5. Magnanimity as Aristotle's Answer to the Paradox

One reason to agree with Kraut that Aristotle could not accept Annas's proposal is that Kraut's moral competition model strongly agrees with Aristotle's own description of "magnanimity" (*meglapsychia*) as a special unifying second-order virtue involving a clear-eyed appreciation of our own character's moral worth along with the desire to be treated accordingly.

The interpretation of this virtue is controversial, since "one who thinks himself worthy of great things" may seem to have one thought too many (in Williams's famous phrase), *even if* he "is really worthy of them" (*NE* IX.3 1123b1–2). Surely some ways of dwelling on one's worthiness can reduce it. Yet Aristotle clearly implies that the virtue of magnanimity depends on other first-order virtues as dispositions to choose other first-order forms of "nobility" for their own sake: he says that "Magnanimity . . . would seem to be a sort of adornment of the virtues: for it makes them greater, and it does not arise without them. This is why it is difficult to be truly magnanimous, since it is not possible without being fine and good" (*NE* IV.3 1124a1–4). Here Aristotle is trying to give this quality—like each of the other virtues he discusses—a deeper moral meaning than it had in the common parlance of his culture (see *NE* IV.3 1124a20–b6): he wants his contemporaries to *transfer* the term they used for a particular kind of pride or sense of honor exemplified by aristocrats (and especially by timocratic warrior-chieftains in archaic times) *and* their admiration for this aristocratic quality to a very different quality that could be possessed by *any* moral person who consistently loves "the noble" (in the philosopher's new moralized sense). His logic is evident enough: since such a person loves the noble in all its forms, and the first-order dispositions to choose various kinds of noble first-order goods are *themselves* noble goods (of persons), he will naturally develop a second-order love of this kind of second-order noble good in himself and in others. (And since this love, which is what Aristotle means by *meglapsychia*, adds to his virtue, it makes his moral worth even greater, which in turn makes the goodness of his character all the more desirable for its own sake to him, etc.)

This conception of magnanimity is crucial to our analysis for two reasons, I think. First, it helps explain why Aristotle believes that the motive of virtue and the desire for eudaimonia are closely related. As a kind of inner sense of one's own worth that is resilient against being dishonored by worthless people, magnanimity is absolutely essential to the mature agent's eudaimonia, helping him be as secure from misfortune as possible and thus as self-sufficient as possible. For example, Socrates exemplifies magnanimity in Plato's *Apology*: his sense of self-worth is insulated from the jury's injustice. The central place of magnanimity in Aristotle's account is a clear indication, then, that eudaimonia is composed *in part* of a kind of reflective awareness of one's own virtue. As a result, the virtues consisting in stable dispositions to choose acts with various kinds of first-order nobility for their own sake will also contribute directly to the agent's subjective sense of his own life going well overall (a key part of his eudaimonia) *when magnanimity is added.* And since this awareness is also a stable disposition to love a particular sort of noble good and thus a virtue in its own right, it might even suggest to Aristotle that the fundamental desire for one's own eudaimonia could just be the desire to be able to be magnanimous, which would be the desire to love the noble in all its first- and second-order forms, or the desire to have all the virtues. This would provide one way of understanding how the desire for eudaimonia could *radiate into* the desire for noble actions, as the eudaimonia thesis requires.

Second, magnanimity, as analyzed here, is also the self-love that Aristotle connects so intimately with friendship, especially in the passages that brought us to the paradox of eudaimonism. In the discussion of friendship, once again Aristotle argues that only the agent who is good in the moral sense (choosing from pure motives) can truly have the excellence of friendship when it is properly understood (as opposed to popular conceptions of it). And he emphasizes that what a morally good person loves in his friend is precisely that friend's *moral character* (as opposed, say, to other features of his personality that might make him interesting or unique to us)—which is why Aristotelian noble *philia* sounds austere to contemporary readers.[44] But this is exactly what the magnanimous person also loves in himself and it is why he justifiably cares for his own good as an end-in-itself. This explains why Aristotle would say that the "decent person" has the same relationship to himself as he has to his friends (only more so) and that the friend is "another himself" (*NE* IX.4 1166a30–32), for the virtue of *philia* is roughly the same motive toward another person as magnanimity is toward oneself, in Aristotle's analysis. In both cases, it is a second-order love of first-order virtues of character. This reading also saves Aristotle from appearing to make the narcissistic claim that we can love only persons who are like us in contingent details of personality; rather he means that *philia* is shared magnanimity.

Magnanimity, the reflexive version of this love for the noble friend, is more fundamental only because Aristotle holds that being wholehearted, unified, self-controlled, secure in one's own identity, and comfortable with oneself (*NE* IX.4 1166a14–29) are prerequisites for being the best friend possible to others. But this is not only because, as Aristotle says, a person without these qualities will tend not to be controlled by desires for noble actions and hence will tend to use her friend for pleasure or advantage (as long as he can supply them) rather than loving him for his character, which is more permanent. It is *also* because a person with a secure sense of her own worth will be less *needy* and hence more ready to be openly giving to others.

There is a significant irony in this for eudaimonism, because it implies that it is precisely those who do not need friends to complete them who find it easiest to be true friends to others. Yet, interestingly, Aristotle inadvertently admits this in defending his answer to the puzzle in the *Lysis* (i.e., that similar persons make better friends than those with opposite qualities). He says, "The friendship that seems to arise most from contraries is friendship for unity, of poor to rich, for instance, or ignorant to knowledge, for *we aim at whatever we find we lack*" (*NE* VIII.8 1159b13–15, emphasis added). Thus friendship of utility is no problem for the erosiac model. By contrast, the person of complete virtue, being magnanimous, is as self-sufficient as a human being can be and hence lacks nothing (or as little as possible), and this is precisely what best suits him to act on a pure motive of *philia* toward his friend. Likewise, in the *polis*, where *philia* is extended to civic relationships, the ideal king (as opposed to the tyrant) "is self-sufficient and superior in all goods; and since such a person needs nothing more, he will consider his subjects' benefit, not his own" (*NE* VIII.10 1160b5–7). This should be compared to Plato's statement in *Republic* I that "no art or rule provides what is a benefit to itself" and that this is why craftsmen have to be paid a wage quite separate from the end of their craft (*Republic* 346E). No wonder, then, that when he tries to apply the logic of magnanimity to solve the puzzles about friendship left by Socrates, Aristotle finds that the tension between eudaimonism and the pure-motive model of virtue becomes harder to avoid.

At any rate, the central role of magnanimity makes clear that Aristotle thinks of conscious desire for one's own eudaimonia not only as *among* the virtuous agent's motives but also as *reinforcing* them through the satisfaction gained in magnanimous love of the enduring states that constitute one's own character, and the deep sense of allegiance to the best part of oneself that this affords. That virtuous dispositions will allow me to feel that I am affirming the best in myself is crucial to our desire for the noble, on this view. But here again, we find the confusion of by-product and intendable goal. For we cannot desire virtuous motivation itself *in order that* we may feel magnanimous about it. As Broadie concludes, if "the great-souled person's self-esteem refers to his other virtues," then it is in an important sense derivative, and so, "insofar as he acts from those other virtues, his actions do not express self-esteem."[45] This is exactly right, but Broadie does not see the problem it creates for Aristotle: the desire for eudaimonia, which is partly satisfied by magnanimity, cannot reinforce virtuous motivation by giving us another reason to be virtuous, as Aristotle apparently thought.

This error lies at the center of Aristotle's own answer to the paradox of eudaimonism.

Yet the importance of Aristotle's account of magnanimity in understanding his account of friendship and its problem is usually overlooked in the critical literature. For example, in his otherwise insightful analysis of Aristotle on friendship, Vasilis Politis questions Aristotle's claim that each person rightly loves himself above even his best friends.[46] Politis accepts the idea that "to aim at being virtuous" is a kind of proper self-love distinct from selfishness since it "involves an important altruistic dimension."[47] But he thinks the claim that one should cultivate such proper self-love as much as possible (which he calls the "weak supremacy thesis") should not lead Aristotle to the "priority thesis," which says that each should love himself *more* than he loves anyone else.[48] Specifically, "aiming as much as possible at performing fine and noble actions is a kind of self-love" since it perfects one's rational soul, which is, for Aristotle, our true self. But why does this intrapersonal perfection of self lead Aristotle to claim at *NE* 1169a34 that the virtuous or excellent person awards himself a "greater share" of noble actions, which requires an interpersonal comparison?[49]

Vasilis argues that the inference from the weak supremacy thesis to the priority thesis is invalid unless some further premise is supplied.[50] He considers but dismisses Kraut's suggestion that Aristotle is endorsing a competition for virtue in which each tries to outshine the other.[51] He also considers the suggestion that one can award only external goods (ones over which there can be a zero-sum competition) to one's friends, but he rightly rejects this because Aristotle insists that we can help each other to become virtuous.[52] Lastly, he considers the point that sacrifice of one's *true* good appears to be impossible in Aristotle—a point that I note follows directly from the formal egoism in Aristotle's conception of human motivation. Politis finds this idea both coherent in itself and rightly attributed to Aristotle but insufficient to justify the priority thesis.[53]

I think we already have the answer to Politis's mystery: since A-eudaimonism implies that ultimately all a human agent's motives are expressions or parts of her embracing desire for her own eudaimonia, there is necessarily an asymmetry between one's concern for elements of one's own eudaimonia (such as virtue) and elements of anyone else's eudaimonia. One can pursue the friend's good, in the end, only if that good itself, or the pursuit of it, is seen as *an aspect* of one's own comprehensive good. I think this explains why it is crucial for Aristotle that friendship is "self-referential, i.e., a friend is *my* friend," as Nancy Sherman has emphasized.[54] Hence it is impossible for the agent to make any sacrifice for the other that she would not see as enhancing her own eudaimonia. Aristotle gives no independent argument for the priority thesis because it follows from his first principles.

However, Aristotle is concerned to show that this implication of his eudaimonism holds up in a phenomenology of friendship; but to square his theory with experiences of altruistic motivation in friendship, he has to attribute to the agent a reflective concern with her own virtue that is highly problematic in its own right, as we have already seen. Although Politis ignores these difficulties, it remains paradoxical to call the virtuous person a self-lover.

6. Why the Paradox Cannot Be Solved by Second-Order Desire Subsuming First-Order Desire

I have argued that Aristotle errs in thinking that the paradox of eudaimonism can be explained by (1) treating the desire for eudaimonia as a second-order desire for certain kinds of pure first-order motives; and (2) holding that the second-order desire *embraces* these first-order desires. But since it is so crucial to my argument, this point deserves further examination to ensure that it is completely clear. I begin by considering Richard Kraut's treatment of eudaimonia in an insightful and justly famous paper in which he argues that for Aristotle, "*Eudaimonia* involves the recognition that one's desire for the good is being fulfilled, and therefore one who attains *eudaimonia* is necessarily happy with his life."[55] He explains how this sense fulfills a desire whose satisfaction is itself part of *eudaimonia*:

> We human beings . . . would never be able to attain our good with any regularity, unless we had effective desires for what we think worthwhile. Since we are creatures with strong desires for the good, as we variously conceive it, it is natural and inevitable for us to develop a deep interest in whether or not such desires are being satisfied. An animal with first-order desires, but no strong second-order interest in whether those first-order desires are being fulfilled, would not be fully human. Put otherwise: no person would choose a life in which he remains continually unaware of whether or not he possesses the good. . . . So a major human good is the second-order good which consists in the perception that our major first-order desires are being satisfied. And this second-order good is one we must have in order to be *eudaimon*.[56]

This description is perhaps slightly misleading, since any orektic desire for an end is *eo ipso* a desire for what is anticipated to *satisfy* the desire; it is not a desire for satisfaction as an effect *distinct* from the object itself but rather a desire for the object *as good for the agent* or *as satisfying* some salient lack (as I have argued). Hence to be distinct, the second-order desire that

Kraut mentions must be something like a desire to *know* that my deepest or best first-order desires are and probably will continue to be satisfied.

It is clear that the satisfaction of this second-order desire could be a major part of human happiness, as Kraut convincingly argues, but it is equally clear that this prospect cannot *itself* be what inspired the relevant first-order desires. On the erosiac model, they must arise from my sense that their ends are either means to or part of my well-being—not from my sense that a *desire for them* is one I can satisfy and know it. For if the latter were my reason, then what I desire is the satisfiable motivation to *pursue* certain first-order ends rather than these ends themselves. But that would be tantamount to desiring$_2$ to desire$_1$ some object X just because I know I can get some X.

This comes close to what Callicles proposes in the *Gorgias* when he argues that the happiest person is the one who constantly desires new things as soon as his prior desires are satisfied, just so that he can have more experiences of gratification (491e–92a).[57] If this were the recipe, eudaimonia could be achieved simply by fostering within ourselves a desire for the most diverse range of objects to which we happen to have easy access (e.g., blades of grass) and no others. But this would amount to a perverse kind of self-manipulation that is almost the opposite of what Aristotle advocates. The mere availability of some X by itself does not make X desirable in any D1-D3 sense. To be moved toward some X without having a prior desire$_1$ for X would imply that I had *projected* X, but it is doubtful that I could do this just because I believe I'll be able to satisfy this first-order motivation once I have it, as Callicles's proposal seems to require. What Kraut says, then, must be interpreted as follows to make sense:

    1. The *eudaimon* person cares about several worthwhile goals for their own sake.[58]

    2. The *eudaimon* person's (prospective and retrospective) knowledge of his success in realizing these goals that he pursues for their own sake contributes crucially to his overall *eudaimonia*.

So put, 1 and 2 can obviously both be true, but 2 still remains practically inert, or incapable of motivating the agent, just as in Annas's solution. For although 2 is a psychological experience from the agent's first-personal perspective, it cannot *explain* the truth of 1 for the agent, because even though 2 fulfills his natural second-order desire (as Kraut described it), the goals mentioned in 1 are by hypothesis *not* pursued because their realization will make 2 true. In other words, these first-order goals are not chosen because recognition of their achievement will satisfy the agent's second-order desire for eudaimonia. Indeed it is only because of their independent significance that the agent's successful pursuit of these goals *does* satisfy this second-order desire: the first-order desire must remain independent of any second-order desire that its own agent-regarding by-products can satisfy, if the successful pursuit of the first-order ends is actually to yield this by-product. In light of this example, we can define an important type of relationship between motives as follows:

> **The Subsumption Relation between Motives:** A first-order motive M_1 (for end X) is *subsumed* by a second-order motive M_2 (for end Y) when Y is either
>
> (a) the mere *existence* of M_1; or
> (b) the satisfaction of M_1 by the *realization* of X.

In simpler terms, the second motive subsumes the first when the process of experiencing, acting on, or satisfying the first motive realizes the goal of the second motive. We can say that the relation between these motives is "open" subsumption when (a) is true, and "closed" subsumption when (b) is true. However, both these relations presuppose that M_1 and M_2 are really distinct desires that could exist independently of each other; otherwise the second-order motive becomes just another way of expressing the first-order motive, in which case the former does not truly subsume the latter. We can explain this notion as follows:

> **The Independence Relation between Motives of Different Orders:** M_1 and M_2 are *motivationally independent* if and only if M_2 does not even partially explain the existence of M_1 by motivating the agent to acquire, develop, or foster M_1 as a means to satisfying M_2.

I can now formulate my response to Kraut more clearly. I have asserted the following:

> **The General Principle of Subsumption (GPS)**
>
> **Part 1:** Subsumption of a first-order motive M_1 under a second-order motive M_2 entails the motivational independence of the M_1 from M_2.
> **Part 2:** Subsumption of a first-order motive M_1 under a second-order motive M_2 entails the metaphysical dependence of M_2 on M_1.

In other words, the first-order motive can arise without the second-order motive, but not vice versa.[59] If GPS is true, it will now be fully clear why treating the desire for eudaimonia as a second-order desire that subsumes various pure first-order desires will not solve the paradox of eudaimonism. Yet GPS is a fairly strong principle because of its generality, and full defense of it is beyond the scope of this book. However, I will defend a narrower version of it that will serve for my present purposes.

Is there any way that Aristotelians could argue, against GPS, that subsumption does not entail independence of the first-order motive from the second-order motive? As we have seen, it makes perfect sense for both of the following propositions to be true in conjunction:

    3. Alfred cares about Jane for her own sake, or as an end-in-herself; and
    4. This caring makes Alfred's life better, happier, or more fulfilled and thus partially satisfies Alfred's natural desire for his own eudaimonia.

But can the truth of 4 somehow function as Alfred's *motive* for caring about Jane in 3? Can his presumably ultimate desire for his own eudaimonia or flourishing motivate or explain his caring about Jane in a way that makes him prepared to sacrifice other good things of his, such as external pleasures, power, or perhaps even his life itself, for Jane's sake?

A simplistic argument that this is impossible starts from the assumption that it is just contradictory for concern about any terminal end involving another's good to be related motivationally to the agent's own eudaimonia. I am not making this unsound argument, since my reconstruction of A-eudaimonism was meant to show why this assumption is mistaken. To say that M_1 somehow depends on M_2 in this case is not necessarily to say that Alfred undertakes the care described in 3 *only as a means* to his own happiness or flourishing—that obviously would be contradictory, since 3 says that he cares about Jane for her own sake. Rather, the relevant issue is whether he can come to care about Jane as an end having intrinsic or terminal value (as 3 says) and yet do this *because* he recognizes that caring about her as a final end will be a constitutive part of his happiness or flourishing (as per 4).

The question, then, is whether *motivation to pursue* agent-transcending goals that constitute no direct part of the agent's eudaimonia (such as Jane's well-being) can itself be caused or brought about by recognition that such a desire (at least when stable and acted on) will be part of the agent's eudaimonia. This proposal, according to which the pure first-order motive is subsumed by, yet also dependent on, the second-order desire for eudaimonia seems to be the best possible way of preserving the eudaimonia thesis without giving up on the possibility of pure motives in virtuous agents. It probably represents the best hope for reconciling Aristotle's erosiac theory of motivation in the *De anima* with the claims he makes in his *Ethics* about the pure motivational structure of the virtues.

Contrary to the assumption in the simplistic argument above, it seems quite possible for me to come to desire some end E as completely final (for its own sake and also not as a means to anything distinct from E) and yet to acquire this desire *because* I realize or judge that this *end E itself* will be an integral part of my good life (in the sense of a happy, fulfilling life that exemplifies the proper use or development of my full human potentialities). In such a case, however, the motivating intrinsic value of E is agent-relative. The belief that achieving E will contribute to my eudaimonia may be sufficient for judging that it has a kind of intrinsic value—namely the kind that triggers D3 desire because it is needed for my completeness. Responding to this kind of intrinsic value does not imply that the end is valued only instrumentally; on the contrary, I judge that realizing this end will make my life *better in the holistic sense*, and no other function it might serve is required to make it desirable to me (even if I recognize that it has other effects that may be good in other senses). In my terms, this just amounts to recognizing that we can have a D3 desire for an end that has an agent-benefiting intrinsic value: we desire it because we see it as a *constitutive part* of our eudaimonia. Thus a D3 desire for E hardly implies that we value E only instrumentally, as a means to the distinct, separate end of our own flourishing.[60] On the contrary, D3 desire is one of the basic ways in which we acquire goals that are desired for their own sake, or pursued as ends-in-themselves. So it is perfectly intelligible that:

    5. Jane values something E intrinsically, or pursues it for its own sake; and
    6. E became an end-in-itself for Jane because she judged it to be a constitutive part of her eudaimonia, that is, her overall well-being or flourishing over a complete life.

There are many instances of E where this conjunction could plausibly hold. And furthermore, we must also grant that they include a number of cases where E stands for some *activity*, for example, running a mile in under five minutes, or studying galactic astronomy, or tutoring foreign students in English. These activities could be pursued as pure (agent-transcending) ends-in-themselves, or instead as parts of Jane's own eudaimonia, or even both (in which case Jane would have two independent motives for these activities). In short, E's having intrinsic value, or being pursuable for its own sake, does not entail that E's value is agent-transcending; for there is also the agent-related kind of intrinsic value that something may have as a direct constituent of one's well-being.

But as we have seen, in the mixed or double-motive case, there is no sense in which the desire for eudaimonia *embraces* the other pure motive; for A to embrace B seems to require the right kind of dependence of B on A. Alternatively, in the second option, a pure motive is not subsumed and dependent on the desire for eudaimonia, because *there is no pure motive at all*; although the agent desires E for its own sake, E is not desired purely, or *as an agent-transcending end*, but rather *as* part of the agent's own eudaimonia. We must be careful not to confuse these two quite different ways of specifying end E that the agent is pursuing for its own sake. So even though E can be pursued as *unqualifiedly* final (not an instrumental means to any other end) and as *part* of the agent's eudaimonia,[61] this does not amount to an agent-transcending end being pursued *qua* part of the agent's eudaimonia; that would be an outright contradiction.

Therefore, although a first-order pure motive to pursue an agent-transcending end E can certainly be subsumed under a second-order desire for eudaimonia, we cannot then make the former *dependent* on the latter by interpreting E itself as part of the agent's eudaimonia. If M_1 toward E is pure, then, by definition, E is not pursued as part of the agent's eudaimonia. Hence M_1 is not dependent on the desire$_2$ for eudaimonia in the way that a desire for Y as a part of Z is dependent on the desire for the whole of Z. This does not suffice to prove GPS but it does strongly support a narrower version of it:

> *The Special Principle of Subsumption (SPS):* If first-order motive M_1 is pure, and M_2 is the second-order desire for eudaimonia as a whole, then if M_1 is subsumed under M_2, it follows necessarily that M_1 is motivationally independent of M_2.

And this is enough to show that no subsumption model can resolve the paradox of eudaimonism.

7. The Existential Solution: Pure Motives as Projects of the Striving Will

We have seen that the eudaimonist cannot preserve the jointure thesis by subsuming first-order motives under the desire for eudaimonia. Hence the eudaimonist instead needs some way of construing the *pure motivation toward and pursuit of* some agent-transcending E as itself an "activity" that she can desire for its own sake, just because it is part of her eudaimonia. Desire for this activity (of being motivated$_1$ itself) would then be dependent in the required way on her desire for eudaimonia. But, unfortunately for the eudaimonist, this does not make sense: a state of pure first-order motivation to pursue E cannot itself be construed as an "activity" for which we can have a second-order D3 desire because we recognize that the state of pure first-order motivation will contribute to eudaimonia. For the reason we can find plausible instances of E in the form given by 5 and 6 above, including some in which E is a familiar kind of activity, is that in these instances the *activity* can be intrinsically rewarding even if it is chosen simply for this reason and *not* purely for the sake of some agent-transcending product-good that this activity helps bring about. For example, activities that are forms of *play* are like this—chooseable just because they are enjoyable—whereas practices are not.

Now, states of virtuous motivation aim at bringing about intrinsically valuable products or results whose value exists quite apart from the agent's eudaimonia. This does not mean that the value of virtues themselves is measured simply by their consequences but rather that an agent acting virtuously must believe that her goal is noble and take this as reason for her action.[62] Virtuous activities animated by such motives are intrinsically rewarding only if the relevant agent-transcendent product or result is chosen purely for its own sake. Virtuous activities are therefore unlike other types of activity that can, without self-defeat, be chosen solely because of their direct psychological benefits to the agent. In these cases, *the self-concerned* form of the activity itself—as opposed to any motives or purposive pursuits that would be internal to a pure form of it—can be chosen as part of eudaimonia. I examine these points in more detail in the next chapter.

Moreover, we should remember that whenever the end E that is chosen for its own sake as part of eudaimonia (as in the conjunction of 5 and 6) is best described as an activity rather than a product, we must still distinguish between *pursuing* E and *E itself*. For we can aspire to an activity and desire to perform an activity without yet being able to perform this activity or engage in it fully or in the right way. In those cases, we are motivated to pursue a given primary activity for its own sake (which can be because it is part of our eudaimonia or not) but we have not yet realized our goal since we are not actually performing the activity. Aspiring actors and actresses are well aware of this important distinction, as are applicants for all sorts of different social roles involving activities and the desires and emotions they characteristically involve. Of course, we could say that the aspiring dancer auditioning for parts in different musicals and operas around the city is indeed already performing a kind of secondary activity, namely, the activity of training and auditioning, which is not done for its own sake but only as a means to E (i.e., the primary activity of dancing in public performances). Her secondary activity is motivated by desire for the primary activity, which could be desired just because she knows she will enjoy doing it (although then it will not be the pure form of this primary activity, as I have suggested). But merely *desiring* some primary activity E cannot *by itself* constitute a "secondary activity."

Certainly some of the secondary activities involved in pursuing activity E might also come to seem intrinsically rewarding or instrumentally valuable for other purposes than securing E. For example, suppose our budding actress discovered that she enjoyed auditioning for the thrill of it and because she enjoyed meeting people in the process, whether or not she got the part. Then auditioning would be desired both for its own sake and as a means to meeting people and to getting parts, and so with these independent motives, she might continue auditioning even once she had lost most of her interest in the activity of playing the part in (say) a movie or drama production. It often happens in human life that what begins as our means to some distinct end becomes an end-in-itself for us, and this may often be a sign that projective motivation is at work (see chaps. 9 and 10). But these are not cases of desiring$_2$ the mere experience of some desire$_1$ for its own sake.

Nor could state A, defined as the mere desiring of some product-like end B, itself count as a primary activity that we could find intrinsically rewarding or desire for its own sake. An independent second-order desire for A as a final end does not compute, because the mere experience of desiring something in the orektic sense is never by itself fulfilling; for by definition it involves the feeling of being unfulfilled or lacking some good.[63] Hence *desiring an end E* cannot by itself count as a desirable activity, whether E is an intrinsically valuable activity or product.

With this in mind, let us return to the schema illustrated by the conjunction of 5 and 6 above. It should be clear now why, in this schema, E can be neither the primary *activity of pursuing* the noble for its own sake nor just the pure *motivation to pursue* the noble as an end-in-itself. We can generalize this point for all self-transcending ends that people typically pursue for their own sake. In all such cases:

A. It does not seem plausible that the end E (whether it is an activity or not) itself adds to the agent's well-being or eudaimonia, since E mainly concerns the state of other persons or other things separate from the agent or not naturally connected to her well-being *prior to* her caring about them. Or if E is naturally connected to (some part of) the agent's well-being, E is not chosen *only* for this reason (i.e., is not simply the object of a D3 desire).[64]
B. But *being motivated to realize* E, pursuing E, and achieving E could (separately or together), as a by-product, cause or constitute part of the agent's eudaimonia.

Such ends cannot be instances of E in the 5 and 6 schema. For the result of substituting them for E in this schema to be intelligible, it would have to be changed in the way illustrated in the following case:

7. Jane cares about Alfred's well-being (E) as an end-in-itself.

8. *Commitment to E and the related pursuit of E* (and possibly the achievement of E as a realized end) contribute directly to Jane's well-being or constitute part of her eudaimonia.

But in this case, 8 cannot explain 7. The conjunction of 7 and 8 can certainly be true, but within this schema, desire for eudaimonia cannot explain how Jane *acquired* her first-order end E or became motivated to pursue it. She cannot pursue *Alfred's doing well* both for its own sake and as a *means* to her own eudaimonia, since it is not *Alfred's well-being* itself (prior to her concern about it) that could serve to promote her *eudaimonia*; rather, it is her *willing and pursuing* Alfred's well-being that may make her a happier person, or at least a person with a fuller sense of *personal meaning* in her life.[65] Nor, as we have seen, can Jane pursue Alfred's well-being as a terminal end just *because* she reflects that being moved by a desire for this end will be good for her or improve her life. For this would be "one thought too many," because it could only mean that Jane really saw Alfred just as an occasion to develop in herself a character trait that is integral to a happy life (perhaps because it can inspire her magnanimity) *rather* than seeing Alfred as an end-in-himself at all.

Yet unless its by-product benefits somehow motivate Jane's first-order motive, then her coming to value and pursue *Alfred's well-being* for its own sake cannot be a result of *orektic desire* at all. For the realization of this end itself, as abstracted from the pursuit of it, is not any part of *her* simple being, and thus she cannot *prepurposively* apprehend its being unrealized as something she lacks, as the erosiac model requires. Once she acquires E as her end, pursuit and achievement of it can certainly have eudaimonistic consequences for her; but this cannot cause any prepurposive desire for this end so it cannot explain how she came to pursue E. Rather—and this is the most striking aspect of these examples—it seems to be precisely *because* her first-order motivation toward E is pure and hence not easily explained on the erosiac model that 8 is plausible. Otherwise put, the truth of 8, which we are commonly disposed to grant in many such cases, presupposes that Jane acquires her goal by projective motivation: rather than responding to any prepurposive attraction to her goal, she *wills it*.

So Annas and others are absolutely right that for Aristotle, virtue must involve certain "pure motives," but, contrary to the impression they give, his eudaimonistic moral psychology is inadequate to explain how these pure motives are possible. It is precisely because his analysis of the virtues correctly perceives the need for pure motives that it leads him beyond the resources of his desiderative theory of motivation and thus into a deep though rarely perceived inconsistency. Hence it is only *half true* to say that "charges of egoism made against ancient ethical theories because of their eudaimonistic form miss the mark completely" and are "radically mistaken."[66] Such theories are not egoistic in content, as Annas says, because they "give virtue a noninstrumental role in achieving happiness."[67] But while this is true, the problem is precisely that the dominant orektic conception of motivation in eudaimonistic theories, which is the *reason* for their formal structure centering on the agent's own highest good, is inconsistent with the existence of just the sort of purely virtuous or moral motivation we find in the content of these theories. Thus modern critics are not entirely to blame for their confusions about ancient eudaimonistic ethics!

8. The Paradox as One of Several Related Objections to Eudaimonism

In light of this critique, it becomes clearer what is required to solve the paradox of eudaimonism: one must provide an intelligible psychological story, or coherent model, that preserves *both* the eudaimonia thesis and the purity of virtuous motivation. The foregoing analyses suggest that this is impossible within A-eudaimonism—although in the next chapter I ask if this system can be varied in any plausible way to address the problem. If the paradox is unresolvable, as I claim, this does not show that A-eudaimonism itself is incoherent, but it does show that A-eudaimonism cannot consistently serve as a foundation for virtue ethics.

In conclusion, it will be helpful to contrast this critique of A-eudaimonism as a traditional foundation for virtue ethics with other closely related objections to the A-eudaimonist system, several of which can be found in Bernard Williams's work, among others. I list the main criticisms of A-eudaimonism as follows:

1. *The Conflict-among-Goods Objection:* There can be no comprehensive highest good for human life as formally defined in A-eudaimonism, because it is practically impossible consistently to pursue all the different first-order final ends it would have to embrace, even if they are prioritized in some principled way.

2. *The Metaphysical Objection:* Defining the virtues as qualities of character that allow us to realize our real interests requires a metaphysical account of the human good as based on objective human nature. The basis for this ideal of normal human functioning could only be in sociobiology or in psychology. But no psychological or sociobiological account could be both independent of the moral content of this ideal of normal human functioning and yet provide a noncircular empirical ground for it.

3. *The Paradox of Eudaimonism:* The pure motive of virtue conflicts with the formal egoism involved in the eudaimonia thesis. Virtuous acts do not aim at eudaimonia, which can at most be an unintended by-product of virtue.

4. *The Moral Luck Objection:* Virtues as Aristotle conceives them cannot be voluntarily acquired or developed by the agent but depend entirely on the surrounding culture and actions of her educators.

5. *The Circularity Objection:* The doctrine of the mean does not provide an independent definition of the noble. Without such a definition, we cannot adequately specify the objects of virtuous motives.

6. *The Apollonian Objection:* the conception of virtues as "intermediate" states of passion and desire is unduly rationalistic and models all virtues on temperance as gratification-postponement and control of the appetites.

These objections are closely related in several cases and hence, unsurprisingly, they have not always been clearly distinguished. Without giving them the detailed analysis they deserve, I briefly explain what each is about and where the existentialist should stand on each.

1. I explore the first objection in another work, where I argue that by itself, this objection provides the existentialist with a strong reason to look for a non-eudaimonistic basis for virtue ethics.[68] An alternative existential model of the will involving projective motivation can hold that achieving *existential coherence* or practical unity among a limited subset of first-order goods to be pursued can be vital among rational desiderata for forming our identity-constituting commitments and cares, and I return to this idea in chapter 14. In his later treatment of this problem,[69] Bernard Williams runs this issue together with objection 2, since these are closely related. He argues that Aristotle's ideal of normal human functioning assumes the possibility of harmony among ends that are instead likely to conflict, so there may be no coherent and complete good.[70] He adds that contemporary psychology will not support the possibility or desirability of coherence among pursuits of radically different kinds of goods, which is "a problem . . . for any program that wants to connect the ethical life with psychological health through notions of integration, or reduction of conflict." Even when possible, Williams says, the reduction of psychic conflict may not always be entirely good for the person anyway.[71]

Now, these objections to the eudaimonist project cut so deep precisely because they refute the jointure thesis, and I know of no successful Aristotelian answer to them. Moreover, Williams's conflict-of-goods objection and the conclusion of objection 3 that virtuous motives are *not* embraced by the single desire for eudaimonia are mutually supporting and confirming. The existential alternative to the jointure thesis tries to show that the right understanding of the striving will by which we form life projects and self-defining commitments reveals reasons (internal to its structure) to value practical coherence and wholeheartedness as elements of an "authentic" life without requiring us somehow to balance or harmonize *every* significant kind of first-order good that humans can pursue.

2. The second objection involves the whole question of a functional analysis of human nature, and the version I give of this objection is Williams's argument against an inference from psychological facts to value-claims.[72] Williams's objection—that we cannot read off the human function from those capacities that human beings alone possess among all the other animals—may be decisive against Aristotle's own version of the function argument if it treats peculiarity to human life as a sufficient condition for being part of our function, but not if it regards such peculiarity only as a necessary condition.[73] In any case, there are other possible ways of defining the human function in terms of rationality: for example, by arguing that the notion of a function is required to make sense of the ineliminable concept of an animal's biological flourishing.[74]

These alternatives have their own problems, but whether the function argument can be defended or successfully reconstructed is a difficult question that I leave aside here. I have suggested before that Kierkegaardian existentialists, at any rate, will not reject altogether the idea that there is a natural human telos: rather, they will define that telos in terms of a more minimal set of conditions than characterize the formal telos as defined in A-eudaimonism.[75] However, this disagreement reflects the fact that existentialism takes persons to be defined essentially by their freedom and hence not to be a *natural kind* definable as a species of the genus "animal" at all; according to all existentialists, persons have no "nature" in that sense. Although there is an essence of personhood in the sense of structural features that are true of all persons *qua* persons, individual persons are *not multiple instantiations* of this "essence" in the same way that either instantiations of substantial forms work in medieval metaphysics or instantiations of essences work in contemporary analytic theories of modality. The existentialist version of objection 2 therefore requires working out an alternative ontology of personhood—a task that has to wait upon an adequate understanding of the striving will and the freedom it must have if it is to make us responsible for our own character, long-term commitments, and life projects.[76]

3. The third objection has obviously been the subject of this chapter, but it is closely related to objections 1 and 2. The paradox of eudaimonism supports objection 2 by suggesting that it will be impossible to ground a virtue ethics on a eudaimonist metaphysics of personhood and, as I said, it supports objection 1 by suggesting that the fundamental project of being a good person, or being moral, may conflict outright with the pursuit of one's own eudaimonia—an idea I'll explore further with Kant. As we saw, my version of this paradox is closely related to remaining questions about how reflection on the role of virtues in one's life can have any practical value for the agent, and this question will be explored in the next chapter.

4. The objection that virtue as a basis for evaluations of moral worth will involve moral luck is also due to Williams,[77] but Aristotle evidently disagrees in *NE* III.5, where he argues that we can exercise some control over the development of our own motivational dispositions. On this point, the existentialist will side with Aristotle in holding that we must have some kind of free control over those aspects of our character that can be *morally* evaluated (or by which our whole self can be morally evaluated). In a recent article, I have sketched one possible version of this libertarian control based on Harry Frankfurt's work on the higher-order will,[78] but the full existential argument for a kind of libertarian freedom in the formation of moral character depends crucially on reconceiving the will to include the striving and commitment-setting functions of projective motivation. For it is mostly through these capacities, I believe, that people are capable of autonomously working on and reforming their volitional character. If so, then here again, Aristotle's view depends on projective motivation without recognizing it.

5 and 6. I mention the final two objections for the sake of completeness and because I think they, too, will support accounting for virtuous motivation in terms of projective willing. But I leave this argument for Chapter 11, in which I consider how the projective conception of a deontic will developed in late-medieval and modern philosophy. Chapter 10, sec. I, also briefly analyzes Aristotle's doctrine of the mean. In chapter 8, I argue that contemporary neo-Aristotelian accounts of friendship, practices, and habituation also implicitly presuppose projective motivation.

8

Contemporary Solutions to the Paradox and Their Problems

Overview. Beginning with two commentaries on Aristotle, this chapter focuses on themes in neo-Aristotelian virtue ethics, including MacIntyre's accounts of practices and common goods. The evaluation of these theories, which shows that they support the existential conception of striving will, is most relevant for anyone interested in this genre of work on ethics and psychology but it is written to be accessible to undergraduates. Several parts of the discussion are also relevant for basic issues in political philosophy.

Introduction

In this chapter, I explore several other ways of trying to resolve the paradox of eudaimonism described in the previous chapter while hanging on to central features of the A-eudaimonist model of human motivation. My critique of these alternative proposed resolutions will help clarify both the nature of the central problem and why postulating the possibility of projective motivation (and thus abandoning the eudaimonia thesis) provides a more elegant solution to the relevant motivational paradoxes. I begin with analyses by John Cooper and Paula Gottlieb, which directly address the paradox of eudaimonism, and I add to the list of possible alternatives my own, Parfitian version of indirect eudaimonism. After critiquing these proposed solutions, I turn to analyses of friendship, practices, and perfectionism by Sherman, MacIntyre, and Watson. These analyses were not written specifically to address the paradox of eudaimonism but they shed light on this paradox in their attempts to steer around its central conundrum.

1. Cooper's Solution: Virtuous Motivation as a Constitutive Means to Eudaimonia

John Cooper addresses substantially the same paradox of pure motivation in his early book responding to D. J. Allan's version of the objection.[1] As he notes, Allan believes Aristotle's theory of deliberation in *Nicomachean Ethics* (*NE*) III includes only what we would today call instrumental reasoning and hence cannot explain how we choose a virtuous action for its own sake.[2] Now, in this book, Cooper accepts that for Aristotle, all practical deliberation begins from a maximally inclusive end:

> We have seen that, according to Aristotle, reasoning that leads to action must start from the assumption of some end to be realized in or by acting, and that ultimately for each person such ends must themselves be means to a single highest end, which in the last analysis all his actions are aimed at achieving.[3]

But since this comprehensive end is the agent's own eudaimonia, we have the problem of explaining how practical deliberation could lead an agent to act "for the sake of the noble."[4] For example, Cooper asks, how could a decision to defend one's homestead against marauders "both be the outcome of deliberative reflection and involve the recognition of moral value inherent in the courageous action itself."[5] Cooper considers the possibility that Aristotle could regard "nobility," or the fine, as a final end quite independent of the agent's other ultimate end (his conception of happiness as maximum pleasure, for instance), but he recognizes that this would probably lead to the kind of conflicts that the virtuous agent's non-maximizing conception of his ultimate end is supposed to avoid. Yet Cooper rejects the idea that Aristotle's comprehensive conception of the ultimate end could be inconsistent with "constant and steady commitment to virtuous action as such," which requires valuing various species of the noble for their own sakes.[6]

Instead, Cooper thinks we can resolve this problem by recognizing that Aristotle's concept of deliberation from given ends to "means" is not narrowly instrumental but also includes what we would call constitutive and specificatory judgments about what an end consists in and what is an instance of it. As Cooper puts it, Aristotle's conception of "means" is broad and includes:

> constituent parts of complex ends and particular actions in which the attainment of some end may be said to consist. Morally virtuous action may then be a "means" to the ultimate end of [the agent's] flourishing, not in the sense that it tends to bring it about, as doing favors for the right people makes a government functionary rich, but

in the sense that it [virtuous action] is one constituent part of the conception of flourishing which constitutes the virtuous person's ultimate end. On this view there would be no contrast . . . between regarding an act of virtue as a means to obtaining one's ultimate end and choosing it for its own sake. For the ultimate end is something desired for its own sake (indeed it is desired for itself *alone*) and if morally virtuous action is one of the constituent parts of this, it . . . will thereby also be desired for its own sake.[7]

Cooper is insightful here; in my judgment this is probably what Aristotle thought he meant, as evidence in his account of friendship suggests. Moreover, Cooper is right to point out that the firm disposition to choose (the different species of) the noble for its own sake, which Aristotle identifies with virtue(s), implies "permanent and inviolable principles" of morality that are inconsistent with any consequentialist definition of the morally right as the maximization of some set of goods.[8] Aristotle is certainly not a consequentialist: he does not (contra W. D. Ross's reading) hold that virtuous actions are only *instrumental* means to the agent's eudaimonia.[9] Instead, Cooper says:

although [Aristotle] does hold that virtuous action is a means to eudaimonia, or human good, eudaimonia is not itself specified independently of virtuous action; on the contrary, eudaimonia is conceived as identical with a lifetime of morally virtuous action (together perhaps with other activities as well).[10]

This explanation finds much support from other Aristotle scholars. For instance, Alasdair MacIntyre writes that for Aristotle, "the virtues are both partly constitutive of the supreme human good and to be possessed not only for their own sake as genuine excellences, but also for the sake of that [supreme] good."[11] In other words, virtue is included *holistically* in eudaimonia. Similarly, Jonathan Lear writes:

The . . . virtues are only virtues because they encourage and help to constitute a full rich life. Thus acting ethically is ultimately in one's own best interest. Acting ethically may involve acting well towards others, but that is because acting well towards others—friendship, citizenship—is part and parcel of human flourishing.[12]

As long as "acting well towards others" means caring about their good for its own sake (or just because it is one species of the "the noble"), then this resolution agrees exactly with Cooper's. Nevertheless, I do not agree with Cooper, MacIntyre, or Lear that this refutes Allan's objection that Aristotle's "recognition of the value inherent in moral action . . . conflicts with his analysis of deliberation" and with the embracing eudaimonist motive it requires.[13]

Cooper is right that one way we can acquire a final end of action X is to recognize it as *constituting* something Y that we already regard as an end-in-itself, or as intrinsically worthwhile objective that we already intend as our purpose. If I want to help a child learn to read, then I should want to help him learn to sound out simple printed words, which is not *distinct* from the activity of reading but is rather its first form. And, closely related to this, another way we can acquire a final end X is by recognizing it as a *specification* of Y in the circumstances. Likewise, we can become motivated to seek X for its own sake because we see it as *part* of some more general end Y that we are already motivated to pursue for its own sake, or we see X as the relevant *specification of some such part* of Y in the present case. Arriving at such judgments about the relation of some X and Y is one important form of practical deliberation. And as far as these relationships go, it does not matter whether the original motivation to pursue the more general final end Y is erosiac in structure or not (whatever kind of motivation it is, it will transfer to X). Therefore the agent's erosiac desire for her own eudaimonia can certainly transfer to some part or specification of this eudaimonia without rendering that part or specification a *merely instrumental means* to her eudaimonia; rather, it can still be desired for *its own sake*. I entirely agree with this, but it will not solve the paradox of eudaimonism.

First of all, the specificatory and part-whole relationships determine the kind of intrinsic value found in the specified end or part end *by* the kind found in the general or whole end: X is intrinsically valuable only *as* a specification of Y or *as* a part of Y and not outside these qualifications. For example, suppose I think that the natural environment or biosphere of the Earth has intrinsic value and there is, generally speaking, reason to preserve it for its own sake (perhaps not always an overriding reason, but *some* reason). Now, I might say that preserving natural biodiversity is *part* of this end, and that saving the Amazon rain forest (with its incredibly rich biodiversity) from further decimation is a specification of this part of my general final end. If this is how I deliberate, then I value "the Amazon" *not* as a singular object (i.e., this particular forest, however vague its borders), but rather as a haven of natural biodiversity and speciation, which, in turn, I value as part of the overall intrinsic value of the biosphere. And this is not trivial, since it is a serious question whether other "parts" of the biosphere that we might value for their own sake can all be coherently valued *together* (without irreconcilable conflict) as parts of a single overarching intrinsic value; those who think not will find themselves holding that the intrinsic value of, say, biodiversity is an *independent* value and *not* just an aspect of some larger intrinsic value of "Nature." In short, there are more and less holistic ways of relating these values, and the serious debate between them has practical implications.

Likewise, in social life, the intrinsic value of my friend's well-being (either as a singular and unique individual or as an instance of the set of "my virtuous acquaintances") may *not* seem to lie in the fact that his good is part of my overall good. In every case where we wish to derive the intrinsic value of the part from the intrinsic value of the whole, we have to hold that the value of the whole is explanatorily (and perhaps metaphysically) *prior* to the value of the part.[14] But it seems impossible to imagine that the "nobility" (a species of intrinsic value) of certain sorts of actions, which makes choosing them for this value count as virtuous, *derives from* its being part of the value of the agent's own flourishing, which each agent values above everything else. If my friend's good were *literally part* of my good, just as my arm's good or my memory's good is part of my good, she would have to be literally *a part of me*, just as my arm and my memory are parts of me.

As soon as we put it this way, we see the mistake. Cooper could doubtless reformulate his claim to say that the agent's *pursuit* of his friend's good for her sake (or as an end in herself) constitutes part of his own good whether he realizes his goal or not. This formulation makes much more sense, but as soon as we put it this way, we are recognizing that the value to our agent is a *by-product* of his taking his friend's good as his first-order final end. And as we saw in our discussion of egoism in chapter 5, such a second-order good (which is constituted just by *pursuing* a first-order good) may not be directly willable at all. It is certainly incorrect to say that we desire for its own sake this by-product advantage to ourselves *in* desiring the first-order final good of the friend, because in the pursuit of her good, our advantage is a by-product. For the relationship between Z and X when

> Z is an intrinsically valuable second-order good that it caused, realized, or constituted *by pursuing* for its own sake a distinct first-order good X;

is completely different from the relationships we considered earlier, in which

> Y is the intrinsically valuable whole of which X is a part or a particular specification.

For in the first case, it is completely wrong to describe X as a specification or part of Z. Except possibly in a narrow and highly unusual set of cases, intelligible first-order goals are not normally parts or specifications of the second-order goods that may derive causally or constitutively from the *pursuit* of these goals.[15]

Sometimes we see both kinds of relationship quite distinctly in a single case. I may see the happiness of a particular relative of mine as having a specific value X because it is *part* of the more general intrinsic value Y of the class of "my family members," and working or sacrificing for her good conceived *this way* may produce a particular result Z in my psyche (for example, further disposing me to help other family members)[16]—whereas had I pursued her good as a value X independently of its relationship to Y, quite a different side effect might have been produced. But I then pursue X neither as an instrumental means to Z nor *as a constitutive or specificatory means to Z (which would be equally self-defeating)*. Rather, Z results from aiming at X as a specification of Y and pursuing Y for its own sake.

Given these distinctions, we can sum up the problem. Cooper's solution requires eudaimonia to occupy the Y place in our schema, with the various forms of nobility that virtuous acts pursue for their own sake occupying the X place. But in fact, Cooper gives us no reason to think that eudaimonia *can* occupy the Y place; its relationship to the values pursued for their own sake in virtuous acts still seems to make sense only if eudaimonia occupies the Z place. But a reflective desire for a final end in the Z place (however comprehensive it may be) *cannot transfer* to desire for any final end in the X place, or the Y place for that matter.[17] This is a more formal statement of the nontransferability of desire for by-product satisfaction. Desire for a final end in the Y place can (and usually does) transfer to desire for a more specific final end in the X place, but this is irrelevant to the problem at hand. We are still left with the paradox: pursuit of eudaimonia as a final end in the Z place of our schema will necessarily be *self-defeating*. As Elster's analysis suggests, to avoid this problem, the desire for eudaimonia must somehow be isolated from the first-order motives and pursuits that tend to fulfill it as a by-product. This is the direction in which Paula Gottlieb looks for a solution.

2. Gottlieb's Solution: Pushing Desire for Eudaimonia into the "Background"

After concluding, rightly, that Annas's proposed solution to the paradox of eudaimonism will not work, Gottlieb comments: "What is needed, therefore, is an account of the desire for happiness which explains how the desire can motivate the agent while not appearing in the forefront of the agent's deliberations."[18] Gottlieb then offers such an account, framed in terms of Aristotle's notion of the practical syllogism. Although some commentators include the agent's operative motives in the practical syllogism when fully expanded, Gottlieb's construction emphasizes the idea that although "Aristotle . . . assumes that any rational agent will have a desire for her own good (*boulēsis*)," this desire itself does not appear as a thought in the cognitive process of practical deliberation that leads to her choice:

Most important, reflection on one's own desires is no part of Aristotle's practical syllogism. The practical syllogism enshrines the information the agent needs in order to act correctly, but not the desires themselves. Thus, although the virtuous person is originally motivated by a desire for her own happiness, the desire itself does not appear as the content of her deliberation. Nor does the desire into which it is channeled, deliberative desire (*prohairesis*).[19]

Given this, Gottlieb thinks it follows that the virtuous agent does not suffer from "one thought too many" in his deliberations. "What counts as the agent's main reasons for action will be those aspects of the situation which he finds salient because he has such and such a character."[20]

This solution misconstrues the nature of the problem. Williams's description of the "one thought too many" objection to utilitarianism may give the impression that we need be concerned only about what occurrent thoughts the agent thinks in justifying her action or coming to intend that action, but this is not the central question in the paradox of eudaimonism. The question is rather: What are the agent's *ultimate motives* for choosing virtuous actions, and can these be made to agree with the core eudaimonist thesis that eudaimonia is our embracing or all-inclusive motive, on any reasonable construal of that thesis?

In a case like the one Gottlieb discusses, where a friend is in need, the agent may be focusing on the friend's good and on the fact that helping her friend is the decent, friendly, or (using Aristotle's generic term) noble thing to do in the present circumstances. As I argue above, this first-order belief involving such an objective judgment that an agent-neutral good is obtainable (in this case, the good of another person who is a friend), as opposed to agent-relative pleasure or advantage/utility, must be part of virtuous motivation for Aristotle. But the agent acting "for the sake of the noble" need not attend to any second-order reflective thought *that it is virtuous* to care in this way about what is noble (e.g., the friend's good) as a final end.[21] So I agree with Gottlieb's suggestion that "From a first-person perspective, the central explanation/justification/motivation [of the agent's choice] will be the thought that the situation called for fine action."[22] *A fortiori*, then, I also agree with Gottlieb that the virtuous agent need not think, nor be moved by, the third-order thought that the virtuousness she displays in caring about the noble for its own sake is going to be beneficial in her own life. For this third-order thought depends upon the presence of the second-order thought about the virtuousness of her motives. But then we face the paradox: How can eudaimonia still function as our embracing or all-inclusive motive, when virtuous motives seem to operate *quite independently* of it?

It is no help to say in response that "the content of the original desire remains in the background" rather than in the occurrent thoughts leading to the agent's choice.[23] For the problem is how this original eudaimonist desire can *motivate* the agent to virtuous action, whether it motivates by entering into his deliberation or not. Note that if it cannot be said in any sense to motivate or stand behind his virtuous action, then it seems that the eudaimonia thesis is false. Gottlieb notes that Kraut seems to be going in this direction, since he concludes that "Aristotle's theory must not be egoistic in *any sense whatsoever*"—including purely formal egoism. Kraut reaches this conclusion, according to Gottlieb, because "Aristotle allows that people can be (and indeed ought to be) influenced by factors other than maximizing contemplation," which Kraut takes to be "happiness *par excellence*" for Aristotle.[24] In terms of my reconstruction, we can say: Kraut holds that maximal contemplation is our *material telos* (M), yet he also holds that virtuous motives aim at ends that are no part of M. As a result, Kraut must hold that for Aristotle, acting upon virtuous motives is not aiming at what constitutes or realizes our *formal telos* (F). But understanding the nature of M would not eliminate these virtuous motives; since morality requires us to act on such motives, human beings are in general capable of developing such motives and sustaining them when enlightened about M. Therefore the eudaimonia thesis is false; some of our final ends are not final because of their role in realizing F.

Gottlieb does not seem inclined to go in this direction, since she rejects Kraut's claim on the grounds that virtuous motivation is, for Aristotle, a necessary condition of being able to contemplate well. Whether this is right or not, however, if *virtue's being* a necessary condition of M is not the motive behind virtuous choices, then these choices aim at ends independent of M, even when M is known as such, and so the eudaimonia thesis is false. Thus Gottlieb has not refuted Kraut's idea that maybe Aristotle's normative ideal of virtue is not egoistic at all. But neither has Kraut shown that this is compatible with A-eudaimonism, since, as Gottlieb rightly says, Kraut's idea that we can just have "the noble" and our own happiness as two distinct ends in virtuous action fails to answer Annas's version of the paradox of eudaimonism.[25] In response to Kraut's own "mixed motive" resolution, I add that there is no problem *per se* with an agent being moved by desire for two (or more) distinct ends in intending a single action. Sometimes agents are even irrationally moved by two (or more) desires for ends that they know conflict with one another—such motivation can happen even if the achievement of either end tends in fact to undermine the achievement of the other end and the agent knows this.[26] The problem is, rather, how one of the ends we are discussing, namely *eudaimonia*, can be the all-inclusive or embracing end. This seems to require us to take the noble as our final end in choosing a virtuous act, and yet to do so *out of* desire for our eudaimonia. It is not merely that two distinct motives exist in a virtuous action but rather the *incorporative or sublative* relationship of one to the other that leads to the paradox of eudaimonism.

If we wish to keep the eudaimonia thesis intact, then, we have to say that the agent's fundamental *boulēsis*, desire for her own happiness in the most holistic sense, *does* somehow motivate the action under its virtuous description and not just an action that is also virtuous under *another* description (i.e., as pure desire for "the noble"). This must be true whether or not this fundamental *boulēsis* motivates by entering into her practical syllogism. But in that case, any species of "the noble" as our final end must be apprehended as *part of* the agent's eudaimonia, valued intrinsically for this reason, and desired for its value to her eudaimonia. And that does not seem to be coherent, because the "nobility" of my act, as a description of it, does not seem to make any essential reference to my well-being. This is why trying to see it as a means to or even as part of my own happiness undermines the finality of "the noble" as an end for me.

The problem is somewhat similar, as Gottlieb suggests, to Parfit's point that consciously taking the maximization of collective human utility as one's ultimate end tends to undermine one's ability to act on "non-utilitarian motives and fixed moral dispositions." Even if utilitarian reasons could provide a functional justification of such motives, which value things *other* than the maximization of utility as ends-in-themselves, once this justification becomes the agent's internal reason, his more particular first-order motives are altered.[27] Before moving on to Annas's formulation of the problem, Gottlieb suggests that this version is solved simply by recognizing that Aristotle does not endorse any form of material egoism, since his virtuous person pursues many things ahead of his own sensual pleasure, subjective desire satisfaction, money, honor, power, and so on. Given that Aristotle rejects material egoism, Gottlieb says:

> the agent's thought that the ultimate justification for virtuous action is that it promotes the agent's happiness will not undermine, in the manner suggested above [in the utilitarian example] the thought that he is acting, for example, generously because it is the virtuous thing to do. The awareness of the rationale for acting virtuously will not make him reconsider and act viciously instead.[28]

Presumably that is right: the virtuous agent will not reconsider. But does that rescue A-eudaimonism? Suppose (1) the Kantian who started to see regularly acting on the "motive of duty"[29] as an effective means to maximizing utility and started to choose her actions for *that* reason would find that her new goal conflicts with her old goal in many cases; whereas (2) if the

Aristotelian who chose actions for the sake of their nobility started to see this as an effective way of achieving eudaimonia, her new and old goals would still point to the same action, and hence her two motives would be mutually reinforcing. This seems to be Gottlieb's solution, if I have understood her correctly.

But in the paradox of utilitarianism, the *material* disagreement between the actions recommended by direct utilitarianism and some alternative deontic standard (whose general observance by the agent happens to increase collective well-being) is not the *only* problem. There is another, deeper problem, namely, that direct utilitarianism, like eudaimonism, allows only *one* ultimate goal or embracing end for human action; a moral person, on this normative theory, must do everything for the sake of or as part of maximizing collective utility. If one sees intrinsic values that are *independent* of collective utility in more particular goals and hence desires them or projects them as final ends quite separate from maximizing utility, then one would already be in violation of the direct utilitarian supreme principle. This would be the case *even if* the same actions would also be chosen by an agent in the same circumstances acting solely on the desire to maximize utility. As a result, indirect utilitarianism can only work if the agents acting for the sake of nonutilitarian standards either do not know about or do not care about the utilitarian justifications for their actions.

The indirect utilitarian, then, faces several difficult objections concerning whether such a scheme is psychologically possible, and if so, whether it could ever be morally justifiable—for example, Williams's objections to "Government House" utilitarianism, and Rawls's arguments for the publicity condition for principles of justice. But the eudaimonist faces a much harder problem as a result of the analogous *formal* (not material) conflict between eudaimonia as our all-embracing ultimate end and the motivation to pursue final ends whose value is apprehended or cognized without any reference to the agent's own eudaimonia. This problem seems unsolvable for the A-eudaimonist because the relationship between eudaimonia and the other ends it purportedly subsumes is supposed to be direct: as MacIntyre said, they are desired at least in part for the sake of the agent's own eudaimonia, and the agent is not ideally meant to be unconscious of their happiness-making role.

3. Indirect Eudaimonism: A Possible Parfitian Solution?

Gottlieb's defense of Aristotle might suggest that the psychological eudaimonist can avoid the paradox by reconstructing A-eudaimonism to mimic the structure of indirect utilitarianism or indirect egoism, as described by Derek Parfit. For Gottlieb wants to push the desire for eudaimonia out of the agent's foreground focus in deliberation and into some kind of "background" (that is, either unconscious, or conscious but not reflected on, or otherwise outside the agent's center of attention).

This recalls the position that I called "external eudaimonism" (or EEu; chap. 7, sec. 4), according to which all our practical reasons are ultimately eudaimonistic, but we are capable of intrinsic concern for first-order goods that are not prepurposively connected to our own eudaimonia. In Gottlieb's version of EEu, knowledge of the conditions of eudaimonia would *indirectly* motivate$_2$ the formation of pure motives$_1$ for the sake of their by-product benefits; agents would arrange things so that they acquire these pure motives$_1$ and lose their previous desire$_2$ for them, which would be self-defeating if it remained. Let us call this version of EEu "indirect eudaimonism" or IEu.[30] This approach contrasts with the other proposed solutions we have considered, since it is developmental rather than structural. Several EEu models try to resolve the paradox by distinguishing historical stages of a sequence in which both the pure motives and their eudaimonistic benefits play significant practical roles in the agent's psychology. Let us construct IEu by analogy with Parfit's construction of indirect rational egoism and indirect consequentialism.

Defending rational egoism against its paradoxes of self-defeat, Parfit famously argued that a consistent self-interested conception of practical reason (S) tells an agent "to cause himself to have, or allow himself to keep, any of the *best possible sets of motives*, in self-interested terms."[31] If this requires him sometimes to have and act on self-denying motives that count as irrational if directly judged by the standards of S, then S tells him to acquire motives that are irrational in self-interested terms. This licenses forms of self-manipulation that may require self-deception, since "It is hard to change our beliefs when our reason for doing so is merely that this change will be in our interests."[32] This could even include giving up active belief in S, in which case S would be "self-effacing," but Parfit denies that this would make S unacceptable.[33] Similarly, in discussing consequentialism (C), Parfit allows that given the central role of love and emotional attachment in human psychology, if all members of the relevant community act directly on the motive of maximizing good consequences (however these are defined), they would probably all enjoy less happy lives as "pure do-gooders." And, given our propensity to rationalize unjustified conduct when it suits our existing desires, we might all be better off if we acted on agent-centered prohibitions, for example, against killing innocents.[34] But C does not fail in its own terms any more than S, because C tells us to cultivate whatever motives have the best overall effects, even if this requires manipulation or cultivation of first-order motives only for the sake of their by-product results, which are by definition not intended by agents acting on those motives.[35]

This defense of S and C depends on Parfit's argument that both rationality and morality are not *level-transitive* as applied to motives; it can, without contradiction, be rational according to some theory T to act on motives that count as irrational on T, or moral according to T to act on motives that count as immoral on T, or blameless on T to act on motives that are wrong according to T.[36] Parfit even argues that in sophisticated indirect forms of consequentialism, C applies to acts of moral judgment and related moral sentiments along with everything else: "we ought to blame others, and feel remorse, when this would make the outcome better."[37] Hence these theories regard acting in a way that is subjectively moral, or blameless given the agent's best judgments in the circumstances, as *merely a means* to the formal goal of maximizing good states of affairs rather than as a substantive goal of practical reason in its own right.[38]

While this might be defensible for S or C, by contrast, all traditional eudaimonistic theories of virtue require that virtuous activities are *not* a mere means to eudaimonia as the best outcome. As Parfit himself acknowledges, on many nonconsequentialist moral theories, "the avoidance of wrong-doing is itself a substantive moral aim."[39] Indeed, for Socrates and Plato, as for Kant, this is an *overriding* substantive aim, trumping the pursuit of any other first-order end or constraining the means by which such ends may be pursued. Now, Parfit argues that treating rational or moral motivation as an end-in-itself, never as a mere means, is not a valid requirement on theories of rationality or morality; but, notably, his argument for this turns on a faulty example. In his case, "Murder and Accidental Death," it seems morally better to save person Z from a forest fire rather than to try to prevent person X (who is himself about to die anyway) from murdering another person Y.[40] This case could be improved if we also assume that Y is about to die of natural causes. Parfit thinks that if moral wrongs can stand in such a trade-off relation with other harms to be avoided, then morality is not an independent end. He is apparently assuming that we can interpret the thesis that morality can never be a mere means to other good consequences as entailing the thesis that we ought always to minimize instances of wrongdoing by anyone in the world, for his example refutes only the latter thesis.

But, as Williams has shown, this latter thesis is certainly not what the Kantian or Aristotelian anticonsequentialists endorse; on their theories, we are *primarily* responsible for the moral quality of our *own* actions and only secondarily responsible for the actions of others whom we can influence.[41] The theory that morality can never be a mere means should not be interpreted, then, as the consequentialist doctrine that wrongdoing by anyone is a bad state of affairs that we must always strive to minimize above all else. It is perfectly consistent with Aristotle's and Kant's views to hold that sometimes it would be better, all things considered, to save one person from accidental death rather than trying to prevent another from doing some grievous wrong, like committing murder. This does not prove, pace Parfit, that "the avoidance of wrongdoing is a mere means"[42] on these theories.

This point shows that an indirect eudaimonist theory would indeed involve a fundamental departure from the traditional eudaimonist project as a justification of the virtues. For IEu would have to hold that (a) what it is most rational for us to do, all things considered, is *whatever* will maximize our (individual or collective) eudaimonia; and that (b) this may sometimes require cultivating and acting on motivational dispositions that are *irrational* since they do not aim at maximizing eudaimonia. Among these could be the dispositions of choice called the virtues. On such a view, virtue could be regarded ultimately as a mere means. We could decide (individually or collectively) to adopt virtue standards for the moral worth of persons and to train ourselves and our children to have and exercise virtuous motives, doing this only because we expect it to maximize our eudaimonia. In order for this to be effective, we might have to *forget* our original motives for launching this program of self-manipulation, so that at the later stage, our concern to do what is right or "noble" (in any of its various species) will be pure—since only such pure motives will have the desired by-product effect, as we have seen. This would show that IEu could be self-effacing but not that it would fail in its own terms, according to this Parfitian reasoning.

Yet this conclusion actually shows only that such an indirect eudaimonist theory is not really in accord with the tradition of rational eudaimonism after all. For it is one of the hallmarks of Aristotelian moral theories that they hold objective-list conceptions of the goods worth having or pursuing, and these lists all include being virtuous and acting virtuously as states and activities that directly improve the agent's life. As Parfit says, for a consequentialist who holds such a theory, acting morally and avoiding wrongdoing are not a mere means,[43] and eudaimonists must be able to say the same if their position is coherent. The paradox of eudaimonism suggests that it is not ultimately coherent, but to avoid this paradox by allowing virtue to serve as a mere means to eudaimonia is to give up one of the distinctive elements of the A-eudaimonist project and adopt a form of consequentialism instead.

This analysis suggests that we should add to the definition of rational eudaimonism a clause expressing a kind of publicity principle: the self-critical capacity for accurate assessment of one's life, or knowledge of one's own eudaimonia, and its secure basis in virtue is essential to enjoying eudaimonia. In rational eudaimonist conceptions worthy of the name, the practical reasons there are cannot guide us toward our material telos through deception about our own being and/or the value of our activities, motives, and psychic states. As we have seen, Aristotle's own account of magnanimity confirms the central role that honest self-assessment independent of peer recognition plays in his conception. The desire to know the truth about oneself may be, as Harry Frankfurt has said, "the faintest passion" in the human psyche,[44] but its virtuous development is nonetheless essential to flourishing on all eudaimonist moral theories.

Thus indirect eudaimonism as a legitimate version of EEu is impossible, since the rational eudaimonist clause in EEu requires that the virtuous agent be able both to recognize reflectively the ways that virtuous activities contribute to his own fulfillment and to endorse and reinforce his virtuous desire for the noble as a result of this reflexive evaluation. This is true for Aristotle but it is perhaps even clearer among later Hellenistic philosophers, of whom Martha Nussbaum writes, "there is in this period broad and deep agreement that the central motivation for philosophizing is the urgency of human suffering, and that the goal of philosophy is human flourishing, *eudaimonia.*"[45] As she explains, the procedure of "therapeutic argument" aimed at shaping a healthier psyche depends on the fundamental assumption that "the ethical truth is not independent of what human beings deeply wish, need, and (at some level) desire."[46] While our actual desires and emotions may be unhealthy or inimical to eudaimonia or opposed to our "nature" in its normative sense, without the underlying desire for eudaimonia, the philosophical therapist would have no "hook" by which to help motivate self-reform in the student-patient. Hence the Hellenistic philosophers, like Aristotle, suppose that reflection on the agent-related benefits and harms of different kinds of desires, emotions, and (in general) motives can play a practical role in shaping the self. This would be ruled out on any indirect virtue ethics, just as it was in Annas's proposed solution. I will consider other versions of EEu in section 5.5 to see if they fare better.

4. Sherman on Friendship

Let us now return to friendship and the practices as contexts in which the practical importance of the paradox of eudaimonism becomes especially clear. I have already argued that Aristotle's account of friendship and kindness implied the possibility of pure motives that are in fact inconsistent with his eudaimonist moral psychology. As Nancy Sherman argues in her valuable study, for Aristotle, "both friendship and goodwill require the non-instrumentality of our beneficence."[47] But she, like most commentators, regards this as consistent with interest in eudaimonia as the ultimate wellspring of human motivation. As she explains, self-sufficiency is a mark of eudaimonia for Aristotle, "But since friends are among the goods which make a life self-sufficient, self-sufficiency is relational and the good life is dependent upon and interwoven with others."[48] To realize the agent-related benefit of these relationships, we must value our friends for their own sakes. In the friendship relation, in particular, this means pursuing ends *together*, developing the "capacity to share and co-ordinate activities over an extended period of time."[49] This sort of loyalty involves a kind of constraint on our acquisition of ends: "Ends are co-ordinated not merely within lives, but between lives. Thus, just as a particular choice I make is constrained by my wider system of objectives and ends, so too is it constrained by the ends of my friend."[50] This means that our friendship involves the joint development of a conception of our *joint eudaimonia*.[51] The "consensus" between friends does not simply precede and ground their relation, as it might for parties contracting for mutual self-interest:

> In true friendship, we might say, friends realize shared ends which develop through the friendship and which come to be constitutive of it. Specific common interests are the product rather than a precondition of the relationship. Together my friend and I develop a love of Georgian houses, having had no real interest in them earlier.[52]

I agree with Sherman's point here: friends often do begin to take an interest in some activity or pursuable object simply because their friend cares about this object or pursuit. The question is whether this development can be explained in terms of D3 desires on the erosaic model. Rather than choosing the friend's goals because I see them as part of my good, it seems more likely that I project these ends on the basis of my friendship and only then, *as a result*, come to regard them as part of my good.

To illustrate this with her own example, let us imagine that Professor Sherman knows her friend has started to take an interest in the history, aesthetics, and architectural characteristics of Georgian houses (perhaps after buying one). This "taking an interest" on the friend's part may itself be (partially or wholly) a projective act or it may result from some prior desire (e.g., a D3 desire based on the evaluation of aesthetic or historical knowledge as valuable for one's mind). Sherman herself, we postulate, has no antecedent desire to learn about Georgian houses: the fact that her friend is taking an interest does not represent a sense on Sherman's part of any lack of well-being or deficiency in her own life (if it did, this would be motivation by envy, competitiveness, or a comparative sense of inferiority rather than by friendship). Instead, in a kind of *freedom from prior desire* for it, Sherman projects the end of learning about Georgian houses, visiting them, and preserving them on the grounds that this will allow her to join in her friend's new activities. It is precisely the absence of any prior attraction to this sort of good which shows that in this case, as we would say, "friendship is the motive." Or better, in terms of the existential conception of the striving will, friendship is rather the ground for motivating oneself to pursue this end.

But, the response comes, does not Sherman's motivation instead derive from the more fundamental desire to pursue joint activities with her friend, which she sees as part of her eudaimonia? At this point, several ways to work out this alternative to a projective explanation confront us, but none of them succeed. First, we could say that pursuing joint activities is valued simply as a means to the terminal end of building the friendship, which the agent values intrinsically as part of her flourishing. This fails because it encounters the paradox of eudaimonism: if *this* were Sherman's real motive, she would not really care about Georgian houses, nor would she be acting in a friendly way after all. If she only wants to be the kind of person who has a successful friendship because this is good for her, then she will not be concerned for her friend's needs and interests for their own sake, that is, in the way necessary to have the sort of relationship that often adds to eudaimonia.[53]

Second, we could instead say that (i) the agent desires ends that she can pursue jointly with her friend for their own sake, which is what is necessary for the real sharing of pursuits constitutive of friendship; and (ii) she came to value these ends intrinsically because of recognizing (perhaps in deliberation with her friend) what *realizing them* would contribute to the good shape of her own life as a whole. This suggestion fails because Sherman's point is rather that our motives are sufficiently plastic that we can conform some of them to our friend's motives just out of friendship and not because we have any prior independent desire for the relevant objects or goals. It is very unlikely, for example, that Sherman thinks becoming an expert on Georgian houses itself will improve her life very markedly or that even if she did, this is *why* she came to value this knowledge for its own sake. In friendship, as Sherman's account makes so clear, it is not so much the particular goals, however independently valuable they may be, but rather *the shared pursuit of them* in joint activities that we regard as especially valuable. This implies that we can will$_2$ to be motivated$_1$ to engage in these activities.

On the erosiac model, the first-order interest would have to be some kind of desire for the relevant knowledge and aesthetic experience, and the second-order motive to cultivate this interest would also have to be some kind of orektic desire. But desiring$_2$ in the orektic sense to experience an orektic desire$_1$ is impossible; feeling the lack of some attractive object cannot itself be something to which we are attracted, something whose absence involves a disturbing sense of incompleteness in our being. We must therefore suppose instead that the second-order motive, at least, is projective in form: the agent projects the end of the first-order motive because of what that motive and the activities it motivates will contribute to a particular friendship.

Finally, the eudaimonist could try the following explanation (another version of the 7–8 schema in chap. 7, sec. 7): (i) Sherman is noninstrumentally motivated to learn about Georgian houses, and (ii) pursuing this end *in conjunction with her friend* will contribute directly to her eudaimonia. This has a good chance of being right, but as I have argued, the truth of (ii) could not be the basis of a noninstrumental *desire* for the learning mentioned in (i), because this end itself is not what is singled out as eudaimonistically valuable (or likely to help complete the agent) in (ii). Instead, the motivation mentioned in (i) is probably projective.

5. Practices, Virtue, and External Eudaimonism

5.1. Four Kinds of Practice

A similar conclusion might be drawn with regard to MacIntyre's well-known treatment of goods internal to practices in *After Virtue*.[54] MacIntyre begins with the notion of a "practice" as a "coherent and complex form of socially established cooperative human activity" that involves a certain kind of *reflexive* attitude, or self-conscious concern about its history and mutual recognition between practitioners. This attitude is analogous, in fact, to the reciprocal recognition of other-regarding interest that Aristotle takes to be a necessary condition of noble friendship. Specifically, MacIntyre says that in a practice, (1) the activity of practitioners is teleologically constituted in the sense that it involves "standards of excellence which are appropriate to, and partially definitive of, that form of activity"; and (2) the goods brought about in trying to realize the ends of the practice in an excellent way, or "trying to achieve those standards of excellence," *include* the systematic "extension" or enrichment of its participants' conception of the ends of the practice, and the goods involved in devoting oneself to them.[55]

Applying this analysis to one of MacIntyre's examples, "Planting turnips is not a practice [but] farming is," because the former activity is not reflexively constituted in the way that the latter is: putting turnip roots into the ground in a customary way is simply a behavior done with the intention of growing turnips, while "farming" is a more complex project that, if we devote ourselves to the end of farming well (and all this involves), will enrich us through a better understanding of what farming can achieve, what its possibilities are, and what joys it can bring quite apart from making a profit. Practices are reflexive in the sense that in addition to their primary aim, they involve a second-order goal, namely, in conjunction with others (both in the past and the present) to redefine and extend the first-order goals that the practice can encompass. Thus the telos of a practice is somewhat plastic: "practices never have a goal or goals fixed for all time."[56]

The reflexivity that distinguishes "practices" from simple or first-order activities depends on the phenomena that MacIntyre calls "goods internal to practices." His famous example of teaching a slightly recalcitrant child to play chess offers a preliminary explanation of this notion:

> Notice however that so long as it is the candy alone which provides the child with a good reason for playing chess, the child has no reason not to cheat and every reason to cheat, provided he or she can do so successfully. But, so we may hope, there will come a time when the child will find in those goods specific to chess, in the achievement of a certain highly particular kind of analytical skill, strategic imagination and competitive intensity, a new set of reasons, reasons now not just for winning on a particular occasion, but for trying to excel in whatever way the game of chess demands. Now if the child cheats, he or she will be defeating not me, but himself or herself.[57]

MacIntyre's example is both plausible and persuasive. In this case, the good internal to the practice of chess is the good of rule-constrained strategic excellence, or *winning through fair and cunning moves*. The child must aim at this goal *for its own sake* in order to count as truly playing chess rather than only going through the moves to get some candy, prize money, or other external reward. Since chess is a game, this requires a kind of "suspension of disbelief," or perhaps "secondary belief," by which we enter into the frame of the artifice and imagine therein that the goal of the game is all-important in its own right. In nongame practices, we must acquire the same conviction about the value of the end in the primary world, outside any artificial contexts more specific than culture itself.

Let us call this producible good G, which incorporates the currently accepted standards of excellence in the practice P and which the agent must pursue for its own sake for her activity to count as engaging in P, *the end definitive of the practice*, since the intention to bring about this end is essential to actions that qualify one as a practitioner. Since practices are defined by their ends, we can draw some important distinctions among types of practices by distinguishing different genera of practice-defining ends.

First, it seems to be distinctive of practices that involve in some kind of *game* or *sport* that their defining end is one with no independent material value to the well-being of the practitioner or anyone else in society. Rather, these ends are purely conventional, set up so that the pursuit of them will require the development of rare talents and the demanding exercise of various human capacities. Checkmating the opponent's king, or winning a marathon, or hitting a small leather ball with a wooden bat and running around some bases does not in itself add much to anyone's well-bring. Rather, we set up these artificial goals because we known that earnestly pursuing them in the right ways tends to generate what Elster called valuable by-product benefits, including, for example, physical and mental health, the enjoyment of practitioners and spectators, and perhaps the camaraderie of teammates and spectators who enjoy each other's company. Notice, however, the crucial point that these good side effects will be lost if they replace the practice-defining ends as the practitioner's intended goals. A showman is usually less interesting to spectators and valuable to teammates than a player motivated to cooperate by his pure interest in playing the game well; "team spirit" depends on striving for excellence in the sport as an end-in-itself.

David Miller calls this kind of practice "self-contained"; by contrast, "practices which exist to serve social ends beyond themselves" he calls "purposive."[58] His point is that the second kind of practice has both a utility and often a crucial function in supporting social structures that make its conception of its definitive product-good (or excellence in producing it) subject to external critique.[59] These are the sort of practices that Plato called "crafts" (*techne*), which have as their defining end some *material social good* that transcends the immediate material interests of the practitioner but serves the good of a larger community, including most proximally the "patients" served by these practices. This is why such practices provide useful examples in Plato's arguments against egoism (e.g., in the famous argument against Thrasymachus in *Republic* I). Socrates' examples of the horseman, the ship's pilot, the doctor, and the statesman show the practitioner as aiming primarily at the good of horses, the safety of the ship and her crew, the bodily health of the patients, and the common good of the entire state, respectively.

In other words, these practices are defined by what I have called *pure* commitments to agent-transcending first-order goods. Plato emphasizes this by having Socrates suggest that no art seeks any "advantage" for itself or its craftsmen, "since it needs nothing" (*Republic* I 342D). Likewise, in his rejoinder to Thrasymachus's insistence that the shepherd fattens the sheep for his own profit, Socrates urges in its pure form, "the art of shepherding . . . cares simply and solely for what it is set over . . . since for itself, all has been sufficiently provided" (*Republic* I 345C). These phrasings certainly suggest that need or lack is not the practitioner's motive; rather, her interest in the end definitive of her practice is *non-erosiac*. This suggests that the artist or craftsman *volitionally projects* his end, but Plato does not recognize this implication. In the case of sports, the practice-defining first-order end is only conventionally a good, so the agent projects participation in the game as her end. In the case of professional arts and crafts, the defining end is some natural good either of individuals or collectives of persons. (In some cases, such as veterinary medicine or environmental preservation, it would be the flourishing of nonhuman animals and plants instead.) The would-be practitioner must presumably recognize this natural value, at least in outline, to project the goals of her practice (although her understanding of these goods will also deepen with experience).

Third, what today we call the social and natural sciences are practices that have as their defining ends various forms of *knowledge*, valued for their own sake. These forms of knowledge may have all sorts of practical benefits to human and nonhuman life, including technical applications to laborsaving devices or to better design of educational systems, and so on. But it is essential to the conception of the sciences that their practitioners should not be motivated primarily by these possible material benefits but rather by the search for truth to fundamental questions about physical and human nature themselves. Experience has shown that over time, this kind of "pure research" often has more profound by-product benefits by way of technology and institutional applications than inquiry that is primarily instrumental in motivation. Indeed, where scientific research is constrained by the special interests of different for-profit enterprises with a financial stake in the outcomes, the unbiased search for truth is compromised and its long-term by-product benefits to the entire human community are thus undermined. A scientist hired by either the coal lobby or the Sierra Club to investigate global warming probably cannot practice climatology in its pure form. This is the main reason why disinterested government sources, along with universities that remain neutral about the outcomes, ought to be the main funders of scientific research related to controversial policy questions that may also impact corporate profits.

Fourth, we might wish to distinguish the fine arts as a group of practices that aim not so much at material goods of individuals or communities but rather at the creation of beauty for its own sake—although human enjoyment of this beauty is generally also taken to be a subsidiary end in these practices, which are therefore essentially *expressive or communicative* in structure. If this is right, a particular fine art such as sculpture will involve two defining ends: the making of a beautiful sculpture (however this may be conceived) and the expression to other human persons of something that only this sort of work can express—something that often cannot be put into words, which is precisely why it must be "said" in a sculpture instead.

Fine arts, as a genus of the practices, would also seem to be distinguished by the fact that beyond the technical skills required for (say) good dancing, or painting, or sculpture, which concern knowing how to work with the "materials" of the art, standards of excellence for the products themselves tend to be much more plastic, fluid, and constantly in contention among practitioners than in the case of other practices. For example, striking out in the ninth inning with the bases loaded, or making a specious argument, or infecting a patient with a poorly cleaned instrument can never count as great baseball, or sound philosophy, or excellent surgery. By contrast, I may think that *Finnegans Wake* is nonsense masquerading as literature or that a Jackson Pollock painting is just random paint spilled on a canvas, expressing nothing but the artist's pretentiousness, yet I know that others will passionately disagree and respond with all sorts of arguments for the excellence of these products. This tends to give the impression that the *objectivity* of evolved standards, which MacIntyre points out as a hallmark of the practices,[60] does not apply to the fine arts.

But the fact that these questions of excellence are not (at least among practitioners) demoted to questions of brute subjective preference (or D2 desire) tends to suggest that an imaginary convergence toward universal standards of excellence does operate as a heuristic ideal in the fine arts, motivating the communicative process of seeking to define and redefine what counts as great art. To the extent that artists seek to persuade us and each other that their works give us good reasons for interpreting excellence in artistic products one way or another, they are not simply trying to impose their tastes by force. The historicity of practices is simply more evident and constantly on the surface in these practices (suggesting that they may involve further levels of reflexivity absent from other practices).

Hence in the fine arts too, the defining product is an agent-transcending first-order good that is internally constrained by standards of excellence, although there are more varieties of excellence and the standards are both vaguer and more contentious than in sports, the social crafts, or the sciences. Here again, pursuit of the defining first-order goal can have several kinds of by-product benefits, but only if the artist pursues beautiful, meaningful, or otherwise excellent art as her primary end. Art produced simply to please a mass market or even to flatter a highly elite market is not fine art at all but merely its simulacrum. It may be that originality is sometimes overvalued in the fine arts as a sign of the purity of the artist's motives, and that too many artists fall into the self-defeating trap of being more concerned about their purity than about their product's values. Yet MacIntyre's analysis suggests that the artist will be more successful and fulfilled if he does not focus obsessively on himself but instead focuses on the work to be made, trying to make it the best it can possibly be.

5.2. MacIntyre on the Structure of Practices

This brings us to MacIntyre's distinction between two different kinds of goods internal to practices—a distinction that really needs more emphasis than it receives in *After Virtue*. He initially distinguishes external and internal goods as follows:

> On the one hand there are those goods externally and contingently attached to chess-playing and to other practices by the accidents of social circumstance—in the case of the imaginary child candy, in the case of real adults such goods as prestige, status and money. There are always alternative ways for achieving such goods, and their achievement is never to be had *only* by engaging in some particular kind of practice. On the other hand, there are the goods internal to the practice of chess which cannot be had in any way but by playing chess or some other game of that specific kind.[61]

But "internality" to a practice does not rest primarily on that practice being the *sole means* to a good. It has to do more directly with the way an internal good is realized. Someone acting much as a practitioner of a given practice, but doing so only to gain an external good, treats the practice *merely* as a means and thus does not *authentically engage* in it. Someone engaged in a practice pursues its defining internal goods by striving to meet standards of excellence for the practice's producible object with their *intrinsic worth* in mind: as we have seen, the authentic participant must pursue such excellence for its own sake. To aim at excellent production of the goods defining a practice, then, is to act on a kind of pure motive, in which eudaimonia is not the agent's direct *aim*. As Iris Murdoch put it in a famous essay that influenced MacIntyre and other authors in the twentieth-century revival of virtue ethics, "In intellectual disciplines and in the enjoyment of art and nature we discover value in our ability to forget self, to be realistic, to perceive justly"—in other words, to *transcend ourselves* toward a world of real values.[62] This is why Murdoch talks about "the absolute pointlessness of virtue" and finds in art "a love which is unpossessive and unselfish."[63] Therefore, *if the agent also benefits from engaging in a practice, this is a side effect of pursuing the goals defining the practice for their own sake.*

Thus we must distinguish between two kinds of goods internal to practices. In MacIntyre's interesting example of portrait painting as a practice, "There is first of all the excellence of the products, both the excellence in performance by the painters and that of each portrait itself."[64] It is by aiming to paint a good portrait (and, at the second-order level, aiming to interpret what should count as "good" here) that the artist realizes another good in himself as agent:

> it is in participation in the attempts to sustain progress and to respond creatively to problems that the second kind of good internal to the practice of portrait painting is to be found. For what the artist

Contemporary Solutions to the Paradox and Their Problems 257

discovers within the pursuit of excellence in portrait painting—and what is true of portrait painting is true of the practice of the fine arts in general—is the good of a certain kind of life.[65]

This agent-related good of "a certain kind of life" we could understand as the fulfillment that comes from mastery of particular skills and their employment in creating particular forms of beauty, together with the relationships (with other artists, with customers, subjects of the portraits, etc.) that this involves. It seems plausible that such an agent-related internal good is possible for virtually every kind of practice—though its realization surely depends in part on the social status of the relevant practice, the just or unjust state of the institutions that sustain it, and how engagement in the practice fits into the individual's overall life. But the crucial point is that the agent-related goods internal to a practice are *not targetable*: they are, in Elster's sense, essentially by-products of targeting the internal goods *definitive* of the practice. It is only via a sustained commitment to the practice-defining internal goods (and their further articulation), which are always agent-transcending in nature, that the practitioner realizes the *agent-related* goods internal to the practice. Calling them both "internal goods" usefully emphasizes their difference from external or commodity goods that are realizable without practices, but it also obscures the fundamental difference between these two types of internal goods.

However, MacIntyre does recognize this difference and also finds it in Aristotle: "As Aristotle says, the enjoyment of the activity and the enjoyment of the achievement are not the ends at which the agent aims, but the enjoyment supervenes upon the successful activity in such a way that the activity achieved and the activity enjoyed are one and the same state."[66] MacIntyre's analysis of practices perhaps warrants a small modification to Aristotle's formula, since MacIntyre shows that not only the *successful* achievement of the practice's defining goals but also the purified *pursuit* of excellences may generate such enjoyment as an agent-related internal good. We can diagram the main distinction as follows, again using single arrows for intention and double arrows for the causation of unintended side effects:

The Structure of Practices

Agent-related goods internal to the practice (personal fulfillment, enjoyment of one's products, companionship, and other goods of the kind of life that centers around the given practice).

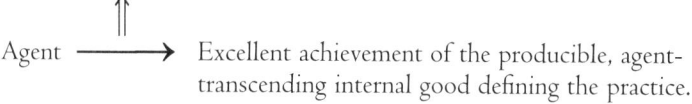

Agent ⟶ Excellent achievement of the producible, agent-transcending internal good defining the practice.

This diagram does not say whether the by-product internal goods related to the practitioner's own eudaimonia are themselves targetable or not, and it seems reasonable to suppose that at least some of these benefits realized in the course of authentically engaging in a practice could also be directly pursued, once their value is understood. Among these, for example, might be the formation of friendships with copractitioners who, given their pure concern for the producible good defining the practice, ought naturally to cooperate in various ways, depending on the nature of the particular practice (another point that Plato makes at *Republic* I 349A–50B). One could easily imagine two copractitioners, on discovering that they had grown into a friendship through cooperation in pursuit of shared goals, performing a "Diotimian switch" and directly willing to develop their relationship as valuable for its own sake, beyond its value for mutual engagement in the same practice. But once again, directly pursuing such a good that was only contingently a by-product of engagement in some practice will require pure motivation to pursue a new kind of agent-transcending final end, which in turn will have other by-product benefits. Thus the structure of friendship looks like this:

The Structure of Friendship

Agent-related goods internal to the friendship (enjoying company, improving one's character, fulfillment in helping the other person, etc.)

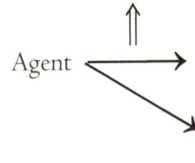

Agent ⟷ The friend's good as an agent-transcending internal good defining the relationship; and

The cultivation of the relationship itself, including any relations with third parties it may involve.

As this diagram suggests, the structure of friendship is analogous to that of practices, except that we probably have to distinguish *two* producible agent-transcending internal goods that define the "quasi-practice" of friendship, the second of which indicates an additional layer of reflexivity internal to friendship. Friendship also lacks the sort of formal institutional framework that sustains the other practices and, being more universal (a quasi-practice that no worthwhile life can lack), its standards of excellence are more fully ethical than are the aesthetic, scientific, and professional standards of the other practices. But beyond these differences, the basic structure is very similar.

It seems plausible, then, that engaging in practices will tend to produce some benefits to the practitioner that are essentially by-products, and among those side effects that can be directly targeted in turn, the most significant of these will, when pursued for their own sake, produce yet further types of second-order satisfaction. This regress must come to an end in side effects that are *essentially* by-products, which can never be pursued as producible goods without self-defeat. However, MacIntyre does not see the problem this implies for his neo-Aristotelian reconstruction of the virtues; the fact that we can engage in practices with the kind of pure motivation needed to realize their agent-related by-product goods is really incompatible with the Aristotelian idea that all of a human agent's motivation is governed (even if only *formally*, as Annas urged) by the flourishing or *eudaimonia* of the agent as her highest good or telos.

5.3. Marx on Unalienated Labor

I have argued that the agent engages in a practice by *dedicating himself* to the pursuit of its defining end products irrespective of any prior need for them rather than pursuing his chosen profession, art, or craft simply because he finds himself *drawn* to it as part of a *eudaimon* life (as in D3 desires). This point is also implicit in one nineteenth-century conception of labor as *vocation* that is among MacIntyre's most important sources: Karl Marx's early work on human nature and alienation. Following Hegel, Marx recognized the will *as Geist* at work in the creation of culture: "In creating an objective world" of institutions and artifacts "by his practical activity, in working up inorganic nature, man proves himself a conscious species being."[67] By this Hegelian term, Marx means that we can aim at social and abstract ends, such as beauty for its own sake. We are therefore also *free* to motivate ourselves in ways not open to other animals: "an animal only produces what it immediately needs for itself or its young. It produces one-sidedly, whilst man produces universally. It produces only under the dominion of immediate physical need, whilst man produces even when he is free from physical need, and only truly produces in freedom therefrom."[68]

In other words, our shared species nature is to engage in what I have called projective motivation; when this is expressed in free labor, we live authentically in accord with our nature and thus also in solidarity with each other. As Erich Fromm says, "work is for [Marx] the active relatedness of man to nature, the creation of a new world, including the creation of man himself." Capitalism alienates the laborer from his products by turning them into private property valued in terms external to the will and self-expression of the worker.[69] In my terms, Marx's view is that capitalism destroys authentic or free labor by forcing the worker to act on D1-D2 desires, making his product only as a means to a paycheck rather than freely projecting his work as valuable for its own sake. Then "labour does not appear as an end-in-itself but as the servant of the wage."[70] As Alan Gilbert says in his impressive chapter on "The Aristotelian lineage of Marx's eudaemonism," Marx inherited from Aristotle the idea that alienation from our human nature arises from "work only as a means of life, not as its varied expression."[71] For Aristotle also, "humans conduct the highest activities—non-productive ones—not under the pressure of necessity but by choice."[72] These activities may produce knowledge, friendship, and beauty rather than material comforts, food, and pleasure.

Marx's original goal, then, is a form of social life that allows the fullest cooperative expression of the striving will in its existential sense. As Fromm says, his main goal is not "the equalization of income" but rather "the liberation of man from a kind of work which destroys his individuality, which transforms him into a thing."[73] It is important to recognize this, even if Marx's goal is actually more difficult to realize than his proposed solutions implied—government ownership of major industries, for example, will not do the trick. In the twentieth century, we have learned that the problems of materialism, consumerism, and status-seeking, which discourage people from projecting more important goals for their lives, cannot be overcome by collectivizing all private property. Radical social reforms may help persons oppressed by poverty get the opportunity to pursue other ambitions besides material survival and help stop the artificial stimulation of acquisitiveness and egoism by ratings-driven media, but beyond that, each individual has to face hard questions in deciding what to live for. We cannot be forced to be free.

Though I have given it an existentialist gloss, Marx's own explanation of his concept of *Homo faber* implies a *eudaimonistic* motive that is ultimately erosiac in form. After talking about motivation free from material needs, he still describes his ideal *eudaimon* man as follows: "The rich human being is simultaneously the human being in need of a totality of human life-activities—the man in whom his own realization exists as an inner necessity, as need."[74]

For Marx, this includes even "poverty" as the experience of dependence on others, for it is valuable for us to experience "the need of the greatest wealth—the other human being."[75] Marx contrasts this proper spiritual need with the artificial appetites that the capitalist tries to create in a consumer "to find satisfaction of his own selfish need."[76] Marx's alternative to such material egoism is thus still an Aristotelian formal egoism of self-realization. The requirements for this kind of self-realization oppose material egoism only because he believes (like Plato) that unalienated work will naturally tend to foster solidarity with others.

Thus Marx runs into the same problem as MacIntyre. His central idea of creative work not motivated by material need is most easily understood in terms of projective motivation, but as a (left) Hegelian, he wishes to interpret it formally in terms of self-realization. Yet in creative work, we are not primarily aiming at self-perfection or even self-expression; although we often do express much of our own mind, thought, and character in our works—and sometimes even intentionally communicate through them—we grow and gain self-worth by expressing our will through our creative work only because when engaged in it, we devote ourselves to values *beyond* our own eudaimonia. The world is not our mirror, not Narcissus's pool; rather, we realize ourselves by mirroring in our devotion the possibilities of value opened for us by the world itself. Why it is that the world offers us such values by devotion to which we can define an authentic self is a metaphysical question of the first order that I do not address in this work. But the existential account of striving will at least allow this problem to come into view, whereas the eudaimonist model obscures it.

5.4. *Rawls on Practices*

The same point applies to Rawls's "Aristotelian principle" (AP) as a criterion for the full deliberative rationality of life plans. AP says that:

> other things being equal, human beings enjoy the exercise of their realized capacities (their innate or trained abilities), and this enjoyment increases the more the capacity is realized, or the greater its complexity.... For example, chess is a more complicated game than checkers, and algebra is more intricate than elementary arithmetic. Thus the principle says that someone who can do both generally prefers playing chess to checkers, and that he would rather study algebra than arithmetic.[77]

Now, AP is a plausible principle for human psychology and it is obviously related to MacIntyre's conception of practices; but as Rawls states it, AP conflates two different kinds of motivation: simple D2 preferences for different kinds of *entertainment* or *play*, and projective motivation to pursue the complex goals of a demanding practice for their own sake. This corresponds to the difference between a casual chess player and grand master or a casual reader of mathematical books and a professional mathematician. We also see this conflation in Rawls's defense of AP:

> Presumably complex activities are more enjoyable because they satisfy the desire for variety and novelty of experience, and leave room for feats of ingenuity and invention. They also evoke the pleasures of anticipation and surprise, and often the overall form of the activity, its structural development, is fascinating and beautiful. Moreover,

simpler activities exclude the possibility of individual styles and personal expression which complex activities permit or even require.[78]

Some of the goods Rawls refers to here are certain kinds of first-order pleasure that also explain why we might prefer to see a new movie rather than one we have seen before or a thriller rather than a documentary. But such desires for entertainment and novelty can take us only so far, and other values in Rawls's description refer to intrinsic goods in the *products* of complex and challenging activities, which are achievable for the most part *only* if we project them for their own sake. Finally, originality of individual style or uniqueness of personal expression is not something that we can desire in the D2 sense of a simple *pleasure*, and if we think of it as part of holistic happiness and thus desirable in the D3 sense, it is not clear how directly it can be pursued. It seems, rather, that the chance for originality and development of one's individual distinctness in an activity would be among the agent-related by-product goods of pursuing a practice in MacIntyre's sense. It could also be among the *grounds* for getting into a practice, without any prior *desire* for it motivating our activities in the practice. Rawls misses this point when he writes:

> If we ask why we are willing to undergo the stresses of practice and learning, the reason may be (if we leave out of account external rewards and penalties) that having had some success learning things in the past, and experiencing the present enjoyments of the activity, we are led to expect even greater satisfaction once we acquire a greater repertoire of skills.

This seems to explain our engagement in practices as the result of egoistic maximization of our rationally expected utility: "there must be some level of achieved ability beyond which the gains from a further increase in this level are just offset by the burdens of the further practice and study necessary to bring it about."[79] But such a calculating motive will be self-defeating; the agent will give up whenever the returns are not forthcoming quickly enough and thus will be unable to *commit himself wholeheartedly* to his endeavor whatever the consequences (within reason). The projective resolve that puts the whole self behind a priority for action is not only non-egoistic but also non-maximizing in form (see chap. 13).[80]

In sum, there is good reason to think that no one can be entirely fulfilled without engaging in some practice-like activities; this is implied by both AP and Feinberg's example of Jones the abstract egoist (see chap. 4, sec. 2.3). But this truth could at most provide some type of retrospective *justification* for getting into a practice, not any prepurposive *motivation* to take up a practice. For the same reason, the fact that life is incomplete without developing one's talents in some practice can provide only an objective, third-personal reason for the virtues that practices require, not any first-personal motivation to be virtuous. An agent reflecting on the *eudaimon* life might be able to see that the virtues, as dispositions of pure motivation in their own right, are essential preconditions of the kind of cooperation required by the pure pursuit of internal goods definitive of the practices; but she could not be *motivated* to become or remain virtuous because this would enable her to gain the fulfillment that comes from engaging in practices. This fulfillment, like the joy of friendship, may be an essential component of human eudaimonia, but these components are experienced only by agents who care about goods unconnected to their eudaimonia. We seem to be left, then, in the same position reached by Annas's proposed resolution to the paradox of eudaimonism.

5.5. *Hursthouse's Habituation Version of External Eudaimonism*

Notably, this is also the position defended by Rosalind Hursthouse, who argues that virtues typically benefit their possessor (at least better than any other "candidate 'regimen'"), and that this provides part of their objective justification.[81] But she denies that this truth provides any part of the agent's internal reasons for virtuous action: "I do not regard their role [in benefiting their possessor] as providing a motivating reason for being virtuous." But this question of motivation, she says, is entirely distinct from the "separate issue" of providing objective justification of the virtues: "So I put the motivation question aside here as a red herring."[82]

This position rejects psychological eudaimonism but endorses rational eudaimonism, which makes it a version of external eudaimonism, like Annas's proposed solution to the paradox of A-eudaimonism. However, Hursthouse's version of EEu is not an indirect eudaimonism; on her account, practical reasons concerning eudaimonia do not recommend any self-effacing manipulation. Rather, they motivate one set of agents to cultivate virtuous motives in another set of agents. While reflection on the eudaimonistic value of the virtues, friendship, and practices may play no motivating role in the life of the flourishing individual (e.g., it does not move him to develop friendships, engage in practices, or reform his vices), this reflective knowledge does play a practical role over time at the *interpersonal* level: persons enlightened by this knowledge are motivated by it to *habituate others* into the virtues, friendship, and practices in order that they may achieve eudaimonia, even though this will not be their motivating goal. These others, in turn, will eventually be able to recognize the eudaimonistic retrospective justification of this kind of life and be motivated by it to bring up the next generation with the types of pure motivation required for their eudaimonia. Call this the habituation version of EEu.

Hursthouse clearly favors this solution; she writes that our knowledge of the agent-relative benefits of virtuous dispositions motivates us, as good parents who "have their children's interests at heart," to modify and redirect our children's self-interested impulses toward more noble ends.[83] We, not they, are motivated by an understanding of the by-product benefits that their virtues will bring them. Thus the parent or guardian in this model is motivated by pure concerns for the child's or student's eudaimonia and for their moral goodness, even when it does not make them happier. Such pure adult motives derive in turn from the habituative care of their parents and teachers in the past. The desire for one's own eudaimonia remains external to the set of motive-states that tend best to bring about holistic happiness or "self-realization" for the individual living a good life.

Now, one immediately obvious question about this habituation version of EEu will be: What is the motive of the teacher who, based on her enlightened reflection on the various kinds of by-product fulfillment essential to human eudaimonia, decides to train others to develop the types of pure motivation that give rise to such fulfillment? Evidently it cannot be *her own* eudaimonia that motivates her; rather, she is acting to help secure her student's eudaimonia. It is compatible with the habituation model to say that the agent's concern (as parent, teacher, friend, etc.) for the ideal psychological development of her subject is a form of pure motivation that she herself developed under the tutelage of a similarly motivated guardian in the past. She is habituated to show loving care for those who need her direction to learn the motives necessary for eudaimonia. By hypothesis, she will certainly understand that this activity—the ethical education of young persons by habituation into the virtues, friendship, and the practices, which is itself another kind of quasi-practice as ubiquitous and essential to flourishing human communities as friendship itself—is likely itself to be highly fulfilling for her overall (though often frustrating in the details and at given moments). And she can verify that in fact the activity of moral education is rewarding in her life.

But this contribution to her own eudaimonia need not be her *motive*; in pursuing the other's ethical education, she may act quite purely for the sake of this agent-transcending end. Rather, this potential to achieve part of her happiness through acting as a good parent or ethical teacher would be part of what motivated her teachers and parents in the past to fit her with the kinds of pure motivation required to engage in this quasi-practice. The objection only applies to this dynamic interpersonal model in the form of the question: How did this whole process get started with *the first ethical teacher*? But the objection in this form is so speculative that it is of little interest; perhaps, for instance, the original (untaught) ethical teachers acquired the pure motives necessary to be good ethical teachers by some kind of accident or by luck or divine intervention?

Leaving this chicken-and-egg conundrum aside, however, there is a more subtle and important objection to the habituation version of EEu that requires attention. It concerns the problem of how, precisely, the ethical teacher is supposed to cultivate the requisite types of pure motivation in her children, students, or (generally) subjects. The habituation model necessarily assumes that this can be done by appealing only to prior desires of the D1-D3 varieties, without requiring the subject actively to project agent-transcending goals for herself. For without this assumption, the theory of habituation ceases to be recognizably eudaimonist and turns into an existential theory describing how to encourage the child's striving will to care about or commit itself to the right sort of ends. This, of course, is the sort of theory of moral education that I think we need.

The objection challenges the assumption that D1-D3 desires can do all the work by arguing that if Aristotle's broadly desiderative (or orektic) moral psychology were correct, it would be impossible for someone to *get into* a practice, or into a virtuous interpersonal relationship, in the right way. The theory of habituation must explain how the young (or uncultivated) subject can transition from motivation primarily by self-interested desire for the external goods contingently realizable through the practice or relationship to an (apparently non-orektic) motivation to pursue the agent-transcending end(s) definitive of the practice or relationship for their own sake(s).

As we have seen, this transition cannot *itself* be motivated by desire for the agent-related goods internal to the practice without becoming self-stultifying, because these internal goods are (at least in part) essentially by-products. So it appears after all that this transition requires a moment of reckoning within the subject when he becomes an agent in the full sense and *projectively motivates himself* to pursue the pure goal, leaving behind interest in the external good as irrelevant, or at least as only of secondary concern. The subject is not learning new motives by rote repetition of actions that a virtuous person would do, nor simply taking a "bait" to act in ways that will awaken higher desires, but rather discovering the desire-independent value of agent-transcending goods and projecting them as his ends or striving toward them.

To return to the example that MacIntyre says is the most important in *After Virtue*:[84] What exactly happens in the crucial transition from playing chess for the sake of getting candy or money to playing it "for its own sake"? It is, of course, plausible that a child who first plays for money might notice certain targetable by-products of doing this, such as the thrill of anticipating the next moves and the pleasure of capturing the opponent's piece, and begin to play more for this kind of excitement or entertainment value or even as a means to build up technical skills. But this will not constitute pure devotion to the goal of the game.

We might imagine that the transition occurs because the child next recognizes that the internal goods of exercising strategic imagination are inherently enjoyable or (more eudaimonistically) that they add to a well-rounded life. But notice the problem with this suggestion: if the transition occurs only because the child recognizes its incompleteness without these forms of second-order satisfaction and conceives what I have called a D3 desire for the difficult strategic engagement that playing chess well provides, and then plays chess for the sake of attaining *that end*, her motives will become self-defeating (in very much the same way that becoming reflectively aware of one's focused concentration on something ruins the whole gestalt of that concentration). The child has to play with *winning fairly*—or perhaps *playing well*—as a terminal end of her activity if she is to realize the full agent-related internal goods, some of which are not directly targetable (or are achievable only in pursuits that are not undertaken for the sake of experiencing or possessing these goods).

As a result, I say that the child learning to play chess must at some point *set himself* the goal of playing chess well as a terminal end if he is ever to rise above playing merely for external reward and enter into the practice in a way that might eventually yield all of its agent-related internal goods. This may not be a fully conscious process and it usually will not be reflectively articulated; he may recognize only later how fundamentally his motives have changed, but the change still requires projective commitment at some level, whether clearly introspected or not. Moreover, the child can have a variety of grounds for doing so, for example, the inherently interesting nature of the challenge involved in chess or the chance to exercise his capacities, to form friendships, and so on, but these grounds cannot consist simply of D3 desires.

Theories of habituation are characteristically vague about this crucial transition of motive precisely in order to finesse the difficulty I have emphasized. If we imagine that this transition occurs by pure conditioning—that there arrives a moment when the chess-playing child has played enough games that he simply begins to play chess for the challenge of playing well and possibly winning through skill—we would have to accept the incredible tutelage thesis, which holds that no one can ever *voluntarily* enter into a practice in such a way as to realize its internal agent-related goods. The emphasis on habituation in MacIntyre's chess-playing child example coheres all too well with this tutelage thesis, which is one of its weaknesses. For even if, in the case of training a young child to enjoy complex activities (like chess), we think that the child can involuntarily acquire pure motives that will be valuable to him, due only to the initiative of others guiding him, this cannot be true in every case of entering into practices in such a way as to realize their internal goods.

To refute the tutelage thesis, consider the example of the agent-transcending value of answering a difficult and important philosophical question as *grounds* for taking up this task, quite independently of any prior orektic desire for it. It is true that participating in the practice of philosophical inquiry and cultivating its virtues may add to my eudaimonia (despite having other more frustrating side effects as well). But my motivation to enter into this practice cannot be explained on the basis of my desire for my eudaimonia (even if this desire is innate in every human being) or any other more specific D1-D3 desire by which I could be encouraged to perform some of the same actions that philosophers perform. For the encouragements I received to engage in this practice, while significant enough, were certainly insufficient by themselves to get me to start pursuing philosophical goals on my own. Rather, I had to transcend these incentives and promptings by deciding to enter into this practice (despite deep concerns about its likely financial effects) and devoting my energies to it.

And such cases are common; entering into a practice often involves a strong sense of risk, which is accepted only because the agent projects the ends to which this practice is dedicated, thinking them important enough to be worth the risks involved in devoting a substantial portion of her life to them. This point is sufficient to refute the tutelage thesis as a universal generalization, but I would venture the stronger suggestion that the tutelage thesis may be false in every case of authentic engagement in practices. Even if one's initial motives for getting involved in a practice were ordinary ones like the desire to follow in a parent's footsteps, or the desire to feel that one belongs to a group, or the desire to learn a lucrative trade, one's motivation for continuing involvement in the practice *becomes* projective in time, and this is the key to realizing the agent-related goods internal to that practice. There comes a point where no further management by others can do more by way of making the goals of the practice seem desirable, and the agent has to move over the threshold by her own will-power. This is precisely because what really makes these goals worthwhile is not any material or formal relationship to her own well-being that could cause her to desire them in the orektic sense. Their intrinsic value is independent of such relations and calls to us without luring or attracting.

Finally, let us take up a case that will help distinguish this projective motivation relevant to practices from closely related D3 desires. Suppose someone becomes involved in a practice because she has D3 desires for the ends that the practice serve; for example, someone resolves to become a doctor out of a desire to reduce death and suffering in her community. This is a D3 desire because it depends on her visceral horror or aversion to needless loss of life and suffering; prior to forming her intentions, she experiences these evils quite personally as a hole in her world, an incompleteness in her happiness. Let us imagine that she also believes she will flourish in the role of fighting these evils. Could these agent-related desires be sufficient for her to enter into the practice of medicine, which requires valuing its internal goods intrinsically?

It seems that they might come close. For she would care about the health of her patients as an end-in-itself, as she would not if she entered medical school simply with the motive of gaining wealth (to satisfy D2 preferences). But her attitude would not be quite right; the battle against disease would be too visceral for her. For she would be drawn toward curing her patients and preventing further disease as a constitutive part of her own eudaimonia—almost as if their bodies were part of her own. But suppose that in time, with success as a doctor, her own happiness starts to depend less viscerally on reducing death and suffering, but she nevertheless remains committed to practicing medicine. Then her motivation for participating in the practice has outlived the satisfaction of the original D3 desire and become projective. She remains dedicated to the goal of medicine because she *wills* that it be her end and not simply because it satisfies an empathetic emotion. We might describe her will as compassionate, but it would be a motive-state quite distinct from empathetic revulsion at disease and injury.

Another person might abhor the same kind of suffering in a rural community, seeing it as wrong and needless, although he does not experience a visceral reaction to it nor any very strong empathetic disturbance that can be returned to equilibrium only by making the community more healthy. He does not *desire* this goal in an erosiac sense; the value of health does not call like a Siren to him, drawing him toward fulfillment of a lack. Rather, he acts on thoughts such as: treating the sick would be a worthy enterprise; I have the opportunity to get into medical school now; and I have no other plans that conflict with this. On these grounds, he projects Hippocratic ends as *his own* goals and thereby motivates himself to enter the practice of family medicine. In the process of pursuing this project, he eventually also develops D3 desires for the internal goods defining his practice, but these desires are, in Nagel's sense, "motivated." He can no longer be fully content if health conditions are declining in his town, but that is because of his volitional devotion to improving these conditions.

This shows how projective willing can motivate an agent's desire for goods internal to a practice, without the agent's initial motive for participating in the practice deriving solely from D3 desires for its ends. If this were impossible, in fact, then the habituation necessary to acquire many of the most interesting and important D3 desires would (as Aristotle may have thought) be wholly dependent on fortunate intervention or benign manipulation by others and could never be self-willed. Accepting this would be a high theoretical price to pay, especially since many moral conceptions of responsibility for character do presuppose that a responsible agent can regard herself as capable of self-reform and ordinary effort to develop her talents and various capacities in better and worse ways without depending entirely on others.

6. Watson's Pure Aretaic Naturalism

Another interesting alternative to A-eudaimonism and its problems is what I will call a "pure aretaic naturalist" account that does not rest the moral importance of the virtues on more basic concepts of eudaimonia or well-being. In his justly famous paper on virtue ethics, Gary Watson offers such a theory. It emerges from his attempt to distinguish what he calls "Aristotelianism" both from "character utilitarianism" (which holds that the right conduct is defined in relation to the virtues, and "a virtue is a human trait the possession of which tends to promote human happiness more than the possession of alternative traits")[85] and from what Rawls calls "perfectionism" (which holds that right action maximizes good outcomes defined as "the development and exercise of the virtues, these being intrinsically good").[86]

Both character utilitarianism and perfectionism (in this sense) are consequentialist and count as instances of "the ethics of outcome." Watson wants to show that virtue ethics, or "Aristotelianism," can be formulated as teleological (giving explanatory primacy to the good) without being consequentialist.[87] In addition to the primacy of aretaic notions, which distinguishes Aristotelian moral theory from deontological theories, an "Aristotelian ethics" should give a naturalistic account of the virtues: "Virtues are (a subset of the) human excellences, that is, those traits that enable one to live a characteristically human life, or to live in accordance with one's nature as a human being."[88] Since Watson relates "flourishing" to "living properly as a human being," the virtues acquire their natural significance "by reference to certain necessities and desiderata of human life, in which case the basic moral facts would be facts about what is constitutively and instrumentally needed for that way of life, facts, in short, about flourishing."[89]

Such a theory is nonconsequentialist in its conception of the good—in one of two senses. The less radical way of explaining this is to conceive the virtues "as constitutive of, not merely instrumental to, flourishing"; whereas for "character utilitarianism, virtues are so identified because of their relation to independent values such as happiness."[90] Virtuous activity is an intrinsic part of the flourishing whole. On this approach, we have an ethics of outcome that is teleological (giving primacy to the good) but nonconsequentialist (yet otherwise like the view that Rawls calls "perfectionism").[91] The virtues get their normative status from their relation to flourishing, understood as the ultimate good outcome.

Here and in other passages, Watson seems to distinguish "flourishing" as an objective evaluation of one's state of being and its relationship to one's "human nature" from eudaimonia as a state that must *at least partly* consist in a subjective sense of fulfillment, sufficiency, or absence of any significant lack in one's life. This is important because while, on every plausible construal, someone can feel happy and believe his life is going well without actually enjoying eudaimonia—since the satisfaction of whatever subjective desires we happen to have is never sufficient for this sort of holistic happiness—it is sometimes assumed in the recent literature on virtue ethics that eudaimonia can be conceived as the object of an entirely third-personal judgment with no first-personal reflexive conditions of recognition or experience of satisfaction *at all.*

But understood this way, eudaimonia is a purely metaphysical, and not a psychological, state. Both *well-being* (construed as not requiring any subjective experience of first or second-order satisfaction, e.g., construed as enjoying sufficient primary goods) and *flourishing* in Watson's sense, as a state of one's motivational psyche that realizes certain natural potentialities, can be understood as the objects of detached or impersonal metaphysical judgments. This does not seem to be the case for "happiness" in any modern sense *nor*, I think, for what anyone in the Socratic schools of philosophy understood by the *eudaimon* life. Hence a tree or an animal incapable of any reflective recognition that its life is going well can be said to flourish. Although there are third-personal speculative judgments about how happy someone may be, their truth-conditions depend in part on phenomena that are essentially first-personal, or inseparable from the practical perspective of agents. Thus Hursthouse also distinguishes between the metaphysical thesis that "The virtues make their possessors good human beings," or flourishing members of their natural kind, and the more psychological thesis that "The virtues benefit their possessor," although she believes that Plato and his followers link these two theses.[92]

On the more radical approach, virtue ethics is nonconsequentialist because the normative status of virtues is not based at all on realizing outcomes *already* conceived as good. Unlike perfectionist theories, which also hold "the fundamental moral facts to be . . . about people's desires, ends, and dispositions," or "to be facts about virtue,"[93] Watson says that the more radical virtue ethics is not an ethics of outcome in which conduct is evaluated by reference to "states of affairs or outcomes deemed to be intrinsically good or desirable on their own."[94] Instead, this theory starts from the idea that "Living a characteristically human life (functioning well as a human being) requires possessing and exemplifying certain traits" or motivational states, and outcomes like misery and well-being take their moral significance *from* the fact that virtuous people care about them in certain ways rather than these concerns being virtuous *because* they respond rightly to states that are "intrinsically good or bad."[95]

I call this view *pure aretaic naturalism* to indicate its radicality in rejecting any basic moral facts about the goodness of certain states, definable prior to the virtues, as a foundation for the normative value of the virtues. As Watson emphasizes, this theory does not even allow any foundational role to "the idea that living a characteristic human life is intrinsically good." It does not hold that the desire for a normal life is virtuous *because* such a life is supremely good and thus to be our highest aim; rather, such a desire is virtuous because it is essential to living a characteristically human life.[96] In other words, while a characteristic human life and flourishing are interdefined, "the evaluation of such a life as a final end is derivative from, rather than foundational to, the theory of virtue."[97] The relevant motivational traits count as virtues because they are constitutive of and instrumental to such a life but not because they help secure or instantiate some independently defined ultimate good. Even flourishing is not such a good, for "On the second account, the theory of ultimate good is dependent on the theory of virtue."[98] As a result, we are not committed to maximizing any good, and so the psychic traits essential to distinctively human life can include observing nonconsequentialist or agent-centered restrictions on various kinds of act.

This sort of pure aretaic naturalism certainly vindicates Watson's hope of showing that there can be non-outcomes-based teleological moral theories, but at a very high price. The central claim in this theory is much stronger than the modest epistemological thesis that there may be no neutral viewpoint from which the egoist and the virtuous agent can agree about the elements of a happy life and proceed to argue over whether virtues do, in fact, on the whole, tend to bring more of these elements to their agents than vices do.[99] For this modest thesis is consistent with holding (as in external eudaimonism) that their value for well-being or eudaimonia (both directly and by way of making possible friendship and engagement in practices) is the primary justification for the moral authority of virtues—although perception or sensitivity to this value will be diminished the more thoroughly one's motives are corrupted by vice. In the most extreme form of aretaic naturalism, which I think we find in Michael Slote's "agent-based virtue ethics," the good is simply defined as whatever virtuous agents may value, and we lose any independent criteria for recognizing what sorts of dispositions make one count as a virtuous agent. His theory has been widely criticized on this basis.[100] Slote also recognizes that this theory is not Aristotelian, since Aristotle grounds the authority of virtues in eudaimonia.[101]

In Watson's version, the pure aretaic naturalist holds that the authority of the virtues derives not from their helping bring about an independently good outcome,[102] but rather from their role in making us fulfill the *good of our kind*. As he acknowledges, this approach faces both the difficulty of providing a sufficiently robust functional conception of the human species (or living a characteristically human life) and the more fundamental objection that unless living such a life is prescribed or endorsed *as good* or valuable by an independent moral judgment, we have no particular reason *to care* about "living naturally" relative to the capacities of our species.[103] This objection could be understood in two ways: (a) as a challenge to the aretaic naturalist *justification* of the virtues holding that it involves an illicit reduction of ethical values to quasi-biological facts or to premoral metaphysical facts; or (b) as the objection that on such a conception, we would lack any clear *motive* for living virtuously (for the possibility is left open that virtue may not make us happy at all).

However, I will not pursue these questions here, since I am not directly concerned in this book with the central problem of moral theory, that is, to explain the kind of justifying rational foundation that should we accept for basic moral norms and ideals of character. Rather, my concern is with the central question of moral psychology (as the indispensable groundwork for moral theory), namely, what kinds of motives exist in the human repertoire? For this purpose, what is relevant is that pure aretaic naturalism neither presupposes nor grows naturally out of the erosiac model of human motivation on which A-eudaimonism was based. Hence this theory poses no real obstacle to my argument in chapter 7 that if human beings are capable of virtuous motivation, then our motives cannot all be formally erosiac in structure and so they cannot all be embraced in the unifying desire for eudaimonia.

Instead, the pure aretaic naturalist would seem to require a motivation to flourish *qua* human, in the natural or premoral sense of doing what is most characteristic or distinctive of our species. This could be construed either as an internal motive for cultivating the virtues in ourselves, or (along the lines of the habituation model of EEu) only as our motive for inculcating them in young persons whom we have in our care. The pure aretaic naturalist could argue that such a motive is itself *innate* in our nature or at least develops automatically if our upbringing is not wholly corrupt. But either way, this would be a strange motive. How exactly could we describe the desire to be natural or to be fully human without invoking some already normative conception of our function as one among rival conceptions? Especially given modern interests in distinguishing ourselves as distinctive and original, who would be inspired by the ideal acting in the standardly human way?

A full positive argument against such radical aretaic naturalism requires developing the alternative, rival, existentialist conception of personhood and a defense of some kind of libertarian freedom as one of the conditions of moral responsibility. I leave this task for later work, since Watson's pure aretaic theory rescues virtue from the paradox of eudaimonism only by rejecting the eudaimonia thesis. This paradox points toward the need for a *non-eudaimonistic virtue ethics*, and pure aretaic naturalism of both Watson's and Slote's varieties will be one species of this genus, which also includes character utilitarianism, intuitionist theories of virtue, Kierkegaardian existential virtue ethics,[104] and Nietzschean theories according to which virtues are those motivational dispositions that best express or embody the will to power or the will to life (as opposed to any formally egoistic desire for my own happiness or eudaimonia).[105]

I include in this genus every type of moral theory that both (a) gives virtues a significant role in normative ethics independent of the right (not reducing virtues simply to dispositions to do one's duty or making ethical evaluation of characters and lives entirely derivative from deontic concepts), and (b) does not seek to base the authority of the virtues, or the criteria of moral worth for characters and lives, entirely on their relationship to the eudaimonia, basic goods, or well-being of individuals and communities. Although the value of virtuous actions is often related to promoting such goods, they are not the whole story, according to non-eudaimonistic versions of virtue ethics.

7. Social Holist Eudaimonism as a Radical Solution?

Finally, I briefly explore the possibility of another radical response to the paradox of eudaimonism, which is based on Aristotle's famous statement that our "complete" good must not only extend to our whole life but must also include the good of other members of our family and community (*NE* I.7 1097b8–14). In the literature on eudaimonism, it is sometimes suggested that Aristotle's conception of our social nature implies that an individual agent's good, rightly understood, *simply includes* the good of family, friends, and perhaps fellow citizens (although not the whole human race). If so, this approach suggests, then the paradox of eudaimonism is an illusion; the virtuous agent's desires for jointly enjoyed communal goods are also validly describable as desires for "his own" eudaimonia, when this is understood in the true, most expansive sense. So the distinction between agent-transcending and agent-related goods is itself transcended in the right conception of eudaimonia.

7.1. MacIntyre's Joint Goods

Something close to this idea often seems to be at work in MacIntyre's *Dependent Rational Animals*, for example, when he writes that

> the practical learning needed, if one is to become a practical reasoner[,] is the same learning needed, if one is to find one's place within a network of givers and receivers in which the achievement of one's individual good is understood to be inseparable from the achievement of the common good.[106]

MacIntyre also emphasizes the idea that there are significant goods that can exist only *as shared*, and thus there are activities "in which the goods to be achieved are neither mine-rather-than-others' nor others'-rather-than-mine, but instead are goods that can be mine only insofar as they are also those of others, that are genuinely common good, as the goods of networks of giving and receiving are."[107] His main point is that we cannot (without self-defeat) seek to sustain and participate in such networks simply as a Hobbesian contract,[108] because we can receive the aid we need in youth, old age, disability, and periods of illness only if we are members of a society all (or most) of whom act virtuously or "who make the good of others her or his good, and this not because we have calculated that, only if we help others, will they help us, in some trading of advantage for advantage."[109] As this makes clear, however, the common good essential to the flourishing of humans as vulnerable, bodily/animal beings emerges from the joint activities of many virtuous agents in a community who are acting on *pure motives*

> to participate in this network of giving and receiving as the virtues require, I have to understand that what I am called upon to give may be quite disproportionate to what I have received, and that those to whom I am called upon to give may well be those from whom I shall receive nothing. And I also have to understand that the care I give to others has to be in an important sense unconditional, since the measure of what is required of me is determined in key parts, even if not only, by their needs.[110]

As an analysis of social virtue, this seems entirely right; we have to regard needs as grounds for setting goals. But it looks as though the easiest way of understanding MacIntyre's proposal is just that the common good of mutual flourishing is *essentially a by-product* of the pure motives of "just generosity" involved in virtue as such.[111] If so, then the common good itself is not the virtuous individual's intended purpose; rather, she aims at more particular goods, as required by circumstances and her place in the network, and thereby helps produce the common good. And to participate in this social system by *making* the good of particular others her own good then requires projective motivation, just as engaging in a given practice requires projecting as one's final ends the goals definitive of this practice. This brings me to three important distinctions.

(1) Projectively Determined Conditions of Eudaimonia

First, as I explained in the discussion of second-order satisfaction in chapter 5, once an agent-transcending goal G is projected as the agent's own, she may then derive satisfaction from achieving it and even see it (somewhat metaphorically) as "part of her own good" since she will be unhappy to the extent that G is unrealized. Such satisfaction depends on a purposive motive rather than being the intentional object of a prepurposive motive. That G contributes to the agent's satisfaction, or to her eudaimonia as a whole, is *psychologically dependent on* her prior volitional projection of G and her striving to attain it; thus this satisfaction plays no initial role in motivating the uptake of G. In *this* sense, then, I readily agree that a virtuous agent "expands" her sense of what her own eudaimonia includes, but she does this by her own striving will and hence not in a way consistent with the eudaimonia thesis. The scope of the agent's eudaimonia, or what sorts of shared goods it includes, is the determined rather than the *determining* variable, as eudaimonism requires.

Thus the paradox of eudaimonism remains, and its resolution still requires the existential capacities of striving will.

(2) Abstract versus Concrete Goals

Second, we ought to distinguish between abstract goals, such as adhering to moral ideals or principles or sustaining social systems of expectations and joint activity, and more particular or concrete goals that agents may pursue either *as* specifications of the abstract goals or as particulars not subsumed under more general concepts. A loyal baseball fan may continue to buy season tickets to his local team after a couple of bad seasons just because he loves the game, not because he believes in the ideal of fan loyalty. However, his doing so may inspire other fans to stick with the team. A venture capitalist acting on a motive with a highly determinate end, for example, to earn a certain amount of money per year by setting up a for-profit company, may also be participating in and helping to sustain a system of market competition that produces certain common benefits, but that is not the capitalist's aim; that he functions this way is a by-product of acting for the sake of other goals, and in general the "invisible hand" of the market is an unintended by-product of the aggregation over time of millions of individual consumer and producer decisions that have no structural economic goal in mind.

MacIntyre is clear that the "common good" is not the aggregate result of this kind of self-interested motive, nor is it simply a mereological "summing of individual goods."[112] Yet MacIntyre's account is a bit ambiguous about when the "common good," as he understands it, can or should be anyone's *intended* goal. It is probably true that "it is only through the acquisition and exercise of the virtues that individuals and communities can flourish in a specifically human mode," as required by our bodily dependencies, our need for love and recognition, and our capacities for independent practical reasoning.[113] But should we think of this judgment as motivating any virtuous agent's actions?[114]

Perhaps we could if we thought of these agents as aiming at the abstract good of sustaining a network of giving and receiving such as MacIntyre describes. But notice what this would mean in a particular instance of, say, aiding an ailing elderly neighbor with no children who needs transportation to doctors and hospitals. It would mean that I help her because I believe that such actions are part of a network from which we all benefit (from which I have benefited and may benefit again), not because I have any special love for her as a particular individual.

Now, such abstract motives do play an important role in human life and should not be discounted. Politicians and educators, in particular, may have to act explicitly with such abstract ends in view. Likewise, a wealthy alumnus of Fordham University may say to himself, "well, I have benefited from the institutions and resources built up by the collective generosity of past alumni, and I ought to carry on this tradition by making a substantial gift to the university's endowment so that future students will be able to get an education, recognize their dependencies, and eventually make their contribution according to their abilities." This would be a perfectly reasonable and admirable ground for such philanthropic activity, and indeed it would count as virtuous, as exhibiting the kind of *asymmetric reciprocity* characteristic of the central virtue that MacIntyre calls just generosity.[115] For, as MacIntyre argues, even though this virtue demands "unconditional care for the human being as such, whatever the outcome," it is "nonetheless in virtue of what we have received that we owe."[116] But still, many of the virtuous activities necessary to sustain the network of giving and receiving are surely not aimed at such abstract goals as those of the philanthropist but rather focus on the good of particular people or organizations or on reforms called for by a particular political issue, and so on. In such attentive care focused on particulars, it seems that the common good as a whole is once again the unintended by-product rather than the goal.

(3) Targetable and Nontargetable Common Goods

For the social holist alternative to get off the ground, then, it has to argue instead that the agent's expanded sense of her own eudaimonia as necessarily including the flourishing of others can motivate her virtuous actions. It is not clear that MacIntyre's analysis, despite its many insights, will support this strong claim. He argues that "participants in networks of giving and receiving are only able to identify their individual goods in the course of identifying their common goods," and because this requires "shared deliberation with those others whose common goods they are," understanding our own flourishing requires political reasoning. Moreover, "my decisions about what part certain goods are to play in my life" will affect my relationships and must depend in part on how my community values these goods.[117]

But although MacIntyre is surely right that no individual could intelligibly understand her own flourishing without relation to networks of giving and receiving in which she is involved from her beginning, to see her good as *joined* with the well-being of any particular range of other persons requires a commitment to them or to the network of relations which is never simply given as part of her facticity. For the person always has the option of defining her good instead as merely *parasitic* on the background of supporting social relationships, which she will make as little sacrifice to help sustain as she can strategically get away with. The eudaimonist can say that this egoistic strategy is mistaken and cannot lead to happiness, but that remains debatable. It seems instead that the gestalt shift whereby the individual comes to see her good as inextricably joined with others in various social networks must depend crucially on her own projective engagement in these relationships for reasons *other* than certainty that her own happiness depends on it. *She fuses* the good of others to her own, deciding in the process which kinds of caring networks are most relevant for her attention.[118]

Moreover, insofar as one agent's eudaimonia is inextricably bound to another's, their joint eudaimonia may not always be directly targetable for either (e.g., in friendship). When joint eudaimonia is a nontargetable common good, it may nevertheless derive in part from the joint action of agents for the sake of other kinds of targetable common goods (e.g., the goods definitive of practices). One *ground* for such a projection of some genuinely common or joint good may be, as Rawls suggests in his account of reciprocity, that others are willing to coproject it with us. For example, a sense of justice (expressed in a public conception of the principles defining fair terms of social cooperation) is such a joint good: one of its key requirements is that everyone can accept it, provided that each knows that all (or enough) others accept it and do so in part because they share this very knowledge.[119]

The motivation for such a joint action must be projective in cases where each party requires the willingness of others as a condition of their own willingness to act, yet no party requires this primarily because they believe the willingness of others promises any direct contribution to their own material or psychic well-being. Unlike egoists making a Hobbesian contract, their joint willingness is seen by each agent as a condition for serving some higher purpose, for example, establishing fair institutions, or ending an injustice affecting some minority, or creating together a legacy for future generations, even if it also promises them some material gain. In such cases, person A is willing to sacrifice for some good G as long as the other person B will sacrifice for it with him, since without their mutual efforts G cannot be achieved—but G still transcends the material welfare of both A and B.[120] Their motive is not self-interest that overlaps contingently with the self-interests of other cooperating parties but, rather, making common cause for a noble goal that extends beyond the material interests of either party.

Many of the most important moral and political goals require such joint or unified commitment, because they cannot effectively be pursued alone. The distinguishing characteristic of such joint ends is that they are only *mutually targetable*. Unlike values that are essentially by-products of activities not directed toward them, these goods can be pursued intelligibly as one's end, but not by a single isolated actor. Think, for example, of building a Stone Age temple, which required raising stones that no would-be builder could have moved at all by himself. Among such goods that can be pursued only in concert with others will be some whose intrinsic value is recognizable quite apart from the well-being of the agents pursuing them, for example, the religious value of the temple, or the beauty of a choir singing in unison, or the dignity bestowed by the rule of law. These are mutually targetable but agent-transcending goods. This also explains why the continuation and deepening of networks of giving and receiving that I recognize can sometimes justly demand much more from me than I will ever receive from them; the joint good of these networks is targetable only by *mutual projection*.

My ground for caring about such social goods, whose fundamental status MacIntyre rightly emphasizes, would seem to be intrinsic values that I, like others who join me in sustaining the networks in which these social goods are realized, can appreciate as valuable quite apart from their (immediate) relation(s) to my own good. It may also be that a complete human life requires a kind of satisfaction that can be gained only from devoting oneself to such mutually targetable goods that often include but still transcend each cooperating agent's interests; for the sense of "fraternity" or "solidarity" that results from being part of such a joint quest is among the most ennobling experiences in human life. But this satisfaction is a by-product of concern for common goods sustained by systems of justice and generosity. Such concern is formed in a willing that is pure of erosiac attraction, although the devoted agent can then see common goods as linked to her own flourishing.

This will be clearer if we consider John Drummond's similar account of intending essentially shared goods, which preceded MacIntyre's. Starting from Husserl's conception of evaluative motives, which are D3 desires in my scheme,[121] Drummond argues that Aristotelian generosity involves "the identification of the good of the other and the good of oneself."[122] This identification appears to be an achievement of the will. Drummond tries to explain its possibility by saying that we recognize goods that

> make their claim on us independent of our particular desires because they are *a priori* goods, and, insofar as part of the sense of these goods is that they are good for humans as such, they also obligate us to seek them not only for ourselves but for all humans.[123]

It is not clear how this obligation can motivate an Aristotelian agent. Intending a good G because I recognize that it is part of the human good certainly commits me to the judgment that it is also good for other persons, but that by itself cannot cause me to desire that they also enjoy G. If my enjoying G will also benefit others, then I might intend it solely for my own sake and regard the benefit to others as a mere side effect. But if G is essentially joint, such that it will benefit me only if I pursue it for the good of others as a *final* end, then pursuing it this way and thus identifying our goods requires projective motivation. Thus if the a priori status of essentially joint components of the human good obligates me to seek them for others' flourishing as an end-in-itself, this obligation cannot be an erosiac motive. It will function more like Kant's categorical imperative, namely, as a ground for setting new ends that transcend the agent.

7.2. *Brink and Spinoza*

If the social holist is to defend his theory as a real solution to the paradox of eudaimonism, he must argue that we are capable of expanding our sense of self prior to and independently of motivation to pursue noble goals defining the virtues and motivation to pursue craft goals defining the practices. The virtues would then find their place in a kind of transformed egoism. Probably the best contemporary defense of this idea is given by David Brink in his analysis of rational egoism as a basis for ethics, which he identifies as "A Neo-Aristotelian Approach."[124] Brink follows Parfit in basing his "egoist justification of other-regarding concern" on controversial models of branching psychological continuity, or fission cases:[125] the good of intimates who share my projects, plans, and commitments is also my good, in the same way that the good of later minds psychologically continuous with mine is my own good.[126] In addition to the dubiousness of this analogy, this model also has the same problem we noted in MacIntyre's account, namely, that it presupposes that I can form projects and plans or commit myself to life goals that others can share. Since such projects or life goals frequently involve agent-transcending goods, however, it seems that projective motivation is required to form them. In that case, a social holism based on Brink's model will not rescue the eudaimonia thesis.

However, there are also prominent examples of the social holist position in the history of philosophy that do not rely on such psychological continuities. The most notable is Spinoza's enlightened egoism, in which moral sentiments are supposed to be modifications of self-interest in a self that ultimately identifies with the Whole (not only with all human beings but with the entire cosmos as the One Substance, of which we are all modes). This paradigm version of metaphysical holism was taken up in the twentieth century by J. Baird Callicott and Arne Naess as a basis for their environmental ethics; according to their accounts, the motive for caring about the Earth and its life-forms as ends-in-themselves is simply part of the self-interest of a vastly expanded self that sees no border between its own identity and the planet (if not the entire universe, as Spinoza would have it).[127]

Technically, if one accepts its premises, this kind of social holism does solve the paradox of eudaimonism by showing how virtuous motives are embraced by the agent's desire for "his own" eudaimonia. It works, in other words, by making trivial or empty the self-reference in "formal egoism." I think this is quite telling, because it helps confirm a crucial genealogical point: Socratic eudaimonism traces its historical origins to the Hindu sages and was always deeply indebted to their ideas about the transcendence of self. Now we see—what was always the case, although it was often forgotten—that for the eudaimonist project to work, it requires something like the holistic metaphysics of the self that stands at the center of the Hindu and Buddhist traditions. This is a much stronger premise than MacIntyre's recognition that a eudaimonist account of the virtues cannot be independent of metaphysics and biology altogether.[128]

However, admitting that social holism can resolve the paradox is not much of a concession, since the metaphysical premises of this view are so radical that they are wholly implausible, at least to most contemporary audiences. It is also clear that most of the ancient Greek proponents of eudaimonism did not accept anything like the kind of radical denial of the separateness and freedom of individual selves that their ethical project really requires. For example, when Aristotle argues in *NE* IX (in the passage that so worried Annas) that in sacrificing for their friends, the virtuous agent gains the greater good, he clearly still recognizes a real difference between the two persons, and so he clearly does *not* mean that the friend as "another self" will *literally* become part of the virtuous agent. That is not his own intended resolution of the problem, even if it may be Spinoza's. If the eudaimonist project requires mystical holism of the strongest metaphysical variety imaginable, then I consider it defeated for all practical purposes in the twenty-first century. As a famous U2 song says, "We're one, but we're not the same."[129]

Moreover, even the radical metaphysical rejection of individuality in the Eastern mystical traditions going back to the Hindu sages cannot be regarded as any *independent* evidence against the existential alternative to eudaimonism. For, as I suggested in chapter 2, that radical metaphysical position was *itself* motivated primarily by moral suspicion of the striving will, whose full capacities and existential significance the existentialist tradition alone has recognized. This radical suspicion is understandable enough, given its time and place of origin: in cultures so full of suffering that any sustained endeavor seemed likely to lead only to the agent's misery by involvement in hopeless causes—cultures so full of corruption by warlords and princes who cared nothing for this suffering of the masses that they would do anything to secure their power. How, in such an environment, could the positive potential in the striving will give any hope for a meaningful life or even be recognized as having any positive significance by reflective persons?

But these historical circumstances are greatly changed today, at least for the roughly 40 percent of human beings not living in the poverty of underdeveloped nations. We can now recognize third-world conditions as those in which the rejection of the striving will in the Eastern metaphysical ideal of non-individuality had a practical point and even made a good deal of sense, despite being in the end simply a form of rational despair. For two thousand years, this kind of metaphysical holism could be placed in a new religious context in which again it might make sense to mystics, and in the eighteenth century, it offered a kind of escape from the endless religious wars and suffering of the modern European *misérables*. But today, outside of these contexts, it makes virtually no sense against the fundamental fact of the distinctness of persons that both Kantian ethics and the existential tradition following Kant take as their starting point. Recognition of this fact need not lead to solipsism nor to a flat denial of Hegel's insight that a sense of our own identity requires social relationships,[130] but it does require admitting that there can be real conflicts of interest and that the individual uniqueness of selves in their freedom is not altogether an illusion.

8. Conclusion: Toward a Rejection of the Transmission Principle

By now it appears likely that the paradox of eudaimonism is unresolvable within the terms allowed by any *metaphysically plausible* variant of eudaimonism, where the minimal conditions of plausibility include recognizing some form of the individuality of persons rather than subsuming all selves into one all-embracing organic whole or Overself. This means that the eudaimonist project of providing an adequate account of virtuous motivation grounded in a eudaimonist account of human nature and motives *must fail*, given its own internal contradictions, on plausible metaphysical premises.

This result has far-reaching implications for theories of well-being and value, for it implies that happiness is not our highest good. As Raymond Belliotti argues, happiness is an important value but it "is not everything" and should not be overrated: "Happiness remains valuable in most cases, but it is not the most important human aspiration."[131] Happiness is not the aim or end in the pursuit of other worthwhile values, such as "truth, art, creativity," and so on. Rather, happiness is largely a by-product of pursuing such values, and some measure of happiness is also frequently sacrificed in such pursuits.[132] The existential view that a meaningful life is more fundamental than a happy life is thus supported by Belliotti's arguments that "we reasonably value a life replete with enduring accomplishment, high creativity, powerful social effects, and unparalleled excellence more than a minimally meaningful, happy life."[133] This view validates the paradigmatically Western conception of the aspiring will as potentially positive and constructive rather than grasping and self-aggrandizing (see chap. 2).

The failure of the eudaimonist project also has implications for normative ethics, since it entails that some other sort of foundation will have to be given for the virtues if we wish to give them a fundamental role in normative theory. The alternative non-eudaimonist grounds for virtue ethics will become clearer in my existential account of striving will. My extended critique of eudaimonism opens the door to the existential alternative by undermining the Transmission principle (TP). This result can be summarized in a natural deduction as follows. Suppose, as is very likely, that despite the failure of the eudaimonist project, we still affirm that:

1. There are pure motives of the sort that Aristotle and his followers praise as virtuous.

It follows from 1 and the paradox of eudaimonism that:

2. The eudaimonia thesis is false.

Yet, as we saw in chapter 6, section 3, the eudaimonia thesis is the conclusion of the valid "A-eudaimonist core argument," which starts from several premises. As a result, it follows from 2 that at least one of the premises in the A-eudaimonist core argument must be false. Looking back over these premises, the most vulnerable or least obviously sound is TP, which, together with the weak erosiac thesis (WET), entailed the conclusion that all human motivation must be formally erosiac in its psychic structure. If TP is the weak link in the A-eudaimonist core argument, then the paradox of eudaimonism probably implies that:

3. TP is false [by *reductio*, from the conclusion of the A-eudaimonist core argument and 2].

A critic might hold that it is the jointure thesis rather than TP that ought to be rejected among premises in the A-eudaimonist core argument. For this reason, it is important to emphasize that 1 and the paradox of eudaimonism together support the rejection of TP in another way, namely by *inference to the best explanation*. As we saw in chapter 4, section 1.2, if we grant the simplifying assumption that all prepurposive motive-states are erosiac in form (WET), but we can find purposive motives that are non-erosiac, then TP is falsified. The best explanation we have found for the paradox of eudaimonism is that virtuous motives aim at final ends (various species of "the noble") that are often materially unconnected to the agent's good and sometimes even to his entire community's good, prior to his forming an intention to pursue these ends. Thus the "noble" cannot attract the agent or cause her to experience erosiac desire for noble action. If the paradox of eudaimonism is best explained by the non-erosiac structure of aretaic motivation, and WET holds, then TP must be false.[134] This opens up the possibility of an existential account of aretaic motivation as a projective effort or activity of the striving will.

Such an account neatly avoids the paradox of eudaimonism by rejecting the idea that we *desire* to do the "noble" (i.e., just, generous, temperate, friendly, etc.); here ordinary language misleads. We do not take the relevant actions that appear to have agent-neutral aretaic value to be *filling up some lack* in our well-being at all (or if we do, we do not choose them for this reason). Rather, we *project* "the noble" itself as our goal, which is to say that we use our self-motivating power of striving will to *set* some species of *kalon* action as our final end. This is what really happens when we resolve to do the noble thing for its own sake. The existence of action done from "the motive of virtue," then, turns out to be a primary piece of evidence both for the existential conception of the will and against the eudaimonist account of willing as *logos-eros*, or rational appetite. This suggests the need for an existential virtue ethics.

Although developing such an ethics is a task for another book, the case studies explored in subsequent chapters help define its parameters. While their primary aim is to illustrate and help clarify the projective model of striving will, the examples generally have ethical significance. We can regard the Levinasian conception of agapé discussed in chapter 9 and the related Kantian conception of duty discussed in chapter 11 as attempts to specify the master virtue of an existential ethic. I argue that these attempts fail because they do not recognize many other kinds of projective willing. Among these are radical forms of malicious motivation, which are analyzed in the existential theory of volitional vice developed in chapter 10. The remaining chapters explore the wider realm of human cares whose normative criteria need to be incorporated into a complete existential virtue ethic. Norms and virtues defining ethically good wills have to take into account the full scope of the will's motive-powers.

III

Case Studies for the Existential Will as Projective Motivation

9

Divine and Human Creativity: From Plato to Levinas

Overview. This chapter describes the emergence of a new concept of motivation from Neoplatonic speculations on why the divine principle generates the physical universe. The first half of the chapter is generally accessible and potentially useful in a philosophy of religion course. The later sections on Arendt and Levinas will be most relevant for those with some background in these philosophers but can also serve as interpretative introductions to some of their main themes. The last section, which is slightly more technical, completes the description of projective motivation in the terms of contemporary action theory, picking up where chapter 3 left off.

I. Thick and Thin Concepts of Motivation

In previous chapters, I have repeatedly suggested that an existential conception of striving will implies a kind of human motivation that (a) *contrasts* with erosiac desire, and (b) violates the Transmission principle (TP), since it arises only within what Pink calls volitional agency, that is, the activities in which intentions, plans, or purposes are set by the agent. Although decision is the paradigm of such activity, forming and executing intentions is not the only function of volitional agency. However, as I note in chapter 4, contemporary theories of motivation in analytic philosophy are usually committed to TP, and they usually ignore the phenomenology of motivation as a subjective experience of the agent, conceiving it abstractly as whatever state plays certain formal roles in explaining or rationalizing intention and action. I call this the *thin* sense of "desire."

For example, in a recent work on value theory, Robert Audi treats experienceable intrinsic value as motivating because it can be the "the object of desires and intentions . . . the experience of hearing a sonata can be precisely what I want to hear, and hence, in prospect, can motivate me to act."[1] This sounds as if the prospect of an aesthetic good moves the agent as in a D3 desire, but the description is too ambiguous to be certain. It could also be that the agent projects the goal of learning a certain style of music and "wants" to hear the sonata as a means to that goal. Both these kinds of motive have the "world-to-mind direction of fit" of practical attitudes;[2] so that it is not enough to distinguish between them. This problem goes back at least to F. H. Bradley's attempt to define volition as "the alteration of existence so as to agree with the idea."[3] Note that this definition applies to any "practical relation" or pro-attitude motivating intentional action. But Bradley fails to see that not all pro-attitudes are autonomous, and hence when the world is changed in accordance with an idea, it does not necessarily follow that this "realises for me my inmost being which before was ideal."[4] This approach identifies the self with all of its motives.

The ubiquitous use of "desire" in the thin sense thus makes it harder to state adequately the existentialist's thesis that the will includes a projective capacity. For the thesis that we can motivate ourselves in "non-desiderative" ways to make sense, it has to be made relative to a *thick* account of "desire," such as the erosiac analysis in the eudaimonist tradition. This is not to deny that, as Pink says, "there surely is . . . a sense of 'desire' that applies whenever we are motivated to act";[5] for we could define "desire" in a maximally formal or abstract fashion as "any state in which an agent is motivated to pursue some goal or end." Similarly, we could conceive "teleology" in a minimally thin sense merely as any psychological state in which an agent "conceiv[es] of the future as including a state of affairs which is an end to be produced, where this end is provided in the propositional content of a belief or desire."[6] For example, Alfred Mele defines "wanting" this way: "to want to A is to have some motivation to A, the content of which features a representation of the agent's (current or prospective) A-ing." As Mele says, this does not differentiate among types of motives, such as "appetitive versus nonappetitive wants."[7] In fact, it says nothing at all about how the motivation is experienced or what kind of representation of the object is involved. In this thin sense, it is *vacuously true* that all motivation is teleological or desiderative.

Hence substantive theses about motivation like Hume's or Aristotle's require the addition of further terms. To express their views, we need thick senses of desire; for example, Hume holds that all motivation derives from D2 desires, relative to which reason plays only an instrumental function, whereas Aristotle holds that motivation includes D3 desires in which reason plays an end-prescribing function.[8] The erosiac model of desire as "lack" that I introduced in chapter 4 also gives a substantive sense to teleology as a *structure* of motivation, or a *way* of having ends; it is not just any type of goal-directed state that could inform intention-setting. Now that the erosiac model and the eudaimonist framework that incorporates it have been explained, we have a sufficiently substantive foil for the existential account. Projective motivation contrasts with "desire" in its classical erosiac sense but not in its contemporary thin sense.

It is perhaps ironic, then, that the original idea of a fundamentally different projective form of motivation can be traced back to Plato himself— although it was much less influential than the erosiac model, and its significance was largely covered over by the more dominant eudaimonist tradition. Historically, the projective idea first developed in theological contexts and passed, by way of Stoic and Franciscan moral philosophy, to Kant's ethics and finally into existential philosophical anthropology and twentieth-century phenomenological realists (Scheler, von Hildebrande, and their disciples). In this chapter, I consider several illustrations of projective willing in this countereudaimonist "tradition," beginning with the notion of divine creativity, and I take up Arendt and Levinas before presenting a general schema for projective motivation. Later chapters will test this schema in case studies involving existential psychoanalysis, deontic moral motivation, radical evil, and contemporary conceptions of caring and identity-forming commitments.

It will be especially useful to trace in outline the original theological inspiration for the idea of non-erosiac or projective motivation—not because the significance of the projective concept for contemporary moral psychology or ethics *depends* on any form of traditional Western theism, but rather because (1) the theological case provides a clear paradigm instance from which we can read off the general form of projective motivation; and (2) as a bonus, it will show why an agapic ethics requires a projective model of striving will. Thus the relevance of this conception of volitional striving for central themes in existential ethics will be clarified by starting with the problem of divine motivation.

2. The Neoplatonic Projective Model of Divine Agapē

2.1. *The Erosiac Thesis and Perfection* in Republic II

The germinal thought behind the countertradition arises from the problem of creation, or the metaphysical relationship between the Divine, as foundation of reality, and the everyday universe we inhabit. That the Divine is in some way the source or basis of this universe's reality is implied in the most primordial archetype of the sacred in all human mythology[9]—a point certainly not lost on Plato, although, of course, there is little evidence that he understood the cosmogenic principle as in any way personal.[10] Yet if the perfection of the divine being (whether conceived as a personal entity or an impersonal principle) implies lacking nothing, or being completely self-sufficient and whole in itself, then it follows from the erosaic model that the divine being would *desire nothing* and hence apparently not be moved at all. But why, then, would less perfect grades of reality emerge from it, since it certainly does not *need* them? Mark McPherran sums up this point as follows:

> [B]oth the early and middle dialogues, and especially the *Lysis*, make it clear that love (as a desire for what is lacking) is irreconcilable with perfection, and that therefore the (perfect) gods cannot love anything. Furthermore, if they cannot love anything, and since all rational activity is rooted in rational love, they cannot act at all.[11]

We can see the theological form of this problem emerging in Plato's conception of what theologians eventually came to call "divine impassibility," meaning that the Divine is not affected or moved in any way by anything outside it or (in Christian theology) by any created substance. For example, in discussing the religious education of his guardians, Socrates (Plato's character) presents a sustained diatribe against the anthropomorphic divinities of Homer's and Hesiod's mythologies, insisting that these gods of the poets completely fail to embody the form of the Divine discerned by the philosopher. For the Divine must by definition be perfect: "But think, God and what is God's is everywhere in a perfect state."[12] Yet the gods and goddesses of the Greek pantheon not only get angry and jealous, and act unjustly, and trick one another; they also change in intrinsic accidental properties. In response, Socrates makes a justly famous argument for divine immutability. Assuming that being changed involuntarily by another is contrary to God's power, then only God could change himself. Yet, Socrates argues, he would have no reason to do so:

> "Does he change himself for the better and more beautiful, or for the worse and more ugly than himself?" "He must change for the worse," said he, "if he does change, for I suppose we shall not say there is a lack in God of beauty or virtue." "Quite right," said I, "and if thus perfect, do you think, Adeimantos, that anyone, God or man, would willingly make himself worse than this in any respect?" "Impossible," said he. "Then it is impossible," I said, "that God should wish to alter himself. No, as it seems, each of them, being the best and most beautiful possible, abides forever simply in his own form."[13]

It is worth reconstructing this argument to bring out its two key premises more clearly. It is tempting at first to ignore the psychological elements in the passage and offer this simple construction:

1. God is perfect [definition of divinity];
2. if God changes, he must change for the better or the worse [premise based on an implicit definition of change as alteration in some intrinsic value-significant property];
3. if God changes for the worse, he would be imperfect [self-evident premise];
4. if God changes for the better, then he improved [definition of improvement];
5. if he improved, he was not perfect before he improved [allegedly self-evident premise?];
6. hence, if God changes for the better, he was not always perfect [from 4, 5, by hypothetical syllogism (HS)];
7. hence, if God changes, he is imperfect [2, 3, 6, by disjunctive syllogism (DS)];
8. hence God does not change [1, 7, by modus tollens (MT)].

But this construction seems to be question-begging, for premise 5 seems to presuppose that perfection is an absolutely static state that cannot grow or develop. There is an alternative conception of perfection as a *process* of ever-expanding richness in which the values that are added are such that they cannot all be realized together from the beginning. On this process view, improvement from state A to B does not entail imperfection at A; rather, God would be imperfect if he did *not* constantly change for the better. This process theory is precisely what Plato's argument needs to disprove. We can come closer to this goal, however, if we add in premises embodying the erosiac model of motivation:

1. God must be perfect [def. divinity];
2. if God changes, he must change for the better or the worse [def. change as alteration in some intrinsic value-significant property];[14]
3. if God changes for the worse, he is imperfect [intuitive premise];
4. if God changes for the better, then either he is changed by another or he changes himself [intuitive premise];
5. if God is changed by another being, he is imperfect [for perfection entails causal independence];
6. if God changes himself for the better, he must be moved to this improvement [no agent-caused change without a motive];
7. if he is moved to change for the better, then there is some possible good that he lacks when moved by this desire [the erosiac premise];
8. but to lack some possible good is to be imperfect [intuitive premise];

9. hence, if God changes himself for the better, then he was imperfect [6, 7, 8, HS];

10. hence God cannot change himself for the better [1, 9, MT].

This argument can be extended to show that God cannot change at all. This second reconstruction is much better, because premise 8 seems to be part of any neutral preconception of perfection that we could non-question-beggingly use as a starting point. At any rate, unlike premise 5 in our first reconstruction, it does not obviously beg the question against the process conception of perfection.[15] Now, however, our new premise 7 seems to be doing most of the heavy lifting (although new premise 5 is also important in the history of conceptions of a maximal or greatest possible being, for example, in Spinoza's *Ethics*). The weight borne by premise 7 in this version of the argument suggests that Plato's conception of perfection as an immutable state rests squarely on his idea that a perfect being would be *motivationally impassible*, since such a being would lack no good that could attract it. The *Republic* interpretation of perfection as immutable and impassible is thus dependent on the erosiac model of motivation.

2.2. Plato's Late Alternative: Overflowing Superabundance as Projective Motivation

The problem with this conception of the Form of the Good, or the perfect being, is precisely its apparent lack of reason for *doing* anything, or initiating any change in itself, on the erosiac model. If we think of it instead as the highest soul, or Demiurgus, then since it is complete in itself, needing nothing, it would seem to have no reason to produce or give rise to anything less perfect than itself. Other things, *if they already exist*, might be moved by the presence of this perfect being (e.g., by being attracted to it), but it could never be moved to create them. Anders Nygren put the point most simply: "An Eros that was rich, that had everything it wanted, would be a contradiction in terms."[16]

Arthur Lovejoy explains this convincingly in his famous William James Lectures: with his first conception of perfect being, Plato found himself unable to explain why there should exist a mundane world of sensible particulars rather than simply an eternal world of Forms or only the highest Form itself. To overcome this problem, in the *Timaeus*, Plato tried to explain why a perfect being would (atemporally) generate a lower-value world of time, which is the moving image of its own higher value, despite the fact that its absolute goodness demands total self-sufficiency:

> The "best soul" would clearly, upon *this* Platonic principle, not be the best if it had need, for its own existence or excellence or happiness, of anything other than itself. Yet when he sets about telling us the

reason for being of this world, Plato exactly reverses the essential meaning of "good" [as self-sufficient]. In part, no doubt, he is taking advantage of the double-signification which the word [*agathos*] had in Greek, as in modern usage. But the metaphor which he employs in making the transition suggests that he was attempting to reconcile the two senses, and indeed, to derive the one from the other. A self-sufficient being who is eternally at the goal, whose perfection is beyond all possibility of enhancement or diminution, *could* not be "envious" of anything not itself. Its reality could be no impediment to the reality, in their own way, of beings other than it, alike in existence and in kind and in excellence. On the contrary, unless it were somehow productive of them, it would lack a positive element of perfection, would not be so complete as its very definition implies that it is. And thus Plato, tacitly making the crucial assumption that the existence of many entities not eternal, not supersensible, and far from perfect, was inherently desirable, finds in his other-worldly Absolute, in the Idea of the Good itself, the reason why that Absolute cannot exist alone. The concept of Self-Sufficing Perfection, by a bold logical inversion, was—without losing any of its original implications—converted into the concept of a Self-Transcending Fecundity.[17]

From this crucial inversion in the *Timaeus* arose the Neoplatonic conception of the One that remains eternally unchanging and unmoved but nevertheless is so "superabundant" in perfection that its own being "overflows" into all those levels of possible reality with lower potential value, actualizing them and thus realizing every possible form of metaphysical value—from highest to lowest—on the ontological scale, or Chain of Being. And, of course, from this in turn comes the abiding paradox in Christian theology of a God who is philosophically conceived as absolutely impassible but who, according to Scripture, nevertheless freely chooses to create a world including creatures made in his own image.[18]

The problem for Christian theology is even greater because, as Lovejoy rightly emphasizes, the Neoplatonists conceived the generative activity of the One as following necessarily from its essence, thus implying the kind of absolute cosmic determinism we eventually find in Spinoza's pantheist holism and arguably also in Leibniz's monadology. In reaching this conclusion, the Neoplatonists were simply reasserting the logic of the erosiac model: everything seeks completeness, only now the complete Whole must be the entire Chain of Being with all its levels of actualizable value, not simply the being at the top of this chain (who acts for the sake of this Whole as much as everything else). For if each level of being is valuable, the whole is incomplete without them all.

So, as Spinoza saw, if instead we take this complete Whole with maximal natural/metaphysical value to be the Divine, the God-substance is once again at rest and impassible. For this reason and others concerning the personal picture of God in biblical scripture, it is now widely recognized that impassibility, as a central feature of the "God of the philosophers," is in deep conflict with key themes in Judaism and Christianity as historical religions—especially those concerning God's love for persons and his care for His creation in general.[19] Impassibility can probably be secured for the necessarily existing source of contingent beings at the cost of not only divine determinism but also pantheistic holism.

However, Lovejoy's analysis implies that the conception of goodness as infinitely self-diffusive and creative really contradicts the conception of goodness as impassible. There is something to this charge if we take impassibility in its strong sense as signifying the property that X has when it is metaphysically impossible for X to be motivated *in any way* to act; for this would rule out overflowing generosity. But it is probably fairer to say that the original idea behind impassibility as a divine attribute is that God cannot find himself *lacking anything* or in need of some good in the way that human beings are when experiencing desires of type D1, D2, or even D3. For, since God is creator and hence divine owner of all things, there is no good that he does not possess, so he could not experience erosiac yearning (except perhaps metaphorically). If it is construed in this weaker sense, then impassibility only entails total absence of all motivation to act if we *also* assume the strong erosiac thesis (SET):

    1. God is (weakly) impassible in the sense good or of not being able to experience a salient lack of some value needed for God's completeness;

    2. but all motivation is generally erosiac in form, that is, caused by the experience of some value-needed-for-the-agent-to-be-whole as lacking or not securely possessed;

    3. so God cannot be motivated to act at all [from 1 and 2 by Barbara syllogism].[20]

Here premise 1 states the weak impassibility thesis, and 2 states SET. It is clear in this argument that we can avoid the unwanted conclusion 3 if we relax SET, which provides the most attractive way out of the theological dilemma. This solution requires us to conceive of *non-erosiac motivation*, that is, a state of motivation to act in which the agent actively focuses on an end or goal, but not because it is desired in the D1, D2, or even D3 sense. If such motivation is based on any reasons concerning its ends or the process of pursuing them, these reasons must be different in kind from the eudaimonistic value of attractive goods seen as "completing" us.

Such motivation would in a concrete sense be *superabundant*, since it would "overflow" the agent's completeness: although initially lacking and hence "desiring" nothing (in the erosiac sense), he would take on a new task or pursuit as an expression of this very perfection and for the sake of any other intelligible value in its goal. Given the obvious resemblance between this sketch of superabundant motivation and the notion of "projective motivation" outlined at the end of chapter 3, we may call this the "projective model" of divine creativity. On the projective model, then, God could be weakly impassible (or immune to desire) and still be self-motivating, concerned about his goals, and active in working to realize them—perhaps by creating or generating worlds and bringing them to their end. So if this is what Plato intended, he can escape Lovejoy's criticism as long as he abandons the strong erosiac thesis.[21]

Some evidence that he did abandon it can perhaps be found in the portrayal of "soul" in several dialogues as *self-moving*, rather than static like the Ideas. T. M. Robinson discusses this idea found in the *Phaedrus* and the *Laws*, concluding that the model that the philosopher is supposed to imitate is now "living and moving, as well as divine."[22] A divine soul can be moving because it is self-motivated or "a source of motion," and, Robinson notes, *Phaedrus* 246B6–7 makes sense of this by saying that "it is a characteristic of any soul that it should care for that which is deprived of soul."[23] If this is so, then divine souls could care for the material world, helping to shape and order it, without having any erosiac need for it. "Caring" as the soul's function may then be a prototype of projective motivation.

Certainly Plato denies that the gods feel bodily pleasures or pains;[24] therefore they transcend the sort of desires (such as hunger and thirst) that depend on these.[25] And this sort of motivation does seem to be the paradigm on which the erosiac model is based; as Socrates says, "When one becomes empty then, apparently he desires the opposite of what he is experiencing; being emptied, he longs to be filled."[26] Socrates argues that all such desire must be experienced in the soul (since bodies cannot by themselves be conscious of what they lack, i.e., the correlate of their emptiness). Thus "it is to the soul that all impulse and desire, and indeed the determining principle of the whole creature, belong."[27] This does not imply, however, that the "determining principle" or motive *must* be erosiac in form, and the conclusions of the *Philebus* in fact imply that there must be motives that do not have this form.

The reasoning is as follows. (1) We know that the divine state must be devoid of erosiac motivation. As Socrates says, the good differs from "everything else" in that "A creature that possesses it permanently, completely, and absolutely, has never any need of anything else; its satisfaction is perfect."[28] This summarizes the same conception we found in the *Lysis* and *Symposium.* But (2) no one would choose to live with only pleasure or intelligence exclusively. So (3) "neither of the two can be the perfect thing that everyone desires, the absolute good."[29] Rather, (4) the divine state must involve a proportionate mixture of intelligence and pleasure, with the latter in the "fifth place." The operations of pure intelligence, then, will not be erosiac in form; speculative thought, in contrast to practical reasoning, will not be motivated by desire for any missing good.

As Nussbaum puts it, "thinking was taken by both Plato and Aristotle to be something one could love and choose, even without awareness of any incompleteness, or pressure of any need"; by contrast, Epicurus took even philosophical reflection to be practically motivated, and so he had to conclude that the gods do not engage even in philosophical thinking.[30]

2.3. Divine Agapē and the Open View of God in Christian Theology

Speculative thinking thus became the paradigm for activity without erosiac motivation in Plato's philosophy. It is the "superabundant" activity that would overflow from the total plenitude of a being lacking nothing. In agreement with this analysis, theological discussions have often portrayed God's motives for creating the world as a kind of "superabundant" motivation, albeit not always with adequate clarity. C. S. Lewis, still operating under the enormous influence of the erosiac model, struggles to suggest how divine motivation differs from human desire, which, given its erosiac structure, can fall into egoism or selfishness:

> The situation implies a need or passion on the part of the lover, and incompatible need on the part of the beloved, and the lover's disregard or culpable ignorance of the beloved's need. None of these conditions is present in the relation of God to man. God has no needs. Human love, as Plato teaches us, is the child of Poverty—of a want or lack; it is caused by a real or supposed good in its beloved which the lover needs and desires. But God's love, far from being caused by goodness in the object, causes all the goodness which the object first has, loving it first into existence, and then into a real, though derivative, lovability. God is goodness. He can give good, but cannot need or get it. In that sense, his love is, as it were, bottomlessly selfless by very definition. . . . Hence, if God sometimes speaks as though the Impassible could suffer passion and eternal fullness could be in want . . . this can mean only . . . that God of mere miracle has made Himself able so to hunger and created in Himself that which we can satisfy. If He requires us, the requirement is of His own choosing. . . . Before and behind all the relations of God to man . . . yawns the

abyss of a Divine act of pure giving—the election of man, from non-entity, to be the beloved of God, and therefore (in some sense) the needed and desired of God, who but for that act needs and desires nothing.[31]

Though, of course, Lewis is not a professional philosopher or theologian and he writes for a popular audience, it is hard to imagine a better summary of the erosiac model and the theological paradox it generated. Lewis's solution is that, unlike us, by actualizing some created good (such as human beings), God *causes* a "lack" in Himself that the values realized by the creature's proper activity (such as our worship) can refill. This is hardly a sufficient answer, though, since it merely pushes the problem back one level: we now have to ask what God's motive could be for "hollowing out" in Himself this "need" for creatures? Lovejoy would surely ask whether God's creative act should be thought of as being moved by the *possible goodness* of some possible combination of entities that He could actualize—a natural or metaphysical value that is *lacking* if not actualized. This is Leibniz's view, and his interpretation of God's will as determined by the Principle of Sufficient Reason very clearly reinstates the erosiac model; as a result, it seems to me that Leibniz's God is not impossible (as he thought) but rather moved by a fundamental desire for metaphysical value outside His own being.[32] What is impossible in the *Monadology* is the whole system of beings, the totality. The alternative to this sort of divine determinism is to say that God's creative act is not motivated by erosiac attraction to the maximal possible goodness in His creation but is rather a superabundant act of self-motivated projection into a realm of totally unneeded potential goods, or values that are in a sense "superfluous" to Him.[33] On this alternative, there is no need to reintroduce by miracle desires with an erosiac structure into the divine mind: the superabundant divine will can love its creations, and hence become subject to happiness or sorrow over their choices and fate, without having literally "to hunger" for them at all. We can say that God needs us as a *result* of God's purposes rather than prepurposively, but this signifies only that God has taken an interest in us, for example, by projecting our salvation as his goal. If creation is a free act unmoved by erosiac desire, then God is capable of projective motivation.

It is not clear that this approach avoids every kind of divine determinism, however. In the most thorough recent treatment of this question, Linda Zagzebski starts from Norman Kretzmann's argument "that God was *not* free not to create because of the Dionysian principle that goodness is essentially self-diffusive," although God "was free to select which possibility to actualize," since he was not moved by desire for a maximal metaphysical good.[34] Zagzebski argues persuasively that such necessity does not make

God's motive nonautonomous; nor does it imply that God "*needs* to create," which would mean that he is incomplete without his creatures, or that "there is some lack in God that creating a world fulfills." For human beings are also essentially active, but not because of our incompleteness.[35] In my terms, then, Zagzebski's view is that God's motivation is non-erosiac, though still metaphysically necessary. Nevertheless, Zagzebski does not understand the alternative positively as *projective* motivation because she thinks that God is just pushed or impelled to create by motives that are essential to his nature without aiming at a result that he already recognizes as good. In this, I think she perpetuates an error that derives from Anders Nygren.

To understand this error, we have to recognize that the Neoplatonic idea of superabundant divine motivation was developed in a theological heritage that extends from the early Franciscans to Kierkegaard, who portrays divine motivation as a type of love that involves volitional *resolve*. In *Philosophical Fragments*, Kierkegaard's pseudonym, "Johnannes Climacus," argues that unlike Socrates, who has a reciprocal relation with his learners since Socrates seeks his own perfection in teaching them, "the god needs no pupil in order to understand himself."[36] Rather, the god appears to the learner because he moves himself; says Climacus:

> But if he moves himself, then there of course is no need that moves him. . . . But if he moves himself and is not moved by need, what moves him then but love, for love does not have the satisfaction of need outside itself but within. His resolution, which does not have an equal reciprocal relation to the occasion, must be from eternity. . . . Out of love, therefore, the god must be eternally resolved.[37]

This description suggests that agapic care for the learner generates its own sense of need "within" the agent. In this eternal resolve, the divine agent motivates himself to teach the learner even before the learner exists. This solution to the paradox of impassibility has been taken up today by the personalist theory of "open theism." For example, Richard Rice argues that

> A well-known feature of the New Testament writings is the use of agapē to express God's love. Unlike other Greek words whose meanings are broadly covered by the English word *love*, agapē has an unconditional element. It refers to affection motivated by the subject, not the object of love. God loves us, not because we are lovable but because he is loving. Spontaneous and unconditional though it is, God's love is not a mechanical outpouring, an inexorable natural process. God's love can never be taken for granted.[38]

According to Rice, then, divine agapē is a state of motivation actively initiated by the agent, and in that sense it is not conditional on anything desirable in the object being presented to the agent in advance (even if it may have other grounds). This paradigm species of projective motivation explains how God can remain weakly impassible (in my sense) and yet act as a *personal* agent: "God enjoys relationships, has feelings, makes decisions, formulates plans and acts to fulfill them."[39] The fact that something similar must be true of human agapē, if it is possible, explains why a scholastic philosophical tradition wedded to the strong erosiac thesis was forced to conclude that human beings could achieve agapic love of our neighbor only by an act of divine grace.

In his analysis, Rice clearly follows Nygren's view that "Agapē is creative love" which imparts value to its object *by loving it*. And Nygren is influenced by Kierkegaard when he calls this sort of love "spontaneous and unmotivated."[40] However, this formulation obscures part of Kierkegaard's insight by assuming that if an action is not orektically motivated, then it is not motivated at all (as the strong erosiac thesis implies). In addition, although he only means that God is not moved by *orektic desire* to acquire a good that God lacks, Nygren's way of putting this unfortunately suggests that agapē can be spontaneous motivation only if the agapic agent is not responding to *any value* that the actual or potential object/goal has prior to being loved.[41] In other words, Nygren assumes that if agapic devotion is formed in light of any value that already exists in its object, then such a value would be attracting the agent, or motivating in the erosiac sense. This is also Zagzebski's assumption when she argues that the only way to avoid implying that God's motivation to create was self-interested is to say that this motive is not "for the sake of an end."[42] Thus, like Nygren, she concludes that "The goodness of the world is consequent to God's creative act."[43]

The problem with this solution is that it makes agapic projection of the goal (i.e., the object's good) entirely *arbitrary* for the agent: the only reason we can give for such agapic motivation is that it is just built into the agent's nature. Avoiding such arbitrariness requires forms of value that could provide a reason for devotion to some end or goal without necessarily causing prior attraction to it by correlating with some need or lack in the agent. Agapic care need not be *motivated* by the object's prior value to involve a rational *response* to that value.[44] Agapic willing can also give the object new personal value to the lover, but only if this personal value supervenes on its intrinsic value prior to being loved (see chap. 14, sec. 4.5). For example, God could see some potential value in the being to be created, prior to willing its actualization, without being moved erosiacally by this value, as in Leibniz's model.[45] Note that this view is compatible with the idea that divine love transcends all *earned merit or moral worth*, because human persons, like other creatures, can have inalienable or constitutive intrinsic value that does not vary with moral worth.[46]

The same problem occurs in Alan Soble's portrayal of agapic personal love, because he follows Nygren's formula. In this type of love, "the attractive properties of y play no role in either the reason or the nonreason causes of xLy [x loves y] (that is, personal love is neither property-based nor reason-dependent)."[47] Soble is correct that motivation sharing the agapic structure is not caused or justified by properties that *attract* in the erosiac sense, but he mistakenly assumes that all relevant properties in the beloved object or person would be of this sort. Hence he concludes, like Nygren, that agapic-type motivation must not be grounded on *any* property in the object: "Since x values y's properties in virtue of loving y, y's valuable properties cannot explain why x loves y. Love, then, is incomprehensible"[48] and lacks any kind of intentionality involving evaluative judgment that could be criticized.[49] Soble's portrayal certainly allows agapic love to be a "pure act of will," but only at the price of rendering it irrational.[50] He is right that this kind of motivation originates within the agent rather than being caused by the object, but he interprets this as implying that the object's qualities can form no part of the agent's grounds or reasons for such motivation:

> In eros love is elicited by the objective merit of the object, while agape is freely given love that creates value in its object regardless of the object's objective merit. . . .
>
> In the second [agapic] view, nothing valuable, objectively or subjectively, about the object is the ground of love; whereas in the first [erosiac] view, whether the lover responds to the objective or to the subjective value of the beloved, something valuable about the beloved figures into the ground of love.[51]

This extreme Nygrenian formulation forces Soble to counterintuitive conclusions, such as that, if "neighbor-love" is based upon some universal objective value in all human beings, then "neighbor-love is erosiac love."[52] What Soble fails to realize is that values in the object could serve as the ground of an obligation, or at least of an optional reason, for devoting oneself to the object without this causing any appetitive or passive emotional response to the object. We revisit this problem with Levinas below.

2.4. The Judeo-Christian Heritage of Projective Motivation

These points about agapic motivation help explain why the existential sense of "striving will" is first philosophically formulated in Judeo-Christian theology, although it is present in prephilosophical notions of heroic courage in many traditions. As Reinhold Niebuhr says in his Gifford Lectures, the concept of creation *ex nihilo* in the Judeo-Christian tradition makes God both "the source of vitality as well as of order." And following the "unity of God's will and wisdom, man is interpreted as a unity of will" ordered by the divine source of value.[53] Similarly, Charles Kahn argues that the "theological concept of will," which "begins with Augustine and culminates in Aquinas and the medieval 'voluntarists'" [i.e., Scotus], models human volition on the divine will.[54] It inherits from the biblical tradition a notion of the will as a kind of *self-unifying motivation*. Kahn summarizes Albrecht Dihle's explanation of the origins of this notion as follows:

> In his recent and extremely valuable Sather Lectures, Albrecht Dihle has adopted the perspective of the theological tradition.[55] His thesis is that the concept of the will as a factor or aspect of the personality distinct from, and irreducible to, intellect and desire or reason and emotion is completely absent from the Greek tradition, but implicit from the beginning in the biblical notion of obedience to the commands of God. . . . The appropriate human response is to be seen neither in terms of rational understanding, nor in terms of emotion and desire, but as a *commitment of the whole person* that calls out for the concept of will for its articulation.[56]

"Commitment" in this existential sense is clearly something more than a speech-act involving a promise, or a pledge to execute a standing plan that borrows its motivation entirely from prior desires that moved the agent to form that plan. As Kahn and Dihle insist, for Augustine and his descendants, the will constitutes a different type of motivation altogether, a type that is *sui generis* although also linked to reason and action. In this tradition, freedom is the liberty of this self-motivating process of setting ends, and such liberty cannot be reduced to the habit of rightly guiding appetite by reason. It is rather a way of drawing oneself together to meet the challenge, steeling oneself to the task, and cultivating passion for one's end—in short, a kind of motivational bootstrapping. In its strongest form, it is the absolute commitment of self, or unbreakable resolve, which is perhaps symbolized in the northern mythological figure of the Valkyrie, a being of pure will. But we can also find this strength of spirit in other less outwardly "heroic" guises: in the quiet perseverance of a single mother caring for her children despite every obstacle; in the patience of a terminally ill elderly man determined to die according to his values; in the inward determination of a disaster victim to rebuild her life, and so on. For in the Judeo-Christian tradition, the heroism of the striving will moves *inward*; it is seen in many forms of spiritual strength, and as Hauerwas says, it is the source of "character" as a set of motive-dispositions that the agent has taken part in forming, rather than a mere set of traits "which simply happen to him."[57]

Because Jewish and Christian theologies regard human beings as made in the image of God, it was natural for thinkers starting from the *imago dei* doctrine to hold not only that we share something like divine freedom but also that we have a capacity for motivation *like* that which is expressed in God's act of creation *ex nihilo*—an act that is not rationally required or desired, as if God would be incomplete without the world, but is instead a voluntary *overflowing* of His perfection. If so, then in our creative work as well, we may find something at least analogous to "superabundant motivation." For example, Martin Buber describes genuine artistic creation as an act of willing resolve by one who "commits himself with his whole being" to the form that confronts him as his Thou.[58] Being true to the form that calls him may require sacrifice, but he is resolved to overcome external difficulties in order to express this form. Similarly, Tolkien once argued that creating fictions for the sake of their intrinsic value—or for sheer delight in their wonder—is part of the natural function and rightful power of human beings as "subcreators": "Fantasy remains a human right: we make in our measure and in our derivative mode, because we are made: and not only made, but made in the image and likeness of a Maker."[59] In other words, invention is a free expression of the creative will.

For these thinkers, creativity is something much more than "the happy choice of the right concept at the right time," aided by a general ability to recognize unanticipated patterns, as Douglas Hofstadter suggests.[60] Programming a computer to get bored whenever it discovers itself in a repetitive pattern of similar actions, or to watch for "interesting" patterns of change in its data structures, or even to watch itself to make sure it is not getting "ruttish" or stuck in its ways would not be sufficient to give it a capacity for true *originality*;[61] that requires the capacity to discover entirely new things to care about and to respond to them in ways not determined by one's past activities. To Tolkien and Buber, that is the divine spark in human persons. Nietzsche is also indebted to this tradition when he conceives art as a primary expression of the will to power and holds that "We are to make ourselves into works of art, self-created," as Charles Larmore puts it.[62] Yet Nietzsche could not recognize agapic love as another expression of creative willpower, the kind that Erich Fromm called the "art of loving." Agapē so conceived is not a "tepid love,"[63] but rather a state of resolve involving a kind of energy and determination similar to that of the devoted artist.

In sum, the notion of divine agapē and its human analogs provided the historical precedent for a countertradition opposed to the classical thesis that all motivation must conform to the erosiac structure.[64] This countertradition reemerged in the work of Duns Scotus and Kant, whom I discuss in chapter 11, and was exemplified in twentieth-century philosophy primarily in three personalist schools: the religious existentialists, the phenomenological realists, and the Levinasian proponents of alterity ethics.[65] Its influence is also clear in the more secular existential philosophy of Hannah Arendt, who wrote the most important work on "willing" in the first half of the twentieth century. In the next two sections, I consider Arendt and Levinas as case studies in this broad countereudaimonist tradition before explaining the general conclusions to be drawn for an account of projective motivation.

3. Arendt on Creative Work

Between Marx's ideal of unalienated labor (see chap. 8, sec. 5.3) and MacIntyre's theory of practices comes Arendt's highly original reflections on creativity in human work and the shape of lived time. In volume II of *The Life of the Mind*,[66] Arendt not only retraces the history of conceptions of willing from Aristotle through Scotus and on to Nietzsche and Heidegger but also proposes a novel view of her own.

Arendt begins with the existential relation of will to time: "the Will, if it exists at all . . . is obviously our mental organ for the future as memory is our mental organ for the past. The moment we turn our mind to the future, we are no longer concerned with 'objects' but with projects."[67] Arendt means "projects" in the literal sense of plans and directives, for example, those spelled out in a "Last Will and Testament." But Arendt follows Augustine and Scotus in conceiving the will as essentially free in a way that (as we will see) requires the possibility of projective motivation: "A will that is not free is a contradiction in terms—unless one understands the faculty of volition as a mere auxiliary executive organ for whatever either desires or reason has proposed."[68]

By contrast, Arendt conceives the will as a motivational faculty that is not merely determined by prior appetite or evaluative judgments. Moreover, she recognizes that volitional motivation cannot have the kind of teleological structure that Aristotle invokes to explain "making or fabrication—*poiein*, as distinct from *prattein*, acting or *praxis*." The problem with Aristotle's account is that the model in which "everything that appears grows out of something that contains the finished product potentially" makes time into a circle, denying genuine novelty:

> The view that everything real must be preceded by a potentiality as one of its causes implicitly denies the future as an authentic tense: the future is nothing but the consequence of the past, and the difference between natural and man-made things is merely between those whose potentialities necessarily grow into actualities and those that may or may not be actualized. Under these circumstances, any notion of the Will as an organ for the future . . . was entirely superfluous.[69]

Arendt suggests in fact that this explains why any notion of the will more substantive than mere voluntary action (intentional as opposed to unintentional acts) is missing from Greek philosophy.[70] This "curious lacuna . . . is in perfect accord with the time concept of antiquity, which identified temporality with the circular movements of the heavenly bodies and with the no less cyclical nature of life on earth."[71]

An open future suggests instead the notion of will as a capacity "that in principle is indeterminable and therefore a possible harbinger of novelty;" it fits with the notion that the entire world had a "divine beginning" and is therefore a radical novelty. It is against the background of the "rectilinear time concept" required by the story of Christ's resurrection and Christian eschatology that, Arendt says, "the Will and its necessary Freedom in all their complexity were first discovered by Paul [the apostle]."[72] And she adds that the continuing resistance to acknowledging this phenomenon, manifested in philosophy from the medieval period to the present, shows how strong the reluctance has been "to grant human beings, unprotected by any divine Providence or guidance, absolute power over their own destiny and thus burden them with a formidable responsibility for things whose very existence would depend exclusively on themselves."[73] Here we see Arendt at her most existentialist; she reads every reduction of the will, including the German idealist tendency to "equate Willing and Being" and the refusal of free will in Nietzsche and the later Heidegger, as episodes of bad faith.[74]

Whatever we might make of her historical analyses of this issue,[75] the innovation in Arendt's own account lies in her development of the theme of novelty. For Arendt, the motivational power of volition, its surplus over desire, is found in its conferring practical meaning on an indeterminate future. In contrast with *liberum arbitrium*, which simply picks from preordained options, "spontaneity" as Arendt understands it is "a power to begin something really new" which "could not very well be preceded by any potentiality."[76] She allows that the end that the will gives itself is logically possible, but denies that it is the agent's potential in the sense of something that is teleologically anticipated and unfolds when triggered. Although she does not contrast the will's creation of new ends with the relative passivity of desires, Arendt forces us to see how implausible it is that all the ends we take up could derive simply from a prior telos: "Can anybody seriously maintain that the symphony produced by a composer . . . existed in a state of potentiality, waiting for some musician who would take the trouble to make it actual?"[77] The sheer complexity and variety of products of human willing, "art objects as well as use objects,"[78] attests to the fact that through will, we conceive goals for ourselves for which there is not necessarily any prior impetus; we conceive new challenges and invent new needs for ourselves.

It is clear how well this fits my description of projective motivation: through projective striving we can work up our own motivation, sometimes over a period of time. Only understanding the will in these terms allows for the innovations through which historical time becomes linear:

> It is not the future as such but the future as the Will's project that negates the given. In Hegel and Marx, the power of negation, whose motor drives History forward, is derived from the Will's ability to actualize a project; the project negates the now as well as the past and thus threatens the thinking ego's enduring present.[79]

I think Arendt is right that nothing truly novel in human affairs could come about, except by sheer accident, if projective motivation were impossible. For the instinctual appetites vary little; the fundamental conditions of overall human well-being remain largely constant, altering only in the means necessary for their realization in different historical contexts; and brute preferences are too subjective or inarticulate about their reasons to extend to complex and incommensurable options: nobody just finds themselves "preferring" to compose a symphony in a new style rather than to watch sitcoms in the way that they prefer chocolate to vanilla. We don't "have a hankering" to compose a symphony; except in pathological cases, we can acquire such a goal only by making it our project, by *willed aspiration to a great work*. Perhaps we can also project ends that are mundane and repetitive, but precisely because the will's resources are greater than this, the suspicion will naturally arise that what we are really projecting is the goal of living in a way that requires such modesty in our pursuits or that expresses our rejection of traditional conceptions of excellence (a project that could be based either on good or bad grounds).[80]

Arendt does not concentrate on the distinction between act and motive, but her remarks on the "tonality" of the will reveal her understanding of the distinctive nature of volitional motivation. There is in Arendt's view a fundamental tension between the mind's two aspects, thinking and willing.[81] She quotes Bergson's suggestion that "In the perspective of memory, that is, looked at retrospectively, a freely performed act loses its air of contingency under the impact of now being an accomplished fact."[82] In thought, which is hindsight, our will's projects seem to flow continuously out of a preceding series of psychic states as if they were necessitated; thus the temptation to reduce the will to something else, although from "the perspective of the willing ego, it is not freedom but necessity that appears as a delusion of consciousness."[83] This "clash between thinking and willing" is also a matter of the opposing tones or moods of these mental activities.[84] Thinking, even in working out difficult questions, is self-contented:

> Rememberance [sic] may affect the soul with longing for the past, but this nostalgia, while it may hold grief and sorrow, does not upset the mind's equanimity, because it concerns things which are beyond our power to change. On the contrary, the willing ego, looking forward and not backward, deals with things which are in our power but whose accomplishment is by no means certain. The resulting tension, unlike the rather stimulating excitement that may accompany problem-solving activities, causes a kind of disquiet in the soul easily bordering on turmoil, a mixture of fear and hope that becomes unbearable when it is discovered that, in Augustine's formula, to will and to be able to perform, *velle* and *posse*, are not the same....
>
> Speaking in terms of tonality—that is, in terms of the way the mind affects the soul and produces its moods, regardless of outside events, thus creating a kind of life of the mind—the predominant mood of the thinking ego is serenity, the mere enjoyment of an activity.... The predominant mood of the Will is tenseness, which brings to ruin the "mind's" tranquility.[85]

As I argued in chapter 4, we could describe the "tone" of desire in Plato's account as a state of unquiet or dissatisfaction attempting to return to harmony and inner equilibrium. What differentiates desire from will in this respect is that in striving volition, the ego *willingly takes on* such tension, disturbance, and the risk of having an unrealized end. By willing in the existential sense, we voluntarily move ourselves from a state of relative pose or quietude into a state of resolute interestedness that risks frustration and disappointment—something that is impossible on the erosiac model. Arendt means to emphasize this point when she writes that

> in flagrant contrast to thinking, no willing is ever done for its own sake or finds its fulfillment in the act itself. Every volition not only concerns [contingent] particulars but—and this is of great importance—looks forward to its own end, when willing something will have changed into doing it. In other words, the normal mood of the willing ego is impatience, disquiet, and worry (*Sorge*) . . . because the will's project presupposes an I-can that is by no means guaranteed.[86]

This statement could be misread as an affirmation of Aquinas's view that the motive for willing must lie entirely in the perceived value of the end to be achieved. What Arendt actually means is that a motivational supplement is necessarily involved in the deliberate formation of any intention to act: there *is* no decision unless the agent is resolved to act in such-and-such a way if possible (even in the face of competing desires). This tension, willingly undertaken, is the projective element in *all* decisions. But it is especially pronounced if the decision involves setting a new end for the sake of which the intended act will be done. Projective motivation is distinguished by the fact that it freely undertakes the uncertainty and tribulation that all motivation involves; through it, we *make* ourselves dissatisfied with the actual states of affairs, or bring about an internal "restlessness"[87] similar to that from which desire starts for Plato.

4. Levinas on Superabundant Will and Volitional Generosity

Emmanuel Levinas follows Plato's late model of divine creative will as "superabundant" or projective and makes this idea the basis of his famous phenomenology of ethical experience at the interhuman level. Levinas does not see God's creative act as ontologically determined by his superabundant nature (since he does not think of God as having a nature at all) but he understands both human moral responses to others and the basic call to respond in non-erosiac terms. The "idea of creation *ex nihilo*" suggests the possibility of a "relationship between strangers" that is not based on need for each other; moreover, such creation implies that the creature is not merely a "part" of its creator, giving it the independence necessary for it to be capable of love not based on neediness.[88]

As I detail elsewhere,[89] Levinas conceives the ideal of agapic love asymmetrically—as a willingness to sacrifice without concern for reciprocity—and he interprets the categorical imperative to love another person in this radical sense as the transcendent quasi-experience in which the very existence of others *as persons* is first made manifest to the self. The person as "neighbor," or the Face that calls me to agapic love, is contrasted, for Levinas, with all objects of erosiac attraction that the self seeks to appropriate or possess in order to achieve its completeness. As a result, the originary experience of responsibility to love another as neighbor must ground an agapic love that is *projective* in form. In other words, Levinas's account requires the existential conception of the striving will.

Levinas himself is not entirely clear about this implicit commitment; at points, he apparently approaches the paradigmatically "Eastern" suspicion that all will is willfulness (see my discussion in chap. 2). But in other passages, he acknowledges the creative power of projective willing that his own phenomenology of ethical experience requires. While there are many dimensions to Levinas's thought, often corresponding to the rival views that he hopes to answer (from Heidegger's ontological philosophy to Hegel's analysis of recognition and intersubjectivity), I will focus only on (i) Levinas's debt to the Neoplatonic countertradition and the associated

Judeo-Christian conception of creativity sketched above; and (ii) his own discussion of willing in *Totality and Infinity* and related essays.

4.1. The Agapic Revelation of Alterity

Levinas's philosophy is built on his argument that our encounter with the other person as a being to whom we owe an absolute responsibility, which he refers to as being called by the other's "Face," has absolute primacy in the structure of selfhood and indeed is presupposed in the possibility of all other experience, knowledge, and action. It is in this encounter with ethical *alterity*—the Otherness of the other person, who is not constructed out of our consciousness nor constituted by our intentional attitudes—that we first encounter reality outside our mind at all. Yet this is not something *added* to a self-knowing consciousness that already constitutes a self; rather, it is only *by being* appropriated into moral duty to others that the *I* arises as a self-aware center of responsible agency at all.

It is helpful to think of this as an inversion of Sartre's quasi-Hegelian conception of the *I* as threatened in its solitary self-absorption by the existence of the other's look.[90] Levinas is specifically opposing the philosophical tradition in which "*conflicts* between the [self-]same and the other are resolved by a theory whereby the other is reduced to the same—or, concretely, by the community or the state."[91] Instead, the Other is originally an ethical appeal or obligation that cannot be assimilated back into the self or mediated in a higher synthesis: in Fichtean terms, the Other is the *Anstoss* through which the *I* comes to have the reflexive capacities of self-awareness necessary for selfhood and agency to begin with.

On Levinas's account, this alterity or absolute difference of another person has both negative and positive aspects (which he tends to equate). Negatively, it consists in the other person's being unappropriable or unpossessable by the subject of conscious experience: the Other is "transcendent" to my experience, unlike all objects and tools, for "the distance at which the object stands" from our mental acts of cognizing it "does not exclude, and in reality implies, the *possession* of the object."[92] This negative thesis depends on a particular conception of mental intentionality as *orektic*.

Levinas follows the notion found in Sartre, but going back to earlier German idealists, of all ordinary modes of consciousness as generically erosiac in form, appropriating the object to the subject by mental acts that aim at constituting it as an object-for-me. Thus, rightly or not, Levinas sees Husserlian phenomenology, in which the content thought is the correlate of the subject's intentional attitude toward it, as analogous in structure to ordinary appetitive motivation *as lack*. On this view, as Alphonso Lingis says, all intentional direction toward "a term" or "object" is "a lack aiming at a content."[93] Just as the object desired is proleptically anticipated by the desire for it, since it is apprehended in terms of its value for the agent's well-being or satisfaction, Levinas believes that in Husserl's model, *all* intentional contents are conformed to the conscious act of the agent (as in Plato's maieutic theory of knowledge, the object known is anticipated in the agent's trace memory of it; thus recollection is analogous to appetition). In classical phenomenology, Levinas believes, we never find in the world anything but reflections or externalizations of what was already within us; that is, we never encounter genuine otherness without constructing it in our own terms.[94]

In contrast to this, our original responsibility for the other "in nowise resembles the intentional relation which in knowledge attaches us to the object"[95] determined by the mode in which the subject intends it, as in classical phenomenologies. The alterity of the "Stranger" or person-as-other exceeds my mental grasp: it is "an idea whose *ideatum* overflows the capacity of thought."[96] This Neoplatonic metaphor of overflowing superabundance is associated with the projective conception of divine motivation, as we have seen. And like Nygren, Levinas sees agapic love as the paradigm of such superabundant motivation not driven by any neediness in the self. Hence, in distinguishing the impact of alterity from all other kinds of experience, Levinas looks to the projective structure of agapē in contrast to eros.

As in agapē, the Other toward which the agent is oriented is not an "end" in the classical sense of a *correlate* that fulfills some deficit in the agent,[97] or that addresses some lack that would motivate a self-interested concern to realize that end. Thus "the vision of the face is not an *experience*" or an absorbing of objects into the self, "but a moving out of oneself, a contact with another being.... The infinite is given only to the moral view: it is not *known* but is in society with us."[98] Similarly, in commenting on Franz Rosenzweig, Levinas describes "revelation" as an "entering-into-relation completely different from the one that corresponds to a synthesis"; since such a revelatory relation is not teleological, it links its terms nonadditively "in a connection for which language or sociality or love is the original metaphor."[99] Likewise, Levinas calls the dependence of personal interiority on revealed responsibility for others and for the human "world" in general a "fundamental non-narcissism."[100] This leads to the positive aspect of alterity.

4.2. *The Projective Structure of Metaphysical Desire*

The comparison with agapē is more than mere analogy, for alterity consists in a moral obligation or imperative not only *not* to possess or enslave the other (not to treat her as a mere thing) but also to show active concern or regard for her being as an end-in-itself. This is the positive aspect of alterity. The original preintentional responsibility to the other is conceived not as a limitation on the agent's freedom of will but rather as the ground of his freedom's possibility *outside itself* (since the I does not ground itself). As Levinas says, "the other absolutely other—the Other—does not limit the freedom of the same; calling it to responsibility, it founds it and justifies it."[101] As in Kant's moral philosophy, the agent's free will is possible only as already constrained by a categorical moral responsibility.[102] Merold Westphal's summary of this point brings out its basic similarity to the duty of neighbor-love in the Judeo-Christian tradition:

> He [Levinas] is claiming that the face of the neighbor confronts us not as a contractual proposal to be negotiated, but as an unconditional obligation. It is unconditional in that its validity depends in no way either upon our agreeing to accept it or in the Other's doing something to evoke or merit our compliance.[103]

This is correct; as Levinas emphasizes, "The will is free to assume this responsibility in whatever sense it likes; it is not free to refuse this responsibility itself."[104] Even when violating our duty, Levinas believes we are unintentionally acknowledging it. As Jeffrey Kosky says, for Levinas, "The self is elect insofar as in responsibility it is chosen for or assigned to itself before being free to choose or commit itself to responsibility."[105]

Levinas describes this unconditional responsibility for the other person, of which their "Face" is the revelation, as a "metaphysical desire for the absolutely other."[106] It so happens that Levinas's choice of terms is singularly unfortunate for my purposes; for, as we have seen, the word "desire" and its cognates inevitably connote the kind of magnetic attraction toward completion that Levinas believes can never reach alterity. Yet, in fact, what Levinas means by "metaphysical Desire" is precisely a *non-orektic* type of motivation, a practical end-directedness that is not a *conatus* in the usual sense of being drawn toward objects to satisfy itself. Like Nygren describing agapē, Levinas characterizes his "metaphysical Desire" specifically by *contrast* with Plato's lack model of erosiac appetition, which, as we saw, Levinas extends even to speculative cognition:

> The other metaphysically desired is not "other" like the bread I eat, the land in which I dwell, the landscape I contemplate. . . . I can "feed" on these realities and to a very great extent satisfy myself, *as though I had simply been lacking them.* Their *alterity* is thereby reabsorbed into my own identity as a thinker or possessor. The metaphysical desire tends towards something else entirely, towards the absolutely other. . . . As commonly interpreted need would be at the basis of

desire; desire would characterize a being indigent and incomplete. . . . It would coincide with a consciousness of what has been lost, a longing for return. But thus it would not even suspect what the veritably other is. The metaphysical desire does not long to return.[107]

The "customary analysis of desire" that Levinas describes here comes straight from Plato's *Symposium* (though Levinas also distinguishes his own unique sense of "eros" that is neither Platonic eros nor agapic response to the Face).[108] Metaphysical Desire, then, is distinct from all erosiac forms of causality, intentionality, or motivation, which Levinas portrays as violent in a quasi-Kantian sense: "the fabrication of a thing, the satisfaction of a need, the desire and even the knowledge of an object" use alterior realities as a means to self-satisfaction or completion.[109]

This claim is hardly uncontroversial. William Desmond, for example, objects that "a teleology of desire" does not "necessitate a totalitarian tyranny of the self over otherness."[110] This is fair insofar as Levinas's references to "violence" suggest material egoism. But Levinas's claim is really that we are capable of motives that transcend formal egoism, while Desmond seems to remain locked in the erosiac model.[111] For he asserts that without ends that can attract and thus cause desire, "There would be purely inert being, wanting nothing."[112] Desmond does not reduce all motivation to "pure bodily urge," or DI desire, but he does see the development of the self as primarily an erosiac process.[113] Levinas's conception of moral motivation is a radical challenge to this kind of Hegelian picture.

Levinas explains his problematic language of "metaphysical desire" in an early essay that confirms that this terminology was inspired by the view that the late Plato discovered a non-erosiac kind of motivation that was already intimated in "the transcendence of the Good with respect to Being" in the *Republic*:[114]

> In the "Canticle of the Columns," Valéry speaks of a "faultless desire." He is doubtless referring to Plato who, in his analysis of pure pleasures, discovered an aspiration that is conditioned by no prior lack.[115] We are taking up this term desire; to a subject turned to itself . . . we are opposing the desire for the other which proceeds from a being already gratified and in this sense independent, which does not desire for itself. It is the need of him who no longer has needs. . . . The desire for the other, sociality, is born in a being that lacks nothing, or, more exactly, it is born over and beyond all that can be lacking or that can satisfy him. . . . The movement towards the other, instead of completing me and contenting me, implicates me in a conjuncture which in a way did not concern me—what was I looking for here?[116]

Here again Levinas clearly contrasts our original ethical motivation to care for the other with all forms of "desire" in the erosiac sense, in which the agent wants his end to restore an equilibrium by making up for a perceived lack in his well-being (see chap. 4, sec. 2, of this volume). Instead, he thinks of metaphysical Desire in specifically Neoplatonic terms as a kind of *overflowing* of an agent who (in this motive at least) *needs nothing* for herself but goes freely out of herself toward an end that she was not *drawn* to realize by any prior apprehension of an imperfection that the end would remedy. As he claims in *Totality and Infinity*, "Alongside of needs whose satisfaction amounts to filling a void, Plato catches sight also of aspirations that are not preceded by suffering and lack, and in which we recognize the pattern of Desire: the need of him who lacks nothing."[117]

In another essay, Levinas explains that he talks about the infinity of metaphysical Desire "to mark the propulsion, the inflation, of this beyond" since it is

> opposed to the affectivity of love and the indigence of need. Outside of the hunger one satisfies, the thirst one quenches and the senses one allays, exists the other, absolutely other, desired beyond these satisfactions. . . . This desire is unquenchable, not because it answers to an infinite hunger, but because it does not call for food. This desire without satisfaction hence takes cognizance of the alterity of the other.[118]

This formula is repeated in *Totality and Infinity*: "Insatiable Desire—not because it corresponds to an infinite hunger, but because it is not an appeal for food."[119] This opaque phrasing may be partly due to Lacan's related notion of desire for otherness, which still conceives desire as a consciousness of absence, but one that can never be filled. As Darius Sleszynski summarizes, "In Lacanian psychoanalysis, that toward which desire is 'directed' has paradoxically a structure of a document of lack. Contrary to needs, desire is never satiated, [always] unfulfilled: it is an eternal call to existence. Desire renews itself."[120]

This in turn reminds one of Heidegger's claim that, as Ben Vedder puts it, "For Dasein, not-having and lacking are structural" or essential to our entire practical attitude as "being after something." Heidegger means that human beings are essentially purposive or volitional beings, and it is unfortunate that he puts this in erosiac terms implying that "lacking, deprivation, and need is inherent in Dasein."[121] But like Lacan, Heidegger holds that Dasein is essentially open to new purposes and hence "can never be regarded as complete and realized."[122] This rules out any eudaimonist conception of our formal telos, but this negation is not enough to get us to the projective model. For it is also compatible with a Hobbesian view that we have no telos but only indefinitely extendable activity moved by insatiable hunger for power. By valuing the possible over the actual, Heidegger means to suggest a nonconsumptive relation to alterity.[123] But he falls into Nygren's error of assuming that if we focus on *realizing* goals rather than contemplating them as possible and letting them be, then we must be seeking to possess them in order to complete ourselves. By contrast, projective motivation is the idea of a non-erosiac striving toward ends.

Hence the language of "insatiable Desire" can be misleading in Levinas and other Continental philosophers. By metaphysical "Desire," Levinas means something closely related to volitional striving or projection in my existential sense, in which we devote ourselves to someone or something for reasons unrelated to any contribution it might make to our well-being. The volitional capacity to become so motivated is in one relevant sense *unquenchable* because through it, we can acquire ever new ends. Since their acquisition does not arise from a sense of lack wanting fulfillment, success does not limit the generation and maintenance of projective motivation. Levinas means something like this when he writes that "It is a desire that cannot be satisfied . . . it desires beyond everything that can simply complete it. It is thus like goodness—the Desired does not fulfill it, but deepens it."[124]

Yet one could misread this as meaning that Levinas still has in mind a kind of mystical eros for an object with which we can never completely join, whose pursuit must ever continue (like the painted lovers in Keat's "Ode on a Grecian Urn"). Levinas indicates that metaphysical Desire does not seek union with the Divine but is rather "a generosity nourished by the Desired, and thus a relationship that is not a disappearance of distance, not a bringing together . . . for it nourishes itself, one might say, with its hunger."[125] Levinas has in mind the idea that our responsibilities are open-ended, so our awareness of them expands the more we try to fulfill them.[126] But the metaphor of food that makes us hungrier is not helpful: it risks suggesting an ever-expanding eros, which sounds like a Dantean torture, rather than providing any positive account of duty to the other as a motive.[127] Rather than trying to turn eros against itself in a figure of speech, it would have been much clearer for Levinas to say that he is proposing a type of motivation that is *non-desiderative* altogether, and then to explain how such motivation is possible.[128]

As I emphasized above, Levinas's descriptions of metaphysical Desire are meant not only to contrast it with Platonic eros but also to associate it positively with agapē (as conceived by Nygren). Although metaphysical Desire is first and foremost the revelation of a *duty* to love the other—a duty to which we freely respond in different ways—Levinas describes this involuntary experience of categorical obligation as if it were *itself* a kind of neighbor-love. Thus he calls it "A Desire perfectly disinterested—goodness. . . . For the presence before a face, my orientation toward the Other, can lose the avidity proper to the gaze only by turning into generosity."[129] This sounds like a love pure even of formal self-interest, unselfish generosity as opposed even to eudaimonistic self-realization.[130] As Levinas puts it later, the "proximity" or relation of the self *for*-the-other "is a *for* of total gratuity, breaking with interest."[131] He even refers to the responsibility that requires substitution of oneself for another—the sacrifice of one's subjectivity—as "love without eros."[132] Such a responsibility "to answer for the other is, perhaps, the harsh name of love."[133]

Similarly, near the end of his famous essay on "Ethics as First Philosophy," Levinas describes our originary sense of responsibility for other persons as "love without concupiscence." In another essay, Levinas describes this as "the binding separation known by the well-worn name of love."[134] He repeatedly emphasizes that the face-to-face relation in which my responsibility is revealed to me has the same structure that Derrida finds in an ideal (or, for him, "impossible") gift beyond all "economy," self-interested contract, or expectation of a return.[135]

Nevertheless an experience of responsibility cannot by itself really constitute generosity, disinterested care, or agapic regard. For, as Levinas says explicitly, in response to "the gaze of the stranger, the widow, and the orphan . . . I am free to give or refuse."[136] By contrast, metaphysical Desire in Levinas's account is primarily a sense of responsibility, a "mauvaise conscience" not arising from any action or intention, an originary guilt that gives us Socrates' "capacity to fear injustice more than death, to prefer to suffer than to commit injustice."[137] The analogy comparing this nonoptional moral call itself with the best optional agapic response to it threatens to obscure the crucial distinction between projective resolve or commitment of the self and the projective motive's *prior ground* or rational basis.

Insufficient clarity about this distinction in turn leads Levinas into the same error that we identified in Nygren's analysis: (1) Levinas imagines that for a motive-state to have a grounding reason must be for it to derive from the attractiveness of its end; (2) but since the latter is ruled out in non-erosiac motives, these must arise without any basis in values subject to the agent's rational judgment. The mistaken first premise is evident when Levinas suggests that since metaphysical Desire involves no erosiac "anticipation" of the Desired, "it goes towards it aimlessly,"[138] as if it has no goal at all. This paradoxical conclusion would be unavoidable if every kind of value that could be "anticipated" in an end or goal were the correlate of some species of *orektic* desire. But if there are other kinds of values to be found in some possible goals of human action, then these values may ground commitment to such goals without *prior desire for these values*. Without some experience of such a grounding value in an end (or in the process of pursuing it), metaphysical Desire would be just a blind and arbitrary thrust into the void.

In fact, Levinas's account avoids total arbitrariness by recognizing the alterity of the other as a kind of "ground" for the agent's projective response. In this sense, Levinas's model is already superior to Nygren's.[139] However, the call of alterity is not treated as a *practical reason* (in the usual sense) for setting oneself the task of serving the other's good or respecting the other's dignity; instead, it is treated as exceeding our rational comprehension. Whether projective willing can be a nonarbitrary kind of response to such a "transcendent" event is an intriguing question, but it is surely not limited to this kind of ground. The existential theory of projective motivation provides a more rigorous and broader conception of Levinas's basic concept. For as we will see, "goodness" or "generosity" in the agapic sense as selfless universal love is only *one* possible species of projective motivation. Nor is it clear that every cognitive assessment of value in the other reduces her uniqueness or does violence to her alterity, as Levinas thinks (see chap. 14, sec. 4, of this volume).

4.3. Levinas on the Will

I have suggested that Levinas's language of superabundance is an apt expression for the phenomena of projective *creativity* in setting and pursuing new ends. For, like Arendt, Buber, Tolkien, and others in the Judeo-Christian countertradition, Levinas recognizes the volitional power of resolve—the power to devote ourselves to tasks and projects whose ends are not proleptically anticipated as needed for our completion. In this sense, superabundant motivation functions *as if* the agent needed nothing, overflowing into agent-transcending objects and goals rather than returning to the agent through reference to his own needs, wants, or drive to self-realization (however enlightened).

Levinas's discussion of the will further demonstrates his place in this genre of thought. It is in willing that we find the individual's most intimate reflexive relation with himself—his capacity to determine the motives on which he acts: "When the will triumphs over its passions, it manifests itself not only as the strongest passion [contra Hobbes] but as above all passion, determining itself by itself, inviolable. But when it has succumbed, it reveals itself to be exposed to influences."[140]

Like Butler and Kant, Levinas holds that the will can transcend all appetitive motivation. Thus the I "can sacrifice to its [metaphysical] Desire its very happiness."[141] But, in keeping with the existentialist emphasis on the factical side of selfhood, Levinas emphasizes that the will characteristic of persons is always exposed to violence from others, such as threats, pressure, coercion, manipulation, hatred that imposes suffering and reifies the will, and even murder.[142] Levinas acknowledges the Sartrean point that the will is not absolutely determined by such attacks (and is in that sense "immune");[143] yet as embodied, it can be influenced: "Violence recognizes, but bends the will."[144] Nor can courage in the face of death give me ultimate independence from the other's will.[145] In a more general way too, our volitional activity is dependent on relations with others who take up the results of our work and can by their own activity give a significance to our efforts that we did not intend. As Levinas says:

> this way a will plays in history a role it has not willed marks the limits of interiority: the will finds itself caught up in events that will appear only to the historian. . . .
> The whole being of willing is hence not enacted within oneself. The capacity of the independent I does not contain its own being.[146]

As John Llewelyn says, "Levinas located will in the lived body," which connects its works to a shared history in which others act on these works.[147] Thus "the will, whereby a being wields itself . . . is by its work exposed to the other."[148] Yet its freedom is restored to the will, paradoxically, by its being called beyond itself in absolute duty, in "will as Desire and Goodness limited by nothing."[149] It is the presence of nonoptional moral obligations that allows freedom to be sovereign for the individual, since without this metaphysical dependence, free choice is arbitrary.[150] Yet this conception does not avoid arbitrariness simply by reducing the will to reason; rather, employing the Neoplatonic metaphor, Levinas says that will requires "the idea of creation which, in God, exceeds a being eternally satisfied with itself."[151] Levinas conceives such purely creative motivation as neither simply cognitive nor affective in form but rather as having its own unique structure that stands in between these two—like Plato's "middle part of the soul."

Occasionally, Levinas seems to portray volition more negatively as need-driven and egoistic. In contrast to Marx and Arendt, he does not see human "labor" (for example in building dwellings) as projective: "Labor characterizes not a freedom that has detached itself from being, but a will: a being that is threatened, but has time at its disposal to ward off the threat."[152] Here willing is conceived as Spinoza's self-interested *conatus ascendi*: "To will is to forestall danger."[153] Unlike Martin Buber, who sees that a work can have its own kind of alterity, Levinas does not clearly recognize the phenomena of projective motivation involved in the practices. When he writes that "Every will separates from its work," he means only that we are exposed to others in our works (as we saw above), not that we produce a work purely for a value distinct from our good.[154] Similarly, he is suspicious that in equating autonomous will with reason, Kant's ideal Kingdom of Ends reduces all others to identical abstract minds whose difference is found only in their separate interests: "The so-called animal principle of happiness, ineluctable in the description of the will, even taken as practical reason, maintains pluralism in the society of minds."[155] Here Levinas probably meant that the desire for happiness is an ineluctable element in *Kant's* description of the human will, not his own. Still, Levinas has sometimes been misread as equating all willing with violence, bringing him into agreement with Luther and "paradigmatically Eastern" thinking.

It easy to see how this misreading gets started. After all, the "revelation" of alterity, or the Face, is distinguished by our radical passivity; this "manifestation Καθ' αυτό consists in a being telling itself to us independently of every position we would have taken in its regard . . . it is present as directing this very manifestation."[156] Thus our engrossment in our own projects is broken by this transcendent "experience" of direct contact by what exists independently of our will. We are no longer in control, directing our attention where we like; rather, we are gripped by a revelation in which our mind does not actively disclose anything, as it does in all other conscious experience.

This may sound a lot like the passivity of receiving grace on the Lutheran model (see chap. 2, sec. 2), with its rejection of all human initiative or assertiveness as willfulness, pride, or misappropriation. But this reading is wrong: Levinas not only rejects predestinarian providence as a totalizing scheme; he also recognizes the possibility of "a will that is not egoist," whose agent is not "the I of need," whose desire "is for the other."[157] He insists that "when I maintain an ethical relation" with another, I am actively doing something in a story of which I am at least part-author, and he denies that this is willful, hubris or "diabolical pride."[158] For the will is active— and in a founded sense, even autonomous—not only in violating the other's interests but also in responding to the neighbor with love: "In the welcoming of the face[,] the will opens to reason."[159] The "rational" rightly understood for Levinas is a discursive relation with others in their plural alterity, not a comprehension of the universal. Finally, without the "inner life" or subjectivity that the will governs, there could be no recognition of the other's infinity, or genuine plurality;[160] for without will, I would just be an extension of the other.

Someone may still object that while Levinas equates metaphysical Desire with an involuntary obligation, a duty that is the very ground of possibility of agency, my prior sketch of projective motivation described it not only as voluntary but even as involving agent-control over motivation itself. But my claim is not that the will is active in the originary revelation of responsibility. I agree with Levinas that agapic love, like all forms of projective motivation, requires recognition of an involuntary or unchosen ground or basis (other than appeal to preexistent desires). This is the grounding thesis that I defend in all the subsequent chapters of this work. Levinas believes the agent's *response* to this involuntary call to the "Face" can be purely motivated precisely because its ground is a categorical imperative. Hence metaphysical Desire plays the same role in Levinas's account as the "inclination to justice" in Scotus's account (see chap. 11); this call to justice, which is itself involuntary, is the basis for the will's *freedom* to pursue ends not given to it by the intellect's apprehension of objects as "good for itself." And just like Scotus, who writes about this ground as if it were *itself* a motive and who characterizes this motive in nonteleological terms, Levinas *transfers* the structure of projective love of neighbor back into his description of the absolute ethical duty that grounds and makes agapē possible.

Hence the only substantive differences between Levinas's position and my own are that (a) my existential conception is clearer about the distinction between the alterity of agent-transcending values and the projective motives they ground; and (b) I have generalized the category of projective motives to include devotion to a whole range of ends *other* than the neighbor-as-Face. Agapē is only the most important species of this genus. The latter difference brings my existential account of striving will closer to the phenomenological realist school. As Norris Clarke writes, Scheler and von Hildebrande held that as an agent, I can respond to a wide range of aesthetic and ethical values "for their own sake, not just for what enjoyment they give to me."[161] Gabriel Marcel writes that "the proper function of the subject is to emerge from itself and realize itself primarily in the gift of oneself and in various forms of creativity."[162] Like Levinas, Marcel sees free response to the appeal of an other as a paradigm occasion for such "self-donation," but he also recognizes the same self-transcendence in the context of vocation or devotion to creative work.[163] Similarly, John Crosby comes close to Levinas's idea of the unique and unrepeatable character of the neighbor, but without limiting self-transcendence to moral motivation in response to the basic dignity of the individual.[164]

Although I cannot do justice to the phenomenological realists here,[165] this tradition provides an important precedent for opening up the category of alterity to include nonmoral grounds for volitional striving.

5. The General Structure of Projective Motivation

We can now return to the point where chapter 3 left off after introducing projective motivation as a type of willing. For we are finally in a position to give a more rigorous formal definition of what projective motivation must be, if it exists. One need not believe in the superabundant generosity of a perfect creator to see that agapic love, divine or human, provides both an ideal counterexample to the erosiac model and a paradigm case through which the structure of projective motivation can be made clear, in contrast with the "lack structure" of orektic motivation. The claim that there are instances of non-erosiac motivation means that a human agent can be motivated to pursue ends *because she has given herself* these ends or adopted these goals as her own rather than because she is drawn by their preexisting appeal or their anticipated contribution to her well-being.

In this largely uncharted structure that I call volitional "projection,"[166] the motivation is caused not by the intentional object but rather by the agent actively taking up this object or state of affairs as the goal of his actions. That is why I have said that such motivation is essentially purposive, arising *in* the formation of specific intentions (chap. 3, sec. 3.4). Irrespective of any prior need for the intended end (or any prepurposive desire for it to fill a felt absence in his well-being), the agent *takes* an interest in it. As Peter Bertocci argues, "the quality of purpos*ive* activity that a person undergoes as a feeling-wanting agent must be differentiated from the quality of purpose*ful* experience whereby he organizes his feelings and wants in accordance with some consciously held goal."[167] For agency to be "purposeful" in this sense, its goal cannot not be fixed *as* the agent's goal or practical object without her participation, both in forming the intention to act *and* in shaping the motivation that endures in that intention.

Lest the paradigm case of divine creativity mislead us, however, it is important to note that projective motivation is not defined as "freely created" in a libertarian sense and it is certainly not conceived as formed for no reason at all. As Bertocci suggests, "will-agency does not occur within a vacuum . . . [since] the person at choice-point confronts habits, attitudes, traits within his acquired nature,"[168] which influence both his projection of new goals and his ability to muster willpower in pursuit of ends already intended. Moreover, projective striving characteristically involves *rational* considerations. Like D3 desires, projective motivation usually has "reasons" in the sense of judgments with objective purport. As we saw in the critique of Aristotle, D3 desires involve an evaluation of the *object or goal* of possible action as "good" in the sense of contributing to our well-being or proper functioning, broadly understood. By contrast, the judgments underlying volitional projections evaluate the *agent-neutral* worthiness or value of projecting this or that *as an end itself*—an evaluation that does not depend (solely) on whether this end satisfies a want or contributes to the completion of the agent's well-being. Hence volitional projection is a *conative* or motivational state of tendency toward an end, which is nevertheless not teleological or "broadly desiderative" in any substantive sense. For as Pink argues, "Desire formation, characteristically, is passive passion, not active action,"[169] whereas projection is *enacted*, actively formed motivation that informs particular intentions or plans of action.[170]

For example, suppose I have motivated myself to work out a philosophical problem through committing myself to this task, or projecting its solution as my end. The intrinsic importance of the problem furnishes reasons for this, but these reasons do not cause a prior attraction to this end. Before making the solution my goal, I do not believe that my well-being will be less without the solution to this question—or if I do believe this for other reasons, and so conceive a D3 desire for the solution, my projecting the solution as my aim is independent of this desire or at least overdetermines my interest in this project. In most other respects, the motivation formed by projective striving functions like a desire; for example, it leads me to form various specific intentions, such as to read an article on the topic in order that I might better understand the problem I am tackling. But the motivation does not have the "lack structure" of an erosiac desire: to put it in dynamic metaphors, the motive originates from the agent "pushing" the goal out in front of her rather than by a beguiling prospect "pulling" her toward it.

This distinction between erosiac desires and projective motives can be framed more rigorously in terms of familiar distinctions in "direction of fit." As we saw in chapter 4, Section I.2, the dominant belief-desire distinction in contemporary action theory makes it appear that cognitive and conative functions are mutually exclusive, since no single state could involve both without having contradictory directions of fit. But *volitional* states as essentially purposive motives are like Platonic *thumos* and Aristotelian rational appetite in respect of being both cognitive and conative in structure; as we saw, the Aristotelian composite version of the middle soul avoids this paradox by distinguishing the rational judgment of value, the attraction to it in D3 desire, and the choices it motivates. For example, John McDowell argues that "a genuinely cognitive capacity can yield at most part of a reason for acting; something appetitive is needed as well." He distinguishes these in terms of direction of fit: "How one's will is disposed is a fact about oneself; whereas a genuinely cognitive faculty discloses how the world is . . . independently of one's will."[171] "Will" is conceived here as the appetitive element, *boulēsis*. But the existential conception of striving will as self-motivating resolve or determination suggests instead an indivisible psychic state of motivation that is formed along with one's intentions or plans of action.

To make sense of this, we have to see that the traditional belief-desire distinction that McDowell employs here is too simplistic: it considers only the direction of fit between the *intentional content* and reality or the *world* and fails to consider the relation between the *agent* of the intentional state and the *content intended*. Even though philosophers of mind typically recognize the important distinction between a state of believing or desiring and the content believed or desired, the idea that this relation also has two directions of fit has not been sufficiently considered in action theory. Yet there is a direction-of-fit distinction to be drawn at the agent-content level, as well as at the content-world level. The erosiac conception of desire is effectively a theory of the agent-content fit in conative intentions; as we have seen, classical philosophers such as Plato and Aristotle recognized the *agent's* being "drawn" or *fit* to the content wanted as the distinctive mark of desire.

Of course, as Aristotle's distinction between speculative and practical attitudes shows, they also recognized the anticipation of fitting the actual world to the content wanted (or changing reality to fit the agent's desire) as the mark distinguishing desire from speculative belief—but this was less central in their analysis than the "lack structure" or *teleological* agent-content fit, which they saw as essential to desires of all kinds (appetites, passions, or rational desires). In all forms of *orexis*, the agent's motivation is *fitted to* the content desired (either by the brute "pull" of delicious appearance or by being drawn toward an objectively judged potential good for the agent). In diagramming this with triangular arrows to indicate direction of fit (e.g., x ▷ y), the element at the base of the triangle (x) is the one moved or changed to agree with, or fit, the element at the tip of the triangle (y). Thus orektic desires have the following schematic form:

Erosiac Desire: Agent   ▷   Content   ◁   Factual World

The agent is drawn toward the content that attracts her (as final cause or telos) and is thus motivated to change the world so as to actualize this desired content, that is, to satisfy her desire.

Despite their doxic (non-conative) content-world fit, factual beliefs are *like* desires in their agent-content fit. Hence classical models of knowledge emphasize the idea that the world "pulls" the mind's fact-tracking sensitivities into agreement with it, into correspondence with "the way things are." If this is right, then beliefs are not usually under our direct voluntary control. Plato and Aristotle exploited this similarity to emphasize the links between desire and beliefs about the human good. As with original (or nonderivative) desiring, the agent's *believing* some content seems to be passively directed by objects or states of affairs in the world impinging on her belief-forming faculties, which consider different contents eligible for belief in light of all sorts of evidence. Hence beliefs and judgments have the following schema:

Factual Belief: Agent   ▷   Content   ▷   Factual World

By contrast, volitional projection is unlike *both* belief and desire in its agent-content direction of fit; in projection, the intended content is "fitted to" or guided by the *agent's active intending of it*, rather than the reverse. In other words, the agent voluntarily *causes* this object to become his end or goal, or to become the intentional content of a purposive motive. Hence we have the following structure:

Projective Motive: Agent   ◁   Content   ◁   Factual World

While differing from erosiac desires in agent-content fit, then, projective motives (or "projects," for short) share their conative (or non-doxic) direction of fit in the content-world relation.

We can now link this to our preliminary sketch (at the end of chapter 3) of projective motivation as the psychological concept required to explain the existential interpretation of heroic striving will. Like all orektic states of motivation, projects can guide the formation of more particular intentions to act. However, because the agent causes the relevant state of affairs (apprehended first as a potential goal) to become his actual objective or end, the formation of such a motive-state is an act of second-order agency in Pink's sense; like decision, and unlike prepurposive appetites and wishes, it will always-already constitute a formed intention of the agent. Prepurposive motives that can simply happen to us without necessarily being taken up into intended purposes must have the passive agent-content fit of erosiac desires. Since projective motives have the opposite agent-content fit, they cannot involuntarily happen to us and thus they cannot be prepurposive; rather, they are essentially volitional motives embodied in actual intentions. Hence "projects" is an apt abbreviation for these states, since they always constitute commitments to pursue some projected end. "Projects," in my existential sense, are commitments to tasks the agent has set herself, not mere yearnings on which she may or may not decide to act.

With two types of fit relations, each having two possible directions, there are naturally four possible permutations, three of which have turned out to match recognized and hypothesized psychic states. For the sake of completeness, we should ask if it is also possible to *project* intentional contents that have doxic or cognitive content-world fit. Perhaps this provides one interesting way of interpreting states of *faith* and their difference from ordinary beliefs (as well as explaining some of the intuitive resistance to accepting the involuntariness of all "beliefs"):

Projective Faith: Agent   ◁   Content   ▷   Factual World

Projects are active in the same way as states of faith so conceived; they differ only in their content-world fit, since states of faith are appropriately about reality as it is taken on faith to be (actually or possibly, now or in the future); moreover, faith is usually about states of affairs that we cannot do anything about and so cannot will or give ourselves as *intention-guiding* ends for action.[172] We may be able to act in response to faith beliefs,[173] but this will require some further D3 or projective motive based on such states of faith. In this respect, states of faith have a doxic function, while projects have a conative one. But both are actively undertaken by the agent and both have cognitive significance in the distinct sense that they will reflect or express the agent's reasons or grounds for such an undertaking. Projective motives share this feature of making an objective validity claim about value with their closest conative relative, namely D3 desires.[174]

This points to the importance of another problem: namely, where to place evaluative judgments in this scheme. The difference between evaluative and factual judgments raises large questions that cannot be solved with the distinctions I have drawn alone. A natural way of diagramming the structure of evaluative judgments would distinguish them from factual beliefs by giving them the conative world-content fit and would distinguish them from projects and faith by making the agent passive in respect to them. The problem is that this results in the same structure as erosaic desire. If we do not think that evaluative beliefs *necessarily* motivate (even prepurposively), then we might instead diagram evaluative beliefs just like factual beliefs, replacing the factual world with the ideal world. The problem with this is that part of the *content* of evaluative beliefs seems to be that the real world should approach the ideal. I suggest the following way of capturing this additional complexity:

Evaluative Belief: Agent ▷ Content ▷ Ideal World ◁ Factual World

However, this may not sufficiently capture the idea that this complex content of evaluative beliefs is itself guided by a "world" of values (whose metaphysical status will be relevant here). Nor does it capture the idea that judgments are more active than mere beliefs.

This is only a sketch of how to conceive evaluative beliefs but it is sufficient to support the direction-of-fit analysis used above in clarifying how projective motivation can be conative without being desiderative and how it can respond to—or be guided by—considerations the agent has *other* than those that typically arouse some type of appetite in him or draw him toward the apprehended content. In a volitional project, the agent's motivational thrust toward the goal she has set for herself is not explained in terms of any kind of prior *attraction* to it, for example, because of its perceived power to satisfy preferences, or its inherent value for her well-being, or its instrumental value for either of these. Rather, the agent's projective motivation to pursue her task (which may vary in strength) is explained by her determination to *make it* her end and by the reasons that inform this projective uptake. For volitional projection never occurs *arbitrarily*, even if the considerations on which it is based are not easily introspected or completely conscious.

For example, I have (what appear to me to be) rational grounds for determining myself to solve my philosophical question: for example, the question is inherently important and has major implications for ethics, a commitment to pursuing it is noble and potentially enlightening even if the question is not adequately resolved, and so on.[175] Similarly, perhaps the needs of other persons can give me grounds for projecting a goal for myself without any prior desire for this goal or for any other end to which this goal is instrumental. But if so, then my reasons for setting myself a task concerning someone else's well-being are not considerations that connect with concern for my well-being or foster any *desire*, even of the D3 kind. Such cases, if plausible, allow us to isolate volitional projection from other, familiar forms of prepurposive motivation, namely D1–D3 states. If we add in the considerations that ground projective motivation, the structure looks like this:

Projective Motive: Agent   ◁   Content   ◁   Factual World
$\qquad\qquad\qquad\qquad\quad\ \perp\qquad\quad\ \perp$
$\qquad\qquad\qquad$Grounding evaluative reasons

I include two symbols for the grounding relation, because the reasons that the agent considers can count in favor of the agent's goal-content directly or in favor of the *process* of pursuing this goal. This structure is related to the diagrams for noble friendship and the practices in chapter 8, although we have to add in single-line arrows for intention and double-line arrows for side effect goods to make this relation clear:

$\qquad\qquad\qquad\quad$By-product Benefits
$\qquad\qquad\qquad\qquad\ \Uparrow$
Projective Motive: Agent   →   ◁   Content   ◁   Factual World
$\qquad\qquad\qquad\qquad\quad\perp\qquad\qquad\quad\perp$
$\qquad\qquad\qquad$Grounding evaluative reasons

This final formulation includes all the key elements of projective motivation in a single schematic representation. *Philia*, agapic love, creative work, and striving for excellence in a practice are all instances of this general structure.

The cases discussed in this chapter, beginning with the idea of a divine creator who lacks nothing, were introduced simply as illustrations of projective motivation or possible examples in which we can easily discern the non-erosiac structure of the striving will. To the extent that they are plausible or believable cases, they help establish the crucial premise 4 of the existential core argument (chap. 4, sec. I.2).[176] The analysis of moral motivation, the "will to meaning," caring, and aretaic commitment in chapters 12 and 13 add even stronger evidence for this premise. My positive argument for the existence of projective motivation is both phenomenological and open-ended, since it depends on adding further examples and arguing that the existential interpretation best explains them.

In the next chapter, I argue that the projective model of willing solves two more long-standing difficulties for eudaimonist moral psychology; namely, the problem of adequately accounting for (1) the phenomena of radical evil; and (2) other experiences of "strength of will." My discussion of these problems is not meant to be exhaustive or definitive but only to illustrate the relevance of the existential conception of willing to these familiar problems and to clarify further the notion of projective motivation.

10

Radical Evil and Projective Strength of Will

Overview. This chapter critiques psychological eudaimonism from another direction, arguing that it cannot explain the reality of several types of "radical evil"—by which I mean not heinous crimes but willing negative goals, including certain kinds of harm (small or large) for their own sake. The discussion begins with Aristotle and ends with Aquinas and Kierkegaard, but the middle sections present a new existential analysis of distinct levels of evil motivation with literary examples. The discussion presupposes familiar distinctions in normative ethics and is not a contribution to moral theory so much as an attempt to face the real volitional strength of evil in its darkest truth. While the beginning and ending sections assume some familiarity with eudaimonist diagnoses of vice, the middle sections should be universally accessible to general readers.

I. Why Eudaimonism Misses Virtue and Vice in Their Most Radical Forms

The idea that actions can be chosen purely for the sake of harm or wickedness has been rejected for different reasons in ancient, medieval, modern, and contemporary philosophy. This chapter critiques such attempts to rule out such "radical evil" and confronts them with motives whose malice does not consist in the mere absence of the appropriate goodness or justice.

1.1. Aristotle's Apollonian View of Virtue as a "Mean"

It is famously one of the implications of eudaimonist moral psychology in its classical forms that vice or ethical corruption of the psyche consists primarily in either ignorance of the good (Plato) or inordinate desires for external goods resulting from intemperate sense appetites and passions for status and worldly success (Aristotle). These motivational problems at best necessitate self-control (*enkrateia*) to keep them in check or (worse) lead to unethical action via "weakness of will," or *akrasia*. This idea is connected to Aristotle's famous doctrine of virtues as "mean" or intermediate states of motivation, with its strikingly "Apollonian" rather than "Dionysian" construal of good character as a kind of balance (to use Nietzsche's famous contrast). Although suggestions of the striving will appear in Aristotle's accounts of courage and magnanimity, they are largely suppressed in a model that acknowledges only practical reason aiming at the agent's good (including joint communal goods) and trained sentiments of the sense appetite as springs of controlled action.

This is unsurprising, since Aristotle's view is that human beings fail to recognize and pursue the good as they ought primarily because they *overvalue* those material rewards, powers, entertainments, and sensual pleasures craved by the lowest part of the soul—so vice consists in inordinate desire for those goods that constitute the part of our well-being most subject to luck and fortune. And this idea in turn derives directly from Socrates and the Eastern tradition in which striving will is condemned, although this view is reconceived in various ways by Plato and Aristotle, the Stoics, Augustine, and Aquinas. In all these authors, the impression persists that the key ingredient in the recipe for happiness in the holistic sense, or distinctively human flourishing, is *to control the appetites and passions*; this becomes the primary function of the moral virtues. Their ideal, as Bonnie Kent says, "is to bring one's passions into harmony with one's values, so that, having acquired virtue, it becomes easy and pleasant to do what one should."[1]

Against this background, it is not hard to see why Freud took the moral training or habituation of our psyche to be a matter of generating an Ego to suppress the Id. Of course, even for Plato and Augustine, the choices of a morally virtuous person would not be those of a *passionless* reasoner. Rather, as we already saw in discussing Aristotle's "intellectual appetite" (chap. 4, sec. 3.3), practical choice requires motivation that comes from desires, but these must be modified to follow enlightened practical judgments about the objective good. This model therefore sees the *primary proximate cause* of ethically ignoble actions as the influence of untrained passions and animal appetites that resist rational desire in the self-controlled (*enkratic*) man and overwhelm rational desire in the weak-willed (*akratic*) man.[2] Yet against this, there is the well-known objection: some *prohairetic* acts of "choice" are wrong not because of recalcitrant D1 or D2 appetites that oppose D3 desire (*boulēsis*) but rather because the rational evaluation on which D3 deliberation or disposition is based is "corrupted."[3] To the extent that Aristotle recognizes this possibility, he seems to suggest that such bad judgment would *itself* result from prior akratic acts, making the agent responsible for his misjudgment of a bad end as noble or as that by which "he will get what is best."[4]

However, it can hardly be said that Aristotle's focus is on this possibility of corrupt *boulēsis* or D3 desires for ends based on erroneous judgments about their good; rather, his account implies that the main difference between virtuous and either incontinent or vicious actions is largely a function of whether or not the agent's bouletic wishes (rational evaluative desires) are able to shape and control lower sorts of motive-states so they always agree with, follow, or support practical reason. As Broadie argues, Aristotle's virtuous agent not only acts on but even forms correct practical judgments in part because his feelings and sentiments have been trained to motivate "intermediate" actions; the "discriminating emotional reaction" in moral virtue thus helps in "hold[ing] the ring against potentially unbalancing impulses, so that a patterned response has the chance to crystallize"[5] rather than being overwhelmed by chaotic appetites and passions. Aristotle's conception of virtue as a whole thus takes his notion of temperance as its model: the virtuous person is one whose practical reason has colonized her *pathē* and *epithumia* (lower appetites), reforming them in its own image. As Broadie insightfully explains, this colonization of sentiment and emotional dispositions is essential to "choice" in the sense of *prohairesis*:

> what characterizes a *prohairetic* state (as distinct from, say, a skill) is that it shows itself in the agent's acting and failing to act because of his feelings. . . . if we do assess someone as a bad performer on the basis of a performance which we know fell short because of fear, lust or anger, then we are assessing his quality as a *prohairetic* agent. Emotional excitements, like physical handicaps, tend to excuse the craftsman, in the sense that his skill is not impugned by performances spoilt by these conditions. But while the *prohairetic* agent may thus be excused by physical handicaps, he is not as a rule [excused] by emotions, pleasures and pains . . . it is, Aristotle thinks, the proper business of the *prohairetic* agent to be in whatever emotional condition is necessary for him to function well.[6]

In short, the prohairetic *orthos logos* is "the type of *logos* whose formation and execution is potentially supported or threatened" by the "basic feelings and impulses which everybody has" in the nonrational part of their soul.[7] This is related to the problematic notion of "virtue as a mean," because:

> a virtuous person is dispositionally neither too fearful nor too cautious, cares about wealth, pleasure, the opinion of others, etc., neither too much nor too little, to make the right responses to particular

situations. It is not that the right responses are themselves intermediate, although Aristotle, as we have seen, falls into this way of thinking at times; but rather virtue itself is a disposition [of choice] such that whoever has it is protected from excesses and deficiencies of feeling and impulse that *lead to* the faulty particular responses.[8]

In other words, Aristotle diagnoses the main species of vicious action as resulting from excessive or deficient amounts or kinds of the feelings, sentiments, passions, and impulses relative to those that ought naturally to be experienced in the agent's situation. The agent either acts from sudden passion or fails to feel the emotions she ought to feel. Aristotle's doctrine depends on the truth of this claim.

Virtually the same conclusion is reached by J. O. Urmson in his account of Aristotle's mean: "in the case of excellence of character both emotions and actions are in a mean, whatever that signifies; in the case of self-control [*enkrateia*], actions, but not emotions, are in a mean; in the case of bad character neither actions nor emotions are in a mean."[9] By reviewing several unacceptable interpretations, Urmson argues convincingly that Aristotle is not proposing an independent sense of "intermediate" actions or sentiments as a *definition* of the noble. Certainly, "moderate" instances of a particular emotion are often inappropriate to the situation. Rather, "Aristotle holds excellence of character to be a mean or intermediate disposition regarding emotions and actions, not that it is a disposition toward mean or intermediate emotions and actions."[10] In other words, the concept of a noble act is more fundamental than the concept of a "mean" state; emotional dispositions are then defined as intermediate, or between excess and deficiency, because they motivate noble action conceived as what the practically wise man will recognize as the right act in the situation.[11]

This analysis implies that vicious acts result from motives that are by *definition* not intermediate. But this does not make the doctrine of the mean vacuous: it tells us that the different species of wrong action each results from a given kind of emotion (or appetite) usurping the role of *prohairesis* and determining our actions without calm forethought. Since each vice involves inappropriate experiences of the relevant emotions and desires called for in the circumstances (e.g., anger when being insulted), the virtues produce noble acts because they bring the experience of these passions and emotions into line with *prohairesis* and its practical wisdom.[12] As Philippa Foot puts it, on this view, the virtues are "corrective, each one standing at a point at which there is some temptation to be resisted or deficiency of motivation to be made good."[13]

But Urmson rightly recognizes that Aristotle has great difficulty proving this claim, especially when it comes to justice, which does not seem to be the contrary of any particular emotion. For unjust actions can arise from all sorts of motives; they are not especially associated with excessive or deficient experiences of a particular kind of passion or sentiment. Greed (*pleonexia*) is one prominent cause, but virtually any other vice can also lead to acts that are unjust (even in the narrow sense connected with property rights).[14] Foot concurs: there is "no corresponding moderation of passion implied in the idea of justice," because "Almost any desire can lead a man to act unjustly, not even excluding the desire to help a friend or to save a life."[15] Similarly, Aristotle's analysis of spite and envy as (respectively) the deficiency and excess of some particular emotion that could have an intermediate (called *"nemesis"*) is unintelligible, and many different emotions can lead to an improper level or kind of concern with others' good or bad fortunes.[16]

1.2. From Vice as Ignorance and Akrasia to Radical Evil

These problems noted by Urmson are just the tip of a large iceberg. We need not detail the difficulties that arise in interpreting each virtue as the right orientation and strength of a particular emotion, but it is important to see that these problems arise because there is a fundamental error in Aristotle's thesis that it is primarily *rational control of the emotions* that leads to virtue—understood not as the difficult "self-control" of the *enkratic* man who can overrule resistant appetites and unruly passions but rather as their full Apollonian colonization, which makes the emotions and appetites into positive allies of practical reason.[17]

Although such rational control of the passions doubtless plays a large role in good character (Aristotle's account surely captures a key *part* of what virtue requires), equating vice with *inordinate emotion or unruly appetite* blinds us to the role of the existential striving will in certain forms of evil motivation and action and consequently also to its role in contrasting forms of virtuous motivation and action. Nor are these omissions corrected by including the state below *akrasia* in Aristotle's hierarchy, which Urmson calls "badness of character, the state of the man who wants to act badly and does so without resistance, thinking it to be a good way to act."[18] For it is here that Aristotle places those forms of corruption that Plato diagnosed as due to inveterate ignorance of the good, which by modern standards would exculpate an agent as either too immature or incompetent to understand right and wrong (unless this incapacity itself is intentional or negligent). As Kenny explains, Aristotle argues that "incorrect volition" (*boulēsis*) is possible because pleasures and pains can bring us to misjudge the noble: "Vicious choice results from the uncontrolled pursuit of the objects of the passions (honor, money, sensual pleasure or the like)."[19]

This means that, according to Aristotle, the apparent goods at which choice (*prohairesis*) aims when misled by corrupt bouletic (D3) desire are all misjudged as noble because *materially self-interested* passions (appetites and temper) make them appear to be intrinsically good or admirable. As Reeve says, unlike the akratic, the fully "vicious person thinks that what he is promoting in his actions is [his] eudaimonia."[20] By contrast, the existential account of human motivation predicts that there will be vices that do *not* result from ignorance about our true good due to poor education or from misjudgment caused by excesses or deficiencies in self-interested emotions and sense appetites, nor from mere *akrasia* in failing to control such inordinate passions. For the existential account holds that agents can devote themselves to malign or destructive ends that do not appear to offer any material contribution to their own welfare and that they even recognize as ignoble relative to some ethical standard. Such projectively willed forms of *radical evil* transcend the classical forms of vice in viciousness of motive.

Blindness to such radical evil is not limited to Aristotelian moral psychology, however, for it is also closely related to the common error in modern philosophy of assuming that the root cause of all evil must lie in selfishness or unlimited egoism. Like most modern moral-sense theorists, Bishop Butler affirms Plato's principles that "no man seeks misery as such for himself, and no one unprovoked does mischief to another for its own sake."[21] Kantians also fall into this error,[22] and it is present in contemporary virtue ethics too. For example, in trying to defend Aristotle's idea that good dispositions are virtues precisely because they correct temptations involving excesses or deficiencies of emotion, Foot suggests that our strong natural tendency toward egoism explains the kind of virtues whose status Urmson questioned:

> With virtues such as justice and charity it is a little different, because they correspond not to any particular desire or tendency that has to be kept in check but rather to a deficiency of motivation; and it is this that they must make good. If people were as much attached to the good of others as they are to their own good, there would no more be a general virtue of benevolence than there is a general virtue of self-love. And if people cared about the rights of others as they care about their own rights, no virtue of justice would be needed.[23]

In other words, Foot maintains Aristotle's general idea that virtues correct problems natural to the human psyche by expanding his one-level picture of this process to two levels. *Particular* virtues modify particular types of desire and emotion, such as fear of mortal threats, lazy aversions to hard work, furious reactions to minor slights, and appetites for rich foods—each of which is self-interested by my Feinbergian definition (chap. 5, sec. 2.2) but still quite distinct, as Butler and Kant saw, from more abstract desires for our long-term material advantage and overall happiness. *General* virtues, on Foot's second level, correct the tendencies toward injustice and failure to aid that arise from these more general egoistic D2 and D3 desires.

The problem with this defense, however, is that there remain other forms of evil that are not vices of self-indulgent appetites (concupiscence), nor of other hostile passions (irascibility), *nor even* of abstract egoism (putting one's own long-term material advantage before "the noble" where this requires significant and possibly irretrievable sacrifice).[24] As Richard Taylor urges in his classic work on ethics, in addition to altruistic motives, "There is another side to this disregard for themselves of which men are capable, and that is the selfless pursuit of and natural satisfaction in injury to others."[25] Hence if we conceive of justice and benevolence as the virtues that specifically counter the corrupting influence of prudential motivation (in Kant's sense as the general desire to maximize material advantages over a complete life), we are still left with forms of malign will that transcend correction by justice and benevolence so conceived, since their root is not egoism, or inordinate love of what Kant called "the dear self."

In such cases of malign will, we encounter *a positive volitional evil* that is not usefully understood on the classical models of a "privation," which refers to a decision to pursue a *lesser but apparently real* good over a higher value out of ignorance or weakness, giving in to sensual appetites or general egoistic desires. By contrast, in cases of resolute malice, no sagacious enlightenment about his own eudaimonia as a cure for axiological ignorance, nor any therapy designed to enhance his self-control or mastery of his appetites, nor even training by example to encourage just and benevolent sentiments will solve the agent's ethical problem. Following Frankl, only logotherapeutic confrontation, encouraging or challenging such a person to find less destructive trajectories for self-expression, to see new goals worth caring about, and to make an unforced effort to change himself (or perhaps religious strategies encouraging repentance), stands any chance of success.

2. Toward an Existential Theory of Radical Evil: Six Forms of Volitional Hatred

My hypothesis is that certain recognizable forms of evil or perverse ends that have long posed problems for broadly eudaimonistic *and* egoistic theories of motivation (e.g., Aristotle and Hobbes) become easier to explain if we accept the possibility of projective motivation. Evil is "radical" in my sense if its negative or harmful goals are agent-transcending ends posited by the agent for their own sake. This is not Kant's sense of "radical evil," nor does "radicality" in my sense imply "horrendous" evil or a high degree of wrongness or *mens res*.²⁶ For horrific crimes of the greatest gravity meriting the most serious punishments one thinks morally permissible have often been done out of simple avarice, lust, or bravado. As Susan Neiman says, "Thoughtlessness may be more dangerous than malice."²⁷ She derives this point from Hannah Arendt's famous thesis that Adolf Eichmann's motives for his evil actions were "banal" careerist interests.²⁸ Although the controversy about Nazi evils arising from Arendt's book was highly influential in twentieth-century thought, only two points about it are crucial for my analysis.

Arendt's insight is that "thoughtlessness," incapacity for free judgment, and narrow bureaucratic mind-sets can combine with such common vices as greed and intemperance to motivate actions resulting in colossal horrors such as the systematic transportation of Jews to killing centers. This is linked with her argument that "the essence of totalitarian government"—like warlord cultures and fundamentalist militias—is to "dehumanize" their operatives so that they hardly realize what they are doing or to leverage quite ordinary human motives to bring about terror and atrocity.²⁹ What is "barbaric" in such phenomena is not the small-minded egoism of the functionaries but rather their systematic manipulation and brainwashing. Thus, as Richard Bernstein argues, when banal motives become the engines of enormous wrongs, this may even *require* direction by a more radical kind of evil.³⁰

Thus Bernstein insists that in *Origins of Totalitarianism* and *The Human Condition*, Arendt rejects Kant's view that evil consists in violating others' dignity to serve self-interest.³¹ Not all architects of genocide are like Eichmann; a society in which average people can willingly participate in crimes against humanity is organized that way by leaders with a will to dominate others so completely that their moral sense, freedom, and "singularity" as a person with individual life goals are stripped away. Making humanity "superfluous" by such "total domination" is the core of radical evil on Bernstein's reading of Arendt.³²

However, this vital insight needs to be situated in a broader account of radical evil to be fully appreciated. For there are other kinds of evil motivation between Arendtian domination and simple egoism, and they are not always manifested in great crimes.³³ Some offenses aiming at relatively minor harms that would merit only a small fine are done because the agent made it his business to upset, shock, or disappoint others just "for the pleasure of it." This is the converse of Arendt's thesis that monstrous acts can have banal motives; it is also true that small cruelties, gratuitous slights, and other acts of minor consequence sometimes reveal willed malice of terrifying potential beyond what Arendt found in Eichmann. Consider an act that is legally permissible yet done out of perverse will: a miserable old millionaire widow gives all her fortune to a worthy charity not for love of its good cause but only to relish during her dying days the thought of her surviving children's disappointment and her hope that they will fight with each other over who is to blame and ultimately become bitter like her. Suppose that she hates her children simply because they are living more exemplary lives than she has, and their greater need for money is partly a result of choosing nonprofit careers promoting public goods. In such cases, we see the intention as shocking because of its radically evil nature, even if the overall moral gravity of the act remains less than violent crimes done simply for monetary gain.[34]

Nevertheless, we typically regard the phenomena of radically evil motivations that require philosophical explanation as always intrinsically *worse in form* than other types of egoistic motivation, even though the particular actions chosen for radically evil reasons can be less bad than those chosen for selfish reasons. As Richard Taylor argues, it "is not the *consequences*" of evil actions that especially appall us, "but what is in the hearts of the agents."[35] The existential account of the striving will helps explain why we intuitively distinguish radically evil motives from "merely" selfish interests and why we regard the former as intrinsically more mean-spirited, nastier, or formally corrupt, whatever the specific content of the intended act. But showing that the existential model can do this important explanatory work does not depend on developing a comprehensive account of how we access the overall moral value of actions, which is not my task here. Even a schematic review of the relevant phenomena is so large a task that I can only survey a few representative examples and suggest how the idea of projective motivation sheds some light on their mysteries.

Following Bishop Butler, Joel Feinberg conceives "malevolent" motivation as a state in which the agent's purpose is to cause material harm to another person just for its own sake rather than as a means to any self-related first-order good such as entertainment or monetary gain. In that sense, he considers it "disinterested" rather than self-interested.[36] A man planning to kill his wife so that he can marry another woman without losing any of his wife's fortune would obviously count as egoistic, not as malevolent, on Feinberg's analysis. To count as malevolent, he would have to intend to kill her just because he *hates* her and wants her to suffer and to lose all her opportunity for future happiness. The "merely" egoistic husband would be quite satisfied if he could magically teleport his wife away to another planet in the universe, where she could live in bliss while a lifeless duplicate of her body remains in the house, apparently killed in a household accident while he was away on a business trip. But this magical solution obviously could not satisfy the malevolent husband, who wants *her* (the very person) dead or deprived of joy, not merely out of the way or out of her role in his life.

"Hatred" in this sense is obviously not *aversion*, by which I mean an appetite in the D1 or D2 sense to avoid something painful or disliked. "Aversion" in this broad sense is just the negative form of attraction and it still has the formal structure of *erosiac* motivation: if I "hate" boiled asparagus in the aversive sense of "hatred," then I have a D2 appetite to avoid smelling (much less eating) it; we could explain this by saying that its presence is felt as a harm to me, and while smelling or (perish the thought) even tasting it, I am lacking the equilibrium I enjoyed without it. Its presence literally makes me sick, and my body wants to distance itself from the asparagus in order to restore its normal homeostasis. "Hatred" in this classical sense as aversion thus fits the classical Greek schema of *orektic desire*, and contrasts starkly with the *volitional hatred* of a malevolent agent who wants to remain near her victim, who may even protect her victim's continued existence so that this victim can be further harmed or deprived again and again. A paradigm case of this kind of hatred is the character Chillingworth in Hawthorne's haunting novel, *The Scarlet Letter*, who lives for nothing but the humiliation and destruction of Dimmesdale, the guilt-ridden minister who has fathered a child with Chillingworth's former wife, Hester Prynne. When Dimmesdale dies, so does Chillingworth, for volitional hatred is (in most cases) parasitic on the existence of the hated person, and the parasite cannot exist without its host.

Certainly, we might ask whether malevolent hatred in this sense is intelligible. It is ruled out not only by eudaimonist accounts but also by some contemporary internalist theories of motivation.[37] Others admit that "Harm can be an end in itself," but imagine this merely as a brute attraction (or D2 desire).[38] Still others insist that such pure malice always turns out to be something else. The abstract idea of pursuing another person's harm or suffering for its own sake seems hard to imagine without more explanation; both in literary examples and even more in real life, something besides pure malice often seems to be going on. However, an account of such cases in terms of projective motivation does *not* require that harming others should be projected as a final end *arbitrarily* or for no reason at all; as we saw in the discussion of Frankl, agents must always have reasons for projecting a goal, but they do not respond to these reasons or values by way of *desire* in the erosiac sense. In order to sort out several potential confusions raised by these complexities, I will divide putative cases of radical evil into six groups with my own chosen labels[39] as follows:

1. *Sadistic Cruelty:* pursuing the harm of other living beings *for sport or entertainment* or for the intrinsic pleasure of seeing them suffer and

try vainly to escape. If this motive is not satisfied unless the agent himself causes the desired harm, then it may also include the desire to discharge his own pent-up aggressions upon an arbitrarily chosen person.

2. *Fanatical Cruelty:* projecting the harm or even destruction of innocent person(s) as a means to some ideologically valued aesthetic, political, or religious cause. The agent can either be totally in the grip of the violence-legitimizing ideology and project personal goals on its basis, or will to be in the grip of such a dogma as a meaning-conferring identity.

3. *Malicious Anger:* the vengeful pursuit of others' material harm (loss, misery, suffering) as an end-in-itself, based on the idea that this expresses or is required by prior reasons for anger at them. This hostility toward them as offenders of some kind is cultivated for its perceived retributive appropriateness. This includes pursuing the harm of other living animals regarded as a final end or *as a means* to harming persons who care about them.

4. *Spite:* an extreme form of malice, in which the agent projects the psychological destruction of her hated other at all costs, the *communication or expression* to the other of her absolute hatred of him, and the other's recognition of this hatred and its success as a reason for his despair.

5. *Malevolence:* projecting the harm or destruction of others as a means to or way of expressing one's superior power to control them, one's absolute domination of them, or even one's possession of them as slaves or mere things. In this case, the will to power makes pure ascendance over others or appropriation of them its final end, and the harm or destruction of others is primarily intended as a way of denying their alterity or enslaving them to one's will.

6. *Demonic Autonomy:* projecting the harm or destruction of others or even oneself just because it is morally wrong or unjust. In this case, the final end is a kind of absolute rebellion against moral requirements or limitations, or perhaps against the God who is thought to embody moral ideals and requirements. As a pure will to rebellion, it is also a will to reject any limits or external demands on the self. It is thus closely related to malevolence, differing only in its qualification of the goal as *moral evilness* of character.

These different types of malign motivation are often confused or conflated with one another, but I will show that there are important distinctions between them that clarify their relation to the existential conception of striving will.

2.1. Sadistic Cruelty

Under this heading, I am not concerned with what is sometimes called sexual sadism (or "S and M"), which seems to supervene in complex ways on desires for sexual satisfaction and other D2 inclinations, in which harm is allegedly desired only as psychodrama rather than in earnest. Rather, I am concerned here only with the pure enjoyment of cruelty outside a sexual context. It is obvious that cruel acts aimed at causing both physical and psychological suffering can be motivated by a nonsexual kind of D2 desire, namely, a perverse preference for witnessing suffering and struggle as a source of amusement, in which some people find a kind of first-order pleasure.

Although it is not especially complimentary, it is a simple fact of human psychology that many people are amused, entertained, or given states of mind they find inherently pleasant (e.g., "thrill" or "shock") to differing degrees by observing violence, explosions, mortal struggles, and sometimes suffering and humiliation quite irrespective of desert.[40] Most people may find these tastes odd or appalling, but in seeking these pleasures, those who crave them are acting in a self-interested, even hedonistic fashion. As a result, several cases that Taylor discusses fail to prove the existence of nonegoistic malice; for example, the fact that people take gruesome satisfaction from watching a hanging may be due to their indulging revenge fantasies or their taste for sheer spectacle. Likewise, the horrible pleasure that some school-age children take in teasing, reviling, and ostracizing a particular child who has problems or is in any way different may be moved by nothing more than a bad habit starting from a desire for some distraction or entertaining spectacle to relieve boredom.[41]

Among his horrifying catalogue of evils, Dostoyevsky describes a "voluptuous pleasure from torturing children."[42] He seems to have in mind a visceral enjoyment of distress and despair: "What excites them is the utter helplessness of the little creatures, the angelic trustfulness of the child who has no where to turn for help."[43] Similarly, we recognize the brutal pleasures of Romans watching early Christians be consumed by lions or gladiators condemned to fight to the death as no more than extreme forms of the same corrupted D2 desires that motivate people to watch boxing matches today.[44] Though these practices go far beyond any kind of violence we find naturally among nonhuman animals (as Dostoyevsky points out), and though they deserve severe condemnation, they are not radically evil in my sense.

Much the same must be said for the strange fascination that somewhat fewer people have for death itself as a spectacle or even, in rare cases, for the *necrophilious* pleasure of watching the destruction, dismemberment, or decay of living tissues. Taylor describes imaginary (but sadly, quite plausible) cases of boys pinning insects to trees or lighting a barnyard cat on fire.[45] Acts of such cruelty should evoke revulsion and horror and deserve the strongest punishments, but the most troubling thing about them is precisely that the agents do them *for fun*, that they find the spectacle of something or someone burning to death in unimaginable agony, for example, to be entertaining—if not sensuously pleasurable, then at least riveting, thrilling, boredom-relieving. How, we ask, could they possibly have a D2 preference or taste for anything like this—yet they do, just like someone who finds gustatory pleasure in drinking urine or sensual pleasure in being pierced by needles. In fact, given the frequency of disgusting burning scenes in popular Hollywood movies, it would seem that an enjoyment of death and suffering have become common in our culture.

The extreme end of this sort of perversion is clinical necrophilia, not just in its sexual form but in its broader sense as delight in witnessing and causing death and attraction to the lifelessness and decomposition of corpses. In his landmark study of this syndrome and its variants, Erich Fromm correlated the cold, dark, and unfeeling antisocial mechanicalness of the "necrophilious character" with the radical evils of Hitler and Stalin[46]—and it may well be that such a set of perverse D2 appetites is often a *result* of a life devoted to radical evil in some of the forms I discuss below. But in its prepurposive motivational manifestation as a basic "taste" for corpses, dismemberment, and decay, necrophilia is just an extremely bizarre type of D2 desire, though it occupies the maximally revolting end on the scale of abnormal visceral reactions.[47] Jeffrey Dahmer, despite committing terrible crimes that made him "monstrous" to most people, was probably not radically evil in my sense but only a person of highly antisocial temperament moved by the most disgusting and harmful kind of compulsive desire. Indeed, such was the strength of his compulsive disorder that it is questionable whether he should even have counted as morally sane or as meeting the conditions required for full legal responsibility for his actions. By contrast, the radically evil agent acts autonomously (and hence ordinarily will be responsible if he also knows right from wrong); for by projective engagement, he helps generate the motives on which he acts.

Hence sadistic cruelty would not require projective motivation unless the agent anticipated no inherent sport, entertainment, or fun in it and was not driven to it by any prior craving for which release of tension could only be found in cruel acts. This covers most cases, but perhaps not those in which the agent decides to try cruelty just out of a kind of curiosity—not out of any prior desire to relieve boredom but merely to exercise his will in some dramatic way that impresses by its power. So he "puts on" the maniacal emotions that he imagines must be felt by people enjoying cruelty; he then plans and tries to execute a cruel act on some randomly chosen victim. Then, of course, having projected the goal of being cruel, he will derive second-order satisfaction from it if he succeeds, but this is not what motivated him. To complete the picture, we have to imagine the curiosity that grounds his projection as simply a belief that this activity will be valuable in some abstract sense not initially related to his eudaimonia: for example, that it will provide important knowledge, or introduce meaning into a meaningless life,[48] or prove to him that he has sufficient strength of will to overcome his own revulsion to suffering or repress a tendency to empathy that he judges as weakness.

In other words, the curiosity that could ground projective sadism is not any D2 desire to know a secret, or to find out more information about an anticipated benefit or harm (e.g., being curious about one's test score), or to "get dirt" on someone that it will be fun and useful to have. Instead, it is similar to the researcher's sense that the goal of her research program is inherently important in some agent-transcending way—because of its value to society or its intrinsic status among questions of science, and so on. It is precisely this kind of pure reason for projecting an end that would, if it became a ground for cruelty, make the agent's motive state radically evil—a pure will to cruelty for its own sake, as Taylor wanted to suggest. If this is imaginable or cogent, then we have already identified one type of radical evil in the existential sense. Let us call it "volitional sadism" to distinguish this motive from the garden-variety sadistic appetites described in this section.

2.2. Fanatical Cruelty and Motive Switches

In approaching this category, we should reiterate that many horrendously evil acts are probably attributable to motives that are explainable in terms of ignorance or weakness, as held in the Aristotelian tradition. In many cases, as John Kekes argues, actions that predictably cause avoidable harm to innocent persons are "nonautonomous" because the agents "fail to understand or evaluate the significance of the alternatives they freely choose. They do evil, but they do not see what they do as evil. . . . They are, therefore, not moral monsters but moral idiots."[49] Similarly, Kekes suggests that evil-producing vices may often result from dogmatic belief-systems that the agents could not avoid and that require ruthlessness, insensitivity, or unbending expediency from them: "The choice for them was between living according to a [distorted] conception of the good life to which they had no acceptable alternative, and failing by the standards of that same conception."[50]

I agree that many kinds of external influences can and regularly do provoke people into hostility toward others that may motivate acts of extreme cruelty or callousness (as we see in Iraq today). But although indoctrination, brainwashing, or overbearing influence of authority figures may produce cruel actions in ways that render the agents less than fully responsible, this does *not* mean that the movement from belief to motivation cannot be *projective* in structure, as I explain below.

In his penetrating study of ways in which ordinary people may come to commit horrific atrocities, Fred Katz cites three important causes: (1) a culture of cruelty, in which creativity in being cruel is valued as an art form; (2) the normalization of cruelty through bureaucratic systems in which functionaries simply "do their job"; and (3) an ideological package or grand mythology justifying evil in the name of higher callings, collective goods, or religious concepts such as fate/destiny or (I add) even the divine will.[51] The first cause refers to the spread of a deviant pleasure in toying with people and being "refinedly and artistically cruel," as Dostoyevsky put it.[52] It is not projective unless the agent acts this way to distract herself from moral concerns, to steel her own psyche against pity, or to create what she regards as pure aesthetic excellence (see below).

To the second cause in Katz's list we might add many other ways in which a culture can desensitize persons to the wrongness of arbitrary violence, thus making it possible to see cruel acts as mere sport (as for the ten-year-old boy with a machine gun who has grown up in the care of an African warlord like Liberia's Charles Taylor and thinks nothing of hacking off another child's hands).[53] Such normalization of violence turns ordinary desires—such as the desire for acceptance by others, success in career, or status and honor—into potential temptations to accept malicious practices. As Katz describes, Rudolph Hess tells in his diary that he lacked the courage to protest the brutality of his first SS boss, Theodore Eicke.[54] His own careerism and discomfort at disobeying authority figures led him *akratically* to accept a regime of cruelty, until his protesting conscience was virtually numbed to its horror.

In these cases so far, we are not forced to cite projective motivation in the explanation. But things are different when we consider Katz's third cause, that is, fanatical adherence to an ethically corrupt ideology that preaches hatred and violence toward innocents in the name of higher values. An agent such as Heinrich Himmler, as Katz describes him, resolves to devote himself wholeheartedly to "that grand Nazi cause, Hitler's vision of a purified and awesomely great Germany, to whose realization these horrendous deeds [of mass murder] made an essential contribution."[55] Similarly, Goldberg reports that "Hermann Göring . . . reluctantly admitted that some of what went on was extreme, but he grandiosely justified the abuses as necessary to carry out his government's long-term policies for solving serious social and political problems."[56]

I view this kind of fanaticism as a movement of projective motivation, because the goals to which the agent devotes himself clearly transcend his own *eudaimonia*; hence he may even see his work as a kind of moral self-sacrifice, a willingness to dirty his hands for a higher cause when others are too squeamish to get the job done. In such cases, we do not find a will to injustice or cruelty *as such* but, rather, a will to do *whatever it takes* to bring about some end conceived as noble through distorted aesthetic, ethical, or religious values. This is projective identification with a corrupt ideology, because the agent is not moved by prepurposive attraction to his ends as pleasurable, advantageous, or intrinsically part of his own happiness. We could also imagine a person who sees the "purification" of his culture as essential to his own happiness, but not every ideologue is this narcissistic. Rather, our agent takes the self-transcending values that the ideology places on her destructive ends as impartial reasons for projecting the ends.

For example, Kekes's "sixteenth-century witch hunter" is devout in his faith; he is supported by authorities, and "he is sincere, dedicated, and as just as he can be in following ecclesiastic law."[57] He suffers none of Hess's doubts, but passionately pursues justice and the purification of his community as he conceives them. Nor need he be in bad faith, using his ideology as a mere rationalization for his sadistic enjoyment of cruelty or for getting rid of opponents—like the Jesuit inquisitor Bernardo Gui in the famous movie, *The Name of the Rose*.[58] Instead, Kekes's witch-hunter is projecting an agent-transcending goal in the same way as someone devoting himself to a "practice" in MacIntyre's sense; he differs in being fanatical because his underlying values are so corrupted and irrational yet he will not question them at all, even when he has reason to. Thus his will blocks the critical rationality that authentic devotion to practices require. In other cases, such as Himmler's, the agent may believe that both his goals and the necessary means to them contravene traditional morality (e.g., prohibitions on killing innocents) yet find other putative values (e.g., racial purity) important enough to justify overriding traditional mores. So he projects ends that require cruel and immoral actions as a means. We call such motivation evil because the values grounding the agent's projective commitment are so corrupt that he must recognize their injustice according to any traditional standard. Nevertheless, he wills to reject these standards.

In both these cases, then, we find a radically evil will in the existential sense: the agent intentionally defines his identity and finds meaning for his life in commitment to corrupt causes. Because he so radically misjudges the value of his mission, our fanatical agent feels called out of mere egoism to a "nobler" set of goals, even though they involve systematic violence toward innocents. This is the problem with contemporary jihadists, who believe that they are permitted to kill anyone of a different faith for their distorted conception of religious purity. In such cases, appeals to the fanatic's own best interests will avail little. Where the agent still experiences internal conflict because of moral doubts, as in Hess's case, he may also strive volitionally to solidify his commitment to the higher cause by repressing or crushing out these moral qualms and emotional reactions of horror and pity.[59] Eleonore Stump has usefully analyzed this as the phenomenon of someone trying to harden his heart against mercy or altruistic sentiment because of his volitional identification with ends inconsistent with these emotions or related moral motives.[60] Arguably in this kind of case, the radicality of evil is greater, because the agent perpetrates crimes in the name of causes that he knows to be morally wrong yet he sets his will against his conscience.

This kind of intentional "hardening of one's heart," even against one's better judgment, may be one species of a broader volitional phenomenon in which people decide to project some end E (or actively work up their motivation to pursue E) *in part* because they have already been acting on a weak desire for E or acting *as if* they had a desire for E. In such cases, people finally decide to throw themselves without reserve into some project or activity, forming for the first time an existential commitment to it, because they feel they are already "involved," or already "in too deep" to do otherwise, or because this project will give more coherent meaning to their previous actions. These are backward-looking grounds for projecting evil ends.

We have already seen something like this in Sherman's account of taking up one's friend's cares and concerns out of respect for the friend (see chap. 8, sec. 4). In such cases, the first reason or ground for positing E as an end lies in *the past*, in the agent's filial relationship (although she may discover new reasons once she pursues E). Such backward-looking considerations are not easily understandable as objects of any D1–D3 desire, for desire in its erosiac forms always looks forward to some *future* consummation or to continuing the possession and enjoyment of some good (object or activity). Backward-looking considerations are not intrinsically related to the agent's expectation of any future gain or satisfaction; hence they count as agent-transcending values or reasons for moving oneself in the relevant way (see chap. 13, sec. 2).

Backward-looking considerations are also important in understanding how a person who does not start with strong sadistic desires or emotions of rage or fury toward innocent victims can be "drawn in" to a system of cruelty and at some point come to feel that she might as well embrace it wholeheartedly, given her past trajectory. This helps explain Katz's observation that "The route to evil often takes the form of a sequence of seemingly small, innocuous incremental steps, in each of which one tries to solve a problem in one's immediate situation."[61] I am suggesting that such a sequence of acts motivated by egoistic desires can terminate in a fundamental *switch of purpose* in which the agent projects as a final end something that she formerly pursued only as means to self-interested goals.

This kind of projective acceptance of one's fate might even have played some role in the subjects tested in the famous Milgram experiment, whose results Katz attributes to the authority of the actors posing as scientists and to the power of special circumstances to deemphasize the importance of moral values that are more salient for persons in average circumstances.[62] To this I add that the incremental approach in Milgram's experiment—getting subjects slowly to increase the force of what they believed to be electric shocks administered to persons on the other side of the screens—succeeded in getting many subjects to feel that they were *already invested* in this experiment, or beyond the point of no return, by the time that the shocks seemed to be inflicting serious pain (from the feigned screams of their "victims"). This is a powerful strategy because it forces the agent into a volitional dilemma. In this dilemma, even willing oneself to trust the charismatic leaders and lay aside reservations may be the "weaker" response, because the only other alternative—rejecting their commands and turning back when one already seems to be deeply involved—requires a heroic strength of will that few can muster.

Sometimes, then, in projective initiative on the basis of prior involvement or even a sense of inescapability, the agent seems to alter his motive from self-interested appetite to volitional commitment. In such cases, part of the agent's reason or ground for projecting his goal is his own past action on the basis of desires for prosperity and social status. When this happens, the desiderative states (D1–D3) precede and *occasion* the projected motives, but without the former *causing* or *motivating* the latter. Rather, the agent has acquired a personal ethos (in part from established patterns of action, in part from the kinds of significance that different persons and objects have acquired for him) which he finally decides to *take as a reason* for investing himself fully in the goals that make the most sense for this way of life.

For example, imagine someone who desires to enrich himself and believes the best means to this end is to start a criminal organization. He dreams of living a life of peaceful luxury and he takes this as a reason to pursue wealth by establishing an effective and ruthless crime ring. But as time goes on, other motivations start to appear. Eventually, he *projects* the success of his crime ring and his pursuit of criminal activities as a way of giving meaning to his life—even though he did not originally desire these activities for their own sake. The work of building his gang did not itself make him happy, and its maintenance remains laborious for him, but he comes to be *dedicated* to it in a way he never initially envisioned. Because this projection of criminal ends is motivationally distinct from the desires for wealth that overshadowed it at the outset, these motives can *coexist* in uneasy symbiosis, or one can remain while the other withers.

Imagine that our gangster has attained a vast wealth, and his desire for riches is sated; or we could imagine that his original dream of living in a Caribbean paradise fades and comes to appear adolescent and uninteresting to him in his old age. Either way, after attaining the status of "godfather," our criminal kingpin loses his initial desire for simple luxury. Yet, notably, he remains more committed than ever to developing the criminal ring's influence. He is no longer moved by a desire for contentment, ease, and sensual pleasures, since now what he "really wants" is to be involved in the day-to-day manipulation of people, the exercise of power, the challenge of planning the next hit, and so on. The thought of retirement no longer arises; he is bent on pursuing his criminal practice. We might say that activities that were formerly a *mere means* to his desired end have taken on a life of their own for him: they have become ends-in-themselves.

This is a common experience that occurs in many different variations, yet it is often not very usefully explained just by hypothesizing a new terminal desire for what was formerly just the agent's method of attaining an end. Rather, the agent has come to value the evils internal to his or her corrupt practice by projecting these activities and their immediate goals as his or her final ends; projective motivation has *detached* itself from the desires out of which it developed. The possibility of such shifts in motive from desiderative attraction to projective striving is also required, as we saw, to make sense of the progression of "habituation" into virtuous motivation (chap. 8, sec. 5.5).

I believe that this sort of dynamic is found in many different contexts in human life because the fundamentally temporal structure of the will maintains motivation toward the future but is ever pregnant with the past and thus disposed and conditioned by its own prior decisions. Ends that are adopted initially as means to satisfy preexisting desires have the tendency to become *projected* for their own sake, pursued because of the inherent meaning the agent finds in this pursuit. Because this enacted motivation is distinct from desires that prepare the way for it, it can take on a life of its own. This helps explain the difficulty that people often have in explaining why they are so committed to the practices in which they are engaged and why they may simply respond, "because this is what I *do*."

Such a motive switch may also help explain the related (but inverse) sense that one has "lost the point of it all" somewhere along the way.

Sometimes this is a misdiagnosis: when people discover that they are pursuing ends they no longer *desire*, they often assume they are caught in a mindless routine, when in fact the explanation may be that they have now *projected* these ends, though the reasons are ones that they do not want to face or accept.[63] Our godfather figure might fall into this category. But sometimes it is a correct diagnosis: a person finds that her persistence in some set of activities is controlled by desires quite distinct from her original projective commitment to an end that these activities are supposed to serve. For example, a police detective who joined the force out of love for his community finds that he now lives only for the thrill of the chase, the glory of big catches, or the vindictive pleasures of interrogation. This policeman has lost his original projected commitment and is now moved only by D2 desires of a dubious sort. In this case, projective commitment to (something like) a practice has decayed into simple appetite, and the agent has abandoned himself to his desires. Still, we would have to rate the policeman's condition as a lesser evil relative to the godfather's passion, which shifted from merely shallow and selfish desires to an active and resolute self-investment in violent disruption and manipulation of human lives.

Of course, such motivational shifts can also occur in more fortunate ways. Harry may adopt the end of becoming Sally's friend on the dubious grounds that he wants to sleep with her, and appearing friendly will increase his chances; but in the process, his initial desire may disappear (or be altered), while his motivation to spend time with her, help her out, talk over ideas and plans, and so on remains, without any sense that it promotes his well-being. Rather, Harry now projects Sally's happiness for its own sake. Perhaps the latter projection can even grow out of the former desire without requiring a clear formulation of some new justifying ground other than the fact that he took on the role of being friendly to her in the past. This suggests that *familiarity* itself may serve as a consideration for the striving will: as in the judicial argument of *stare decisis*, that something was sought in the past may itself become *a* reason (if not the sole or controlling reason) for projecting it into the future.

It should now be obvious why such motive shifts are relevant for understanding fanatical loyalty and unwillingness to "see" or believe evidence of atrocities (even when, as for Hitler's followers, such evidence surrounds one). Those who do not simply follow but, rather, earnestly commit themselves to a monstrously evil regime have usually willed this state of being because the *difficulties* of willing justice and truth are in the circumstances so much greater. The former alternative is not less "painful" or more satisfying in any sense that appeals to *orektic* desire but it is less demanding on the striving will.[64] Yet it is still a (weaker) projective commitment of the self, and so it can move the agent to sacrifice for "the cause." Consider, for example, the Fedayeen militants still loyal to Saddam Hussein in 2004 and killing innocents in his name long after they must (at some level) have known how terrible a tyrant he was. Even after his regime's fall, they were too far gone to stop. The striving will does not easily give up even when beaten or revealed as devoted to evil goals. Likewise, despairing of his "charmed life" when all the witches' prophecies betray him, Macbeth still summons the will to fight to the end, and forces himself to face Macduff:

> Though Birnam Wood be come to Dunsinane,
> And thou oppos'd, being of no woman born,
> Yet I will try to the last.[65]

If we sense a vestige of spiritual nobility in this moment, despite Macbeth's atrocities, it is because he has the will to embrace completely the self he became incrementally by succumbing to his wife's goadings and his own fears. He thus shares a volitional quality found in true heroes. Yet he lacks real courage, because it would have taken still greater strength of will to repent—as we see in the resolve that Raskolnikov musters by the end of *Crime and Punishment*.

2.3. Malicious Anger

So far, we have identified two major sources of evil devotions: a sense that one is already compromised beyond the point of return, and a willingness to subordinate traditional moral norms to a distorted conception of greatness or purity. In my view, however, the most common origin of projective malice is resentment of perceived wrongs. In other words, this kind of evil is a perversion of the will to justice.

However, "anger" is a multifaceted phenomenon. Sometimes anger at an individual or group depends on fanatically projected loyalty to a corrupt ideology—as when a church mob savagely slaughters a former nun, her lover, and a baby thought to be theirs, in Kleist's "Earthquake in Chile."[66] We might think of anger in its simplest form as involving both a judgment that some wrong (or culpable harm) has been done and a desire to express this judgment to the perpetrator. So understood, the latter could be a D3 desire to engage in expressive or communicative acts, and the agent may feel somewhat better after getting it "off her chest." But often such judgments about responsibility for wrongs done and the moral emotions of resentment or indignation they evoke may become grounds for projecting the goal of retributive punishment (so that wrongs do not benefit their perpetrator) and/or getting the wrongdoer to repair in some way (or to the extent possible) the harm done. Such motives are not necessarily vengeful in any pejorative sense, but important distinctions must be drawn here.

It is often assumed that retributive motives are egoistic or that they somehow aim at satisfying or calming the agent by restoring the psychic equilibrium she lost when harmed; but when the end really is just deserts, this cannot be correct. Since they are based on backward-looking considerations and seek to bring about a just state conceived (abstractly) as one in which the wrongdoer gets what he *deserves*—which can mean either that a wrongdoer does not benefit from wrongs or that the wrongness of his acts is forcefully communicated to him and he is invited to repent[67]—pure retributive motives seek an agent-transcending end for its own sake. This end could be described as an aspect of justice, that is, the state of affairs in which wrongs do not pay, or it could be described as the communication and upholding of moral requirements such as fair treatment for all. In its pure form, then, this motive does not seek anything *for* its agent other than the satisfaction of seeing justice done—and it is therefore on a par with the motive of duty, which (as I argue in chapter 11), can only be projectively willed, not desired in the D3 sense.

The pure will to fair retribution, then, is in principle neither malicious nor vindictive; it is, rather, simply a specification of the will to justice. Given human nature, however, when the will to justice motivates retributive purposes toward others, it is always in *danger* of corruption, always liable to *become* malicious. It does so through another subtle kind of motive switch: the agent stops seeking the (perceived) offender's harm *only as* just punishment or justice-restoring retribution according to impartial standards and starts seeking it merely as *harm suffered by this particular person (or group)* who has offended me or damaged something I care about. The will to the abstract end of redressing wrongs then becomes the essentially particularistic *will to vengeance* against this person (or group) just because I have an excuse and opportunity for using my willpower this way.[68]

A person willing vengeance thus almost hopes to be wronged so she can find justification for striving against a wrongdoer; she will delight in making her hated target suffer some similar harm—not simply because it is just but only because it is *this despised person's* suffering. Even worse, in what I call spiteful vengefulness, she may especially desire that the person on whom she is taking revenge *know* that she is enjoying his suffering and suffer further abasement in this knowledge.[69] Of course, this may be rationalized as simply what the victim deserves, given his past wrongs, and so on, but the agent's true purpose is no longer simply justice, even as it appears to her distorted judgment (we could say that she aims at a conception of justice twisted beyond recognition by her absolute will to vengeance, but a misconceived notion results from her will).

The literary paradigm for this kind of evil is Madame Defarge in Dickens's *The Tale of Two Cities.* "Citizeness" Defarge is not primarily actuated by the extreme Jacobin ideology of her group but rather by a will to infinite vengeance against the Evrémonde family. Although she came from a coastal peasant family and despises all "aristocrats," that is because the Evrémondes belong to this class. Her inexhaustible hatred, it is finally revealed, began when two Evrémonde brothers killed several members of her immediate family.[70] Throughout the long years, she cultivated and nourished that hatred into a will to "pursu[e] this family to annihilation," down to the last woman and child.[71] As Dickens says, she does not care that the husband, wife, and child she is scheming to execute are innocent of "the sins of their forefathers"; she aims to extirpate every last vestige of that family's being from the earth.

Were she to succeed, one suspects that even then she would rationalize the guilt of some new victim (e.g., anyone who had ever helped an Evrémonde) on which to vent her limitless wrath against the world. The disproportion of her malice to the original crime, as heinous as it was, reveals the contribution of her own will. Dickens describes her as possessed of "a strong and fearless character, of shrewd sense and readiness, of great determination" to see her purpose through, and finally as "absolutely without pity."[72] Madame Defarge is malice incarnate. Indeed, her strength of will would almost be an obscene testament to Nietzsche, if she were not finally mastered by the more poignant determination of Miss Pross to protect Lucie and her child: "Miss Pross, with the vigorous tenacity of love, always so much stronger than hate, clasped her tight."[73] Thus Dickens affirms the classical priority of the Good, but only after revealing the true nature of radical evil.

From the natural law perspective, in which pure, retributive conceptions of criminal punishment are usually defended, when retribution instead licenses expressions of hatred, it corrupts a citizen's character by weakening her concern for justice or her focus on whether the act that caused the harm being avenged was really a *wrong* or morally blameworthy. If this attitude becomes pervasive among enforcers of the law or citizens in general, then concern for both proportionality and appropriate modality of punishment also weakens. Then citizens may feel no shame in publicly expressing delight at the thought of convicts being tortured; they may engage in revelry at public executions. This phenomenon is not limited to extreme contexts like the French Revolution; it has a subtle presence in our own culture, which now accepts a high probability of rape in prison as a normal part of the correctional process; everyone laughs at frequent jokes about this "penalty" on talk shows and in popular movies. Family members of convicts, who often suffer enormous losses of emotional and financial support despite being entirely innocent, are reviled in public, denied welfare benefits, and treated like criminals themselves by the bureaucracies involved in the prison system.

These are signs that a culture of vengefulness has set in. Righteous anger at the crime has become hatred of the criminal himself and even open public enjoyment of such hatred and advocacy for its expression. Even disgust at a repeat criminal bears the seed of this psychological danger within it. This is why, in *The Lord of the Rings*, Gandalf warns us to remember that flawed mortal beings with finite intellects should err on the side of caution when pursuing retributive justice: When Frodo says that Gollum deserves death, Gandalf responds, "I daresay he does. Many that live deserve death. And some that die deserve life. Can you give it to them? Then be not too eager to deal out death in judgment."[74]

Tolkien's insight is that vengeful passions are easily converted into intending harm to others whom we dislike for any reason; almost any slight becomes a ground or basis for projecting a crusade against them. Eventually, such a will to vengeance can so consume a person that she becomes a spiritual parasite more focused on others' faults than her own flaws and on humbling and debasing others than on pursuing the positive basic goods achievable with her own talents. Vengeance, like other kinds of volitional hatred, is thus a perversion of the existential will itself, a focus on negative grounds for committing oneself to destructive projects rather than on the many available positive grounds for committing oneself to creative projects, like friendships, the practices or professions, and the fostering of flourishing communities.

Many cases in literature and life in which it seems that the agent maliciously pursues another person's harm or suffering as an end-in-itself seem to conform to this model: they begin with anger at the other for some actual or perceived harm done, but they move beyond simple desires for expression and redress involved in such anger and become a self-sustaining will to a potentially limitless campaign against the offender rather than against the offense. This involves projective willing, because rather than letting anger be exhausted by its expressions in speech and punishment along with the other's attempt to respond by making some restitution (if any), the agent *cultivates* his anger, makes sure to keep it alive against anything that might threaten to satisfy it. Then the last thing he wants is for the offender to try to make restitution or seek to restore right relations between them. For his hatred has to be maintained now as part of a larger project that transcends its initial basis; it has become central to his identity. For example, in Hawthorne's *The Scarlet Letter*, Chillingworth certainly begins with some (limited) justification for being angry with Dimmesdale, but he takes up a project of deception and mental torture that extends far beyond anything that could be explained by desires for his wife or his lost marriage or by any legitimate concern for his own well-being and fair treatment. The classical notion of an "irascible" or "splenetic" character obscures this distinction between righteous anger seeking restitution and hatred that transcends any interest in right relation with the offender.[75] But the existential conception of the striving will clarifies the difference: Chillingworth resolves with his whole being to destroy Dimmesdale and from thereafter lives only for this end. He *is* only the project of driving Dimmesdale mad with guilt and fear. Thus he no longer loves Hester Prynne, his lost wife; he is interested only in Dimmesdale, the adulterer.

We find another literary case fitting this pattern in *Moby Dick*: Captain Ahab's absolute determination to destroy the whale certainly begins as anger at past offenses (though since the whale is a nonrational animal, its responsibility in Ahab's mind requires a certain personification). But this anger progresses to a self-destructive personal quest in which *nothing else matters*, so entirely is Ahab's will bent upon the sole purpose of his enemy's death. In this kind of case, unity of purpose involves not only volitional strength but also fanaticism, since the agent distorts his own awareness of values outside his purpose, or simply wills to ignore them, in order to strengthen his motivation to the maximum degree possible for his nature. As Jean-Luc Marion writes, "revenge prefers anything to no longer avenging itself," and thus is essentially suicidal: better death than reconciliation.[76]

2.4. *Envy, Superiority, and Spite*

I reserve the term "spite" for malicious anger in its most extreme form. The extremity of this motive may be indicated by contrasting it with two attitudes that focus on *relative differences* between my holdings and yours rather than on the intrinsic value of my holdings absolutely taken.

The first of these two attitudes has been called "envy" in recent social theory and moral psychology. In this context, "envy" has come to mean a preference for lowering *relative inequalities* in holdings, even if this can only be done at the price of lowering the absolute amount of social goods (on some set of indices) distributed to the envious agent—in short, envy in this sense favors greater equality even at the price of "leveling."[77] As Rawls puts it:

> we may think of envy as the propensity to view with hostility the greater good of others even though their being more fortunate than we does not detract from our advantages . . . we are willing to deprive them of greater benefits even if it is necessary to give up something ourselves.[78]

The "advantages" Rawls refers to here are simple (noncomparative) first-order goods, like food, clothing, land, and education. Rawls is worried about envy because if the worst-off agent were envious, he would not choose the difference principle (which allows for relative inequality if it improves the absolute level of primary goods held by the worst-off person). To make this more precise, we must say that *the motive* in envy is to reduce the comparative differences *per se*, not because they are unjust or simply because we wish those better off to suffer as a final end, but only because they *are* better off than us—that is, there are evident differences in holdings. Thus, as Rawls says, envy is not a "moral feeling" toward the other; rather, "we are downcast by their good fortune and no longer value as highly what we have." By contrast, resentment *is* a moral feeling or evaluative attitude in which "we think that their being better off is the result of unjust institutions."[79] The goal of envy is instead to bring about *relative* equality with the other, even at the price of an absolute loss to both oneself and the other. Thus envy and resentment are formally distinct, though they often coexist.

As I noted in chapter 5, social envy in this sense is a problem for broadly Hobbesian theories of rational decision, which presume "simple egoism" as the desire to maximize absolute preference-satisfaction without any concern about the preference-satisfaction of others unless it interferes with one's own. As we saw, Rousseau was the first thinker in the contract tradition to explore this kind of problem in depth. But although he discussed envy, he focused on "the universal desire for reputation, honors, and preferences, which devours us all," leading to an alienating "furor to distinguish oneself" as superior in power and right to others. This *desire for superiority*, as I call it, is similar to envy in its focus on relative differences in material holdings or status (or other objects of simple D2 desires) but different in seeking maximum comparative *advantage* rather than equality.[80] The superior elite revels in its status, while the masses grovel "in obscurity and misery . . . because the former prize the things they enjoy only to the extent that the others are deprived of them," rather than for their own sake.[81]

Although Rousseau traces most social evils, including tyranny, to this kind of comparative second-order desire to possess X because significant others both desire and lack X, the desire for superiority can still be considered complexly egoistic rather than radically evil. Its perversion lies primarily in seeing intrinsic value in having *more* of some mutually desired goods than others have (when there is no natural value in such comparative advantage) rather than in positing harm or suffering as an end-in-itself. Thus, in principle, it could be satisfied without the other knowing or caring about her inferior possessions or status. This changes, however, if the motive turns into the direct enjoyment of the other's abasement or misery itself, and the agent seeks comparative advantage only as a means to make the other suffer envy. "Envy-enjoyment" usually refers to such an essentially social emotion in which the intentional object includes the victim's painful envy. Rousseau sometimes conflates envious comparative desires with such spiteful "pleasure of domination," in which the masters "thought of nothing but the subjugation and enslavement of their neighbors" as an end-in-itself.[82]

Around the same time, Scottish Enlightenment thinkers also made some progress in distinguishing these complex motives. A few years after Rousseau, Thomas Reid argued that "all the malevolence that is to be found among men" can be traced to the misuse of two natural motives, which he calls "emulation and resentment."[83] Reid follows Butler in dividing "resentment" into the animal instinct to sudden anger in response to any harm and the more "deliberate resentment" based on rational judgment of "injuries" or wrongs done.[84] He does not clearly distinguish this from what I call malicious anger or vengefulness.[85] By emulation, Reid means "a desire for superiority to our rivals in any pursuit,"[86] which he distinguishes from "ambition" as the noncomparative desire for power.

In keeping with the Western paradigm, Reid argues that emulation or ambition is an engine of progress, motivating human beings to great works, and when "it is under the dominion of reason and virtue, its effects are always good."[87] Here Reid conflates the desire for superiority as a comparative good with pure concern for "excellence" and the volitional strength that it gives to "every noble and manly pursuit."[88] Thus he concludes that the desire for superiority leads to vice only when it focuses on material comparisons. What Reid fails to see is that rivalry in the practices is derivative from the pursuit of excellence for its own sake (because one way to measure excellence is by reference to the performance of other trained practitioners), whereas the desire for superiority is an egoistic motive aiming at a "good" that cannot be shared, competition for which is a zero-sum game.

Radical evil is often reduced to envy or a desire for superiority. Colin McGinn has argued that apparently pure interest in another's pain may, like seduction of the chaste or browbeating persuasion of the unwilling, appear attractive as a way of making another person abjure his values (at the extreme, even the value of his own life). This in turn may satisfy the agent's "deep existential envy" of others for enjoying lives happier than his own: "His life-project . . . is to reduce the well-being of others to his dismal level."[89] This account plausibly describes some malicious persons, but not all. Coercing a person to give up or invert her values does not seem necessary to attaining the goal of envy; it suggests a deeper will to domination of her spirit. Nor is causing pain a necessary or sufficient means to this end: prolonged suffering may cause a person to stop *applying* the value of life to his own existence but not to deny this value altogether. Finally, the purely envious agent does not care if the reduction of the other's well-being occurs through his own agency or by accident: as McGinn says, "painful illness" may bring this about by bad luck. But a spiteful agent will not be satisfied by this kind of misfortune in the other's life: he wants to bring about the victim's suffering *himself*.

Therefore spite is more radical than desires for superiority or envy that take comparative "goods" as final ends. The spiteful agent intends harm to the other person, but not in order to gain something they have or to punish them for having it, nor simply to reduce relative differences or gain comparative advantages over them. Rather, in spite we hate the other person for who they are inwardly, for their very character; we despise their very *self*. Thus spite ordinarily focuses on particular individuals (although it can be directed toward small groups), whereas envy is often directed against large groups or whole social classes. Spite relishes not only the other's envy but all her painful emotions (envy, dread, hate, despair) and communicates this enjoyment to the victim.

The despiser shares with the envier a willingness to suffer significant loss of assets or noncomparative goods in bringing the other down; but unlike the merely envious agent, the spiteful agent does not essentially focus on reducing the *relative differences* between his holdings and those of his target in areas such as financial assets, affections of desirable friends, social position, political power, or cultural dominance. The spiteful agent's goal is not relative equality or superiority but, rather, *the other's absolute loss* (at virtually any price). To bring harm, misery, and despair to her target, she may even be willing to *increase* relative differences between their holdings of various noncomparative goods in the process of making her despised victim worse off than she was before. For instance, imagine a woman who is willing to go into personal bankruptcy in order to deprive her despised rival of the lavish wedding she was planning (say by a lawsuit that costs her rival $100,000). After paying $150,000 in fees to her own lawyer, our agent ends up even poorer relative to her rival than she was before:

	Wealth Before	*Wealth After*
Agent	$150,000	$0
Rival (victim)	$200,000	$100,000
Difference	$50,000	$100,000

In this circumstance, the agent's preference for the scenario following her lawsuit would seem irrational to the envious agent who prefers simple leveling, since the predicted outcome involves a *larger* relative difference between her holdings and her target's holdings.

Thus spite is not compatible even with complex versions of psychological egoism that make room for self-interested desires for relative or comparative goods even at the cost of some loss in noncomparative goods. The despiser cannot be explained as a complex egoist; she really does *sacrifice* her natural interests just as much as a charitable agent who intends no indirect benefit to herself. But the goal of her sacrifice is the true opposite of a charitable agent's goal; namely, to cause her victim a significant loss as measured absolutely—in my example, to deprive her of her dream wedding. Spite is like this; it wills to deny the victim his deepest hopes, fondest dreams, or most important pursuits in order to bring him to despair. It aims to destroy whatever its victim cares about most, just to spite her.

If spite is a motivational state in which the spiteful agent is bent on harming another person in this way, even if he can only achieve a little harm at great cost to everything else that should matter to him in life, no non-self-deceived judgment about his own happiness can produce such motivation. *Once* he is spiteful, of course, the agent can draw satisfaction from inflicting harm on his target, but only because he is antecedently committed to doing personal damage to his victim, even at a steep price to himself; thus the anticipated satisfaction is a by-product and cannot itself be the cause of this commitment. His spiteful motivation is pure in a way similar to the purity of agapic love: he is prepared to sacrifice his own well-being absolutely for the sake of his goal, and his goal is usually focused on the unique selfhood of another individual. For he attends with care to the details of the other's psyche—so as to personalize the harm all the more piquantly. It is difficult to see how such a goal could become anyone's end except by projective willing: spite is a *volitional* state. Still, the agent starts from reasons for such a project. The spiteful agent's mission against the other person cannot be for no reason if it is autonomous; it must have some grounds, however inadequate they might seem to third parties. This can be illustrated by a series of popular examples.

(I) Shakespeare's King Richard III utters many memorable lines, the first of which is: "since I cannot prove a lover / To entertain these fair well-spoken days / I am determined to prove a villain."[90] Though it seems unlikely that anyone would so explicitly formulate their negative project, we could diagnose Richard's problem as a simple case of *envy*: since he is deformed, he thinks that he cannot enjoy the goods of peaceful times, so he decides to deprive others of their happiness and cause war. At first glance, this seems to be just a case of complex (comparative) egoism: "Richard loves Richard; that is, I am I."[91] But if this character (who is quite unlike the historical king) is believable at all, then something beyond envy must be at work in him. For although outwardly he seems to be working to secure political power and a sexual partner, inwardly he seems to despair:

"Uncertain way of gain! But I am in / So far in blood that sin will pluck on sin."[92] So he becomes haunted and paranoid, drives away Buckingham unnecessarily, and goes on to crimes that are not essential to his apparent purpose. His spite is apparent in this, and how much he relishes the sorrow they cause. He seems happier in drawing others into guilt than in cultivating their friendship. His initial envy develops into despising others with abandon.

(2) The agent's grounds for spite may *initially* be the same as in less extreme cases of "malicious anger." Consider Max Cady (played by Robert de Niro) in the remake of *Cape Fear*, who does not want to build any kind of life for himself after getting out of prison but only wills the destruction of his attorney, Sam Bowden (played by Nick Nolte) and his family. Cady's terrifying determination to pursue this end at all costs is based on his conviction that his attorney betrayed him at his rape trial years before. This is a typical background circumstance for spite: we believe that the other did us an injustice, or the other wrongfully succeeded where we failed or in some other way indirectly harmed us or someone or something we care about. But then repaying the harm or requiting the injustice becomes only the occasion for a more radical project; for spite transcends the circumstances out of which it is first born and wills infinite vengeance.[93]

(3) Likewise, in the film *Amadeus*, Salieri begins with jealousy of Mozart's superior musical abilities and he judges that God has wronged him, since he is more virtuous and deserving than Mozart.[94] As a way of punishing God, he decides to destroy the musician who has received God's special grace so undeservedly. However mistaken this judgment may be, eventually Salieri's main motive develops beyond this purely retributive project of punishing God for his alleged injustice; he comes to despise *Mozart himself* (rather than God) for his flippancy, for his open sexual infatuation with his wife, for his financial neediness, for his spontaneous tendency to suggest improvements in others' work, and so on. Through intense concentration on Mozart to see if he could possibly be worthy of the evident genius he's been given, Salieri finds in the complete gestalt of Mozart's personality a new basis for projecting the deception and destruction of Mozart—quite apart from getting even with God. That is, Salieri comes to anticipate and hate every mannerism, every gesture, every way of being that Mozart embodies. He has to become a kind of connoisseur of this individual, in order the more perfectly to despise poor Mozart for his every distinctive trait and even finally to *relish* this activity of despising as his highest purpose in life. Of course, Salieri continues to rationalize his project as retribution for God's unfairness. But in fact, hating Mozart becomes Salieri's comprehensive final end, to which misrepresenting himself as a friend, destroying Mozart's confidence, and worsening the illness that hampers Mozart's work,

are his chief means. Hence after Mozart dies, Salieri has nothing left to live for except the memory of his triumph.

In addition to the motive switch it exemplifies, this example also illustrates how far volitional hatred is from the classical model of an aversion: for Salieri must become more and more closely involved with Mozart not only in order to betray him more profoundly but also to build up his spite by focusing on every nuance of the character he cannot stand. In this respect, he is like Chillingworth in *The Scarlet Letter*, who needs a kind of intimacy with Dimmesdale in order to fan the flames of despite or to harden his heart as much as possible against his victim. This strange way in which the despiser draws near to his despised cannot be a simple attraction nor a perverse D2 desire to see the victim suffer in some particular way fetishized by the agent.[95] For in true spite, there is no level of damage, including even death, which could "satisfy" the despiser or restore him to an affective equilibrium; each success he experiences in inflicting harm on his target only provokes him to deeper hatred and thus to drive the knife in further and further. Hating the other—*the pursuit* of the other's suffering as a final end—is projected as an activity of intrinsic value that may be even more important than the other's despair and demise.

Thus perhaps the ultimate despiser would prefer to keep his victim alive indefinitely in order to go on hating him all the more perfectly—much as the ultimate romantic lover finds the activity of loving his partner worthwhile in itself and strives to love her ever more perfectly.[96] For the ultimate despiser actively and wholly *identifies* with his pursuit of the other's emotional destruction and lives completely in the experience of acting on his hatred; he relishes it and sustains it by volitional effort, as seen in his search for ever new ways of expressing it. Thus, unlike any erosiac desire, spite is *open-ended, without any definite consummating end*, which is why it can never be satisfied with just reducing the differences between the agent's well-being and someone else's. This can make spite seem like an insatiable obsession, as if it were an uncontrollable or compulsive addiction, but it is not. For the person with a compulsion or obsessive disorder finds her autonomy compromised and she is at least temporarily placated by performing her ritual or experiencing that with which she is obsessed. By contrast, the spiteful person *wills* to remain obsessed with his victim and maintains this focus for its own sake. Spite is thus a bottomless volitional obsession from which there can be no relief without a volitional change in his identity-defining commitments.

If the spiteful person could be fully honest with himself, then, he would have to recognize that he does not quite know "what he wants" to do to his intended victim. Although he imagines all kinds of humiliations and harms, none of these will seem like fully satiating prospects, because what he really wills is simply to go on despising indefinitely and to bring about infinite or endless anguish. In that sense, Socrates would have to say that he wills his mental "sieve" to have enough holes that it can constantly be refilled with sweet revenge without ever overflowing and losing any of that nectar.

Yet, paradoxically, this infinity of spite also demonstrates how dependent the despiser remains on the presence and alterity of the other. The other is hated for his concrete otherness—his unique self, his individual identity—yet this implies that his otherness has to be sustained if volitional hatred is to have its object. Thus spite is volitionally contradictory in much the same way as the self-hating will to inferiority (chap. 12, sec. 9). In destroying its despised victim, the spiteful will inevitably harms its own spirit. Salieri ends up insane; Chillingworth dies without Dimmesdale; Cady, Ahab, and Defarge all unwittingly destroy themselves. Thus radical evil in this form remains parasitic on the good, but its dependence is different from that of a mere privation.

2.5. Malevolence, Torture, and the Will to Misappropriation

In spite, then, there is no delimitable final goal. The nearest we can come to it would be to say that the spiteful agent intends to destroy the victim's very identity, or to cause her to hate and reject herself for being who she is (the person with this particular history). In many cases, this involves trying to show the victim that the despising agent has a certain kind of *power* over her—not just to harm her physically but to affect her very psyche (ideally, forcing her to lose all confidence, to give up on all her hopes, dreams, and meaningful purposes, abandoning her existential identity). The other killing herself out of loathing for her own powerlessness is an image that approximates the despiser's real target (though his true end cannot be specified). This is why spite in its purest form requires cultivating a personal relationship with the intended victim, and the despiser is willing to sacrifice material welfare or sometimes even his life to gain control over his victim's psyche.

In this limit form, spite comes close to malevolence, in which the agent aims at the domination of others as a pure expression of his own ego. The crucial difference is that the malevolent agent, unlike the spiteful agent, need not begin from some kind of anger at his victim's past actions as a basis for projecting spiteful ends. Instead, the malevolent agent finds in his own volitional capacity to appropriate, possess, or control things a sufficient reason for trying to turn everything and everyone into his possession or slave. In malevolence, the agent's will to power makes pure ascendance over others the final end, and the harm or destruction of others is simply a way of denying their alterity or enslaving them to one's will. This is the kind of radical evil that Arendt originally recognized. I approach it indirectly, beginning with the difficult jurisprudential problem of defining torture and distinguishing it from other crimes.

Torture, even more clearly than the killing of innocents, has often been held to be unjust or morally illegitimate for any purpose.[97] It would be hard to see why this is so if merely causing intense physical pain without permanent maiming is sufficient for torture, and it has proven difficult to draw behaviorist boundaries on this crime. After all, battlefield surgery without anesthesia is intensely painful but obviously not torture. However, the *proximate* intention in the case of torture is different from other crimes, and this may be the clearest way to set it apart.

For whatever ultimate purposes it is employed, torture involves trying to bring about a special kind of mental result via physical mechanisms. Through inflicting agonizing pain, bodily deprivation, terror, repeated or random shocks to mind or body, or other means of destabilizing the victim, torture aims to destroy her sense of *bodily integrity*, the most basic level of psychophysical security on which the victim's sanity and ability to act depends. The torturer tries to accomplish his ultimate goal (e.g., extracting information, getting a confession, beating down resistance to the regime, etc.) by robbing his victim of the corporeal security necessary for autonomous choice and self-direction. At the extreme, torture aims not just to "break the will" of the victim (in the sense of making him disclose information or cease unwanted political activity) but rather to repress that victim's very sense of being a free agent capable of making moral choices. Torture is an attack upon the victim's ability to retain his individual identity—his sense of personal priorities, values, and capacity for initiative—even if it doesn't kill or permanently injure his body. At its limit, torture aims to create—whether more subtly or more explicitly—an enslavement of the mind to terror through lack of control over one's own body, a sense of total powerlessness. All this is what we mean when we say that torture is "dehumanizing," and arguably it explains why torture may be a crime even more grave than manslaughter.

In this brief analysis of torture, we have a clue about the kind of volitional hatred I called "malevolence." Torture as I define it may often be used merely as a means to some further end, like getting valuable information from the victim or forcing some action. But a person who pursued *for its own sake* the dehumanization of others that is the proximate goal of torture (distinguishing it from other actions causing physical suffering) would count as "malevolent" in my existential sense. A powerful illustration of such an agent is found in the movie version of the play, *Death and the Maiden*, in which the heroine (Sigourney Weaver) has been tortured years before by a doctor (Ben Kingsley) when she was a political prisoner. This doctor reduced her to his plaything, thereby almost destroying her capacity for agency and a sense of coherent identity, simply *because he could.* As we discover at the film's dramatic conclusion, the doctor did not rape his victim for ordinary sexual satisfaction, or for sadistic first-order pleasure, or for sport, or to gain information, or for any other external end. Rather, he says that he found himself placed in circumstances in which he discovered his capacity to will *the absolute domination* of a human person, and he did this just for the sake of affirming his ability to *exercise power with impunity.* Such torture for its own sake, or dehumanization as a final end, is a paradigm species of the will to exercise absolute power over others; it aims to strip them of their alterity and independence, reducing their being to a mere extension of our will—like an instrument whose functions we can direct, which will do our bidding at our command. Here we approach the very essence of evil in its existential sense.

However, torture is only one way in which such a will to the enslavement or domination of others' freedom can be expressed; there are more subtle methods than dividing a victim from control over his own body. But the malevolent agent's goal is always to assert his ascendance over others' powers of self-direction; so the victims must succumb *unwillingly*, or else the element of resistance necessary for conquest is lacking.[98] Here is the essence of tyranny—observable in men such as Nero and Napoleon—which Plato and the Sophists mistakenly thought was motivated by material greed and bodily lusts and which even Hegel interpreted in eudaimonistic fashion as merely a mistaken attempt to gain the free recognition from others that is necessary for full self-consciousness.[99] On the contrary, this radical goal of dominating the wills and minds of others by force or holding them in bondage to one's whim cannot be the object of any erosiac desire, because there is no prepurposive way to see this as part of our own well-being. Rather, it can only be projected by the striving will.

But *why* would anyone do this? What considerations could the malevolent agent regard as reasons for pursuing such an end? Remember that in asking this question, we are not presupposing, as a Humean must, that there is some *further desire* that answers the "why" question. If apparently malevolent action has an unconscious or ulterior motive, such as a sublimation of the desire for open love or friendship or an attempt to cover up feelings of inadequacy, then it is not volitional malevolence after all, but only its simulacrum (just as apparent friendship driven by some hidden motive is not real friendship). When we are dealing with the real thing, there is no other desire underlying the limitless assertion of one's own *power to appropriate,* or take things as one's possessions, to be employed, deployed, or disposed of at will.

The grounding reasons for such a projective will to domination are twofold, I believe. First, like the making of artifacts, dwellings, and artworks, turning bits of the world into possessions through work or claim is natural to us. Appropriation is an essential power of human nature—its development and proper exercise is part of our existential telos (see chap. 12, sec. 3). This fact is sensed by all persons with the minimum mental capacity and opportunities to make, build, and appropriate. Even the one-year-old baby grasps a blanket, stuffed animal, or other familiar object as "her own"; toddlers proudly display a crayoned squiggle or juxtaposed blocks as a masterpiece. Hegel is correct to this extent: we express ourselves in our works. Second, this power also has an inherent ontological limit: we cannot *make alterity* nor determine by our creative powers the existence of freedom in beings independent of ourselves. Nurturing our children is the closest we can come to this distinctive mark of the divine, but children are not and should never become our artifacts.[100] The things that we make cannot escape their ontological status as subordinate to their human maker; they remain human artifacts even when we give or throw them away. Most of all, they can never acquire a will of their own; to have that would be to resist appropriation, to face us and answer us as respondents rather than tools. Hence nothing with this kind of alterity can be our artifact.

This ultimate limit to our creative power is also obscurely sensed in all responsible human agents,[101] and there are two basic responses to it. On the one hand, most people accept this limit and some even interpret it in religious terms: nothing absolutely and finally belongs to us but only to the Creator from whom all being comes. On this view, we are stewards whose ownership is derivative and provisional; life and being are loaned to us. So we must release any absolute claim to sovereignty over the products of our art and work, or our "subcreative" activities, as Tolkien called them.[102] On the other hand, we can rebel against this limit and try to reject the order of appropriation etched in the ontological limits of our volitional powers, to insist on the absolute sovereignty of our creative will.

This is what Sartre has somewhat misleadingly called the "desire" to be God.[103] It is in fact the will to claim the uniquely divine right to *create and own* beings that are nevertheless also secondarily independent of the power that created them—beings able to face that power as free respondents. But we cannot succeed in creating beings independent of our will or *other* than ourselves; our works remain extensions of our minds. So we assert our will to divine power by trying to appropriate, dominate, or enslave the freedom of other creatures that we have not made, trying to own them while making them keep their alterity. This futile endeavor is the topic of Sartre's famous analysis of "concrete relations with others,"[104] whose ideal is a being Y who is other/free in relation to X yet still owned/appropriated by X. If this relation is possible for any X, then X is divine. But we are not capable of bringing about this paradoxical relation.

Combining these points, the reason why the malevolent agent projects his radically evil end is that (a) he is *not* God, that is, he cannot create alterity, yet (b) *others exist* in their freedom and alterity, which together imply (c) that he did not create these others and so cannot own or possess them. The malevolent agent takes these ontological truths as negative, as intolerable offenses to his ontological status, and projects the goal within his power that comes nearest to tearing down these ultimate laws of being. If this is right, then there was a good deal of insight in Augustine's idea that the malevolent will is based on sheer rebellion against God. However, this is not rebellion in the sense that a typical adolescent resists oppressive parental authority; rather, it is the rejection of any limits to one's being, the will to *infinite appropriation* of anything that is not already oneself, the rebellion against the scandalous possibility of difference, the offense at discovering that one is *not* the whole of Being. Augustine's view tends to make him suspicious of any human self-assertion, but it also makes him better than virtually all other thinkers in the eudaimonist tradition at recognizing the radicalness of some kinds of evil.[105]

The clearest examples of such malevolent willing comes from fictional depictions of the devil or other demonic figures—naturally enough, since they are artistic expressions of this phenomenon, purified by the imagination. For instance, in Tolkien's *Lord of the Rings*, the dark lord Sauron (a fallen Maia or angelic spirit) seeks to dominate the minds and wills of his slaves and his opponents through the creation of the One Ring, into which he has placed a great part of the spirit or willpower that is native to his being. As a result, the Ring enhances his ability to possess others and control their thoughts—while paradoxically *objectifying* Sauron himself, linking him with a material object that can be destroyed.[106]

Sauron's malevolence is clearly not any kind of ignorance nor *akratic* concupiscence or irascibility; he is a tyrant but he is not ruled by sensual appetites or lusts for material gains. His fundamental crimes are perpetrated for their own sake: the destruction of natural beauty, the twisting of all life to his malign purposes, the imposition of his will by torture, terror, mind control, and (most subtly) seduction to submit to his spirit rather than make the volitional effort to resist, are all inherently pleasing to him because they help maximize his power and ascendancy, which he projects with almost infinite strength of will. His ultimate goal is appropriation of all independent life: thus Gollum accurately says that if Sauron regains the Ring, he will eat up the whole world. The will to power and the will to possess or dominate are identified in Tolkien's striking portrait of malevolence in its absolute form.

2.6. Demonic Autonomy

Malevolence, then, turns out to be based on the rejection of any limits to one's will or its power to possess, appropriate, or control. It is just this perversion of the striving will which, as I argue in chapter 2, the ancient Hindu and Daoist sages most feared as the root of violence and tyranny—although, ironically, they were also the first to obscure its true source by mistakenly diagnosing its cause as untamed sensual appetites and overattachment to material things and particular people (among other goods subject to time and fortune).

Milton sees more clearly than these Eastern sages when he portrays Satan as willing the destruction of God's creation and the corruption of human beings precisely *because* this is a way of interfering where he has no right, or doing something intrinsically wrong. "Demonic autonomy" in this sense is the will to *moral* wrong or misappropriation for its own sake. But again, this end is not projected arbitrarily; it is chosen because it expresses an absolute rejection or refusal of any moral requirements or limits. The will to illegitimate acts just for the sake of their moral wrongness is intelligible only as an attempt to go "beyond good and evil," or to *defy* (at any cost) the authority of moral norms or their source. Milton, of course, was drawing on Augustinian ideas concerning how to explain the "fall of the devil"—a long-running "disputed question" in Scholastic philosophy. Near the end of his dialogue *On Free Choice of the Will*, Augustine suggested that perhaps the devil turned from God to himself just because he is a distinct being and therefore he could will allegiance to himself before God.[107] Similarly, Tolkien represents Morgoth (the highest archangel) as falling because he wills to create in *absolute independence* from God, and this is denied to him. The creaturely status that other angels take as a reason for worship he takes as a reason to set his will against the metaphysical law that all being has its ultimate source in God.[108]

In Christian theology, as these literary portraits suggest, the defiance involved in willing evil *per se* is often interpreted as an expression of pure rebellion against God. Since, however, it is also possible for atheists to achieve this form of will, I define it more widely as an explicit rejection of any moral limits on the self or its rights to own and control. Such an agent presumably fixes on moral requirements as the particular object of his defiance because, in demanding virtues of character, these requirements reach to the very heart of the self's identity. The demonic attitude interprets these requirements of fairness, justice, and virtue as heteronomous impositions on the self rather than as autonomous expressions of his will's own implicit commitments, and rejects them in a will to freedom *from* morality. For example, the infamous murderers Leopold and Loeb are commonly thought to have killed their victim just to prove that they could flout moral standards of decency—allegedly, they had nothing else to gain from it and no other ulterior motive.

I conclude this taxonomy of evil by considering the necessary Arendtian objection. As Bernstein shows, Arendt's later view that "evil is never radical" or spiritually deep, but only "extreme" in its effects,[109] was inspired by Karl Jaspers's insistence that the Nazis be seen "in their total banality." Jaspers understandably feared that talk of radical or even "satanic" evil would imply a kind of "greatness"[110] that would actually appeal to people raised on the highly distorted version of Germanic mythology disseminated by the Nazis, and Arendt agreed. Thus they would object that my analysis may "mythologize the horrible."[111]

My response is that Jaspers and Arendt obscured important truths in effort to prevent evil seeming heroic: in fact, the *same kind* of willpower that is essential to moral heroism can be turned to pure destruction, open-ended spite, or rebellion against alterity and pluralism. This spiritual reality has to be faced if we are to deal with these forms of evil. Someone may regard such radical evil as heroic in a quasi-Nietzschean sense, but at least we will understand that some types of malevolent motivation start from bases *similar* to genuine heroism. Value concepts and ideals of the same categories that ground noble and decent projects are used, in deficient forms, as the grounds for evil projects; considerations of justice, beauty, knowledge, self-reliance, practical autonomy, and even metaphysical finitude can be twisted into reasons for evil devotions. But in radical evil, this is not due to brain-washing, irresistible ideology, or other involuntary malfunctions of the practical intellect. Rather, it is the will that forces negative ends to be regarded as noble, or adopted as pure maxims: as Milton's Satan says, "evil, be thou my good."[112]

3. Aquinas and Kierkegaard on Evil: A Response to MacIntyre

The preceding remarks are obviously no more than a sketch of a complete existential theory of radical evil. A full argument for my thesis that the reality of radical evil proves the existence of projective motivation would require, in addition to the existential hypotheses account sketched here, a rebuttal of the most sophisticated eudaimonist explanation of malice, namely, Aquinas's. I believe the above analysis supports my suggestion in an earlier essay that Aquinas's eudaimonist moral psychology cannot adequately explain these phenomena.[113] In response, MacIntyre has recently argued that Aquinas can explain the intentional choice of evil actions as based on inordinate desire for some temporal good, which can lead an agent to choose unjust or wicked actions despite *knowing* that he is sacrificing spiritual goods in the process.[114]

The problem with Aquinas's argument is twofold. First, its hypothesis that "evil is nothing other than the perversion of some good" requires tracing all corrupt motivation to an overvaluing of some positive intrinsic or instrumental value (e.g., wealth, honor, sensual pleasure, etc.). This is precisely what the existential analysis of volitional hatred says is implausible; experience reveals agents who seek some harm or loss of well-being for its own sake, *not* as a good apparently related to their own eudaimonia in ways that could attract orektic desire. Second, Aquinas acknowledges only that persons can *accept* evil (i.e., the privation of a spiritual good) as a *side effect* or necessary cost of pursuing some temporal good to extremes or in unjust ways; he does not concede that they can *directly pursue* the destruction of their own spiritual goods just in order to reject them or rebel against them.[115] Even in his later discussions of malice, as Carlos Steele says, for Aquinas, "no one intends to do evil for the sake of evil. Evil can only be intended by a rational agent for the sake of obtaining another good or avoiding another evil. If it were possible to obtain a good without the evil or immorality, everyone would prefer to do so."[116] Yet our examples of spite, malevolence, and demonic autonomy suggest that Aquinas is wrong: our volitional powers do extend to such extremes.

Similarly, Steele suggests that Augustine's famous experience of stealing pears shows the incompleteness in Aquinas's model: minor though the transgression was, it was an "experience of wickedness with no other motivation than wickedness, the fascination for the nothingness of evil."[117] It was not done to satisfy hunger, or for profit, or just for sport, or to annoy homeowners against whom his friends had a grudge, but rather for the sake of gratuitous injustice. Unsurprisingly, Steele turns to Kierkegaard for an explanation of the sinful will as intentional defiance of the good.[118] In contrast to Kierkegaard's idea that evil can be willed as a "position" in its own right, not just as a negation of the good, "for Thomas, sin remains fundamentally what it was for the Greeks: a *hamartia*, to miss the mark, to fail in one's purpose, to go wrong, to make a mistake, to err, a shortcoming, a defect, a privation."[119] Evil remains a malfunction for Aquinas, even though, as MacIntyre says, he recognizes the corrupt will as akratic and self-deceiving rather than merely ignorant about its goal.

Kierkegaard's critique of this classical diagnosis in *The Sickness Unto Death* is supported by cases like the pear theft, in which misappropriation or violation of right is the final end, and by what he calls self-conscious forms of despair. Defiant despair is not weak or fearful of selfhood; rather, it wants to create itself entirely without prior metaphysical direction: it "recognizes no power over itself."[120] Hence it tries to bootstrap value into its goals by sheer will, but its resolve is undermined by the arbitrariness of this enterprise.[121] Understood as sin, radical evil has to be interpreted as a "position," rather than as "something merely negative—weakness, sensuousness, finitude, ignorance, etc."[122]

Radical evil is a "leap" of the will in Kierkegaard's sense, and this simply means that it involves the projection of ends that are *new* to the agent's standing stock of motives, which include both prepurposive desires and already formed purposes. Such a volitional leap would have to be arbitrary or criterionless on Aristotelian assumptions, for according to A-eudaimonism, choice of actions is rationally motivated *only if* it is *prohairetic*, or moved by rational appetite (the specification of D3 desires according to the circumstances). As we saw in chapter 5, deliberative choice in this sense simply *transmits* general appetite for one's good into appetite for this or that fully particular act; at the highest reflective level, it channels our embracing desire for eudaimonia into motivation to select concrete means to this holistic end.

Aquinas shares this view: reason can motivate only by conveying appetite for one's good into an indefinite number of particular acts.[123] That is false according to Kierkegaard's argument that the commitments we form and pursue with our wills change our practical character or alter what Bernard Williams called our "subjective motivational set."[124] Kierkegaard's "stages" of existence (the aesthetic, ethical, and religious—and their many substages) can each be understood as a distinctive kind of motivational set or constellation of motivational dispositions. Hence his idea that our will can move us from one stage to another, and have intelligible grounds for doing so,[125] implies that we can posit new ends or generate new motives on the basis of recognized practical reasons *without* these putative grounds for self-motivation having antecedently stimulated our desire.

On Kierkegaard's conception of the will, then, a choice can fail to be motivated by any desire that is formally erosiac in structure, including Aristotelian "rational appetite" or *boulēsis*, but *nevertheless* be grounded in considerations whose objective rational significance the agent antecedently recognizes. This is simply to say that the will can project new motivation based on values and consideration that do not themselves already *move* the agent in the usual prepurposive sense. Only the leap gives full subjective force to these considerations as ones on which the agent resolves to act.[126] In other words, it is through such projective leaps that the agent autonomously changes practical reasons "external" to her motivational set into reasons that are "internal" to this set. This *internalization* of practical reasons, giving them a motivational role, is grounded but not determined by these external reasons themselves and their cognitive relation to the agent's existing dispositions and plans.

Thus Kierkegaard's pseudonymous books suggest that the will is a faculty with a creative power lacking in Aristotle's and Aquinas's conceptions. Significant life choices that change our inner character do so by generating and cultivating new motives for action. Though they are radical in *this* sense, such choices are neither causally *ex nihilo* nor rationally arbitrary; they are both conditioned by tendencies arising from past choices and informed (although not erosiacally drawn) by other kinds of reasons and considerations available to us, which may or may not conflict with the tendencies of our acquired character. Neither our existing dispositions nor available rational grounds for possible new motivations *determine* the leap, which allows for novelty even in our deepest motives or longest-term commitments. This is not "voluntarism" in its Ockhamist sense, that is, the total subordination of reason to will, but it does transcend the relation assumed by Aristotle's model of the practical syllogism (i.e., choice *determined* by prior states internal to the agent's motivational set along with the entire gestalt of the choice circumstance). Kierkegaard posits a new relationship between will and reason that is more subtle than those recognized by either the voluntarist or eudaimonist pole of this classical dichotomy. It is precisely this new relation that we have to work out to understand in more detail how the existential will functions. This chapter points out some kinds of considerations or reasons that can ground projective motivation without already constituting or causing orektic desires in the agent, and the full range of such values is developed in chapters 11 to 14.

4. Projective Strength of Will versus *Enkrateia*

Because they ignore the role of projective motivation in human psychology, eudaimonist accounts of moral character remain incomplete in two closely related ways. In addition to reducing vice to ignorance and weakness in the face of appetitive temptations and strong emotions, eudaimonist accounts reduce existential strength of will, or uprightness of character, to simple *enkrateia*—the self-control that is the logical complement of *akrasia*. "Strength of will" in this classical sense as self-restraint and repression of the Id is supposed to be transcended in virtue through rational sculpting of the passions. But this negative conception obscures the true nature of volitional strength in human beings.

4.1. Kierkegaard and Kupperman on Character

As I suggested in introducing the idea of projective motivation in chapters 2 and 3, we are already familiar with a *positive* sense of "strength" of character that we find in persons who show great loyalty to their friends and ideals and who display persisting or even aggressive determination in pursuing their goals. Such persons display what I call the "proto-virtue" of "constancy" or existential courage, which Kierkegaard called "earnestness" and regarded as a prerequisite to both good and evil character in their fullest sense.[127] This thesis is central to existential moral psychology and reveals one of its deepest differences from the eudaimonist tradition. Kierkegaardian existentialism recognizes that heroic character is something more than the self-controlling capacity to resist great longing or ravenous appetite. Nor is it simply another strong emotion; when Kierkegaard speaks of heroic "passion," he means caring, "concern," or the "prodigious strenuousness" of devotion.[128] It is a mode of "spirit,"[129] not in the sense of *thumos* but rather of volitional activity. Agents displaying existential courage are *moving themselves*, rather than being moved by need or desire. They are not oppressed but, rather, liberated by the motives that drive them with such passion. This explains why such existential strength of will (rather than *enkrateia*) is more apparent in cases where prepurposive desire for the goal is unlikely or even unintelligible. For example, someone deeply engaged in a practice or profession that demands sacrifice or someone thoroughly devoted to a political cause with little apparent relation to his own material well-being exhibits such strength of will.

As we saw, this kind of constancy and volitional determination is also exhibited by persons passionately bent on malevolent purposes from which they stand to gain little if anything that could have *prima facie* instrumental or natural value for them prior to being desired. Such malicious obsessions do not have the character of a bizarre D2 preference (like the desire to eat some mud) nor a woefully misinformed D3 desire (like the conviction that God will love us for suicide bombings aimed at civilians). They seem instead to display a hatred that is in one sense quite "unnatural"—or which transcends natural self-interest—since it may even involve full knowledge of its own self-destructiveness. This helps explain and justify Joel Kupperman's assertion that:

> Strength of character is independent of goodness of character, in that deeply wicked people have strong characters. Indeed, a strong character is required to be either extremely good or deeply wicked. It is possible to have a strong character and yet to be fickle or unreliable. . . . However, it is not possible to have what we would call a strong character and to have no ongoing concerns or commitments whatsoever.[130]

In other words, character-strength in Kupperman's sense is incompatible with wantonness; the "deeply" evil person *autonomously* wills wicked ends at least in part for the sake of their intrinsic wrongness. Thus Kupperman, like Kierkegaard, holds that character has less to do with *what* goals we are committed to and more to do with *how* we are committed to them: "Character has a great deal to do with how we are prepared to maintain, modify, or abandon a structure of goals and commitments."[131] For example, a person of strong character will exhibit tenacious "loyalty to commitments and projects" and change life goals "only for her own reasons" (not simply to please others).[132] Character in this existential sense is not a sum of traits nor even a sum of goals, projects, and commitments; it picks out the *way* that an agent forms, maintains, and modifies these elements over time, or the characteristic volitional dispositions underlying this process. The mode of strong character is resilience, integrity, and wholeheartedness.[133]

4.2. Roberts's Analysis

Despite its great importance, this kind of character strength is rarely recognized or discussed in contemporary philosophical literature, which tends to fall back on the *enkratic* conception. For example, Robert Roberts divides virtues into (a) those that are morally "substantive and motivational" (involving intrinsically moral motives), such as "honesty, compassion, justice, generosity, promise-keeping, and kindness"; and (b) "virtues of willpower," which include patience and courage.[134] Only the latter, he argues, are essentially "corrective" of passions and desires whose extremes interfere with "moral and prudential life."[135] This distinction is insightful, and Roberts is surely right that dispositions like courage and patience can be displayed by persons in pursuit of immoral purposes. I also think he is correct that some degree of by-product satisfaction is essential to sustaining the substantive moral virtues, but not necessarily when exercising "self-mastery."[136]

The problem is that the sense of "will" involved in these virtues of "willpower" remains negative on Roberts's account: it "designates not motivations but a family of capacities for *resisting* adverse inclinations."[137] By "motivation" here, Roberts apparently means erosiac desire; he does not regard "efforts" of self-mastery as a different kind of *motive* generated by one's agency. Thus he assimilates all the virtues of willpower to "self-control" in the *enkratic* sense; they are "(in large and basic part) the capacities to manage our inclinations, when they are wayward, to flee dangers and seek pleasures." Willpower in Roberts's sense is an essentially appetite-corrective capacity, rather than an end-setting one.[138]

This misses the positive sense of willpower as strength of commitment or resolve. People are assessed as heroes and villains not only for their willpower in the sense of self-control, as Roberts suggests,[139] but even more for their focus on the tasks at hand and their determined effort to succeed. For example, what Randall Helms calls Aragorn's "force of will" in his mind-battle with Sauron and his ability to lead men through mortal danger is something more than the power to control his own fear;[140] it is a sustained direction of volitional energy on the goal of saving the city of Minas Tirith. Even an agent who has a pure heart in Roberts's sense, since he does not need virtues of self-control to exercise substantive moral virtues, may be counted more heroic for demonstrating such positive volitional strength (as we saw in chapter I, the idea of heroic will contains the idea of self-motivating effort). A moral "saint" like Mother Theresa is that not primarily because of her great capacity to resist temptations but rather because her temperance aids her unyielding devotion to her noble cause.

By contrast, a virtuous person in Aristotle's sense, whose moral dispositions are too strong to need the support of enkratic self-control, might still fail to exhibit projective willpower in pursuit of greater social goods that we regard as essential to the highest state of moral heroism.[141] Although such an agent would not count as "weak-willed" in the akratic sense, nevertheless she would still lack existential strength of will. Gaining it requires not merely the training of passions to follow wise practical judgment but also an effort to exercise the fundamental human capacity of motivating oneself toward an end because of its value. This may be experienced as difficult or as involving inward struggle, not primarily because of the resistance of opposing inclinations and emotions but rather because (a) the task is inherently daunting, or (b) the agent has not exercised this fundamental power of her agency enough before now, or (c) both. When the agent is not used to sustaining earnest dedication to worthy goals, which are often hard to achieve, awakening from what Kierkegaard calls "aesthetic" slumber of the will is an effort to rouse a basic spiritual power. But even for those whose character is marked by long devotions and cares, sustaining these choices of purpose always remains an effort, no matter how heroic they become.

Hence the existential account of projective willing solves the long-standing puzzle about why volitional striving or effort seems to characterize moral heroism, even though a fully virtuous person should not need to exercise self-control against recalcitrant passions. The explanation is simply that there is a different sense of volitional struggle, the need for which never disappears in a state of virtuous habits. This sense of "willing" is not recognized within eudaimonist models because they reduce all human motivation to erosaic desire. Only the existential model offers an adequate explanation of this positive, *non-enkratic* sense of willpower and its crucial role in developing our character.

Roberts is correct that struggling against temptations or "psychological adversities" helps strengthen the will enough to make possible "an abiding passion for justice."[142] But that is because of a complex feedback relation between enkratia and existential will-strength: (a) trying to gain control over one's prepurposive appetites and passions is itself a work of the striving will, even though it is no longer necessary for the virtuous person; and (b) some level of self-control or (better) rational sculpting of one's desires and emotions is a necessary precondition for earnestly setting and pursuing noble self-transcending ends.[143] This enkratic precondition is not, however, a *sufficient* condition for positive caring: the agent must also muster the volitional resolve to devote herself to the task, which reinforces her control over opposing first-order inclinations.[144]

This brief discussion has not surveyed all the main conceptions of strength of will in contemporary moral psychology; several can be evaluated only in the context of a broader analysis of autonomy and the different species of weakness that undermine it.[145] But the examples above are sufficient to explain why medieval thinkers before and after Aquinas turned away from eudaimonism in search of a more volitionalist conception of moral motivation, as we will see in the next chapter.

11

Scotus and Kant: The Moral Will and Its Limits

Overview. This chapter argues that medieval critics of Thomism began to see the free will in which virtues develop as having the power to generate moral motivation. Kant inherits from Scotus this idea of projective motivation in the moral realm. Although the chapter is primarily historical and accessible to nonspecialists, the analysis of Kant's conception of the motive of duty reconstructs key arguments as natural deductions that may be useful in teaching the *Groundwork*. The discussion of libertarian freedom in Kant presupposes some knowledge of Kant's metaphysics.

I. The Medieval Shift away from Eudaimonism: Scotus and the Moral Will

The positive existential idea of volitional strength described in the previous chapter suggests the possibility of conceiving virtuous character in ways that, unlike Aristotle's Apollonian conception of virtue (chap. 10, sec. I), contrast directly with radical evil on its own volitional level. As accounts of the virtues of justice and charity developed in medieval philosophy, a fundamental shift away from the Apollonian conception occurred; it became clearer that to will the good wholeheartedly requires something more than the right disposition of sense appetites. A radically good will is not just a corrective to strong or misdirected passions and habits that can lead to cowardly, ungenerous, dishonest, or intemperate actions.

Thus the key insight in this medieval turn away from eudaimonism is that the virtues of a good will are not all structurally analogous to temperance; in some cases, virtue requires bringing ourselves to *care more* than we are naturally inclined to about selfless ends of several kinds rather than just desiring self-interested goods less strongly. That the former will not automatically follow the latter was not emphasized by Socrates and Plato, whose psychological and ethical analyses were primarily focused on the problem of government. They rightly saw that the *polis* is ruined by leaders who are too timocratic, avaricious, or intemperate to control their own selfish lusts or to place justice and the common good above their private pleasures, profit, and glory. The practical philosophy of Socrates and Plato was from first to last a response to this great disaster for the state, which still haunts us today. But being a good person turns out to require *more* than the character traits that we need to cultivate in future leaders in order to ensure that they will tend away from tyranny and toward philosophy and ideal guardianship. It extends to radical generosity beyond concern for harmony in one's own soul.

1.1. From Aquinas to Scotus: Kent on Virtues of the Will

The move toward a positive volitional conception of virtue has some roots in the Roman Stoics and St. Augustine, but it begins in earnest in post-Thomistic medieval philosophy. In her invaluable study, Bonnie Kent explains that Aquinas's placement of temperance and courage in the sense appetite as opposed to the will (where he placed justice) was hardly universal: "In the later thirteenth and early fourteenth centuries, more than a dozen thinkers," including "Bonaventure, Henry of Ghent, Peter Olivi, Gonsalvus of Spain, and Duns Scotus," defended the view that only "habits of will," as opposed to dispositions of sense appetites, can count as virtues.[1] Initially, these authors still conceived the will, in contrast to the irrational or sense appetite, as the faculty of prohairetic choice flowing from intellectual appetite. But as Kent points out, following Augustine, "will" in this bouletic sense (*voluntas* in Latin) was no longer restricted to good persons: "Augustine presented *voluntas* as the potential expression of either virtue or vice and so helped lay the foundation for later conceptions of *voluntas* as a faculty of the soul."[2] As we'll see, this provides the basis for one of Scotus's arguments for the autonomy of volitional motivation.

Augustine attributed libertarian freedom to *voluntas* and employed this concept in explaining how the will can pursue ends with different moral values. Since virtue and vice are the basis of moral worth, and moral worth is now related to libertarian freedom, virtues must rest in the faculty endowed with such freedom: "It is by the will that we lead and deserve a praiseworthy and happy life, or a contemptible and unhappy one."[3]

This line of thought is developed by Bonaventure, for example: "Because merit is rooted in free decision, Bonaventure argues, the cardinal virtues must belong to those powers that share in free decision"; hence temperance and courage must reside in the will along with justice.[4] It might be, as Aristotle clearly suggests in *Nicomachean Ethics* III.5, that agents can exercise some kind of control over the development of their own virtues; but as Kent rightly notes, "he demonstrates an indifference to the 'moral luck' necessary for that noble upbringing his theory of the virtues evidently requires."[5] By contrast, for theological reasons, Catholic medieval philosophers had to conceive virtue and vice as states for which the agent could justly be held responsible—and therefore as distinct in kind from personality traits that could be fixed by individual nature or nurture (such as habits of the sense appetite).

Hence Bonaventure "consistently emphasizes that virtue must lie within the scope of free decision; it must, in effect, be within the agent's control."[6] Kent, like Bernard Williams, attributes this condition on moral virtues to the "Stoic restriction of morality to what lies within the agent's control," or the exclusion of luck-dependent traits.[7] But, as I have argued, the tendency in this direction is already present in Plato, and Aristotle also sees virtue as the most luck-resistant component of our happiness. In that sense, Bonaventure was simply taking to its logical limit Socrates' rejection of the archaic Greek belief that a person's value is primarily a function of their birth caste.

Aquinas answers this argument by maintaining that every power that participates directly or indirectly in reason must have virtuous states (in which it functions rightly) and vicious states (in which it malfunctions). As Kent explains, for Aquinas, "the sense appetite, in being conformed to reason, can have moral virtue begotten in it," and thus the will can help make the irascible and concupiscible powers virtuous through its "politic rule."[8] Yet as Urmson argued, Aquinas seems to recognize that Aristotle's Apollonian account, implied in his doctrine of the mean, is incomplete (see chap. 10, sec. I.1):

> Aquinas does not attribute all moral virtues to the sense appetite. . . . the sense appetite needs only those virtues that moderate the passions. Because temperance and courage produce an internal order, no additional virtue of the will is needed [for these states to exist]. . . . Aquinas posits justice in the will because it moderates actions, thereby ordering the agent's relations to others rather than to her internal condition.[9]

In other words, those virtues that are *not* correlated with particular passions or emotions that can lead to extreme or inordinate actions (which reason judges according to the individual's temperament) go into the will. Hence justice is not a mean between two vices for Aquinas,[10] and the radical implications of its distinct status are developed by Scotus in his account of the will to justice. Nevertheless, as Kent emphasizes, Aquinas answers the familiar argument that "moral virtues, as habits of choice, must belong to the will" by insisting that "[t]he right intention of an end concerning the passions comes from the good disposition of the sense appetite."[11] This is the key issue in the dispute, because Aquinas is denying to the will as rational appetite the power to choose between different completely final ends. Our only ultimate end, eudaimonia, is fixed by our nature, and our essential desire for this formal telos is directed into desire for particular final ends (as constitutive of our happiness) by the state of our sense appetite and the practical judgments it influences; "choice" is *prohairetic*, only determining our selection of particular acts as means to such desired ends. This is exactly where Scotus thinks that Aquinas's account goes wrong.

In this he is anticipated by Walter of Bruges, who, according to Kent, holds that the "habits" of willing that constitute virtues are inclinations rather than determinations to choose rightly. Moreover, "Walter argues that the will needs virtues because it is not determined to act in accordance with reason even when reason discloses what is good."[12] In other words, it retains the power to choose the worse act even knowing it is worse—something that Aristotle can attribute only to appetite overwhelming reason but not to self-corrupting *boulēsis* itself. Likewise, Henry of Ghent replies to Aquinas that the sense appetite was not naturally rebellious before the Fall, but "The will, by contrast, needs virtues by its very nature, for by its very nature the will is indeterminate" in its motives.[13] He also agrees with Walter that "Because it can choose against the judgment of right reason, it needs more than a natural inclination to the good"; in other words, the will needs virtues that it develops through its own pattern of free choices.[14]

This shift results in a new account of the unity of virtues. Just as Plato, Aristotle, and the Stoics regarded *sophia* or *phronesis* as master virtues that allow all other abilities and qualities of character to be used rightly or deployed for the good,[15] both Walter and Henry take the will's virtue as primary, without which the sense appetite's virtues lack moral quality.[16] It is also possible to have real virtue in the will without perfect conformance of the sense appetites and passions:[17] an agent with volitional self-control may possess the most essential element of full virtue, lacking only its adjunct reflection in a perfectly conforming set of appetites and emotions.

Similarly, Peter Olivi gives supremacy to virtue in the will: "Habits in other powers are virtues only *secundum quid*, that is, only in connection with related virtues of the will."[18] Habits of the sense appetite are never enough without rightly willed choices, because "beasts and madmen . . . may have the same habits of the sense appetite that are found in the virtuous" but without acquiring any moral worth from them.[19] If its factual premise is true, this seems like a particularly strong argument against the Thomistic view. If nonhuman animals and incompetent human beings can indeed display temperate or courageous appetites and aversions without exercising rational will in forming or acting on their motives, then either they should count as morally praiseworthy agents (which is absurd) or the actual virtues of courage and temperance require something *more* than these states of sense appetite. Habits of the sense appetite are insufficient for virtue because they lack direction by "a good will," which takes over the role of rational prudence (or *phronesis*) in Aristotle's account:

> Olivi accordingly argues that the chief part of prudence, insofar as prudence signifies a virtue worthy of [moral] praise and reward, is in the will. Only through the *will's rectitude* is the intellect rightly applied; only through the virtue of the will does the intellect come to discriminate properly between good and evil.[20]

This emphasis on rectitude in the will becomes central in Duns Scotus's moral theory as well. As an addendum to Kent's account, I suggest that the notion of volitional rectitude as the supreme virtue (or *sine qua non* for all the others) grows out of the earlier idea that justice could be the master virtue qualifying all other candidate states as virtues. We find hints of this unification theory in Aristotle's idea that boldness in pursuing an unjust cause is not true bravery[21] and in Plato's conception of justice as the rule of wise reason over appetites with the help of spirit.[22] As Robert O'Connell has argued, Plato sometimes presents Socrates as arguing that he should never do what he knows is intrinsically "disgraceful and dishonorable" (such as betraying his "divinely appointed duty" in Athens).[23] But Plato never moved from this to the Franciscan idea of a just will as one concerned with something *other* than happiness as its ultimate goal, because Plato believed in a "perfect coincidence" between fulfilling our deontological obligations and attaining eudaimonia.[24]

Scotus, as Kent shows, appropriates and develops all the earlier arguments for virtues as dispositions of choice in the will itself, emphasizing the point that the will can moderate or redirect excessive or corrupt desires and emotions more effectively than the sense appetite can, since it has no access to rational evaluation of ends.[25] Someone may object that teachers and parents train a child's sense appetite using their reason as a guide, and that the resulting dispositions influence how the child judges practical options. The Scotian response is that any direct conditioning of the sense appetite (e.g., operant or Pavlovian conditioning) could not possibly constitute a disposition that qualifies the agent as a morally good person. What gives us this distinction is neither reason as speculative discernment of the good, nor sense appetites, but rather the will that operates *between* them and generates its own disposition to choose rightly.[26] Since this disposition of free choice is a motive that the will gives itself, it seems that the leading medieval Franciscan philosopher gives the will what I call a projective power. This becomes clear, however, only once we see that Scotus believes that the will's self-generated disposition to choose rightly does not trace to D3 desires for the agent's own well-being.

1.2. Scotus on the Will to Justice

Duns Scotus's conception of the will is, of course, a subtle matter, but I need to touch on only a few of its most important points. Unlike my own arguments for the existence of projective motivation, several of Scotus's arguments depend on libertarian assumptions about the freedom required for moral responsibility and a closely associated rejection of moral luck. I am not interested in defending these premises here but only in showing that Scotus's conclusions constitute a dramatic move away from eudaimonist moral psychology toward an existential conception of the striving will and its liberty. I begin with Scotus's well-known indeterminism and move to his underlying theory of motivation, which is less widely appreciated.

First, in his famous *Oxford Commentary on the Sentences of Master Lombard*, Scotus explicitly rejects the notion that "will" (*voluntas*) properly so called is determined by prepurposive motives or desires that exist prior to the agent's intention. He attributes this mistaken view to Aristotle: "In Book III of the *De anima* Aristotle lays down an order of what moves and what is moved, thus: the desirable object is an unmoved mover; the appetite is a moved mover, moved, that is, by the desirable object."[27] Citing Augustine, Scotus argues instead that "it is in the power of our will to have *negative* and *positive* attitudes to a *single* object. Therefore these cannot be produced by an agent naturally; and therefore not by the object, which is a natural agent."[28] We can view this as an argument that in exercising libertarian freedom to pursue or reject a given intentional object, the agent (or his will) cannot be moved to turn one way rather than the other merely by the attractiveness or repulsiveness of the object itself; therefore, the will turns one way or the other through its own *projective activity*. Pursuing this interesting argument would bring us into contemporary discussions about how to explain libertarian control as more than mere chance or arbitrary swings of will. Scotus's position, like Kierkegaard's, implies that there cannot be a complete contrastive explanation or sufficient reason for choosing this option *rather than* that one prior to the choice itself, if we are to avoid teleological determinism.

Second, Scotus agrees with Aquinas that the will controls the intellect by being "able to move the intellect to the consideration of this or that"; but in reply, he argues that these shifts of attention cannot be *determined* by the will's natural and involuntary orientation toward the Good, or else "it will no longer be in the power of the will so to command the intellect concerning the consideration of this or that any more than was the first act" of desiring the Good in general.[29] Like Augustine, Scotus concludes that "nothing other than the will is the total cause of volition in the will"; he regards the will as an indeterministic cause of action[30] and, unlike Aquinas, he does not rest this indeterminacy in the intellect's power of attention to this or that particular good: "There is a different form of potency which is still undetermined after the object has been presented to it, which is *perfect*, and *not diminished*. The will is of this kind."[31] Clearly, Scotus conceives the will in terms of what Pink called a second-order executive agency, in which nothing but its own decisions are sufficient to *cause* it to form intentions to act. He also effectively conceives this as agent causation, with reasons for the various options informing but not determining the choice. As Allan Wolter explains, for Scotus, "even by his absolute power, God could not force the human will to elicit an act of volition or nolition," since this is metaphysically impossible.[32]

There is evidence that Scotus amended his teachings on the relation of will and intellect in later lectures given after his first move from Oxford to Paris, which were not originally part of his *Oxford Commentary*.[33] In these lectures (as recorded by reliable students), Scotus no longer holds that the object of the will is merely a *causa sine qua non*, but teaches instead that the object is a *partial* cause of the will's movement toward its end.[34] The free decision and the object or goal that the will decides to pursue are independent causes of the action in the sense that neither depends on the other for its role in influencing the outcome, but free choice remains "the principal cause."[35] Yet even with this modification, Scotus's position remains original, as Wolter explains in his discussion of Scotus's fifteen questions on Book IX of Aristotle's *Metaphysics*.[36] In these questions, the Master challenges Aristotle's principle that "Whatever is moved is moved by another."[37] As Wolter summarizes:

> Among other instances of "self-movement," Scotus singles out the human will's ability to determine itself. As an active potency, this will is formally distinct from, but really identical with, the soul substance, and is either the exclusive or at least the principal efficient cause of its own volition. The volition in turn is an immanent action that falls under the Aristotelian category of quality . . . [so] one can correctly say that the soul "moves itself" from a state of indeterminacy to a positive state or decision.[38]

Wolter suggests that this notion of the "superabundant sufficiency" of the will to determine itself refers to a state "more suitably called 'positive indeterminacy' rather than 'negative indeterminacy,'" since it is not arbitrarily determined, but rather determines itself in the light of considerations presented by the intellect (including moral reasons) that nevertheless by themselves underdetermine its choices.[39] As Kent argues in a recent essay, Scotus regards the will as always choosing for reasons; the ability to do otherwise does not make the choice random: "It means that the agent herself determines which of various reasons will guide her action."[40]

Formally, Scotus still follows older Aristotelian definitions of the will as "rational appetite."[41] He admits the existence of motivating desires and appetites that are simply natural to the human species, the principal of which is will's necessary and thus passive appetite for "happiness" in general, in which the "infinite good, as man's ultimate end, occupies the first place."[42] But as a free power, the will can also choose to pursue an evil end (thus *making* it into "an apparent good") because:

> it can choose any being as the object of its desire and make it an ultimate end, were it not for any reason other than its own pleasure in abusing freedom and performing an evil act. Thus a rational creature, with full knowledge of what it is doing, can hate God and find satisfaction in such a hatred, not because God is hateful or because the hatred of God is not something evil, but because of the pleasure that even such a hatred can bring to a rational creature in the form of an apparent good.[43]

This description of a radically evil will implies the kind of projective motive I described as "demonic autonomy" in chapter 10. Note how Scotus retains the letter of the doctrine that what the will seeks must always be apprehended as an apparent good (or under the aspect of value in general), but rejects this doctrine's eudaimonistic spirit. For he implies that the radically evil will's goal G will appear good to it *not* because the will's free choice itself is motivated or drawn by its natural tendency to happiness, and G antecedently appears as a means to or some part of happiness, but rather because whatever end the will gives itself *thereby becomes* an apparent good for it. In other words, that the agent apprehends his evil goal as a good for him is not the *prior motive* for his choosing it but rather the *posterior result* of his motivating himself to pursue it in the very choice that forms his evil intention. The pleasure he experiences in pursuing his end G is a by-product of projecting this corrupt goal, rather than an attractive cause of erosiac desire for G. As Arendt says, it is "a delight inherent in the willing activity itself as distinct from the delight of desire in having the desired object, which is transient."[44] Hence, while Scotus can still describe the will as an "appetite" for value, his account implies that it can value and project ends without any prevolitional apprehension of their contribution to the agent's well-being.

Bonansea notes that this puts Scotus in opposition to Aquinas's theory that "no specific distinction obtains between the natural appetite [for the good] and deliberate volition, since the latter is for him merely an application to a particular good or the original movement of the will towards good in general."[45] As Bonansea explains, Scotus's main counterargument rests on the point, which Aquinas concedes, that in its free acts, the will can divert the intellect from particular goods or prevent the agent from knowing them; then, "since the will is free in directing the intellect towards its final end, or happiness in general, it is also free in its tendency towards happiness as such."[46] Similarly, against Aquinas's theory, Scotus objects that if, in its free or "elicited" acts, "the will tends of necessity towards happiness as its final end, and it is within its power to apply intellect to the consideration of that end, it will do so at all times and necessarily." But we know from experience that the will does not continually force the intellect to consider the agent's happiness.[47]

As Wolter explains, for Scotus, this means not only that every elicited act of the will is "free in the sense of its being an act of self-determination elicited contingently and not deterministically,"[48] but also that the will has different possible highest *motives*. Following Anselm, Scotus argues that in addition to the natural appetite for happiness or the agent's eudaimonia, the will has an inclination toward the "good" in a radically distinct agent-neutral sense, so that it has *two* different highest or fully complete ends. This means that Scotus rejects A-eudaimonism: there is no single all-embracing motive or *ultimate* end (see chap. 6, sec. I.1). Aside from the natural desire for the agent's own happiness, which we share with other animals, there is a motive that exists only in moral agents capable of *free* elicitation of their acts.[49] As Wolter says, in addition to the freedom present in any voluntary intention, whatever its motive, Scotus holds that

> there is a prior sort of "liberty" or "innate freedom" possessed by the will, a liberty that frees it from the need to seek self-perfection as its primary goal, or as a supreme value. It consists in free will's congenital inclination towards the good in accord with its intrinsic worth or value rather than in terms of how it may perfect self or nature. Anselm calls this higher inclination the will's "affection for justice," or *affectio iustitiae*. In virtue of this . . . the will is able to love God for his own sake as a supreme value. But it also inclines the will to love other lesser goods . . . in terms of their intrinsic worth rather than in terms of how they perfect one's individual person or nature.[50]

This means precisely that Scotus rejects the requirements of formal egoism; the will can directly pursue first-order ends as valuable in themselves without first perceiving in the pursuit or achievement of them *any relationship* to its own well-being. Hence Scotus can hold that *purposive motivation* toward certain final ends (e.g., God's glory) can be *good in itself*, whether or not these purposes seem to promise anything to the agent in return. John Boler puts this aptly: for Scotus, "morality cannot be an extension or refinement of a project of self-realization and/or eudaimonism . . . but requires precisely going beyond it."[51] The motivation to justice is non-erosiac in form; in acting on this motive, the agent is not seeking her own completeness. If Scotus had made this distinction clearly, he would have said that the "justice" of certain active loves or self-initiated pursuits can give the will *grounds* for projecting them rather than an "appetite" for them. Framed this way, the moral appropriateness of an action becomes an agent-neutral ground for projecting its end rather than a reason for being attracted to this action as a means to (or as part of) the full development or expression of one's nature.

Scotus still calls the two highest innate potentialities in the will its two fundamental "inclinations" and describes them as "the affection for justice and the affection for the advantageous,"[52] thus verbally following Augustine's notion of lower and higher "loves." But I think this Anselmian terminology is misleading; it suggests a structural similarity between the two fundamental motives, when in fact Scotus conceives the *affectio justitiae* as a radically different kind of motive. We see this when we try to understand Wolter's key point that the *affectio justitiae* is more closely associated with the will's libertarian freedom for Scotus. The appetite for advantage or happiness is the motive natural to all animals as part of their kind-essence: it is "simply the inclination the will has towards its own perfection, just as in the case of other things that lack free appetite"; indeed, it is the tendency toward its flourishing or full development that any "nature" must have in order to *be* a nature.[53]

Scotus also clearly understands the natural appetite for happiness or advantage according to the lack model of desire; he describes it as "the inclination the potency has to *tend* towards its proper perfection. . . . It is imperfect unless it possesses that perfection to which this tendency inclines this power." By contrast, when the will "tends freely and actively to elicit an act," it is self-moving rather than passively drawn by its object, since it *posits* the tendency toward the end rather than merely *being* a tendency caused by the need to have this object to realize its own perfection.[54] So in arguing that the agent's own happiness is not "the rationale behind all willing," Scotus sums up the two types of motive as follows: "There is a twofold appetite or 'will': one, namely, that is natural [i.e., necessary], another that is free."[55]

Although this passage might make it sound as if actions done in pursuit of happiness are unfree, Scotus is actually referring here to the more autonomous nature of the motivation toward justice. He believes that in agents with libertarian freedom, the will must consent to the *affectio commodi* to form an intention to act for the sake of the agent's happiness.[56] Although in nonhuman animals, the appetite for *eudaimonia* or for the realization of their natural telos may directly *cause* an intention to be formed or an act to be done, in moral agents whose will "has the 'superabundant sufficiency' necessary for free agency," the will must consent to this natural motive to act at all.[57] So if the act is freely elicited whichever fundamental motive the will follows, why should the *affectio justitiae* be more closely associated with freedom? The difference is that acting on this motive means choosing ends to which the agent is not *naturally* drawn at all. Thus the *affectio justitiae* is not really a form of desire in the *orektic* sense. This is John Boler's insight when he writes that for Scotus, to be a rational agent is to be able to transcend the mere realization of one's nature, and "[o]ne must be careful, therefore, not to treat the *affectio justitiae* as a higher appetite that realizes a higher nature."[58] Aquinas treats the will simply "as a special kind of natural appetite: i.e., the appetite of a rational nature," whereas Scotus's moral psychology is distinguished by its thesis that:

> the will, precisely because of its dual *affectiones*, escapes all limitations of natural appetite. This constitutes a radical break—at least with the like of Aquinas. Scotus is not saying just that the rational will has a higher and lower appetite; he is saying that the normal (Aristotelian) scheme, in terms of appetite and proper object, for explaining how an agent comes to move itself is not appropriate for will.[59]

The distinction Boler wants to draw can be captured precisely by saying that whereas the inclination to happiness divides into multiple D2 and D3 desires, what Scotus calls the "inclination" to justice is really the will's function of *projecting goals* because of their intrinsic rightness. Thus Arendt is right to emphasize that for Scotus, the will's power extends beyond desire; a person can "discount happiness altogether in making his willed projects."[60] The terminology that Scotus inherits from Anselm obscures this distinction by making it sound as though he is simply talking about two kinds of *prepurposive* motive, to either of which the will can respond by eliciting an intention or not. But what Scotus really means is that the *affectio justitiae* is an essentially volitional motive (see chap. 3, sec. 3.4)—a motive that arises from the will in the formation of intentions to act for particular purposes. Hence it would be better to call it "the *will* to justice," since this motive is generated by *the will itself* in deciding on acts that respond to reason's discernment of the right, decent, or just in particular cases.

This requires, as Boler rightly notes, that "the intellect must be able to determine what is good in itself or 'just' prior to the operation of the will."[61] Neither the justice of its goal nor the resulting "rectitude" of the will is an attractive object toward which the agent is lured in any prepurposive form of appetite. For all erosiac appetites can be experienced by the agent as alien, or moving him against his will, whereas the *affectio justitiae* could not be experienced this way. In modern terms, we would say that action on this motive is *essentially autonomous* for Scotus, and this is why such action expresses the will's native freedom more clearly or counts as "freer" (see the extract quoted below) even though action on either fundamental *affectio* is freely elicited. Thus we have a kind of *motivational* freedom that is obscured when the will is reduced to *prohairesis*. Arendt sums this up crisply: "The Will's freedom does not consist in the selection of means for a pred.-termined end—*eudaimonia* or *beatitudo*."[62]

This existential interpretation of Scotus's doctrine doubtless crystallizes distinctions that Scotus himself failed to clarify fully, but I think it reflects the trajectory of his ideas, deriving from Augustine's belief that the will has the reflexive power to will its own goodness. Augustine's reason for giving such power to the will thus has to do with his conception of morality. As we saw, Scotus gives some arguments that assume that libertarian freedom is a requirement of moral responsibility, but I agree with Boler that Scotus's primary reason for believing in non-eudaimonist motivation derives from his view that moral requirements in general do not acquire their authority or objective moral necessity from the natural requirements of human flourishing. The *affectio justitiae* must exist because we are aware of moral demands whose obligatory status transcends any such natural justification: hence, for Scotus:

> it seems clear that *affectio justitiae* is needed if the rational agent is to be capable of moral action at all. For example, if eudaimonist or self-realization schemes are limited by their structure to the analysis of an agent's "natural" potential, it follows that they operate only within the range of *affectio commodi* and so simply fail to capture what is essential about morality as such and not just Christian morality.[63]

If the moral law (knowable by nature) requires such "disinterested" motivation, then it must be possible for us.

For example, Scotus thinks that the practical principle that "what is best must be loved most" is self-evident to natural reason,[64] yet "the intellect could not rightly dictate something to the will that the natural will could not tend toward or carry out naturally."[65] Hence Scotus holds that agapē, as love of God and neighbor for their own sakes, is a possibility built into the will's natural capacity, whereas the A-eudaimonist has to regard it as a miracle requiring special grace (since in agapē the will would transcend its formal egoistic structure and desire something completely beyond its own eudaimonia).[66] As Wolter summarizes, "Scotus, in contrast to many of his contemporaries, believed that man by his natural powers could love God above self or any other created good, and that this capacity was not something he possessed only in virtue of some special grace or the infused theological virtue of charity."[67] Rather, natural agapic love is an expression of the will to justice:

> The affection for justice is nobler than the affection for the advantageous, understanding by "justice" not only acquired or infused justice, but also innate justice, which is the will's congenital liberty by reason of which it is able to will some good not oriented to self. According to the affection for what is advantageous, however, nothing can be willed save with reference to self. . . . To love something in itself [or for its own sake] is more an act of giving or sharing and is a freer act than is desiring that object for oneself. As such, it is an act more appropriate to the will, as the seat of this innate justice at least.[68]

Pure love in this sense must consist in projective motivation, for it aims at the other's good irrespective of the value to the agent of realizing this good or even of seeking it: "it is not necessary that the will seek whatever it seeks because of its ultimate end as a source of happiness."[69] We see this even more clearly in Scotus's description of charity (*caritas*) as the theological virtue that perfects the natural will to justice. For charity "is distinct from hope, because its act does not desire the good of the lover" but rather "tends to the object [God] for its own sake, and would do so even if, to assume the impossible, all benefit for the lover were excluded."[70] Thus the aspect of God that is first loved in charity is God's essence rather than God's loving us in return or God as the source of beatific fulfillment. Scotus explains this by analogy with friendship between human beings:

> For just as in our case someone is first loved honestly, that is primarily because of himself or herself, and only secondarily because such a one returns our love, so that this reciprocal love in such a person is a special reason of amiability over and above the objective goodness such a person possesses, so too in God.[71]

Secondarily, we love God "because he shares himself," and only thirdly because of "the satisfying happiness God gives as our ultimate end," which is "a natural consequence of the elicited act of loving him."[72] Thus the ultimate end in Aquinas's system turns out to be a by-product of projective love on Scotus's analysis. Conscience, as *synderesis*, is the ground of such love in the intellect, but it does not necessarily move the will.[73]

Likewise, we recognize moral obligations to love persons or institutions without regard to our own happiness (e.g., the duty to risk death to save our country), and so we must have the power to love these objects for their own sake rather than for the sake of our own virtue or good.[74] Thus, in the tradition of existential agapē ethics, Scotus agrees with Buber and Levinas, who also hold that we have a natural capacity to care for others as final ends not formally assimilated to our own egos.

According to Scotus, the virtue of charity infused by grace simply increases the effect of the will's own striving effort.[75] For as we have seen, Scotus conceives the will not just as a faculty of decision but also a source of motivation; Wolter describes it as capable of "emotions of varying intensities," in which the "solidity or firmness" of commitment to its end is the measure of its strength or the intensity of its resolve.[76] Perhaps because of his northern cultural background, Scotus began with the heroic sense of "striving will" that I describe in chapter 2 rather than with the generalized, eroticized, and domesticated version of Platonic *thumos* that Aquinas called intellectual appetite.

Unfortunately, however, like Anselm before him and Kant after him, Scotus sees the will's distinctive functions (i.e., setting new ends and enhancing our resolve to pursue already-intended purposes) as operative only in positing and committing oneself to distinctively *moral goals* whose rectitude is based on principles that are self-evident to the intellect or knowable *a priori* for all agents. Since his primary reason for believing in projective motivation concerns the pure nature of moral ends, it is only the pursuit of this kind of value that Scotus recognizes as projective; actions chosen for any other reason must ultimately trace their motivation to the appetite for eudaimonia or the natural conatus toward self-realization. It is undoubtedly because the inadequacy of eudaimonism is most apparent in trying to explain our response to pure moral requirements (of noble character, fairness to others, and duty to God) that only these became the province of projective motivation in the Stoic-Augustinian-Franciscan tradition. But as I argue below, this first revolt against the dominant eudaimonist paradigm, while certainly bold for its time, still claimed altogether *too little* for the striving will and thus failed to grasp the full existential significance of projective motivation. For the striving will can form many different kinds of life goals and devotions to ideals that make for a meaningful life as a whole.

2. Kant and the Projective Motive of Duty

2.1. From Scotus to Kant

The great significance of Scotus's analysis can be seen in the answer it provides to Aquinas's main criticism of Augustine's conception of the will. In Question III of the "Treatise on Happiness" in his *Summa Theologica*, Aquinas argues that our eudaimonia (as material telos) consists in speculative intellectual vision of the divine nature and not in the operation of any lower faculty. In the process of excluding the operations of each lower faculty, he comes to the will in the fourth article, where he considers Augustine's neo-Stoic view that happiness consists in willing well (or ordinately) whatever first-order ends we will.[77] Augustine's idea is that since it wills this second-order end of rectitude in the first-order will, the good will can satisfy itself by its own ordinate love of each first-order object.[78] Aquinas seems not to understand this idea of a higher-order will to rectitude,[79] and he responds that:

> the will is directed to the end both as absent and as present—absent when it desires it; and present when it delights in resting in it. Now it is clear that desire for the end is not attainment of it, but a movement towards the end. Now delight is in the will as a result of the end being present; but the converse is not true, that a thing becomes present because the will delights in it.[80]

Aquinas's argument here manifestly presupposes the erosiac conception of will as intellectual appetite, and he correctly infers from this premise that simply desiring an absent end cannot produce fulfillment in the eudaimonistic sense. But suppose instead that Scotus is right that human persons can will *as a final end* that their acts be just or that their first-order purposes be ordinate. Now, Aquinas is correct that simply willing this internal state of affairs hardly guarantees its realization (and Augustine would add that this requires grace). Nevertheless, Augustine would insist that my intention to ensure that my first-order purposes are just cannot fail to exist if I so decide; for in that sense, willing is directly in the will's power.[81] And a special kind of fulfillment derives directly from forming a good higher-order will in this sense or simply from *sincerely pursuing* rectitude in our first-order intentions. The will to rectitude can be a source of its own satisfaction in this manner. Hence we can reject Aquinas's claim that in every case, "the object of happiness is something outside the soul."[82] A person has an internal source of dignity in the just ordering of her own will. This Stoic idea finds its way through Augustine into the Franciscan tradition, receiving particular emphasis in Scotus.

Moreover, the object of the higher-order will to rectitude should not be "thought of as attracting desire for it," as Aquinas says all goals must.[83] Although a good will may be a necessary condition for happiness,[84] it does not reject corrupt first-order motives for the sake of happiness but rather for the sake of meeting an ideal standard of right intention. Hence Aquinas misleads when he says that "rectitude of the will consists in being properly ordered to the ultimate end"; while a just person may "love whatever he loves in subordination to God," as Aquinas argues, willing this ordering is *distinct* from willing to see "the essence of God."[85] Scotus's analysis allows us to see that the value of a good will is not reducible to its part in establishing union with God, as Aquinas's approach presupposes.

2.2. Kant and the Will's Highest Function

To defend the value of the will as distinct from the beatific vision, we can follow Scotus's thesis that eudaimonia is not our formal telos after all. If the common notion of our telos is identified with our will performing well its highest function, then, according to Scotus and perhaps some of Augustine's Stoic ancestors, the will's natural function is to will "justice" for its own sake. This is also what Immanuel Kant has in mind when he argues in the *Groundwork* that the proper function of practical reason is not to let the agent secure happiness but rather to make his will good. Kant's function argument, as we may call it, involves three premises:

1. "[N]o organ is to be found for any end unless it is also the most appropriate to that end and the best fitted for it";[86]
2. Since reason has been imparted to us "as a practical power" that can influence our will,[87] it must have a natural purpose or telos;
3. Yet practical reason does not guide us sufficiently in satisfying our needs and desires or in attaining happiness generally; instinct would be a more secure guide to eudaimonia;
4. Therefore, practical reason is not designed to make us happy [from 1 and 3].

It follows from 2 and 4 that practical reason must have a non-eudaimonistic telos. But the only other candidate is the Franciscan one:

5. "[I]ts true function must be to produce a *will* that is *good*, not as a *means* to some further end [e.g., eudaimonia] but *in itself*."[88]

The first two premises express Kant's teleological conception of nature; his third premise derives from the Romantic tradition (which conceived "the common run of men" as happier because such peasants supposedly live "closer to the guidance of mere natural instinct").[89] This premise is probably unsound, but it is Kant's conclusion in which I am interested here. He says that if our "highest good" (or formal telos) is to form a good will, then

> we can easily reconcile with the wisdom of nature our observation that the cultivation of reason, which is required for the first and unconditioned purpose [i.e., the right ordering of the will] may in many ways, at least in this life, restrict the attainment of the second purpose—namely happiness—which is always conditioned [by the requirement of the right]; and indeed that it can even reduce happiness

to less than zero without nature proceeding contrary to its purpose; for reason, which recognizes as its highest practical function the establishment of a good will, in attaining this end is capable only of its own peculiar kind of contentment—contentment in fulfilling a purpose which in turn is established by reason alone.[90]

This passage introduces Kant's famous thesis that the Right (or "justice," broadly speaking) is morally prior to the Good (or happiness, broadly speaking, including the pursuit of one's desired ends). The special contentment that he mentions here refers to *moral self-respect*—the good that can at least partially be secured by the will's direct initiative, according to Augustine and Scotus. Kant's thesis is not a wholesale rejection of teleology, as is often assumed, but rather a rejection of the erosiac concept of our formal telos (chap. 6, sec. 3) in favor of the alternative concept derived from the Franciscan tradition, that is, *rectitudo*, or the good will. This concept retains the idea that our formal telos specifies the function implicit in our natural design but rejects the idea that the motivation associated with this telos must be formally egoistic; for a person to realize his natural design may just be *good*, rather than good *for him* (in any nontautological sense).[91]

Kant differs from Scotus and Anselm only in giving a different material conception of what really constitutes the formation of a right or just will or satisfies our non-erosiac formal telos. For Kant, this involves willing that one's first-order intentions are universalizable, consistent with respect for the inviolable or superordinate intrinsic value of rational free willing itself; whereas for the Franciscans, what makes first-order intentions and acts just, right, or charitable, is not apparently measured by this kind of universalizability test. These are different material conceptions of the same non-erosiac concept of our formal telos, just as Aristotle and Aquinas offer different material conceptions of what complete happiness as our formal telos really consists in or how it can be realized.[92]

Given this connection, it should not be surprising that what is called "motivation by specifically *moral* reasons" in the Kantian tradition fits the structure of projective motivation. In explaining the good will, Kant famously argues that we see this phenomenon most clearly in cases where a person makes a sacrifice or does the right thing neither for the sake of long-term self-interest (prudence) nor to satisfy more particular desires (e.g., the gout sufferer's D2 appetite for fine foods or the suicidal person's instinctual D1 aversion to death) but "for the sake of duty alone."[93] As in the case of Aristotle's notion of action for the sake of the noble, Kant is proposing a form of pure motivation; the agent-neutral goal is that one's first-order ends and the means one intends to use in pursuing them (together constituting an intended plan of action) conform to formal criteria of rightness or (what Kant takes to be the same thing) respect the intrinsic dignity of individual persons as a value trumping all other values, *irrespective* of the effects this may have on the happiness of the agent or others he cares about. Interestingly, he even proposes that the agent's proper happiness (limited by conformity with the moral law) can itself be *one* of the intrinsically valuable ends projected for this reason, that is, because pursuing it in certain ways, within certain limits, conforms to the moral law.[94]

Officially, Kant's argument for this self-motivational power is that this motive of duty must be universally available to all morally responsible agents, whereas other appetites and even sympathetic emotions are not always available or sufficient to move us to action (Kant postpones the final proof of the possibility of acting for the sake of duty until Part III of the *Groundwork*). But whether or not Kant's ought-implies-can argument for the universal availability of this motive of duty is convincing, his conception of this motive clearly frames it as one *kind* of projective motive, which we can call the will to rightness. For, as Murphy (following Donagan) notes, Kant means to claim that persons themselves rather than other "producible" goods (including the various components of human welfare) are our highest end.[95]

More precisely, for Kant, strict loyalty to the existence and inherent dignity of persons (as free rational agents) ought to be our highest end; thus we always have a trumping reason to choose a plan of action that coheres with the requirements of justice or fairness to all persons as distinct individuals. But all our desires in the *orektic* sense (D1-D3 states) are appetites for producible goods of one sort or another (i.e., states of affairs related to our welfare in some way), and therefore the motive of duty is no such appetitive state at all. Acting for the sake of persons themselves means projecting their existence and dignity *qua* free, rational agents as a good that trumps all first-order product-values and doing so *because* the moral law requires it, given the inviolable value that moral personhood has.

This point is clarified by Kant's key distinction between the "purpose" [*Absicht*] of our action, which we may understand as our intended end or goal, and the "maxim" or principle on the grounds of which we decide to form our first-order intention. Although Kant does not use the word "intention," this is roughly what he means by "volition" [*Wollen*]. So his distinction is between:

> **A first-order intention I:** perform behaviors B1 to Bn to bring about purpose P, and
> **A principle or maxim:** a reason for deciding to form I in circumstances of kind C.

Kant thinks of the principle that grounds our decision to form a given first-order intention as mentioning reasons for this intention, which will include a sense of its intended purpose as having value for us as either a proximate or final end. Since different principles endorse different reasons for forming intentions, two agents could form the same first-order intention on the basis of quite different principles. The reverse is also true: the same principle or maxim could also ground different intentions in different circumstances. Korsgaard applies this analysis to Kant's distinction between the person who aids another out of sympathy or pity and the person who aids on the motive of duty: "They have the same purpose, which is to help others," but this becomes their intended final end on the basis of different maxims that respond to distinct springs of action.[96]

This sheds light on Kant's otherwise confusing second proposition in his argument that only the good will has unconditional moral worth:

> An action done from duty has its moral worth, *not in the purpose* to be attained by it, but in the maxim in accordance with which it is decided upon; it depends therefore, not on the realization of the object [or goal] of the action, but solely on the *principle of volition* in accordance with which, irrespective of all objects of the faculty of desire, the action has been performed. That the purposes we may have in our actions, and also their effects considered as ends and motives of the will, can give no unconditioned moral worth is clear from what has gone before [i.e., the four examples].[97]

This passage has traditionally confused students because it sounds as though Kant is saying that it does not matter what results or consequences a good will aims to bring about, which would be highly counterintuitive. What Kant actually means is that if the particular goal or purpose P in our first-order intention (e.g., helping a friend in need) were *all* that made our will good, then taking any appetite for P as a sufficient reason for intending P would give us a good will. And that cannot be true for two reasons: first, because it would mean that pursuing P by *any means* necessary in the circumstances could be morally legitimate, which is counterintuitive; and second, because in other possible circumstances where we have a duty to form some intention aiming at P, yet we lack any prior inclination toward P, we must still be capable of deciding to form this intention on other grounds.

Kant develops this second point immediately following the passage stating the second proposition in the overall argument of *Groundwork* I. He begins with the distinction between formal and material maxims/principles for deciding to form any intention that is in accordance with the moral law:

> Where can this [unconditional moral] worth be found if we are not to find it in the will's relation to the effect [or purpose] hoped for

from the action? It can be found nowhere but in *the principle of the will*, irrespective of ends which can be brought about by such an action; for between its *a priori* principle, which is formal, and its *a posteriori* motive, which is material, the will stands, so to speak, at a parting of the ways; and since it must be determined by some principle, it will have to be determined by the formal principle of volition when an action is done from duty, where, as we have seen, every material principle is taken away from it.[98]

A material maxim or principle is one that transfers preexisting desire for the result or end of the possible action into the intention that makes this end our express purpose P to be realized by the intended performances. By contrast, a formal maxim or principle is a reason for forming a first-order intention that is *independent of any prior attraction to its purpose* or intended goal. Such a reason is not based on the agent's having any prior orektic desire for the intended result P. Thus a will that decides on the basis of such a formal principle *projects* its purpose (in the existential sense), *taking* an interest in P by its own activity.[99] Kant's modal argument that the motive of duty must be projective in this sense can be reconstructed as follows:

> 1. If some plan of action or intention I (which aims at purpose P) is morally required in circumstances of kind C, then it is right for any free, rational being (or person) in C-like circumstances to choose I [from the meaning of moral necessity].[100]
> 2. For any intention I that is morally necessary in C, it is possible that some free, rational being in C-like circumstances lacks any inclination or appetite for P and thus lacks a material principle for choosing I [given the psychological contingency of orektic desires].
> 3. Thus it is possible for a being without any material or desiderative ground for choosing I to have a moral duty to choose I [conjunction of 1 and 2].
> 4. But if any personal agent A *ought* to choose I, then A *can* choose I [the ought-entails-can rule].[101]
> 5. If any personal agent A can choose I, then A can recognize, accept or identify with, and act on some maxim or principle that can ground the choice of I [The Kantian principle of action as rational decision (KP)].[102]
> 6. Thus if A ought to choose I, A can recognize, accept or identify with, and act on some maxim or principle that rationalizes or explains the choice of I [from 4 and 5 by hypothetical syllogism].
> 7. Thus it is possible for a person without any material or desiderative ground for choosing I to recognize, accept or identify with,

and act on some maxim or principle that can ground the choice of I [from 3 and 6 by *modus ponens*].

8. Thus it is possible for some responsible agent to act on a formal maxim for choosing I [from 7 and the definition of formal maxims].

Since the condition in premise 2 applies to *any* morally responsible agent, the argument can be generalized to all persons. And since forming an intention on the basis of a formal maxim is equivalent to projecting one's intended purpose on the grounds specified in the maxim, as we have seen, the conclusion is that morally responsible agents can project purpose P whenever they recognize sufficient moral grounds for pursing P in the intended way. At least this argument tries to establish that such a formal principle (which will be *a priori* in its most general formulation) for choosing intention I must be available whenever the agent recognizes that choosing I is morally required.

This, in turn, explains Kant's conclusion that the motive of duty must involve choice or the formation of intentions on the basis of such a formal maxim or principle, which he calls *reverence*: "Duty is the necessity to act out of reverence for the law."[103] Like Scotus's notion of the "affection for justice," respect for the law is described as a "feeling," and this can sound like a prepurposive motive. But Kant means a motive generated in the agent's will in the process of forming a given intention because this intention will satisfy the requirements of morality. Whatever its emotional by-products, respect is fundamentally a volitional activity of projecting conformance with the moral law as one's highest-order end—an activity with moral obligation as its ground.[104] Hence Heidegger is incorrect, for example, to interpret Kantian respect as a type of "*oreksis*" (although he rightly sees it as a kind of "striving" like that involved in forming a project).[105]

Kant adds to this powerful deduction what is really a separate argument for the distinctive status of this moral motive, which also makes sense once we understand formal principles as grounds for projective motivation. He claims that an intendable goal or purpose by itself cannot be the object of reverence "precisely because it is merely the effect, not the activity, of a will,"[106] and he adds that any result (defined by its intrinsic properties)[107] that we could take as our intended purpose could, in principle, be realized through other causal processes:

> Thus the moral worth of an action does not depend [solely] on the result expected from it, and so too does not depend [solely] on any principle of action that needs to *borrow its motive* from this expected result. For all these results (agreeable states and even the promotion of happiness in others) could have been brought about by other

causes as well, and consequently their production did not require the will of a rational being, in which, however, the highest and unconditioned good can alone be found.[108]

This argument suggests that the value of a good will cannot lie simply in its intended consequences or its tending to produce certain results by intending these as its purposes.

A reconstruction of this argument must include the supposedly self-evident thesis at the opening of *Groundwork* I, namely that only the good will is unconditionally good. Scotus and most of the Franciscan tradition also affirmed some version of this thesis, which I dub "the Augustinian premise." As we saw, Kant's function argument provides support for this thesis, but I am not evaluating Kant's defense of it here.[109] With this premise, his second argument for the distinctive status of moral motivation can now be stated as follows:

1. Any causal process that derives all its value from its consequences C has only instrumental value, which can be no higher or more valuable than the intrinsic value of C [the derivative nature of instrumental value].

2. If the value of a good will (W) were simply its instrumental value in bringing about its intended purposes or ends, then its value could not be any higher than the value (V) of its ends or products considered independently of how they were produced [instantiation of 1].

3. In principle, it is possible for some other non-volitional process (N) to cause the same results or consequences as the realized purpose of an intention formed by the good will (W) [uncontroversial causal premise].

4. Thus N could only have an instrumental value equal to, or lesser than, the intrinsic value (V) of its products [from 1 and 3].

5. If the value of a good will (W) were simply its instrumental value in bringing about its intended purposes or ends, then W could have an instrumental value no higher than the value of N—that is, a value equal to V [from 2 and 4 by substitution of N for V].

6. The good will is the object of unique reverence, which means that necessarily, its value is higher than that of any causal process not involving the second-order agency of the will [the Augustinian premise].

7. Thus the value of a good will (W) must be higher than the highest possible value of N [from 4 and 6 by transitivity].

8. Thus the value of W transcends any instrumental value it has in virtue of bringing about its intended purposes or ends [from 5 and 7 by *modus tollens*].

This second argument is a bit more awkward but it establishes that the good will has an intrinsic value that can exist only in persons capable of second-order agency, which transcends the value of the will's intendable purposes or end products. In the third premise, Kant specifically has in mind that prepurposive appetites or inclinations could desire the same results or consequences that happen also to be the intended purpose of some volition adopted by the good will; therefore these PPMs would share any value that the good will derives merely from its tendency to bring about its intended goals or "material" ends. Hence, if the four famous examples of *Groundwork* I support the Augustinian premise by showing that motive of duty has a moral value that we do not find in other maxims that "borrow" their motive from prepurposive inclinations attracting the agent to the same goals, then the intrinsic value of the good will has to transcend the product-value of these intendable goals.

Hence the second argument shows the same conclusion as the first, namely, that the good will can have its unconditional worth only if it *motivates itself projectively*, independently of all prepurposive desire. Contrary to Humean intuitions, as Ameriks says, "such willing is precisely not necessitated by any ... desires in the agent's prior 'motivation' set."[110] This conclusion makes sense if we see the exercise of projective willing for moral reasons as having an inherent value in its own right that is distinct from the product-value of the ends that it can will.

Scotus and Kant support this intuition by treating projective motivation as *freer* (in the sense of more "autonomous" or "self-determining") than desire, in which the agent depends on passive attraction toward the perceived object. If this is right, then even an evil project that sets some kind of harm to another person or society as one's absolute end is, while far more corrupt than conquest motivated by simple lust for riches, still metaphysically nobler in its greater inherent autonomy. Of course, Kant follows Scotus in imagining that the natural/metaphysical value of our capacity for projective motivation lies solely in making possible the will to justice, since this is the only kind of projected goal Scotus and Kant recognize.[111] But the existentialist who recognizes a much wider range of projective motives can still endorse their conclusion that the capacity for striving will in the projective sense does have an intrinsic natural value all its own because it makes possible autonomy and lets us become subcreators of our own identity. This value is distinct from the terminal value of the various possible goals or ends that provide some of the possible grounds for pursuing them.

For Kant, the good will must also be seen as projective because of the higher-order regulative function it exercises over all action grounded in particular desire or the appetite for happiness in general. He concludes from the four examples in *Groundwork* I that the pure motive of duty is fundamentally unlike any appetite for particular states of affairs or results and distinct from the general desire for happiness that can be specified in so many different ways according to different tastes, cultures, and worldviews. The moral motive does not simply focus us on any end or result to be maximized; rather, it is concerned about how (and within what limits) *other* first-order ends may be pursued. This higher-order function suggests that the motive of duty can operate *in addition* to other first-order desires. At the level of imperfect duty, it also operates to require that certain goods that the nature of our will implicitly commits us to valuing in our own case (such as assistance in pursuing our legitimate projects and self-development) are valued for other agents as well. To act on the motive of duty or the will to justice is, therefore, first, to *project* certain second-order restrictions on the ways and extent to which one acts on natural and learned first-order motives; and second, where the requisite inclination or emotion is lacking, to project particular self- and other-regarding first-order ends as well (e.g., when not feeling empathetic, still projecting the goal of contributing a just amount to worthy charities because respect for the personhood of others demands it).

This regulative function helps explain why the motive of duty is "something which is conjoined with my will solely as a ground and never as an effect—something which does not serve my inclination but outweighs it or at least leaves it entirely out of account in my choice."[112]—which is to say that it cannot be the object of natural desire. For the complex second-order good that is the goal of the good will is both a minimum-threshold requirement of decency and a side constraint on the pursuit of first-order ends; thus it is structurally unlike any goods that we typically apprehend as naturally attractive (D1), as brute-preferable (D2), or as part of our eudaimonia (D3). For our inclinations and desires are always for states of affairs or activities that can be pursued or done in different ways, but the good will aims at a qualitative modification of such first-order pursuits to bring them in line with justice and respect to persons as ends-in-themselves. As Augustine failed to grasp but Scotus saw, the second-order end of pursuing first-order purposes ordinately, or in the right way, or subject to the requirements of fairness to all is an end that can only be *projected*.

This existential interpretation of the good will—as a regulator that projects the second-order goal of holding our pursuit of other ends to formal conditions of fairness—also explains why Kant thinks that we can have a "reverence" for an agent acting on the motive of duty (or for a will *generating motivation* according to the moral law) that we can never have for any prepurposive desire or inclination, including even the general desire for happiness that all human beings share. For "reverence" is described as a feeling that is not "received through outside influence, but one *self-produced* by a rational concept, and therefore specifically distinct from feelings of the first kind, all of which can be reduced to inclination or fear."[113] In other words, reverence is an emotion that responds specifically to projective striving of the will.

Kant's description of reverence certainly recalls Scotus and Anselm on the *affectio justitiae*: it "demolishes my self-love" because its object is apprehended as based neither on appetite nor on aversion but rather on a *law* to which we are subject "without any consultation of self-love."[114] In particular, the desire for eudaimonia and objective requirements for attaining it (if these can be discerned, about which Kant is skeptical)[115] cannot be the objective basis for the authority of this law. Instead, Kant thinks that this law arises from the nature of our will and therefore can be considered self-imposed. Hence our ground for projecting obedience to this law (or conformity of our intentions to its requirements) lies in *our own constitution*: we are already implicitly committed to this law in valuing ourselves just for being free, rational agents capable of moral responsibility (rather than as agents for whom happiness is possible).

In choosing a plan of action simply because it is morally required or at least in part because it is morally legitimate, we motivate ourselves by projecting the second-order end of rectitude in our will (or reverence for the law, as Kant expresses it) rather than acting on any *orektic* desire for conformity to the law: our reason for obeying the moral law is quite *independent* of any relation that the required or permitted actions may have to our eudaimonia; hence it is not the kind of thing we can "desire" in the classical Greek sense.

In this analysis, I am not defending Kant's claim that the objective authority of the moral law is autonomous—although I find much merit in Christine Korsgaard's own defense of this conclusion.[116] Nor am I endorsing Kant's argument, which follows immediately upon the passages we have been considering, that from the unique projective form of the motive of duty, we can derive (at least in outline) the supreme norm or moral principle that guides the will acting on this motive or provides its ground. Kant's suggestion is that we can tell *what* our duty is, at least in abstract, from *how* our motive to do our duty is structured.[117] I call this the "elimination argument" for the categorical imperative in *Groundwork* I, and I reject the dichotomy on which it rests. But my goal here is only to show that Kant's remarks on the motive of duty, which he contrasts with all desires or inclinations for outcomes or results (as the "material" or end of our maxim), become more cogent when understood as arguments that this motive is projective in form—like Scotus's will to justice. Kant exaggerates what can be derived at the normative level about the requirements of duty from the insight that this pure motive has a structure unlike the appetites recognized in eudaimonist moral psychology, but he must at least be credited with the recognition that there are fundamentally different intentional structures here.

Like Scotus, Kant manifestly struggles to find an adequate vocabulary in which to formulate his insight precisely because he sees that the will to justice is *not* appetitive in structure; but neither the resources of traditional (eudaimonist) or modern (Hobbesian) moral psychology provide him with philosophical terminology suited to expressing this distinction. For in this case, the theory-influenced history of psychological language itself had covered over the rift that Kant was attempting to expose. Like Scotus, who writes as if the will to justice were an appetite or inclination, Kant also calls pure practical reason a "higher faculty of desire," but here the term signifies "all that contrasts with mere belief," or motivation in general.[118] He calls it "higher" to distinguish it from refined desires that he considers still essentially self-perfective—such as intellectual stimulation, intelligent conversation, the desire for power, the development of talent, and the enjoyment of challenges.[119]

The lower faculty of desire aims only at agent-relative objects: "the determining ground of choice consists in the conception of an object and its relation to the subject, whereby the faculty of desire is determined to seek it realization. Such a relation to the subject is called pleasure in the reality of an object."[120] In other words, Kant thinks that all motives *other than* the motive of duty (formed by pure practical reason) aim at pleasure in their consummation. As the analysis in chapter 5 suggests, it would be better to modify this into the view that lower desires all aim at some self-related first-order good or some good that is apprehended at least as appropriable by the self.[121]

We find the notion of projective motivation implicit again in Kant's compressed reconstruction of this analysis of the good will in the *Critique of Practical Reason*, where he argues that desire for the end or goal of our action is not always its motive. In Theorem III, he writes that "The material [or end] of a practical principle is the object of the will. The object either is the determining ground of the will or it is not."[122] The material object or goal "determines" our will or furnishes the motive for our intention (or "volition") when we decide to act on prior desire, inclination, or attraction toward this object; when we do not, our will is moved by something *other* than appetite for the goal of its intended action. However, this alternative kind of "determination" of the will by a "practical law," or a formal maxim (having a universalizable form), does not imply that resulting intention to act has *no* end in view (or "material") at all. Kant clearly affirms, "Now it is certainly undeniable that every volition must have an object and therefore a material, but the material cannot be supposed, for this reason, to be the determining ground and condition of the maxim."[123] This just means that in some cases, appetite for the intended end is not the motive.

Without this point, one cannot adequately understand Kant's later discussion of the "Highest Good" (i.e., happiness in proportion to virtue, or nature conformed to the moral law) as the end or object of the will when it is determined by pure practical reason:

> The moral law is the sole motive of the pure will. . . . Consequently, though the highest good may be the entire *object* of pure practical reason, i.e., of a pure will, it is still not to be taken as the *motive* of the pure will; the moral law alone must be seen as the ground for making the highest good and its realization or promotion the object of the pure will.[124]

In other words, the highest good is projected as the end when the agent forms intentions on the basis of moral reasons or wills moral motivation. While it is true that for Kant, without "reference to outcome, to results, to *materia*, to ends," there can be "no willing,"[125] this does not mean that all motivation is erosiac or desiderative in this substantive sense. Rather, it means only that intentional action must always be goal-directed. But the *adoption* of the intention or "volition" [*Wollen*] can involve projection of ends for which we have no prior appetite; a certain class of pursuable ends can be projected on grounds *other* than their potential value for the agent's happiness.[126]

Underlying this view is a conception of the will and a theory of action that though not fully articulated, radically resists older erosiac models of motivation.[127] It can be summarized in three points. First, as Ameriks argues, it is central to this theory that there be gaps between desires for some state of affairs S, reasons for pursing S, and the formation of any actual intention to pursue S. Even when the agent has an all-things-considered judgment that it is best to do A in pursuit of S, her will "still has the task of determining itself in that direction."[128] This commits Kant to the idea that intentional purposes are actively formed by decisions that are themselves an active/agentive process (see chap. 3, sec. 3.3).

Second, willing always has some normative content; agents form intentions through their "will, i.e., [a] faculty of determining their causality through the representation of a rule" or "according to principles."[129] These intentions will always have a form such as "I will do A in order that X, because . . ." When Kant says that "we must make it our maxim to act on [a] desire," he means, according to Korsgaard, that "the reflective mind must endorse the desire before it can act on it: it must say to itself that the desire is a reason" for it.[130] This is right as long as we remember that even immoral action can be "endorsed" in the sense required for the intention to count as self-formed by the will, though it cannot count as fully autonomous.

Third, Kant seems to see all purposive motivation (on which the agent acts intentionally) as projective in the *minimal* sense that it is never simply caused by prepurposive desires combined with beliefs. Often, as in maxims following from the principle of happiness, "an object of choice is made the basis of the rule and therefore must precede it."[131] Yet even in such heteronomous acts, in which desire for the object is taken up into the agent's purpose, the desire is first sanctioned in cognitive form by the will. Hence decision adds something not present in the inclinations or impulses on which it works: "the will is never determined directly by the object and our representation of it; rather the will is a faculty for making a rule of reason the motive of an action that can make an object real."[132] Thus the decision-as-agency model, combined with the normative conception of decision, suggests the idea that between prepurposive motives and intended purposes there is always a (weaker or stronger) projective supplement. This supplement is conceived theoretically as "spontaneity." In some cases, it only incorporates a desire into an intention; in others, it generates the moral motivation (in place of prepurposive motives) for the intention.

Since Kant distinguishes practical "rules" from "laws" (i.e., rules that are rationally universalizable or that enjoy lawlike form) and likewise distinguishes "will" from "pure will" (which is motivated only by laws), his remark that the will is never determined *directly* by its object clearly applies not only to action from the motive of duty but to heteronomous acts as well.[133] The operation of the will is thus the domain of spontaneity, which, as Henry Allison says, "concerns rational agency in general, that is, the capacity to determine oneself to act on the basis of general principles (whether moral or prudential)."[134] This idea is sometimes expressed by saying that Kant does not even regard prepurposive desires and inclinations as constituting motives to act but only as *grounds* for possible motives;[135] only when the will gives them the discursive form of *reasons* do they acquire motivating force.[136] In his insightful review of Barbara Herman's work, Paul Guyer summarizes this point:

> On an empiricist [i.e., Hobbesian/Humean] conception of agency, feelings, desires, and other naturally occurring and empirically given conditions are, as such, motives, functioning as causes for action. So here the idea of action in the absence of feelings or desires does not make any sense to begin with, and actions can instead be expected to arise only from an agent's strongest feelings or desires in any particular situation.... Kant's conception of moral worth seems paradoxical, Herman suggests, because we approach it with such a picture in mind,

but Kant's conception of agency is not at all like this. For Kant, no naturally occurring and empirically given condition such as a desire or inclination is ever itself a motive for action; a motive reflects an agent's "reasons for acting," or his decision, for example, to accept a desire as an adequate ground for action in light of his underlying principles and other relevant circumstances.[137]

This will seem surprising to English-language philosophers accustomed to using the term "motive" in its *prepurposive* sense. Does Kant imagine that animals which lack a "will" in the sense of decision-making or intention-forming agency but which have quite sophisticated desires do not have any *motives* strictly speaking? Even if such animals are naturally determined to act on their strongest desires, as Hobbes suggested of human beings, we can intelligibly speak of their motives to act.[138] So Herman's gloss makes sense only if we take "motive" in the more restrictive *purposive* sense, as the motivation on which the agent is actually trying to act in intentional action. Herman does not make this distinction explicitly, but she implies it:

> Kantian motives are neither desires nor causes. An agent's motives reflect his *reasons* for acting. An agent may take the presence of a desire to give him a reason, as he may also find reasons in his passions, principles, or practical interests. All of these, in themselves, are "incentives" (*Triebfedern*), not motives, to action. It is the mark of a rational agent that incentives determine the will only as they are taken up into an agent's maxim.[139]

Thus "incentives" (*Triebfedern*) are like "prepurposive motives" or Davidsonian pro-attitudes, except that they cannot simply combine with beliefs to cause intentions; they have to be adopted by the agent to become purposes.

This clarifies Kant's reasons for holding that heteronomous action is also spontaneous or free in the transcendental sense, since it is never directly determined by prepurposive desires along with instrumental beliefs. As Charles Nussbaum puts it, "Though heteronomous and conditioned, empirical practical reason is spontaneous, even if not, strictly speaking, autonomous."[140] Similarly, Allison argues that for Kant, it is essential to the very *concept* of a self that we actively form our purposes through the agency of the will: "To think of oneself as a rational agent requires presupposing that one is capable of projecting ends, acting on the basis of self-imposed general principles (maxims) and in light of objectively valid norms."[141]

For Kant, this implies that nothing moves us to intentional action until it is adopted or formed by the will as our purpose, and thus our intentions are always underdetermined by our prepurposive incentives; as Allison says, "It is not that one's desires are irrelevant to the determination of what one chooses to do (they are obviously the source of reasons to act); it is rather that they are not *sufficient* reasons."[142] Or, as we might better put it, our desires *become* practical reasons or motives for us only through spontaneous incorporation. In that weak sense, all the motivation that informs settled intentions is projective; decision is inherently projective in function.

The existential conception of willing that I defend does not need to endorse this Kantian claim that the "transfer" of prepurposive appetites or inclinations into intentional purposes *always* involves the projective adoption of a rule with normative content. In some cases, it might involve no more than tacit consent to act on immediate impulse (or utterly singular prescription, at best). But Kant's view that all human purposes adopted by the will in forming intentions are minimally projective includes one insight, namely, that various types of incentives, such as D1–D3 desires, and emotions involving such desires, in addition to drawing us toward objects or states of affairs, may *also* serve as the grounds for projecting various ends. For one thing, when a desire plays a negative role in our lives, this can be a reason to project its alteration or even its elimination.

But we also sometimes take the existence of certain desires as positive reasons for projecting desired ends or lending our volitional support to these desires. For example, when someone desires (D2) to obtain a college degree in order to have more opportunities to get higher-paying jobs, the fact that this end *draws her*, in combination with other considerations (such as the value of challenge), could give her grounds to *project* this end as well. In that case, she no longer merely desires it but also commits herself to this goal on the ground or basis of some more agent-neutral consideration such as "it is healthy to want a good job employing one's best talents." Through such resolve, she aims to gain admittance to a good college and to graduate as a means to her projected end. We could regard this as a case of overdetermination, in which the agent has two different types of motive to pursue this goal of graduating. It would be more Kantian to regard her as having only one purposive motive, which combines prepurposive desires and other considerations as its grounds.

2.3. *The Limits of Deontic Projection: Kant's False Dichotomy and Practical Identities*

If this reading is right, then the idea of projective motivation permeates Kant's account of moral agency. As Otfried Höffe summarizes, "Practical reason, as Kant says for short, means the capacity to choose one's action independent of sensible determinations such as instinct, desires, passions, and sensations of pleasure and pain."[143] But interpretative care is needed here, for there are two different senses in which actions might be motivated "independently" of impulses arising from our sensuous nature as an empirical being.

In the first sense, as we have seen, even *heteronomous* acts are independent of causation by desire, since they make inclinations into motives only by incorporating them voluntarily into the maxim on which our intention is based or by accepting the satisfaction of these impulses as our end.[144] In the second sense, which corresponds to Kant's notion of *autonomy*, to be independent requires that our intention to do A for end E not be derived even in this indirect fashion from inclinations for E or desires for happiness arising from our sensuous nature.[145] This reading agrees with Frederick Rauscher's argument that the "freedom" found in any empirical will involving "transcendental decision" is distinct from a stronger sense of freedom that applies to the will "only when it is following the moral law."[146]

Yet, as Rauscher says, Kant's equation of will with pure practical reason (which may or may not fully determine the subjective will) tends to obscure this distinction and to give the impression that only moral motivation is independent of natural inclination in any sense. Hence readers often think that for Kant, autonomy just *means* motivation by pure practical reason, and only autonomous motivation is "projective" in the weak sense of not being caused by prior desires for the ends of one's actions. Although this is not the correct reading, it accounts for the frequent misunderstanding that only action done for the sake of duty counts as "free."[147] Even Korsgaard, for example, writes that "the will must be autonomous: that is, it must have its own law."[148] This is right only if "autonomy" is used in its contemporary sense to mean "self-determined" (which is included in what Kant calls "spontaneity"), *not* if it simply means "motivated primarily by duty." For although the moral law ought to be our primary motive, we often act on conflicting nonmoral motives that still count as "autonomous" in the contemporary sense and that Kant would count as spontaneously accepted. The will may have the capacity for autonomy in Kant's sense, but it does not always employ it when voluntarily forming intentions or incorporating motives into its maxims.[149]

Even with this clarification, however, a serious problem remains in Kant's account of autonomous motivation. As Allison points out, it seems that some actions whose motive or grounding maxim is neither derived from desires nor from strictly moral considerations could be "strongly independent" of sensuous impulses.[150] This undermines Kant's "exclusivity postulate," that is, his implicit assumption that autonomy, or strong independence, occurs only in the form of *deontic* motivation, that is, adoption of a maxim because of its universalizable form. Yet this premise—that projective motivation responds exclusively to deontic grounds—underlies the key dichotomy in the elimination argument for the categorical imperative in

Groundwork I.[151] Likewise, this exclusivity postulate is presupposed in the argument by dilemma in the second *Critique*, which says that since the end or object of an intention or volition cannot determine the will in moral motivation, only the lawlike *form* of the maxim remains as a ground for the intentions formed by the dutiful will:

> Since the material of the practical law, i.e., the object of the maxim, cannot be given except empirically, and since a free will must be independent of empirical conditions (i.e., those belonging to the world of sense), and yet be determinable, a free will must find its ground of determination in the law, but independently of the material of the law. But besides the latter there is nothing in a law except the legislative form. Therefore, the legislative form, in so far as it is contained in the maxim, is the only thing which can constitute a determining ground of the [free] will.[152]

This passage says that if a motive is strongly independent of "empirical conditions" such as natural appetites or inclinations toward objects, then this motive can only be concerned with lawlike form. But the argument for this point seems to beg the question.

It is easier to see the problem if we translate Kant's dichotomy into my terms: he holds that an intended purpose can be volitionally *projected* only if an evaluation of its maxim's deontic form is the primary ground for its projection; all other intentions borrow their motive from *orektic* desire. Let us call moral motivation based on a rational evaluation of possible maxims by formal nonconsequentialist criteria of justice (such as universalizability tests) "deontic projection." In deontic projection, the agent intends some act A as a means to some intelligible first-order end E and forms this intention because doing A as a means to E is universalizable in his circumstances (or because it is just to all relevant parties, or for similar formal reasons). If the authority of such reasons for deontic projection rests on the implicit commitments essential to all free rational willing, then deontic projection may be considered a special case of projective motivation in which the grounding reasons are neither forward- nor backward-looking but rather transcendental.

This translation has the advantage of clarifying that "autonomy" for Kant is a concept distinct from the motive of duty; it signifies strong independence from the contents of prepurposive desires. But then why think that deontic projective motivation exhausts "autonomy" in this sense? Kant seems uncritically to take over the Franciscan dichotomy: if the motive isn't based on the *rectitude* of the act, then it is derived from appetite for the material goal. My own account diverges from Kant's on this crucial point: although deontic projection constitutes *one* important kind of projective motivation,[153] I hold that it is hardly the *only* kind. Kant deserves credit for being the first philosopher to try explicitly to formulate the notion of projective motivation, but he links its structure with the derivation of a formal principle of morality and hence he tends to suggest that *all* other motives aside from deontic ones are formally self-loving because appetitive in form, or even materially hedonistic. Kant's crucial error lies in supposing that the *only* alternative to the will's choosing first-order ends on the basis of their attractiveness to the agent's prepurposive inclinations is for the will to choose them on the transcendental basis of their universalizable form. By ignoring agent-transcending but non-deontic values, Kant repeats Scotus's mistake.

This exclusive focus on moral duty as the sole motive that escapes eudaimonist strictures prevents Kant from exploring in any detail the manifold other considerations that are neither objects of desire nor moral considerations in his strict formal sense, but which can supply grounds for projecting ends. Hence the world did not learn from Kant about projection as a broad type of motivation with subcategories that are *neither eudaimonistic nor essentially deontic*. In eliding the possibility of autonomous volitional projection without a formal deontic ground, Kant prevented the full potential of his break with the eudaimonist paradigms of Greek antiquity from being realized. The Scotusian-Kantian dichotomy in which every motive is assimilated either to justice or to happiness as our highest ends obscured the practical importance of many other non-egoistic, agent-transcending values that can ground volitional projection of practical ends.

Korsgaard effectively concedes this point in her account of "practical identities" that are formed in large part by particular commitments and social roles whose normative authority for us is *only partially* grounded in the deeper normative authority of our universally shared moral identity as persons capable of socially conditioned practical identities.[154] Such an identity functions as "a description under which you value yourself, a description under which you find your life to be worth living and your actions to be worth undertaking,"[155] which can include a wide variety of value-descriptions. As she says, "Part of my intention in invoking the concept of practical identity is to break down Kant's overly harsh . . . division between natural impulses that do not [automatically] belong to my proper self and rational impulses that do" (i.e., moral motives).[156] Practical identities occupy a middle ground; they consist in large part of commitments that are typically neither deontic in ground nor merely the expression or development of sense-appetites or other appropriative desires.

Yet Korsgaard still fails to provide any substantive account of the non-deontic grounds for such thick practical identities. She argues effectively that communitarians must recognize that the obligations arising from the particular ties and loyalties defining their selves-in-community ultimately depend on the universal importance to all human beings of developing such group memberships: "Someone who is moved to urge the value of *having* particular ties and commitments has discovered that part of their normativity comes from the fact that human beings need to have them."[157] But beyond this point, she uncritically accepts Sandel's picture of such socially constituted identities as radically contingent: "You are born into a certain family and community, perhaps even into a certain profession or craft. You find a vocation, or ally yourself with a movement. You fall in love and make friends."[158] The contrastive fact that *this* family, community, religion, craft, lover, friend, political identification, and so on, *rather than* others, are constituents of your practical identity seems to be largely a function of chance of birth and temperament, on this picture. Korsgaard admits (as her picture of human agency requires) that these ties and the projects and relationships they involve are open to critical reflection. But other than considerations of consistency and prudence, she offers no substantive reasons for endorsing and maintaining them or rejecting and changing them. The only objective requirement she mentions is the need for some conception of your practical identity, without which "you will lose your grip on yourself as having any reason to do one thing rather than another."[159]

Thus Christopher Gowans rightly complains that Korsgaard does not explain how practical identities can be fully normative rather than just morally permissible or "weakly normative":

> from the standpoint of the agent deliberating about how to live, a standpoint that is central to Korsgaard's entire argument, choices have to be made among the weakly normative practical identities that are possible [for us]. Moreover, in thinking about this, we do not ordinarily suppose that any such identity is as good as any other: we believe there is more to a good life than a morally permissible life.[160]

Gowans defends this claim with examples contrasting apparently important and challenging undertakings with relatively trivial activities aimed at entertainment. He concludes, naturally enough, that for practical identities to be more strongly normative, they must be not only morally permissible but also "truly valuable."[161] Without such an objective basis, "the will provides no critical force" in shaping our practical identities; they end up determined, like desire in Kant's account, "by contingent circumstances outside the will."[162] Gowans suggests that the solution is to look for "some objective understanding of values," perhaps grounded in a variety of realism, that can support the diverse kinds of identity-components that Korsgaard mentions.[163] He goes on to consider and critique Rawls's constructivist solution to this question in his theory of "good plans of life."[164]

In short, it appears that Korsgaard recognizes the lacuna in Kant's moral psychology but does not find within her own tradition the resources needed to fill it. This is not her fault. Two hundred years after Kant, moral philosophy and psychology have made many advances, but a detailed phenomenology of different grounds for projective motivation has never been rigorously worked out, precisely because Kant's approach led later philosophers to take it for granted that deontic projection is the *only* conceivable alternative to those moral psychologies that uphold both the strong erosiac thesis and the Transmission principle—for example, traditional eudaimonism, Hobbesian egoism, and Hume's mixture of egoistic and altruistic sentiments (which formed the basis for utilitarian moral psychology).

Today, ideas relevant to mapping out the rational bases for projective willing are scattered throughout discussions of other questions in moral psychology, normative theory, virtue ethics, and the theory of autonomy. The diverse realm of possibilities comprehended under the basic motivational structure of projection has remained largely uncharted because philosophers since Kant have assumed that any motivation supposedly transcending the erosiac structure of desire could only be what Habermas calls "the weak force" of impartial reasons, with its (frequently alleged) unappealing abstractness. As a result, it is also now commonly assumed that among systematic theories of ethical norms, the field is exhausted by Kantian deontology, utilitarianism (along with more complex forms of consequentialism), and neo-Aristotelian virtue ethics. Hence mainstream philosophy ignores the possibility of a rigorous existential agapē ethics that could be developed on the basis of a more adequate moral psychology recognizing the full range of projective motivation. This large preliminary task must precede any rigorous development of an existential theory of good lives.

I approach this problem in three stages. First, in the final section of this chapter, I survey questions about the freedom of deontic projection that are inevitably raised by Kant's account, as by Scotus's. Second, in the next chapter, I take up contemporary ideas in psychoanalytic theory that bring us to the question of what grounds human beings may find for projective motivation. Some possible negative grounds are indicated in the analysis of radical evil in chapter 10, but in subsequent chapters I am more interested in positive grounds for constructive and creative projects rather than grounds for destructive willing. Third, in Chapters 13 and 14, I argue that contemporary accounts of caring and their problems reveal the importance of objective axiological reasons for projective motivation. In sum, my defense of existential objectivism attempts to provide some answers to Gowans's pressing questions.

3. Projective Willing and Libertarian Freedom

3.1. *Projective Motivation Is Not Necessarily Libertarian*

Following Thomas Pink, in Chapter 3 I argue that the *ability to will* that is distinctive of persons is the capacity for second-order agency through which persons not only form intentions to perform first-order acts but sometimes in the process also generate new motivation for their intentions (or sustain existing motives) by projecting ends quite independently of pre-existing desires and incentives. Although I argue that such self-motivating agency always has reasons or grounds for positing the final ends on which it decides, I also suggest (contra the rationalist tradition) that projection is not an automatic result of practical reasoning and its evaluations. Given this, it might look as though my thesis is that projective motivation means *freely* giving oneself a practical end in some suitably libertarian sense of "freedom." The claim that Kantian moral motivation is a paradigm kind of projective motivation makes the question of freedom inevitable since it is linked so closely to the motive of duty in Kant's analysis. In this section, I briefly consider this issue.

It is not my thesis that the distinction between "desire" in the Greek sense and projective motivation is primarily a contrast between the involuntary formation of *orektic* desires and the *metaphysical spontaneity* of projective commitments. Although I think it is natural enough to interpret projective motivation in terms of some theory of "agent causation," as we see in Scotus and Kant, I am not defending any such metaphysical explanation here. Moreover, I have emphasized that we always project ends for ourselves for reasons that do not themselves depend for their status *as grounds* on the very same projective efforts of striving will. Contrary to the familiar Humean picture, we recognize the importance of various sorts of reasons and values—deontic, informally ethical, aesthetic, religious, and other personal or existential considerations—that transcend our existing set of motives, and the projection of new ends is never without some rationale or basis of these sorts.

The distinction between erosiac desires and projected motives is recognizable in *the way* this motivation is experienced, whatever metaphysical account we give of its emergence from prior reasons/grounds. For projective motivation does not involve the experience of attraction that we find in *orektic* motivation because of its different agent-content direction of fit (chap. 9, sec. 5). By itself, this seems to be compatible with an intentional account of agency according to which, given the grounds she had (including internal features of her character, such as personality, dispositions, and past commitments, as well as features of the world), a competent human agent could not have projected otherwise than she did.

Thus the phenomenological distinction I draw between important classes of motive might be explained by their having different sorts of causal origin; for example, one might hold that a projected motive is distinct from a desire (and from other types of motivating emotional states) because it is agent-caused, whereas desires and prepurposive passions typically are not. Similarly, a libertarian who does not explain how free choices count as *self-determined* by recourse to a concept of agent causation might still hold that in the case of projective motivation, the agent could have motivated herself otherwise. But my analysis does not depend on adopting either of these explanatory strategies, and it remains at least facially compatible with the possibility that even though we might never know how, our projective efforts of striving will could be determined by the initial state of the universe along with the laws of physics and laws governing any emergent properties at the neurochemical and mental levels. I hold that an analysis of the conditions of responsibility for character might show that such psychological determinism is incompatible with responsibility for the sort of person we will to be, but that requires a separate argument. In other words, the phenomenological analysis of projective motivation should not beg the question against every form of compatibilism; otherwise it cannot provide evidence for the metaphysical level of explanation.

Further phenomenological analysis of reflexive projections (in which we commit ourselves to establishing and maintaining certain first-order psychic states rather than others in our motivational character), along with an analysis of the conditions on responsibility for character, will probably support the hypothesis that the striving will generally has the capacity for a significant range of alternative identity-defining commitments, and that this *liberty* of the projective will[165] distinguishes it both from rational deliberation *per se* (which may not motivate) and from desiderative motivation.

Others have already taken steps in this direction. For example, Pink argues that the main reason for accepting a second-order agency account of the will is to recognize the ordinary intuition that we have alternate-possibilities freedom not only of action but also of the will or decision-making.[166] This freedom of the will is transferred to the level of action; we "always retain a continuing freedom not to act as we have decided," because "decision-making is a method of future action control which is essentially non-manipulative," or freedom-preserving.[167] Thus Pink holds that the will is not a deliberative but an "executive agency,"[168] since the intentions that it forms

> are quite distinct from practical judgments. One can form intentions which are not accompanied by any conviction that what is intended is desirable. One can form intentions which are not actually explained

by concomitant practical judgments at all. Nevertheless, the capacities for practical judgment and intention are still possessed together, because the core function of intention formation is to apply or execute our practical judgments about how we should act.[169]

In other words, the fact that one "can decide akratically" goes along with the fact that "It is very much more intuitive that we have freedom of decision than that we have a freedom of practical judgment."[170]

Similarly, in his own less sophisticated but still interesting treatment, the neo-Hegelian Rudolph Steiner holds that the most important question about freedom cannot even be framed unless we talk in terms of decisional agency and its motives for forming intentions:

> Should it matter to me whether I can do a thing or not, if I am *forced* by the motive to do it? The immediate question is not whether I can or cannot do a thing when a motive has influenced me [freedom of action] but whether only such motives exist as affect me with compelling necessity. . . . The question is not whether I can carry out a decision once made, but *how the decision arises within me*.[171]

On this basis, Steiner is skeptical, for example, of Eduard von Hartmann's model, which holds that the motives determining our decisions follow from the interaction of our environment with the individual "characterological disposition" that makes us who we are. Hartmann's theory is a precursor of contemporary psychological models of action as a function of "personality type" (clusters of dispositional traits) and situational variables. Such models leave us no liberty in the determination of our basic motives, whether or not we enjoy liberty in transferring these motives into specific intentions or in acting on them.

But it does not follow analytically from my existential conception of the will as a decision-making agency that forms intentions and projects new ends that the will normally enjoys libertarian freedom (in the agent-causal or leeway senses). That such freedom is required for the existential will to play its distinctive role in the ethos of a person requires a *further* argument going beyond the proleptic phenomenological analysis in this book. Such an argument will have to contend with the objection that if the will not only operates as executing agency in making decisions but also forms the primary *motive* for some intentions, libertarian freedom at this level would result in a regression that is unstoppable except by arbitrary choice. While I have tried to forestall this objection by introducing the idea of grounds for projective motivation (rooted in such aspects of personhood as the agent's historical acquisition of character and volitional dispositions, her moral reasoning, and the kinds of missions or purposes that she can find meaningful), it remains to be shown that grounds sufficient to avoid arbitrariness in projective motivation are compatible with libertarian freedom of the will.[172]

3.2. Allison and Ameriks on Freedom in Kant's Practical Philosophy

In support of this distinction between phenomenological and metaphysical levels of analysis in motivation theory, it will help to consider how far my reading of Kant is consistent with two others which address Kant's argument that human motivation is both projective and free in a libertarian sense that would be impossible if temporal nature (as a causally closed deterministic order) were the whole of reality. In his critique of novel interpretations by Henry Allison and Allen Wood, Karl Ameriks argues that although "Allison does a good job of showing how Kant himself was attached to this conception" of agent freedom,[173] neither Kant nor Allison provide sufficient grounds for this conception against compatibilist alternatives.

I briefly evaluate three aspects of Ameriks's argument in light of my analysis of projective motivation. First, I consider his argument against Allison's view (following Kant) that the conception of ourselves as agents who act for reasons requires us to conceive our acts as involving libertarian freedom. Second, I consider Ameriks's reasons for holding, *pace* Allison, that even if it could be established, the practical necessity of postulating libertarian freedom cannot stand by itself without prior metaphysical conditions (which, for Kant, are provided by an ontological rather than merely epistemic version of transcendental idealism). Third, I consider Ameriks's argument that actions that seem to us not to have desiderative motives could in fact still be determined by unconscious impulses (and this issue is divided into three subpoints). While I am largely sympathetic to Ameriks on all three issues, I raise questions about each in hopes of clarifying the kinds of freedom to which the existential analysis of striving will is committed.

I. Projective Agency versus Libertarian Spontaneity

Ameriks recognizes that Kant interprets transcendental freedom as leeway-liberty: as Rauscher puts it, "we must have been able to have chosen otherwise to be subject to praise or blame."[174] But Ameriks maintains that Kant's own argument that leeway-libertarian freedom is required by the common or ordinary understanding of conditions for moral responsibility is inadequate.[175] Thus he agrees with Allison about

> Kant's basic belief that, even if humans do universally seek pleasure, they are still rational and in some sense spontaneous agents who do

so because of maxims that they have a ground for in a non-mechanistic sense. We can even agree, as Allison also stresses, that Kant believes these maxims have an expression in our empirical, temporal being, and that, as Kant says, this expression takes the form of "laws of freedom" (A802/B830), e.g., about what ought to be done even for the sake of prudence. But we need *not* agree that the mere capacity to act according to such laws already defines us as having free agency in an *incompatibilist* sense.[176]

In my terms, Ameriks's point is that being moved by giving oneself maxims as opposed to being moved directly (or *"brutum"* in Kant's sense) by desires and impulses is to be "spontaneous" *only* in the sense of projective self-motivation, which does not necessarily imply libertarian freedom, either as leeway to project alternative maxims or as the power to initiate an uncaused causal sequence. That "on the Kantian theory of agency, one's maxims must always be not sheer givens but 'taken as one's own'"[177] only requires that maxims are willed responses to incentives and practical reasons that give them at least a minimal normative status.[178] Hence a general capacity to form intentions and project their ends does not by itself entail libertarian freedom. In fact, the notion of projective motivation helps clarify the crucial distinction between three different senses of freedom:

Sense 1. That intentions are not efficiently caused by prior motives, since these have to be incorporated into maxims (the weak projectivity of decision as executive agency);

Sense 2. That motivation is actively generated without derivation from prior desire (full projective motivation, which I follow Kant in labelling "autonomy");

Sense 3. That one acts as an ultimate cause in making decisions or adopting maxims (Kant's primary sense of "spontaneity" as "transcendental freedom").

Rauscher agrees with Ameriks that the moral law's arising *a priori* does not require the "will as power of decision to be transcendentally free. Kant fails to exclude the possibility that the moral law can motivate a determined will in inner sense within the confines of a deterministic nature."[179] Yet Rauscher does not fully distinguish the weak independence of executive agency and the strong independence of "autonomy" from both libertarian freedom and moral motivation. Thus he does not consider that an *a priori* ground or reason for acting may at least entail that the will possesses the power to transcend naturally given motives through projection of new ends. The gap in Kant's account is between "autonomy" in this sense and libertarian spontaneity or transcendental freedom.

Since Ameriks's critique was published, Allison has acknowledged that "the practical necessity of acting under the idea of [libertarian] freedom leaves in place the epistemic possibility that I am deluded in believing that I am acting," and this is a doubt that "cannot be exorcised by any theoretical means."[180] But though this correctly reflects Kant's view that the practical perspective cannot provide us with metaphysical knowledge, it does not explain why the idea of oneself as a rational agent capable of adopting maxims even requires one *to think of oneself* as free in an incompatibilist (rather than merely projective) sense. Which sense of freedom is required by the practical standpoint of agency itself? As Allison himself said in an earlier essay, "Why, after all, should the capacity to project ends, act on the basis of reasons, or even independently of desire, require the assumption of a mysterious contracausal faculty? Could it not rather be the outcome of a cognitive process that is completely explicable in naturalistic terms?"[181]

Allison's response to his own question is that libertarian freedom is not "introduced in an attempt to provide something like the best explanation for the 'phenomenon' of rational agency," but rather is *conceptually* essential to the idea of an agent who deliberates and chooses maxims.[182] This conception of ourselves as agents requires not only that our decisions are projectively independent of "passions or overwhelming urges" but *also* that they are "not . . . merely causal consequences of our antecedent states."[183] In effect, then, Allison claims that the first sense of freedom in my list, which is essential to the standpoint of agency, also entails freedom in the third sense. But since he does not explain why this additional condition follows from our volitional capacity to incorporate given desires or inclinations into the maxims on which we act, he leaves it unclear why libertarian freedom should be vital to our sense of ourselves as responsible agents.

As a result, Ameriks is right: Allison has not shown that the conditions of moral agency require us to regard ourselves as free in any libertarian sense. Like Kant, Allison has not given "adequate attention to the possibility of a sophisticated compatibilism."[184] This result supports my claim that the phenomenology of projective motivation does not include or directly require libertarian metaphysical premises. But it leaves the door open to other arguments that the standpoint of agency requires the idea that our decisions involve libertarian freedom. Consider the following sketch of an argument from the epistemology of modality:

The Modal Argument for Leeway-Liberty

1. The ability to see ourselves as projecting our purposes for deontic reasons is essential to the standpoint of moral agency [shown by Kant].

2. Deontic projection would be impossible if the significance of *moral* necessity were not accessible to us [shown by Kant].

3. Yet in order for the concept of moral necessity to have meaning for us, we must be able to apprehend the modal significance of counterfactual possibilities of action and motivation [from possible-worlds semantics of modal concepts].

4. Such counterfactuals would be epistemically inaccessible to us if we did not enjoy leeway-libertarian freedom [from?].[185]

5. Therefore the standpoint of moral agency requires libertarian freedom [1–4, hypothetical syllogism].

One might be able to defend the crucial fourth premise as follows: since awareness of moral necessity depends on seeing some volitionally possible motives in the circumstances as required, some as permitted, and some as not permitted, moral necessity would be unintelligible to us unless we were able to see both moral and nonmoral motives (and related intentions) as volitionally possible for us in a given circumstance—which is just to see ourselves as enjoying morally significant libertarian leeway. To see our different options only as physically or nomologically possible would be insufficient to provide a basis for our understanding of *moral* possibility and necessity, which concerns volitional possibilities, i.e. possibilities of motivation and action that are voluntarily accessible to us. If this is right, then we must at least see one moral and one nonmoral purpose (along with their different grounds) as volitionally possible for us whenever we see ourselves as responsible agents aware of moral modality, rather than simply as nodes in a causal nexus. In Allison's terms, our incorporation of a desire or incentive can be morally significant only if we act under the idea that we can also refrain from forming our actual intention or its maxim and form others instead.

Note that this proposal does not interpret premise 4 as a version of the ought-implies-can principle (although that would be another strategy). Rather, the idea is that the *epistemic* conditions of responsibility include being able to use the concepts of moral necessity and possibility, which in turn include the concept of volitional modality—and in particular the idea of nonactualized volitional possibilities.[186] Hence to satisfy the epistemic conditions of moral responsibility is to act under the idea of leeway-liberty: the standpoint of agency is incompatible with psychophysical determinism. This is only a sketch of a transcendental deduction of leeway-liberty from the concept of moral obligation, but it is clearly Kantian in spirit.

2. Practical and Metaphysical Standpoints

Along these lines, one might be able to rescue Kant's deduction of libertarian spontaneity from the basic "*faktum*" of moral obligation, on the premise that moral necessity has to be a significant concept for us. This transcendental deduction would still leave open the possibility that our concept of moral necessity, along with the "practical point of view" to which it is essential, is an illusion.[187] But what of Allison's neo-Kantian position that we can focus on how persons who take themselves to be moral agents must regard themselves and ignore the metaphysical question of whether their actions and motives *really are* undetermined by the past and the laws of physics and psychology? Ameriks argues convincingly that for Kant, even if we can demonstrate a practical requirement to regard ourselves as having liberty, this would not be enough if theoretical metaphysics did not leave open the *possibility* of undetermined agent-causation: "surely, any actual determining must itself be regarded ultimately as either caused naturally or not so caused. If nature is the closed system that Allison allows, then the latter option appears excluded, even if, as he claims, we 'can't help' but think ourselves free 'regulatively' in a practical respect."[188] Thus, for Kant, a practical requirement to regard ourselves as having liberty can have a grip on us only if we can independently establish that *ontologically* there are "two aspects" to reality, including a "timeless" noumenal aspect in which freedom can underlie spatiotemporal causal processes.[189] Ameriks clarifies this point in a more recent paper:

> Kant properly indicates that, at the common sense level, even positive unanimity [about our liberty] from the practical perspective could not save the claim of our freedom *if* it were to come into conflict with what can be established about nature, either by science or metaphysics (*KrV* Bxxviii–xxix); in this one respect there is precisely not a "primacy of practical reason." . . . The doctrine of transcendental idealism is especially significant for him here because it means not merely that there *might* be some "non-natural" room for uncaused causing; it shows that there always *must* be some such "room," given the antinomies that arise from taking determined spatio-temporal nature to exhaust reality.[190]

This is correct as an interpretation of Kant, and it also seems right more generally that if our knowledge of nature is not ultimately dependent on our practical perspective,[191] any alleged practical requirement to regard our actions and motives as involving liberty depends for its pragmatic force on its consistency with metaphysical and scientific knowledge.[192] It is less clear that we need a metaphysical *guarantee* that scientific evidence can never undermine the practical standpoint, as Kant thought. If there is a sound argument that responsibility entails a form of libertarian freedom incompatible with psychophysical determinism, then perhaps we can only say that our *a priori* knowledge of moral obligation entails that determinism must be false.[193]

3. Moral Responsibility Entails Projective Capacity

But in responding to Allison, Ameriks also challenges Kant's evidence that regarding ourselves as moral agents implies accepting our capacity for projective motivation (whether or not projective motivation would in turn require us to regard ourselves as free in an incompatibilist sense).[194] Ameriks says that despite Kant's "great reversal," his error in *Groundwork* III is similar to his mistake in the *Critique of Practical Reason*. In the former, Kant invalidly infers

> from the *psychological* absence of a particular causal *content* in one's intentions (i.e., one doesn't see that one is acting as the "mere" effect of a particular force [or desire]) to the *metaphysical* absence of any natural cause as the *efficient* ground of the act which has that content. Similarly, in moral contexts, the fact that certain maxims involve a rule whose content makes no essential reference to human desires still does not show that the actual adoption of such maxims . . . is not in fact caused by desires. . . . The compatibilist hypothesis is not that "rules" about sensible ends, or even beliefs about such rules, need be what cause our actions, but rather just that there can be desires present which in some, perhaps totally hidden, way are their ultimate efficient cause.[195]

Three things are suggested here. First, even if heteronomous and autonomous motivation appear to be alternatives of projective agency or existential willing, the experienced choice of either alternative may in fact be determined by hidden causes, for all we know: "The 'phenomenal' fact that the maxims permeating our moral life appear as 'self-imposed' rules hardly settles the question of whether this imposition is free of natural determinism."[196] Second, intentions grounded in pure moral considerations might not really be projective; they might have *desires* as their hidden causes. Third, Ameriks demands proof that viewing ourselves as agents who can respond to moral obligation requires that "there is moral autonomy in the sense of 'motivational independence' from all our needs as sensuous beings"[197] (i.e., full projective autonomy). In response to the first point, I agree that Kant's argument fails to rule out the possibility that decisions are really determined by hidden causes; moreover, the agent's *full grounds* for setting various ends and striving to reach them may be only imperfectly introspectable—even though deciding to intend a first-order act is itself something *done* for reason(s), and therefore the agent must always (however unreflectively) have something "in mind" in forming any intention—including those in which the end is posited projectively rather than suggested by prior desires. The agent must have in mind reasons or values that make her intended act voluntary under one set of descriptions (or intentional designations) and not under others.[198] But the sense of "having reason R in mind" in which this is true does not entail that the agent can successfully introspect R or identify all its contents as her reason for projecting some end that informs particular intentions. She may not even recognize that the intentions on which she acts are motivated by interest in this projected end.

In response to Ameriks's second point, it is important to note that not just any kind of hidden causation by desires can serve the compatibilist's purpose, for some will obviously undermine responsibility. If desires cause my intentions by way of deviant causal chains, or if my intentions are often caused by desires that I cannot recognize, which are therefore completely beyond the reach of critical reflection, then my intentions might not be sufficiently responsive to practical reasons for me to count as morally sane. Similar doubts would arise, I think, if all my apparent activities of projective motivation were illusory because my ends were all being set by unconscious desires.[199]

In any case, projective motivation is certainly not *compatible* with causation by hidden desires; for in such instances, I do not really act on a maxim whose *true* content is independent of prior desires. The projective status of a motive M aiming at end E requires that M is caused by an agentive process that can operate in nearby possible worlds where the agent lacks prepurposive desires for E. But I agree with Ameriks that this requirement does not entail that the agentive process that sets new goals and/or consolidates existing motivation must also be an *ultimate* cause involving transcendental freedom. The compatibilist is better off emphasizing this point rather than the suspicion that hidden desires may be operative everywhere or that projective motivation may always be illusory.

Moreover, Ameriks has not shown any incoherence in distinguishing the psychological grounds of decision and/or projective end-setting from their *efficient cause* in the classical sense; the reasons and values one has in mind (introspectably or not) when coming to commit oneself to some moral principle, political cause, professional excellence, or any final end whose significance transcends one's material interests may *rationalize* one's volitional resolve to strive for these life goals without *causing* or necessitating the psychological processes involved in this striving. Kantians and existentialists may regard the generation of this volitional effort in our psyche as simply uncaused (in the sense of natural event-event causation), although it is an activity of the same executive capacity that makes decisions;[200] or they may regard projective willing as *agent*-caused, as suggested above.[201]

As Allison suggests, holding that our decisions and acts are not "causal consequences of our antecedent states" is *not* to "deny that there is any connection between an agent's antecedent condition or underlying character and the ensuing action, but it is to deny that the connection can be understood in *strictly causal terms*."[202] Choice need not be indifferent between the agent's options for it to involve a casual "leap." Of course, if decisions and projective motives are not "caused" in this nomological sense it remains possible that they can be determined in some nonphysical way by noumenal states of affairs—for example, our fixed atemporal character, or divine decree, or God's choice of the maximal compossible set of monads that make up the actual world, and so on.

I have not tried to rule out such Leibnizian scenarios; although I hold that the conditions of moral responsibility for one's volitional character require libertarian freedom at least in the higher-order will (understood in existential terms as the capacity for reflexive projection of ends concerning our own motives or first-order dispositions), I do not defend that claim here.[203] However, in response to Ameriks's third suggestion, I do defend the weaker claim that the practical standpoint requires us to see ourselves as capable of projective motivation in the formation of intentions whose purposes are independent of prior motives that we did not actively shape. For this follows directly by the ought-implies-can principle if Kant is right about the pure content of our moral obligations and their universal scope of application (as I argue in sec. 2.2 above).[204]

Finally, even if the compatibilist were right that moral responsibility for a given act does not require anything more than that its maxim is freely adopted in the first sense (i.e., decision as an act distinct from desiring/ believing), there might still be *other* reasons for positing libertarian freedom. For example, our capacity to form intentions standardly seems to superintend multiple and often conflicting motives: if we can adopt maxims with either autonomous or heteronomous motives (or both), this suggests *leeway* in deciding which first-order intentions to form and for what reasons. Since even an act required by duty may be chosen for self-interested reasons, the guidance of intentions by maxims seems to include the practical alternative of heteronomous or autonomous motivation—even if responsibility did not require such alternatives.

Kant's position in the second *Critique* reflects this: he "tries to show that our absolute freedom must be clear from (and solely from) our commitment to maxims that involve (*either through acceptance or rejection*) specifically moral ends."[205] Ameriks is right that the projection of either kind of motive by itself does not imply leeway-liberty, but the phenomenological evidence that motives of both kinds seem available in the same choice circumstance does lend support to the thesis that it is part of the standpoint of agency in general for human beings to regard themselves as at liberty to act on motives with different moral worth. This kind of evidence will be crucial for any further analysis of the freedom-conditions of responsibility.

Conclusion

As explained in the preface, establishing libertarian freedom as a condition of moral responsibility in general (and of responsibility for character in particular) is an essential component of an existential theory of personhood. However, a phenomenology of the values to which the striving will can respond together with an account of how the will responds to them by projecting ends and motivating the agent's pursuits must precede any viable argument for existential liberty. For until we know what *willing* is, how can we understand freedom of the will? Hence on the existential approach, an understanding of the will rooted in reflections on human motivation in everyday experience is prior to any argument that liberty is a condition of moral responsibility. In particular, we have to understand the role of striving will in shaping the agent's practical identity through cares and loves and the way that devotions central to one's personal ethos generate a unified sense of one's life as meaningful or worthwhile. These themes are explored in existential psychoanalysis (chap. 12) and in contemporary moral psychology (chaps. 13 and 14).

12

Existential Psychology and Intrinsic Motivation: Deci, Maslow, and Frankl

Overview. This chapter surveys developments in psychological theory that support the existential account of projective motivation and applies the distinction between targetable and by-product goods to these debates. It critiques recent theories of intrinsic motivation and self-actualization on this basis and interprets Viktor Frankl's "logotherapy" as a projective theory. It also applies the goal versus by-product distinction to the problem of self-regarding attitudes such as various types of "self-esteem." The discussions are not technical and connect familiar themes in psychoanalysis with the work of well-known philosophers such as Rawls, Noddings, and Frankfurt.

I. Twentieth-Century Psychological Theories of Motivation

The debate we have traced between egoistic, eudaimonist, and existential theories of human motivation can also be found in twentieth-century psychology and psychoanalysis, where we now find support for the existential model of striving will. I will focus in this chapter on only a few among several areas of important work in contemporary experimental psychology. For the theories behind these experimental approaches often uncritically take over the Transmission principle and focus mainly on the etiology of long-recognized states of prepurposive motivation—for example, whether altruistic or sympathetic feelings could be evolved responses. As Edward Deci says, the fundamental disagreements between "metatheories" guiding different empirical methodologies (for example, concerning whether inner experiences are merely epiphenomenal or play a causal role in voluntary action and whether human action is ultimately determined or involves liberty) result from philosophical hypotheses that cannot be directly tested.

"The research does not substantiate the assumptions" that constitute the metatheory but simply coheres with the framework used to interpret the results.[1]

Deci provides a useful summary of the main approaches to motivation in twentieth-century psychology,[2] which include:

I. Mechanistic Theories which hold that behavior is a direct response to stimuli, while thoughts, feelings, and choices are epiphenomenal, playing no causal role in behavior.

(A) Early psychoanalysis (Freud, Adler), which held behavior to be caused primarily by unconscious drives, conscious desires, and environmental stimuli.
(B) Extreme behaviorism (Watson, Skinner), which ignores conscious processes and intentionality altogether.
(C) Behaviorist drive theory (Hull), which focuses on internal associations between stimuli and behavioral responses.

II. Organismic Theories which hold that behavior is primarily caused by conscious internal processes, including cognitive and affective states, and thus generally counts as voluntary action.

(A) Affect arousal theories (McClelland, Young, Atkinson, Clark, and Lowell), which hold that behavior follows quasi-mechanistically from positive or negative affects or feelings caused by past experiences and aroused again by similar environmental cues.
(B) Cognitive theories (Vroom, Hunt, etc.), which hold that actions are caused by choices that are determined in turn by beliefs and desires (or in general, pro-attitudes).
(C) Humanistic psychology (Buhler and Allen, Maslow, Laing), which adds free will to a cognitive picture of motivation, with a special emphasis on personal experience.

To clarify their similarities and differences, it may also be helpful to picture the relation between these theories on a two-dimensional table:

Motivation Theories	Noncognitive Causes/Motives	Cognitive Causes/Motives
Nonconscious Causes of Behavior	Extreme behaviorism (Skinner); James-Lange theory of emotion	
Unconscious Causes	Early Freudian psychoanalysis	
Conscious Causes	Drive theory (Hull); Affect Arousal theory	Cognitive theories; Humanistic theories

In this chapter, I will be interested primarily in ideas from theories in the bottom-right cell of the table, since the others proceed from assumptions now largely rejected in philosophical action theory (chap. 3). When they allow conscious states to play a causal role in generating behavior, these theories also tend to be absolutely egoistic. For example, affect-arousal accounts imply that all motivation flows ultimately from the drive to maximize positive feeling and minimize negative feeling,[3] as per the reward-event theory (see chap. 5, sect. 2.2). Similarly, Hull's system conceives the telos of all desire as physiological "equilibrium," with drives as disturbances in this equilibrium that have to be reduced by behavior. In this version of behaviorism, "Drives activate stimulus-response associations, and drive reduction strengthens stimulus-response associations," as the organism learns what kind of behavioral responses will reduce the unpleasant feeling of the drive by returning it to homeostasis.[4] On this theory, actions motivated by emotions such as pity would have to be regarded as energized by the agent's desire to quell his own distress. Pure or non-egoistic motives are ruled out *a priori*.

The dominant influence of such egoistic models is obvious in Douglas Mook's leading textbook on motivation in contemporary experimental psychology, which lists as main topics all the following:

- under "Biological Motives," hunger, thirst, sex, aggression, homeostatic feedback mechanisms involved in these motives, cultural and cognitive processes related to these, and the neurological and chemical realization of these states in our nervous system;
- under "Energy, Arousal, and Action," theories of habit and drive, and Freud on arousal and drives;
- under "Acquired Drives and Rewards," theories of avoidance conditioning, Pavlovian conditioning, imprinting in early infancy, and opponent-process theory;
- under "Reinforcement Theory," the behaviorist account of operant conditioning; rational decision theory, its relations to criminology, and problems with maximizing, and so on.[5]

It is only in the last quarter of Mook's textbook that we come to issues closer to the central problems of philosophical psychology, including the cognitive processes involved in human motivation (e.g., reducing cognitive dissonance); theories of emotions as motivating states; love and altruism as forms of "social motivation" and "attachment"; and finally a brief look at "long-term goals."[6] As this indicates, the origin of the most important motives in human psychology—those most central to the *ethos* of a person—

has until recently been addressed only in post-Freudian psychoanalysis and humanistic psychology, while more "scientific" approaches focused on motive processes that human beings share with other animals. As Joel Kupperman points out, there is so little good experimental work on "character" and other key concepts in moral psychology (such as ultimate ends) because it is extremely difficult to conduct experiments in these areas without violating the rights of test subjects or conducting expensive and logistically challenging longitudinal studies of individuals over many years.[7] Even when experiments can be done, they either use animal models or limit test subjects to college students, and the experiments often proceed by way of collecting stories, diaries, and so on (which must then be parsed according to subjective criteria). Thus the more speculative contributions of psychoanalysis and humanistic psychology have been able to contribute more to literary and philosophical debates about the content and sources of ultimate human motives.

To illustrate this point, consider one recent example in the post-Freudian psychoanalytic tradition. A scholarly workbook for therapists using "ego-strengthening" techniques, including scripts for suggestion under hypnosis, relies on a conception of the "ego" as "the agent or organizer" of the self that is capable of what the authors call "inner strength."[8] They never mention the word "will"—an example of the lingering effects of Freud's effort to dispense with the will. But they start from a notion of "inner strength" which they take to be "part of the vernacular of the common man," referring to a "psychic structure created through ordinary maturation and development."[9] They attribute extraordinary powers to this "structure," which their primary script describes to the patient as feeling "like the very center of your being."[10] In particular, the script suggests that

> when you are in touch with this part of yourself, you will be able to feel more confident with the knowledge that you have within yourself all the resources you really need to take steps in the direction that you wish to go . . . to be able to set goals and to be able to achieve them.[11]

This part of the psyche described here as "inner strength" obviously plays the roles that I have attributed to the will as the capacity for projective motivation. To the extent that focusing patients' attention on this source of willpower and resolve helps them gain confidence in themselves and overcome obstacles, it is a testament to the existential theory. Yet these authors start from a theoretical framework that obscures any deeper understanding of what this faculty of "inner strength" really is.[12]

2. From Drive Theories to Intrinsic Motivation

This example illustrates how far some psychoanalytic conceptions of motivation have come from Freud's basically Hobbesian model (with Helmholtzian mechanisms). Psychoanalysis has been influenced by developments in empirical psychology, starting around the middle of the twentieth century, spurred by recognition that many animals have an innate interest in exploration of novel spaces and objects.[13] Such motives do not seem to be "drives" according to the classic erosiac conception, that is, energies seeking reduction of some physiological "deficit" in a "consummatory" experience.[14] For, among other things, curiosity is often open-ended (aiming at no particular object) and can even motivate activities that seem to *increase* or stimulate it (such as seeking novel stimuli).[15] As we have seen, an agent cannot be motivated by erosiac desire to induce a motivating lack or deficit in herself. Yet evidence shows that human beings may seek new experiences even at the cost of increasing anxiety and dissonance with current cognitions.[16] Hence, as the Wallachs note:

> A great deal of what we want and strive for has always seemed to some psychologists just too remote from sex or aggression to be accounted for in terms of Freudian drives. In the early days of psychoanalysis, Jung felt this way about strivings for religious values, for meaning, and for self-realization; Adler felt this way about strivings for power and superiority.[17]

They also note Gordon Allport's point that activities originally motivated by basic drives may "become ends in themselves" for us, and Asch's thesis that "certain forms of experience and activity—for example, music, dancing, and painting—are simply interesting or desirable in their own right from the start."[18] Much the same might be said for activities involved in other practices, from chess to ecological science, even when their pursuit becomes difficult.

The inadequacy of Freud's gray-tone palette to produce the colorful array of actual motives we find operating in human experience first became apparent to many psychoanalysts in Hartmann's argument that young children do many things that function to develop their motor, speech, and cognitive capacities without trying to satisfy basic needs for food and comfort. Hartmann saw the "energy" used by the "ego" to motivate such activities as coming from itself, not from the Id.[19] This clearly moves us toward the Aristotelian idea that beings tend to enjoy the development and exercise of their natural capacities in activities with no (other) utility. As Piaget noted of the infant's experimentation with objects, "The activities tend to be engaged in and enjoyed precisely when they are just in the process of being mastered or of producing new and interesting effects—circumstances in which they afford more challenge and provocation."[20]

Of course, I am not suggesting that very young children exercise their will to self-motivate; infants have not developed the rational capacities to recognize values as reasons for projecting new ends. Since all psychologically healthy children who are given the opportunity do engage in such play, the motivation for it is both innate and instinctual (nor is this instinct limited to human beings). Kierkegaard's aesthetic young man describes it as the drive to avoid "boredom" and says that "As long as children are having a good time, they are always good."[21] Although seeking relief from boredom by "the interesting" is a movement away from a kind of stasis, this is not enough to make it projective. Still, although our instinctive aversion to tedium is not a willed motive, its goal becomes harder to target directly the older and more reflectively aware one becomes: for to succeed, we have to forget that we are trying to avoid boredom or (better) stop trying to avoid it and start exercising our volitional power to set new goals worthy of our developed capacities.

Hence the baby's play instinct points indirectly to the latent projective power of the will, for both enable the human being to act on motives that do not seek their own reduction. Activity motivated as willed striving differs from the infant's non-erosiac play motive in actively seeking to sustain or enhance the motivation involved. But their kinship helps explain why, as I suggested in discussing the practices (chap. 8, sec. 5), human persons tend to find value simply in novelty and in an activity's being challenging (in the sense of requiring skill and sustained effort), whatever its other effects. Mild novelty and challenges of the most rudimentary sort are instinctively enjoyed by the toddler, but the adult can recognize in complex forms of novelty and challenge a set of values that at least *contribute* to making the relevant ends worth willing for their own sake. Even if these values are rarely sufficient by themselves to ground projective motivation, they are ones to which projective striving can respond. At this stage, they are not sought simply for *amusement*, nor just as arbitrary distractions to save us from boredom, but rather because setting ourselves to work on challenging problems and novel tasks (even when we have no prior need for their goals) is our natural volitional function, and we find its exercise inherently meaningful—at least when applied to goals or objects that are important apart from their mere difficulty (e.g., because they produce recognizable goods in some way).[22]

This point also applies to the development of personal identity in social relationships. As Alan Gilbert notes in his study of individual selfhood in democratic theory, an Aristotelian-Hegelian influence is found "in the modern psychoanalytic conception of the self offered by Heinz Kohut, Harry

Guntrip, and Alice Miller." For "[i]n contrast to the misguided instinctual determinist strain in Freud's view, Kohut focuses on the social formation of the self in the contexts of its early relationships."[23] He finds that even persons who have suffered deprivation in childhood can form healthy "integrated" selves via the practices: for instance, "through participation in intrinsic goods—painting, music, friendship, nurturing and the like."[24] As the Wallachs also recognize, social motives aimed at direct contact with others, participation with them in activities, and belonging to groups can be more powerful than primary biological drives—even in nonhuman mammals.[25] After reviewing experimental evidence, they suggest the possibility of motives that point beyond the agent's own good:

> Perhaps concern for other individuals also exists without having to be based on the biological needs or competence development of the animal or person showing the concern. Typically, when we are attached to people, we not only want to be near them and to interact with them, but we also seem to care about their welfare. Perhaps such caring is also real and direct, rather than necessarily derivative from one's own needs and welfare.[26]

On this view, care for others is not simply driven by a need to reduce one's own empathetic distress, since this reduction is only a concomitant effect of caring. This idea is hardly surprising to philosophers, but it was a difficult step for a human science so dominated by Hobbesian assumptions about motivation.

This crucial break from Hobbes, Freud, and behaviorist drive theories led psychologists back to the old idea of "intrinsic motivation," which Mook summarizes as "performance motivated by pleasure in the task itself, rather than by external rewards offered for performing it. Think of the difference between a man who works on a car as a hobby, for the joy of it (intrinsic), rather than as a job (extrinsic)."[27] Unsurprisingly, the leading twentieth-century proponent of this idea, Edward Deci, drew explicitly on Aristotle's thesis that human beings are intrinsically motivated to pursue knowledge or understanding:

> Intrinsically motivated activities are ones for which there is no apparent reward except the activity itself. People seem to engage in the activities for their own sake and not because they lead to an extrinsic reward. The activities are ends themselves rather than means to an end. This . . . serves quite adequately as an operational definition of intrinsic motivation.[28]

However, one problem with this definition is that it does not distinguish agent-transcending from egoistic ends. If I take a walk in the park simply to enjoy being outdoors and take in some scenery, that activity is pleasurable in itself and so would count as intrinsically motivated, on this definition. So would any activity that directly produces some kind of first-order pleasure or entertainment.

Yet Deci clearly has in mind the kind of higher aspirations that Maslow included within "self-actualization."[29] He and colleague Richard Ryan now present "self-determination theory" (SDT) as an account of roughly the same phenomena that I have described as resulting from striving volitional engagement:

> The fullest representations of humanity show people to be curious, vital, and self-motivated. At their best, they are agentic and inspired, striving to learn; extend themselves; master new skills; and apply their talents responsibly. That people show considerable effort, agency, and commitment in their lives appears, in fact, to be more normative than exceptional.[30]

Thus Deci and Ryan describe intrinsic motivation as sustained by agentic effort and as including "great volitional persistence."[31] Although they do not identify "the will" as a *cause* of such motivation, they associate intrinsic motivation with a higher level of voluntariness, "a feeling of volition that can accompany any act" felt to emanate from the self rather than from external pressures.[32] Thus they relate intrinsic motivation directly to personal autonomy (although they use the term "authenticity" instead): "Comparisons between people whose motivation is authentic (literally, self-authored or endorsed) and those who are merely externally controlled" show the former to "have more interest, excitement, and confidence, which in turn is manifest both as enhanced performance, persistence, and creativity."[33] The existential account would explain this as a result of the inherent autonomy and resilience of projected motives.

It is also apparent that Deci and Ryan limit the use of "intrinsic" to *certain kinds* of final ends whose value is recognized independently of any material contribution to the agent's good (whereas if "intrinsic" just meant "final," then any voluntary or goal-directed action would have to involve *some* intrinsic motivation, as Aristotle argued). "Intrinsic aspirations" include "goals such as affiliation, personal growth, and community" or relationships, while "extrinsic aspirations" aim at things such as "wealth, fame, and image"[34] that constitute "tangible rewards."[35] For example, Ryan and Deci contrast acting "from a sense of personal commitment to excel" with "fear of being surveilled" or being bribed.[36] Thus "intrinsic" and "extrinsic" ends in SDT largely map onto MacIntyre's better-defined concepts of "internal" and "external" goods, rather than onto the universal distinction between final and nonfinal goals, as Ryan and Deci sometimes suggest.[37] We see this in more substantive definitions of intrinsic motivation as a "natural inclination towards assimilation, mastery, spontaneous interest, and exploration." An intrinsically motivated agent seeks out challenging and novel goals even in the absence of specific material rewards.[38] Given that the intrinsic-extrinsic contrast in this literature really marks an (intuitive) distinction among different kinds of *final ends*, what is meant by "intrinsic motivation" would be better captured in the existential concept of projective motivation.

However, this conceptual problem in "self-determination theory" is rooted in what I see as a deeper explanatory error that leads Deci and Ryan to construe "intrinsic" or internal goods in an agent-relative way. Although I regard their new, humanistic approach within the family of cognitive theories as more insightful than any other model found in empirical psychology today, SDT still does not recognize the projective function of the human will, because its explanation of the "psychological basis of intrinsic motivation" retains too much of the structure of the drive theories that SDT was meant to replace. Deci recognized that his initial operative definition of intrinsic motivation did not contain a causal explanation[39] so he sought to develop one that would subsume earlier drive-theoretic explanations ranging from "secondary reinforcement," "optimal stimulation," "optimal incongruity" or dissonance, "optimal arousal" and "the reduction of uncertainty,"[40] to drives for "achievement" or excellence, self-actualization, and "meaning" (conceived by Maddi as a need to symbolize, imagine, learn, judge critically, distinguish oneself as an individual and become self-reliant).[41]

Deci's own proposal is most indebted to White's concept of "effectance motivation," conceived as the drive to "competence and efficacy,"[42] which includes Kagan's "motive for mastery" in relation to high standards and the "motive to reduce uncertainty" or be in control of one's fate.[43] To this complex idea of competence, Deci adds both a basic social drive for affiliation with significant others and an intrinsic concern for "self-determination" or autonomy, in the broad sense of acting from an internal locus of control.[44]

Thus Deci and Ryan now describe SDT as "an organismic metatheory that highlights the importance of humans' evolved inner resources for personality development," based on empirical research identifying these three "innate psychological needs" as universal and their satisfaction as essential to normal growth and development of human personality.[45] Much as Aristotle sought to embrace all motivation in the desire for happiness, Ryan and Deci now explain all intrinsic motivation as differentiating out of *formally self-regarding* needs, or what I would call quasi-drives: "We have thus proposed that the basic needs for competence, autonomy [or self-determination], and relatedness must be satisfied across the span of life for an individual to experience an ongoing sense of integrity and well-being or 'eudaimonia.' "[46]

This explanation results from a dialectical subsumption of earlier drive theories (such as Hull's) that nevertheless leaves intact their most basic (and commonly invisible) premises; namely (1) that there must be *some* reward or perceived benefit to the agent involved in causing all motivation; and (2) that the prospect of this benefit explains the energy involved in intrinsically motivated activities, since no activity can *literally* be its own reward.[47] It follows from these assumptions that intrinsic motivation exists because of the goods that it tends to produce for its agent, which SDT identifies as psychic development, autonomy, competence and competence-based security, fulfillment, excitement, and so on. In other words, SDT starts from the erosaic concept of our formal telos (see chap. 6, sec. 3), and interprets the substance of that telos as including a triad of innate and irreducibly psychological needs, the drives toward which cause intrinsic motivation to arise (and eventually to be channeled into particular pursuits, projects, and relationships).

The eudaimonist form of SDT is evident in another article, in which Deci and Ryan say that it is part of the natural function or "adaptive design of the human organism to engage in interesting activities, to exercise capacities, to pursue connectedness in social groups, and to integrate intrapsychic and interpersonal experiences into a relative unity."[48] They equate performing this natural function, or attaining our natural telos, with psychological health or holistic well-being: the Hullian definition of the three psychological needs as "organismic necessities" assumes "a fundamental human trajectory toward vitality, integration, and health."[49] This seems to imply that a fundamental desire for eudaimonia motivates the activities that fulfill these needs. This is explicit in Deci's first book, which replaces his initial operative definition with the following formula: "Intrinsically motivated behaviors are behaviors which a person engages in *to feel* competent and self-determinated."[50] Yet Deci and Ryan now acknowledge that an intrinsically motivated pursuit

> does not have to be aimed at need satisfaction *per se*, it may simply be focused on interesting activity or an important goal if they are in a context that allows need satisfaction. However, if need satisfaction is not forthcoming while they are acting, nonoptimal or dysfunctional consequences typically follow.[51]

This phrasing is ambiguous: it suggests that satisfaction of one (or more) of the three basic psychological needs is sometimes only a by-product of some intrinsically motivated activity A; but it adds the caveat that if this contribution to the agent's well-being does not soon follow, then the intrinsic motivation for A will be counterreinforced and will wane. Thus "A direct corollary of the SDT perspective is that people will tend to pursue goals, domains, and relationships that allow or support their need satisfaction."[52] This turns SDT into a formally egoistic model like Aristotle's: activities not motivated by acquisitive or consumptive appetites are still driven by the agent's own need for fulfillment. Yet this seems to be refuted by the inherent resilience of intrinsic motives, their tendency to be sustained even through "dry spells" where the usual fulfillment fails to follow.

3. An Existential Reinterpretation of Intrinsic Motivation

I argue here that intrinsic motivation is better understood in terms of projective striving that is not formally egoistic in structure. Carefully specifying the role of by-product fulfillment will lead us to a fuller articulation of our existential telos, as an alternative to the three quasi-drives identified in the Deci-Ryan model. To clarify this alternative, let us return to the example of character-friendship as a type of intrinsic motivation.

One leading account of friendship (which SDT includes in the intrinsic good of relatedness) helps illustrate the Deci-Ryan view that agent-related benefits of intrinsic motivation are crucial to their continuance. Neera Badhwar argues that even when benefits to the agent are an "unintended result" of an activity as Bishop Butler said, "it may well be that the tacit expectation of self-benefit—based on past experience, or even just on the natural teleology of our biological constitution—is necessary for sustaining the activity."[53] Applying this idea, she argues against Nygren that for the object I contemplate in love to "further evoke the love" rather than quench it, the happiness I derive from the contemplation "must serve to perpetuate the love of the other who is its source."[54] Alternatively, we might explain this idea in terms of what Korsgaard, following C. I. Lewis, calls "inherent value," which is "the value that characterizes the object of an intrinsically good experience."[55] In these terms, Badhwar's claim is that we can perceive the inherent value of a person who is loveable for herself only in enjoying or delighting in that perception.[56]

While it is plausible that delight and similar agent-related benefits act as *reinforcers* for end-friendship and other types of intrinsic motivation, it is as plausible that my friend's delighting me is an essential *component* of the intrinsic value I see in her—or is an integral part of what I love or am devoted to. In general, the staying power or commitment that is characteristic of intrinsic motivation is difficult to square with final ends that have agent-related benefits built into them, because joy is not always present in the activities explained by intrinsic motivation. In fact, the greatest sense of fulfillment or meaning often requires persistence through dry spells (both initially and later on), during which we still recognize the value of our goals and continue to strive for them. Sometimes the usual joy in loving our friend is missing; sometimes the intrinsically worthy task involves so many negatives that the real sense of satisfaction in its pursuit comes only after a long time of sustained devotion without reinforcing delight.

That many people are not stoical enough to pursue such "thankless" but valuable activities for long enough to fully appreciate them is no argument for the Aristotelian account. The situation is similar when the agent-transcending goal of intrinsic motivation is an objective standard of excellence rather than the qualities of some figure or the good of some person. As Albert Bandura and Dale Schunk suggest:

> By making self-satisfaction conditional on a certain level of performance, individuals create self-inducements to persist in their efforts until their performances match internal standards. Both anticipated satisfactions for matching attainments and the dissatisfactions with insufficient ones provide incentives for self-directed actions.[57]

But notice that these "inducements" are *generated by* appropriating some conception of excellence as one's personal standard; on pain of circularity, the volitional activity of setting and maintaining the standard cannot itself be motivated by the anticipated satisfaction of a job well done. Once again, this hoped-for delight can act as a reinforcer only *after* the goal of meeting one's standard is projected. This reinforcer can be necessary for continued pursuit of the goal beyond some point, because the agent can tolerate only so much frustration in the pursuit of the relevant kind of excellence. This is why "A sense of personal efficacy in mastering challenges is apt to generate greater interest in the activity." Thus motivation training has to (a) get the agent to see the intrinsic value in a goal; and (b) tolerate enough lack of success in pursuing it to get to the point where some effectiveness can be experienced.[58]

Hence the existential account of intrinsic motivation does not require that the agent-related by-product goods remain motivationally irrelevant or play *no* supporting role. On the contrary, such benefits may often help the will sustain its efforts by providing some of the necessary psychic preconditions for volitional striving or outward-looking cares (since a miserable agent may have trouble keeping volitional focus). By-product satisfactions may also provide personal reasons for valuing the caring process that support and complement the agent's independent reasons for valuing her outward goals. For the striving will, though, these agent-related and process-based reasons for pursuing goals with agent-transcending value are not themselves attractors or erosiac motives; the vital functions of by-product benefits remain *dependent* on the primary operation of the striving will in projecting ends without regard to self.

Hence the existential account can agree with Deci and Ryan that major parts of human happiness depend on the by-product goods of intrinsic motivation, or as they put it: "a critical issue in the *effects* of goal pursuit and attainment concerns the degree to which people are able to satisfy their basic psychological needs *as* they pursue and attain their valued outcomes."[59] We should therefore design our schools, trades and professions, civil society, and family life to support and encourage the inherent human tendency to develop intrinsic motivation in various domains of life. But we should remember that these effects emerge from pursuing certain kinds of "valued outcomes" for their own sake and *not merely as occasions* for developing competence, relatedness, and autonomy. Thus it is not these "spiritual" needs that initially "give goals their psychological potence."[60] Rather, the pursuit of potential goals can meet these needs only if these goals have recognizable agent-transcending values independent of these needs, for the sake of which the agent can posit or set them as her own.

This central tension in the Deci-Ryan theory of intrinsic motivation results from trying to account for non-drive-like motives in an explanatory framework that still assumes the Transmission principle: *all motives* on which people act, whether learned or innate, are originally prepurposive, can compete with one another prior to intention-forming choices, and thus may or may not be acted on. SDT pictures intrinsic motivation as already *there* in the psychic needs, nascently waiting to be expressed and differentiated, rather than as generated by the existential will—the will conceived as an innate *capacity* to generate various types of intrinsic motivation. The SDT model of prepurposive intrinsic motivation thus implies that the basic triad of innate psychological drives interacts with environmental variables to *determine* the development of particular intrinsic motives in the individual. But if that were true, intrinsic motivation could not play the autonomy-making role that the authors attribute to it, for it would arise without the individual's agency.

From the beginning, Deci did distinguish the motive structure of the quasi-drives for competence or effectiveness and autonomy from that of Hullian physiological drives. He notes White's point that "Effectance motivation is persistent in that it is always available"[61] and not slaked or reduced by success in the pursuits that it motivates. Hence in "intrinsically motivated behavior, however, the goal will be attained and the behavior will be rewarded, but the need will not be reduced. Rather, the need is ever-present, so it will remain, and other goals will be set."[62] Yet surely this would be an infinitely frustrating process, like Sisyphus rolling his stone or

Plato's leaky sieve, rather than a fulfilling one if competence and autonomy were really motivating "needs." To explain why intrinsic motives do not aim at goals that reduce the intrinsic motivation, how they can be self-sustaining, and why activities they motivate can be fulfilling even when *not* successful in attaining their final ends, we have to postulate instead that these motives do not seek their ends as agent-relative *rewards* at all. Even if the agent usually derives by-product benefits from pursuing and/or achieving these goals, the relation between intrinsic motivation and these by-products is contingent and the motivation is internally structured to continue in their absence (within the limits of the agent's tolerances, beyond which agent-fulfillment *is* a necessary condition for persistence); if it were *not* so structured, then these by-product benefits would have no chance of following from the activity.

This requires a non-erosiac conception of our formal telos and hence a radical break with all drive models. Deci and Ryan recognize that the needs they postulate to explain intrinsic motivation do not seek a *homeostatic completion*, but they do not see all that this implies:

> From the [drive theory] perspective, needs are understood as physiological deficits that disturb the organism's quiescence and push the organism to behave in ways that were learned because they satisfied the needs and returned the organism to quiescence. Thus in drive theories, the set point of the human organism is quiescence or passivity; need satisfaction is a process of replenishing deficiencies.... By contrast, in SDT, the set point is growth-oriented activity ... [people are] naturally inclined to act on their inner and outer environments, engage in activities that interest them, and move towards personal and interpersonal coherence.[63]

Though this formulation is insightful, the problem with it is that psychological "growth" does not identify any "set point" at all; it specifies an *open-ended* by-product of volitional devotion to other goals. This alleged telos in SDT differs in three striking ways from the equilibria of drive theories. First, there is a direction toward increased effectiveness, autonomy, differentiation of interest, and so on but *no rest point* at which we could say that a "satisfaction" internal to the aim of the activity has been reached. This means that the real aim is not rest, completion, or satisfaction at all. Second, it follows that the motivational telos (or *teloi*) of intrinsic motivation would have to be the agent-transcending goals that human agents can take as sustainable final ends (or some relation among such ends), whereas the natural/functional telos of a human person would be her functioning so as to pursue such agent-transcending ends. So an agent's motivational telos can no longer be identified with her natural/functional telos. Third, since well-being or eudaimonia is a by-product of such pursuits, there is also a gap between performing one's design function well or realizing one's natural telos, and attaining happiness, fulfillment, integration of self, and so on. The agent's holistic good, in this sense, thus stands at *two* removes from pursuing her true motivational *teloi*. They may be related such that, if the by-product benefits that the agent normally derives from pursuing her motivational *teloi* are blocked and fall below some threshold, then some of the necessary preconditions for intrinsic motivation are missing. But, as I said in reply to Badhwar, such a threshold is not the end-point of the motivational telos, which exceeds it and remains infinitely open to new goal-setting.

These three features together present a working *existential concept of our formal telos*. The existential approach breaks up the erosiac formal telos (see chap. 6, sec. 3) into three distinct concepts with different extensions: (1) our highest ends, (2) our natural function, and (3) our flourishing. This is a more detailed description of the non-erosiac formal telos that we found in both Scotus and Kant, although they do not fully agree about its substantive content or requirements (chap. 11). Within this tradition, different material conceptions of our existential telos are distinguished by the content they specify for our highest ends or, equivalently, the order of agent-transcending goods that it is our natural function to will for their own sake. For example, I will present a material conception of our existential telos that is more inclusive than either Scotus's or Kant's conceptions (chap. 14). Any such account of our existential telos remains normative, because it excludes as bad some significant ends that it is possible for human persons to project. But it does not make this discrimination simply by asking which among projectible ends it is most fulfilling, integrating, or self-actualizing to will.

4. Maslow's Eudaimonism

To clarify the importance of these distinctions, it will also be useful to consider Abraham Maslow's theory of self-actualization. Maslow's theory is less sophisticated than Deci's and Ryan's, which builds in Maslow's idea of an innate motivation to growth and development of creative talents that awakens "higher needs."[64] But given his place in the tradition of humanistic psychology, Maslow's account is much better known among philosophical audiences and more clearly exhibits the problems with eudaimonist meta-theory.[65] Maslow proposes that human needs come in a lexical hierarchy, ranging from our most basic biological requirements, through our social dispositions to affiliation, to the most distinctively human goals, in the following order:

1. physiological needs (nutriment, shelter, care in infancy);
2. safety (protection from physical danger and stability in one's lifeworld);
3. love and belongingness (relationships with friends, groups, spouse; attachment in childhood);
4. Esteem (recognition from others for our personality and for our productive/useful work);
5. self-actualization ("realizing their capabilities fully, being all they could be").[66]

This theory certainly recognizes a range of possible ends like those suggested in Aristotelian philosophical theories. Maslow still thought of these motives as drives that are innate in human nature, although the higher ones emerge only when the lower ones are largely satisfied.[67] And since even the highest goal of "self-actualization" is understood formally in terms of the agent's flourishing or full development of psychic health, all our motives remain formally egoistic in this model.

Maslow's account of the self on a stagewise quest for its eudaimonia remains too mechanical, conflating how we ought to be moved with how we will in fact be moved. As Mook argues, it predicts that "the more a person is deficient in a given need, the more important it should be. And the more the needs at each level are satisfied, the more important the needs higher in the hierarchy ought to be." Yet in survey studies, "[t]here was little support for either prediction in the data."[68] This is unsurprising, since Maslow forgot that many people never outgrow what Frankfurt called wantonness, or what Kierkegaard called the "aesthetic" stage of existence:[69] they are contented with the satisfaction of their existing D1–D2 desires without making any strong evaluations about values that could motivate D3 desires, let alone projecting agent-transcending goals necessary to engage in practices or cultivate noble friendships. After winning the lottery, they would happily just sit in their mansion and watch movies on TV all day long.[70]

That said, even if there is an innate disposition to higher intrinsic motives such as exploration, creative work, and achievement, we could reconstruct Maslow's lexical ordering as a thesis about how *some level* of physiological satisfaction, physical security, and basic acceptance may function as preconditions to willing higher ends. It is certainly compatible with the existential approach to hold that projective willing has necessary preconditions that are not part of the goals it adopts. Physical deprivation, chaos in civil society, terror, or mental abuse may undermine our capacity to set and strive for worthwhile ends. Ryan and Deci cite extensive research showing that "a secure relational base" needs to be in place for children to develop their capacities for intrinsic motivation.[71] Indeed, we might regard all the evidence they present that nondominating, autonomy-encouraging family and school environments help facilitate the development of intrinsic motivation as supporting this reconstructed hierarchy thesis.

However, given its eudaimonistic character, Maslow's theory is also subject to the crucial objection that it confuses intentional goals and by-products. As Mook notes, the best support for Maslow's ideal of self-actualization in empirical studies is found in the growing literature on intrinsic motivation. I have argued that such motives are best understood as concerns about first-order goals whose value is intelligible to the agent independently of any feedback relation it may have for the agent's own psyche (at least within her limits of tolerance). Maslow should agree, since he emphasizes that "self-actualized" persons are focused outwards on problems to be solved, not on themselves.[72] They tend to be "caught up in the tasks and challenges per se, and not in the extrinsic rewards of performing them" (as MacIntyre also suggested). Yet, as Mook notes, such "intrinsic motivation is fragile . . . extrinsic rewards for an activity can turn play into work. . . . Anxiety about someone else's evaluation can do the same."[73]

These observations suggest that what Maslow calls "self-actualization" is essentially a by-product of pursuing other worthwhile first-order goals for their own sake—a side effect that is especially pronounced when the activity aims at highly valuable agent-transcending ends, like those of the practices, noble friendship, just political causes, and so on. If Maslow's representative individuals, such as Einstein, Thomas Jefferson, and Eleanor Roosevelt, had been focused on becoming self-actualized or building self-esteem rather than on working out general relativity, creating a new democratic republic, or solving the problems of poverty generated by the Great Depression, they would never have become self-actualized.

In fairness, this confusion may be more attributable to our idioms for expressing intrinsic motivation rather than to particular theorists. For example, like Maslow, Robert Cavalier describes "self-actuation" as a form of motivation in which "individuals seek ways to fully express their interests, talents, and potentials as free human beings. . . . They find joy in doing, in creating, in performing, in experiencing themselves as people through their work and accomplishments."[74] Readers easily distinguish this kind of motive from, say, painting as a means to wealth and fame; but the phrasing is still misleading, for it implies that the agent's intended goal is a kind of joy in experiencing the power of their talents. This would reduce the goals of their craft to mere occasions for self-discovery or opportunities to test their abilities, when they are rather the opposite: self-discovery and joy in developed talent happen in activity aimed at something else. The agent may recognize these goods that emerge in the process as *reasons* for continuing their devotion, but that is distinct from being moved by a desire or drive for these goods.

The same distinction also needs to be made—but usually is not—in studies on "personal achievement" as a long-term goal. For example, Mook describes David McClelland's theory of achievement motivation as follows:

> People high in need for achievement (*nAch*) are likely to choose occupations that entail independent decision-making and rapid, concrete knowledge of results. McClelland's group has gathered evidence that across societies over time, industrialization and economic growth are associated with the prevalence of achievement motivations.[75]

However, we must distinguish someone who considers "achievement" (in the sense of success in school, success in a high-status job, or success in starting a business, along with the recognition these normally entail) to be an intrinsic part of his well-being and thus acquires a D3 desire for it, from someone who cares primarily about the agent-transcending purposes of her studies, profession, or even a for-profit business and *projects* excellent realization of these purposes as her final end. In the latter case, it is misleading to say that the individual has a "need for achievement" and so is formally seeking her own well-being in striving to excel. Rather, she actively pursues something for which she has no prepurposive need at all. In doing so, she may display "drive," but this is the resoluteness of her will, not her "ambition" in the sense of seeking something to add to her resume. (Resumes tend to be more impressive when their contents are mostly a side effect of goals *other* than building an impressive resume).

Of course, in everyday life, we can find it hard to distinguish this D3 desire for merits and the projective striving for ends that may (as a side effect) count as meritorious or as "achievements." Often a person may act on both kinds of motives, to a greater or lesser degree in each case, and I do not believe that the ambitious D3 desire must always defeat the pure projective motive; in a single psyche, the two can often be mutually supporting, despite their different purposes. But they will tend to come apart in cases where a determined effort to bring about some agent-transcending result may bring no immediate worldly success or may even hamper one's chances of gaining social recognition as a high achiever. This is where we see the difference between a person of strong will and McClelland's highly achievement-motivated agent, who needs continual feedback confirming success and recognition of the merits or status he is accruing.[76]

By contrast, imagine a mathematician who is so certain of the importance of the problem on which he is working that he pursues it even when colleagues whose support he needs dissuade him and see no value in it. Indeed, the value of such work may sometimes become apparent to others only after the agent's death. For example, in 1919, the "little-known Polish mathematician named Theodor Kaluza from the University of Köningsberg" sent Einstein a paper suggesting that in addition to the three recognized spatial dimensions, our universe could have another, smaller, curled-up, fourth spatial dimension.[77] After some initial enthusiasm, Einstein became skeptical; although Kaluza's paper was eventually published, it was largely ignored for decades.[78] But now it has become the foundation of string theory, the leading contender today for the ultimate unification of physics! Sadly, Kaluza never got a Nobel Prize or appointment to the Institute of Advanced Studies in Princeton, but he could still have been self-actualized.[79] In sum, the "drive for achievement" can be interpreted either so that Kaluza satisfied it or so that he did not, and this implies two quite different kinds of motive.

5. Frankl's Existential Will to Meaning

5.1. *Meaning as a By-Product of Self-Transcending Devotion*

These criticisms of Maslow's theory, which parallel my critique of Aristotle, were famously made by the existential psychoanalyst Viktor Frankl. In his book *From Death Camp to Existentialism*,[80] reprinted under the best-selling title, *Man's Search for Meaning*,[81] and in later works, Frankl argues that the "will to meaning" is a "primary concern" of persons.[82] While imprisoned in Auschwitz and other concentration camps, Frankl found that when people were stripped of dignity and treated as mere objects to be used and finally exterminated, their practical egos (or sense of being a continuing self defined by its values) tended to collapse.[83] Under these terrible circumstances, "only a few kept their full inner liberty and obtained those values which their suffering afforded" by achieving spiritual growth.[84]

This was in large part, Frankl judged, because their dehumanization cut prisoners off from the goals that had formerly given meaning to their lives and the hopes that gave significance to their future: "A man who could not see the end of his 'provisional existence' was not able to aim at an ultimate goal in life. He ceased living for the future, in contrast to a man in normal life."[85] In other words, these conditions made it almost impossible to exercise the striving will in projective motivation. "A man who let himself decline because he could not see any future goal found himself occupied with retrospective thoughts," tended to turn inward, and eventually to find everything "pointless."[86] Then the crisis would come in which the prisoner simply gave up and refused to get up or do anything, until he became sick and died.[87] In human beings, the phenomenon that Martin Seligman has called "learned helplessness"[88] often involves existential despair or loss of will.

The only way to "restore a man's inner strength" when he reaches such despair is "to succeed in showing him some future goal,"[89] to change his attitude by focusing him on life's challenge "to fulfill the tasks which it constantly sets for each individual."[90]

Frankl generalized these findings into a theory of motivation that led to "logotherapy," a method for helping those with "noögenic neuroses" that do not come from trauma or repression of appetites but rather from lack of sufficiently meaningful purposes to which to devote themselves. This theory recognizes the distinction between the projective motives of the existential will and what I call D1-D2 desires:

> Logotherapy deviates from [Freudian] psychoanalysis insofar as it considers man as a being whose main concern consists in fulfilling a meaning and in actualizing values, rather than in mere gratification and satisfaction of drives and instincts, the mere reconciliation of conflicting claims of id, ego, and superego, or mere adaptation and adjustment to the society and environment.[91]

Frankl also distinguishes the proper functioning of what I call the striving will from all erosiac motivation, including D3 desires. For he recognizes that in finding intrinsic values in different possible goals and devoting ourselves to them on these grounds, we "may arouse inner tension rather than inner equilibrium."[92] To explain this remark, it helps to recall that from Plato's point of view in the *Symposium*, it would seem that by projecting goals for which we had no prior appetite or attraction, we would be *creating* need or lack in ourselves, or making ourselves *less satisfied*. Frankl describes this as moving from a state of motivational equilibrium or psychic stasis to a new state of tension caused by *caring passionately* about something. "However," Frankl continues, "precisely this tension is an indispensable prerequisite of mental health."[93] We can even recognize this and realize that we *enjoy* the tension caused by our enthusiasm for the tasks at hand. To paraphrase Senator John McCain, another war camp survivor, we find meaning by devoting ourselves to "causes greater than our self-interest."[94]

Hence Frankl explicitly rejects "those motivational theories which are based on the homeostasis principle"—the psychoanalytic version of Plato's lack model of desire, according to which "man is basically concerned with maintaining or restoring an inner equilibrium."[95] This was Freud's principle, but Frankl thinks that it is refuted by Allport, Maslow, and Bühler, who found that "propriate striving" resists equilibrium and maintains motivational tension.[96] So Hobbes and Callicles turn out to be right in a sense if we restate their objection to Plato in existential form. There may be no value or sense in stimulating additional D1-D2 desires (which, according to Socrates' famous analogy, would be like making holes in our psychic sieve), but there is certainly a point to creating a wholly different kind of "dissatisfaction" in our mental economy by setting demanding goals for ourselves. As Frankl puts it, our mental health always requires

> the tension between what one has already achieved and what one still ought to accomplish, or the gap between what one is and what one should become. . . . What man actually needs is not a tensionless state but rather the striving and struggling for some goal worthy of him. What he needs is not the discharge of tension at any cost, but the call of potential meaning waiting to be fulfilled by him.[97]

If so, then it seems that the strong erosiac thesis is wrong; not all our motivation arises from attraction toward completeness, however broadly interpreted. It is our nature to be ready to suffer as long as that suffering has a worthwhile point or meaning.[98] By contrast, a person who believes that happiness is our ultimate goal must see unhappiness as "a symptom of maladjustment" and therefore experience second-order unhappiness or shame *about* his or her suffering or unhappiness.[99]

Frankl also considers serious existential commitment to real values beyond ourselves to be the mark of psychological *maturity* in human persons: "the Freudian pleasure principle is the guiding principle of a small child; the Adlerian power principle is that of the adolescent; and the will to meaning is the guiding principle of the mature adult."[100] In other words, mature agency is typified by projective response to an array of important moral and nonmoral values. Frankl also rejects Nietzsche's and Freud's hermeneutics of suspicion, which contend that behind all apparently noble, virtuous, or other-regarding commitments of the self there must lurk repressed, ulterior, self-serving motives. After noting Allport's remark that Freud specialized in interpreting motives that "cannot be taken at their face value," Frankl adds, "The fact that such motives exist certainly does not alter the fact that by and large motives can be taken at their face value."[101] Psychological egoism can be defended against such counterexamples only if it is taken as an *a priori* dogma—as when C. S. Lewis's wonderful Nietzschean devil, Screwtape, rejects the "cock-and-bull story about disinterested love" and insists that all this "talk about Love must be a disguise for something else."[102]

Because he recognizes that projective motivation is necessary for mental health and that the neuroses of the "existential vacuum" result without it, Frankl still speaks of "man's desire for a life that is as meaningful as possible,"[103] and he calls such meaning a "higher need."[104] But "desire" and "need" stand here for motivation in general, not any kind of erosiac attraction. Objectively, we can be said to "need" the meaning provided by existential willing, since this is our natural function (which is one part of our existential telos), but that does not mean that projects are undertaken by persons *on the motive* of satisfying a desire for meaning or of gaining happiness. As a result, the phrase "will to meaning" is misleading if it is taken as implying that meaning itself is our intentional target; rather, Frankl employs it to contrast with the will to power and the will to happiness.

For, as Frankl himself insists, finding meaning requires an outward focus on values "found in the world rather than within man or his own psyche." Hence he rejects the formal egoism of Maslow's theory: "Self-actualization is not a possible aim at all, for the simple reason that the more a man would strive for it, the more he would miss it."[105] This point is obviously similar to my critique of A-eudaimonism: "like happiness, self-actualization is an effect, the effect of meaning-fulfillment . . . if he sets out to actualize himself rather than fulfill a meaning, self-actualization immediately loses its justification."[106] This paradox of Maslow's eudaimonism results from the psychological fact that the agent's sense of his own self-worth depends on what Jaspers calls "that cause which he has made his own"; as Maslow himself admits, we realize our "selves" primarily "via a commitment to an important job."[107] More generally, a person can become his "true self" only through concerns that are directed to persons, standards, and issues *outside* himself or unrelated to his own material interests:

> He becomes so, not by focusing on his self-actualization, but by forgetting himself and giving himself, by overlooking himself and focusing outward. . . . What is called self-actualization is, and must remain, the *unintended effect of self-transcendence*; it is ruinous to make it the target of intention. . . . It is the very pursuit of happiness that obviates happiness.[108]

This parallels my Elsterian critique of eudaimonism as self-defeating, because eudaimonia is essentially a by-product of virtues, practices, and pure relationships.

The concept of self-transcendence, which is at the heart of Frankl's theory, also corresponds to my description of agent-transcending first-order motives (introduced in chap. 5, sec. 2.2). Frankl emphasizes self-transcendence precisely because he recognizes the point (which we also found in Feinberg and Williams) that a fulfilling and meaningful life depends on forming commitments and undertaking endeavors as valuable for their own sake. Hence in logotherapy "the typical self-centeredness of the neurotic is broken up instead of being continually fostered and reinforced," as in the introspective methods of Freudian psychoanalysis.[109] This agrees with Frankfurt's paradox that there is something liberating in the experience of being "seized" or "captivated" by an object of our love, through commitment to which we move out of ourselves (and toward focus on others or the world).[110]

The relation between projective motivation and existential meaningfulness is therefore not usefully explained or analyzed in terms of a *desire* for meaning. If we could be motivated to take up a demanding task just by the simple longing to have something to do or to avoid boredom or to find "some meaning or other" for our life, then we would be able to satisfy such a desire just by picking any end *arbitrarily*. But such randomly chosen ends could not be projected or pursued with serious devotion and volitional resolve. For they would not be *responding* to any perceived importance; either there would be no substantial grounds for valuing these ends or, if there were, we would not be choosing them for these reasons. As a result, we could only *play at* pursuing them. If our ends lack the requisite gravitas or intrinsic importance for us, we find it possible on a whim to reverse our interest in them—which is just to say that we are not able to form a real commitment to them or to fully invest ourselves in them.

5.2. The Alterity of Values to Which the Will Responds

Frankl's existentialism, like my own, thus presupposes the possibility of real values outside us in the world to which we can respond. As Frankl argues, if "the meaning that is waiting to be fulfilled by man" were just an invention of his mind, like Narcissus's image in the pool, "it would immediately lose its demanding and challenging character; it could no longer call man forth or summon him."[111] On this basis, Frankl rightly rejects Sartre's notion that we invent values by choosing our projects; Sartre gets the relationship backwards.[112] This is what he means by saying that one cannot just "will to will" without the perception of meaning or significance that could provide an objective reason for forming a serious project.[113]

Without nonarbitrary grounds, then, existential projection would be self-undermining and fail to generate personal meaning. This is why "subjectivism and relativism" about values undermine our capacity for existential resolve, or "erode idealism and enthusiasm" of the spirit.[114] Moreover, to furnish grounds for projective motivation rather than only D3 desires, these values must have a certain *alterity*, otherness, or separation from the agent's good. This independence of the agent is implied in the concept of self-transcendence, which Frankl explicitly takes from Buber: "The essentially self-transcendent quality of human existence renders man *a being reaching out beyond himself*."[115]

In this respect, Frankl's theory agrees with Nel Noddings's conception of caring, which is crucially influenced by Kierkegaard, Buber, and Marcel. She conceives caring for "living things" as including an effort to attend to "their natures, ways of life, needs, and desires."[116] Without this focus on the other's reality, we could not understand their good well enough to help them. Thus the caring agent focuses on the other rather than on herself "as caretaker" or on how burdened and caring a person she is.[117] In particular, Noddings emphasizes that caring involves "engrossment" in the other, or "a displacement of interest from my own reality to the reality of the other." Moreover, she adds that a "genuine caring for self . . . for the *ethical* self, can emerge only from a caring for others."[118] Thus, although there is a secondary place for concern about the coherence and value of one's cares, at the ground level, "caring is always characterized by a move away from self,"[119] or a *nonreflexive* focus. There is a convergence here with Frankfurt's claim that caring is liberating because of its "selflessness."[120] Caring as a motive state requires this intrinsic interest in something or someone transcending the self: "At bottom, all caring involves engrossment. The engrossment need not be intense nor need it be pervasive in the life of the one-caring, but it must occur." Without it, Noddings says, there is no love in Buber's sense of direct contact with the other-as-*thou*.[121]

Existential willing therefore requires an *Anstoss*, or experience of a reality that is not merely an ideal construct in the manifold of one's own consciousness. Echoing Buber, Frankl writes: "The world must not be regarded as a mere expression of one's self. Nor must the world be considered as a mere instrument, or as a means to the end of one's self-actualization."[122] In projective motivation, I will my movement toward persons, objects, and states whose value I do not seek to possess, experience, or appropriate into myself (even in a reasonably extended sense). It is this *alterity* or *alienness* of its ends that makes existential willing essentially *non-narcissistic* in its general form, in strict opposition to formal egoism.[123] As Frankl puts it, the human person "reaches out for something other than itself."[124]

We cannot create *ex nihilo* any basic or underivative values with this kind of alterity or difference from our own being, as Sartre's approach would require, because we are not God. Our inventions and artifacts are doomed to remain extensions of our minds; we rightly see them as expressions of ourselves, and our love of them (even when justified) remains formally narcissistic, for they cannot become free beings whom we can meet or to whom we could devote ourselves in fully self-transcending will (this is the dream of which Pinocchio becoming "a real boy" is a classic expression).[125] As the existential theory of divine creativity in chapter 9 suggests, the ability to create *alterity* itself—to bring forth separate beings that are not mere property or equipment of the maker but free of his or her control—would be a distinguishing mark of the divine.[126] Indeed, Levinas (a Jewish author) reminds Christian theologians that

> The great force of the idea of creation such as it was contributed by monotheism is that this creation is *ex nihilo*—not because this represents a work more miraculous than the demiurgic informing of matter, but because the separated and created being is thereby not simply

issued forth from the father, but is *absolutely other* than him. Filiality itself cannot appear as essential to the destiny of the I unless man retains this memory of the creation *ex nihilo*, without which the son is not a *true other*.[127]

Thus God, on Levinas's "open" conception of the divine, is the only one who can give distinct being itself to the value aimed at in projective willing, and this is the right way to understand creation *ex nihilo*.

Of course this general point about the need for non-arbitrary values to ground projective motivation does not depend on theism, nor does it tell us *which* values can play this role. But it does clarify why worthwhile purposes, according to Frankl, are not all formally egoistic or agent-relative in their content. Frankl tends to interpret this altruistically, like Noddings, who writes that "Our motivation in caring is directed toward the welfare, protection, or enhancement of the cared-for."[128] Yet Frankl's structure of self-transcending motivation could also be instantiated by evil volition; as Jeffrey Blustein says, "we can devote ourselves directly to the destruction or diminishment of something," and such caring is "negative in tenor."[129]

Perhaps the significance to be found in such negative projects is in some interesting ways less enduring or shareable or fulfilling when pursued. But that it is possible at all puts in clear relief the crucial distinction between existential *meaning* (i.e., subjective/personal significance and practical coherence) and *eudaimonia*, which the radically evil agent may lack. As an agent-related good deriving *from* volitional projection or as an *effect* of a life with self-transcending motivation, existential meaning is more fundamental than eudaimonia. For a *eudaimon* life is necessarily a life with existential meaning, but the converse does not hold: a life full of existential meaning is not necessarily *eudaimon*, both because it may be subject to serious ill-fortune and injustice and because it could be devoted to negative ends that are either contingently harmful to the agent or even intrinsically self-destructive (on this point, see sec. 9 below).[130]

Thus even if the reflective patient does take an interest in finding existential meaning through projective willing, she would not be acting on a *eudaimonistic* D3 desire. If meaning itself is an indirectly targetable end for us, as Frankl sometimes seems to suggest, then our motivation to pursue it would still not embrace all other motives in the way that the drive to eudaimonia is supposed to, according to the Eudaimonia thesis. Rather, it would constitute what Blustein calls one type of "care about caring," namely a basic commitment to being engaged meaningfully in the world:

> The person who cares about caring in . . . [this sense] is emotionally invested in being a caring person, that is, a person who takes an interest in and devotes him or herself to things, activities and people

in his or her world. A person who cares about caring . . . may deliberately take measures (perhaps with the assistance of others) to find something to care about or to keep alive a sense of purpose and attachment to life.[131]

As Blustein says, such a search for meaningful roles or worthwhile values to care about normally sees caring as an end-in-itself. If it is conceived only as a means to a self-interested end like showing off superior abilities or perhaps maintaining an image of oneself as caring, then it can become hollow and self-defeating.

Noddings also affirms that "As human beings, we want to care and to be cared for. Caring is important in itself."[132] But she tends to construe our response to the intrinsic value of caring in more erosiac terms, for example, as the "longing for relatedness,"[133] and to suggest that genuine "presence" to the other requires an *affective* response from the one caring, so that the cared-for "feels her warmth in both verbal and body language."[134] It is debatable whether volitional devotion to individuals must always involve this kind of affective component. In many cases, the projective efforts of the will may entrain emotional dispositions, but the same dedication to a shared purpose may find quite distinct emotional expressions in different personalities. Yet the deeper problem lies in Noddings's suggestion that our "longing for goodness"[135] or "our longing for caring—to be in that special relation" is the wellspring of ethical motivation.[136] She may well be right that "the joy that accompanies fulfillment of our caring" can bolster our allegiance to the ethical ideal of caring response. But caring cannot begin from such a motive: Buber is clear that I-Thou relations are not directly targetable. Noddings's error here is like Badhwar's: she conflates a reinforcing condition that can become a necessary condition of continuation with an initial incentive for caring.

6. How Caring Benefits the Agent: Frankfurt on Means and Ends

We have seen that existential meaning is not usefully conceived as the target of D3 desire, since it is founded on devotion to ends in view of intrinsic values that are *at least* partly independent of the by-product goods that the agent derives from pursuing these ends, such as the feeling that her life is important in virtue of its engaging in significant pursuits or maintaining caring relations. This position can be contrasted with a closely related analysis offered by Harry Frankfurt in his essay "On the Usefulness of Final Ends"[137] and further developed in his recent book, *The Reasons of Love*.[138] Frankfurt's concern, like Frankl's, is with what makes an agent's life meaningful, not in the third-personal sense of indicating or representing something to others, nor in the consequentialist sense of having a major impact on the world, but rather in the essentially first-personal sense of being experienced as significant by the agent living it.[139]

More clearly than Frankl, Frankfurt recognizes that while it is good for life to have this kind of existential significance, this is not the only important good, since a life that is meaningful to its agent could still be unhappy or evil.[140] Still, the meaningfulness a person finds in her life is a very important good that depends, in Frankfurt's view, on (1) how important the goals of her activities seem to her; and (2) whether she finds the means to her ends or the activities involved in pursuing them intrinsically interesting and well suited to her personality. This shows that the meaning-value of *working toward* a final end is more than the terminal value of the state of affairs sought as the final end, and this surplus may be realized even when the end is not achieved:

> when *is* activity important to a person? It is important to him only when he is devoted to something that he cares about. Thus a person's life is meaningful only if he spends it, to some considerable extent, in activity that is devoted to things that he cares about. It is not essential that the activity he devotes to the things he cares about be successful. The extent to which life is meaningful depends less upon how much it accomplishes than upon how it is lived.[141]

Thus Frankfurt rejects the traditional view that "the only value that a final end necessarily possesses for us, simply in virtue of the fact that it is a final end, must be identical with the value for us of the state of affairs which we bring about when we attain that end." For having and pursuing final ends gives personal meaning to our activities, which is an existential value distinct from that attained in the end.[142] In some cases, the quest itself is so rewarding that we are almost sad when the end has been attained and the journey toward it is over.

The distinction to which Frankfurt is drawing attention here is the one that I have characterized as the difference between the *product*-value of end E and the derivative values realized in pursuing and possibly achieving E (existential meaning, challenge, solidarity with others involved, self-esteem, etc.). Simply for heuristic purposes, I summarize these relations in the following schema:

$$(\text{Agent } A \rightarrow E) \Rightarrow M$$
$$\perp$$
$$V$$

where $\rightarrow$ indicates intention, $\Rightarrow$ indicates efficient causation, and $\perp$ indicates a grounding relation of rational support.

In this schema, agent A intends E as a final end, and this is grounded by E's terminal value V, and pursuing E for this reason causes personal meaning (M) and other goods in A's life. I have argued that A's motive for intending E must be projective where V is an agent-transcending value; for M is an effect on A that derives from pursuing E on the basis of V (or having E among his active final ends) rather than part of E. I have also suggested that such existential meaningfulness is not itself a directly targetable goal; it can be pursued effectively only by looking for objective grounds for caring or seeking out realizable values worth caring about that supply reasons for projecting final ends.

Frankfurt instead takes this distinction as a reason to question the traditional relation between "instrumental value" and "terminal value," and the "fundamental asymmetry" between means and ends in Aristotle's moral psychology. He summarizes Aristotle's position as follows:

> [First,] A means derives its instrumental value from the relationship in which it stands to its end, but an end derives no value from the relationship between itself and the means to it. . . . [Second,] A means derives no terminal value from being useful. . . . Of course, what has instrumental value may have terminal value as well. But it cannot have the latter by virtue of the fact that it has the former.[143]

Frankfurt believes that this Aristotelian approach is too "impersonal," since it "diverts attention from the fact that every end is the end of an agent" and plays a complex role in her life.[144] Human agents posit ends, Frankfurt says, not just for their terminal value but also so that their activities (and thus their life) can be meaningful for them.[145] This suggests, in terms of my schema above, that end E can be chosen in part for the sake of M:

> Final ends are possible states of affairs, which someone values for their own sakes. It must not be supposed that the measure of how a life is lived is given by the value of his final ends. Rather, how a life is lived is a function of what it is like for the person to *pursue* them. The problem of selecting final ends is not the same, then, as the problem of measuring the inherent or terminal value of possible states of affairs. . . . The goals that it would be most desirable to achieve are not necessarily those that it would be best to seek.
>
> This is not only because there are differences in the probabilities and in the cost of attaining various goals. It is also because there are differences in the kinds of activities, and in the patterns of activity, by which various final ends may be pursued.[146]

In other words, the required means to a final end have a lot to do with the existential value of pursuing that end. For example, Frankfurt suggests it is possible that pursuit of some highly noble end might (for a particular individual in his circumstances) require very little challenging activity, whereas pursuit of a different end with more modest product-value "might require invigoratingly complicated and wholehearted attention" that "would fill the person's life with meaning and purpose."[147] I agree that the fulfillment an agent gains from pursuing worthwhile ends is partly a function of her means to that end (including relationships involved and necessary preparations), and that considerations about the means can function as reasons for taking up a final end E that do not focus on the product-value of E. This is one species of what I will call *process-focused* grounds for projecting ends. E's existential value, or the meaningfulness of pursuing it, is in part a function of these important considerations about the processes by which E can be sought.[148]

Yet, as the title of his article indicates, Frankfurt instead concludes that final ends have a kind of "instrumental value" for making life meaningful: "our final ends derive a certain instrumental value from the very fact that they are terminally valuable."[149] This is a category mistake like the one that leads to the paradox of eudaimonism: meaning is construed as an embracing end that we desire (or existential boredom becomes the object of an embracing aversion), and we choose final ends because of their "instrumental value" as a *means* to this end of leading a meaningful life. Frankfurt repeats this view in his lectures on love: "Despite the air of paradox, we may fairly say that final ends are instrumentally valuable just because they are terminally valuable"; for example, the lover cares about his beloved "for its own sake," but in addition "what he loves necessarily possesses an instrumental value for him, in virtue of the fact that it is a necessary condition of his enjoying the inherently important activity of loving it."[150]

Frankfurt clearly senses the tension in this proposed solution, for he asks us to consider

> a man who tells a woman that his love for her is what gives meaning and value to his life. Loving her, he says, is for him the only thing that makes living worthwhile. . . . From his declaration that loving her fulfills a deep need of his life, she will surely not conclude that he is making use of her.[151]

Assuming that this man is sincere, Frankfurt is surely correct—but only because the woman will understand that the existential value that loving her contributes to the man's life is primarily a concomitant effect of devotion to her rather than *the motive* for his attention to her and his concern for her well-being. For if she thought the latter, she *would* feel used, like a mere ornament in the man's narcissistic (and self-deceiving) project of constructing and maintaining an image of himself as a loving being. Frankfurt seems both to recognize this point yet to obscure it:

The appearance of conflict between pursuing one's own interests and being selflessly devoted to the interests of another is dispelled once we appreciate that what serves the self-interest of the lover is nothing other than his selflessness. It is only if his love is genuine, needless to say, that it can have the importance for him that loving entails. . . . Accordingly, the benefit of loving accrues to a person only to the extent that he cares about his beloved disinterestedly, and not for the sake of any benefit that he may derive either from the beloved *or from loving it*.[152]

While correct, this last sentence surely implies that the loving agent is *not* pursuing his own interest (even if his volitional state does in fact promote it); therefore the conflict is *not* resolved. Frankfurt's phrasing suggests that his analysis gives comfort to eudaimonism, when really it does not.[153] There is also something misleading in Frankfurt's interesting and closely related argument that because "living a meaningful life is important to us for its own sake, useful activity possesses for us not merely instrumental value but terminal value as well."[154] As Frankfurt explains, his point is not just Aristotle's idea that "activities may be desired as final ends and not merely as means to ends other than themselves." Of course activities themselves can be desired as ends because of their "intrinsic character." But "Aristotle does not recognize that [activities] may possess terminal value precisely because they are instrumentally valuable,"[155] that is, because they are experienced as meaningful work that helps produce an end whose realization is valuable for its own sake.

Frankfurt's point could be expressed by saying that there is a unique form of terminal value that attaches to the very *pursuit* of many ends; thus "it is inherently important for us to engage in activity that is devoted to advancing our goals," even aside from the product-value of the goals themselves.[156] This is the intrinsic existential value that useful activities have independently of the value of the ends that define these activities. Existential value in this sense is unlike the terminal value that activities can have for Aristotle when they constitute an intrinsic good. For even those activities that are only means to such goods rather than constituting part of the human good still have Frankfurt's existential value above and beyond the product-value of the ends when achieved. This is an insightful response to Aristotle but it neglects to mention that when an activity acquires such terminal existential value because it is at least partially constituted by disinterested commitment to the final end, the agent cannot choose this activity as a *means* to such existential value, or initially be moved by erosiac desire for such existential value.

In general, Frankfurt misses the fact that not all terminal value is targetable and what generates nontargetable terminal value should not be described as *useful* for causing such nonintended by-product value. His analysis conflates the existential value of final ends (their power to provide an object for meaningful endeavor) with a kind of instrumental value and thus reinscribes caring within precisely the eudaimonist framework that he has criticized as leading to an inadequate picture of selfhood. The traditional distinction between ends and means may be inadequate, but the problem is not solved by blending them. Considering process-focused grounds for taking up a final end E—such as how interesting the means involved in the task may be or how pursuit of E is likely to affect one's character—cannot amount to regarding the whole process of *pursuing E as final* as what we ordinarily call *a means* to a separate end. As I argue in chapter 7, even when our final end is itself an activity involving the pursuit of other things, the terminal value of this activity for the sake of which it could be intrinsically desirable is quite distinct from the *derivative* benefits of taking the activity as final. Potentials for meaning, interesting work, full employment of one's talents, or fulfilling engagement with a diverse range of goods operate here *neither* as ends nor as means but, rather, as *grounds* for willing both the final end and its requisite means. The introduction of this third term allows us to solve the problems that Frankfurt identifies in the traditional Aristotelian doctrine.

So while I agree with Frankfurt that the process of pursuing final ends can add to the agent's life a kind of value distinct from anything the agent believes to be inherent in the end-state pursued, I deny that *desire* for this agent-related value can be what moves the agent to set and strive for such ends. Her own will must motivate the agent if her effort is to generate the highest kinds of existential value for her own life. Another way of saying this is that if they are not to be self-defeating, agent-relative process-focused considerations can enter into the selection of final ends only as *grounds for projecting them*, not as attractors that cause an appetite for the pursuit of these ends. When they function as grounds, such process-focused considerations are not already operative as *motives*; hence they cannot compete with any other motive for pursuing the relevant end for its own sake. Moreover, they can serve as agent-relative grounds for projection only *in conjunction* with more agent-neutral grounds focused on the product-value of the final end. For recognizing that a final end has some terminal value that could justify anyone projecting it is quite consistent with judging that the pursuit of this end is also supported by considerations concerning what this project would be like in a particular individual's life, given his circumstances, history, other projects, and so on.

Hence I argue that the sort of consideration to which Frankfurt draws attention in this part of his work in fact helps explain why, contra Frankfurt's own position, caring is grounded on objective reasons. Our projected life goals can give meaning to our lives only because they are grounded by our awareness of values that are *important to care about* independently of their power to satisfy preferences, contribute to our eudaimonia, or make life interesting. I defend this "objectivist thesis" in chapter 14.

7. Self-Esteem as By-Product

At this point, we might imagine some contemporary psychologists countering that a meaningful life in Frankl's sense is motivated by the ultimate or embracing desire for strong "self-esteem." For it seems that a sense that our life is worth living must involve some positive evaluation of our own character and social roles. But we must be wary of conflating existential meaning with other reflexive psychic states, especially when their concepts have several senses. If self-esteem is simply a matter of achieving one's goals whatever they are, then anyone with very low self-expectations could achieve it through meeting his very modest targets. Conversely, someone who demands much of herself for worthy ends may enjoy a rich sense of meaning in her endeavors even while remaining frustrated by lack of adequate accomplishment. After all, some endeavors may be worthwhile even though there is very little real chance of attaining the goal; for example, counseling death-row inmates to come to terms with their lives and themselves; doing everything possible to save or comfort a terminally ill child; trying to broker peace in the Middle East; or running for president in the United States on a platform of social justice, financial sacrifice for the common good, separation of church and state, and a new federation of democracies with our allies. There is a superlative kind of self-esteem that would come from succeeding at any of these tasks, but it is not based on reasonable expectations of oneself. Not all kinds of "self-esteem" should be important to us, nor are all forms of it that are inherently valuable also directly targetable.

"Self-esteem" is often recommended as a crucial goal by therapists to their patients, by teachers to students, and by parents to children. In moral theory, a number of thinkers follow Rawls in treating "a sense of our own self-worth" as both a human good (something it is rational for all persons with a rational life plan to want) and as a "primary good" (or precondition for carrying out rational life plans) for the purposes of determining basic justice.[157] For example, as Joel Anderson explains, Alex Honneth develops from Hegel a conception of ethical life in which individual autonomy "depends crucially on the development of self-confidence, self-respect, and self-esteem," all of which require "recognition by others whom one also recognizes."[158] I am sympathetic with Honneth's analysis, but it also points to important distinctions. For example, while he treats "self-respect" as a matter of possessing universal dignity shared with all persons, he understands "self-esteem" as involving "a sense of what makes one special, unique, and (in Hegel's terms) 'particular'" in a valuable way.[159] As this suggests, we need to distinguish between at least four different kinds of positive self-regarding attitudes:

1. The first derives from social recognition of our *constitutive status* as a competent moral agent capable of responsible action, or as a person capable of forming and pursuing a conception of her good, or as a citizen capable of exercising rights, and so on.[160]

2. The second derives from other people (our caregivers first and foremost) believing in our innate and acquired *abilities* to do things that should earn us respect and recognition over and above what we deserve merely as competent agents and rights-bearers.[161]

3. The third, when reality-based, derives from actually *doing* these things; it thus depends on the desert or merits we *may or may not* acquire by our choices, efforts, and projects. Since these merits arise from accomplishments measured on some *absolute* scale of excellence (whether discounted relative to individual abilities and circumstance or not), in principle everyone could acquire high merits and the reflexive attitude that properly depends on them.

4. The fourth kind of positive self-evaluation properly depends instead on merits defined *comparatively* according to the differences between individual accomplishments as measured absolutely in 3. Merits of this last kind cannot even in principle be achieved equally by all.[162]

Since usage is fluid in this area, it does not matter much what labels we give to the different kinds of positive self-regard that arise in these four ways. I will call the first "basic self-respect," or a sense of our "intrinsic dignity," and the second "faith in ourselves," or confidence in our own potential. The third, which I call "self-honor," or pride in our accomplishments measured absolutely, comes closest to Aristotelian "magnanimity" (see chap. 7, sec. 5). The fourth, which I have already called the "desire for superiority status" and "pride in distinction" (chap. 10, sect. 2.4), has an important place in human life but is also dangerous; the desire for this kind of pride is what Hobbes calls "glory" and what Nietzsche celebrates as the will to ascendance over others.

Now, it is clear that if a child's "self-esteem" or "positive self-image" refers to either justified self-honor or pride in distinction as defined here, it is irrational to try to produce it directly. For unless they are to rest entirely on illusions about oneself, these kinds of self-esteem must be mainly by-products of activities undertaken for reasons *other than* building self-esteem. Hence it is not surprising that one study of 642 college freshman by Jennifer Crocker of the University of Michigan Institute for Social Research found that students trying to improve their looks or get good grades for the sake of self-esteem were more likely to become frustrated and experience anxiety—thus lowering their confidence in themselves. "An obsession with external markers of self-worth, Dr. Crocker believes, leads to self-absorption," and this "focus on the self" is also off-putting to others.[163] Frankl's existential approach seems like a plausible solution to this common neurosis: what is needed is *more will directed outward at worthwhile causes, relationships, works, and ideals.* It is hoped that pride in genuine accomplishment will follow.

Rawls's conception of "self-respect (or self-esteem)," which combines what I have labeled "self-honor" and "confidence in oneself," has the same implication. For he describes its two aspects as follows:

> it includes a person's sense of his own value, his secure conviction that his conception of the good, his plan of life, is worth carrying out. And second, self-respect implies a confidence in one's ability, so far as it is within one's power, to fulfill one's intentions. . . . It is clear why self-respect is a primary good. Without it, nothing may seem worth doing, or if some things have value for us, *we lack the will to strive for them.*[164]

Rawls is not concerned to explain how this striving will functions, but he thinks it is undermined both by a lack of worthwhile goals and by pervasive social impediments that make it impossible to pursue worthwhile projects. In this first respect, self-esteem is clearly dependent on the goods that are available for the agent to care about. Like Honneth, Rawls also thinks that this requires some level of interpersonal recognition of the value of our life goals and activities; in addition to internal coherence, it requires "finding our person and deeds appreciated and confirmed by others who are likewise esteemed and their association enjoyed."[165] Like Frankl's analysis, this suggests that the goods we care about must have a kind of objectivity, although Rawls rejects the strong objectivity of perfectionist doctrines of excellence.[166]

Rawls's student Thomas Hill, Jr., develops this idea beyond moral self-respect. He argues that in addition to basic respect of oneself as a moral agent, some people develop respectable nonmoral standards, values, or goals for their lives, whereas others lack "a sense of minimum non-moral standards."[167] It is possible for a person in the latter category to satisfy basic deontic moral requirements yet think and act wantonly within these limits.

By contrast, a person in the former category cares deeply about values beyond respecting basic moral rights and feels self-contempt in violating these values. Hill summarizes: "This form of self-respect would require that one develop and live by a set of personal standards by which one is prepared to judge oneself even if they are not extended to others."[168] Let us label this fifth kind of positive self-regarding attitude *ethical seriousness*. A person who is ethically serious has a more demanding scale on which to judge herself than a person who is not.

On Frankl's account, once again, this kind of self-respect is also derivative from identifying worthwhile objects of attention and concern and devoting oneself passionately to them. For example, someone fully engaged in a practice in MacIntyre's sense would obviously derive some appreciation of her own ethical seriousness as an agent from this. Moreover, like Rawls, Hill recognizes that needed for values and standards broadly ethical self-respect cannot be selected arbitrarily but must have significance for others too. For one can *lack* respect for oneself as an ethically serious agent in at least three different ways: (1) by remaining wanton; (2) by setting respectable standards and goals but failing to live by them; and (3) by setting standards that one recognizes as arbitrary or caring about values that one sees as insufficiently important. In this last case, "It is as if one's interests, projects, and plans seem worthless even to oneself."[169] If this negative self-judgment is justified, then this constitutes one kind of noögenic neurosis in Frankl's sense. The best therapy is to care more devotedly about more valuable goals and ideals—a topic that I explore further in chapters 13 and 14.

8. Willed Carelessness: Emily Fox Gordon's Case

Frankl's central point that certain kinds of self-absorption can block passionate devotion to self-transcending ends or block volitional investment of the self in intrinsically rewarding activities goes a long way toward explaining one especially revealing kind of noögenic neurosis, in which the agent quite intentionally avoids the volitional effort required for any ambitious undertaking. For illustration of this neurosis, we might turn to Dostoyevsky's Underground Man or Shakespeare's *Hamlet*. But since they receive variant interpretations—and so many different diagnoses of Hamlet's "problem" are possible—a less ambiguous autobiographical case will serve better.

In a shockingly self-critical piece on her personality as a writer, Emily Fox Gordon begins, "I am a gormless woman. My life has been characterized by an extreme and pervasive failure of agency."[170] Coming from the best-selling author of *The Mockingbird Years*, this is a little hard to believe at first. But she proves her point by describing how, into her thirties, she cultivated disengagement from her own life and a snobbish disdain for others happily engaged in theirs—such as Marcy, the chipper wife of a fellow graduate student. On Marcy's hokey calendar, plans were listed in detail (and with obvious zest for life) for each day of the current month, accompanied by absurdly enthusiastic cartoons drawn by Marcy and her husband.[171] Perhaps this calendar so filled with tasks and interests got to Gordon because it represented the kind of planning described by Michael Bratman as extending "beyond simple purposive agency" to deeper commitments.[172]

Gordon admits that she defaced this calendar during a party at Marcy's house while making fun of the calendar with friends. She diagnoses the "vehemence" of her reaction as due to the existential challenge she sensed in Marcy's down-to-earth Midwestern spontaneity: "Marcy's proactive grip on her life called into question my own attitude of fatalistic detachment. . . . I was forced to ask myself a painful question: If she cared so much about her life, how was it that I could care so little about mine?"[173] Her approach to life had been the opposite of Marcy's: she had tried to "avoid acknowledging any ambition or aspiration" in order to "stay potential" and avoid any commitments that would fix significant aspects of her future. This attitude, which Kierkegaard called aestheticism, Gordon figures as follows: "Nor would I allow myself to inhabit my life fully. Instead, I'd stand waiting in the doorway, half in, half out."[174] Gordon finally discovered the personal essay as the genre best suited to her temperament, because it allowed lengthy introspection, irony, and taking the stance of passive observer toward one's own experiences. "Unproblematically self-assured types" like Marcy would not make good essayists, but self-tortured aesthetes like Kafka would. This essay form "granted me the paradoxical authority of self-deprecation."[175]

As Frankl's theory predicts, Gordon found that when circumstances finally gave her the chance to write her memoir, and she had to focus on this task rather than on her own psyche, it was fulfilling: "Having a job to do, and a limited time to do it in reminded me of my pregnancy twelve years earlier—I felt the same sense of being pulled towards the future."[176] She ought to have tried this earlier since, as her memoir tells, she already recognized that undergoing too much traditional psychotherapy in her adolescence had been destructive because it encouraged morose self-involvement, and she was saved, interestingly, by the "anti-psychiatric psychoanalyst Leslie Farber"[177] (whose ideas on unwillable states of character and self-defeating ways of pursuing them were among Jon Elster's chief inspirations—see chap. 5, sec. 2.4). But by Gordon's own account, the work of writing her autobiography was not enough to overcome her essential barrier to meaningful engagement in life. Since this book itself focuses on her adolescent years in self-stultifying therapy, it marginalized her more modest adult activities: "my studies; my motherhood; my marriage; the pleasures, pains, and struggles of my daily life" were all consigned to obscurity in the memoir.[178]

In her *American Scholar* essay, Gordon diagnoses this as part of her continuing failure to value her role as participant in ordinary daily activities; instead, she tended to value speculative reflection on herself—even on her own disillusionment with therapy and its inward focus.[179] Thus acknowledging the regret she felt in Marcy's kitchen more clearly recognizes the need for existential engagement than the memoir did: there "it occurred to me that there was something to be said for planning to make a life instead of planning to make a story of my life."[180] Her conclusion is both poignant and philosophically significant:

> What was I regretting as I stood in her kitchen? Almost everything: I regretted the way I had exiled myself as an observer rather than a participant, regretted the exceptionalism I had used to console myself since childhood. . . . How many times have I comforted myself with the old saw about how the unexamined life is not worth living? In Marcy's kitchen it occurred to me that the reverse might well be truer—that the unlived life is not worth examining.[181]

This response to Socrates could serve as the motto for my new version of existentialism, as long as we remember (as I noted in discussing Elster) that authenticity still requires something more than totally unreflective spontaneity, which only leads to wantonness. Instead it requires a kind of practical self-critique and volitional self-control that seeks existential coherence while avoiding the self-defeating aspects of speculative and introspective evasions. And this will always require commitments regarding our own character that cannot be followed through merely by *writing an essay*, however sincere. Notice that having written a memoir that was itself largely a reflection on the dangers of too much therapeutic reflection-on-self, Gordon went on to critique her memoir as inauthentic, but she did this by writing *another* self-reflective essay about the process of writing a memoir and its seductions.[182] In other words, she achieved *fourth-order* reflection on the possibilities of self-deception in reflecting on the dangers of therapeutic reflection! Even Proust never managed this feat.

Gordon does not tell us *to what* concrete purposes she will now commit herself, although her studies, her relationship with her spouse, and her relationship with her children are possible candidates. An abstract resolve to form some commitment or other will not work, as Frankl's analysis implies—we need to let ourselves encounter values that transcend us in their alterity, because *particular* commitments are a response to values that strike us independently of our will. We cannot have such an I-Thou encounter with meaningful values simply in writing an essay about our existential regrets; that is still too reflexive an activity.[183] As an emotion, regret at most opens us up to encountering values that we might positively embrace in willed resolve. (That important values may sometimes only be discoverable this way at least implies that a life without any regrets may be condemned to a certain ignorance and should not be regarded as an ideal). Regret over ignoring or rejecting worthwhile goods is thus a possible *ground* for projecting more concrete goals involving these values, as long as one does not *wallow* in regret. As the saying goes, if you feel sorry, *do something* to make amends.

9. Willed Inferiority: Sartre

Whereas Gordon willed her state of noncommitment or aesthetic wantonness, there are (probably) even more dramatic cases in which *dissatisfaction itself* is the agent's primary goal. In such cases, lack, deficiency, and incompleteness would become final ends (not so that the agent could consume more, as Plato's Callicles imagined, but just so that she would be punished for her self-perceived inadequacies). In such an intended purpose, where the opposite of fulfillment is the goal, virtually by definition the motive must be non-erosiac: such a goal could only be projected. For example, consider Sartre's argument, against Nietzsche's reduction of all motivation to "will to power," that "We can choose ourselves as fleeing, inapprehensible, as indecisive."[184] Indeed, Sartre argues that an "inferiority complex" consists at bottom in the will to take one's being-for-others as a basis for self-abhorrence:

> the inferiority that is felt and lived is the chosen instrument to make us comparable to a *thing*. . . . But it is evident that it must be lived in accordance with the *nature* which we confer on it by this choice—*i.e.*, in shame, anger, and bitterness. Thus to *choose* inferiority does not mean to be sweetly contented with an *aurea mediocritas*; it is to produce and assume the rebellion and despair which constitute the revelation of this inferiority. For example, I can persist in manifesting myself in a certain kind of employment *because* I am inferior in it. . . . It is this fruitless effort which I have chosen, simply because it is fruitless—either because I prefer to be the last rather than to be lost in the mass or because I have chosen discouragement and shame as the best means of attaining *being*.[185]

Such a project is paradoxical because it requires the agent to project a recognizable task or role such as being a great artist (and strive to achieve it) yet to select such a goal *because* it guarantees failure. The project becomes a mere means for the agent to prove her worthlessness or lack of merit. Such a state is no mere expression of "infantile dependency." Rather, it is one manifestation of what Izenberg calls "a will to unfreedom or self-abnegation."[186]

If it really is possible for an agent to be so motivated, then she clearly cannot *desire* her inferiority in any orektic sense. Nor could her problem be a separate second-order desire to experience *unsatisfied* desires for approval and success, because as we have seen, second-order desire must be independent of the satisfaction *or frustration* of the first-order desires to which it refers. Sartre's agent does not even want any second-order satisfaction in being regarded as inferior; ironically, her aim would be stymied if she were happy as a by-product of attaining it.

Sartre imagines an existential ground for such a project that is perhaps intelligible: the agent is desperate enough to see inferiority as a viable way to be assured of *some* definite meaning in her life, some individual *distinctness*, no matter what the cost in happiness. In addition, we might suggest as grounds for such a project that after years of neglect and abuse by others or the failure to develop ambitions she can earnestly pursue in good faith, the agent decides in self-hatred that the only thing to which she can devote her whole self with all her volitional capacity is the denial of her value as a person and the denigration of her agency—and *better this than nothing!* In this way, she will spite those who destroyed her hopes or discouraged her, or she will punish herself for past failures.

If Kant is right, then the volitional capacity that this agent engages to will her own worthlessness also inevitably expresses its own inherent value in the very process of motivating her to strive for her perverse goal. This implies a kind of pragmatic contradiction in the existential project of inferiority. For the ground or basis for her projection is the importance of some meaning rather than none, or the value of individual expression via existential projection rather than pure passivity, and this seems to commit the agent to the inherent value of her own will. But the specific content of her goal is to deny this value.[187] The will to inferiority is therefore self-contradictory in the sense that violates the categorical imperative and it can also be regarded as a form of radical evil, or willed cruelty to persons. It is directed inwardly at the self rather than outwardly at others, as in the forms of radical evil I discussed in chapter 10.

Perhaps this kind of self-hatred is often connected with a malign will toward others; perhaps some agents who define themselves in terms of despising others cannot believe themselves capable of more positive contributions or relationships. Since they do not believe themselves capable of willing genuine goods, in despair they throw themselves into evil purposes instead.

Conclusion

At this point, we have identified the objective status and alterity of values or practical reasons that can serve as grounds for projecting related ends. We have also identified some particular examples of such values or reasons serving as a basis for projective willing: for example, in the good will to justice or duty and (oppositely) in the various forms of radical evil, willed carelessness, and the will to inferiority. These are all states of the existential striving will with strong moral properties, ranging from moral virtue to extreme moral corruption. In between, however, there is a large range of projective endeavors that are morally neutral (in the narrow deontic sense), being morally permissible within limits required by justice, but which have broader ethical significance arising from nonmoral values to which they respond.

In chapter 8, I suggested that we find grounds for engaging in practices in aesthetic values, theoretical values of knowledge, and other social goods, while we find grounds for engaging in friendship in the values of individual personalities and character on the basis of which we commit ourselves to friendships. In the next two chapters, I return to this question of broadly ethical or non-deontic grounds for projective willing. We will see that the existential theory of striving will requires not only a conception of the right but also a conception of the good.

13

Caring, Aretaic Commitment, and Existential Resolve

Overview. This chapter argues that caring and commitment—concepts central to both analytic moral psychology and ethical theory—are best explained as projective phenomena of the striving will. Although the chapter surveys a wide set of recent developments in moral psychology, it focuses on work by Harry Frankfurt, Bernard Williams, and Jeffrey Blustein. The discussion is rarely technical and can also serve as an introduction to this genre for the general reader.

Review

The previous chapters in Part III have advanced three main theoretical goals.

1. They have provided substantial evidence that the primary function of the striving will is the active projection of new motives. For they argued that virtuous motivation as Aristotle conceives it, Kant's motive of duty, Levinasian agapē, and vices involving radical evil cannot adequately be understood except in terms of projective motivation and the corresponding existential conception of volitional strength.

2. These examples, along with others from existential psychotherapy, suggest that projective end-setting and striving are always responses to strong evaluative judgments concerning intrinsic values. Like D3 desire, projective willing involves practical validity claims concerning pursuable goods; but unlike D3 desire, projective willing responds to such goods as at least partially agent-transcendent, or initially unrelated to the agent's own well-being or perfection, however broadly conceived.

3. Analysis of these case studies suggests a working taxonomy of the different kinds of intrinsic values to which projective volitions can respond, which extend beyond the formal considerations of fairness and justice that ground deontic projection.

This chapter completes the case for I by arguing that the closely interrelated concepts of care, commitment, and personal projects—which play such vital roles in contemporary theories of the self, its obligations, and the conditions of a meaningful life—cannot adequately be understood without the projective model of striving will. Goals 2 and 3 are completed in the next chapter.

I. Frankfurtian Care as Projective Motivation

In the last thirty years, the fields of ethics and moral psychology have absorbed several closely related critiques of egoistic, utilitarian, and Kantian moral theories. From Humean, Aristotelian, feminist, or even Nietzschean perspectives, critics have converged on the idea that classical modern theories of moral norms do not fit with the most important motives operative in human life. Arguments offered by Bernard Williams, Michael Stocker, John Kekes, Harry Frankfurt, Nel Noddings, Annette Baier, Virginia Held, and several others imply that human beings are capable of projecting a wide variety of goals for themselves, including but going well beyond moral considerations of justice or fairness.

Yet as impressive as this convergence is, the main motivational concepts on which these arguments rely remain largely unexplained. In my view, the crucial role played by cares, commitments, and ground projects in forming a person's practical or volitional "self" and their difference from ordinary prepurposive forms of desire can be adequately understood only in terms of projective motivation. Without the existential conception of the striving will, we cannot make sense of how an agent is active in forming her ground projects or shaping her self-defining commitments. The alternative, which holds that the cares and devotions around which our life is structured ultimately arise from contingencies that are beyond the agent's control, undermines the *autonomy* of these states, without which they cannot have as much importance in moral theory as is commonly thought.

At the end of chapter 3, I suggested that only the existential conception of the will as both second-order executive agency *and* the capacity for projective motivation can explain the crucial role of striving will in determining *the ethos of a person*—that is, his personality, but especially his character, what he stands for, the narrative unity or fragmentation of his life's "subplots" and its development over time, and in general the whole way in which he experiences (or fails to experience) his life as meaningful or imbued with significance. Any human life that develops from infancy acquires such a personal ethos, for better or worse, and it is crucial for the existential conception of personhood that what we might call the *practical depth* of this ethos—the profundity of meaning and the extent to which it is self-determined—is distinct from its happiness.[1] The existentialist claims, then, that one acquires a personal ethos with practical depth primarily through projective willing—that is, through resolving on projects and purposes that have significance both in their producible ends and in the pursuit of those ends. Frankfurt's analysis of caring, developed over several years in a number of works, seems to be closely related to this existential view in several respects, though several important differences will emerge as well.

1.1. Care and Self-Unification over Time

First and most importantly, Frankfurt clearly understands "caring" not as a prepurposive motive but rather as a settled or plan-like purposive state that actively guides the formation of more particular intentions over time. Unlike many short-lived inclinations (including many of what I have called D1 and D2 desires), what a person cares about "coincides in part with the notion of something with reference to which the person guides himself in what he does with his life,"[2] and thus "The outlook of a person who cares about something is inherently prospective: that is, he necessarily considers himself as having a future."[3]

This point connects caring with Bernard Williams's well-known concept of "ground projects" as motives that give an agent reasons to go on living since they are "categorical" in the sense that they do not "operate conditionally on his being alive, since [they] settle the question of whether he is going to be alive."[4] Like Frankfurt, Williams says that we can understand the practical unification of the self over time through its interest in its own future agency, given "the idea of a man's ground projects providing a motive force which propels him into the future, and gives him a reason for living."[5] However, Williams seems to think that to provide such temporal unification, ground projects must involve goals we would be willing to die for if circumstances required it. Cares as Frankfurt describes them do not necessarily have to motivate this level of self-sacrifice; different cares can have higher or lower priority for the individual agent, and only the highest-priority cares might fit Williams's definition.

Yet Frankfurt seems to be right that it is essential to cares—not only cares for which we would die—to endure through time in a way that desiderative states need not. When an agent genuinely cares about something (as opposed to just paying it lip service or wishing it well), then she is already committed to acting for it in some way as circumstances may allow; and this activated motive tends to preserve itself over time. Its stability arises by the agent's design or activity, whereas when a desire influences someone's conduct over a long period of time, its persistence may be due to chance alone (e.g., imagine someone who has enjoyed evening television for years but who can drop it without much regret when his Army Reserve unit is called up). Thus the persistence of desires does not by itself entail that the consciousness experiencing them understands its past, present, and future as related or unified by that consciousness's own activity in positing goals and planning actions aimed at them. Frankfurt puts this point in a way that suggests connections to Heidegger's analysis of the distinctively human experience of temporality:

> Desires and beliefs can occur in a life which consists merely of a succession of separate moments, none of which the subject recognizes—either when it occurs or in anticipation or memory—as an element integrated with others in his own continuing history. When this recognition is entirely absent, there *is* no continuing subject. The moments in the life of a person who cares about something, however, are not merely linked by formal relations of sequentiality. The person necessarily binds them together, and . . . construes them as being bound together, in richer ways . . . a person can care about something only over some more or less extended period of time. It is possible to desire something, or think it valuable, only for a moment. Desires and beliefs have no inherent persistence.[6]

To *guide oneself* through caring, then, is not simply to exhibit a pattern of actions over time that can be intelligible to third-party interpreters in terms of ongoing motives; it is *to will* an ongoing understanding of one's activity in terms of certain lasting goals, projects, or ideals.

Here again Frankfurt's account converges significantly with Nel Noddings's (remarkably enough, since neither Frankfurt nor Noddings cite the other's work). For Noddings argues that the most essential elements of caring, as experienced from the inside, are "The commitment to act on behalf of the cared-for, a continued interest in his reality throughout the appropriate time span, and the continual renewal of commitment over this span of time."[7] Like Frankfurt, Noddings understands caring as outwardly focused yet involving an active effort to sustain the motivation: the caring agent repeatedly "renews his resolve."[8] However, Noddings does not clearly recognize that the active effort through which first-order motives persist in cares is distinctively volitional; instead, she treats it as basically affective or emotional and as an extension of "natural inclination."[9] To this view, Frankfurt's account is a useful corrective.

1.2. Caring Involves Reflexive Volitional Attitudes

Thus Frankfurt's first thesis about the function of cares in the temporal structure of the self depends on his second main thesis, namely that to care about some X, the agent must identify with this care (and with other desires and emotions that caring about X may involve). In his most developed treatment of caring, Frankfurt reaches this conclusion through a series of steps. He begins by arguing that in equating happiness with the satisfaction of desires, Hobbes fails to recognize that "people may be misguided in what they want."[10] Whether or not desires may be objectively wrong, Frankfurt claims that getting what we want may not make us happier because "some of the things that people want, or prefer, are things they do not really care about."[11] He points out that even if it is important to us to avoid frustration of strong desires, this can be done either by satisfying such desires or by eliminating them, which is not true of cares.[12] Of course, we often say things like "I wish I didn't care what she thinks of me," but our desire for another's praise here does not refer to a volitional devotion.

On the other hand, if we are engaged in trying to alter some first-order devotion, then this must be motivated by some *other* care(s). A care in Frankfurt's sense cannot motivate its own elimination. This is also true of D3 desires because they involve strong evaluations of agent-relative goods to be realized in action; this was Gary Watson's chief insight (see chap. 5, sec. I.2). Hence it is natural to assume that caring differs from ordinary first-order desire in part because it also involves strong evaluative attitudes. Frankfurt does not accept this explanation, but I will postpone discussion of this issue until chapter 14.

Instead, Frankfurt suggests that caring about some goal or person means (1) being disappointed or feeling loss if X is not realized or things do not go well for X; (2) that the agent *continues* to care about X even when giving some other purpose higher priority in a decision; and (3) that this motivation "must endure through an exercise of his own volitional activity rather than by its own inherent momentum" or "affective inertia."[13] In other words, caring involves higher-order volitions that aim at preserving the desires, emotions, and other attitudes involved in serving the object of our care and attenuating or eradicating first-order motive-states that conflict with our care. For example, Frankfurt says that an agent's caring about attending a concert

> implies that he is disposed to support and sustain his desire to go to it even after he has decided that he prefers to satisfy another desire instead. Foregoing the concert would frustrate his first-order desire to attend the concert . . . [but] it would fail to touch the higher-order

desire . . . that this first-order desire not be extinguished or abandoned. His caring about the concert would essentially consist in his having and identifying with a higher-order desire of this kind.[14]

This passage clarifies the relationship between identification and caring that was less clearly indicated in Frankfurt's first essay on caring, where he avoids directly defining caring in terms of his controversial notion of volitional identification:

> A person who cares about something is, as it were, invested in it. He identifies himself with what he cares about in the sense that he makes himself vulnerable to losses and susceptible to benefits, depending on whether what he cares about is diminished or enhanced. Insofar as the person's life is in whole or in part *devoted* to anything, rather than being merely a sequence of events whose themes and structures he makes no effort to fashion, it is devoted to this. . . . Thus caring about something is not to be confused with liking it or with wanting it; nor is it the same as thinking that what is cared about has value of some kind, or that it is desirable.[15]

Perhaps Frankfurt hesitated to define caring in terms of volitional identification because of Gary Watson's well-known objection that identification could not consist simply in a higher-order "desire." In introducing the concept of caring, Frankfurt was looking for a motive-state that would be clearly distinct from mere desire because it is inherently autonomous or expressive of the agent's will. But the concept of caring could not solve this problem if it were defined in terms of higher-order desires. The idea was to explain in some other way why cares are autonomous or inalienable. Identification would then become intelligible as part of the process of caring. Hence Frankfurt suggests that in the profoundest type of caring, which he calls "volitionally necessary" caring (or "love"), the agent "does not experience the force of volitional necessity as alien or external to himself" because it is partly constituted by "desires which are not merely his own but with which he actively identifies himself." This active support of the first-order motives involved in his care helps him "avoid being guided in what he does by any forces other than those by which he most deeply wants to be guided."[16] Such cares are experienced as inherently autonomous.

Along the way, Frankfurt has also explored other ways of analyzing volitional identification to solve Watson's objection, such as the model of decisive identification,[17] and the model of identification as satisfaction with one's desires.[18] The latter model of "identification as acceptance" allows Frankfurt to say that identification with some desire is insufficient for caring about it: "Since I may identify with desires that I consider to be quite trivial, such as a desire to have some ice cream, identifying does not entail caring."[19] This is problematic,[20] but even if it is true, it does not entail that there is no "essential linkage between identification and caring," as Frankfurt suggested here.[21] For even if identification does not entail caring, the converse might hold. And indeed, Frankfurt affirms this in *The Reasons of Love* when he explains why caring cannot be constituted simply by a certain intensity of desire:

> When a person cares about something . . . he is willingly committed to his desire. The desire does not move him either against his will or without his endorsement. He is not a victim; nor is he passively indifferent to it. On the contrary, he himself desires that it move him. . . . Besides wanting to fulfill his desire, then, the person who cares about what he desires wants something else as well: he wants that desire to be sustained. Moreover, this desire for his desire to be sustained is not a merely ephemeral inclination. It is not transient or adventitious. It is a desire with which the person *identifies himself* and which he accepts as expressing what he really wants.[22]

Hence caring about X entails identification with desires for X's good (if X is a person) or upholding X (if X is a principle), just as alienation from (or counteridentification with) a desire entails *not caring* about the desired object.

Yet Frankfurt's phrasing here clearly recognizes the so-called *ab initio* problem that Watson first raised against the simple hierarchical account of identification: an ephemeral higher-order desire or brute second-order preference will not do. Frankfurt might now suggest that to identify himself with the higher-order desires involved in his care, the agent must be *satisfied* with them. But this formulation leaves out the idea that the agent who cares about some X is *committed* to it (in the relevant sense) and hence committed to the first-order motives and evaluative attitudes that devotion to X requires. I propose that it is because the higher-order volition(s) involved in caring about something or someone themselves consist in a firm commitment *of the striving will* that they are distinct from types of motive-states (such as desires) which in themselves are wanton and merely sequential over time unless the agent endorses them or otherwise makes them autonomous. The concept of projective willing supplies what Frankfurt needs to complete his account.

1.3. Caring Is Based on Volitional Commitment

Several passages in Frankfurt's work move toward this idea that a kind of volitional commitment is the central element in caring that distinguishes it from lower-order desires and assures its autonomy in the agent's motivational life. In his 1999 essay on caring, following the argument that caring involves higher-order volition, Frankfurt suggests that although "beliefs, feelings, and expectations" may often reliably indicate what someone cares about,

> What is at the heart of the matter is not a condition of feeling or of belief or of expectation but of will. The question of whether a person cares about something pertains essentially to whether he is committed to his desire for it in the way that I have suggested. . . .
>
> Being committed to a desire is not at all equivalent to simply approving of the desire or to merely endorsing it. Commitment goes beyond acceptance of the desire and hence willingness to be moved by it. It entails a further disposition to be active in seeing to it that the desire is not abandoned or neglected.[23]

In other words, caring about something involves more than identification *understood as mere satisfaction*; it involves the agent's proactive effort to keep this care alive and informing her choices. Here my notion of striving will as not only projecting new ends but also strengthening the agent's motivation to pursue existing projects and priorities suggests itself as an explanation of this ongoing intrasubjective effort. The agent's reflexive contribution to caring seems to consist primarily in a resolve that focuses her willpower on building up the "right" sort of affective and motivational dispositions and breaking down the "wrong" sort, where right and wrong are determined by the needs and/or content of what she cares about.

Frankfurt's insistence that care and love are "volitional" phenomena requires such a projective explanation. In his first essay on caring, Frankfurt says that "The fact that someone cares about a certain thing is constituted by a complex set of cognitive, affective, and volitional dispositions and states,"[24] but he emphasizes the volitional: "the fact that a person cares about something is a fact about his will."[25] But the relevant sense of "will" here cannot be what Frankfurt has routinely called the "first-order will," signifying the desire on which the person acts;[26] for the unwilling addict's first-order will is to get heroin. Certainly the addict "cares" about his heroin in one sense but not in the sense of deeper commitment or resolve that Frankfurt has in mind. Nor is Frankfurtian caring "volitional" in the sense of being a "decision," which Frankfurt analyzes as an "iteratively self-implementing" act that forms a specific intention.[27] For he emphasizes that cares function like entrenched dispositions in a person's character that are not easily altered and hence not subject to "decision" in this familiar sense: "the fact that a person decides to care about something cannot be tantamount to his caring about it," as we see in Sartre's famous example of the young man.²⁸ Contra Sartre, Frankfurt says that the young man might decide to choose the option that he truly cares about less and then find himself *unwilling* "to carry out his intention."²⁹

I agree with this argument up to a point, because the commitment on which caring is based must involve a kind of investment of the self that significantly binds the agent's first-order motives going into the future; no attitude toward X could count as commitment to X if it is just as easy to abandon X or reverse oneself after adopting this attitude as it was before. I am more skeptical about Frankfurt's claim that this binding can amount to "volitional necessity," or that it is ever totally outside the reach of the agent's control, unalterable by her initiative.³⁰ However, the present question is rather: What kind of "will" or "unwillingness" is determined by whichever option the young man truly cares about most in his "volitional heart" (even if he does not introspect it accurately)? Frankfurt says:

> If a person's will is *that by which he moves himself*, then what he cares about is far more germane to the character of his will than the decisions or choices that he makes. The latter may pertain to what he *intends* to be his will, but not necessarily to what his will truly *is*.³¹

Consciously or not, Frankfurt is appealing here to the existential conception of striving will, which functions at a level deeper than its surface decisions—a level at which it is an active source of new motivation as well as a shaper and sustainer of existing motivation. In the very process of forming particular intentions on the basis of existing motives, it also reaffirms and expresses its own unique type of motivation, which Frankfurt calls "caring." This existential interpretation explains why Frankfurt wants to say that caring is a mode of *willing* even though it is not an act of "decision," or what Kant would call the legislation of a subjective maxim.

This existential interpretation also explains why Frankfurt can insist that agents express themselves in their cares, as well as why agents experience "love," in his volitional sense (as an especially strong species of care), "as actually enhancing both their autonomy and their *strength of will*."³² For caring is an ongoing effort of will, and the volitional commitment upon which it is based is the paradigm achievement of a will strong enough to posit demanding goals and to keep in place the focus of mind and energy to pursue them. The projective explanation also makes sense of Frankfurt's frequently repeated claim that caring strongly about morality is one particular kind of care that does not arise from pure reason alone; for recognizing rational justifications for justice or fairness is not the same thing as a personal commitment to these ideals as overriding all other goals.³³ The latter, as I argue with respect to Kant (see chap. 11), is one kind of projected motive that the agent forms on rational grounds that do not move him without his will's participation.

Finally, the projective account of caring sheds light on how cares can autonomously "guide" us while not themselves simply consisting in a decision or set of decisions. First of all, to be "guided" by one's care is for it to function as a standing project in one's practical life:

> To care about something is not merely to be attracted by it, or to experience certain feelings. No one can properly be said to care about something unless, at least to some degree, he guides his conduct in accordance with the implications of his interest in it. This means paying attention to it and to what concerns it; it means making decisions, taking steps. Thus, with respect to those things whose importance to him derives from the fact that he cares about them, the person is necessarily active.[34]

Hence cares are "active" in *something analogous* to the way that decisions are active: by forming intentions, decisions guide first-order action (mental or bodily acts other than decision); by caring, the will guides the motives that inform decisions. In decision, as I argue in chapter 3, "the will" is no more than the executive agency (or perhaps "power") that takes up some preexisting motives and forms a particular *purpose* motivated by them. But caring does not simply select in this way among already present motives in order to define the agent's purposes; it also guides his particular purposes by *dedicating* the agent to a cause, person, or ideal and thus forming a distinctive kind of motive. Thus *to care about some X* is not just voluntarily to form, on the basis of prior desires, an intention to achieve X, to promote X's well-being, or do what X requires. It is to have what I call an "essentially volitional motive" (chap. 3, sec. 3.4), i.e., one *generated by the will's resolve* in the process of forming the specific intentions.

Although this is clearly my explanation, not Frankfurt's, it coheres well with his insistence that caring is not governed by "decision" in the ordinary sense; for the striving will as the capacity for projective motivation musters resolve, sustains commitment, and shapes the agent's most central motives rather than simply forming particular intentions. Something like the intensity of such efforts at dedication or sustained devotion may perhaps be felt in *making* a decision in the ordinary sense, especially when this requires *resolving* a contest between competing preexisting motives.[35] But the power of the striving will, whose exercise we sense in making any significant intention-forming decision, is much more strongly felt in projecting motives or (we may now say) in *forming cares*—even though this is a process not achieved in an instant nor always played out in fully articulated reflective awareness of what we are doing.

So, although it does not feel much like a "decision" in today's sense of that term, the formation of cares is a voluntary movement of agency. It is often a slow and quiet buildup, sometimes culminating in a great moment of personal commitment but often simply growing into an established engagement and concern with a project or relationship. For example, in the film *Tombstone*, Wyatt Earp never seems to pass through a moment of deeply fraught and conflicted decision.[36] How this works is an interesting question that deserves more attention in philosophical psychology.

1.4. Volitional Love as Nonappetitive Motivation

So far, I have argued that caring in Frankfurt's sense is best understood projectively because it is a persisting motive-state that involves higher-order management of one's first-order desires, and a state that is distinct both from ordinary desire and from decision. Of course, since it is a kind of motivational disposition, caring could be called a "desire" in the thinnest or maximally formal use of this term (as in Davidson, Mele, Lewis, and many others). But Frankfurt rightly complains that "desire" as a catchall synonym for "motive" is not very useful as a philosophical concept because it tends to obscure or downplay important distinctions among different kinds of motives.[37] As I argue in chapter 4, to clarify how the states produced by striving will differ from other kinds of motive, we have to contrast them with "desire" in the Greek erosiac sense. In this section, I argue that this distinction is implicit in Frankfurt's treatment of "love" as the existentially deepest kind of care.

Among the many "different *ways* of caring," Frankfurt holds that "The most notable of these are perhaps the several varieties of love."[38] In his important paper on "Autonomy, Necessity, and Love," Frankfurt clarifies that the kind of "love" that he has in mind is a distinctively *volitional* state:

> As I deploy the concept, it has a very wide scope: love is a species of caring about things, and its possible objects include whatever we may care about in certain ways. . . . To love differs from having feelings of a certain type, such as those of powerful attraction or of intense desire or compelling delight. It is also not equivalent to or entailed by any judgment or appreciation of the inherent value of its object. To love something is quite different from considering it to be especially appealing or precious. . . . Of course, love does ordinarily involve various strong feelings and beliefs that express, reveal, and support it. The heart of love, however, is neither affective nor cognitive. It is volitional.[39]

This distinguishes volitional love from D2 appetites (such as "loving" chocolate), from D3 desires (such as "loving" the feeling of security provided by a good retirement plan), and from complex emotional states composed of D2 and D3 states (perhaps romantic love is an example, if it includes both sexual attraction and an appreciation of the partner as complementing our own personality). And as we have already seen (in sec. I above) Frankfurt takes loving some X in the volitional sense to involve regarding X (or X's good) as an end-in-itself. This helps explain his intriguing thesis that the "commands" of love can be "categorical," just as Kant claimed the commands of morality must be.[40]

Yet, as Frankfurt argues, Kant denies that motives that are affected by "contingent personal features" and varying circumstances "that make people distinctive and that characterise their specific identities" are autonomous, because "personal interests" that are affected by such contingencies "are not integral to the essential nature of a person's will."[41]

I agree with Frankfurt that Kant is mistaken on this point; he seems to have conflated those constitutive properties of rational free willing that are universally shared by all morally responsible beings because they are essential to moral personhood (a general "essence") with those commitments and character traits that are essential to the practical identity of an *individual* person. Kant's goal is to show that based on its universal nature, the free rational will is always-already implicitly committed to the fundamental norm of morality, namely the overriding value of the existence and effectiveness of free rational willing itself. But even if Kant is right about this (as I think he his), these universal implicit commitments of free rational will *as such* cannot define the whole of what Korsgaard calls a person's "practical identity." Hence other more specific motives may be autonomous for the individual.[42]

Frankfurt understands the core of a "practical identity" to consist in the agent's volitional loves; hence action motivated by such loves must count as autonomous:

> A person acts autonomously only when his volitions [or intentions] derive from the essential character of his will. According to Kant, a person's volitions are related to his will in this way only insofar as he is following the austerely impersonal dictates of the moral law. In fact, however, the same relation between volition and will holds when a person is acting out of love.[43]

To defend this claim, Frankfurt then argues that the motives of love are structurally analogous to the Kantian motive of duty in important respects. Since I have already shown that the motive of duty as Kant conceives it has a projective structure, it should come as no surprise that this is what Frankfurt's analogy implies about motives of love as well.

Frankfurt draws this analogy by arguing that volitional love is "active" in much the same way that Kant believed the will to be active in resisting temptation for the sake of duty or treating persons as ends. By contrast, Frankfurt characterizes as "passive" all other types of "love" in which the motive is erosiac (and hence formally egoistic) in structure:

> In many of its instances, love is fundamentally passive. It is passive when the lover is motivated by an expectation that obtaining or continuing to possess the object of his love will be beneficial to him . . . his love is conditional upon his attribution to his beloved of a capacity to improve the condition of his life.[44]

This description clearly encompasses what I have called D2 and D3 types of desire, including the global desire for eudaimonia and all the forms of *eros* that this involves. Volitional love, on the other hand, is not even formally egoistic in structure:

> But love need not be based upon self-interest. It may be fundamentally active, differing from passive love in the nature of the lover's motivation. . . . Loving of any variety implies conduct that is designed to be beneficial to the beloved object. In active love, the lover values this activity for its own sake instead of for the advantages that he himself may ultimately derive from it. . . .
>
> This must not be understood to mean that what motivates him is the inherent appeal of the activities in which loving leads him to engage [e.g., their enjoyability], considered entirely apart from their effects on his beloved.[45]

This formulation seems to me clearer than those I critique in chapter 12 (sec. 6) as unwittingly reintroducing formal egoism into the account of volitional love; for here instead Frankfurt emphasizes the *agent-transcending* nature of the agent's purpose. The example he introduces to illustrate this point—which reappears in all Frankfurt's discussions of love—is a parent's "wholly active and unconditional" love for her child. He suggests that caring for the child may involve many activities that are inherently enjoyable in themselves (though I add, based on personal experience, that it certainly includes some that are *not* so pleasant too). But either way, the activities involved in caring for the child are chosen for the child's good as the final end: the loving parent's "interest in the child is entirely disinterested. It can be satisfied completely and only by the satisfaction of interests that are altogether distinct from and independent of his own."[46]

"Disinterestedness" in this sense is the same quality that I call "purity" of motive: the agent has sufficient motivation in first-order goods that are not materially connected to his own good. In his long essay on caring, Frankfurt worries that the term "disinterested" may not be adequate, however: although it expresses the idea that "the lover's concern for his beloved . . . must have no ulterior aim whatsoever," it may sound "colorless and lacking in personal warmth," whereas in fact volitional love usually involves "a kind of passion and urgency that *disinterestedness* appears to preclude."[47] I note that the existential account of the striving will explains this intuition because it tells us that *love* in Frankfurt's special sense consists primarily in an *ongoing volitional effort* and secondarily in the first-order emotions and desires that this striving cultivates. In projecting and maintaining personal ends, volitional striving is experienced as a kind of *pathos* that is unlike passive emotions, which is precisely why the Greeks called it *spirited* or full of heart.[48]

This reading fits well with everything Frankfurt says except his claim that disinterested self-love can be achieved by desiring one's own well-being as a final end.[49] The projective model of volitional love certainly allows for the possibility of *projecting* one's own happiness as a personal end, but it requires us to distinguish this clearly from natural *desire* for one's own eudaimonia. For even one who, through despair or some other emotional dysfunction, has lost the natural love of his own life could still *will* to become happier and to recover this natural concern for his well-being.[50] This would constitute a kind of *care of self* that is quite distinct from any egoistic state of mind.

Love is "active" for Frankfurt, then, when its motive is "disinterested," or *pure*, in my sense, which is to say when it is not caused by external attractors that trigger appetites but, rather, is actively energized by the agent's own will. And this is why such actively willed loves are experienced as essentially autonomous, unlike passive first-order appetites: in contrast to those "passions" that "have no inherent motivational authority" for us because we can either identify with them or alienate them, "Love is not an elementary psychic datum" that we can accept or reject. "Since love is itself a *configuration of the will*, it cannot be true of a person who does genuinely love something that his love is entirely involuntary."[51] The existential account explains such configurations of the will as established dispositions of projective or self-motivational activity itself.

Frankfurt instead offers what I think is a less plausible explanation for such states of will: for him, they are parts of the "essential identity of an individual," one's personal essence.[52] On this view, love-motivated action is autonomous in the strongest metaphysically conceivable sense: "Thus, despite the fact that unconditional love is a personal matter, what a person loves may be among his essential volitional characteristics," giving them not just personal authority but even volitional necessity for the agent.[53] Although this formulation allows Frankfurt to maintain a parallel with Kant's notion of rational necessity as a basis for categorical authority in motives, it seems unnecessary to me. The individual agent's loves, or strongest cares, can have an unconditional personal authority based on his unconditional commitment to them, which in turn finds justification in the grounds for his projective resolve without this personal authority constituting a form of *necessity* analogous to logical truth.

Hence I do not see that personal authority or the autonomy of the agent's motive could be rooted only in an absolute identificational *destiny* or volitional essence that is uniquely her own. To make a case for this claim, Frankfurt has to argue not only that the activeness/autonomy of volitional love is distinguished by its selflessness or the absence of prior attraction to the beloved, but also that the personal authority of volitional character is not compatible with leeway-libertarian freedom.[54]

I am concerned here with only the first of these two theses, which amounts to the claim that volitional love is an especially important form of projective motivation. Indeed, Frankfurt's insights become clearer in light of the existential analysis of the striving will. Volitional caring can play the crucial role that Frankfurt gives it in establishing the ethos of a person— what the person stands for and "who he is" in the practical sense—because caring is the primary function of the willpower that distinguishes human persons from all other animals. So it turns out that Frankfurt was correct when he wrote that "one essential difference between persons and other creatures is to be found in the structure of a person's will"[55]—but not only because of our capacity for higher-order volition. Rather, it is our capacity for projecting self-defining commitments, combined with the ability to reflect on ourselves, that makes us persons.

2. Aretaic Commitment and Backward-Looking Considerations

2.1. *The Concept of Commitment*

In the foregoing sections, I used the term "commitment" loosely as an analog to caring and ground projects. But we can isolate a more precise sense of "commitment" that is directly related to the projective phenomena of volitional resolve. The term "commitment" has been used in many different ways in recent analytic philosophy. Most often, it simply refers to a normative epistemic connection between something an agent already believes and what follows from this. It can also be used in this sense to say that an agent is implicitly "committed" to some norm or principle by things that she does or says (e.g., this is the sense in which Kantians say that the employment of the will commits agents to the principle that the free will has inviolable intrinsic value).

Another usage comes a bit closer to the sense of "commitment" I am interested in: it takes committing as an *act* with the same intentional content as promising or contracting: the agent *binds* himself to do, say, or deliver something. Crucial to this sense of "commitment" is the idea that it creates a *backward-looking* consideration for decisions and action in the future. Thus W. D. Ross argues correctly against utilitarianism that "the fact that we have made a promise is in itself sufficient to create a [*prima facie*] duty of keeping it, the sense of duty resting on remembrance of the past promise and not on thoughts of future consequences of its fulfillment."[56] But considered this way, "commitment" is a kind of speech-act, or its equivalent, that gives other persons some sort of claim on us.

The existential tradition suggests that commitment in this speech-act sense is possible for us only in virtue of our capacity for a more fundamental kind of commitment that rests *in the will itself*.[57] Commitments of this most primordial kind are volitional in nature; although they are commitments *to* something or someone outside the self, they also involve a reflexive or intrasubjective relation-to-self. The agent binds herself not to others (as in promises) but, rather, to *herself*, forming the sort of higher-order volitional disposition that proves central to caring, on Frankfurt's account. As we saw, to care about something (or someone) involves acquiring the beliefs, judgments, emotions, and dispositions that should come from willing its (or their) flourishing. *S cares about X* entails that S identifies with

1. whatever first-order desires, emotions, and other evaluative attitudes are required for (or fit with) promoting X's well-being (if X has interests) or living up to X's demands (if X is a principle or an ideal);
2. dispositions to express care for X, to endorse the value of X, and, when appropriate, to encourage others to care about X as well.

This helps explain the sense in which caring about something or someone involves commitment to develop or maintain one's own psychic economy in a certain state over time. Without such commitment, as Frankfurt says, "We would have no settled interest in designing or in sustaining any particular continuity in the configurations of our will" or the motives on which we act.[58]

Hence the sort of commitment we are isolating is the kind that stands at the core of every volitional care. Since they partly define the character or overall ethos of the agent, I will call these "aretaic" commitments. In addition to their reflexive element, such commitments are distinguished from appetites and inclinations by their *consequence-transcending content*; prepurposive motives in general arise as attractions to various outcomes or states of affairs (usually involving the agent's possession or consumption of some object), but an aretaic commitment is a motive-state that *expresses* or affirms values that are irreducible to first-order states of affairs (not only of the agent's own well-being, but in general).[59] To commit himself to this kind of value, the agent's resolve must be in an important sense unreserved: his commitment cannot be conditional on success in bringing about the outcomes or consequences at which he aims as part of the expression of these values.

This is already suggested by the familiar (prephilosophical) sense of "commitment" as crossing a threshold, often described as a "point of no return." For instance, a textbook on aeronautics may say that once the airplane reaches the V-1 velocity for the runway, the pilot is "committed" and must lift off (since not enough runway remains to abort the takeoff). Similarly, once you jump from the tower with the bungee cord, you have "taken the plunge," and there is no way back.

Through these colloquial expressions, "commitment" is associated with *irreversibility*, with full investment of oneself in an activity, or even with staking everything on a single bet. But the sense in which aretaic commitment is unconditional or absolute does not entail that it must be *literally unrevisable* or that the agent who commits herself in this special sense can never reconsider her commitment (perhaps in light of criticism or new experiences); it entails only that the committed agent cannot disengage simply to save herself trouble, or to maximize her own happiness, or *even* to promote the good states of affairs whose realization she is committed to pursue. This last qualification, which puts the essential structure of aretaic commitment in clearest relief, emerges from ideas found in MacIntyre, Kierkegaard, Williams, Anderson, and Blustein.

2.2. *MacIntyre and Aretaic Commitment*

For example, MacIntyre has pointed out that to engage in a practice is not simply to pursue the first-order good it produces (e.g., health as the good produced by medicine) as a final end; it is also to be committed to standards of excellence internal to that practice, which limit the means by which its first-order good may be produced. So the doctor must care about her patient's health, but not as a good consequence to be maximized by any means whatsoever; the values expressed in caring about the patient's health transcend these consequences, and aretaic commitment to them is *unconditional* in the sense that it cannot be violated even to cure illness. Even the nonmoral conceptions of excellence involved in every practice are distinguished by this consequence-transcending quality; for instance, performance-enhancing drugs may increase a runner's speed, but excellence in sprinting consists in more than achieving the fastest possible speed (even when one is not competing against other athletes in formal competition, and issues of fairness do not arise). This becomes even clearer when the standards of excellence in practices are extended to include the virtues on which practices depend:

> It is of the character of a virtue that in order that it be effective in producing the internal goods which are the rewards of the virtues it should be exercised without regard to consequences . . . although the virtues are just those qualities which tend to lead to achievements of a certain class of goods [components of social well-being] nonetheless unless we practice them irrespective of whether in any particular set of circumstances they will produce those goods or not, we cannot possess them at all.[60]

For example, courage may tend to overcome obstacles to human flourishing both for individuals and communities, but the courageous person remains brave even when no first-order human good seems likely to result; it is in that sense uncompromising. Likewise, justice tends to produce trust and coordination among persons who need to cooperate, but the commitment to give people what they deserve according to fair criteria cannot be turned off or on whenever such changes in our psyche might produce more just outcomes; loyalty to the principle of justice has an intrinsic value that transcends its instrumental value as a *cause* of just outcomes.

2.3. Williams against Consequentialism

Similarly, Bernard Williams uses "commitment" in the practical sense for one broad species of project, namely "those with which one is more deeply and extensively involved and identified."[61] Commitments are lasting pursuits that give intelligible shape to a sustained course of activity requiring some perseverance, thereby providing much of the personal meaning our lives have for us. This is why, in agreement with Feinberg's argument against egoism, Williams adds that "It may even be that . . . many of those with commitments, who have really identified themselves with objects outside themselves, who are thoroughly involved with other persons, institutions, or activities or causes, are actually happier than those whose projects and wants are not like that."[62] Like Frankl and Frankfurt, Williams clearly recognizes that a devotion to worthwhile projects generates much of the value and fulfillment in human lives. What he adds is the insight that these effects arise precisely because *existential devotion* to a project, principle, or person is not simply a specification of desires for good consequences; this is why a consequentialist ethic would inevitably break down or divorce us from such commitments.

As we saw, Williams thinks of "ground projects" as one species of care, namely, the kind that forms the *core* of one's personal ethos because it involves commitment to our highest ends embodying our ultimate reasons for living. Thus ground projects are manifested in what Kierkegaard calls "infinite" passion, and this puts some limits on the type of goals that one can reasonably pursue as ground projects; for "It is a contradiction to be willing to sacrifice one's life for a finite goal."[63] Ground projects will also help determine what other, less central or fundamental commitments are volitionally possible for a person. Whether they are pursued in pure immediacy or involve reflective evaluation, the infinite commitment of the will that characterizes ground projects is incompatible with a utilitarian attitude toward one's subjective ends.

As Williams argues, a man's "decisions as a utilitarian agent are a function of all the satisfactions which he can affect from where he is: and this means that the projects of others, to an indeterminately great extent, determine his decision."[64] Of course, sometimes it is reasonable for our projects to give way when they conflict with the more important projects of others or with communal needs, and we have to be sensitive to this. But loyalty to our deepest commitments cannot vary with every change in the social context that may (given how others will react) alter the net effects that are likely to follow from our pursuing these principal life goals. As Williams asks:

> how can a man, as a utilitarian agent, come to regard as one satisfaction among others, and a dispensable one, a project or attitude around which he has built his life, just because someone's else's projects have so structured the causal scene that this is how the utilitarian sum comes out?[65]

To expect someone to abandon his ground projects whenever doing so would maximize collective utility is, as Williams says, "to alienate him in a real sense from his action and the source of his actions in his own convictions."[66] The point here is not that a morally responsible agent can never recognize reasons to change his or her ground projects or be open to changing them or willing to suspend them when necessary;[67] nor do ground projects require the agent to ignore all possible consequences of actions.[68] Rather, Williams's point is that a human life cannot have a narrative structure and robust personal meaning without being held together by some commitments that are regarded as worthwhile for their own sake and not just as ways of maximizing good results.

Thus some commitments with an aretaic structure are necessary for a well-unified life-narrative. Ground projects usually direct us toward realizing some state of affairs, but this is hardly all they do; if we could permanently secure that state of affairs simply by pushing a button on a superpowerful machine, then the ground project could not play its existential role in giving our life-narrative shape. But since what consequentialist principles directly enjoin is the maximizing of some state of affairs (S), as opposed to directly enjoining certain forms of action, attitude, or purpose, a consequentialist concern to maximize S cannot replace a ground project that involves caring about S. As Williams was the first to explain in detail, the consequentialist version can even require the agent to do something counter to S if this will cause other agents to take steps that will maximize S-states,[69] whereas *caring* about S usually cannot have this implication.

I suggest that this is because volitional caring involves an aretaic form of commitment that rules out resorting to strategies that betray that very commitment as a *means* to pursuing its ends. For example, a parent who is committed to her children will not consider doing them some serious harm on the assurance that others will then give them some benefit that greatly outweighs the harm. For this would communicate to them and others that she sees her love for them *only* as a means to their good, not as important in its own right. But what their good most requires is a loving devotion that plays a stable and central role in the ethos and life-narrative of the parent. This is true of all cares involving interpersonal relationships, of the practices, and of devotion to principles.

What about commitment to direct utilitarianism or some other "extremely impersonal moral perspective?"[70] Owen Flanagan suggests that Buddhists, for example, may believe that the collective good of all persons trumps any attachment to personal projects.[71] Yet Flanagan recognizes that "if Buddhism said that persons ought to realize a moral personality that involved no attachments whatsoever, it would be an impossible and self-defeating theory, since it would then . . . prohibit attachment to its own tenets."[72] This is correct if we understand "attachment" as willed devotion, for setting oneself to pursue a goal is an inherently self-sustaining projective activity. Thus if "commitment" to a consequentialist ideal entails being willing to erase the beliefs and motives involved in this commitment whenever one reasonably believes that doing so will maximize the likelihood of the outcomes preferred by this ideal, then this cannot be "commitment" in the volitional/projective sense. Pure consequentialism cannot, then, be earnestly willed in a self-sustaining manner that stabilizes the significance of future options for the agent.

For instance, a person who has, by volitional effort, set himself wholeheartedly to the task of (say) maximizing average income in his nation would have to see something inherently noble in this cause. If he respects this value and wants this respect to be reflected in his life, then he could hardly will to take a mind pill that makes him into a political libertarian if this would somehow get the right redistributive tax laws passed to maximize average income. Subjecting himself to a false political ideology as a means to his goal would betray his own sense of what gave meaning to his life. The motive-power of commitment is undermined if the agent sees volitional striving as having only instrumental value. Perhaps this basic fact of human psychology holds because human willing is, as Kant thought, an essentially self-respecting process.

This point is worth further elucidation. Respect for X is a relation that by definition cannot be a mere means to X's benefit or to anything else. Aretaic commitment involves respecting the intrinsic value of principles, persons, excellences, and worthy causes as having a kind of significance that ought to be recognized and expressed in human identities, not simply promoted by those identities. To respect them *is* to regard our volitional response to them as more than a mere means to actualizing them or to realizing the product-value of our goal. Thus aretaic commitment always implicitly affirms its own *existential nobility* as a respectful response. For the object of such commitment is taken to have a kind of value that cannot be served by betraying the intrinsic value of one's volitional agency in treating the will as a mere means.[73] Hence, beyond a certain point, which only prudence in the classical sense can ascertain, *to care* in the sense of volitional devotion is *to refuse to calculate certain consequences any further*, to bracket some possible outcomes as irrelevant, and to rule out certain ways of producing cared-for outcomes. To illustrate this kind of identity-shaping devotion, Kierkegaard contrasts two politicians. The first has only what Kierkegaard calls a finite passion for his goal, though (comically) he wants to be heroic, considers himself inspired, and deceives himself into believing that he is willing to sacrifice his life for his cause. "But he is sagacious enough to perceive—something that is hidden from the more simple—how important his life is for the state, that if he lives a long time no one is going to be in want, but inspiration this is not."[74] The other dies for his cause without trying to calculate the consequences of his absence on the public good.[75] His commitment is what Kierkegaard calls "infinite."

2.4. Anderson, Frankfurt, and the Priority of the Object

The conflict between caring devotion to personal projects and consequentialist theories of practical rationality has been widely acknowledged, even if its origins in the projective nature of care or commitment to tasks and persons has not been clearly recognized. This is in part because commitment is frequently based on what Elizabeth Anderson calls "backward-looking" reasons: "agents often choose an alternative not because it maximizes expected future payoffs but because the alternative bears an appropriate relation of narrative unity to prior action."[76] Anderson uses this feature to show that her own principle of respect for persons recommends ends for reasons different from those generated by alleged consequentialist equivalents. For instance, a forward-looking consequentialist principle that "fulfilling [past] commitments to oneself is intrinsically good" recommends maximizing the state of affairs that commitments are kept, and so would encourage people to "make commitments willy-nilly, just so that more commitment-fulfillments can exist in the world."[77]

Moreover, on any consequentialist principle recommending that we bring about some state of affairs E, the motive for pursuing E is always such that "there can be no rationale for avoiding E-violations when they would bring about more instances of E."[78] Thus no principle R defining what is reasonable or good in terms of "agent-centered restrictions" can be captured by a putative consequentialist equivalent calling on us to maximize the state of affairs that R is realized.[79] Thus nonconsequentialist motives involving agent-centered restrictions, such as Kant's motive of duty, do not aim simply at *promoting* ends but, rather, at pursuing ends in *certain appropriate or legitimate ways*.

Anderson takes the "attitude" of love to be a backward-looking commitment in her argument against the adequacy of a consequentialist principle P, which says "Act so as to *promote* the state of affairs: that my actions adequately express my rational attitudes towards persons."[80] Anderson argues that this principle, in asking us to maximize a certain state of affairs, implies the wrong motives for actions regarding our beloved:

> In acting on P, I take my own desire to be a loving person as my reason for action. In taking this to be my reason for action, I do not act out of love for my husband. . . . What makes sense of my taking my husband's needs as my reasons for action is that I love him, not that in so taking them I make myself a loving person.[81]

This point is also related to the reflection problem that we noticed in Elster's analysis (chap. 5, sec. 2.4): genuine love or care is a purposive motive focused on an agent-transcending object; it is distinct from the desire to validate a certain *self-image* of oneself as loving, which might be measured by how much apparently loving activity one exhibits. As Blustein argues, my caring about a person or principle "is not reducible in any simple way to caring about my own satisfaction or advantage, or more particularly, to caring about an image of myself as caring about these" persons or principles.[82] The latter motive would be concerned only about the consequence that I act lovingly, as recommended by a principle like P. But action on this motive is not genuinely loving; it is a neurotic and potentially narcissistic perversion of true devotion. By contrast, if the agent takes the satisfaction of her husband's needs as intrinsically valuable and on this basis *projects* the end of satisfying these needs (in reasonable ways), then her motive is loving in Anderson's sense.

Such a projective commitment could even make her willing, in certain circumstances, to undercut her self-image as "the person lovingly devoted to this man," if she saw that this was necessary to promote his good. This might happen if, for example, she found that for his own good, she had to *disengage* from pursuing his good through direct interaction with him.[83] The projective structure of volitional love explains how it is possible for a true lover sometimes to sacrifice such loving activity itself *out of love*. By contrast, a desire (in the substantive *orektic* sense) can never motivate one to abandon pursuit of the desired outcomes except as a temporary postponement in service of future gratification. I cannot permanently sacrifice my enjoyment of some object or end on the basis of my desire to possess this object or be completed by reaching this end. But projective devotion to some end or person *can* sometimes motivate me to abandon direct pursuit of this end or to give up direct relation to the person for their sake (thus promoting a good that I cannot experience as its direct cause but can, at most, appreciate from a distance). To be strong-willed in the existential sense does not mean always asserting oneself as an agent who has to be active in every significant development or who has to be centrally involved in the life of things and persons she cares about. Sometimes it takes volitional strength to withdraw, leave things or persons alone when that is best, or let others achieve a noble end that we could secure (see "Conclusion: The Danger of Willfulness Revisited).

This seems to be part of what Frankfurt means when he writes that "the value of loving to the lover derives from his dedication to his beloved," for, in spite of the by-product benefit that the object of love may have for the agent (by making it possible for him to enjoy "the inherently important activity of loving it"), his active pursuit of the beloved's good is motivated *purely* by the intrinsic importance of the beloved's good. Thus "the activity of the lover is subordinated to the interests of his beloved."[84] This entails that he is willing to disengage from direct involvement with her and thereby *lose* the by-product benefits of his interaction with her if this is what her good requires. But it does *not* entail that the agent's caring devotion could motivate him to *give up his commitment* to his beloved—to cease caring about her entirely or even to cultivate hatred of her—as a means to promoting her good. We have seen why this kind of manipulation of self and other is inconsistent with loyalty to the values that makes her worth caring about. *What* he wills is not only her good but also his respect for her value (and thus for the value of her flourishing). Thus his volitional loyalty to her cannot merely be instrumental to her good. By contrast, a consequentialist principle like P could motivate Anderson to despise and harm her husband if this would make her more loving toward him or make him better off in the long run.

Thus Williams's insight really points out a distinctive mark of aretaic commitment in opposition to consequentialist motivation toward end-states, product-goods, or results in general. Although it can certainly motivate disengagement from direct pursuit of the valued end or suspension of active relations with the beloved person, aretaic commitment to some end E cannot motivate its own elimination *as a means* to promoting E; nor can it motivate its own violation or repression as a means to its longer-term cultivation. Aretaic commitment is uncompromising in two senses: it gives priority to its object rather than to itself, but it also cannot be self-effacing. Both these features reflect the overriding importance of remaining true to the values that make the object worthy of devotion. Thus, once formed, aretaic commitment always serves as a backward-looking reason for its own preservation and active expression (even though this must sometimes take the form of disengagement or hiding one's love) and so it rules out the kinds of self-manipulation that indirect consequentialism is notorious for justifying.

It is because ground projects and volitional cares in general involve aretaic commitment that they cannot be explained simply in terms of a motivation to optimize certain results or to bring about the best states of affairs (even the state of affairs that one is loyal to one's commitments). Rather, to care is generally to be subject to agent-centered constraints in *the ways* that intended results may be pursued, where these constraints express both (1) respect for the intrinsic value of one's object, and (2) proper respect for the authenticity of one's own will. These constraints govern the actions, attitudes, and attention that we render to the object of our care, giving our devotion to it an essentially nonconsequentialist structure.

It follows from this analysis that aretaic commitment to some X is reflexive in the sense that it is always also a commitment to its own purity; its goal is not simply the first-order value of X's flourishing or being upheld, but also the second-order value of its own respect for X's value. This second-order value is the nobility that a volitional state derives from taking the sincere expression of first-order values in the world as its regulating principle. Commitment in this strong sense can only be projective for the same reason that Kant's motive of duty must be projective: its full aim transcends the consequence-only focus of *orektic* prepurposive motives.

2.5. *Blustein on Commitment*

The relation of commitment to caring is clarified in Jeffrey Blustein's thorough treatment of these concepts. Blustein considers commitment central only to a subset of cares, because he recognizes several kinds of "caring," following common usage:

1. "caring for" some X as "liking, having affection for, being drawn or attracted to" X;
2. "having care of" somebody or something, that is, being in charge of them or it;
3. caring about something or someone X: the agent's well-being is tied up with X;[85]
4. "caring that" something X is the case or happens: the agent is invested in X.[86]

Senses 3 and 4 are closely related, because caring about something or someone usually involves caring that some propositions are true or false and/or that some states of affairs obtain or do not. For example, caring about my son might involve hoping that he has not died today in Iraq. However, Blustein argues convincingly that caring about X can be quite independent of caring *for* X. Positive caring about X requires only that "S wants to do something that will benefit X, or be welcomed by X, or that will enhance it in some way, or keep it from being harmed."[87] It does not require that the agent enjoys X or the pursuit of X.

So Blustein follows Frankfurt in emphasizing that caring about something or someone involves risking distress and loss; for example, "close friends are strongly, durably, and deeply invested in each other's well-being." But, unlike Frankfurt, Blustein recognizes that this kind of attachment to another person or investment in her well-being can also be self-interested: "I may positively care about you because I am dependent upon you for advancement of my own interests," as when an employer cares about an employee only *qua* worker.[88] In these cases, the dependence of the agent's well-being on the well-being of her target *precedes* and motivates the care relation rather than following from it. Thus Blustein distinguishes self-interested and other-regarding "caring about," calling the latter "disinterested care."[89] In such disinterested care I actively "take an interest in things and people I care about when I make their condition my active concern because I identify myself with them."[90] This clearly corresponds to Frankfurtian caring, in which the agent's well-being depends on the beloved's flourishing as a result of his projecting her good as his end.

However, Blustein also argues that even some disinterested cares do not embody deep commitments or give "deliberative priority to projects" involved in the care.[91] Caring without commitment occurs in cases of *akratic* caring against one's will (or against one's central values);[92] it also occurs in the case of personal projects such as "hobbies" that the agent "could forego with relative ease, even if not without any personal disappointment or pain."[93] Here the absence of commitment seems to be marked in two ways, according to Blustein. First, hobbies are not ground projects; the agent would not die for them, and they are not even vital to her identity. Second, the agent can see the hobby's value as purely "personal," or derivative from his caring about it. These two aspects of such existentially peripheral cares are related:

> Perhaps when one cares seriously about something that one values, one must suppose it to have a kind of value that does not simply derive from one's own individual caring about it. . . . It is only in connection with what we might call deep-seated caring that the one who cares must see the value of what he or she cares about as lying both within and without him or her. In cases of peripheral caring, this is not necessary. . . . The projects that have personal value for us must at least be seen to be innocent in themselves, apart from their relation to us, and in the case of deep-seated caring, personal value must also be sustained by the conviction of impersonal value.[94]

This seems largely correct, for there is an evident distinction between projects that are more central and those that are more peripheral to one's identity, and hobbies may by definition fall into the latter class.[95] I would amend Blustein's analysis only by allowing that caring about something because of its objective or impersonal value need not make our care deep-seated or give it a high degree of deliberative priority in our lives. For this reason, it seems possible that projects such as hobbies may also be taken by their agents to be responses to forms of value that are not only morally innocent but also interpersonally recognizable as goods, although they are only optional and not obligatory. For example, I might see some objective value in maintaining a Web site on local history; I do it "for fun," as we say, but it is fun because the history has some genuine interest rather than being absolutely trivial.

This minor quibble aside, Blustein's great insight is that the commitment involved in cares that play a deep role in the agent's personal ethos must be experienced as a serious response to values that stand over against the agent, whose high importance should be intersubjectively recognizable. This thesis fits well with my further claim that these values must be experienced as consequence-transcending (or not exhausted by the product-value of the relevant end-states). For it is only to values of this kind that we can be aretaically committed, and only this kind of commitment defines the agent's volitional identity in the deepest way, making strong narrative unity possible and giving value to integrity as a kind of second-order loyalty to one's commitments. By contrast, in projects motivated only by the value of the likely consequences, our volitional devotion to the goal, as well as to our own resolve and the sense of enduring meaning that it produces in our lives, functions only as contingent means to the goal itself. Our volitional identity, as defined by this kind of project, is in principle dispensable. This is a deficient form of projective willing, whereas aretaic commitment is the will's highest function.

Blustein recognizes that integrity in our projects or cares is at issue only if they involve commitment to impersonal values,[96] but he does not rule out consequentialist values as grounds for the identity-defining commitments of a stable and integrated self.[97] He writes, "If we think of integrity in a formal way as what is manifested in a person maintaining his or her principles or deep commitments in the face of temptations or trials, then it is not clear why the utilitarian must lack integrity."[98] I agree with Blustein that a utilitarian can regard his project as having primacy in his own deliberations and that real human agents could enthusiastically pursue a project such as increasing the collective happiness of some group—appropriating it as their own and making this goal personally important to them.[99] But this project cannot constitute an aretaic commitment; for if the agent judged that the world would be improved by giving up his commitment and teaching others not to hold it, he would have to do this.[100] This amounts to denying that the value of collective happiness deserves ongoing respect and hence denying the intrinsic value of willing the utilitarian project; only its outcome would have such value. But, as Blustein has helped to show, the striving will's natural relation to its ultimate grounds is respect, which implies *continuing* affirmation. Thus the existential analysis of volitional commitment puts the integrity critique of utilitarianism on a new footing.

This is only a sketch of an existential argument against utilitarianism; its full development requires an analysis of integrity as a proto-virtue of the human will (as well as further distinctions in value theory).[101] However, we have seen both that the existential role of aretaic commitment has significant ethical implications and that only the existential account of striving will can explain how aretaic commitment is possible. Our analysis of this phenomenon has identified the following main elements:

The Existential Conception of Aretaic Commitment
(from Blustein, with my additions)

I. Active Direction toward an End: Commitments are *states of our agency* (not something that simply happens to us), and they are motivational states aiming at (usually self-transcending) objects of concern. Commitments may be to principles (propositional maxims) or directly to persons or to other kinds of valuable ends.[102]

2. **Investment of Self and Staying Power:** Commitments involve personal engagement in a relationship, or *personal appropriation* of an ideal or set of values. Apathy or detachment defeats commitment, as does the absence of sincere conviction in its objective value or importance. Because they embody respect for objective value, commitments are motivational dispositions through which we are engaged in a way that is difficult to reverse: *we cannot disengage* "at will" just to please others or ourselves or whenever it might be convenient.[103]

3. **Backward-Looking Significance:** Thus aretaic commitments shape the volitional feasibility of future options for us. Such a commitment is always a backward-looking reason for future action in circumstances where it is relevant. Thus aretaic commitment to something is inconsistent with a pure consequentialist attitude toward the future:[104] it is never sufficient to justify changing or suspending my commitment that doing so will allow me to cause more of the outcomes that I am committed to pursuing.

4. **Self-Sustaining Significance:** Commitments are self-sustaining in the sense that they always give us a personal reason to preserve them and to remain loyal to them, given the alterity and endurance of the values that they respect. This is a reason that can be defeated only by conflicting commitments or by evidence telling against the evaluative attitudes on which they are based. Thus it is essential to aretaic commitment that *it* can never directly motivate us to abandon it, betray it, or alter it.

5. **Reflexive Resolve and Resilience:** Commitments involve devotion of oneself to the end because of its intrinsic values but also involve an effort to mold related desires and emotions in accord with our commitments. As a result, commitments are resilient against non-cognitive resistance from other experienced motives; in strong-willed agents, they are swayed only by evidence bearing on rationality of the goal (i.e., the reasons for valuing the end intrinsically) or the rationality of one's route toward it (i.e., the reasons for believing that one's pursuit of the goal is feasible and fits coherently with other commitments). Thus commitments do not change easily, on a whim, or merely as a means to producing other desirable consequences.

6. **A Basis in Strong Evaluation:** This suggests, in turn, that the judgments (or other cognitive attitudes) on which commitments are based tend to be strongly evaluative in nature and hence sensitive only to evidential reasons for altering the evaluation rather than to

nonevidential reasons (such as D2 desires) for adapting one's commitments to convenience or expediency. Yet the committed agent should entertain rational critique of her commitments since her respect for their grounds implies that she does not want them to be based on falsehoods.

7. **Strength of Will:** Commitment to some X implies the ability to act for X's sake and some significant level of success in doing so (whether or not X is attained), which is incompatible with a high degree of *akrasia*.[105] Thus commitment is a phenomenon of *volitional effort*, liking "trying," but concerned with setting and sustaining ends rather than merely attempting to enact intentions once formed. This effort of will is not just in response to adversity, for exceptionally resolute persons have little difficulty in acting on their commitments;[106] that is because they have already made the effort to bring other motivations into line, and active effort to maintain their end or goal is now a lasting disposition of their will.

One advantage of this conception is the way it makes sense of our intuition that "strength of will" is enhanced by firm commitment. Following Ronald Milo, Blustein suggests that an irresolute person "does not make a sufficient effort to preserve strength of resolve even though this could have successfully been done had the person exercised powers of self-control."[107] It should be apparent now that the "resolve" lacking in such cases is a projective effort of self-motivation.

In conclusion, this chapter shows that several concepts playing central roles in late-twentieth-century ethical theory and moral psychology cannot adequately be explained without the existential conception of striving will. In particular, the key concepts of care, volitional love, identity-conferring commitments, and integrity are clarified by the existential approach to personhood. It remains to be shown that this approach is compatible with an objective conception of the values worth caring about, as suggested by Blustein's rich analysis and the concept of respect to which I have appealed. That is the task of the next chapter.

14

An Existential Objectivist Account of What Is Worth Caring About

Overview. This chapter develops the idea introduced in chapters 12 and 13 that an existential conception of the will as an end-setting and motivation-sustaining capacity is compatible with moderate objectivism about the values that give us reasons to set ends, initiate new projects, and form deep commitments. The chapter begins with a review of the importance of this question about the nature of good lives for contemporary political philosophy, and then develops an existential response to Harry Frankfurt's subjectivist interpretation of the worth of what we care about. The analysis does not try to establish the metaphysical status of values but it does have normative implications (in particular in the concluding taxonomy of grounds for caring).

Introduction

This chapter concludes the argument for the book's first main thesis by showing that the existential conception of the will is compatible with an objective account of practical reasons for willing and so escapes charges of arbitrariness or irrationalism. Against Harry Frankfurt's subjectivist account of practical normativity, I argue that when caring is understood in terms of projective commitment, it always depends on objective (and even, in a weak sense, "universalizable") grounding value-judgments. Nor are these reasons for caring entirely derivative from already-existing cares or loves. There must always be grounds for the projection of any goals, yet these grounds do not necessitate action and need not themselves constitute prepurposive motivation.[1]

Consistent with the account of aretaic commitment in the last chapter, I also maintain that the grounds for caring about something X are not generally exhausted by the product-values involved in realizing X or bringing about X's good; for there are often other goods related to the process of pursuing X that can (without self-defeat) provide at least *part* of the basis for devotion to X. Moreover, some grounds for caring about X may be accessible or salient only to particular agents, depending on contingent features of their personal history, including past choices and standing projects or relationships. This chapter concludes with a preliminary taxonomy of grounds for projective willing, which plays the same role in an existential virtue ethics that a list of basic goods plays in "new" natural-law theories of practical reason.[2]

I. Existential Objectivism

In chapter 13, we saw that the existential account of caring and volitional love explains and supports Frankfurt's theory on all but these two points: the existential conception of the striving will does not require that the core of the self be constituted by "volitional necessities" that, in turn, are determined by contingencies beyond the agent's control; nor does it imply that the agent's ultimate grounds for caring are *inscrutably* personal or subjective. My goal in this chapter is to show that an existential theory of the will does not imply that the volitional constitution of our life goals or ground projects is ultimately arbitrary or without interpersonal justification. By contrast, in explaining the structure of projective motivation (chap. 9, secs. 4 and 5), I introduced the Grounding thesis, which says that goals and ends are projected upon objective grounds. This implies what I call *existential objectivism* (EO):

> EO: The goal-setting and goal-pursuing activity of the striving will (projecting new final ends, modifying existing motives, and consolidating or focusing the motivation behind intended purposes already decided on by the agent) is always performed *in light of* values or goods that (appear to the agent to) *ground* or at least partially justify the motives formed by volitional commitment and resolve, independently of any relation between these goods and the agent's existing D1-D3 desires. In general, these values have the *broadly ethical* character of tending to provide *intersubjectively accessible* reasons for ways of life, modes of caring, or different types of personal ethos.

This kind of existential view clearly rejects Sartre's signature thesis that my practical orientation toward goals, relationships, and concerns that inform my actions is an "original projection of myself . . . which causes the existence of values, appeals, expectations, and in general a world" of practical significance to exist for me.³ Whether or not we exercise libertarian control over projective motivation in my sense, it does not experience itself as utterly unjustified or anguished due to lacking any foundation for its purposes. Rather, existential objectivism is analogous to the old eudaimonist formula that the will always aims at some good; but it is liberated from the idea that the first-order good(s) at which the will aims must be part of the agent's own eudaimonia or even the collective eudaimonia of the agent's community.

Despite its sharp departure from Sartre's early theory of values,⁴ EO has a well-established place in the tradition behind my existential conception of the will. We have seen that Scotus and Kant are objectivists about specifically moral values as overriding grounds for projective motivation (chap. 11) and that Frankl is an objectivist about a much broader range of potential "meanings" to be found in potential causes, purposes, or undertakings (chap. 12). This is unsurprising, because at the *normative* level, quite apart from metaethical questions about value-realism, there are several reasons to think that the proper functioning of the human will presupposes objective values (of multiple kinds) and requires volitional agents to be at least moderately able to recognize and track such goods, taking them to be realities *independent of* their own subjective states, including especially their desires.

Today, an interesting array of figures in both analytic and Continental thought provide support for this view. In recent moral psychology, perhaps the most impressive is Jeffrey Blustein, who argues that "not all care is, all things considered, *good* care or equally good care."⁵ He presses this point in order to show that one cannot build an ethic solely on the formal structure of the caring attitude, as Nel Noddings once suggested.⁶ Some personal projects are immoral, and others are "excessive," focusing obsessively on one cause or principle while ignoring others to which the agent ought to attend.⁷ Cares can be criticized not only according to deontic standards but also according to other broadly ethical standards about what anyone ought to care about: "Plausible candidates are things that can be identified as fundamental and important human goods: knowledge, life, play, aesthetic experience, practical reasonableness (including morality), and sociability (love and friendship)."⁸

Blustein's list focuses on human goods, whereas EO recognizes grounds for projective motivation beyond the human realm, for example, in natural values like the flourishing of nonhuman species and ecosystems, good essences (among ersatz entities), and possibly divine being. But Blustein agrees that such objective values provide a key part of the evaluative framework in which we can undertake "critical scrutiny of our fundamental carings and core commitments," which in turn is crucial for "autonomy" in our deepest identity.⁹

As we will see, such an objectivist approach has to be qualified in several ways to stand up to Frankfurt's arguments for the opposite position, which we might call *existential subjectivism* (ES). Since Frankfurt draws together several antiobjectivist and antirationalist arguments from other thinkers, focusing on Frankfurt will help to show how EO can be made sufficiently flexible to capture the features of human psychology on which subjectivists focus, without abandoning key aspects of objectivism that reflect ordinary prephilosophical intuitions about the relationship of cares and values. In the next section, I put this project in historical context by arguing that recent political philosophy reveals the need to find some acceptably objectivist understanding of norms concerning good lives.

2. Caring and the Good in Recent Political Philosophy

As I suggested in chapter 2 (sec. 4), the question of whether there are objective ways of understanding goods that can inform individual and group decisions about how to live was raised in the twentieth century by communitarian and Aristotelian responses to neo-Kantian political theories. The revival of virtue ethics reopened questions about good character and good lives that were underemphasized in moral theories aiming primarily to provide criteria for justice in liberal societies. As we see most clearly in John Rawls's *Political Liberalism*, these theories aimed to define justice in a way that would be neutral between many (although certainly not all) rival comprehensive conceptions of happiness for individuals and communities.

The hope of both pragmatist and more rationalist versions of the neo-Kantian project is to show that there are grounds (either in the nature of practical reason and agency itself or at least in personhood as conceived in some political traditions) for principles of duty, justice, and individual rights that are largely *independent* of other values we may pursue in life. Hence without threatening the objectivity of morality and the foundation of political justice, citizens can disagree not only about *what* other values should regulate our long-term goals or highest ends but also about whether these values are entirely subjective (defined only in reference to agents' brute preferences) or objectively based in human psychology, sociology, religion, or in some other dimension of reality. It is, of course, this sought independence from any comprehensive doctrine of "the good" that makes "morality" in the neo-Kantian sense narrower than "ethics" in the broad, classical sense of a practical inquiry into what goals are worth pursuing for their own sake and what ways of life are superior.[10]

Yet several twentieth-century authors, such as Elizabeth Anscombe, Alasdair MacIntyre, Bernard Williams, and Michael Sandel, have made different criticisms of this neo-Kantian project, both as a goal for moral theory *per se* and as a way of grounding political philosophy. In every case, their criticisms are driven by a desire to refocus attention on the question of how we can argue for the superiority of some forms of shared life and some kinds of personal goals over others. The principles required for such a broad, ethical evaluation of political institutions and social life (the state, civil society, and the personal endeavors they support) unavoidably involve "thicker" conceptions of the good than a neo-Kantian conception of justice can provide. Thus an adequate political ethics cannot abstract entirely from the values that guide the selection of individual and group life goals.

But belief that this question needs a systematic answer, part of which may include an account of the virtues or perfections of character that make possible the pursuit and perhaps attainment of the best form(s) of life, is, interestingly, *not exclusive* to those who reject the possibility of moral principles that are neutral between at least a large range of comprehensive accounts of the good. In recent years, a significant number of other authors who are not as pessimistic about the neo-Kantian project of finding an ethos-independent basis for political philosophy have suggested that we also need substantive conceptions of "the good" and have looked for values that can ground ways of life or justify personal devotions. In addition to Blustein, authors as diverse as Owen Flanagan, Joel Kupperman, Thomas Hurka, Stephen Darwall, and others have asked whether we have any objective criteria for what is worth caring about. Their work in moral psychology intersects with a growing feminist literature that attempts to base normative ethics on an account of caring. Some of the authors in this tradition see their project as complementary with neo-Kantian accounts of justice, and others do not. Moreover, similar themes have for decades concerned Continental philosophers writing on ethics, such as Buber, Sartre, Jaspers, Arendt, Levinas, and Ricoeur.

The main problem with all these recent attempts to revive ethics in its broader sense is that they lack a conception of the will adequate to the task. As far back as 1960, Elizabeth Anscombe told us that before significant progress could be made in ethics, we would need to address several more basic problems in moral psychology.[11] Since then, following her lead, philosophers have devoted much attention to explaining the notions of intention, action, decision, and practical reason as well as to clarifying the differences between consequentialist and nonconsequentialist moral theories. Yet, as we saw in chapter 3, these developments led to a conception of "will" that covers only decision or the formation of intentions—which at most is conceived as a special kind of agent-causal process that occurs in selecting among multiple options.

Thus twentieth-century moral psychology failed to reach the heart of the problem that Anscombe recognized. Without a sufficient understanding of the will's unique motivational function, proponents of the broad ethical approach could not adequately explain how human persons form and sustain long-term commitments, identity-defining cares, or governing personal goals, the pursuit of which gives life not only its narrative shape but also a large part of its personal meaning or practical significance for the agent living that life. That is the lacuna I have tried to fill.

My existential conception of the will supports the recent idea that a value-objectivist response to this question of "practical normativity"[12] can be compatible with holding that a neo-Kantian analysis of the Right is a better basis than comprehensive conceptions of the Good for understanding the basic requirements of social justice and legitimate constitutional structures. It is possible to favor a deontological conception of basic duties and political rights without holding that the plurality of "comprehensive conceptions" of the good in contemporary societies shows that objective ethics at this level is impossible. One could simply hold that the concept of the Right is the *primary* criterion for evaluating the basic structure of society, with rival theories of the Good playing at most a secondary role in justifying a given society's public conception of political justice (it is the common point of reference in constitutional debate).

If this is correct, then fundamental principles for political justice are determined by ideals that are definable and defendable largely in abstraction from the values that inform concrete life goals or existential projects, although these might play a secondary role by justifying some differences between just constitutional schemes across different societies. One can hold this, as Kant clearly did, *without* thinking that the question of the best life or what goods we should value is merely subjective, or without taking a relativist view of the Good. As a result, one can accept that at least the formal structure of the Right is analyzable largely in independence from the Good, without accepting the implausible further claim that the particular content of political rights and democratic lawmaking can be understood *wholly* without reference to our substantive views about what human beings need and what ends and goals are worth pursuing for mature moral agents. For it is difficult to interpret the scope of rights and to justify even the weakest types of legal paternalism (such as state support for the arts or prohibitions on polygamy) without reference to thick goods.

Such a combination of political deontologism and ethical objectivism contrasts sharply with two theses recently defended by Jürgen Habermas (but also present in Rawls and other neo-Kantians): (1) that substantive accounts of the goods to be valued in human life always depend on some form of "metaphysics" that illegitimately presupposes appeals to religious faith or to discredited essentialism in a theory of human nature; and (2) that "philosophy no longer has the right to intervene" in debates about substantive goods, since the "legitimate pluralism of worldviews . . . prohibits any form of paternalism in the area of genuinely ethical advice."[13] In my view, these theses are both profoundly mistaken. The first is refuted by the plain fact, proven again and again in creative philosophical and literary work, that philosophers (along with novelists, playwrights, and screenplay writers) *are* capable of a descriptive phenomenology of different goods worth being valued and pursued, along with a critique of such values and their social conditions, without recourse to anything more "metaphysical" than reflection on human experience, critical psychology, sociology, and history—though they sometimes appeal to faith.[14] Disagreements about thick goods within literature and film are really analogous in philosophical status to disagreements about what is politically just: they are articulated with relevant examples in search of reflective rational consensus.

Habermas's second thesis commits a fallacy of misplaced neutrality, for the idea that persons must to some extent be free to form and pursue goods as they conceive them is itself a *substantive* deliverance of a theory of the Right—as is any position concerning what issues the state should leave up to individual choice (and thus also to market forces). Moreover, philosophical analysis can at times even give direct advice about the goods that inform life plans and ways of life without violating political freedoms. The liberal approach to political justice cannot reject this, because neo-Kantian theories of justice obviously depend on a conception of the person as a willing agent who values goods and pursues life projects in their light. This metaphysical conception implies that the problem of *what* to will, or what values we should commit ourselves to pursuing, is in principle at least partially answerable in terms other than sheer personal preference (or D2 desire), arbitrary selection on a whim, or blind acceptance of some traditional authority. As Joel Kupperman has convincingly argued, the liberal idea that persons should be free to pursue their own subjectively preferred values and goals, as long as this violates no moral requirements, *does not* entail that we cannot or should not judge, condemn, reproach, or praise their choices and activities or argue with them about their priorities in terms external to their own "system of desires." In fact:

> Such extreme reluctance to judge, from the outside, the lives of others (apart from those small areas that are subject to moral judgment) lends itself to a sense of one's own life as having no relation to standards of excellence. From this it is a short step to a sense of one's own life as essentially meaningless.[15]

This is correct and it can also be defended from the opposite direction. Imagine a person who explains to a friend or relative the long-term goals upon which she has resolved or the highest values to which she has devoted years of her life and unquantifiable amounts of blood, sweat, and tears. Now consider the effect when her interlocutor responds with no more than "well, whatever turns you on," or "that's nice, I suppose," or "if that's what you wanted, I'm glad you were free to pursue it." Such empty responses constitute only the most hollow form of "recognition"; they implicitly dismiss the agent's strivings as no more than an expression of her brute private preferences, which cannot have any further significance beyond her own subjective enjoyment of her projects—though that is certainly not why she thought them worth so much effort. In short, the concerns and priorities around which our agent has built her life are implied by her interlocutor here to be *no concern of his at all*, as if the fact that they mattered so much to her couldn't be any evidence that he should consider their importance as well.

But if his view is justified, then what was their point for her? What her interlocutor implies is far worse than if he had criticized her goals or questioned the wisdom or adequacy of her projects. At least then they would be recognized as having some universal human significance, however inadequate it might be, in his judgment. This would be a far more reassuring recognition of her agency. By comparison, pure toleration based on the implication that the question is a matter of mere personal taste is necessarily offensive when the question concerns the core of one's practical identity. The meaning our identities have for us requires them to matter in the broadly ethical sense and to be subject to broadly ethical judgment or be based on objective grounds.

3. Three Initial Reasons for Objectivism

When Frankfurt first tried to explain the importance of caring in human life, he seemed to recognize some of the reasons sketched above for an objectivist analysis, yet he also insisted that in many cases, the only "importance" that our cared-for object or goal has is that which we *give* it by caring about it. Although the latter theme has come to dominate his recent treatments of caring, in his 1982 essay Frankfurt aids the objectivist by noting that, given the centrality of cares to our character and our concern about the value of our character, "a person may care about what he cares about"—a question naturally related to "evaluation and justification."[16] At the very least, he thought that it makes sense to *ask* "what ends to set for ourselves and what sort of character to strive for," and thus to *look* for a "genuinely objective sort of reasoning by which a person can establish or validate his ends."[17]

3.1. Caring about the Worth of Our Cares

Indeed, the force of this point is far stronger than Frankfurt lets on: although some measures of character may be primarily reflexive (like integrity or loyalty to one's own projects), most measures refer to standards that are thought to be widely held or in principle even universally shareable, such as moral, aesthetic, or broadly ethical norms and ideals. If it makes sense to worry about *how worthy* our character is in these senses, this could only be because we believe that, in principle, we have access to some objective standards for the worthiness of our character. To the extent that this question of merit is a function of *how worthwhile* our cares and loves are, it suggests that there must be objective grounds for or against caring about certain objects or caring in certain ways. So higher-order caring about one's volitional character, or reflexive concern to understand and approve of what one cares about, is most naturally construed in objectivist fashion as caring that one's first-order cares are well grounded or sufficiently guided by the real values there are in the world, which are not created by one's own will.[18] In other words, it is caring$_2$ about the axiological adequacy of one's cares$_1$.

In *Saving Private Ryan*, this is what the elderly Ryan means when he asks, at the Normandy graveside of Captain John Miller, "Have I lived a good life?"[19] This question is intensely personal, and admittedly the standards for judging it are difficult, complex, and, as his case makes unusually clear, historically conditioned in unrepeatable or individually unique ways.[20] Nevertheless, Ryan's question is interpersonally intelligible, and his wife understands that it means more than "Have I cared deeply about something or someone, no matter what or who?" For it includes, among other things, the question: Were my cares adequate responses to the sacrifices to which I am indebted?—which in turn involves: Were the objects of my care the sort of things that it is good to care about, given the individual sacrifices made so that I had a chance to live and had material conditions necessary for caring about things beyond myself? No advanced philosophical education is required to understand what Ryan means when he asks his own less abstract, more existential, version of Socrates' eternal question, "How should one live?" The audience understands immediately and intuitively that Ryan could have done better or worse, and the movie reinforces the natural presumption that this objective difference *matters*—not just for Ryan but for anyone (especially in reference to the past sacrifices of others).

This example illustrates why some kind of axiological objectivism is required to capture in philosophical theory the intuitive prephilosophical outlook of most persons on the relationship of caring to values. If people naturally look for values that can ground, explain, or justify their cares, and this is what they ordinarily take themselves to be attending to in caring$_2$ about whether their cares$_1$ are good, adequate, or responsible, then the burden is clearly on the subjectivist to explain how caring$_1$ can make sense or be meaningful to its agent without such objective grounds. Frankfurt seems to recognize this when he admits:

> The fact that what a person cares about is a personal matter does not entail that *anything* goes. It may still be possible to distinguish between things that are worth caring about to one degree or another, and things that are not. Accordingly, it may be useful to inquire into what makes something worth caring about—that is, what conditions must be satisfied if something is to be suitable or worthy as an ideal or as an object of love—and into how a person is to decide, from among the various things worth caring about, which to care about. Although people may justifiably care about different things, or care differently about the same things, this surely does not mean that their loves and their ideals are entirely unsusceptible to significant criticism of any sort or that no general analytical principles of discrimination can be found.[21]

In this crucial passage, Frankfurt originally acknowledged that even if there is wide latitude in the scope of cares that could be reasonable for a person, given her circumstances, that is compatible with some objective limits. For example, he recognizes here that it is not worth caring about "avoiding stepping on cracks in the pavement,"[22] and that "there is a well-established and valuable usage" according to which the preference of Hume's man who prefers the destruction of the world to some minor damage to his finger is not only unreasonable but even "crazy."[23] Frankfurt suggests that this man's "defect is volitional,"[24] but he does not clarify that the volitional error in this case consists in caring too little about something of enormous importance and too much about something of infinitesimal importance by comparison. Such a person's cares seem to be so unguided by real value that we might question whether he meets the cognitive conditions required for moral responsibility. Or if he does recognize these value-differences but simply ignores them, then we might well ask whether he meets the motivational conditions for moral sanity.

In sum, then, the first reason for existential objectivism about the broad range of values relevant to personal projects, relationships, and goals concerns the widely held conviction that *one sense* in which a final end or object of care can be "important" is what we might call the *normative worth* sense (NW): some things are *worth* caring about in such a way as to justify normative judgments of cares as *worthy*. NW importance, in other words, functions as the truth-maker for a certain kind of evaluative judgment that, even in the age of abstraction from comprehensive conceptions of the good, still plays a vital role in interpersonal, broadly ethical assessments of characters and lives.

3.2. *The Intersubjective Intelligibility and Criticizability of Cares*

In the crucial passage quoted above, Frankfurt accepts another point in favor of objectivism: we generally presume that people's cares, loves, and ideals are intersubjectively evaluable, and even if we reject particular evaluations of our life goals and projects, we cannot intelligibly reject the very possibility of such critique. As Charles Taylor has persuasively argued, following Hegel, "No one acquires the languages needed for self-definition on their own."[25] Precisely because our volitional "identity" (consisting centrally of our cares and long-term devotions) is so important, "We define this always in dialogue with, sometimes in struggle against, the identities our significant others want to recognize in us."[26] Even in dialogue with ourselves, we have to understand our practical identity as "the background against which our tastes and desires and opinions and aspirations make sense."[27] And to make sense to us, they must, at least *in principle*, be capable of making sense to others as well; hence to "define ourselves" through personal commitments or cares, "we have to take as background some sense of what is significant,"[28] or what values have sufficient intrinsic importance to merit attention from any relevantly situated human agent.

Thus in Taylor's view, as Joel Anderson explains, "There are grounds for disputing one's sense of what is personally important that go beyond the experience of internal conflict," or subjectivist norms of "internal coherence."[29] We must articulate any robust self-conception in a "vocabulary of values" that cannot be a private language game.[30] Without such a vocabulary, as Taylor says, we could not even ask "what constitutes a rich, meaningful life—as against one concerned with secondary matters or trivia."[31] Moreover, the importance of many pursuits cannot be described without invoking the kind of aretaic values and contrasts (between noble and base) that Taylor terms "strong evaluation."[32]

Thus our practical identities can be significant to us only within a horizon of intersubjectively intelligible values. If this were not the case, then the normative worth of our endeavors, relationships, and life goals could not form the basis of what Taylor calls our personal "dignity" or "our sense of ourselves as commanding (attitudinal) respect."[33] Although Taylor is surely right that popular views about what activities are worthwhile or command respect have changed radically since the warrior culture of Homeric Greece and now emphasize possibilities available in "ordinary life" much more than in earlier times, our pride in our activities and purposes still depends on interpersonal evaluations in public space. "The notion is never that *whatever* we do is acceptable. This would be unintelligible as the basis for a notion of dignity."[34] (See the related discussion of self-esteem in chap. 12, sec. 7.)

3.3. Goods Internal to Practices Are Worth Caring About

A third important argument for existential objectivism comes from the analysis of the practices already given in chapter 8. The goods at which a practitioner must aim for their own sake to count as engaging in the practices are objective social goods that are important for the flourishing of human individuals, communities, and other living beings.[35] Although different individuals will differentiate their attention to and enjoyment of these social goods, this hardly requires them to deny that (for example) public health, different types of scientific knowledge, and the various types of beauty created by fine arts and crafts are objectively good (even if their goodness is incommensurable or impossible to compare on a single scale). Moreover, the various nonmoral types of excellence and standards for great products of the practices can also count noncontroversially as objective goods.

These excellences that arise in the process of pursuing the objective goods definitive of the practices are usually related to various kinds of *difficulty* resulting from the concrete conditions of human life. The existential account of projective motivation as the primary function of willing explains these material conditions as objective (process-based) grounds for striving for ends that are hard to attain, because they constitute *challenges* that can help make life interesting and meaningful. If full and rich human lives involve some level of devotion to goods internal to practices that are not easy to master (as well as other kinds of interpersonal relationships that demand sustained effort from us), then a meaningful life depends on projecting goals in part because they are challenging. Sport practices are distinctive in that they are specifically designed around this thin reason for taking up a goal that can test and hone human talents (even if the goal is contrived or has no terminal value outside the game-context).

The value of challenge is also evident in the familiar notion of a "dream" or a personal aspiration that can require our greatest talents and efforts. Thus in her famous song in *The Sound of Music*, the Abbess of Salzburg tells Maria to choose a way in life that will draw on her great capacity to love: "A dream that will need all the love you can give, every day of your life, for as long as you live!"[36] This advice is based on objective considerations that ought to be important to the projective will. Although the development of talent or full use of distinctive personal qualities is a relatively thin ground for projecting a purpose, it remains interpersonally intelligible and does not depend on the romantic faith that if we search our hearts, we will discover what we already care most deeply about. Maria cares about the abbey, the mountains, music, Captain von Trapp, and his children; she cannot make her decision by simply introspecting her emotional response to each. But, as the Abbess gets her to see, a life with the von Trapp family is clearly the better "fit" for her; the family needs more of what she can give best.[37] To care in the volitional sense about something is always to challenge ourselves in some important way, and thus the possibility of caring depends on the same background conditions of human finitude as do practices with their own internal goods. As Margaret Tate has insightfully argued, developing Frankfurt's analysis, "It is a necessary condition of things that we value highly and about which we care deeply that those things are scarce, fragile, and ephemeral. This is true of both animate and inanimate objects of caring, as well as activities about which we care."[38] I would add that some objects of our care, such as individual persons, are not merely rare and precious but irreplaceable.

In the case of activities, Tate adds that activities to which we devote ourselves would be of no interest "if everyone could do everything perfectly that he/she desired with no effort or no danger or no fear of failure."[39] The point is not that we can care about or invest ourselves *only* in achievements that will distinguish us comparatively from others—although the possibility of distinguishing oneself is another thin process-focused ground for projecting certain ends. Rather, the point is that the difficulty of realizing an end or the scarcity or uniqueness of some valuable object provides opportunities to *give ourselves* challenges where none necessarily existed from prior desires. It is not always wise to do so, but we can make virtually any limitation the occasion for motivation by positing an end that is only realizable with struggle against this limitation.

For example, Christopher Reeve's heroic efforts to maintain his muscle tone and recover some bodily control despite his quadriplegia surely went far beyond anything attributable to natural desire for these goods. In an AP interview not long before he died, Reeve said "I refuse to allow a disability to determine how I live my life. I don't mean to be reckless, but *setting a goal* that seems a bit daunting actually is very helpful toward recovery."[40] Likewise, we surely do not *need* to reach the top of some high mountain; even if we have an appetite for a good view, or pleasant air at the top, or the exercise that climbing will involve, it may be the difficulty of the ascent that we have in view in willing ourselves to make it to the summit. The goals definitive of sport practices, like many hobbies, typically have their difficulty for an average or unapprenticed person among the process-focused reasons for projecting them.

Of course, the scarcity of other things that we do need for survival, such as food and water, or the scarcity of social objects that form generic means for other ends, such as money and professional degrees, may also heighten our (direct D1 or derived D2) prepurposive desires for these things. But their objective importance to us, both individually and communally, can also be a reason for making them the goals of various practices. Thus a practice like gourmet cooking starts with the objective need for food as its most basic ground but increases the difficulty of the goal by adding other kinds of gustatory values to nourishment as a basic good.

4. Frankfurtian Arguments for Subjectivism and Objectivist Rebuttals

4.1. *Two Kinds of Importance*

In considering Frankfurt's arguments for subjectivism, it is helpful to begin with the distinction he draws between (a) something's being important in what I called the sense of having "normative worth," or *deserving* consideration whether or not the agent already has any motivated interest in it; and (b) something's being important to a particular agent because he cares about it, in which case, as Frankfurt says, "caring about something makes that thing important to the person who cares about it."[41] The (b) sense is *agent-relative*, whereas the (a) sense is *agent-neutral* in its basic content (though it may have agent-relative specifications, as we'll see). The existential objectivist should certainly accept Frankfurt's point that there is a kind of "importance" that *derives from* caring rather than operating as a prior ground for caring. We might call this *personal importance* (PI) to signal that it arises from the attention that the agent directs toward her object or goal or from her *personal appropriation* of some possible task or relationship as her own.

Blustein describes this "personal value" as the "value that we give to the objects of our care by caring about them."[42] In this sense, following my earlier example, Maria made it personally important to her that Captain von Trapp's children gain the liberation they need to flourish. It is also personally valuable or important to Maria to be a loving wife to the captain once she has wholeheartedly embraced that goal (having overcome her earlier volitional ambiguity about erotic love).

According to existential objectivism, the agent-neutral (normative) sense of importance and the agent-relative (personal) sense of importance are always related as follows: the agent projectively devotes herself to some goal, ideal, or relationship because she believes that this possible final end *deserves* her care or is worth caring about and thus she makes it personally important to her. In other words, "personal" value derives from the volitional uptake of impersonal value.[43] This view can accommodate Frankfurt's claim that for the person who cares about not stepping on cracks in the sidewalk, this goal is really important to him: "his error consists in caring about, and thereby imbuing with genuine importance, something which is not worth caring about."[44]

This way of putting the matter is fine, as long as we clearly distinguish the two senses of importance involved: avoiding the cracks may be *personally* important to this neurotic agent, but it is not (in the agent-neutral or normative sense) *worthy* of attention. Hence when Frankfurt insists that an object's importance to an agent can be "fully genuine" although it depends on his already caring about it,[45] this observation proves no more than that personal importance is a real phenomenon distinct from objective value. It tells us nothing about the possible bases of personal importance and thus it does not count in favor of subjectivism; for objectivism is refuted only if agents can, by their own will, make something personally important to them without any thought whatsoever about its worthiness to be an object of care or any judgment concerning the normative worth of caring about it.

One cannot easily get such an example out of everyday cases in which agents devote excessive attention to unimportant trivialities, because the objectivist will respond that either the agent mistakenly sees normative worth in his goal (when there is none), or he just perversely desires this goal rather than caring about it in the distinctively volitional sense (which is compatible with EO).[46] On the other hand, the subjectivist faces the objection that her agent seems to care quite arbitrarily or on a mere whim, which in turn would seem to undermine the seriousness of the agent's care or the authenticity of his devotion. If he is brought to see his project as the result of a compulsive disorder or a mere delusion, his resolve will be undermined. As Blustein says, if someone or something "is deeply important to me, I must believe that it matters, that my devotion is to something that is worthy of it."[47]

For example, irrespective of any concern for future sales, it must matter to a budding novel writer what an intelligent reader in her target audience thinks of her story draft. It must matter to a scientist that his project has some basis in existing science and potential for new discovery. A young couple deciding to have children cannot think that they are doing nothing but adding to the world's population problems. This tether to objective value is also necessary to the experience of volitional dilemma. Blustein cites Loren Lomasky's example that a woman's struggle to balance raising her children with pursuing her career would be trivialized "unless she supposed that some value inheres in her childrearing and her career ambitions that is independent of the fact that she cares about her children and a career."[48] Finally, Blustein notes that when people do come to believe that pursuits to which they have devoted much time and energy were pointless or unworthy, their sense of misjudgment about the grounds for caring may render them "unable to summon up enough conviction or interest to care deeply about anything at all."[49]

These points all support the essential role of objective values as grounds for the projective motivation in caring. Many of the common tensions involved in caring about concrete particulars would not exist if the only experience of value essential to caring was the kind that is bootstrapped into being by caring. Yet Frankfurt sometimes implies that the very existence of personal importance and its difference from agent-neutral importance or normative worth are sufficient to show that caring is a process of creating new value that transcends any possible guidance by rational deliberation about values independent of the will. For example, although he accepts that moral obligations are *objectively* important in the NW sense (they are *worth* caring about), Frankfurt suggests that in cases of personal dedication to an ideal with moral content, the agent is "probably not being moved most immediately by objective moral considerations"; rather, he is moved by his own "commitment" to this ideal, or his giving it special emphasis in the structure of his life.[50]

My projective analysis of caring clarifies the error here: Frankfurt is confusing *personal appropriation* of some moral value (which is the willed response to it) with the *ground or basis* for this movement of the striving will. Frankfurt means to deny that pure reason simply causes a desire to act morally and means to hold instead that caring about morality transcends such prepurposive desire. But a moral obligation need not function as a prepurposive *motive* in order for it to serve as the justifying reason in light of which the agent commits himself to live by an ideal embodying or expressing this moral value. In doing so, he may go beyond what it requires universally of all agents, but the moral value still grounds such a supererogatory response to it. As I have argued in explaining Kierkegaard's notion of the existential choice, the objective ethical force of some value or norm must be distinguished from the personal act of *embracing* that value or norm, making it the basis for one's goal-setting and intention-defining volitional activity.[51] Even if caring is a distinctively resolute mode of such personal response to perceived values or norms, this could hardly entail that the agent does not have these values or norms in mind (reflectively or tacitly) as justifying reasons in so strongly taking them to heart.

That Frankfurt does not understand agent-neutral normative importance and agent-relative personal importance as *interdependent* in this way is clear when he writes that either kind of importance can function as the agent's ground for caring about something:

> He might claim that the thing is independently important to him and that it is worth caring about for this reason. Or he might maintain,

without supposing that the thing is antecedently important to him at all, that he is justified in caring about it because caring about it is itself something which is important to him.[52]

This last clause is ambiguous, but Frankfurt explains it by saying that when the object or goal's importance derives *only* from caring, "the only way to justify doing this is in terms of the importance of the activity of caring as such," which "serves to connect us actively to our lives in ways which are creative of ourselves."[53] In other words, Frankfurt holds that, in some cases at least,[54] caring for some particular X needs no justification beyond the value that the process of *caring about anything* in general has for the agent because it lets him engage in meaningful willing that gives narrative shape or "thematic continuity" to his life. This is what Frankfurt means when he writes that

> the significance to us of caring is thus more basic than the importance to us of what we care about. Needless to say, it is better for us to care about what is truly worth caring about. . . . However, the value to us of the fact that we care about various things does not derive simply from the value or suitability of the objects about which we care. Caring is important to us for its own sake, insofar as it is the indispensably foundational activity through which we provide continuity and coherence to our volitional lives.[55]

This is correct, because the *process* of caring involves a personal appropriation of values by the will which takes them as grounds for its projective endeavors; in doing this, the will is performing its natural function, or realizing its *existential telos*, in a deeper way than it does in making superficial decisions: it is helping to shape the agent's volitional character and thus his practical identity. This "good" of engaging willpower transcends the product-value of the ends projected, to be sure, but it also relates itself to these and other objective values as grounds for its activity rather than simply bootstrapping value into its activity or serving as its own ground. Thus the idea that a rich, autonomous personal ethos as the by-product existential value of caring in general could serve as the primary ground for whatever cares the agent discovers in himself (see chap. 12, sec. 6) was really developed to provide a generic agent-relative ground for caring when objective grounds are either absent or insufficient. Frankfurt thinks there are such cases, as we will see.

4.2. The Nygrenian Fallacy

Frankfurt's idea that loving or caring can be its own ground seems remarkably similar to Anders Nygren's conception of divine agapē as a love that is unmotivated by any possible value in the persons or things it loves. As I suggest in chapter 9, Nygren errs by arguing that:

(i) if any objective value in the object X explains or grounds love of X, then
(ii) this value in X must cause that love by attracting the lover, in which case
(iii) his love is erosiac rather than agapic (or, more generally, projective) in structure. Hence
(iv) if a love is agapic (or non-erosiac), then it has no objective grounds [i, iii, contraposition].

As we saw, (ii) is an erroneous premise: values can inform the will in ways other than appetitive attraction or prepurposive motivation of any kind. Yet Frankfurt seems to make an error identical to Nygren's: he treats erosiac motivation or appetite-love and self-justifying love/care as *dichotomous* alternatives:

> The loving activity of the passive [erosiac] lover is motivated essentially by a self-regarding interest in sustaining or enhancing the likelihood that the object of his love will be useful to him. In active [projective] love, the lover is not motivated by any interest of this sort in the utility to him of his beloved. Rather he is motivated by *an interest in loving itself.*[56]

This dichotomy suggests that the "active" nature of loves—their independence from prior desires, including self-interested appetites—entails their independence from all objective grounds, or their self-justifying status. This is just Nygren's fallacy. Thus it is especially noteworthy that Frankfurt footnotes Nygren's *Eros and Agape* at the conclusion of his first essay on caring:

> According to one theological doctrine, divine love is in fact bestowed without regard to the character or antecedent value of its objects. It is God's nature to love, on this view, and He therefore loves everything regardless of any considerations extrinsic to Himself. His love is entirely arbitrary and unmotivated—absolutely sovereign.... When a person makes something important to himself, accordingly, the situation resembles an instance of divine agape at least in a certain respect. The person does not care about the object because its worthiness commands that he do so. [Rather] the worthiness of the activity of caring commands that he choose an object which he will be able to care about.[57]

This crucial but rarely noticed passage reveals how Nygren's failure to understand the real structure of projective motivation in analyzing divine agapē provided a key inspiration for Frankfurt's subjectivism. He takes from Nygren the idea that absolute autonomy is determination solely by what is intrinsic to the agent, which entails lack of prior motivation, which entails unresponsiveness to values that exist prior to the agent's willing. In his most recent book, Frankfurt pushes this conception of divine agapē to its most Spinozistic extreme: "God loves everything, regardless of its character or its consequences." Thus divine love is totally unconcerned about merit or any other kind of objective criterion.[58] Echoes of this description of divine agapē are clearly heard in his emphatic summary of the existential subjectivist view:

> It is true that the beloved invariably is, indeed, valuable to the lover. However, perceiving that value is not at all an indispensable *formative* or *grounding* condition of the love. . . . The truly essential relationship between love and the value of the beloved goes in the opposite direction. It is not necessarily as a result of recognizing their value and of being captivated by it that we love things. Rather, what we love necessarily *acquires* value for us because we love it.[59]

I conclude that Frankfurt is led into this position by a misunderstanding of what makes love volitionally active or autonomous—a misunderstanding that derives from a highly influential misconstrual of agapē in the counter-eudaimonist tradition. The result is an ES theory of willing according to which our fundamental cares are 'brute" motives, just like brute D2 preferences, with no strong evaluative content: "[T]he fact that a person cares about something . . . need not derive from or depend on any evaluations or judgments that the person makes or accepts. . . . It may simply be a brute fact, which is not derived from any assessment or appreciation whatsoever."[60] But, thus far, Frankfurt's arguments for this view are preempted by the existential analysis of willing as projective motivation.

4.3. *The Rejection of Strict Proportionalism: Wolf's Analysis*

Existential objectivism is compatible with different metaethical views about the status of objective values. For example, EO does not require an extreme realist view that something has objective value only "if it would be a good thing for it to exist even in a world without conscious, desiring beings, even if it were never experienced by anyone." EO can conceive objective value instead as "interpersonal or intersubjective value."[61] Nor does EO require that my carings are arranged in a hierarchy that exactly mirrors "their ranking in some impersonal scale of values I accept."[62] The values to which the striving will responds need not be conceived as rigidly ordered; they can be open to legitimately different ways of taking them up and embracing them as personal values. For EO includes a moderate version of the idea that what Blustein and Nagel call "the personal point of view" is vital to human agency and must be respected by any viable moral theory or conception of good lives.

This insight is central to Susan Wolf's critique of Frankfurt. She correctly notes that his reliance on the existential import of caring in general recommends that "we care about whatever it will be most fulfilling, rewarding, and satisfying to us to care about."[63] Yet this implication reintroduces a formal egoism seemingly at odds with Frankfurt's insistence on the disinterestedness of volitional caring; it also allows anything we may enjoy caring about, however immoral. However, Wolf also presents another putative argument for subjectivism that we can find suggested in Frankfurt's writings. This argument works by rejecting a strict proportionalist view that "one's love of a person or object or activity should be proportional to its value or worthiness to be loved. One should love most that which is most deserving."[64] That it involves such a strict desert criterion is a familiar objection against Aristotle's account of noble friendship, and Wolf rightly rejects such a criterion as "pompous, stiff, self-righteous, or naive, foolish."[65] Even if there are objective differences in the (moral and nonmoral) merits of different individuals, loving devotion to them should not be keyed precisely to such measures: "Just imagine the parent who loves one child more than another because one is better (smarter, perhaps . . .)."[66]

Parental love serves as a paradigm case in subjectivist arguments: Frankfurt points out that we love our children before we have "any relevant information about their personal characteristics or their particular merits and virtues,"[67] and he argues that this is "the species of caring that comes closest to offering recognizably pure instances of love."[68] I take up this example again below, but my initial response is that important evaluative judgments *do* play a crucial role in "unconditional" love; one is the negative judgment that with close friends, and even more in the case of our children, certain kinds of objective criteria of merit *ought not* to guide our caring. The right attitude involves what MacIntyre calls "a *systematic* refusal to treat the child in a way that is proportional to its qualities and aptitudes," and a determination instead to provide them with unconditional love.[69] As MacIntyre argues, this attitude can be systematic because there are objective social grounds for this egalitarian attitude; without it, the practice of parenting is hindered in realizing those social goods of nurturance and cultivation of ego security in the child that only the childrearing art can provide.

Thus the rejection of strict proportionalism is a *principled* rejection of one possible kind of ground for love in a certain context, not a determination that practical reason should play *no* role in guiding the will in forming cares.

If it were the latter, then it would validate a parent who loved only one of his two children and entirely ignored the other, *not* because the first scored higher on objective talent or performance scales of any sort but just as a totally *brute fact*. Imagine a father who said, "I just find in myself a deep love of Tim, but no love at all for Jeff. I don't know why, but after all, I have to follow my heart!" Anyone who would try to use the valid objections to proportionalism as a basis for defending this parent would quickly see how limited those objections are; he would be immediately suspect to anyone with even a moderate degree of parental virtue. For obviously, this putative defense entirely misunderstands the reasons why proportionate regard is out of place in this context and substitutes totally arbitrary whim for the values that govern parental love. Of course, it can also happen that a parent who wills equal love for all his children finds himself unable to come near to the mark, and not for lack of volitional effort on his part, either. But when this is not due to *akrasia* or other vices, we consider it a tragedy, not a psychological fact that determines who he ought to love.

This is sufficient to show that the inappropriateness of merits as a ground for strictly proportional care responses in many contexts does not entail existential subjectivism (quite the contrary, since this inappropriateness itself has objective grounds). Wolf's response to Frankfurt is more modest: she suggests that "the role worth plays in determining what to care about is to set a minimal condition" or threshold of value beneath which an object or end cannot fall if it makes sense to care about it.[70] Yet she does not simply say that above this threshold all options are equal. The grounds for caring may not call for maximizing product-value or for fine-tuning the level of our attention to degrees of merit, but they include different kinds of *excellence*. Thus Wolf notes the relevance of the familiar advice, "You can do better." This does not mean, for example, that only the *very best* partner, job, hobby etc. is worthy of devotion,[71] but rather that "as long as one has or is in a position to cultivate having more options, there is something to be said for aiming higher for a more interesting or virtuous or appealing partner, or a more challenging or responsible or socially useful job."[72]

Wolf also rightly notes that a rich diversity of interests is a criterion for caring, especially for those optional pursuits and hobbies that ought not to be the primary focus of someone's attention: "Being a fan of a sports team, a bridge player, a lover of musical comedies, adds interest and variety to life. . . . Interests like these are good and healthy—but they can take more time, and demand more sacrifice than they are worth."[73] We would presumably not say this about causes of great moral importance (such as devoting part of one's life to working for Doctors Without Borders) or relationships of love in families and a few other cases in which we think single-minded devotion to the exclusion of almost everything else can be justified (at least for a time).

In addition to such agent-neutral criteria for care objects and ways of caring, Wolf identifies a very important type of agent-relative consideration that begins to explain how agents may choose between different care options that all fall within the acceptable range on agent-neutral criteria. This is what she calls the agent's "affinity" for a particular care object. I suggest that we understand affinity as including the fit between a potential project, goal, or object of care and a person's talents, emotional dispositions, and less central aspects of his personality. The importance of affinity, as Wolf says, explains why "the fact that one activity, object, or person is not objectively as good or better than any number of others may pale in importance before enthusiasm for that particular one."[74] For example, we saw that in *The Sound of Music*, Maria has more affinity for the von Trapp family than for the abbey, though she loves both. One may simply find oneself drawn to one kind of practice more than to competing options, even if the latter involve social roles that one's family, friends, or significant others expect one to play.

The tension between personal affinity and social expectation is a familiar theme in literature and film. A useful illustration is provided by the movie *Bend It Like Beckham*, in which Jess Bhamra, a British girl of Indian ethnicity and Sikh faith, finds herself powerfully drawn to soccer; her aptitude and affinity for this sport, along with the opportunity to play it professionally, provide ample grounds for projecting her serious engagement in soccer as a practice—even though it conflicts with the traditional ideal of a marriageable young woman in her culture.[75] However, it is crucial to recognize that although affinity itself is always agent-relative, the *importance* of affinity as a valid ground for volitional devotion is universally applicable and so objective in authority. The importance of this criterion for authentic willing relative to other cultural considerations is precisely what Jess's father has to learn in *Bend It Like Beckham*, and its function as a valid ground for the will has significant ethical and political implications. Affinity may include D2 desires and related emotional tendencies, but for the will, it functions not as brute attraction but, rather, as an interpersonally recognizable and (within limits) defensible reason for projecting purposive motives that go well beyond any preexisting appetites and emotions that are part of the individual agent's prior personality.

This is not to say that culture-based expectations of significant others regarding the roles we should play are of no relevance or have no objective weight for the will. For example, any child of an Old Order Amish family starts life with a weighty reason for cultivating an appreciation of those values that the life of the Amish realizes in distinctive ways. But the judgment that considerations of this kind are generally less important or weighty than (often competing) considerations of personal affinity is a distinguishing mark of modern as opposed to strongly traditional culture. To assert the objective superiority of this aspect of modern culture is therefore to judge that it better reflects the *true relation* between the values of personal fit versus fit with rigid or highly specified cultural prescription regarding what roles and relationships are appropriate to whom.

I regard it as a theoretical advantage of EO that it makes such intercultural comparisons possible and perhaps even requires broadly ethical assessment of cultures. For it does not seem that our access to values that ground caring is entirely determined by a cultural frame that we can never critique or assess. We can assess cultural attitudes both with respect to how well they promote and sustain the central elements in human flourishing and whether they make possible fully meaningful lives for individuals. Both these approaches must pay special attention to how a given cultural outlook or worldview either clarifies or obscures the grounds for caring or volitional devotion that there are in the world and their relative weight or significance. We should want a conception of practical normativity that makes it possible, for example, to support Bill Cosby's often-repeated argument that a culture that privileges machismo, violent self-assertion on the model of the gangster, disdain for learning and courtesy, and conspicuous consumption is a corrupt culture that destroys many of its members and radically levels off their ability to appreciate much of what is most worth caring about in human life. It is difficult to see how an axiological subjectivist like Frankfurt could support such a critique of the life idolized by gangsta rap or of the wider American culture of crass materialism and status-seeking out of which this highly influential subculture grows.

4.4. *Does Optionality Entail Subjectivity?*

The importance of personal affinity brings us to another major argument that Frankfurt offers for ES: namely, that it follows from the *rational optionality* of many cares or loves. By this I do not mean that Frankfurt thinks we can form cares or loves "at will"; he clearly rejects this as implausible. But he does argue that "Caring about something differs not only from wanting it" but also "from taking it to be intrinsically valuable. Even if a person believes that something has considerable intrinsic value, he may not regard it as important to himself."[76] I agree with this distinction, for we can think of many cases in which someone recognizes intrinsic value in some possible goal, relationship, or activity yet does not make it *her own* end. In *The Sound of Music*, the Abbess tells Maria that married life is also sanctified, but she hardly takes this judgment to require that she give up her own cloistered life and go find a husband. I may recognize that golf is an interesting game requiring difficult skills and that it tends to give its players physical exercise, social interaction, and relaxation in the midst of peaceful (if rather sculpted) greenery—all good reasons to play golf. Yet I may focus on tennis, or skiing, or biking instead. Hence, as Frankfurt says, recognizing significant intrinsic value in something does not rationally require that someone cares about it. At most, "it commits him to recognizing that it *qualifies* to be *desired for its own sake*, and to be *pursued as a final end*."[77]

In other words, some end E can have significant intrinsic value while remaining *rationally optional*. Any X is rationally optional in the sense I mean if it is true *both* that it is rational for agents (meeting certain background conditions C) to pursue X for its own sake, giving it a certain priority (P) in their lives, *and* that it can also be rational for agents meeting conditions C not to devote any attention to X, or at least to give it a priority lower than P. Clearly many of the pursuits, causes, activities, and relationships that people typically care about fall into this category. Frankfurt considers the success of a basketball team to be an optional object of caring attention in this sense: neither fans nor those with no interest in the team are guilty of any error in practical reasoning or choice here.[78] Rational optionality will be evident whenever we care deeply about something or someone but do not believe that this entails that *everyone else* (meeting the same background conditions) ought to care about it as well (or care as much as we do). The fact that I love my best friend very dearly ought not (and usually does not) involve any evaluative judgment to the effect that anyone in circumstances roughly like mine ought to love this person as I do. Thus Frankfurt concludes that, unlike universal principles of reason, love is personal in the sense that the agent "does not thereby commit himself to supposing that anyone who fails to love what he does has somehow gone wrong."[79]

From this, we can start to see how someone might try to construct an argument from rational optionality to ES. The general idea is that since it would not be *unreasonable* for a given individual *not* to care about X, if he does come to care about it, this cannot be explained by or grounded in any objective value that X may have. This argument could be formalized as follows:

> 1. If A's caring for X were justified by *universalizable* values V associated with X itself and/or with the process of caring about X, then V would require any agent (situated similarly to A) to care about X.
> 2. But caring about X is optional: for some agents (situated like A) it is reasonable not to care about X. In other words, V does not require all agents (situated like A) to care about X.

3. Therefore, since the consequent of I is false, the antecedent is false [by *modus tollens*]: A's caring about X is not justified by universalizable values.

The argument is valid; so, given that premise 2 is true in many cases of caring, if I were a conceptual truth, 3 would follow, at least for those cases. However, premise I falsely assumes that a value cannot *justify* caring about X unless it universally *requires* of all similarly situated agents that they care about X. This narrows the concept of justification or grounding to its strongest form. Values and practical considerations can rationally *support* caring about something or someone without universally *requiring* that all relevantly similar agents do likewise, on pain of irrationality if they do not. Hence I is false, and the argument is unsound. Frankfurt is correct that recognizing inherent value in some goal does not entail "that anyone has an obligation to pursue it as a final end."[80] But this does not support ES; it is compatible with EO.

Another way to see the subjectivist's error here is to recognize that caring about X can involve or commit the agent to a validity claim that is significantly *weaker* than the demand that everyone similarly situated care about X as much (or in the same way) as he does. Suppose, as the existential objectivist maintains, that caring about X necessarily involves an evaluative judgment J concerning the significant intrinsic value of X, or the significant intrinsic value of the process of caring about X, or both. Then, as Frankfurt himself suggested, the claim that these values exist (objectively, for all) may commit the agent to no more than the judgment that anyone (similarly situated) *rationally could* care about X. This is still an important evaluative judgment: it says that a person will have *good grounds* for caring about X, if she chooses to do so. Minimally, this means that X does not fall below the acceptable threshold; one would not be wasting one's time on X.

Beyond this, personal affinity may make all the difference. More robustly, the judgment could extend to the claim that persons relevantly situated ought to consider X carefully, or *pay serious attention* to X as a viable candidate for their concern, even if they pass it up for other options. For example, at a time when the nation lacks sufficient numbers of highly qualified teachers, a talented college student with an affinity for children has the imperative to consider teaching in our public schools as a valuable calling to which he ought to give serious consideration. This leaves the personal devotion required for such a career quite optional, but it says *more* than simply that a person who devotes his or her life to teaching in public schools has not wasted their potential. As Wolf sees, the objectivist can content herself with this kind of an objective validity claim in cases of rational optionality. The values that an agent caring about X cites as her grounds are indeed universally relevant, even if not taken up by all persons. Sometimes (as in the case of a career, political activity, or friendship), the judgment may be that X is one instance of *a type* of which it is rational to have at least one in our life. Frankfurt recognizes an analogous phenomenon when he explains the possibility of disjunctive needs, no one of which is indispensable to us, although we must have at least one of the disjuncts.[81] In other cases (as with a sport or a hobby), the judgment may be weaker than that: one should strongly consider playing *some* sport or having at least one hobby, although it may not be irrational entirely to exclude such pursuits if other callings demand all one's attention.

Frankfurt seems to resist this view when he argues that "We can think of many things that might well be worth having or worth doing for their own sakes, but with regard to which we consider it entirely acceptable that *no one* is especially drawn to them and that they are never actually pursued."[82] He suggests a life devoted to meditation or to "courageous feats of knight errantry" as examples. Yet normally, it seems that in recognizing something X as having volitionally optional intrinsic value, we judge that although it is not unreasonable for any single individual to pass it up for the sake of other cares, still (a) caring about X would be more reasonable than caring about nothing at all or being wanton; and (b) it would be a shame if no one in the world devoted significant time to X, even in the past. Surely the human race would be collectively poorer (in a nonmoral but broadly ethical sense) if King Arthur's knights had never ridden across old Britain on their noble quests—at least in story? History would also be less interesting without persons of great meditative devotion (as the fascination with such characters in popular film and literature shows). In any case, there may be some level of intrinsic value that we can recognize as significantly supporting some endeavor or undertaking, without judging that our community is poorer if it does not include even one person who cares about it. This would still constitute an objective value judgment in favor of such a care, should anyone decide to take it up.

Thus EO only requires a *loose* fit between cares and the objective value of what is cared about. It does not demand caring strictly proportional to merit, and it is compatible with multiple rational options. As Blustein writes:

> Actual caring should align to some extent with what ought to be cared about by anyone.... Conversely, there is much that people care about of which it cannot plausibly be said that anyone ought to care about it.... But if this caring generates personal value that is sufficient to support a sense of meaning and that implicates one's integrity, the one who cares cannot see the value of what he or she cares about as emanating simply from within.[83]

My account explains these observations by saying that the values that are personally appropriated by the striving will as its reasons for projecting goals have normative significance for the agent, but in many cases, she may be committed only to the claims that they are important candidates for agents like her to consider and that others should recognize that her devotions have a basis beyond her own brute preferences. Others may disagree with her, but they are then disagreeing about substantive axiological judgments relevant for willing.

Moreover, EO includes a *complexity caveat*: some objective grounds for caring about something may be relevant only if the agent does or does not already have certain *other* cares. For example, having children may be rationally optional, but for a person who has embraced the value of raising children and has taken up this task, the individual value of each child is not rationally optional: he ought to care about each of his children (and in a way not proportional to merit alone, as we saw). Similarly, Wolf's criteria of greater interest, appeal, or challenge may not be (as) relevant to someone once they are committed to a particular partner, career, and so on. But the fact that some criteria for caring take on new importance while others become less relevant as we change our cares (or alter what is personally important to us) does not mean that these criteria are merely subjective or derive all their authority from the agent's existing motivational set. On the contrary, they come with certain volitional territories or narrative environments (and not others), whether the agent likes it or not. Such practical worlds are generally self-sustaining but not totally self-enclosed; they may include values that give the agent good grounds for forming new cares, some of which would take her into *different* axiological territories or narrative spaces. This reflexive relation between the rational grounds for caring and the current state of our will is part of any sufficiently complex existential objectivism.

4.5. *Does Essential Particularity Entail Subjectivity? Raz's Analysis*

It might be suggested that individual friends, close family members, or loved ones are an exception to the objectivist account I have sketched for rationally optional cares. Sometimes a romantic will go to the extreme of pretending that the lover need not care in the least whether anyone else in the world sees the slightest bit of value in his beloved. As Tracey Ullmann sings in her (one) hit song, "I tell the others 'don't bother me,' 'cause when they look at you, they don't see what I see!"[84] While it is sometimes quite admirable to ignore the opinions of certain other people, taken to an extreme this view becomes a fiction, for it generally does tend to undermine what Frankfurt calls our "confidence" in our love to recognize that *everyone* whose judgment we respect thinks we are crazy. Thus, we generally *do* want others (especially significant others whose character we value) to recognize at least some of the values in our friend or lover that would make loving them intelligible; that is, we want these people to see at least *some* of what we see, even if we know that they could not see it all without actually loving this person just as we do.[85] Otherwise put, we do not mind mysteries of value that are revealed only to us, once we have already volitionally embraced more basic values; but we still believe that some *part* of these values should be intelligible to wise, value-sensitive persons who are not initiated into our personal mysteries. When even those whose advice we respect completely deny that our love has any rational basis, we have to be quite sure that they are wrong—that we *do* have solid objective grounds for our care—to strengthen our will against the resulting doubts.[86]

Nevertheless, the argument for subjectivism with the widest appeal today is based on our familiar experience of what has come to be called "essentially particularistic love." Michael Stocker introduced this idea into contemporary moral psychology by arguing that utilitarian and deontological accounts do not call us to love a particular person in his uniqueness but only to consider his instrumentally or intrinsically valuable properties (such as happiness or rational freedom):

> What is lacking in these theories is . . . the person. For love, friendship, affection, fellow feeling, and community all require that the other person be an essential part of what is valued. The person—not merely the person's general values nor even the person-*qua*-producer-or-possessor-of-general-values—must be valued.[87]

Stocker's insight has been taken up by Bernard Williams, who argues that moral theory never provides reasons for loving particular individuals as unique, but only gets in the way. Nel Noddings draws similar antitheoretical conclusions from her even stronger claim that the basic form of care is essentially particularistic. Given "the uniqueness of human encounters," she rejects any universalizable principles, since these "function to separate us from one another."[88] She conceives caring for unique persons as "essentially nonrational,"[89] which makes it impossible to conceive of universal caring, except as a readiness to care for "whoever crosses our path."[90]

Here again, Noddings converges with Frankfurt, who argues that volitional love of an individual person is not "a response to the perceived worth of the beloved."[91] In the case of children and friends, he argues, our love is unlike "impersonal" benevolence directed at categories or types of needy persons.[92] Rather, the agent (volitionally) loves the particular individual as *irreplaceable*: "There can be no equivalent substitute for his beloved." That is because the person as a unique individual is loved, and she cannot be unique in virtue of possessing multiply instantiable properties. Thus "[t]he significance to the lover of what he loves is not that his beloved is an instance or an exemplar" of various valuable properties: "Its importance to him is not generic; it is ineluctably particular."[93]

I accept that such essentially particularistic love occurs—and although Frankfurt considers it basically nonmoral in significance, I would suggest that some conceptions of agapē make it a moral requirement to cultivate precisely this kind of focus on the person as properly named or as absolutely individual.[94] The problem is whether we should think of all essentially particularistic love, agapic or otherwise, as arbitrary generosity. As Barbara Herman notes with respect to Frankfurt's view, "in loving, the support for reasons is not any value inherent in the loved person or the loving relationship. The welfare of the loved other is reason-giving for me because, and only because, I care about him."[95] According to ES, the unconditional authority to me of considerations related to my beloved's well-being derives *completely* from a subjective condition of my psyche. As in other internalist theories, "the value of what we care about does no work in the generations of reasons" that move us;[96] it is not the object's own value, but rather our *valuing* this object that gives the normative status of reasons to the considerations that move us.[97]

This implies a radical *asymmetry* in caring relationships: all essentially personalistic love becomes a blind gift that is entirely unmerited by the beloved. But this is just as offensive as reducing a person to iterable properties. Suppose one answered Stocker's question by explaining to one's friend in the hospital: "Honestly, nothing about your personality or character gave me any reason to care about you; it is just my nature to care about you, though I have no independent reason to do so." Would the friend be any happier about this explanation than a Kantian or utilitarian one?

To avoid both extremes, we need some way of grounding essentially particularistic love in the *beloved's* real value, but without reducing this value to a mere *instantiation* of some pattern or participation in some ersatz form. If objective value could consist only of repeatable properties that would require us to love equally anything exemplifying the same properties, then this subjectivist argument would succeed; the particularistic caring that exists in our life would have to be entirely ungrounded. But this is not the case, as several philosophers in the study of normative particularism have recently argued. Among them, I will focus briefly on Joseph Raz's insightful analysis, which makes possible an objectivist account of essentially particularistic love.[98]

Raz begins by endorsing rational optionality in the sense that I have already explained: a legitimate diversity of ends arises from "the partiality of people to some people or goals which are all valuable, but to which some people are attracted and committed, whereas others are indifferent."[99] Raz has also developed at length the point that rational optionality makes sense as long as we do not conceive practical reason as an exclusively *maximizing* enterprise that could never ground more than one option in any choice circumstance. My account differs only in that I do not take "attraction" to be what motivates personal commitment or caring itself. What I call the broadly ethical importance of having rational grounds for one's cares, Raz calls practical respect for value: "partiality is permissible so long as it does not conflict with respect for what is valuable."[100]

Raz also defends the distinction between personal "attachment" to objects of love or devotion and the objective criteria of "suitability" that make such attachments worthwhile. "Attachment" here refers to what I (following Kierkegaard) call *personal appropriation*; as Frankfurt argues, this implies a kind of value that is essentially agent-relative or particular because *it derives* from the agent's attachment, caring, or volitional appropriation itself. Raz calls this special kind of value "personal meaning:" "Meaning is invested in the world by our attachments."[101] In my view, the will has the power of creating this special kind of value, which "depends on the person's attitude to the object or objective of the attachment."[102] But the values that give us reason to attach ourselves to goals in this way are not similarly derivative. People can form attachments based solely on personal affinity, but "these are highly unusual cases"; normally we believe that "the people we love are suitable objects of our love. Otherwise the love is demeaning to us," and its autonomy is undermined.[103] The normal relation is that "our attachments appropriate (impersonal) value, and make it meaningful for us."[104]

This is also what the projective model of the will implies: an agent responds to a range of worthwhile values by devotion to some of them or some instances of them, thus taking them up in to the personal fabric of her life. My existential theory differs from Raz's in emphasizing that the impersonal values can be appropriated by volitional resolve without these values having to link up with any natural appetites for the agent's own well-being. Yet the idea of projective motivation is implicit in Raz's language: "By assuming duties, we create attachments," thus generating a "meaningful life."[105] Thus, as Frankl also argues (see chap. 12, sec. 5), Raz maintains that "The personal meaning of objects, causes, and pursuits depends on their impersonal [agent-transcending] value, and is conditional on it. But things of value have to be appropriated by us to endow our lives with meaning."[106] This formula captures the two conditions for existential meaning according to EO: the first sentence expresses the objective condition, and the second sentence expresses the existential condition (requiring volitional incorporation through projective motivation).[107]

Within this framework, particularistic love can be grounded on the basis of an agent-relative criterion that differs importantly from personal affinity, which was defined relative to non-volitional features of the agent's personality. The new criterion is backward-looking: it consists in a complex set of *historical relationships*, including the agent's past involvement with the potential object of care and relations with other persons who have cared about this or related ends or who have cared about goals or activities contrary to this object's interests, and so on. Sometimes these relationships in themselves have powerful ethical implications: I suggested that Private James Ryan has a historically unique relationship with Captain John Miller that could not be repeated without the two agents *being* the same temporally developing persons. We are all caught up in a web of debts to the past that we did not voluntarily choose, which often create backward-looking reasons for focusing on an irreplaceable object of care or devotion specified in a way that is unique to our shared history.[108]

Raz focuses on the beautiful case of Saint-Exupéry's Little Prince, who is mortified to discover that the single rose whose looks so charmed him is not unique in appearance at all. But the Little Prince refuses to conceive maturation in Diotimian fashion as *only* a movement from the particular to the universal form that it instantiates:

> He believes in the importance of uniqueness. He believes that uniqueness is of the nature of love, which is for him the paradigm of all special attachments to people and to objects. He believes that both meaning and understanding, misery and happiness, arise out of one's special, particular, non-universal attachments.[109]

Clearly this is what Stocker and Frankfurt believe too (maybe they read *Le Petit Prince*). But when the Little Prince devotes himself in a new way to his rose, he bases his love on "their common history," which itself originated from aesthetic attraction.[110] The Little Prince sees his rose as unique because of the efforts he has already made at cultivating her.[111] Thus agent-relative historical considerations help explain why (as noted in chap. 13), appetitive motivation can sometimes transmute into projective motivation; in some cases, actions in the past that were motivated by ordinary desires establish a historical sense of involvement or investment that the agent can then take as grounds for projective devotion.[112] As MacIntyre says, this also happens with the practices: "Someone may become a physicist or a physician or a baseball player" merely for money or out of altruistic desires; but once involved, he starts to see the importance of the profession's unique type of excellence and to care about meeting these standards. Similarly, according to the complexity caveat (above), standing commitments to impersonal ends may happen to bring us closer to particular individuals, giving singular importance to their unique personality and interests.

Raz actually argues that individuals who are the object of essentially particularistic love can become "irreplaceable" in two ways: the first is "de facto" uniqueness due to certain aspects or features that *happen* not to occur in this combination in others (often because of their complexity); the second is "logical uniqueness . . . and a common history is the only way to ensure it."[113] This factor can explain parents' particularistic love for a child who is temporally unique, even if its clone were born at a later time.[114] Likewise, presumably Stocker's friend in the hospital would *not* be offended if, on asking Stocker why he cared enough to visit, Stocker reminded him that they had grown up as next-door neighbors, had shared good and bad times, and developed a friendship like none other in their lives. Historical contingencies that generate such agent-relative reasons are not problematic; rather, they are a familiar indicator of what Heidegger called the essentially temporal nature of human caring.

Similarly, though less exclusively, many grounds for attachment to a particular heritage or traditional way of life are temporally contingent and apply only to certain individuals.[115] It may be the intersection of such shared traditions with other factors, such as career interests, hobbies, political or religious ideals, and other causes of emotional affinity that singles out a given individual as uniquely important for us to care about (prior to our particularistic devotion to her). Alternatively, we could think of the uniqueness as located in the agent X's *access* to the value of another individual Y: although Y's worth is in principle accessible to others, in fact only X knows Y well enough to see it. This idea is familiar in popular culture; for example, Cindy Lauper sings: "I see your true colors; that's why I love you."[116]

Whether the grounds for such attachments are historically unique in themselves or unique in their accessibility, they may not at first glance seem to be universal in normative force since they will be salient to only a few or maybe just one agent in certain circumstances. Indeed, the gestalt complex of reasons that individual X has for loving individual Y, as opposed to anyone else, may be relevant only to X because he shares a certain metaphysically unique trajectory through the web of historical relationships with Y (which include individuated grounds for caring about Y).

But Raz points out that if we move up one level of abstraction from these particulars, we recognize them as token instances of *types* of considerations or grounds that are universally important to all agents and that serve as legitimate reasons for anyone to form particularistic cares (within moral limits). Thus "recognition of the value of unique attachments meets the condition of universalizability" as a requirement on values, and indeed "public recognition of personal attachments can be impartial."[117] For we can each recognize the relevance to others of many particularistic grounds for projective motivation that apply to them as a result of the historical facts of their lives, including their own previous actions, the actions of others to whom the agent is related, and their consequences.[118] Thus we can judge, for instance, that Chief of Staff Marshall is not being unfair to other soldiers in risking so much to save Private Ryan, because of his unusual situation. Likewise, we judge that the child we mothered, fathered, or adopted is bound to us in an intimate reciprocity that grows from the date of his or her arrival, distinguishing the child as uniquely precious in our life.

Thus the love of persons as unique individuals—as that which we signify by their proper names rather than definite descriptions of their features—fits within a sufficiently nuanced version of existential objectivism that recognizes backward-looking, historically conditioned grounds for caring. An essential feature of personhood is the capacity to will another person's good on such a basis. Without this, the kind of singular encounter with another person as *Du* or "Thou," which Martin Buber calls the "I-Thou" relationship, would be impossible.[119] More generally, Raz's analysis seems to answer Joel Anderson's question for Charles Taylor, namely, how is a "pluralistic notion of something having special value for me (and not for you) to be squared with the general prescriptive and motivating character that Taylor attributes to the good?"[120] The general perspective is individualized by *volitional uptake* and the historical development of selective involvement with some projects and persons (rather than others) occasioned by such personal appropriation of general values.[121]

4.6. Do Objectivist Values Lack Noncircular Grounds?

At this point, we can return to cases that are easier for the objectivist to handle. Although "the realm of values is both complex and pocketed with indeterminacies,"[122] Wolf suggests that the objective importance of values such as truth should be obvious: "we do not want to be deluded about the things that we love and care about," even when the truth is painful.[123] Although some people do prefer delusion, the normative value of truth has also been supported by Nozick's Experience-Machine argument and the related theme in the *Matrix* movies.[124] Frankfurt's own critique of "bullshit" as an attitude that harms communicative practices through wantonness toward truth values also supports this point.[125] Similar remarks, it seems, would apply to beauty, basic components of human welfare (much discussed in new natural-law theories), and also environmental goods: persons who are entirely numb to such values seem even more deficient than those who recognize these values but neglect them for material gain or pleasure.

These likely candidates may explain why, at various points in his career, Frankfurt was more optimistic about identifying universalizable grounds for caring. In addition to moral values, Frankfurt suggested that "imperatives of tradition, of style, of intellect" (which would surely include knowledge) "or of some other mode of ambition" (perhaps types of excellence) would make sense as "ideals."[126] This search for grounds is important, even though we do not exercise immediate executive control over our cares, because "From the fact that what binds us to our ideals is love, it does not follow that our relationship to them is wholly noncognitive. There is considerable room for reason and argument in the clarification of ideals and in the evaluation of their worthiness."[127] And even though I can love someone as an unrepeatable particular without thinking "that anyone who does not do the same is making a mistake," it does not follow that our loves are mere givens, "brute facts with respect to which deliberation and rational critique have no place."[128] This is surely right if our will is not entirely blind to reason or entirely lost in fanaticism. We can change our cares, and do so in light of reasons intelligible to others. Why, then, does Frankfurt finally reach the conclusion that our identity-defining loves are inscrutable givens, and the practical question of how one should live "is inescapably self-referential and leads us into an endless circle"?[129] I suggest that this error has three main causes.

The first is that when he considers possible criteria for judging ends worth caring about, Frankfurt tends to focus on putative goods that are agent-relative, or conceivably part of the agent's eudaimonia. In order for someone to judge between ways of life,

> it must be clear to him how to evaluate the fact that a certain way of living leads more than others (or less than others) to personal satisfaction, to pleasure, to power, to glory, to creativity, to spiritual depth, to harmonious relationship with the precepts of religion, to conformity with the requirements of morality, and so on.[130]

Without reliance on a metaphysical account of the human telos, any justification of such agent-relative values might seem to assume existing concern or desire for them. Of course, Frankfurt recognizes that the value we find in our cares transcends the agent-relative value of their goals. As he wrote in 1982:

> The varieties of being concerned or dedicated, and of loving, are important to us quite apart from any antecedent *capacities for affecting us* which what we care about may have. This is not particularly because caring makes us susceptible to certain additional gratifications and

disappointments. It is primarily because it serves to connect us actively to our lives in ways which are creative of ourselves and which expose us to distinctive possibilities for necessity and freedom.[131]

The problem with this is the implicit dichotomy: agent-relative benefits (such as emotional fulfillment) and existential by-product goods (such as developing one's practical identity) exhaust the alternatives. The possibility of agent-transcending goods in the end-product to be sought seems to be excluded from the start. Yet it is in such values that many of Frankfurt's contemporaries have looked for meaning. For example, Robert Nozick says:

> The particular things or causes people find make their life feel meaningful all take them beyond their own narrow limits and connect them up with something else. Children, relationships with other persons, helping others, advancing justice, continuing and transmitting a tradition, pursuing truth, beauty, world betterment—these and the rest link you to something wider than yourself. The more intensely you are involved, the more you transcend your limits.[132]

Thus Frankfurt looked in the wrong place for objective criteria of normative worth.

The second problem is the demand for *procedural and contrastive* justification. In 1993, Frankfurt wrote that more philosophical attention is needed to what features our ideals must have and to explaining "the basis on which a person can reasonably make a choice from among various worthy ideals."[133] This way of posing the question asks for too decontextualized a reason for caring: It supposes that having *any rational ground* for positing some worthwhile activity or social cause as an end or for motivating oneself to pursue some ideal or the welfare of some particular person requires having a contrastive justification for spending time on this one goal to the exclusion of all other possible candidates. On this view, there cannot be objective values that ground caring unless they provide an agent volitionally engaged in a given ethos "reasons good enough to justify him in living that way" as *opposed* to any other possible ways.[134]

This is an old fallacy frequently featured in critiques of libertarian accounts of moral freedom; it insists that choice is irrational or arbitrary if it is not made by some algorithmic method or decision procedure that determines a single best outcome, or at least on the basis of reasons that single out one option as the exclusive best.[135] This demand for a sufficient contrastive explanation leads to the conclusion that nothing is an objective ground for caring if it cannot explain, in terms free of all singular references, why the agent cared about one ground project rather than another or why she devoted loving attention to one unique individual as opposed to others who rank the same or even higher on ahistorical criteria. On this view, even Platonic ideals such as social justice, beauty, or truth, whose importance is apt to seem most evidently objective or universally applicable, lose their objective status, for "it is not generally considerations of value that account for the fact that a person comes to be selflessly devoted to one ideal or value rather than to some other."[136] This is misleading, for personal affinity and historical relationships cannot do all the work of grounding our cares and life projects on their own.

Third, Frankfurt's subjectivism reveals Bernard Williams's influence, for it amounts to the thesis that every proposed reason for caring about anything is implicitly hypothetical or has to appeal to some care that is *already* in our "internal set." One cannot in advance identify "criteria on the basis of which" the question of what to care about can be answered without affirming definite answers to the question.[137] Yet this circularity should be troubling only if we start from the radically antitheoretical assumption that *rational* justification of values (including those that give normative worth to our cares) has to have a *procedural* structure, like Rawls's theory of justice, in which we first isolate a method for deciding the question that is in reflective equilibrium with our considered convictions then apply this criterion to uncontroversial instances, refine it, apply it to harder cases, and so on. The question of grounding values may be too fundamental to be answered in that way, but this would not make it "systematically inchoate" or inscrutable; this is the kind of circle, untroubling to phenomenologists, that we always encounter when we can do little more than describe our experience of basic values and try to make clear the natural properties on which they seem to rest.

For instance, in his famous diary of wilderness experiences, the American naturalist (and father of ecocentric ethics) Aldo Leopold writes the following about his communion with a crane marsh:

> Our ability to perceive quality in nature begins, as in art, with the pretty. It expands through successive stages of the beautiful to values yet uncaptured in language. The quality of the cranes lies, I think, in this higher gamut, as yet beyond the reach of words. This much, though, can be said: our appreciation of the crane grows with the slow unraveling of earthly history.... When we hear his call we hear no mere bird. We hear the trumpet in the orchestra of evolution. He is the symbol of our untameable past.[138]

This may seem closer to poetry than philosophy, and indeed, the study of philosophical theory is hardly the primary route to an appreciation of basic values.[139] One may need to experience the crane marsh firsthand (in combination with many related experiences). One may also need a certain amount of biological understanding to "see" in the cranes the value-gestalts that Leopold perceives. It may also be true, as the *Symposium* teaches, that higher value-gestalts in different domains worth caring about become more apparent to us only after we have *started* to care about the lower ones. For example, a child who had already acquired at least a moderate love of charismatic mammal species (especially domesticated ones like dogs or cats) might find it easier to follow Leopold on the journey toward an appreciation of intrinsic values in wild animals, entire species, wilderness ecosystems as organic wholes, and so on.

5. The Reciprocal Relation between Value Insight and Volitional Resolve

To escape from Frankfurt's circle, we have to remember the medieval insight that there is a reciprocal relation between the development of volitional and of cognitive aspects of one's personality. In this chapter, I frequently portray this relation in its simplest form as an unconditioned value insight grounding a volitional response. The actual relation is usually more complex, because beyond early childhood, the agent has almost always projectively willed some ends and acquired rudimentary cares. In the narrative process of human lives, such prior volitional activity (whether recognized or not) always, to some extent, affects and colors how various possible grounds for further projective willing appear to us; sometimes it even limits the range of grounds that we can consider.

But this stagewise dynamic in what we might call "broadly ethical education of human sentiments" hardly implies that all reasons for caring about anything new to us must be agent-relative or derive all their (potential) motivational force and direction from what we already care about. Frankfurt has offered no compelling reasons to accept his conclusion that it is impossible "for a person who does not already care at least about *something* to discover reasons to care about anything. Nobody can pull himself up by his own bootstraps."[140] Surely people sometimes do change from leading relatively "wanton" lives with no serious volitional cares or aretaic commitments to anything (even to their own pleasure).[141] If young children count as "wanton," then this transition from wantonness to passionate devotion through the formation of ground projects is probably even part of the normal course of human development; as Kierkegaard's famous transition from naïve "aestheticism" to "ethical" seriousness also suggests, people can pass from uncaring disengagement or superficial busyness to deep engagement through volitional caring.

Are we to conclude that the agent's sensitivity to objective values—or his practical reason in its most extended sense—cannot guide this process at all, that it is entirely blind or only a matter of discovering proto-cares already given within the proto-self? These alternatives are far less plausible than the straightforward explanation that in response to an awareness of values that she did not create (however reflectively this awareness is articulated), the agent projects *new* final ends for herself? "Bootstrapping" cares into being is not problematic; it is the will's natural function. By contrast, the idea that all *values* are bootstrapped into being by self-defining cares is highly counterintuitive since it is a radical revision to the ordinary practical standpoint of nonphilosophical agents. So the intelligibility of "bootstrapping" depends entirely on what boots are being pulled up by what straps.

To put the matter another way, existential objectivists will agree that most people already care about something (even if only halfheartedly) that can be appealed to in getting them to care about something else. For example, if they care about their shiny new Yamaha sports bike, then they will care about reducing motorcycle theft in their neighborhood, and no new projective motivation is needed to explain the latter; it is simply instrumental to preserving the initial object of their concern. But it is quite different when an existing care for X encourages, facilitates, or leads to a new care for Y that is motivationally independent of the first care. It can do this if caring for X *opens* the agent to see logically independent grounds for caring about Y or makes these grounds more salient, better understood, or appreciated. This is a common experience, which I have already mentioned in connection with friendship (see chap. 8, sec. 4): love of some person P is likely to get us to pay more attention to what P cares about and to think about what the grounds for those cares might be. But taking up my friend's interests or practices need not be (only) instrumentally motivated for the sake of the friendship; these interests or practices can become important to me in their own right. Likewise, two people who both care about the same goals or ideals may start to care about each other directly rather than merely as cooperators in a joint quest. This newly formed love may be able to survive the lapsing of some or perhaps even all of the cares that led to it.

Relations between one kind of care and grounds for others in its "practical vicinity" are complex. Suppose that I already enjoy nature photography and have taken it up as a hobby—I visit exhibits focusing on wilderness photographs, read articles about new ultra-high-density mountain shots, and print my own pictures of rivers and streams. Let us further suppose that I got into this hobby from the classroom rather than the field: my grounds for taking it up came from studying aesthetic theories in a photography class, which helped me appreciate the aesthetic values of fine composition and use of natural light in nature photography. I was never really a nature lover; I was more a lover of formal aesthetic theory and the art of photo composition. Still it would be entirely unsurprising, almost predictable in fact, that once I had pursued this hobby for a couple years, the experience of being in settings of awesome natural beauty would *awaken* me to natural values that are related but not identical to aesthetic values in human expressive artifacts or artworks. The objective values of pristine deserts, jagged mountains, and prairie landscapes might have been accessible to me before taking up nature photography, but they become more salient or evident to me as a by-product of my creative pursuit of photography based on an appreciation of aesthetic values realized in photos.

Suppose I respond to these natural values so strongly that I eventually drop nature photography altogether and spend my spare time as a naturalist in the field or as a lobbyist for environmental preservation. This development in my will would be anything but arbitrary; it would make narrative sense in my life story. Yet it could not be explained according to Williams's conception of internal reasons nor according to Frankfurt's similar model of reasons that depend on my existing cares, because it involves the generation of a new final end that transcends my present motivational set.

This kind of "leap" from one care, aretaic commitment, or ground project to another is a very familiar feature in human biographies. Sometimes the emotional dispositions involved in the first care alter the agent's sensitivity to values that are relevant to the normative worth of other cares. For example, suppose that a nurse's devotion to very sick children in a pediatric cancer ward has generated a strong emotional reaction to children's suffering. This in turn leads her to read about issues concerning child welfare and eventually to switch to a career as a social worker with the Division of Children and Youth or as an advocate with a foundation that works to reduce child abuse. Here the connection is obvious enough. But the links between earlier and later cares can involve all kinds of twists and indirect connections that no general theory could reduce to a short list of motifs. Suppose our nurse instead becomes a facilitator for parents struggling to care for children with disabilities; somehow her sympathy for children with cancer has made her more aware of obstacles faced by parents whose children have a different kind of problem. Maybe the explanation would involve a particular family that she got to know in her first line of work.

Given such *narrative complexity*, we can only say that in each case, activities involved in devotion to present goals and relationships have by-product effects on the agent's broadly ethical sensibilities. That is because cares are like peaks in a figurative landscape of practical interest and motivation. In this topological analogy, imagine the horizontal x-y directions as value variables and the vertical z direction as the volitional variable. Our natural desires and learned tastes can move us horizontally along the valleys, and even from there we can see a few mountains worth climbing. But we have to work ourselves up the slopes (against volitional inertia and natural lassitude) to get a better view. Hence the paradox that agents who care sincerely about something worthwhile are better able to discern many other things that would be worth caring about, while agents who care about little can discern few reasons to care about anything. From our present peak, we can get a good view of surrounding peaks and the grounds on which they stand. Thus to educate the will, one starts by getting children to care about something whose value they can already appreciate, however humble, and then one helps them to recognize the new value vistas that their initial effort opens up for them.

But this metaphor fails in one respect: in volitional life, one does not necessarily have to move through a valley to get to another peak. One can sometimes leap from the top of one mountain to the slopes of another. The topological metaphor also fails to capture the fact that intensive cares or loves can sometimes occlude the importance of other potential objects of care, even when contingencies of history and affinity would suggest them. Some volitional peaks are shrouded in clouds of different colors that filter our ethical vision. Caring passionately about something can obscure from our view personally relevant universalizable considerations in favor of caring about something else. For example, years of work prosecuting sex offenders might diminish a person's ability to appreciate the value of the erotic, even to such an extent that it creates relationship problems. Or years of work as a prison guard looking after violent criminals might make it harder for a person to appreciate the importance of mentoring, better opportunities, and second chances for adolescents headed in the wrong direction. Note that it would be oversimplistic to assume that such a person just lacked an "affinity" for caring about impoverished youth; he might have been emotionally and temperamentally well suited for this role, but, given the devotion he put into his corrections work, the reasons for projecting a mentoring role might have become almost invisible to him.[142] This is one of several reasons why our nonmoral endeavors and relationships need to remain nested within a more fundamental devotion to ethical wisdom and virtue ideals that keeps our *phronetic* capacities attuned to values from which our personal projects might otherwise cut us off.

As complex as the effects of the striving will can be on ethical sensitivity to worthwhile values, perhaps in a few areas, an existential version of Diotima's ascent is possible: caring about a more highly specified activity or end awakens us to values of a more general or embracing kind. In such ascents, new values open to us at each stage that transcend the reach of those we already care about. Whether we pursue them or incorporate them personally into our lives depends on our will. Yet these values are not mere fantasies of our will, phantom shadows of our existing motives displayed on the screen of the world. They could not make personal meaning possible for us if they lacked the *alterity* that Frankl emphasized. This is how Susan Wolf puts the same point:

> In addition to wanting to live in the real world, we want to be connected to it—that is, we want our lives to have some positive relation to things or people or ideas that are valuable independently of us. This, I believe, is at the core of the desire to live a meaningful life.[143]

Thus Wolf, Nozick, Raz, and Blustein all give us similar reasons to favor existential objectivism. If they are right, EO does imply one remarkable conclusion: the willing that is most distinctive of personhood and through which life becomes personally meaningful is possible only because the world we inhabit is already "meaningful," full of domains of value worth caring about.[144] In that sense, human autonomy is also dependent on a world of values it does not create. As Larmore argues in response to Nietzsche, self-determination requires authoritative reasons and hence some values that "exist independent of our will . . . our lives cannot be ones of limitless self-creation. . . . Our lives must instead rest on respect for the claims that the world makes on us."[145]

6. Toward a Taxonomy of Significant Grounds for Caring

In this chapter, I have argued that a sufficiently nuanced objectivist conception of values as grounding cares fits well with the projective explanation of caring supplied by the existential conception of striving will. Of course, this is far from providing a direct defense of objective values themselves. This task would require analyzing a wide-ranging and insightful body of recent literature in the "rebirth" of analytic axiology, such as Chisholm's *Brentano and Intrinsic Value* and Nozick's *Philosophical Explanations*. In different ways, the authors in this broad movement[146] lend support to some version of the objectivist idea that

> in order to explain commitment and in order for an individual's commitment to remain stable over time and to fulfill its roles in the governance of action, enhancement of self-understanding, and constitution of identity, one must assume the truth of moral realism and so make room for the possibility of moral facts.[147]

Although I do not take on the burden of defending a complete objective list theory of values or any metaethical account of value realism, it will be helpful to assemble in systematic form all the different types of values that I have mentioned at various points as possible grounds for projective motivation, especially in the form of ground projects, self-defining commitments, or cares. Organizing the table according to types of grounds rather than types of ends yields a taxonomy with a much clearer structure and order than the sort of goal hierarchies presented in the best available work on this topic in empirical psychology.[148] This taxonomy serves as a sketch of an existential theory of "basic goods."[149]

Worthwhile Objects of Care and Other Grounds for Commitment

I. Agent-Transcending Product-Focused Reasons. Such reasons are independent of:

- the agent's prior cares, commitments, or desires and emotions in the agent's internal set;
- objective conditions for the agent's individual well-being, flourishing, or happiness (the material elements of the agent's welfare);
- higher-order goods of existential coherence and subjective meaningfulness (process-goods for the agent).

1. The moral worth of an end E (or the moral status of some way W of pursuing E) irrespective of the positive or negative impact of realizing this end on agent's own flourishing:

   Ia. E or W is required under a formal or deontic standard of universalizability or fairness or justice, given the intrinsic value of each individual (e.g., keeping a promise or protecting innocent persons from lethal threats when possible).

   Ib. E or W is inherently good according to nonformal ethical standards; for example, W is a virtuous action aimed at E as a species of "the noble" as defined by an authoritative list of virtues of character.

   Ic. Under such standards, taking an interest in E or caring about E is morally required of any person in the situation in which the agent finds himself or herself.

   Id. Devotion to E is itself an inherently worthy state according to nonformal criteria of moral worth, such as the duties of agapē as a universally caring response to neighbors and strangers; for example, E is the goal of showing mercy to a wrongdoer, or forgiving one who has wronged us, or reconciling persons who have been enemies.

2. The broadly aesthetic value of an end E, irrespective of its value for the agent's well-being:

2a. E is an end whose realization would create some kind of made beauty in human works or communicate something important through art—which, in most cases, makes it the object of an *artistic practice.*

2b. E is some form of natural (not made) beauty or harmony in chemical, mineral, or geological phenomena, land forms, or ocean environments that can be destroyed or preserved according to human choices.

2c. E is an end whose realization would develop the conception of beauty or aesthetic value in a tradition or practice in which the agent participates.

2d. E is an end whose realization is difficult or challenging for human beings, which thus presents an opportunity for developing and testing certain talents or capacities. These tend to be ends definitive of *sports* practices.

2e. E is a standard of excellence concerning the way in which difficult or challenging goals are properly pursued, which is internal to some practice.

3. The broadly ethical value of an end E, which is not simply a function of the positive or negative impact of the intended outcome on the agent's well-being:

3a. *Social goods.* Although not an object of justice deontically conceived, E is an important component of the common good of individuals as parts of larger groups or communities—which, in many instances of this type, makes E the end definitive of some practice; for example:

- knowledge or theoretical unification as the goals defining *scientific practice*;
- the dissemination of such knowledge and understanding and the apprenticeship of persons into practices in general, as the goals defining *practices of education*;
- public health and the bodily and psychological health of patients, as the goals defining medicine and counseling;
- wise political decisions regarding the use and administration of public resources.

3b. *Cultural goods.* The devotion of groups of persons to E is part of a living tradition of human activity that fosters a sense of communal identity or creates some other cultural good; for example, preserving one's heritage and the monuments and works that embody it, or connecting persons to shared ethnic roots, or fostering civic fraternity.

3c. *Filial and romantic love.* E is part of the flourishing of a person whose entire personality we apprehend as uniquely valuable or who has some other historically unique relationship to us and who is thus an apt target for essentially particularistic love.

3d. *Parents/guardians.* E is (some part of) the welfare of family members or others who provided the nurturing, upbringing, and parental love that enabled our growth and emotional maturation and to whom we therefore have duties of fidelity.

3e. *Environmental goods.* E is part of the flourishing of some non-human form of life, such as particular animals or plants, animal or plant species, biodiversity itself, or environments and ecosystems that sustain species and biodiversity.

4. The religious value of an end E, irrespective of the impact of commitment to it on the agent's well-being:

4a. E is taken to be the authoritative will of a divine being, or part of the good of a divine being.

4b. Pursuit of E is demanded by a sense of religious "calling" or revelation from the divine that goes beyond ordinary requirements of morality or ethical living.

4c. Commitment to E is apprehended as part of one's destiny, fate, or place in a divine order.

4d. E is bound up with a sense of mystery that transcends ordinary life and bears on questions of ultimate meaning (such as the origin and purpose of the universe, the significance of death, or eschatological goods beyond death).

II. Agent-Relative Product-Focused Reasons. Two qualifiers about this category:

- It does not mention considerations that bear directly on the agent's own well-being (since we assume that each agent desires his own happiness and in this case the desire is global enough to provide reason to care about any significant material conditions of his welfare).
- Specific reasons in the subcategories below may not hold as practically reasonable grounds for caring for all persons; the most we could say is that every person will find *some* reason(s) in each of these categories that pertain to them and would provide a reasonable basis for their commitments.

1. Retrospective reasons for caring about E:

    1a. Commitment to E responds to something deeply personal in our past, such as a trauma or loss suffered by ourselves or significant others. By commitment to E, we can transcend this experience as simply a harm or meaningless absurdity, bringing to it a new and positive meaning that it did not have initially (thus bringing a complex good out of it).
    1b. E is required or suggested as a possible creative response, beyond any strict duty of fidelity, to particular individuals or groups:

        (i) to whom we are significantly indebted for technically unrepayable gifts;
        (ii) whose wrong actions it is valuable to repudiate by corrective action or other communicative response;
        (iii) to whom we, as offenders, may make some kind of significant restitution, apology, or offering of reconciliation (this consideration is related to I.1d above).

2. Prospective reasons for caring about E:

    2a. E is effectively pursuable only as a *joint end* with others, who will not commit themselves to it unless we do so as well, on the same terms. (Many social goods that at least partially transcend the good of individual agents, e.g., possibly requiring uncompensated sacrifices from them, are pursuable only as goods to which multiple such agents are jointly committed, each person's commitment being contingent on the others' reciprocation. See chap. 8, sec. 7.)
    2b. E is the end of a *possible hobby*, which is like a practice but usually less complex and demanding and produces a good less widely shareable, or with less social or intrinsic significance.

III. Agent-Relative Process-Focused Reasons. Such reasons are not based on the agent's desire for her own eudaimonia or flourishing, but of all the grounds for projective motivation, they come closest to this. These considerations are based instead on the psychological requirements that living a coherently meaningful life, or living autonomously, puts on the process of caring. Concern for these existential "goods," however, cannot accurately be construed simply as concern for one's own happiness. Although well-being in the broadest sense may involve these goods, in the cases that concern us, the action is not motivated by the prospect of these goods *desired as* part of eudaimonia; rather, the agent does not pursue them directly at all but only sees the pursuit of other possible ends *in light of* these considerations as existential grounds for positing, sustaining, and/or ordering these other ends as final for her. As this analysis suggests, these grounds are not ones that can function entirely on their own; rather, they become relevant only in combination with other considerations relating to the value of the product to be willed as one's final end. That is, they properly arise as qualifying, amending, or reinforcing considerations, not as primary considerations in favor of projecting end E (see chap. 12, sec. 3).

1. Prospective reasons concerning the process of caring about E:

   1a. The stars align: we find ourselves with a fortunate opportunity to pursue E with likely success.[150]

   1b. Structural opportunity: commitment to E is psychologically possible for us, culturally possible, valued and endorsed by significant others in our life, is likely to win cooperation, and so on.

   1c. Replacement: commitment to E provides a sense of purpose and can fit into or enhance a coherent pattern of caring that generates existential meaningfulness in the agent's life.

   1d. Liberal breadth: E is significantly different in kind from our other identity-defining commitments and personal projects, and/or pursuit of E requires activities and draws on talents or capacities that are not as well employed in the pursuit of our other governing life goals—thus promoting the process-good of *intrapersonal practical diversity* in our life.

   1e. Innovation and individualization: the particular instantiations of E that we seek and the activities involved in pursuing them are novel and/or different in interesting ways from those pursuits and goals that shape the distinctive character of significant others in our life—thus promoting the process-good of *individual distinctiveness and originality* in our life.

2. Retrospective reasons concerning the process of caring about E:

   2a. *Stare decisis*: our pursuit of E first developed for other reasons, such as its power to satisfy various desires, and now this pursuit appears outwardly to be an established part of our character on which others trust and rely. We feel too involved with E to turn back now without feeling disloyal and possibly also directionless.

2b. *Existential coherence*: commitment to E is required by, reinforces, or at least fits well with other prior commitments we have made and the shape of our life to date; for example:

- E is the welfare of the child (by former marriage) of the person we are marrying;
- E is valued and pursued by friends to whom we have committed ourselves;
- caring about E is, given the circumstances of human life, practically implied by caring about some other end F to which we are already devoted (for instance, caring about our children's education requires caring that they not be bullied in school).

2c. *Personal affinity*: we find that our commitment to E can be wholehearted or unreserved, unifying what were previously conflicting aspects of our will or preserving us against such disunity—thus promoting the process-good of *practical unity* in our volitional life.

2d. *Innate orientation*: in our quest for self-discovery, we find that our devotion to E is volitionally necessary for us as a volitional disposition that we cannot will to reject and that we were destined to express, given our personal essence or the unique volitional character that individuates us. This devotion is our individual *ergon*, our "personal function."[151]

The basic goods in this list fall into three out of four quadrants of a simple two-by-two matrix:

Agent-Relative Product-Focused Reasons	Agent-Relative Process-Focused Reasons
Agent-Transcending Product-Focused Reasons	[empty]

I have not listed any agent-transcending process-focused grounds in the fourth quadrant, because second-order goods realized in the process of pursuing first-order goods typically pertain to (or are directly realized in) the agent who is in this volitional process. For example, the coherence of his pursuits and the meaningfulness of his life are agent-relative goods and hence are related to his history and circumstances in ways that agent-transcending goods are not. So rather than invent practical considerations for the fourth quadrant or force some into it for the sake of artificial architectonic completeness, I have left it empty. By contrast, existential subjectivist accounts can accommodate only some of the considerations included in the top-right quadrant.

Although many grounds for different types of cares are accessible to reflection in human beings with the necessary experience or knowledge by acquaintance, this existential objectivist account certainly does not claim that all the grounds on which our actual cares or ground projects are based are known to each of us or even that with sufficient introspection, they can all be known. Sometimes the status and content of our cares and ground projects themselves are misunderstood by us, and sometimes we are (to an extent) self-deceived about them. The grounds or considerations to which we respond in projecting some end may also not be ones that *really* justify pursuit of this end (as is always the case with radically evil projects but also with some morally neutral or good projects too). The objective grounds for caring included in my list are reasons that agents do consider in projecting final ends and can *take as* sufficient bases for their cares or commitments; but agents are sometimes wrong in this regard. My claim is only that each item on my list can sometimes serve as part of an adequate ground for setting a particular end.

A theory of authenticity is, in part, a systematic normative treatment of these issues. Even when we do understand what our purposes are, and they were formed on the basis of adequate reasons, these reasons may not be entirely known to us. This does not entail that the volitional commitment involved in these purposes is inauthentic. Indeed, the opposite view is advanced in the Emersonian and Marcelian traditions. As Henry Bugbee writes in his mid-century classic:

> It is the essence of authentic commitment that it be grounded behind the intellectual eye and not merely in a demonstrable basis which we can get before us. The ultimate meaning of service lies just here: we cannot gain command of what grounds our action; there can only be an unconditional basis of action in so far as we are at "its" disposal and not our own.[152]

It is for this kind of reason that category I.4 is included in my list; it is surely true that some "callings" are categorized as religious because their grounds are mysterious and not fully knowable to their agent. But Bugbee and Marcel do not restrict their thesis to religious callings, and Levinas would extend it to moral motivation, which he thinks is a response to a value that transcends human cognition (the infinity of the other). Even if we do not agree that all authentic commitment must be formed on the basis of a "calling" whose ultimate source is hidden from us, it is an interesting question whether some of the more passionate and intense types of human caring or ground projects are generally grounded in this veiled way. Here I will say only that the main elements of existential objectivism as sketched in this chapter do not decide this issue one way or another. Answers to these questions are further refinements or additions to the basic EO framework, which is flexible enough to include a range of views that recognize the alterity of values grounding the self-motivational activity that is human "willing" in its most primordial sense.

Nor is my subdivision of grounds for volitional projection into aesthetic, ethical, moral, and personal reasons meant to be exhaustive; aside from tradition and culture, mere social convention and popular opinion are also sometimes taken as grounds for projective motivation. But this is usually a *mistaken* judgment or perception of normative worth. Aside from the personal grounds mentioned in the list, factors such as religious background, revelations, disturbing events, and many other distinctive experiences not catalogued here, can become the bases for the resolve in which a person steels herself projectively to new ends. My list is also limited to *positive* grounds that can in the right circumstances *validly* support the agent's volitional response to them through care or personal devotion. It does not include those negative grounds that I survey in chapter 10 as reasons-in-view for projecting radically evil ends or any other reasons that it is *always* erroneous to take as grounds for caring. (Many of the considerations in my list *could* be taken as reasons to form projects that would be morally wrong in certain circumstances, but they are distinct from corrupt grounds that the will can *only* take as reasons for forming evil or destructive projects.)

This existential taxonomy of values worth caring about embraces but transcends the insights of the eudaimonist tradition and Frankfurt's alternative. It gives proper place to agent-relative process-focused considerations such as existential coherence and mutually reinforcing relationships among an agent's projects, for example, between friendship and other activities.[153] Concern for process-focused reasons referring to the goods of effectiveness and practical coherence in one's own life is not egoistic, because these goods are required for volitional stability or sustainable devotion to any worthwhile first-order goals. Too much cognitive dissonance or conflict among goals undermines commitment to any of our goals.[154] Likewise, as the psychological study of intrinsic motivation has shown, confidence in a minimum level of control over one's environment and conditions of life is a precondition for strong volitional devotion to anything. Feeling that one is utterly at the mercy of forces beyond one's control is a strong predictor of depression and general demotivation.[155] A heroic agent may be able to pursue good ends even with little prospect of success, but only if she retains confidence in a *minimum effectiveness* of her agency in the world. My existential account denies that adjusting one's ends in light of such considerations is rooted only in desire for eudaimonia. For such process-focused considerations do not by themselves generally provide sufficient reason for willing a first-order end; their relevance piggybacks on the presence of product-focused reasons for forming or continuing various first-order projects. For example, a significant opportunity for success in a career as an engineer becomes relevant to me only if the goods produced by excellent engineering are already worth willing in themselves.

My tentative summary of the main positive reasons for projective willing is also "pluralist" in the sense defended by both Jeffrey Blustein and John Kekes. As chapter 7 made clear, unlike A-eudaimonism, my existential objectivism does not claim that *every* worthwhile good can be balanced in a unified narrative structure within in a single life. Hence I agree with Blustein that "no particular configuration or ranking of . . . basic human goods follows from the claim that living a life that combines these goods in a coherent, harmonious structure is intrinsically good." There are many different ways of balancing goods worth caring about.[156] Similarly, Kekes writes that "Living a good life requires the achievement of a coherent ordering of plural and [often] conflicting values, but coherent orderings are themselves plural and conflicting."[157]

The incommensurability of many nonmoral values and the fact that only limited combinations of them in different priority ordering are practically compatible fits with several features of EO: (1) It helps explain the existence of rational optionality in judgments concerning what is worth caring about. It also explains the reality of what we might call soft dilemmas, in which we are forced to choose between things we have cared about equally or without relative priority up until now. (2) It fits with the fact that moral reasoning about fairness/justice is not the only source of insight into values worth caring about. (3) It also supports the idea that although reasonable life plans are not instantiations of a single recipe, there are objective limits: "not all possibilities are reasonable."[158] In particular, there are "primary values" that determine what count as harms and benefits for all normal human persons, which are culturally invariant.[159] In my opinion, we should also limit the "conditionality" of nonmoral values[160] by giving overriding significance to strictly moral values (deontic requirements). But a defense of this claim goes beyond the scope of my present analysis.[161]

Conclusion

This chapter shows that the existential conception of striving will fits well with moderate objectivist approaches to the problem of practical normativity within contemporary analytic philosophy. It provides a theoretical basis for broadening our view of basic goods beyond those recognized by neo-Aristotelian natural-law theory and thus shows how to fill the lacuna in Kantian moral psychology without reverting to eudaimonism. Thus it is possible to develop an explanatorily powerful non-eudaimonist conception of willing without the dangers of irrationalism, subjectivism, and empty formalism. The resulting existential conception of personhood provides a better basis for a substantive ethic of the good life that can live within a broader deontological framework for moral norms.

Conclusion
The Danger of Willfulness Revisited

> [M]any persons strive for high ideals;
> and everywhere life is full of heroism.
> —Max Ehrmann, *Desiderata*

> Life is what happens when you're making other plans.
> —*Opus*, November 2004

My defense of striving will as key part of the new existential account of personhood started with the contrast between "Eastern" and "Western" attitudes toward willing in its heroic sense. In fixing the concept of willing to be explained by the existential theory of projective motivation, I argued in chapter 2 that it is possible to formulate a moderate version of the positive "Western" attitude toward heroic willing, which the subsequent existential analysis clarifies and supports. We can now ask whether that analysis has shown that heroic willing can play a positive role in the formation of robust practical identity and a meaningful life.

In taking stock of what the previous chapters imply for our original question, it is clear that some "Eastern" worries that the striving will is too Promethean or violent have been recognized as valid in the limited context of radically evil willing. I also acknowledged that decision may frequently be egoistic, taking its goals from self-interested desires. Yet we have also found several reasons to think that human striving will is not essentially violent, metaphysically rebellious, or inherently bent on misappropriation, illegitimate power, or dominance. While it is not a mere privation or result of ignorance or mere weakness in the face of desires for lower goods, radically evil will is still a *deficient mode* of the striving will, not its natural state.

Although the projective capacity of our striving will indeed makes radical evil possible, without it, agapic love and moral virtue in general would also be impossible, great undertakings could not begin, the practices could never have developed, and human beings could not muster the staying power required for long-term devotion to the kinds of goods necessary for a flourishing society. Hence the "Western" attitude has been vindicated to this extent: human beings cannot realize their existential telos without developing the strength of will necessary for authentic caring and the kind of aretaic commitment that makes for strong practical unity among one's motives over time (and ideally throughout one's life).[1]

Moreover, our new existential account makes clear that volitional "resolve" is not mere "choice seemingly devoid of criteria," as Frank Schalow expresses this common worry about Heidegger's concept.[2] Rather, "resolve" is a response to possibilities of value-realization, "the freedom which corresponds to our entry into a domain of praxis." As Schalow argues, this includes entry into social relationships, or possibilities of *Mitsein*.[3] Perhaps such resolve requires some recognition of our mortality—our having only a finite time to devote ourselves to what matters most in our circumstances.[4] Then authentic willing is the very opposite of a blind "will to will" or pure self-assertion; rather, it requires a sense of "guardianship" or responsibility to respond to beings beyond our agency or even to Being itself.[5]

These ideas must be developed in a full existential conception of authenticity that does not confuse being true to oneself with the ground of all moral requirements. However, there is one crucial worry about projective willing and its role in the ethos of individual selves that has not been yet been addressed or allayed. The worry is that even an agent willing worthwhile goals as parts of a coherent ethical life, within limits set by her higher-order will to justice or universal respect, can take the pursuit of her agenda to exhaust the meaning to be found in human existence. What if strength of will, as a magnificent obsession with one's long-term "to do" list, actually blinds us to more objectively important things (such as needs) that come along unexpectedly? Even worse, what if the deepest kind of relationship with other persons is *blocked* by reducing everything in "my world" to the significance it has in *my* hierarchy of cares, personal projects, or long-term commitments?

Such an attitude could involve a subtle kind of existential narcissism, even if my cares are altruistic or my projects consist entirely of devotion to worthwhile agent-transcending goods. Even though I do not violate the categorical imperative by reducing other persons (or ideals such as scientific truth, the value of nature, or human-made beauty) to "mere means" to my ends, I might still see everything through the lens of my "ownmost" project or interpret the significance of each thing or person in terms of its practical relation to my highest ends (as Heidegger's analysis of *Dasein* in *Being and Time* arguably implies). What if opening myself to other persons in their alterity, or experiencing them as they really are, requires an encounter with them as *transcending* the web of concerns constituted by my existing volitional devotions? Indeed, Martin Buber's *I and Thou* seems to suggest that agapic love of another person requires *putting aside* my agenda or suspending my will in order to open myself unconditionally to the other. This is why Nel Noddings writes that caring for persons "involves stepping out of one's personal frame of reference into the other's."[6] Thus contemporary alterity ethics may show, after all, that "Eastern" suspicions of the striving will contain an insight not yet sufficiently addressed in my analysis.

The objection that concerns me is succinctly and straightforwardly developed in a recent book by Robert Ehman (though in response to Heidegger). Ehman rejects the idea that our distinctive identity is revealed when we are "absorbed in our tasks and roles." He thinks of the authentic self as something that transcends the everyday contexts in which "The self is defined in terms of its status, roles, achievement, virtues, purposes, not in terms of its unique personality."[7]

Ehman does not sufficiently distinguish between someone who loses himself in roles and hides behind a "superficial public" face and one who is deeply devoted to the values served by his social roles.[8] As Gabrielle Taylor argues, there is a crucial difference between an agent who is wholeheartedly committed and an aesthete who uses "being busy" as a way of avoiding full engagement and ignoring the question of what is really worth caring about.[9] Yet this distinction is suggested by Ehman's admission that an authentic person need not "oppose the everyday world or retreat from it." He recognizes that Heidegger's idea of "authentic resoluteness which projects upon a single end right up to our death" contrasts with "the unauthentic 'curiosity' and frivolousness of everyday being in which we flit from one affair to another."[10] This agrees with Frankfurt's distinction between wanton and volitionally engaged agents. But Ehman rejects the existential idea that a person is defined by "a unity of purpose, a fundamental project"[11] as too technological or instrumental, reducing the person to a goal-pursuing engine.

Some of the emptiest people, Ehman says, are "resolute in their fulfillment of a single goal in terms of which they give meaning to their lives."[12] He considers living a "dedicated" or "strenuous" life, in which "one performs one's tasks seriously and responsibly," to be a Calvinist or utilitarian ideal that defines an individual in a way that makes her, in principle, replaceable.[13] For it is possible (he assumes) that another individual could have the same purposes or even pursue the same goals in the same way. Yet the personality gestalt that is uniquely individual is too all-encompassing to be the object of a project. The value of a personality is not a possible object of will and action. While the person himself as well as others might attain an inkling of his personality, it is beyond his control. He can only respond emotionally to it, not change it.[14]

Now, this critique assumes that the existentialist typically makes her own personality into an intentional target or goal. This is not necessary to an existential conception of the will, as my account makes clear. Although I have suggested that autonomy, authenticity, and virtues of character must be at least indirectly targetable reflexive goals (chap. 5, sec. 2.4), I regard volitional character as primarily a by-product of first-order strivings. Moreover, in my existential conception, our cares and long-term commitments define only the core of a personal ethos, not the entire gestalt. Each individual will pursue his or her ground projects in uniquely distinguishing ways, and, given the historically conditioned grounds we have for fine-grained cares, a volitionally engaged agent is also usually *de facto* irreplaceable in those pursuits. Thus my model is compatible with Ehman's conception of unique personalities as well as with his thesis that authenticity is not identical with moral goodness,[15] and with his conception of persons as essentially interpersonal and expressive beings.[16]

But Ehman's complaint against the existential approach goes deeper than this. He follows the Levinasian view that "In the face of the otherness of a genuine other, we cannot feel at home." Thus a "personal encounter with another in the depths of his personality" displaces our focus on our own heroic quests and strivings: "we must open ourselves to the strangeness of the other and be willing to explore his otherness. In so doing we must suspend our own everyday projects and purposes, must see the other apart from his functional and instrumental roles, must see him as an end in himself."[17]

This suggests that my earlier treatment of friendship and love relationships as quasi-practices that can be willed fails to go deep enough: a fundamental relationship with an irreplaceable other cannot be a willed project. Rather, it is something that *happens* to us, suspending our agenda and transcending "the competitive teleology of our everyday life."[18] Nor does Ehman restrict this to the context of essentially particularistic love, for he thinks it holds true for the most primordial kinds of "encounter" with other values, too. Contra Sartre's theory of value, Ehman says:

> all of us have moments when we suspend our projects in an appreciation of beauty, truth, personal worth. The very choice of our projects depends in fact upon our experience of the values of things independently of projects, since we engage in projects to bring about something that we already find of value. . . . the intrinsic value of things determines our projects.[19]

Conclusion: The Danger of Willfulness Revisited 543

We see here that Ehman's objection to defining a person in terms of her willed goals turns mainly on his dissatisfaction with subjectivism: the willing agent is responding to values that she did not posit, recognition of which may even interrupt her volitional activity. Thus his insight is already incorporated into existential objectivism: the value of persons and other goods worthy of devotion is not *itself* willed but rather encountered. In that sense, Ehman is entirely correct that existential authenticity built on volitional devotion is dependent on "a world of values and meanings" that have significance prior to or "apart from all purpose."[20] In particular, as I emphasize in discussing Levinas, our moral responsibility to care about persons as ends cannot be autonomous in the sense of being *voluntarily willed*; rather, it precedes all willing.[21]

But Ehman, like Levinasians in general, tends to underrate the existential importance of the *agent's volitional response* to such values. After all, he admits that an encounter with the unique alterity of the other leaves open the possibility of loving, hating, and other responses. Encountered values must be personally appropriated through the projective activity of the striving will; even if this is not experienced as a separate moment of decision, an active embracing attitude is synthesized with passive discovery. The requirement to respond to values certainly puts ethical limits on our egoistic pursuit of power or self-interest but admits the need for volitional response in general. Moreover, a full appreciation of other individuals often requires laying aside our agenda precisely because their personal ethos is defined at its center by *their own* goals, projects, and strivings. This stands in sharp contrast to pure moral respect for the other as a moral agent or end. Hence I have to reject Ehman's claim that "objective, public, universal criteria" cannot enter into our grounds for loving persons as unique individuals.[22] If in part we love them for their devotion to objectively valuable goods, then our evaluation of their character must have some objective criteria as well. This is compatible with Ehman's claim that the self transcends its "interests" and includes its whole way of being in the world,[23] and with his claim that individuals have the right to live lives that we would not judge as good.[24]

My deeper response to this alterity critique of existential willing is twofold. First, while it recognizes the positive and vital role played by the striving will in defining the core of one's personal ethos, my new existential theory of personhood, authenticity, and practical coherence is not committed to the extreme claim that strength of will or depth of commitment is *all* that matters or even to the weaker thesis that projective motivation is the most important requirement of an authentic and/or good life. My sketch of a moderate existential objectivist position in chapter 14 suggests that deeply willed cares can both open us to new values (beyond those which grounded these cares) and sometimes obscure or close off other values from our attention. Because our dedication to our projects can blind us to other important values, in order to attend properly to persons that we ought to care about or other potential goods or harms that we should consider, we may sometimes have to suspend our pursuits, set aside our agendas temporarily, and be willing to modify them in light of new insights. Existential strength of will does not require fanaticism; nor does practical unity require monomania.

Therefore, there is room within an existential objectivist account for the idea that we should sometimes *let things be* without drawing them into the orbit of our projects, or attend to them without viewing them only in terms of their relation to our strivings. Since existential coherence requires caring about the worth of our cares (chap. 14), we have good reason to let ourselves be guided toward values by realities that are independent of our missions. This idea has been central to the Romantic tradition since Wordsworth. Heidegger tells us that our highest dignity is to be witnessing poets, "keeping watch over the unconcealment" of beings.[25] Mary Oliver, the great contemporary American nature poet, says: "To pay attention, this is our endless and proper work."[26] But this is one-sided, for it is not our telos merely to be passive observers of being. Making and building, working the world of nature into culture, and subcreating, in Tolkien's sense, are also essential parts of our natural function. After *Gelassenheit* comes volitional response, ever interrupted by further attending and leading to further alteration of the will (sometimes taking up new purposes, sometimes laying old ones aside).

Of course, sometimes the very earnestness of our dedication to projects and roles can distort our views or hinder requisite axiological attentiveness, but that is the risk we must take. It cannot be avoided by Eastern-style disengagement; while separation from the superficial values of mass consumerism may clear our minds, detachment from the profound values of life cannot lead to a more meaningful life. The danger of blindness to values outside our projects can be addressed only by blending passionate devotion with a willingness to hear objections and remain open to perspectives alterior to our own.

Hence I believe that the right existential conception of authenticity must articulate the required balance between volitional engagement in projects—including the practices, social roles, and relationships that make up culture—and the ability to withhold from pursuits or suspend our will in a way that (at least partially) makes it possible to transcend our present practical horizons.

The second point is that this very withholding, by which we put aside our agendas and let alterity interrupt our volitional trajectories through our shared lifeworld, *is itself a higher-order work of the striving will*, grounded in our recognition of alterity and our own epistemic finitude. This is what Edward Mooney calls "receptive willingness."[27] He argues that sometimes the agent can grow only if his will is humbled by phenomena that transcend him without presenting a particular "task," realities that "bend," check, or even transform his will.[28] But this is not sheer coercion; rather, to be humbled, we must make an inward effort to put our projected ends in abeyance or even be willing to alter them for the sake of the other person (following Buber and Levinas) or perhaps for the sake of nature (following Oliver) or for religious hope (following Kierkegaard).

This "willingness" is the right alternative to the dangerous "will to will" or sheer delight in one's projective powers and ability to make a mark on the world;[29] it is the will, when necessary, *not to will* (for a time) those ends to which one is committed or those roles and relationships in which one is engaged. Through willing$_2$ such volitional disengagement from first-order projects, we are sometimes able to see more clearly the values to which we ought to be responding, or to remember why we set out on the course we were taking, or understand more profoundly the values for the sake of which we began questing in the first place. In this way, we acknowledge that the process of volition in which our practical identity is defined is *not entirely our own*; the grounds on which we will our personal ends are informed not only by friends and tradition but also by regestaltings of our world through strangers, novelty, alterity—perhaps even the divine. Our true self is as much "received" as invented.[30]

In my conception, then, the striving will is not essentially always on a mission or permanently locked into heroic-quest mode. It can stop itself, sometimes to smell the roses, sometimes to remember the past, sometimes to enjoy all that has been won or given, and sometimes to respond to alterities that may turn it aside from its intended path. The will is the heart of planning agency, which can initiate breaks from the status quo, keep focus against distractions, and press on against resistance; but it can also suspend its plans for the sake of the other. To alter one of Bernard Williams's examples, consider an artist who devotes years of her life to an enormous work, like carving Mount Rushmore. But now imagine that she discovers that her partially finished work sits on the last remaining part of lands once holy to a Native American tribe. If she is sufficiently sensitive to these values, then despite her wholehearted devotion to her project, she could change her goal, stop carving, or perhaps rework what she had done into something more acceptable to the original stewards of this land. Because it is a response to objective values, aretaic commitment can be altered without loss of self or volitional integrity when one's perception of the relevant values change. The greatest freedom of all is the power to change one's mind for good reasons.

That is why in great epics, the quest never proceeds directly; for the authentic end can never be reached except by way of what seem at first to be digressions. Much of the final meaning of a life-narrative may lie in these twists and turns (while the perfectly straight road would miss most of what makes life worth living). The higher-order will to digress from one's intended path when necessary is a mark of maturity in human agents. Failure to respond to unexpected needs and problems, even at great cost to one's prior agenda, can mean passing up what were really opportunities for the most meaningful and fulfilling engagements or efforts in our lifetime. The single-minded will to stay "on-task" no matter what the potential "distractions" sounds like a great formula in superficial self-help books but it rejects the conception of agapē at the heart of an existential ethic worthy of the name.

In conclusion, human agapic love is this balance between an attentiveness that transcends prior agendas and, in response, passionate engagement in pursuit of good ends. The agapic will, at our human level, is the higher-order will to balance the need for *Gelassenheit* with sustained effort to make the world more just, more beautiful, and richer in knowledge and wonder for all. So understood, the agapic ideal combines what is best in both the "Eastern" and "Western" traditions: the serenity of LeGuin's sage Ogion must be joined with the dedication we see in progressives such as Francis Bacon, Immanuel Kant, and Gene Roddenberry. A will committed to finding out the good work that needs to be done and resolved to do it is the true ideal of existentialism.

Notes

Preface: The Project of an Existential Theory of Personhood

1. Sandel, *Liberalism and the Limits of Justice*, 57.
2. See Rawls, *Political Liberalism* I.5, "The Political Conception of the Person."
3. See Cadava, Connor, and Nancy, *Who Comes after the Subject?*
4. This is why Cicero emphasizes Plato's procedure in the *Phaedrus* of beginning with a "preface" providing an initial definition of the concepts from which to start analysis; see Cicero, *On Moral Ends*, Book II, sec. 3, 27. See also Heidegger on the "forehaving" in *Being and Time* I.5 section 32.

I: Introduction

1. Hammarskjöld, *Markings*, 71.
2. Yalom, *Existential Psychotherapy*, 289–90.
3. Hence thick conceptions of volition offer differing theories, explanations, or interpretations of will in the motivational sense but they share the same *basic concept* of what it is they are attempting to explicate. This basic notion of the will as the capacity for a particular kind of self-motivation is not itself a "theory" of the will. Thus if this thick basic concept represents our "folk-psychological" notion of volition, folk psychology does not on this account give us any *theory* or determinate *conception* of the will. It only proleptically demarcates or identifies the phenomena that such theories, are supposed to explain. This function of setting basic concepts rather than theories or determining the *explananda* that developed conceptions try to explain is the usual role of "folk psychology"—or, more accurately, of the complex hermeneutic background of inherited ideas and settled usages affected by past theoretical interpretations, for which "folk-thinking" is the shorthand in contemporary analytic philosophy.
4. See my discussion of this theme in "The Ethical and Religious Significance of Taciturnus's Letter in Kierkegaard's *Stages on Life's Way*." This is the same sentiment that finds expression in Kierkegaard's notion of "infinite resignation." Also see the discussion of aretaic commitment in chapter 13.

5. On this topic, see Davenport, "The Ethical and Religious Significance of Taciturnus's Letter in Kierkegaard's *Stages on Life's Way*."
6. Tolkien, "The Homecoming," 151–52.
7. Tolkien, "*Beowulf*: The Monsters and the Critics," 21. The same passage from Ker, (*The Dark Ages*, 58) is also cited in Wright's Introduction to his prose translation of *Beowulf*, 12.
8. Ibid., 23.
9. Ibid., 26.
10. Tolkien, *Lord of the Rings*, Book VI, chap. 3, 211.
11. Auden, "The Quest Hero," 40–61.
12. Hauerwas, *Character and the Christian Life*, 12.
13. Ibid., 15. On this point, Hauerwas cites Nicolai Hartmann, *Ethics II*, trans. Croit (London: George Allen and Unwin, 1963), 287.
14. As Hauerwas notes, the strength of will implied in "having character" is compatible with an evil will (*Character and the Christian Life*, 17). Also see my essay, "Towards an Existential Virtue Ethics."
15. Ryle, *Concept of Mind*, chap. 3, 68.
16. Ibid., 73.
17. Ibid., 68. Nor is the "particular exercise of tenacity of purpose" that we mean by an "effort of will" reducible to fear of irresoluteness, as Ryle suggests (73). The singularly unpersuasive nature of Ryle's regress arguments is taken up again in chap. 3.
18. Pippin, "Review Article: Horstmann, Siep, and German Idealism," 87. However, this existential conception of willing can be detached from Fichte's idealist view that self-positing will is also the ground of knowledge.
19. Breazeale, "Check or Checkmate?" 93.
20. Ibid., 97.
21. Yalom, *Existential Psychotherapy*, 291.
22. Frankfurt, "Freedom of the Will and the Concept of a Person," 12–13.
23. G. B. Wilson, "Goals—Or Ideals?" 33.
24. A large literature has emerged on this topic in the last fifteen years, prompted primarily by the groundbreaking work of Edward Deci and his colleague Richard Ryan. See their Web site on "Self-Determination Theory" at http://www.psych.rochester.edu/SDT.
25. I say "most clearly" because it is possible, on my view, for agents to project ends related to their own well-being, which they may also desire. But in these cases the agent may have more than one operative motive, so the volitional element of self-projection is not as clearly isolated.
26. For this point and other valuable comments on a draft of this book, I am particularly indebted to Mark LeBar.
27. Obviously, the phrase "A-*psychological*-eudaimonism" would be too awkward, so it must be understood throughout that A-eudaimonism is my construction of an ideal version of psychological eudaimonism.

2. The Heroic Will in Eastern and Western Perspectives

1. *Ten Principal Upanishads*, VII Book 2, sec. 8, 73.
2. Ibid., VII Book I, sec. 3, 32.

3. See Davenport, "A Phenomenology of the Profane: Heidegger, Blumenberg, and the Structure of the 'Chthonic.'"
4. Lao Tzu, *Tao Te Ching*, I(38) 3.
5. Reps, "No Attachment to Dust," in *Zen Flesh, Zen Bones*, 72.
6. Huxley, *Perennial Philosophy*, 133.
7. From the Katha Upanishad, *Ten Principal Upanishads*, III Book 2, sec. 2, 36. And this Self, which seems ironically similar to the Nietzschean Übermensch who embraces the *amor fati*, is certainly meant as a model for the detachment of the sage: "Should he do wrong, or leave good undone, he knows no remorse. What he does, and what he does not, is sanctified" (*Taittireeya Upanishad*, VII Book 2, sec. 9, 74).
8. Kupperman, *Character*, 120–21.
9. *Tao Te Ching*, 7(44), 12.
10. Ibid., 11(48), 16. And we could add many similar passages. For example: "Stopple the orifices of your heart, Close your doors; your whole life will not suffer. Open the gate of your heart, Meddle with affairs; your whole life you will be beyond salvation"; ibid., 15(52), 21.
11. *The Phantom Menace*, episode I of the *Star Wars* movies, dir. George Lucas (Twentieth Century Fox, 1999). This theme is repeated many times in the *Star Wars* movies, in which the Jedi are taught to renounce all worldly attachments. Yet the portrayal of the Jedi ideal is ambiguous, since they are also portrayed as persons of unyielding devotion to their purpose in the galactic order, whose strength in using "the Force" seems to proceed at least partly from the passion of their commitment. Anakin, the Emperor, and Luke are thus the strongest wielders of the Force, precisely because they do *not* take Yoda's advice to practice detachment! That something is fundamentally wrong with the Eastern ideal—that it stops the source of spiritual strength and emasculates the heart—is also implied in Stephen Donaldson, *The Power that Preserves*, when the new lords discover that their oath of peace itself is the source of their weakness in wielding the Earthpower.
12. *Dhammapada*, chap. 6, no. 83, 46.
13. Ibid., chap. 6, nos. 88–89, 47.
14. Ibid., chap. 7, no. 91 and no. 93, 48.
15. Ibid., chap. 8, no. 105 and no. 112, 50–51.
16. Ibid., chap. 18, nos. 244–45, 71.
17. Gowans, *Philosophy of the Buddha*, 182.
18. *Bhagavad Gita*, chap. I, verses 29–47, 46–47.
19. Ibid., chap. 2, verses 11–27, 49–50.
20. Ibid., verse 41, 52.
21. Ibid., verse 47, 52. We encounter this idea again in the analysis of practices in chapter 8.
22. Ibid., verse 56, 53.
23. Blustein, *Care and Commitment*, 63.
24. One sees many elements of the more archaic heroic/timocratic honor code in a very old work like the *I Ching*. For example, in hexagram 13, "Fellowship with Men," we read "The perseverance of the superior man furthers" (56). Although the later Confucian commentary says that "True fellowship among men must be

based upon a concern that is universal," requiring us to put aside "personal and egoistic interests" (*I Ching*, 57), the need for a will to fellowship to accomplish this is recognized.

25. Gowans, *Philosophy of the Buddha*, 32.
26. See my discussion of Plato on the Divine in chapter 9.
27. Nussbaum, *Therapy of Desire*, 251.
28. Ibid., 41 (emphasis added).
29. Ibid., 92.
30. Ibid., 250.
31. Ibid., 94.
32. Again, see Davenport, "A Phenomenology of the Profane."
33. See Nussbaum, *Therapy of Desire*, 87.
34. Cicero, *On Moral Ends*, Book II, sec. 32, 37.
35. Ibid., Book III, sec. 1, 65.
36. Ibid., Book III, sec. 59, 84.
37. Ibid., Book III, sec. 49, 81.
38. Augustine, *On Free Choice of the Will*, Book II, sec. 19, 68.
39. Ibid., Book III, sec. 24, 120.
40. Ibid., Book III, sec. 25, 122.
41. Milton, *Paradise Lost*, Book I, 262.
42. Augustine, *City of God*, Book I, Preface, 5. For the importance of this point, I am indebted to Brian Harding's doctoral thesis on Augustine (Fordham University, 2004).
43. Ibid., Book I, chap. 31, 42.
44. Ibid., Book XIX, chap. 15, 874.
45. Ibid., Book XIX, chap. 12, 869.
46. Ibid., Book XII, chap. 8, 481.
47. This is discussed in Davenport, "Augustine on Liberty, Foreknowledge, and Providence," the currently unpublished sequel to Davenport, "Liberty of the Higher-Order Will: Frankfurt and Augustine."
48. Luther, *Bondage of the Will*, 110 [*Weimarer Ausgabe* edition, 632].
49. Ibid., 110–11 [*W.A.* 632] (emphasis added).
50. Ibid., 111 [*W.A.* 634].
51. See Taylor, *The Ethics of Authenticity*, chap. IX, 103 and 105.
52. Ibid., 104–5.
53. Rawls, *A Theory of Justice*, sec. xx.
54. From an obituary in the Lancaster *Intelligencer Journal*, May 26, 2003, B3.
55. In a powerful scene near the end of the film *Blade Runner*, directed by Ridley Scott (1982), Tyrell, the human master of biochemistry who created artificial human beings (or "replicants") with built-in "termination dates" to serve as slaves, tries this Nietzschean argument on the rebel replicant leader who has come back to Earth to destroy his creator. When he crushes Tyrell anyway, we hear echoes of Nietzsche: he has killed his god. But, ironically, the god he kills and utterly rejects in this scene is Nietzscheanism, the Nietzschean philosophy of life. For Tyrell stands for Nietzsche's will to power.

56. Solomon, "Virtues of a Passionate Life," 97.

57. And we should not forget here the utterly Hobbesian character of Spinoza's account of the structure of human motivation. Of course, for Spinoza, unlike Nietzsche, this portrayal of our natural egoism is simply a new version of the paradigmatically Eastern description of the worldly person struggling for success amidst endless rivalries, which the sage entirely transcends in achieving volitionless peace. So Spinoza is really using Hobbesian moral psychology against Hobbes's own worldly ideal and in favor of the Eastern ideal.

58. Tolkien clearly recognized this distinction. He once wrote that his One Ring symbolizes the Nietzschean will to domination and ascendance over all, "the will to mere power, seeking to make itself objective by physical force and mechanism, and so also inevitably by lies"; see his Letter to Milton Waldman (1951), in *The Letters of J. R. R. Tolkien*, 160. Likewise, Tolkien condemned the distortion of the Norse mythos by "that ruddy little ignoramus Adolf Hitler . . . [r]uining, perverting, misapplying, and making forever accursed that noble northern spirit . . . which I have ever loved, and tried to present in its true light"; see Letter to Michael Tolkien (June 9, 1941), ibid., 54.

59. See Menand, *The Metaphysical Club*, 16–22.

60. Bacon, *Advancement of Learning*, Book 2, XIII.I, 122.

61. Bacon, "Preface to *The Great Renewal*," in *New Organon*, 9.

62. Ibid., 13.

63. Yovel, "Kant and the History of the Will," 283.

64. Ibid., 284.

65. Ibid.

66. Ibid., 283–84.

67. Ibid., 284.

68. Ibid., 285.

69. Le Guin, *Wizard of Earthsea*, 26.

70. John Casey, *Pagan Virtue*, v–vii.

71. Ibid., vi–vii.

72. Nancy, *Experience of Freedom*, 3.

73. Ibid., 36.

74. Ibid., 5.

75. Ibid., 7.

76. Ibid., 18. By this, Nancy means a will that simply *represents* various possibilities to itself and then intends one of them. Instead, "existence" is a state lacking "an essence" that could be "represented or intended," and so its possible ways of being are not given to it beforehand; they do not even become *intelligible* to the person except through its free decision to posit them. On this view, will is the way that existent beings go out of themselves toward what is unknown or unanticipatable; existential will makes its end or goal meaningful only through commitment to it. This radicalized version of projective willing owes debts to Levinas (see chap. 9), but in Sartrean fashion, it rules out rational grounding of willed ends.

77. Ibid., 40, 43.

78. Lieberman, *Acts of Will*, 30.

79. Rank, *Truth and Reality*, 19.

80. Lieberman, *Acts of Will*, 358–59. It is notable that Rank explicitly rejects the ideal of "Buddhistic will-lessness" that so appealed to Schopenhauer (358).

81. Rank, *Truth and Reality*, 20–21. That said, Rank follows Nietzsche too readily in the assumption that "pedagogy is obviously a breaking of the will as ethics is a will limitation and therapy will justification" (20). In his proximity to Freud and Nietzsche, Rank did not attain Frankl's insight that the authentic will requires values not of its own making, which ethics, pedagogy, and therapy should help the agent to discover. In his idea that the will cannot be authentically one's own unless its ends come entirely from within the self without any external influence, Rank approaches Emersonian individualism.

82. In bringing out this implication, I will often have to refer to ideas developed in the context of an argument for a specific interpretation of autonomy, authenticity, happiness, character, etc. But rather than address their main conclusions, I will be more interested in what their approach implies about the phenomena of willing and their role in human life.

83. See Frankfurt, *The Importance of What We Care About*; Frankfurt, *Necessity, Volition, and Love*; and Williams, "Persons, Character, and Morality."

84. Thus I disagree with Owen Flanagan's claim that empirical psychology gives us a clear and unbiased sense of what is possible for creatures like us that can guide the development of moral theories; see Flanagan, *Varieties of Moral Personality*, 32.

85. Frankfurt, "The Importance of What We Care About."

86. Frankfurt, *The Importance of What We Care About*, 92–93; see also Frankfurt, "On Caring," and *Reasons of Love*.

3. From Action Theory to Projective Motivation

1. Ryle, *Concept of Mind*, chap. 3, 64. Ryle thinks that for the concept to be valid, people would have to be able to count the volitions they enact. This blithely assumes an atomistic conception of actions at odds with the narrative-holist conception in ascendance since MacIntyre. Ryle also thinks that willing cannot be a distinct mental operation unless someone would commonly say things like "he performed five quick and easy volitions" this morning (64). This is intellectually on a par with claiming that there is no such thing as "blindsight" because blind folks do not speak of "seeing things" or that the modern physiology of the eye is wrong because ordinary people do not speak of stimulating their "rods and cones." With arguments this bad, it is no wonder that even philosophers who take naturalism as an article of faith have turned against Ryle.

2. See, e.g., Eysenck and Eysenck, *Personality and Individual Differences*. See also the Myers-Briggs personality-type inventory, which is based on a theory of personality types deriving originally from Carl Jung's work in the early twentieth century, which was in turn influenced by Freud.

3. Yalom, *Existential Psychotherapy*, chap. 7, "Willing," 288.

4. Hobbes, *Leviathan*, Part I, chap. 6, "Of the Interiour Beginnings of Voluntary Motions; commonly called Passions. And the Speeches by which they are expressed," 127.

5. Ibid., 127–28.
6. See Descartes, *Meditations on First Philosophy*, Meditation IV.
7. Oberdiek, "The Will," 471.
8. Pink, *Psychology of Freedom*, 26–27.
9. Oberdiek, "The Will," 472.
10. Hume, *Treatise of Human Nature*, Book II, part 3, sec. 1, 399.
11. Ibid., 402–3. The argument here is a direct precursor of the kind we now find at the foundation of personality-type theories, which begin by holding that statistical consistencies in behavior patterns relative to situations reveal the existence of *traits*. Similarly, Hume appeals to the idea of stock character types in saying: "No union can be more certain, than that of some actions with some motives and characters." Indeed, irregularity in behavior is a sign of madness (ibid., 404). Actions are a function of "motives, temper, and situation" (ibid.).
12. Ibid., 405.
13. Ibid., sec. 3, 413.
14. Ibid., 414: "Tis from the prospect of pleasure or pain that the aversion or propensity arises toward any object."
15. Ibid., 417.
16. See Oberdiek, "The Will," where he described J. S. Mill's Humean notion of the will as "that moment in a series of associations of ideas terminating in action," or the immediate mental antecedent to action (474).
17. Smith, *Jonathan Edwards*, 66.
18. Ibid., 64–65.
19. Oberdiek, "The Will," 472–73.
20. See Cudworth, "Treatise on Freewill," in *A Treatise Concerning Eternal and Immutable Morality*, 168. Though Edwards could not have been influenced by this work, since Cudworth never published it in his lifetime, similar questions motivate Edwards's Lockean compatibilist treatment of liberty in his famous treatise on free will.
21. Ibid., 171.
22. Ibid., 173.
23. Ibid., 168.
24. Ibid., 174.
25. Ibid., 177.
26. Ibid., 178. In this respect, it seems to me that Cudworth's view tends away from Edwards's determinism toward the existential conception (developed in Schelling and Kierkegaard) of free will as endowed with liberty but working on itself as a substantive dispositional character whose freedom is always influenced by its own past and never chooses in arbitrary indifference.
27. Oberdiek, "The Will," 475.
28. Hume, *Treatise of Human Nature*, Book II, part 3, sec. 3, 416, (emphasis added).
29. Ibid., 417.
30. Joseph Butler, Sermon II: "Upon Human Nature," in *Five Sermons*, 35.
31. Korsgaard, *The Sources of Normativity*, Lecture 3, 100.

32. Reid, *Essays on the Active Powers of the Human Mind*, Essay II, "Of the Will," 58.
33. Ibid., 73.
34. Schopenhauer, *On the Freedom of the Will*, 16. Schopenhauer argues that self-consciousness testifies with immediate certainty to freedom of action.
35. Ibid., 14.
36. Ibid., xvi–xvii.
37. See James, *Principles of Psychology*, vol. 2, chap. 26, "Will," 486–594.
38. Ibid., 486.
39. Ibid., 487.
40. Compare O'Shaughnessy, *The Will*, 1:248–50.
41. James, 489–93.
42. Ibid., 493–516. At the end of all this, James concludes by saying: "On the whole, then, it seems as probable as anything can be, that feelings of innervation do not exist" (516). The issues at stake in this debate are related to contemporary theories of action in what Audi calls the "volitionalist" category, but have little direct relevance for my analysis.
43. Ibid., 518.
44. Ibid., 521.
45. Ibid., 522.
46. Ibid., 523. Compare O'Shaughnessy on what he calls "sub-intentional actions": *The Will*, vol. 2, chap. 10.
47. Ibid., 526. As he says, "Every pulse of feeling which we have is the correlate of some neural activity that is already on its way to instigate a movement. Our sensations and thoughts are but cross-sections, as it were, of currents whose essential consequence is motion" (526). This refers, of course, to James's famous dynamistic theory of consciousness.
48. Ibid., 527.
49. Ibid., 528.
50. Admittedly, James goes on to give a much more complex analysis of such deliberation, distinguishing five types of decision and different experiences of "will" that go along with them, but they all adhere to his basic Hobbesian paradigm.
51. Oberdiek, "The Will," 477.
52. James, 528.
53. Ibid., 529.
54. Oberdiek, "The Will," 478.
55. Hume, *Treatise of Human Nature*, part 3 sec. 1, 399.
56. Ryle, *Concept of Mind*, 67.
57. Wittgenstein, Brown Book, in *Blue and Brown Books*, II, no. 11, 151.
58. Ibid., no. 11, 150.
59. Ibid., 151–52.
60. On these points, see the helpful summary in Scott, "Wittgenstein's Theory of Action."
61. See Wittgenstein, *Philosophical Investigations*, II, xi, 213.
62. Scott, 363.

63. Wittgenstein, *Philosophical Investigations*, I, no. 613, 159.
64. On this point, see also Winch, "Wittgenstein's Treatment of the Will."
65. Wittgenstein, *Philosophical Investigations*, I, no. 627–28, 162e. Of course, we can try to move our arm and discover that it is strapped down. But if I read him right, Wittgenstein means that there is no separate act of initiating the arm movement that will either succeed if physically unimpeded or fail if the arm is held; for if there were, then this separate act would also be something that we could try to do and succeed or fail in trying. But we do not experience this in voluntary acts such as intentional bodily movements. This may or may not be compatible with a theory like O'Shaughnessy's, which simply unpacks the experience of intentional first-order action to show that it always involves at least a weak sense of trying to perform the intended act. But Wittgenstein's aim is to deny that we try to form first-order intentions themselves, as Kane and Pink maintain.
66. See Wittgenstein, *Remarks on the Philosophy of Psychology*, no. 1040, 181e.
67. Ibid., no. 766, 137e. Actually, Wittgenstein often uses "trying" in the more specific sense of making a focused effort against resistance, since he says that in ordinary cases, "when I walk, that doesn't mean that I try to walk and it succeeds" (ibid., I, no. 51, 13). This explains why he says that although an experience of effort is the paradigm, it is not essential to volition, since it is lacking in voluntary acts such as handwriting or moving the eye to look at an object (Brown Book, II, no. 13, 152–3). Moreover, it is crucial to Wittgenstein's view that the kinesthetic sensation we feel in, say, moving our hand while drawing is not something we anticipate and decide to bring about; at the most basic level in voluntary action, there must be motions or changes that are part of the "matter" of the action but are not themselves specifically selected in advance by deliberate choice (ibid., no. 13, 154).
68. Wittgenstein, *Philosophical Investigations*, I, no. 618, 160–61.
69. Ryle, *Concept of Mind*, 67.
70. Kane, *Significance of Free Will*, 4 (emphasis omitted).
71. Ibid., 27.
72. Ibid., 21.
73. Ibid., 27.
74. Aquinas, *Summa Theologica*, I–II Qu. 6–8. Of course the details of Aquinas's account are actually much more complex, but this rough summary is not too misleading. I have discussed the location and nature of libertarian freedom in Aquinas's model in more detail in Davenport, "Aquinas's Teleological Libertarianism."
75. Kane, *Significance of Free Will*, 22.
76. Ibid., 26–27.
77. Ibid., 125.
78. Ibid., 126.
79. Ibid., 127.
80. Ibid., 128–33.
81. Ibid., 4.
82. Ibid., 152.
83. Ibid., 25.

84. There is admittedly *a strand* in so-called "existentialist" literature that does provoke this common attribution of a reductive conception of will to existentialists. This strand, which sometimes appears dominant in Sartre (though even in *Being and Nothingness* it does not totally exclude more substantial kinds of volition) may ultimately derive from Fichte's claim that since "nothing pertains to the I which it does not posit," its feelings of limitation must also be posited or self-given (a position Fichte shares with Reinhold). See sec. 6 of Fichte's summary, "The Major Points of the *Wissenschaftslehre* of 1789–1799," in *Foundations of Transcendental Philosophy*, 69.

85. Van Inwagen, *Essay on Free Will*, 8.

86. If we add in the requirement that the alternative courses of action at least involve intentions, then van Inwagen's definition is consonant with the second concept of the will described below.

87. At this point, Dennett quotes Anscombe's complaint that there is no univocal sense in which I can "will" my arm to move but not will a matchbox to move—see Anscombe, *Intention*, 48–49. This sort of view is the main target of O'Shaughnessy's work, but interestingly, its secondary thesis that action is intentional only under certain descriptions is reaffirmed in the context of later executive action theories of the will (see sec. 3.3 below).

88. Dennett, *Content and Consciousness*, 171.

89. Ibid., 172.

90. Ibid., 173. Dennett equates conscious "awareness" here with verbal expression of the information that the brain is processing. This elimination of sentience continues to be a problem in all his later work in the philosophy of mind.

91. Ibid., 173.

92. As it happens, there is now much empirical evidence against Dennett's eliminativist treatment of willing. See Miller, *Inner Natures*, part 2, chap. 3, "The Impetus of Self: Action and Volition." Miller argues that it is portions of the frontal lobe that control "the overall regulation and evaluation of thought and behavior" (44). Damage to this part of the brain leaves more particular abilities intact but destroys regulation of their sequences:

> In such cases, the individual's very capacity for autonomous volition seems to have been sucked right out of him . . . the impression is not unlike that of a robot with a faulty guidance system: The patient does little on his own, but once prompted, seems incapable of stopping what he's already doing or shifting to something else without explicit outside guidance. (45)

In my view, such cases suggest that there are brain centers responsible for (among other things) the function of decision or intention-formation, without which the human being is reduced to an automaton.

93. Moya, *Philosophy of Action*, 106.

94. Ibid., 145–46.

95. Nevertheless, as Moya argues, for Davidson this causal relation requires that an adequate version of physicalism be true: beliefs, desires, and actions must be identical with physical events of some kind, e.g., neurological events. See ibid., 111–12.

96. Kane, *Significance of Free Will*, 27.
97. O'Shaughnessy, *The Will*, vols. I & II.
98. Audi, *Action, Intention, and Reason*, chap. 3, 74.
99. Ibid., 75.
100. Ibid., 76.
101. Ibid., 76.
102. Ibid., 77, quoting Ginet, "Voluntary Exertion of the Body: A Volitional Account," 234.
103. Ibid., 78. Yet Audi draws the wrong conclusion when he infers from the thinness of this agreement that "There may be no ordinary conception of volition, or willing, or even trying, which is being analyzed and used to understand action" (79). Rather, all these accounts are explanations of willing in the thin sense as whatever makes our acts voluntary. This moral concept is what remains after the historical degeneration of the notion of will in the empiricist tradition from Hobbes through William James.
104. Ibid., 79.
105. Kane reconstructs this traditional formula in terms of four conditions: act A is done voluntarily iff the agent (1) has reasons or motives for doing A, (2) wants to act on these motives more than on any others at the time, (3) does A for these reasons, and (4) the agent's doing A and willing to do A for these reasons are not coerced or compelled. The first three conditions thus capture doing A intentionally, in Kane's view. See Kane, *Significance of Free Will*, 30.
106. Oberdiek, "The Will," 464.
107. Ibid., 466.
108. Ibid., 466.
109. Ibid., 469.
110. Ibid., 470.
111. Ibid., 485. He also notes that "Descriptions under which an act is voluntary are not always descriptions under which they are intentional" (484), since an act is voluntary under a description of consequences that are foreseen, but foreseen consequences may not always be intended. For example, I voluntarily caused my mouth to hurt when I went to see the dentist, but this was a side effect of my intended goal of fixing my tooth. This suggests that intention, unlike voluntariness, makes implicit reference to the *motives* for which an act is done; these motives pick out a subset of the descriptions under which an act is intentional.
112. Ibid., 483.
113. Pink, *Psychology of Freedom*, 17.
114. Gert and Duggan, "Free Will as the Ability to Will," 206, n. 2.
115. Ibid., 210.
116. Ibid., 211.
117. Ibid., 213.
118. Ibid., 211.
119. Ibid., 209, n. 5.
120. Moya, *Philosophy of Action*, 18.
121. Ibid., 20.

122. Ibid., 21.

123. Ibid., 23. Moya here cites O'Shaughnessy's early essay, "Trying (as the Mental 'Pineal Gland')," 365–86.

124. Moya, *Philosophy of Action*, 24–25. I am not convinced here by Moya's argument that "trying" to do some nonbasic action can itself only consist in other actions in the ordinary sense, e.g., "trying to start a car is doing such things as taking the key, putting it in the lock, turning it, etc." (24). On the contrary, it seems to me that all these bodily actions are experienced as the outcome of a mental trying in O'Shaughnessy's sense. My efforts to do each specific component of the large act, for example, trying to pick up the key, trying to get it in the lock, and trying to turn it, are experienced *as parts* of my larger effort to execute the intention to start the car, or to drive to town, or whatever I am trying to do.

125. Ibid., 25–26.

126. Ibid., 37.

127. Ibid., 46.

128. Ibid., 50. Note that the account of voluntary action that Scott reconstructs from Wittgenstein's manuscripts is similarly holistic, focusing on the "environment" or context of the action, which in many cases is needed to make it intelligible (Scott, "Wittgenstein's Theory of Action," 362–63). But Wittgenstein does not sufficiently develop the notions of intentional action and meaning-communicating action that are needed to make this holistic point clear.

129. See Habermas, *Theory of Communicative Action*, vol. I, chapter I.3. In particular, Habermas rejects Danto's theory of certain bodily movements as "basic actions"; referring to Wittgenstein's theory of rule-governed games, he argues that communicative acts in particular depend on an intersubjective, background, normative context regulating the pragmatics of language use in making validity claims (97–101).

130. Moya, *Philosophy of Action*, 64.

131. See MacIntyre, *After Virtue*, chap. 15.

132. Pink, *Psychology of Freedom*, 3.

133. Ibid., 29.

134. Ibid.

135. Kahn, "Discovering the Will," 238.

136. Ibid., 240.

137. Ibid., referring to Aquinas, *Summa Theologica*, I.83.4.

138. As Pink suggests, many types of higher animals are probably capable of intentional actions, while the capacity for decision or second-order agency is more closely tied to personhood.

139. Pink, *Psychology of Freedom*, 3.

140. Ibid., 12. Pink thus hopes that his account will be neutral on the question of whether moral responsibility is compatible or incompatible with natural determinism.

141. Ibid., 16.

142. Ibid., 8.

143. Ibid., 10. He assures this agreement with a restriction that he calls "Reason-Apply."

144. Ibid., 15.

145. I treat Pink's account of decision as his conception of willing, although he rejects the term "volition" since it has been used since Locke to name "an undifferentiated category" mistakenly combining "trying" to perform an act and "deciding" to perform it (ibid., 261), or amalgamating "conation and will," as he says earlier (55).

146. Ibid., 20. Pink allows that intentions can also flow directly from habit but argues that this does not crucially affect his account, because "all intentions are governed by rationality in the same way" (21), and so intentions formed by habit are as "'active'" as those formed by decision.

147. O'Shaughnessy, *The Will*, vol. I, 29.

148. Ibid., 32–34.

149. Pink, *Psychology of Freedom*, 9.

150. Ibid., 17 (emphasis added).

151. Ibid., 17.

152. Harry Frankfurt has defended a very similar position in his paper on Descartes's notion of the will's "infinite" capacity: "Concerning the Freedom and the Limits of the Will." He says that the distinction between "choosing to do something and doing it" is absent when "the object of the choice or decision is itself a specific choice or decision" (126), and hence "*the will is absolutely and perfectly active. . . . All the movements of my will—for instance, my choices and decisions—are movements that I make. None is a mere impersonal occurrence, in which my will moves without my moving it*" (127). Contra some of Pink's doubts, this clearly confirms that Frankfurt shares Pink's notion of decision as second-order agency.

153. Stampe and Gibson, "Of One's Own Free Will," 530.

154. Ibid., 530, n. 3.

155. Ibid., 529–30.

156. Ibid., 532–33.

157. Granted, the extreme agoraphobic may not deliberate about this, since she is seized with an overwhelming fear at the bare thought of opening the door and cannot contemplate it. But Stampe and Gibson allow that "a decision need not be an act of deliberation, and it need not be conscious" (530, note 3).

158. Ibid., 532. In general, Stampe and Gibson say, freedom of will requires the ability "to make the rational decision even if the circumstances were relevantly different from the way they actually are—e.g., just different enough that the rational decision would be something other than the one that is rational in the actual case" (532). But they overlook the problem that one of the most important ways in which the circumstances can vary is for the agent's *desires* to change, or for the motives controlling one's intention-formation to alter. If the will can be involved in bringing about such changes, as I argue, then its freedom can hardly be defined according to whether the decisions it would form in a range of possible circumstances would be rational relative to the strengths of desires *given* in these different scenarios.

159. Ibid., 533.

160. Science-fiction fans may consider the example of Angus, a cyborg in Stephen Donaldson's novels *A Dark and Hungry God Arises* and *Chaos and Order*. Angus's

mind has been "welded" to a minicomputer in his back that controls a whole net of minielectrodes in his brain, and these in turn control his every bodily action in accordance with prewritten instructions. Angus does not act like an unconscious machine; he forms *intentions* and even whole plans of action that are always subjectively rational relative to his enforced desire to achieve his programmed goals. But he very clearly does not form these intentions *freely*: his will helplessly rebels against the continual coercion, leaving Angus in a state of never-ending mental torture. The second-order agency that is Angus is powerless before the non-agent machine that forms intentions in him, or forms conscious practical thoughts that are executed as actions of his body.

161. See Frankfurt, "Freedom of the Will and the Concept of a Person," and later essays.

162. Kane, *Significance of Free Will*, 23.

163. Ibid., 24.

164. Ibid., 25. I have summarized only part of Mele's list of six important functions that intentions play in our practical life. He also holds that intentions explain and sustain intentional action, help coordinate action over time and with other agents, and help guide and motivate further deliberation.

165. Moya, *Philosophy of Action*, 53.

166. Ibid., 55–56.

167. Ibid., 58.

168. Ibid. It should be pointed out that there are two distinct senses of "plan." In the first sense, which Moya uses here, a "plan" is a standard for the achievement of something. In the second sense, a "plan" is a genuine commitment of the agent to following a series of steps toward the outcome. The first sense is purely normative, whereas the second is volitional.

169. Ibid., 60.

170. Ibid., 59.

171. Ibid., 141.

172. Ibid., 131. However, this clam might have to be qualified with respect to dolphins and certain species of ape, if current literature on their mental capacities is accurate.

173. Ibid., 148.

174. See Davidson, "Intending," 98. He allows that forming an intention might be a kind of action (89) but holds that intention-judgments can arise without any act of decision (99).

175. Moya, *Philosophy of Action*, 150.

176. Ibid., 153–54.

177. Ibid., 156–57.

178. Ibid., 169.

179. Christine Korsgaard, *The Sources of Normativity*, sec. 3.2.1, 93.

180. Ibid., Lecture 9, 229.

181. Ibid., 120–21.

182. This appears to be the main thesis of Alexander Pfänder's classic 1900 work, *Phänomenologie des Wollens* (Leipzig: Barth, 1900). See Pfänder, *Phenomenology of Willing and Motivation*, 3.

183. Korsgaard, *The Sources of Normativity*, 96. Of course, for Kant it is not only "desires" that provide such suggestions but also purely rational considerations such as the universalizability of a given maxim for beings like us.

184. Ibid., 97.

185. See Moya's point that from his criterion of agency it follows that "there are some descriptions of actions which are in some sense privileged ones, namely those under which the action was intentional" (Moya, *Philosophy of Action*, 55). And as we saw, being voluntary or imputable (in the most basic sense) roughly comes to being done intentionally without being coerced.

186. Kane, *Significance of Free Will*, 28–30.

187. *American Heritage Dictionary*, 1382.

188. Rank, *Truth and Reality*, 17.

189. Rank, *Will Therapy*, 112 n. 1. However, in my view, there is no need to accept Rank's hypothesis about the "original negative nature of will power" as a reaction to control by parents (see *Truth and Reality*, 49). This part of Rank's view shows the long shadow of Freud and Nietzsche, which is overcome in my conception of positive projective motivation as a response to value-alterity.

190. Murdoch, *Metaphysics as Guide to Morals*, 300.

191. Hauerwas, *Character and the Christian Life*, 86.

192. Ibid., 89.

193. Ibid., 113.

194. This is what Hauerwas means when he says, "By acting under one description rather than another the agent not only determines what he will do, but also the kind of person he will be" (ibid.).

195. Ibid., 51.

196. In this respect, as Pink notes, decision is unlike seeking to ensure that we stick to our diet by telling friends that we are going to lose weight in order to "bring the fear of losing face in as a further motive to induce ourselves to eat less in the future" (Pink, *Psychology of Freedom*, 5). Tactics like this are ways of twisting one's own arm, whereas decisions constitute a noninstrumental (or nonstrategic) form of self-control.

197. Ibid., 6.

198. Ibid., 23. This follows from Pink's view that the will is not simply a deliberative faculty but rather an executive faculty distinct from the capacity for practical judgment which it serves.

4. The Erosiac Structure of Desire in Plato and Aristotle

1. I provide some historical evidence for this hypothesis in chap. 4, sec. 2, and chap. 5, sec. 1.

2. Williams, "Internal and External Reasons," in *Moral Luck*.

3. Ibid., 104. Williams actually says that practical deliberation can "add new actions for which there are internal reasons, just as it can add new internal reasons for given actions" (104); but he means only that deliberation can do this by correcting false judgments or extending the agent's imagination about the consequences.

4. Alfred Mele, *Autonomous Agents*, 39–40.
5. Sverdlik, "Motive and Rightness," 338.
6. Ibid., 335.
7. Ibid., 336.
8. On this idea, see the concept of D3 desire developed in chapter 5.
9. Sverdlik, "Motive and Rightness," 336. The example Sverdlik gives is envy, which "gives rise to the desire to remove the envied object from another person." He acknowledges that some emotions, such as grief, may not give rise to desires, but says that they then fail to constitute motives. However, the idea that emotions are usually motivational is not uncontroversial. For example, it is rejected by Richard Wollheim in *On the Emotions*, 128.
10. Ibid., 336.
11. Ibid., 337.
12. Ibid., 339.
13. As explained in the introduction, I focus on the motivational aspects of Platonic and Aristotelian eudaimonism, since this is the aspect that embodies TP. The question of whether some form of rational eudaimonism that rejects TP is plausible is postponed until chapter 8, secs. 3 and 5.5.
14. Davis, "Two Senses of Desire," 64–65.
15. WET remains a simplifying assumption for this book, because some contemporary theories do recognize non-erosiac desires among prepurposive motives. For example, Ronald de Sousa distinguishes "consummatory" from "ludic" desires "that come with a desire for indefinite continuation." As paradigm cases of ludic motives he mentions desires for play and contemplation (*Rationality of Emotion*, 216). Because the scope of "consummatory" desire is narrower than that of "erosiac" motivation as I conceive it, not all de Sousa's ludic desires are non-erosiac. However, some may be, and we find similar non-erosiac PPMs in other contemporary theories. But such motives generally lack the complexity and connection to evaluative judgment that would make them (like D3 desires and projective motives) possible candidates to explain the phenomena on which my account focuses. So I think they can be included in a more complicated and disjunctive version of WET, but I leave this extension of the Existential Core Argument for future work.
16. Vedder, "Heidegger on Desire," 354.
17. See the Latin dictionary at http://www.sunsite.ubc.ca/LatinDictionary/.
18. See the Notre Dame Latin dictionary at http://www.nd.edu/~archives/latgramm.htm. This lexicon also lists the more specific military sense of *desidero* as "to lose" something.
19. Ibid.
20. See the entry in the LSJ lexicon at http://www.perseus.tufts.edu/cgi-bin/resolveform. There is also a useful discussion in Earl Jackson's "The *Phaedrus* Kit," which I hope will become available again on the Internet.
21. Nussbaum, *Therapy of Desire*, 82, citing Aristotle's *De motu animalium*, chap. 7.
22. Nussbaum, *Fragility of Goodness*, 273.
23. Ibid., 276.
24. Ibid., 274.

25. Nussbaum now recognizes this irreducibility to event-causal mechanism as essential to Aristotle's project (*Fragility*, 278), but she is misleading in describing it as "more active than passive: it is a going for, a reaching after . . . , as opposed to a being-overwhelmed" (274). This description makes it sound as though orektic states are all autonomous, which is false, and it obscures the key difference between *projective* "going for" and erosiac being-drawn-toward.

26. See, e.g., Plato's *Phaedrus* 255c: "even so the stream of beauty turns back and reenters the eyes of the fair beloved" (Plato, *Collected Dialogues*, 501).

27. Plato, *Cratylus*, 419e–420a (emphasis added), trans. Fowler, Loeb ed. 167.

28. Gould, *The Ancient Quarrel between Poetry and Philosophy*, 63.

29. Ibid., 64.

30. Nussbaum, *Therapy of Desire*, 259–60, citing Lucretius, *De Rerum Natura*.

31. Murdoch, *Sovereignty of the Good*, 102–3. This essay is also reprinted in part in Crisp and Slote, *Virtue Ethics*, 99–117. In this anthology, see 117 for the quoted passage.

32. Thus, although Nussbaum's expertise in this area far exceeds mine, I must disagree with her view that Plato's account lacks Aristotle's insight into "what is common to all cases of animal movement" (*Fragility*, 275). Aristotle introduces *orexis* to overcome the tripartite soul (as discussed in the last section of this chapter), not to introduce a new schema for motivation unknown to Plato.

33. Soble, *Structure of Love*, 17. He actually writes "erosic," but I follow Robert Solomon in adding the "a" to enhance the distance from "erotic."

34. Ibid., 4. In my judgment, this error results from defining the erosiac thesis as the negation of the agapic thesis as Nygren misconstrues it (as the claim that x can love y without *any reas*on concerning y at all; ibid., 4). See the discussion of Nygren in chapter 9.

35. This problem frequently reappears in postmodern discussions of "identity" and "difference" in friendship: see, e.g., Watson, *Tradition(s)* II, 72. In responding to Levinas, Watson is Aristotelian or Hegelian enough to want to reduce the distinctions between "self and other, egoism and respect" (68). But Levinas's account points to an alterity beyond complementarity that avoids the paradox in erosiac conceptions of friendship.

36. Plato, *Lysis* 215a–b, in *Collected Dialogues*, 158.

37. Moreover, it is much easier to understand in this light why Aquinas wrote in his *Summa Theologica* that with respect to the "perfect happiness we will have in heaven, friendship is not a necessary requirement for happiness since man has in God all the fullness of his perfection" (I–II Qu. 4, Art. 8, Respondo), and likewise, "The perfection of charity is essential to happiness as regards love of God but not love of neighbor" (ibid., Rep. 3).

38. This is how Vlastos portrayed the contrast in his well-known essay, "The Individual as an Object of Love in Plato," 3–42; reprinted in Soble, *Eros, Agape, and Philia*, 96–135.

39. Plato, *Lysis*, in *Collected Dialogues*, 218c, 162.

40. Ibid., 216e; 160. We have to remember here that "evil" translates a word meaning harmful or dangerous.

41. *Meno* 78A–B, in *Great Dialogues of Plato*.

42. See Plato, *Gorgias* 492d–4b; 65–7. It is instructive to compare Gorgias's statement, which reflects the archaic view of nobility and glory that Plato is trying to overthrow, with Thomas Hobbes's thesis that our felicity is found only in the continued struggle for ever more power and challenges, ending only in death (*Leviathan*, 130 and 139). Hobbes puts the same idea as follows in *De homine*: "For of goods, the greatest is always progressing towards ever further ends with the least hinderance" (*Man and Citizen*, 54). As my analysis in the introduction suggests, these formulations are all distorted versions of the right conception of the heroic will, with its inherently projective structure.

43. Plato, *Lysis*, in *Collected Dialogues*, 221d; 166.

44. Ibid., 222a; 166.

45. Ibid., 222b; 167.

46. Irwin, *Plato's Ethics*, 53.

47. Ibid., 54.

48. As Irwin notes (44–45), in the *Laches*, the thesis that virtue must be beneficial is ambiguous about who benefits, but the *Apology* and *Crito* are clearer that his virtue must be the most beneficial or advantageous state for the agent himself.

49. Ibid., 62–63.

50. Ibid., 53.

51. Ibid., 63.

52. Ibid., 116.

53. Ibid., 33.

54. Plato, *Republic* IV, 437b–c; *Collected Dialogues*, 679. The Rouse translation reads:

> thirst and hunger and desires in general, and again to wish and to be willing ... the soul of the desirer always wants that which he desires, or is attracted to that which he wishes to have; or again, inasmuch as it wants something to be provided for him, it nods "yes" to itself as if someone had asked the question, reaching forward to the production of the thing. (*Great Dialogues of Plato*, 236).

55. *Republic* IV, 437e, *Collected Dialogues*, 679.

56. *Republic* IV, 437d–e, 679.

57. *Republic* IV, 438a–b, 679–80.

58. *Republic* IV, 439a, 681 (emphasis added).

59. Hampton, *Pleasure, Knowledge, and Being*, 52.

60. Auden, "Quest Hero," 40. Quests, on the other hand, require higher cognitive and volitional powers, according to Auden.

61. MacIntyre, *After Virtue*, chap. 15, 218–19. I consider *After Virtue* especially Platonic because of its emphasis on the motives involved in crafts and practices as both an analog of the virtues and a site of their application. Although this analogy is also found in Aristotle, it is arguably more central to Plato's analysis of the virtues than to Aristotle's, which instead begins from common definitions of the virtues and then revises them in light of the doctrine of the rational mean stated in *Nicomachean Ethics* II.

62. Plato, *Meno*, 77c–78b.
63. Watson, "Free Agency," in *Free Will*, 97.
64. Ibid., 98.
65. Ibid., 99. In support, Watson cites *Phaedrus*, 237e–238e.
66. Irwin, *Plato's Ethics*, 210.
67. Ibid., 211.
68. *Republic* IV, 439a–b, 681.
69. Commenting on Plato's *Phaedrus*, Earl Jackson, Jr., argues that:

> Eros for the lyric poets was a condition that insinuated itself into the cognitive system of the beloved via the rays of desire emanating from the eyes of the lover gazing upon the beloved. This condition was ecstatic and rapturous but rarely if ever good news. The vision (in two senses) of the beloved is affected, and a searing emotion of need or longing for the lover ensues. Thus it is a "disease of the eye."

This is from his informal essay, "The Lexica of Desire in Plato's *Phaedrus*," which I hope will become available again on the Internet.

70. Plato, *Symposium* 193a, 545. Compare this to an earlier proposal that we desire what is complementary, in *Lysis* 215e.
71. Ibid., 199d, 551.
72. Ibid., 200d–e, 552.
73. Ibid., 207a, 559.
74. See Annas's Introduction to Cicero, *On Moral Ends*, xxv.
75. Aquinas, *Summa Theologica*, I–II Qu. 2, Art. 6, Rep. 1; quotations from the *Treatise on Happiness*, trans. Oesterle.
76. Ibid., 200e, 553.
77. See Payne's useful discussion of such objections by Stokes, Reeve, and Nussbaum in his article, "Refutation of Agathon," 246–47.
78. And this would explain why there is something perverse in the Narcissus complex taken literally as sexual interest in oneself: for one cannot really lack nor therefore desire one's own bodily beauty; one can only desire the image of it alienated from oneself (and such a desire therefore essentially requires self-deception).
79. Payne, "Refutation of Agathon," 243.
80. Plato, *Symposium* 205d, 557.
81. Thus I disagree with Payne's claim that "When we consider rational, good-dependent desires at *Symposium* 204–206 we are still dealing with *epithumia*" (Payne, 243, Greek transliterated). This cannot be right, since in the *Republic*, *epithumia* as D1 or D2 desire is clearly distinguished from D3 evaluative desire. When Plato talks about D3 states of *orexis* in terms that are peculiar to *epithumia* among other forms of *orexis*, I take him to be speaking metaphorically. However, I emphatically agree with Payne's suggestion that the main point in Agathon's argument concerns "the lack which afflicts a lover" rather than Nussbaum's idea that the lover should focus on "repeatable instances of a property" (Payne, "Refutation of Agathon," 249).
82. Payne, "Refutation of Agathon," 251.
83. Plato, *Symposium*, 202b–d, 554–55.

84. Ibid., 203b, 555.

85. And Diotima's analogy here nicely squares with the image of Love as a trickster-figure: "he brings his father's resourcefulness to his designs upon the beautiful and the good, for he is gallant, impetuous, and energetic, a mighty hunter, master of device and artifice—at once desirous and full of wisdom" (ibid., 203d).

86. Ibid., 204a, 556 (emphasis added).

87. See Plato, *Lysis* 217e–218a; 161–62:

> when it is not evil as yet, though evil be present with[in] it, this very presence of evil makes it desirous of good, but the presence which makes it evil deprives it, at the same time, of its desire and friendship for good. . . . On the same ground, we may further assert that those who are already wise are no longer friends to wisdom, be they gods or be they men; nor, again, are those friends to wisdom who are so possessed of foolishness as to be evil, for no evil and ignorant man is a friend to wisdom. There remain, then, those who possess indeed this evil, the evil of foolishness, but who are not, as yet, in consequence of it, foolish or ignorant, but who still understand that they do not know the things they do not know.

In reading this, we must recall here that "good" and "evil" do not have a modern deontic sense but rather refer to what helps or harms us, aiding or detracting from our well-being.

88. This idea is perhaps clearest in the *Phaedrus*, when, upon seeing his beloved, the Charioteer's memory "goes back to that form of beauty" that he had glimpsed as a disembodied soul in his former life (245b, 500).

89. Plato, *Symposium*, 204c, 556.

90. Ibid., 205b, 557.

91. Ibid., 205e, 558.

92. Ibid., 210c, 562.

93. Ibid., 210d, 562.

94. Gadamer, *The Idea of the Good in Platonic-Aristotelian Philosophy*, 110. In this passage, Gadamer is clearly also alluding to Kierkegaard's enigmatic thesis in *Either-Or* that ethical choice begins in or depends upon the fundamental choice to be a chooser.

95. Ferrari, "Platonic Love," 251–52.

96. Ibid., 252.

97. Ibid., 253.

98. Ibid., 255.

99. Plato, *Symposium* 206e, 558.

100. Ibid., 207d, 559.

101. Ibid., 212a, 563.

102. I take this idea that the *Symposium* involves a proto-version of Aristotle's function argument from Andrew Payne's insightful essay, "Practical Reason and the Comparison of Lives in the Speech of Diotima," 4. The idea that Aristotle derived his conception of teleology in general from Plato's *Symposium* and *Phaedo* was taught by Thomas Gould in mentoring my senior thesis in 1989.

103. Gould, *The Ancient Quarrel*, op cit., 9.

104. Aquinas, *Summa Theologica*, I–II Qu. I, Art. 5, Respondo.

105. Nygren, *Agape and Eros*, 175.

106. Vlastos, "The Individual as an Object of Love in Plato," reprinted in Soble, *Eros, Agape, and Philia*, 110.

107. Ibid. John Bretlinger has challenged this point in his reply to Nygren titled "The Nature of Love," reprinted in Soble, *Eros, Agape, and Philia*. But his argument depends on denying the possibility of love as essentially particularistic care, and he mistakenly suggests that Nygren's criticism depends on attributing to Plato the view that "if a person loves x because he believes x to have the property G, he must be using x as a means to G" (Soble, 141). While this principle is indeed false, the formal egoism of Platonic *eros* is not based on making the loved object *instrumental* to the agent's good. Rather it is found in Plato's understanding of *what it is* for an agent to desire some good for its own sake. On the erosiac model, desiring something X as a final end *just is* desiring unity with the value of X as part of one's own completeness. My analysis shows how Diotima's speech confirms this. Bretlinger misses this point entirely when he writes that "All men are alike in trying to satisfy their desires, and thus it shows nothing about the egocentricity of a concept of love to show that it involves desire" (141). For Nygren's point is precisely that Plato's concept of *desire* itself, including desire for final ends, is formally egoistic.

108. Aquinas, *Summa Theologica*, I–II Qu. 3, Art. 1, Rep. 2; in the *Treatise on Happiness*, trans. Oesterle, 28.

109. Ibid., I–II Qu. 5, Art. 4 (Oesterle, 59).

110. Ibid., I–II Qu. 2, Art. 4 (Oesterle, 19–20).

111. Aquinas, *Summa Contra Gentiles*, Book IV, chap. 19.3, 117. I am indebted to Daniel Moloney for this reference.

112. An obvious example pertinent to Diotima's analogies would be the case where a young couple have sex out of mere instinctual desire and nine months later find themselves proud parents.

113. Aquinas, *Summa Theologica*, I–II Qu. 4, Art. 2, Obj. 2 (Oesterle, 42).

114. Ibid., Qu. 2, Art. 6, Respondo (Oesterle, 23).

115. Although (c) refers to any by-product good, whereas "delight" or psychological satisfaction is only *one kind* of by-product good.

116. Aquinas, *Summa Theologica*, I–II Qu. 4, Art. 2, Respondo (Oesterle, 42).

117. Ferrari, "Platonic Love," 256.

118. Ibid.

119. Ibid., 257.

120. Ibid., 258.

121. Ibid., 259–60.

122. An alternative terminology would be to call them "pursuable" goods, but this might give the wrong impression that we mean to pick out those goods that are practically feasible or probably attainable in our circumstances.

123. Rist, *The Mind of Aristotle*, esp. 182–88.

124. Annas, *Morality of Happiness*.

125. Watson, "On the Primacy of Character."

126. Frankfurt, "Identification and Wholeheartedness," 171.

127. Mele, *Autonomous Agents*, chap. 1.

128. Thus, for example, we might place Alexander Nehamas's studies of Plato largely in the second category, though he also writes in the third category; and whereas MacIntyre's reconstructions of Aristotle in *After Virtue* largely fit in the third category, his analyses in *Whose Justice? Which Rationality?* are closer to the second category.

129. Heroic courage as a model for striving will reappears later (but only in distorted form) in works related to political theory that remain more or less at odds with the traditions of philosophical ethics stemming from Socrates—for example, in Machiavelli and Hobbes.

130. I am not here considering the difficult question of whether Plato remained committed to a tripartite moral psychology in later works. On this, see the helpful discussion in Robinson, *Plato's Psychology*, chap. 7. However, I am suspicious of Robinson's hypothesis that the soul appears as tripartite in the *Republic* only to help facilitate the political theory of the three classes (121). I agree with John Cooper that it is more likely the reverse, that is, that the division of classes is modeled on a psychology Plato already believes on independent grounds: see Cooper, *Reason and Emotion*, 120. Angela Hobbs also responds to Robinson in *Plato and the Hero*, 4–5.

131. It is true, however, that in *Laws* IX, Plato distinguishes the sort of motivation arising from anger and other passions from the sort arising from desire for bodily or sensual pleasures of several kinds. But this does not mean that the passions that threaten justice are identified with *thumos*.

132. Oberdiek, "The Will," 465. Thus Oberdiek sees Plato as "offering, for the first time in Western philosophy, the materials and suggestive metaphors out of which modern notions of the will evolved" (464).

133. *Republic* IV, 439e (in Shorey's translation), or "the desiring temper" (in Rouse).

134. Cooper argues persuasively that Plato sees this desire as fundamentally of the same kind as our basic biological urges for food, drink, and sex. Although Leontius's urge apparently arises from imagination, "it is nonetheless a brute fact about the way his being is affected by the physical world," rather than stemming from any rational insight into the good (Cooper, *Reason and Emotion*, 129). Unlike Cooper, I distinguish between D1 desires, which are fixed in their generic end by instinct, and D2 desires, which are brute preferences in Cooper's sense but for more specifically conceived objects. Many D2 desires will be *specifications* of D1 inclinations (or "transformations" of them, as Cooper puts it, 128); however this D2 category also includes other brute preferences as well. Some of these will be desires arising from imaginative specifications of other more variant urges, like the desire to see violence, or enjoyment of shock or thrill, or even "necrophilious" inclinations (in Fromm's broad sense of the term). My taxonomy thus largely agrees with Cooper's but makes a few more distinctions.

135. See C. Taylor, "Responsibility for Self."

136. Vander Waerdt, "The Peripatetic Interpretation of Plato's Tripartite Psychology," 300.

137. Plato, *Republic* IV, 440d.

138. For this point, I am indebted to Meyer, "*Thumos*, Endurance, and Emotion in Plato's *Republic*."

139. As Terence Irwin and other commentators have argued. However, this interpretation is challenged by David Engel, who argues that Plato never does admit that a person can willingly do wrong because Plato's standards for knowledge of the good are so high: see his paper, "Plato's Denial of Willful Wrongdoing."

140. Carr, "The Cardinal Virtues and Plato's Moral Psychology," 189. Carr assimilates Plato's middle soul to "will" rather quickly, but clearly what he means by "will" here is not the process of forming specific intentions to act but rather a distinct motivational process related to self-control, courage, and endurance. My point, of course, is that this kind of effort also represents a crucial sense of "willing" that is lost in contemporary action theory.

141. Plato, *Republic* IV, 440c.

142. Plato, *Republic* IV, 441a. Since the main point in this section is to show that the high spirit is something other than reason, Socrates follows this example with a quote from Homer in which reason chides the heart, standing for the middle part of the soul. Because it is an independent source of motivation, this middle part can come under rational criticism, even though, rightly trained, it strengthens the agent's desire to follow reason's purposes.

143. And there is a good deal of insight in this: in my experience, even from the age of fourteen months or so, children can display what can only be described as a spirited will to autonomy to prove that they can "do it themselves," or be successful by their own efforts (though some display this disposition more than others). And if Plato is right, then a smart parent will do well in trying to channel this energy in productive directions rather than just trying to crush this fledgling spirit entirely (as the "Eastern" attitude discussed in chapter 2 would evidently have us do). Nor should the wise parent inflame this fledgling spirit by mocking the child for its weaknesses. Too much control or shaming can damage the child's future confidence in her abilities and her developing sense that her efforts acquire at least some intrinsic value just from being her *own*.

144. Williams, *Shame and Necessity*, chap. 2, "Centres of Agency," 21.

145. Ibid., 26 and 24.

146. Ibid., 32.

147. Ibid.

148. Ibid., 33.

149. Ibid., 34.

150. Ibid., 36.

151. Pink, *Psychology of Freedom*, 28. Thus Pink dismisses Williams's "special scorn" for "the idea that decision-making is a second-order executive agency" with the rejoinder that "What is more plausibly a peculiarity of 'bad philosophy' . . . is the attempt to conceive the freedom and agency of our decision-making in [purely] deliberative terms, as a freedom and agency of practical judgment" (31–32).

152. Williams, *Shame and Necessity*, 36.

153. Ibid., 37–38.

154. Ibid., 39–40.

155. Ibid., 41.

156. Ibid. As we will see, this error itself derives from Kant. Ironically enough, Williams takes it over uncritically, making a straw man out of his notion of the modern will.

157. The existence of several rival bipartite theories and the influential misreading of Plato in the *Magna moralia* 1182a24–26 (which attributes a bipartite theory to him) is very helpfully explained in Vander Waerdt, "The Peripatetic Interpretation of Plato's Tripartite Psychology."

158. Aristotle, *Nicomachean Ethics*, I.13, 1102a33–b28. Unless otherwise noted, all citations are to the Ross translation in *The Complete Works of Aristotle*, vol. II.

159. This would explain for Aristotle why Plato suggested a few times that the middle soul is always reason's ally: Aristotle could accommodate this within his framework by assuming that Plato was thinking in these cases of the virtuous *thumos*.

160. Aristotle, *Nicomachean Ethics*, I.13, 1102b33–34.

161. Since Aristotle also goes on to compare this kind of exhortation and reproof to that which a child receives from its father, we have another analogy for the parts of the soul implied here as well: the fetus and infant are purely vegetative; while the child from a young age (perhaps four to five) through the beginning of adolescence exhibits rational appetite; and in the young adult abstract speculative reason finally blossoms.

162. Aristotle, *Nicomachean Ethics*, I.13, 1102b29–31.

163. Broadie, *Ethics with Aristotle*, 62.

164. Ibid., 63–65.

165. Ibid., 66. In the cases where there is resistance, the rational part seems to operate half by browbeating and charismatic influence and half by appeal to trust and personal bond (which has to be fostered first). This is without doubt the case in getting very young children to begin doing what is right with some minimal voluntariness on their side. And the same thing can be necessary with an adult in volitionally difficult circumstances: for example, think of Gandalf persuading Bilbo to give up the One Ring in Tolkien's *The Lord of the Rings*.

166. As Broadie says, in the virtuous person, "It is as if the nonrational [desiring] part is, from itself, a practical tabula rasa" (ibid., 66). What she means is that in Aristotle's virtuous person, the only felt PPMs that get taken up into purposes or become "incipient actions" are those that cohere negatively and positively with practical reason's favored ends. Yet, as she notes, this kind of perfect harmony is also possible in principle even when practical reason's vision of the good is thoroughly corrupted (67), which may be a problem for Aristotle.

167. Oberdiek, "The Will," 466.

168. This idea of a generic faculty of erosiac motivation is perhaps even more clearly formulated by Thomas Aquinas, and one finds it in every thinker who closely follows his moral psychology, e.g., C. S. Lewis, *Abolition of Man*.

169. And it is in this form, of course, that we see the "middle part of the soul" as a true *composite* of two subdivisions of the two most basic psychic faculties on a fundamentally bipartite taxonomy.

170. Aristotle, *Nicomachean Ethics*, III.3, 1113a11.

171. Cooper, *Reason and Emotion*, 239. In order sharply to distinguish Aristotle's view from that of the Stoics, Cooper attributes to Aristotle a kind of vector-sum model in which the strongest desire *will* initiate action or cause a voluntary movement. But this sort of determinism is problematic, and we should want to rescue Aristotle from such a view if possible. For one thing, the agent has to have some way of specifying the means to her end, or the particular action she will do in order to realize her goal. And *prohairesis* plays this specificatory function in Aristotle's scheme. If *prohairesis* can be motivated by nonrational desires rather than *boulēsis* without reflective practical reasoning employing objective value-criteria, then Aristotle's position would still be recognizably different from that of the Stoics, who held that all the motivation involved in the purposes behind our voluntary action can be turned off or on by different practical judgments. Perhaps one can move Aristotle a bit closer to the Stoics' more developed model of intention-formation without committing him to their intellectualism.

172. Broadie, *Ethics with Aristotle*, 79.

173. Cooper, *Reason and Emotion*, 240.

174. See the *Summa Theologica*, I–II Qu. 6–Qu. 8.

5. Aristotelian Desires and the Problems of Egoism

1. Cooper, *Reason and Emotion*, 241. I have expanded Cooper's abbreviated titles in this passage. I also find it curious that he treats the *Magna moralia* as a work by Aristotle, since the scholarly consensus now seems to be against this.

2. Hauerwas, *Character and the Christian Life*, 53.

3. Ibid., 55.

4. I am not sure that this is Hauerwas's complaint, because a passage about right reason as judging ends according to their pure measure (58) seems to be in tension with this reading of Hauerwas.

5. See Aristotle, *De anima*, II.3, 415a6–7: "Again, among living things that possess sense, some have the power of locomotion, some not" (560).

6. In general, it seems that *consciousness*, as opposed to powers of soul and the epistemic capacities of sense and mind (*nous*), simply does not occur to Plato, Aristotle, and their predecessors as a separate problem. Something like the notion of *subjectivity* is included in the Eleatic distinction between appearances and reality, and it motivates later skepticism, but consciousness as a phenomenon does not seem to get distinct treatment until Augustine.

7. Aristotle, *De anima*, III.9, 432b15–20. See also III.10, 433a, and III.11, 434a1–2.

8. Nussbaum, *Therapy of Desire*, 81.

9. Consider the famous example of the *Sphex* wasp, presented in Daniel Dennett, "Mechanism and Responsibility," from *Essays on Freedom of Action* (1973), reprinted in *Free Will*, ed. Gary Watson, repr. 162.

10. Although the wasp's behavior is triggered by various sensations, it is not unreasonable to assume that there is no *phenomenal experience* of these sensations, i.e.,

that they are mere physiological reactions without there being anything that "it is like" to be the wasp.

11. See, e.g., Miller, *Body Question*, 39:

> Our nervous system is designed to emphasize what's going on in the outside world.... The inside of the body—blood vessels, heart, intestine, lungs, and bladder—is literally studded with instruments capable of registering changes in pressure, temperature, and chemical composition. But none of these meters has any dials: they are not meant to be read by human consciousness, but are linked up with reflex systems which obey automatically.

12. Aristotle, *Nicomachean Ethics* (trans. Ross), III.1, 1109b35: "Those things, then, are thought involuntary, which take place under compulsion or owing to ignorance."

13. Lear, *Aristotle: The Desire to Understand*, 141. Note that Lear uses "desire" for *orexis* in general, and "appetite" for *epithumia*. He rightly argues that the Oxford translation is misleading, since it uses "appetite" both for lower urges (*epithumia*) "and for the word that is standardly translated as 'desire' (*orexis*)" which is more general (142, n. 110). The Smith translation of the *De anima* unfortunately employs "appetite" throughout for the general concept (*orexis*) and "desire" for lower appetites, which is the inverse of Lear's translation. In order to avoid confusion I have simply noted the Greek terms in square brackets.

14. *De anima*, II.3, 415a7–12. However, the possibility of a conscious computer would cast doubt on this thesis.

15. Thus D1 desires cannot count as emotions. I suggest that emotions typically require D3 desires that include some value-judgment, even if the agent does not assent to the judgment or identify with the emotion. Nussbaum tries to explain this distinction, e.g., between startle (which is not an emotion) and fear (which is) by arguing that the latter involves actually holding a value-belief (*Therapy of Desire*, 84–85). Since Robert Roberts has critiqued this account, it may be better to look at the distinction between D3 and other kinds of desire to explain this difference.

16. Desmond, *Desire, Dialectic, and Otherness*, 18.

17. MacIntyre, "How Moral Agents Became Ghosts," 303.

18. Ibid., 302–4.

19. In order to compare the relative strengths of D2 appetites, one may qualify them as "buffer-free" in Mele's sense (see *Autonomous Agents*, 38–40).

20. It is an interesting question whether some D2 appetites can also develop in relative independence from any underlying instinctual drive. Perhaps this is more likely the more fine-grained the D2 preference is. For example, I may have a very crude musical inclination for classical over pop, or a very refined preference for Mozart over Beethoven over Brahms, without any basis in aesthetic evaluation. More radically, Levinas argues that our "enjoyment" of the "elements" of the material world includes pleasures that have no instinctive basis: "there is a non-systematic accumulation of occupations and tastes," such as desire for cigarettes, that are neither moral nor instinctual (see *Totality and Infinity*, 133–34). However, some of the things Levinas would include in this category could also be interpreted as D3

desires involving aesthetic judgments, such as tastes for "the fine cigarette lighter, the fine car" (140).

21. This is an implication of Mele's version of the thesis that we act on our strongest desires—specifically his principle P1n (*Autonomous Agents*, 40).

22. C. Taylor, "Responsibility for Self," 116.

23. Ibid., 114.

24. See C. Taylor, *Ethics of Authenticity*, 37–39.

25. However, I do not mean to import into the definition of D2 desires anything like the formal apparatus of restrictions on preferences which rational decision theorists have evolved.

26. Cooper, *Reason and Emotion*, 243.

27. Watson, "Free Agency," 101.

28. Murphy, *Natural Law and Practical Rationality*, 75–76.

29. Watson, "Free Agency," 101.

30. MacIntyre, "How Moral Agents Became Ghosts," 304.

31. This is directly connected to the kind of "practical ultimacy" or "categorical nature" of the evaluative imperatives involved in *prohairesis* that distinguishes them from the hypothetical imperatives of skill according to Aristotle; see Broadie, *Ethics with Aristotle*, 89.

32. This may be the agent herself or someone else who is an expert in her evaluative tradition and its underlying theory of rationality.

33. D. Lewis, "Desire as Belief II," 304.

34. Ibid., 303.

35. Ibid., 304.

36. Ibid., 305. Of course, the sort of externalism about ethical motivation that Lewis espouses here is not itself accepted by Hume, who (as noted in chap. 3, sec. I.3) would rather say that no one could have "our" evaluative convictions about joy, knowledge, and love without having our desires for these things. But Lewis's position remains Humean in the broader sense that he sees motivation as *external* to the purely cognitive element in our practical syllogisms.

37. Ibid., 306. According to Lewis, this would make the necessity a merely conceptual or definitional one rather than "any *de re* necessity in nature" (306). Thus if you fail to care about objective value or ethical reality, the only danger is that "your inner states will fail to deserve folk-psychological names" (307). But that would be true only if "desire" had such a definitional role in folk psychology by mere convention, rather than *because* our folk concepts track psychological necessities of human nature or requirements for the flourishing of persons as such.

38. Ibid., 308–9.

39. For this reason, several debates about desire today start with the understanding that something's being desir*able* for an agent is distinct from his actually desiring it, and focus on various possible deliberative or communicative conditions for desirability. For example, Morton White interprets desirability as "what we ought to desire or have a moral duty to desire," and attributes to John Dewey the position that "a thing is said to be desirable just in case we know the causal antecedents and consequences of desiring it" (M. White, "Desire and Desirability,"

230–31). Against this, White objects that if my desire not to smoke opium originated from considering it in a normal state of mind, and I knew the consequences of smoking it, this would hardly make the desire morally obligatory. He also holds that desirability cannot depend on our actually *desiring* the consequences of having the desire (231–32), and that the distinction between desire and desirability is not analogous to the distinction between apparent and real qualities. Thus a pragmatic reduction of "This apple is really red" cannot be transferred to "This apple is desirable" (236–37). These are the kinds of semantic questions raised by D3-type desires. The notion of objective desirability required for D3 desires need not be restricted to "moral desirability," although it is limited to well-being. Both D3 desires and projective motivation have often been discussed under the ambiguous heading of "desirability."

40. Mele, "Moral Cognitivism and Listlessness," 734.
41. Aristotle, *De anima*, III.9, 597, 432b27–34.
42. Ibid., III.10, 598, 433a15–17.
43. Cooper, *Reason and Emotion*, 241–42. Cooper indicates some ambiguity over whether *prohairesis* always involves *boulēsis* as its motive engine or whether it can also take some form of nonrational desire (see Cooper, 242, n. 4). I think it is clear that Aristotle usually thinks of *prohairesis* as involving *boulēsis*.
44. John McDowell, "Virtue and Reason," 345. McDowell acknowledges the distinction (see 335).
45. Aristotle, *De anima*, II.2, 558, 413b21–23.
46. Ibid., II.3, 559, 414b12.
47. Ibid., III.11, 599, 434a1–3: "Clearly they have feelings of pleasure and pain, and if they have these, then they must have desire." So these feelings are *sufficient conditions* for desire.
48. Ibid., III.10, 433b7–9.
49. This is not to deny that "cultural" factors in the most general sense will usually play a role in *how exactly* an instinctive urge is specified or what objects we fix on, since D2 inclinations are open to a large amount of adaptation and social molding, as the influence of television advertising shows (even the desire for chocolate ice cream may be influenced by seeing others we admire preferring it to vanilla). Moreover, I do not deny that there will be borderline cases between the clear domains of these two subdivisions.
50. Watson, "Free Agency," in *Free Will*, 104.
51. Ibid., 105.
52. Ibid.
53. Sober and Wilson, *Unto Others*, 211.
54. In other words, epithumetic desires would count as what Jon Elster calls "visceral" states, including "drives such as hunger, thirst, and sexual desire" (*Strong Feelings*, 1–2), or what Craig Delancey calls "affect programs" (*Passionate Engines*, 5–6).
55. Aristotle, *De anima*, II.3, 559, 414b1–5.
56. Ibid., III.9, 596, 432b5–8.
57. Ibid., III.10, 598, 433a22–27.

58. Lear, *Aristotle*, 143. Again, by "desiring," Lear means what our translation of the *De Anima* means by "appetite."
59. Aristotle, *Nicomachean Ethics*, Book I, sec. 13, 1102b.16, 1741.
60. Ibid., 1102b.26–31, 1742.
61. And as Lear explains, in the *Nicomachean Ethics* "deliberated choice" (*prohairesis*) or decision follows:

> only after a process of deliberation. Aristotle's theory of deliberation (*bouleusis*) is a theory of the transmission of desire. The agent begins with a desire or wish (*boulēsis*) for an object. The object of wish appears to be good to the agent. But the appearance helps to constitute the wish itself . . . an agent's awareness that he wishes for a certain end is itself a manifestation of that wish.

(Lear, *Aristotle*, 143).
62. Aristotle, *De Anima*, III.10, 598, 433a18–20 (emphasis added).
63. Lear, *Aristotle*, 142 (emphasis added).
64. Ibid., 149.
65. MacIntyre, *Dependent Rational Animals*, 69.
66. Ibid., 68–69.
67. Ibid., 66.
68. Ibid., 67.
69. Ibid., 70. Notice the clear reference to the agent's own good in this formulation, as opposed to a later formulation on the same page, in terms of the question: What is it best for me to do? This latter formulation is ambiguous between what it is *best that* I do (which, for Kant, might be determined by deontic standards of justice) and what it is best *for me* that I do. For MacIntyre, unlike Kant, these judgments must agree, but that is because he grounds the former normative judgment in the latter eudaimonistic judgment.
70. Ibid., 71.
71. Ibid., 72.
72. Ibid., 74.
73. Ibid., 75.
74. Ibid., 76.
75. Ibid., 85–86 (emphasis added).
76. Ibid., 87.
77. Bernard Williams, *Ethics and the Limits of Philosophy*, 32. This also relates to the question of justifying the virtuous life to egoists "from the outside," which I treat in the discussion of Hursthouse in chapter 8, sec. 5.5.
78. Jensen, *Motivation and the Moral Sense in Francis Hutcheson's Ethical Theory*, 17.
79. Ibid., 15.
80. Ibid., 16. However, Hutcheson offers *other* arguments against psychological egoism that may be more successful against formal egoism, such as the argument that people sometimes act from purely altruistic motives that are not reducible to sympathetic passions (17–19).
81. Tillich, *Love, Power, and Justice*, 33.
82. Ibid., 25.

83. Ibid., 29. Nor, unfortunately, does it seem that Tillich's treatment of agapē in chap. 7 exempts agapic love from this formal structure.

84. In *Principia Ethica*, chap. III, sec. 59, G. E. Moore nicely distinguishes between getting something that is good and the goodness of my getting or possessing it (98). But he obscures the agent-relative character of the latter value by insisting that in *both* cases we are really talking about an agent-neutral good to whose goodness it is irrelevant that it is coming to *me* (as an indexical referent to the deliberating agent). From this confusion, he reasons that the egoist who says that his possessing some beneficial X is good is committed to the thesis that anyone's possessing X is good, and therefore egoism (formulated in agent-neutral terms) as the view "that *each* man's happiness is the sole good" is self-contradictory (99). If only it were this easy to refute egoism!

85. Sidgwick, *Methods of Ethics*, 91–92.

86. Ibid., 95.

87. Annas, *Morality of Happiness*, 129.

88. Ibid., 28.

89. Ibid., 35.

90. Ibid., 35.

91. Nussbaum, *Fragility of Goodness*, 275.

92. Ibid., 35.

93. Ibid., 30.

94. John Oesterle, introduction to Aquinas, *Treatise on Happiness*, xiii.

95. As Christine Korsgaard has shown, this is the root of serious problems with moral egoism as a doctrine of practical reason that is supposed to show that (1) egoistic principles are naturalistic constructions based on what seems naturally or *prima facie* good (e.g., the satisfaction of our desires); and (2) egoistic principles can have normative force. See Korsgaard, *The Myth of Egoism*.

96. Oesterle, introduction to *Treatise on Happiness* (trans. Oesterle), xiii.

97. Nussbaum, *Fragility of Goodness*, 276.

98. Thus moral egoism does not entail psychological egoism. It is often thought that the inverse obtains, but see note 110 below.

99. See Robert O'Connell, S.J., *Plato on the Human Paradox*, 10–11.

100. Rawls, *A Theory of Justice*, sec. 86, 568 (emphasis added).

101. Feinberg, "Psychological Egoism," in *Reason and Responsibility*.

102. Ibid., 547–48, sec. 4b.

103. Ibid., 549 (some emphasis omitted). The truism Feinberg cites may not be analytic in the sense of logically tautologous, given the meaning of the terms, but it may be metaphysically necessary, given the concept of action.

104. Korsgaard, *The Myth of Egoism*, 17.

105. Ibid., 24. Korsgaard is responding here to Williams's analysis of egoism in "Egoism and Altruism," in *Problems of the Self*.

106. This kind of self-absorption, e.g., in demanding that we be the one to find the cure, rather than just willing that a cure be found, is also the heart of the problem in perverse romantic attitudes, as I have argued in Davenport, "The Ethical and Religious Significance of Taciturnus's Letter," 226–27.

107. Korsgaard, *The Myth of Egoism*, 23. Korsgaard makes an interesting argument that desires as natural items in our psychology may often aim at results that are patently *not* good for us or that only seem by rationalization to add to our well-being (16). This supports an intriguing argument that rational egoism is a dogmatic realist doctrine. My construction of psychological egoism does not conflict with this argument, since it requires only the idea that desires as natural items can aim at first-order objects that are seen in *some way* as good for the agent. It does not require that the agent sees every such object as a *net* benefit or as causing an *overall* improvement in her well-being.

108. Moore, *Principia Ethica*, 97–98.

109. Bernard Gert has argued that Hobbes himself did not really hold this kind of psychological egoism; see Gert's Introduction to Hobbes, *Man and Citizen*, 4–12. But whether or not this is right, Hobbes as traditionally read has come to represent a paradigm version of egoism in the sense defined here.

110. For a general account of MME as a maximizing principle, see Parfit's account of "the self-interest theory" of practical reason (or *S*) in *Reasons and Persons*, chap. I, 3–4. See also Sidgwick, *Methods of Ethics*, Book II, chap. I, which defines "egoistic hedonism" as the doctrine that "each individual should aim at his own greatest happiness," and attributes this position (paradoxically, I think) to Bentham (119). Also compare Kraut's insightful distinctions among three MME doctrines that differ in the kind of consideration they allow us to give to the interests of others; see Kraut, *Aristotle on the Human Good*, chap. 2.1. All three include a maximizing imperative. For instance, "All legitimate reasons for actions, according to pure egoism, must take this form: this act will maximize my own good" (78). This conception of "pure egoism" directly applies the maximization test to each act, while Parfit's *S* does not. There are other imaginable imperatives that give the interests of others zero weight or less weight than our own interests without requiring us to maximize our own interests. But because they may allow the agent to harm his own greater interests or even to prefer a very minor pleasure for himself that requires the death of others to a great good that he could have secured at no cost to others, such imperatives might better be called *perversely* egoistic than *rationally* egoistic.

111. And for this reason, psychological egoism does not entail rational egoism or moral egoism if these must include a maximization requirement. The psychological egoist says that all our actions are ultimately motivated *only* by the desire to secure some self-related first-order good (or perhaps also some self-related second-order good, in complex psychological egoism), and this rules out an independent desire for the good (or harm) of others as final ends. But believing that human beings are naturally concerned only with their own welfare does not entail the judgment that such beings should be rational maximizers of their welfare or should not be irrational or thoughtless egoists. If the MPE theorist endorses any theory of practical reason, it will probably have to be some version of MME; but she might without any logical inconsistency endorse no theory of practical reason at all. Or she might endorse a nihilistic morality on the grounds that if MPE is true, life is so absurd that it does not matter what we do.

112. Feinberg, "Psychological Egoism," 550–51.

113. Ibid., 551.

114. Caputo and Derrida, *Deconstruction in a Nutshell*, 148 (emphasis in original). Note that by "the medievals," Caputo must mean Aquinas, for certainly Scotus and several others would protest most vehemently against the view he expresses here.

115. Feinberg, "Psychological Egoism," 550 (emphasis in original). Feinberg's distinction is not exactly the same as mine here, since I include entertainment and the satisfaction of DI desires as first-order pleasures. Also, Feinberg does not clearly link his "paradox of hedonism" to the pragmatic contradiction of directly pursuing second-order satisfaction (554). But my reconstruction will bring out this connection.

116. Ibid., 552–53.

117. Morillo, "The Reward Event and Motivation," 171. Morillo misconstrues these as arguments against PE itself; in fact they are only alleged defeaters to *arguments for* PE.

118. Sober and Wilson, *Unto Others*, 212.

119. Rousseau, *Discourse Concerning the Origins of Human Inequality*.

120. Ibid., Part II, 77.

121. Ibid., Part II, 64.

122. Morillo, "The Reward Event and Motivation," 174–75. Morillo here refers to famous studies on the electrical stimulation of parts of the limbic system in rats and their remarkable motivational effects, and to similar anecdotal evidence from the direct stimulation caused by smoking crack cocaine.

123. Ibid., 177.

124. Ibid., 178. In my view, this may be true for many objects of our attention that are important both for our survival (like food) and for the survival of our offspring (like tending infants) but it becomes much more tenuous when extended to goals like the friend's good, or the creation of beauty, or the acquisition of speculative knowledge with no evident technical application-value.

125. Ibid., 176. Morillo suggests here that ultimately the aesthetic pleasure of Mozart is made of the same "stuff" as the pleasure of eating, drinking, or having sex.

126. Ibid., 180.

127. As Morillo says, "this is a kind of deep monism, which could be expressed by saying that there is only one basic motive and only one basic object of motivation" (182).

128. Ibid., 178.

129. As Sober and Wilson note, "what begins as a purely instrumental desire may get transformed into a desire that is functionally autonomous"; see Sober and Wilson, *Unto Others*, 221. They cite Slote (1964) and Kavka (1986) in support of this point.

130. In *Utilitarianism*, chap. 2, Mill talks about the pleasures of challenging work and the development of one's talents as "excitement" and suggests that we need a diverse range of such excitements to balance out the other fundamental

component of happiness, which (following Epicurus) he calls "tranquility." In these two poles of Millian happiness we can see the Eastern and Western attitudes pulling in diametrically opposite directions.

131. Feinberg, "Psychological Egoism," 551.

132. Ibid., 551–52.

133. Ibid., 552.

134. See Mill, *Utilitarianism*, chap. 2.

135. Parfit, *Reasons and Persons*, 6–7.

136. Ibid., 27–28.

137. Williams, "Critique of Utilitarianism," 110.

138. Ibid., 113–14.

139. Frankfurt, "Rationality and the Unthinkable," 178–80.

140. Technically, Parfit's agent acting on or following theory S is not necessarily a simple material egoist in my sense, since S does not limit her to the pursuit of materially self-related goods, i.e., to what Parfit calls "selfishness." Rather, S can be interpreted on the desire-fulfillment theory of well-being to count as "self-interested" in the pursuit of agent-transcending ends when the agent happens to desire these for their own sake, e.g., out of love for others (Parfit, *Reasons and Persons*, 5). But if this agent chooses E *because* (1) she just happens to desire E (in the D2 sense), and (2) she believes her happiness consists in the satisfaction of her D2 desires, and (3) she is committed to principle S, then E cannot be a *purely* agent-transcending end for her. If E is her beloved's good, for example, then she acts not on her desire for his well-being but only on this taken together with her policy of trying to fulfill her desires in order to maximize her own well-being (understood here as satisfaction of her desires). Her beloved might then reasonably complain that she really sees him just as an occasion for her desire-fulfillment. Indeed, in this application of S, it seems that it would be in her interest to arrange it so that she has D2 desires for all and only those ends that are most easily realized. But choosing them in this way is not choosing them for their own sake.

141. We could imagine this machine producing wave after wave of orgasmic pleasure as often as possible to maximize the pleasurable feeling without damaging the brain and with whatever variation would be necessary to avoid diminishing pleasurable returns over time, etc. One early instance of this familiar kind of objection to the most brutal form of hedonism is Socrates' response to Polus that the life of a "catamite" (a boy prostitute/slave) cannot be the best life (*Gorgias*, 494e). This point also stands behind Aristotle's remark that the life that many people think constitutive of happiness is "completely slavish" and is really "a life for grazing animals" (*Nicomachean Ethics* I.5 1095b20–21). It is partially to avoid this banality objection that Mill introduces his infamous distinction between "higher" and "lower" pleasures.

142. Korsgaard, *The Myth of Egoism*, 26.

143. Batson, *Altruism Question*. For this reference, I am indebted to John Neubauer's dissertation, *The Role of Feelings in Kant's Moral Philosophy* (Fordham University, 2004), chap. 1.

144. Elster, *Sour Grapes*, chap. II, 43.

145. Ibid., 44–50.

146. It is useful to compare this to Kant's distinction between the "contradiction in concept" and "contradiction in willing" versions of the universal law formula (*Groundwork*, II, Ak 423–24). Of course, Kant is concerned about what either an individual or all relevant moral agents who interact in the same world-system could rationally will as a law for *all possible moral agents* without practical self-defeat—as opposed to what an individual could will for himself alone. But his distinction exists at the individual level as well, as Elster's analysis shows.

147. Elster, *Sour Grapes*, 50.

148. It will therefore be part of the intended sequel to this volume.

149. Elster, *Sour Grapes*, 51. Elster mentions belief but does not explain why such doxastic states are essentially by-products.

150. See Elster's fascinating and extremely insightful discussion of such cases in *Sour Grapes*, sec. II.4, 60–66.

151. See Elster's three responses to this suggestion, 56–60. I return to some of the problems with indirect strategies in later chapters. However, in previous work I have in effect argued that volitional *wantonness*, in Frankfurt's sense as the complete absence of higher-order evaluative attitudes toward one's first-order motives, cannot be intentionally produced even by indirectly self-erasing will (see *Sour Grapes*, 58). Thus there is no return to naive aestheticism or the innocence of moral ignorance for the "awakened aesthete."

6. Psychological Eudaimonism: A Reading of Aristotle

1. See Plato, *Gorgias* 465a.

2. An obvious problem, though, is that in Book X, Aristotle considers that speculative science could be higher than political science. For other problems with this notion of "a ladder, or pyramid of ends" involved in different crafts, see Hardie, *Aristotle's Ethical Theory*, 14–16.

3. Stephen White, *Sovereign Virtue*, 6. White lays particular emphasis on the natural hierarchy among crafts as Aristotle's primary basis for claiming that there is a single highest end.

4. Hill, "Two Perspectives on the Ultimate End," 100. My analysis will focus on what Hill calls the subjective or "internal perspective" on the ultimate end taken by the *Ethics* (106) rather than the "external perspective" that she argues is found in the physical and metaphysical works. However, as I will suggest later, the metaphysical conception of the ultimate end as the animal's "actualization of its form" (101) supports a holistic understanding of the way in which this end includes all others.

5. White implies nonholistic inclusion when he says that for Aristotle, the highest good is such that "we want it only because of itself, whereas we want all the other ends because of it" (*Sovereign Virtue*, 9). White rightly cites the passage at the start of the anti-regress argument in support of this reading. But elsewhere, he implies that the end of politics holistically includes other ends: "The notion of inclusion operating here, then, is hierarchical: the end of politics is to oversee and coordinate the pursuit of a given range of other ends" (7).

6. Aristotle, *Nicomachean Ethics*, trans. Irwin, Translator's Commentary, 174.

7. It is also false that the non-mereological whole is always superior in intrinsic value to its parts, though this is harder to see (G. E. Moore is one of the few to note this point). My activity of breaking the code on some lock could be intrinsically valuable as a display of rare skill, yet it might be a non-mereological part of the larger activity of stealing some poor widow's retirement savings from her safe, which as a whole has negative intrinsic value.

8. Yet the critique of the life of pleasure seems to rely on a criterion of the ultimate good—namely its comprehensiveness, which in turn requires that it involve the full use of our most valuable capacities—that is only established later. So either Aristotle's lecture is disorganized or, more likely, our text does not exactly reflect Aristotle's order of presentation, let alone a mature "fine copy" or completed edit by Aristotle himself.

9. See *Summa Theologica*, I–II Qu. 2, Art. 3, Obj. 3 and Reply 3.

10. Ibid., Qu. 2, Art. 8, Respondo.

11. Cf. Williams, *Ethics and the Limits of Philosophy*, chaps. 3 and 10. In *Fragility of Goodness*, Nussbaum qualifies this claim by noting that all the Greek thinkers she discusses recognize "that the good life for a human being must to some extent, and in some ways, be self-sufficient, immune to incursions of luck" (3). But in chaps. 10 and 11 of *Fragility*, I think she underestimates the extent to which Aristotle tries to minimize the influence of luck.

12. Bostock, *Aristotle's Ethics*, chap. 1, 13.

13. Specifically, Bostock says that the phrase "most complete" in the Function Argument probably "just *means* 'all-inclusive,' as it appeared to do earlier when he was speaking of an end or goal that is 'most complete' (1097a28–b21)" (20). This derives from Bostock's reconstruction of the "more complete" relation (22), whose two conditions are comparative rather than maximal versions of the two conditions in my definition of "most nonholistically inclusive." However, Bostock does not distinguish this from what I call holistic inclusion relations.

14. *Nicomachean Ethics*, Commentary, 184. Irwin calls this the "exclusive" as opposed to the "comprehensive" reading of this passage, which I discuss below. I think it is clearer to describe this distinction in terms of two types of "inclusion": the holistic or comprehensive relation of end parts to the whole end and the nonholistic or instrumental relation.

15. Ironically enough, Richard Kraut offers one such model as Aristotle's considered view; see his highly nuanced and impressive book, *Aristotle on the Human Good*, chap. 1. I discuss a few of Kraut's ideas in sec. I.4.

16. On White's reading, for example, the claim that "happiness is the only thing we want *solely* for its own sake" (*Sovereign Virtue*, 10) seems to be based primarily on the empirical fact that politics is the only science that has a "comparably general end" (8).

17. White describes the nonholistic and holistic alternatives this way: "Although we all have several ends we choose 'because of themselves' [i.e., as final], we might also choose each of them for some one of them that we choose *only* because of itself [unconditional completeness]. Or this supreme end might be the

set of those ends as an organized whole" (ibid., 11). White is right that the holistic alternative cannot "be all-inclusive" in the sense of a simple conjunction or mereological sum of all fully final ends; rather, "it needs a criterion or standard" for ranking them (7).

18. Of course, this agrees with the earlier thesis that politics is the highest craft, whose goal is our highest end. But there is a limit to the sociality of our highest end implicit in the idea that it is the complete good appropriated or possessed by a single individual, bringing him total practical harmony in his own psyche.

19. "Things, then, that are called complete in virtue of their own nature are so called in all these senses . . . because they lack nothing in respect of goodness, and cannot be excelled and no part proper to them can be found outside [them]." (*Metaphysics* 16 1021a30–33).

20. In this light, I find surprising the exclusivist reading of this passage advocated by Heineman, White, and Kenny, as described by Bostock:

> a rival interpretation takes the point to be that eudaimonia does not already include all goods, but may be considered as one among many goods, and when so considered, it is the most choiceworthy of each of them taken singly. But we can count "count it together" with those other goods, and in that case it must of course be admitted that eudaimonia + x is more choiceworthy than eudaimonia by itself, where x is a good (however small) that is not already included in eudaimonia. (Bostock, *Aristotle's Ethics*, 23–24)

This is precisely the conclusion that Aristotle regards as *absurd* (given the sufficiency criterion) and thus as a *reductio* of any noninclusive conception of eudaimonia! For as Bostock points out, Aristotle clearly endorses the argument, borrowed from Plato's *Philebus* 20d–22c, that "x cannot be 'the good' if x + y is better than x by itself" (ibid., 24).

21. *Nicomachean Ethics*, Irwin's commentary on I.7, sec. 5, 181–82.

22. Irwin, *Plato's Ethics*, 67.

23. Thus Irwin argues (69) that Plato can answer his own objection in the *Hippias Minor* by saying that in practice virtue as the supreme craft will never be misused, despite the logical possibility of its misuse.

24. Ibid., 73.

25. White finds support in Aristotle's *Eudemian Ethics* and *Rhetoric* for the idea that other final ends such as pleasure and justice can be seen as "parts of happiness" (*Sovereign Virtue*, 13).

26. Lear, *Aristotle: The Desire to Understand*, 157, 160 (emphasis added).

27. See Davenport, "Towards an Existential Virtue Ethics," 293.

28. Bostock, *Aristotle's Ethics*, 21. Bostock adds that such an inclusivist understanding of the highest good is clearly found in the *Eudemian Ethics*, according to general consent.

29. *Nicomachean Ethics*, Irwin's Commentary on I.7, sec. 3, 181.

30. Davenport, "Towards an Existential Virtue Ethics," 291–92. See also the discussion in n. 91 (318–19), which puts in capsule form what I argue in chaps. 6–8 of this book.

31. Aquinas, *Summa Theologica*, I–II Qu. 1, Art. 6, Respondo (Oesterle, 10–11), 10–11. Aquinas also endorses the holistic interpretation of completeness in Qu. 3, Art. 2, Reply 2, where he approvingly cites Boethius's idea that happiness as "a general notion" is the complete "'aggregation of all goods.'"

32. Lewis, "Weight of Glory," 28–29.

33. Ibid., 30.

34. Bostock, *Aristotle's Ethics*, 26.

35. Hence it is important to emphasize that the weak version of Trans does *not* say that if X is a "fully final" or "unqualifiedly complete" end (pursued *only* for its own sake), then X must also be nonholistically all-inclusive in the sense that every other final end is also desired as a means to X. For, as we saw, weak Trans does not follow just from the idea of a fully/unqualifiedly final end, of which it is conceptually possible for there to be several. The contrapositive of weak Trans does, however, say that if X is *not* all-embracing or comprehensive, then it is *not* fully/unqualifiedly final. Should we understand this to mean that any noncomprehensive final end must also be desired as an *instrumental means* to the embracing good? Since, on this reading, weak Trans would be most implausible, we should reinterpret it to say only that a noncomprehensive final end must be seen as part of the one comprehensive good—not that it must be the subject of *mixed* motives, being desired both for its own sake and also as an instrumental means to some quite distinct end. For weak Trans to make sense, then, there must be *two ways* to fail to be fully final: the nonholistic way (by being also desired as an instrumental means) and the holistic way (by being final only as an integral part of the highest final good). If we take "not fully final" in the first way, as requiring mixed motives, then weak Trans will be implausible. But when we take this negative term in the second way, weak Trans becomes only a little more than a tautology and hence clearly far weaker than Plato's version of Trans. Weak Trans, then, can do little work in Aristotle's eudaimonism: all the heavy lifting is done by the criteria of self-sufficiency and comprehensiveness.

36. Aristotle himself notes that (2) follows from (4) when he argues that because "happiness lacks nothing, but is self-sufficient," it must also be "choiceworthy in its own right," or such that it is not done as a means to anything else (*NE* X.6 1176b5–7).

37. Lear, *Aristotle*, 155.

38. Bostock apparently agrees, since he says of the self-sufficiency criterion, "There is no ambiguity here, and it is very difficult to see how a single 'dominant' end, such as theoretical activity, could satisfy this description" (i.e., being sufficient all by itself); Bostock, *Aristotle's Ethics*, 23. Interestingly, Hardie agrees with this, although he thinks it does not obviously square with the distinction between "two main forms" of happiness in *NE* X.8. Hardie eventually attributes a dominant-end view to Aristotle only because he sees that the inclusive view requires "a plurality of ends," but he mistakenly thinks this is incompatible with one end being "most final" (Hardie, *Aristotle's Ethical Theory*, 22–23).

39. Kraut, *Aristotle on the Human Good*, 25.

40. Ibid., 7.

41. Ibid., 5.

42. This is also clear in n. 13 (8), where Kraut denies that happiness "includes" (holistically) the external intrinsic goods, although he affirms that a happy life will "contain" (nonholistically) these goods.

43. But Kraut does not clearly make this formal-material distinction (maybe because Aristotle is also often unclear about it, despite implicitly requiring it).

44. It is important to beware of a possible confusion here. Kraut is not proposing that Aristotle holds both practical and intellectual virtue (or their related goods) to be ultimate; that would be a contradiction. If both of them are completely or unqualifiedly final (not subsumed under any other as a means to it) then there is no ultimate end in the sense of a maximally nonholistically inclusive goal.

45. Ibid., 8.

46. Purinton, "Aristotle's Definition of Happiness," 264.

47. Kraut, "Aristotle on the Human Good: An Overview," 79.

48. One version of this would be the view Kraut describes as follows: "Here is another possibility. The goal of the best life is a mixture of philosophical and political activity, with more emphasis going to the former rather than to the latter." Kraut rejects this notion of an ideal balance in favor of the formula that the most *eudaimon* life is "the one that has the greatest amount of philosophical activity" (*Aristotle on the Human Good*, 51).

49. Kraut, *Aristotle on the Human Good*, 10–11.

50. Ibid., 84–85. Note that Kraut's formula for weak egoism is ambiguous about whether the benefit that accrues to the agent from his practically virtuous action is part of his motive. However, it must be according to formal egoism. Thus Kraut does not clearly ascribe formal egoism to Aristotle.

51. It is also hard to square the self-sacrificing view that Kraut ascribes to Aristotle with Aristotle's Diotima-like claim that "as far as we can, we ought to be pro-immortal, and go to all lengths to live a life in accord with our supreme element" (*NE* X.7 1177b34–35).

52. Here, as Kraut notes, we must insert whatever further conditions would ensure that the *phronimos* would clearly judge this to be a case where helping the parent is the noble thing to do in the circumstances.

53. Hardie, "The Final Good in Aristotle's Ethics"; and Hardie, *Aristotle's Ethical Theory*, chap. I: "The Final Good for Man."

54. Ackrill, "Aristotle on Eudaimonia."

55. Purinton, "Aristotle's Definition of Happiness," 260.

56. Ibid., 263.

57. Ibid., 260–61.

58. Ibid., 265.

59. Ibid., 265–66.

60. Ibid., 269–70.

61. Ibid., 271–72.

62. Ibid., 285–86. However, Purinton's and Kraut's rejection of the mixed model of eudaimonia in X.7–8 does make it harder to square this part of Aristotle's text with a holistic inclusivism (whether maximal or restricted to human virtues). My own guess is that Aristotle means to be describing study or

contemplation as the most important activity in the complex whole of human eudaimonia, and that he emphasizes its separateness (*NE* X.8 1178a23) to agree with his account of the separable intellect as our divine element in the *De anima*.

63. Irwin, *Plato's Ethics*, 65, referring to Aristotle's *Eudemian Ethics* 1214b24–27.

64. On this point, see Mark Murphy's helpful account of final causation models in his reconstruction of Aristotle's function argument; Murphy, *Natural Law and Practical Rationality*, chap. I, sec. 2.

65. Copleston, *Medieval Philosophy*, 380–81.

66. Although, as we'll see (perhaps surprisingly), it is unclear how within A-eudaimonism this sort of reflective knowledge can actually help our pursuit of F.

67. Aquinas, *Summa Theologica*, I–II Qu. 5, Art. 8, Respondo.

68. In this respect, Aquinas is more insightful, since he perceives that the jointure thesis and the eudaimonia thesis both require some defense, quite apart from the more specific argument that M involves supernatural union with the Divine.

69. In other words, we can distinguish two versions of this thesis. In its *unsaturated* form, the jointure thesis asserts the existence of a highest motive that is the holistic union of all our motives, or an ultimately final end that embraces all our final ends, but it leaves the concept of F *open* beyond that. So this unsaturated formulation does not require that the comprehensive or all-embracing motive be erosiac. In its *saturated* form, the jointure thesis asserts the existence of a good answering specifically to the erosiac concept of F: in this formulation, it has the strong erosiac thesis as a corollary.

70. *Nicomachean Ethics* I.7 1097a37.

71. Hill, "Two Perspectives on the Ultimate End," 107. Thus Hill shares my view that the function argument is the key to Aristotle's account of M rather than to his account of F.

72. Williams, *Morality: An Introduction to Ethics*, chap. 7: "Moral Standards and the Distinguishing Mark of Man," 64–65.

7. The Paradox of Eudaimonism: An Existential Critique

1. Note that, as Annas herself argues in *The Morality of Happiness*, almost all ancient ethical doctrines are eudaimonistic in form.

2. Aquinas, *Summa Theologica*, I–II Qu. 2, Art. 3, Rep. 1. The point here is that virtuous works are not done for the sake of honor, for then "this would no longer be virtue but ambition." Honor is properly a by-product of virtuous works. But it is not clear why one's own happiness is a more virtuous incentive than honor.

3. By this Aristotle is apparently referring to the Platonic idea that a person with a virtue must know the *good* aimed at by that virtue, for he goes on to downplay the significance of this cognitive condition relative to the importance of the disposition of choice produced by practicing virtuous acts. So understood, this cognitive condition says that understanding the agent-neutral moral value of one's act is essential to virtuous motivation, although simply reflecting speculatively on its good will hardly be sufficient for virtuous motivation. But Aristotle may also be referring to the point made later in his discussion of voluntariness (*NE* III.1)

that to be held accountable, the agent must *know* the circumstances of his act sufficiently for him to intend it *as* this particular act under one description rather than another description of his behavior; we are obviously not virtuous if the description under which our behavior would be a virtuous act is not the one we intend in performing it.

4. Aristotle, *Nicomachean Ethics*, II.4, 1105a.29–33, Ross/Urmson translation.
5. Ibid., III.6, 1115b.13–14.
6. Aristotle may have this point in mind when he argues that:

every excellence both brings into a good condition the thing of which it is the excellence and makes the work of that thing be done well; e.g., the excellence of the eye makes both the eye and its work good, for it is by the excellence of the eye that we see well. Similarly, the excellence of the horse makes a horse both good in itself and good at running . . . the excellence of man also will be the state which makes a man good and which makes him do his work well. (Ibid., II.6, 1106a.15–23)

A horse does not perform well just *in order to* qualify as a good horse; when it needs constant incentive, it is not yet a *good* horse. But when it performs well for no other end than performing well, it is good. Similarly, human persons are properly functioning and thus "happy" in the fullest sense only when they are purely motivated to act for the sake of the noble.

7. On the latter issue, see Williams, *Ethics and the Limits of Philosophy*, 38.
8. Ibid., 36.
9. Von Wright, *Varieties of Goodness*, 142 and 145.
10. Ibid., 143.
11. Broadie, *Ethics with Aristotle*, 93.
12. Ibid., 94.
13. Ibid., 94.
14. Edmund Pincoffs, *Quandaries and Virtues*, 112, citing Dewey, *Human Nature and Conduct*, 7.
15. On this topic, see Frank, "Is Subjectivity a Non-Thing, and Absurdity [Unding]?" See also Henrich's essay, "Fichte's Original Insight," and of course Sartre's discussion of prethetic self-consciousness in *Being and Nothingness*, Part I.
16. Broadie, *Ethics with Aristotle*, 94–95.
17. I think it is an open question whether all the kinds of ethical evaluation that go into discerning different kinds of "nobility" in actions are really "welfarist" (in the broad sense of being concerned about human well-being generally). I strongly doubt that they are, although this is left unclear in Aristotle's arguments that the *kalon* is not the warlike, the bold, the powerful, or the aristocratic but rather the balanced and harmonious. Normative theory in the natural law tradition has tried to make up for this large gap in Aristotle's account by basing norms and virtues on considerations about human well-being impartially considered; see, e.g., Mark Murphy, *Natural Law and Practical Rationality*. In "new natural law" theory, however, this approach seems to assume the possibility of impartial concerns about the good of all persons that may not be embraced by any fundamental desire

for one's own eudaimonia. To that extent, such normative theories are no longer psychologically eudaimonist.

18. Annas, "Self-Love in Aristotle," 14.
19. Ibid., 2.
20. *NE*, VIII.13, 1163a24, McKeon edition. Irwin's translation reads: "the controlling element in virtue and character lies in decision." The Ross/Urmson translation reads: "for in choice lies the essential element of excellence and character."
21. Annas, "Self-Love in Aristotle," 5.
22. Ibid., 8–9.
23. Ibid., 9: "In the way he presents the altruistic choice as a choice of the heroic over the humdrum, Aristotle seems to be assimilating it to a familiar Greek tradition of heroism that is distinctly self-centered in its desire to shine and excel for a brief and glorious moment." Throughout the *Nicomachean Ethics*, in fact, we should recognize that Aristotle is drawing on his readers' timocratic values and trying to reconstruct them into desire for his own purified version of "the noble." This is especially clear in the sections of Books III and IV on courage and magnanimity, which are ethically transformed or "moralized" versions of older timocratic conceptions of these concepts as aristocratic qualities of fearlessness in battle and grandeur in relations with others. The transformation occurs with rivalry between gentlemen of the patrician class in this discussion of friendship.
24. Ibid., 11.
25. Ibid., 12.
26. Richard Kraut, "Comments on Julia Annas's 'Self-Love in Aristotle'," 22.
27. There are complex questions in contemporary theories of motivation concerning such counterfactual conditions for the purposes operative as motives in our intentions that I am ignoring here (because these questions demand a separate treatment in their own right that would require a long digression).
28. And again, we should not be surprised nor blame Aristotle for this, for he worked out by far the most sophisticated analysis of human motivation in his time. Many distinctions that are clear to us today are naturally enough not clearly made by Aristotle, who worked near the historical beginnings of systematic moral psychology.
29. Gottlieb, "Aristotle's Ethical Egoism," 5.
30. MacIntyre, *After Virtue*, 2nd ed., 197: "As Aristotle says, the enjoyment of the activity and the enjoyment of the achievement are not the ends at which the agent aims, but the enjoyment supervenes upon the successful activity in such a way that the activity achieved and the activity enjoyed are one and the same state." But whether this idea of "one and the same state" can resolve the paradox of eudaimonism is what I am investigating in this section.
31. Annas, "Self-Love in Aristotle," 12 (emphasis added).
32. Similarly, in our previous example the woman might take her business associate out for a celebratory meal only for the sake of pleasing him but find later that this has also encouraged him to continue his business relationship with her, even though bringing about this result was no part of her original intention. In

this case, there would be no mystery about how to reconcile two motives in our agent because there would in fact only *be one* motive and one unintended by-product result.

33. Annas, *Morality of Happiness*, "The Good of Others," 223. I should note here my view that this book is a monumental achievement in scholarship on ancient ethics in general. Although I take issue with this one aspect of Annas's multifaceted work, I am largely persuaded by her main thesis that ancient ethics concerns largely the same things that moderns mean by "morality" and that despite major structural differences in approach, the gap is not as large as both sympathizers with ancient ethics (such as Williams and MacIntyre) and its legion of critics have made it seem.

34. See Parfit's memorable discussion of this well-known puzzle in game theory in his book, *Reasons and Persons*, chap. 1, sec. 8.

35. Annas, *Morality of Happiness*, 223.

36. Ibid., 224.

37. Ibid., 127. In fact, I want to say that "an ethics of virtue" need not *by definition* be eudaimonistic at all. Holding even a radically aretaic theory of ethical norms for judging character, actions, institutions, and so on, does not by itself commit one to a eudaimonistic metaethics (i.e., a eudaimonist psychological and conceptual justification of one's normative system). As I argue in *Kierkegaard After MacIntyre*, we should not assume that a eudaimonistic moral psychology is the only possible or plausible kind of objective grounding or foundation for a virtue ethics, for a Kierkegaardian-existentialist moral psychology might also do the job.

38. Annas, *Morality of Happiness*, 223.

39. Gottlieb, "Aristotle's Ethical Egoism," 12.

40. Kraut, "Comments on Julia Annas' 'Self-Love in Aristotle,'" 22–23.

41. Williams, *Ethics and the Limits of Philosophy*, 35.

42. Ibid., 39.

43. The question is *not*: Could we part company with Aristotle by rejecting eudaimonism altogether on this issue and regard the agent's reflexive fulfillment in virtue as a pure by-product? For clearly we could do that, but it would mean granting that the strong erosaic thesis is false and thus opening the door to an existential account of striving will. So anyone who takes that route is conceding the conclusion I am working to establish. The question here is rather whether Annas's proposal offers a way of *avoiding* this conclusion.

44. Thus Aristotle's ideal *philia* is "impersonal" in a way that contrasts with the essentially particularistic care that Michael Stocker describes as a love for a single individual just for his or her unique identity; see Stocker, "The Schizophrenia of Modern Ethical Theories," 71–72.

45. Broadie, *Ethics with Aristotle*, chap. 2, 121, n. 29.

46. See Politis, "Primacy of Self-Love in the *Nicomachean Ethics*."

47. Ibid., 153.

48. Ibid., 154.

49. Ibid., 157. This claim concerning the comparative priority of one's own virtue seems to suggest that it is better that x virtuous actions be done by me than

2x quantity of such actions by my friend. Although Politis notes Irwin's failure to include this priority claim in his widely used 1985 translation, Irwin still omits it in his new edition; see *Nicomachean Ethics*, 2nd ed. (Hackett, 1999), IX chap. 8, sec. 8, 148.

50. Politis, "Primacy of Self-Love," 161–62.
51. Ibid., 164–65.
52. Ibid., 166–69.
53. Ibid., 170–72.
54. Sherman, *Fabric of Character*, 145.
55. Kraut, "Two Conceptions of Happiness," 174.
56. Ibid., 172–73.
57. We should not be surprised that Callicles' macho ideal involves a rejection of the erosiac conception of happiness, since it is simply a distorted version of the concept of heroic will that so radically opposed the paradigmatically Eastern ideal of perfection as a completeness in which all motivation reaches stasis.
58. Note that Kraut does not specify that ends we consider "good" or "worthwhile" must refer back to our own well-being; he leaves open the possibility of motivation pure of self-interest, as Annas also insisted.
59. This is the sense in which we can say that the second-order motive is metaphysically secondary to, derivative of, or "supervenient" (in a loose sense of that tricky term) on the first-order motive.
60. This does not mean, however, that some D3 desires are in no sense "egoistic." For valuing something instrumentally or only as a means to one's own interests is not the only way to value something egoistically.
61. Since, as we saw above, being a constitutive part of X, where X is a holistic relationship of its constitutive parts, is quite different from being an instrumental means to X.
62. This is similar to Bruce Brower's claim that certain virtue concepts include reasonableness; e.g., "an act is courageous only if the goal one hopes to attain is worth the risk involved in performing the action," or one *believes* it is worth the risk (see "Virtue Concepts and Ethical Realism," 682). I do not agree, however, with Brower's view that being reasonable or worth doing can be cashed out in terms of maximum utility in the likely results. On rival conceptions, an act could be *kalon* even if the agent knows that the good at which the act aims is inaccessible, or even if he believes that some other act might have maximized utility.
63. Thus if anyone ever did decide to pursue for its own sake the pseudo-activity A of *merely desiring* some other end B—which would be bizarre but I do not say impossible—then his motive for A could not be any kind of desire in the orektic sense. Rather, he would have to be projecting A for some reason (e.g., perhaps because he just wondered what it would be like). I discuss such curiosity as a basis for projection in the analysis of sadistic cruelty in chapter 10.
64. This will include both purely altruistic ends, such as the well-being of a stranger, and many others, such as the ends pursued by those practicing different arts or sciences in their pure mode.
65. I discuss the distinction between eudaimonia (which seems desirable in the D3 sense) and personal meaning (which is not desirable in this sense) in the later sections of chapter 12.

66. Annas, *Morality of Happiness*, 322.
67. Ibid., 322.
68. See Davenport, "Towards an Existential Virtue Ethics," sec. IV, 291–94.
69. See Williams, *Morality*, 60, for his early version of the conflict-among-goods objection.
70. Williams, *Ethics and the Limits of Philosophy*, 43:

> He believed that all the excellences of character had to fit together into a harmonious self. Moreover, he was committed to thinking that the highest developments of human nature, which he identified with intellectual inquiry, would fit together with the more ordinary life of civic virtue, even though they represented the flowering of rather different powers, theoretical rather than practical reason. He was not very successful in showing this.

71. Ibid., 47.
72. Ibid., 45–46.
73. See Kraut, *Aristotle on the Human Good*, 317–19.
74. See Mark Murphy's analysis of natural functions, which is based on Mark Bedau's work, in *Natural Law and Practical Rationality*, chap. 1, sec. 2.
75. See Davenport, "Towards an Existential Virtue Ethics," 301–9 and n. 30.
76. Witness the fact that Sartre runs together all these different senses of "essence" (as functional essence of a natural kind, as Molinist haecceity or individual monadic essence, as character-essence constituted by one's life projects and long-term goals, etc.) in his famous argument that the "existence" of human persons precedes their essence; see Sartre, *Existentialism and Humanism*.
77. Williams, *Ethics and the Limits of Philosophy*, 34–35.
78. See Davenport, "Liberty of the Higher-Order Will."

8. Contemporary Solutions to the Paradox and Their Problems

1. John M. Cooper, *Reason and the Human Good in Aristotle*. Allan deserves credit for giving the first clear statement of the paradox of eudaimonism.
2. Ibid., 2–3.
3. Ibid., 76.
4. Ibid., 78.
5. Ibid., 79.
6. Ibid., 80–81.
7. Ibid., 82.
8. Ibid., 83.
9. Ibid., 86–87; see Cooper's n. 113 referring to Ross's account in his book, *Aristotle* (Meridian Books, 1959).
10. Cooper, *Reason and the Human Good in Aristotle*, 88.
11. MacIntyre, "Virtue Ethics," *Encyclopedia of Ethics*, 1276.
12. Lear, *Aristotle*, 170.
13. Cooper, *Reason and the Human Good in Aristotle*, 87.
14. And the value of the general end must likewise be prior to the value of something we regard as its specification. This is true whether or not we think G. E.

Moore (to whom Cooper refers, 82, n. 110) is right that some wholes can have values that transcend the values of their parts (some of which Moore thinks might be essential to a whole without themselves having any value when isolated). Moore's entire analysis of organic holism in value is confused precisely because it makes no sense to contrast the value of a whole with the mereological sum of the "separate" values of its parts if their individual values are entirely a function of their being parts of this whole. See Moore, *Principia Ethica*, chap. I, secs. 18–23.

15. Perhaps it is possible to imagine cases in which the first-order goal is part of the good that results from its very pursuit. If so, then these pursuits would be *self-reinforcing* in an unusual sense. For example, suppose the student government leader's goal is to promote more student involvement in campus activities and get more students to be visibly or publicly involved in outreach efforts. Now, her engaging in the specific activities she selects as instrumental means to this goal might at the same time constitute part—at least a small part—of the very thing she is after, since she would be at least one student visibly involved in a public campus activity. Her efforts might work instrumentally (by the persuasive force of what she says) and by example, directly showing the value of the kinds of engagement of which this is one instance. Such cases do seem intelligible, but notice that in this kind of case, the part-whole relation between the agent's activities and the goal she is pursuing cannot *transfer motivation*. She is motivated to her outreach activities because they will get other students involved (i.e., because of their instrumental value) and not because they constitute one instance of the sort of involvement she is generally seeking. So such a model cannot help explain how desire for eudaimonia could be transferred into desire for other-regarding goals.

16. Alternatively, we can also see the part-whole relationship at the second-order by-product level in some complex cases.

17. Since Cooper compares Aristotle's view to Kant's, which also refuses to define the right in terms of any maximization of goods, it is worth noting that a formal principle like Kant's categorical imperative may occupy the Y place in a process of reflective deliberation that identifies some particular maxim X as a *specification* of the categorical imperative. If this works, then the motive to do our duty can be specified as the motive to select this specific maxim in the circumstances. Thus Cooper's model may work for a moral principle other than realizing the agent's own eudaimonia.

18. Gottlieb, "Aristotle's Ethical Egoism," 12.

19. Ibid., 13.

20. Ibid., 14. And Gottlieb supports this by reference to Aristotle's *De anima*, III.11, 434a16.

21. Later, the agent might think this second-order thought as part of reflection on her own magnanimity. I believe Aristotle thinks that this potential could even be part of her motive in acting for the sake of magnanimity (as one special species of "the noble"), for example, in rejecting some offer to speak at an exclusive club with which she wants no association, whatever the stipend, because some of its prominent members are corrupt. But this is a special case that presents special problems not present in other, garden-variety virtuous motives.

22. Gottlieb, "Aristotle's Ethical Egoism," 14.
23. Ibid., 13.
24. Ibid., 7, citing Kraut's *Aristotle on the Human Good*, chap. 2.1.
25. Ibid., 10.
26. For example, say the agent has not or cannot decide which of these ends he desires more or which of these desires he identifies with. But he sees that either way, there is a particular action that will bring him *closer* to both ends (though it will not actually bring about both ends—it could hardly do that, since we have supposed that they are logically or causally incompatible states of affairs); for example, I want both X (a Democrat) and Y (a Republican) to be elected president, so I do not want Z, who seems about to do well in a Democratic primary in New Hampshire. So I leak some damaging information about Z, although my two motives for doing so remain conflicted, ambiguous, inconsistent with themselves, or otherwise irrational.
27. Gottlieb, "Aristotle's Ethical Egoism," 10.
28. Ibid., 11.
29. For purposes of this example, we can understand acting on the "motive of duty" to mean choosing one's act because it seems intrinsically right, fair, or just according to some deontic standard distinct from the maximization of happiness or well-being for the agent or for larger collectives. I investigate this idea in chapter 11.
30. It is important to emphasize that the defense of eudaimonism I consider in this section does not derive from Derek Parfit himself but is entirely my own creation. But I make it as robust as possible, not a mere straw man.
31. Parfit, *Reasons and Persons*, 8.
32. Ibid., 19.
33. Ibid., 24.
34. Ibid., 27–28. Cf. R. M. Hare's defense of such a prohibition against torture in *Freedom and Reason* (Oxford University Press, 1963), 44, his more general defense of Mill-style indirect utilitarianism, 130–36.
35. Ibid., 28.
36. See Parfit's discussion of principles G1, G2, and G4. I note that it is much harder to accept Parfit's theses for morality and blame than for rationality, for *moral* praise and blame have been held to be level-transitive on virtually all traditional forms of deontological and virtue-based moral theories—something that reflects their embodiment of a publicity principle as a requirement of fairness in making moral judgments or in feeling moral emotions.
37. Ibid., 35.
38. Ibid., 37.
39. Ibid., 37.
40. Ibid., 47.
41. See Williams, "A Critique of Utilitarianism."
42. Ibid., 47.
43. Ibid., 48.
44. Frankfurt, "Faintest Passion," 5–16.

45. Nussbaum, *Therapy of Desire*, 15. On Aristotle's own acceptance of the analogy between ethical philosophy and medicine, see 42, 48–50, and 59–60.
46. Ibid., 23.
47. Sherman, *Fabric of Character*, 138.
48. Ibid., 128.
49. Ibid., 132.
50. Ibid., 134.
51. As Sherman puts it, "One takes on, if you like, the project of a shared conception of *eudaimonia*" (133). And the eudaimonia so conceived is not only my own: the decisions I make are affected by my sense of their implications for my friend. So "what is relevant to the decision goes beyond the *eudaimonia* of a single, isolated individual" (134). My motivation is thus not egoistic at bottom.
52. Ibid., 133.
53. Children sometimes encounter this problem when they set out too explicitly with the intention of making friends as a means to personal satisfaction, for example, to alleviate loneliness. Approaching others in this needy fashion signals to potential friends that this is a person who will not be committed to them purely or simply in the joy of projecting such a commitment but who is instead moved by a feeling of lack that he believes *having a friend* will fill. And this of course hinders the child in developing real friendships.
54. MacIntyre, *After Virtue*.
55. Ibid., 187. Note that this is my own way of breaking down and partially analyzing the definition of "practice" that MacIntyre presents in a more compact form, but I believe it is true to his meaning.
56. Ibid., 193. MacIntyre refers to this reflexive feature to distinguish "practices" in his sense from technical skills "even when directed towards some unified purpose and even if the exercise of those skills can on occasion be valued for their own sake." Taken by itself, the employment of skills to some fixed end is only *part* of a practice; it lacks the historical sense of itself and reflexive ability to extend its purposes in light of this self-awareness necessary to constitute a practice.
57. Ibid., 188.
58. David Miller, "Virtues, Practices, and Justice," in *After MacIntyre*, 250. Miller's primary concern is with the inadequacy of MacIntyre's account of justice.
59. However, this difference does not run very deep, for games are also subject to external critique, and practices retain standards of excellence *as aretaic requirements* only if they are totally reduced to utilitarian criteria concerning "the needs and purposes that predominate in a particular society" (Miller, "Virtues, Practices, and Justice," 252). In other words, to remain practices, they have to retain some autonomy in interaction with wider social concerns, criteria, and sources of critique.
60. MacIntyre, *After Virtue*, 190: "The standards are not themselves immune from criticism, but nonetheless we cannot be initiated into a practice without accepting the authority of the best standards realized so far" [in the history of the practice].
61. Ibid., 188.
62. Murdoch, *Sovereignty of the Good*, 90. This essay is also reprinted in part in Crisp and Slote, *Virtue Ethics*, 99–117. In this anthology, see 108 for the quoted passage.

63. Ibid., 86 and 88; in *Virtue Ethics*, 105 and 106–7.
64. MacIntyre, *After Virtue*, 189.
65. Ibid., 189–90.
66. Ibid., 197.
67. Karl Marx, "The Economic and Philosophic Manuscripts of 1844," in *The Marx-Engels Reader*, 2nd ed., ed. Robert Tucker (Norton, 1978), 76.
68. Ibid.
69. Erich Fromm, *Marx's Concept of Man*, 47.
70. Ibid., 79.
71. Gilbert, *Democratic Individuality*, chap. 7, 269.
72. Ibid., referring to *NE*, 1105a30-b4.
73. Ibid., 49.
74. Marx, "The Economic and Philosophic Manuscripts," 91.
75. Ibid. One might usefully compare this point to MacIntyre's emphasis on the virtues of receiving care and generosity in *Dependent Rational Animals*.
76. Ibid., 93.
77. Rawls, *Theory of Justice*, sec. 65, 426.
78. Ibid., 427.
79. Ibid., 428.
80. I have said more about this point in Davenport, "The Ethical and Religious Significance of Taciturnus's Letter."
81. Rosalind Hursthouse, *On Virtue Ethics* (Oxford University Press, 1999), 173.
82. Ibid., 180.
83. Ibid., 175.
84. More precisely, at a colloquium on his work at the University of Notre Dame during (I believe) the spring semester of 1997, MacIntyre said that he hoped and believed the chess-playing-child example and the related analysis of practices would stand the test of time even if flaws were found in all the other historical arguments in *After Virtue*.
85. Watson, "On the Primacy of Character," 449–69, 455.
86. Ibid., 457.
87. Ibid., 450.
88. Ibid., 455.
89. Ibid., 456.
90. Ibid., 457.
91. Watson, "On the Primacy of Character," 460–61.
92. Hursthouse, *On Virtue Ethics*, 167. Notably, Hursthouse attributes the claim that the metaphysical thesis defines Aristotelian naturalism to Williams and Watson (169).
93. Watson, "On the Primacy of Character," 456, 457.
94. Ibid., 458.
95. Ibid., 459. For example, "The benevolent person will be concerned that others fare well. But the moral significance of this concern stems from the fact that it is part of a virtue, not from the fact that misery and well-being are intrinsically

or ultimately bad and good respectively" (459). On the radically aretaic view, then, the benevolent person is concerned for the well-being of others simply because he judges that this concern is normal or natural: he sees such caring as part of a characteristically human life. Watson thinks that this radical view provides a "truly naturalistic" grounding for moral virtue, while the eudaimonist view does not (461). I disagree; the eudaimonist approach gives the virtuous person practical reasons for caring about noble ends, while the radically aretaic approach gives her only the descriptive judgment that she is exemplifying human nature or doing what paradigm cases of virtuous persons do. Anyone who took this as their reason for benevolent actions would, in my view, not really be acting on benevolent motives at all but rather on perverse metaphysical aspirations.

96. Ibid., 459–60. This has the odd implication that the characteristic good of humankind includes virtue, which in turn includes intrinsically valuing a characteristically human life, but not *because* it is good in some prior sense.

97. Ibid., 460.

98. Ibid., 460.

99. See Hursthouse, *On Virtue Ethics*, 178–87. I strongly agree with Hursthouse, against McDowell and Slote, that the thesis that virtues bring eudaimonia should not be treated as simply analytic or necessarily true within the outlook of a person reliably motivated by noble ends. The question remains significant, not automatically answered, and there is usually enough common ground with the egoist that arguments concerning the likely results of virtue and vice can have some rational/justificatory purchase. As I have argued in past work, something analogous to this is crucial to Kierkegaard's view that ethical criticism of aestheticism can have practical value, although ultimately a gestalt shift in the agent's attitude is required to make the transition.

100. Slote's theory has been criticized along these lines by Murphy, *Natural Law and Practical Philosophy*, 212–17. In a review essay on this book, I suggest that Slote's theory may be understood as analogous to a pure (ontological) divine command ethics, with the virtuous agent in place of God; see Davenport, "Review of Murphy." Watson also anticipates this criticism in a long note (n. 24).

101. Michael Slote, "Agent-Based Virtue Ethics," 240. However, Slote seems to think that this is problematic, since Aristotle also considers virtuous activity to be "the primary component in eudaimonia" (240, n. 2). Watson recognizes that there is no inconsistency in such view and builds it into his first version of virtue ethics; but he does not clearly admit how un-Aristotelian his second version of virtue ethics is.

102. I note that Watson apparently assumes that a teleological virtue ethics founded on a conception of eudaimonia, welfare, or (in general) good outcomes for human agents would necessarily be maximizing in its normative deliverances. I do not believe this is correct; without automatic inconsistency, one could argue that virtues involve non-maximizing moral attitudes and still say that their value comes from being essential to eudaimonia as the highest intrinsically good outcome. To achieve this, such a theory need only say that eudaimonia consists in part of holding to certain nonconsequentialist standards of action and therefore is a

good we can only strive to achieve as a holistic union of parts rather than something that comes in degrees with a maximum point that we could directly seek. This is not the same as construing eudaimonia merely as a threshold concept, which I think is foreign to the eudaimonist project (see *Kierkegaard After MacIntyre*, 292).

103. Watson, "On the Primacy of Character," 463.

104. See Davenport, "Towards an Existential Virtue Ethics."

105. For Nietzsche's theory as a species of non-eudaimonistic virtue ethics, see Christine Swanton, *Virtue Ethics*.

106. MacIntyre, *Dependent Rational Animals*, 113.

107. Ibid., 119.

108. Ibid., 114.

109. Ibid., 108.

110. Ibid., 108.

111. Ibid., 120. This conception of "just generosity" seems to be simply a nontheological version of agapē or pure neighbor-love, although MacIntyre relates it to pity, or *misericordia*, as "one of the effects of charity" and distinguishes it from charity as a state that requires grace (124–26). However, MacIntyre's analysis of just generosity does, in fact, provide a model for understanding agapē that is superior to others on the philosophical market today, including the model proposed by Emmanuel Levinas, which I criticize in past work.

112. MacIntyre, *Dependent Rational Animals*, 109.

113. Ibid., 112.

114. MacIntyre says that practical reasoning sometimes has to make reference to flourishing and thus bring explicitly into view the further end to which virtuous actions are also a means (ibid., 112). But if this means reasoning from the joint flourishing of a community, this cannot become an individual practical reasoner's goal without projective motivation.

115. Ibid., 99. It also fits the role MacIntyre gives to Marx's conception of justice, with its emphasis on desert and need, in defining the common good; see 130.

116. Ibid., 101. This idea of historically conditioned responsibilities is the central theme of a lecture series I gave in January 2002 titled "Time and Responsibility," which I hope to publish in the future.

117. Ibid., 140.

118. As MacIntyre puts it, the individual "must make" the goods of the community "her own" (ibid., 109). This is not something that follows passively from desire for one's own eudaimonia. Thus the state in which we are "neither egoists nor altruists" but committed to joint goods essential to shared flourishing (160) is an achievement of the will.

119. See Rawls, *Theory of Justice*, sec. 1, 5. One could also consider Thomas Scanlon's notion of the moral motive as directly aiming at reciprocity, or "aiming to find principles that others, *insofar as they too have this aim*, could not reasonably reject"; see Scanlon, *What We Owe to Each Other*, 191 (emphasis added). It is a common error to imagine that all contract theories conceive joint willingness as

relevant only when it can factor into self-interested motives, i.e., when joint consent can produce a good that adds to each party's material well-being.

120. Notice that major fund-raising campaigns for charitable causes or college reunion class gifts tend to employ this kind of dynamic: a number of persons (N) are willing to contribute or sign on, but only if they think that a sufficient number of other alumni (hopefully less than N) are likewise willing, and thus leading gifts may help attract a critical mass of others. It is especially noteworthy that in such cases, it is precisely the fact that others have already been generous or are willing to be if enough members of the group are that grounds the agent's commitment to participate in realizing a good that cannot be attained without such cooperation. In such cases, I believe, projective motivation is at work, since the goal lies beyond most of the participants' own simple well-being; however, the grounds for projecting the goal include not only its inherent value but also the existence of others who are willing to strive for this goal either independently or if others are. This may be in part because our belief that some goal has significant enough value to be worth projecting it depends on others not only validating this value but making it their goal along with us.

121. Drummond, "Agency, Agents, and (Sometimes) Patients," 148.

122. Ibid., 154.

123. Ibid., 150.

124. David O. Brink, "Rational Egoism, Self, and Others," 349.

125. Ibid., 352–53.

126. Ibid., 354.

127. See J. Baird Callicott, "The Conceptual Foundations of the Land Ethic"; and Arne Naess, "Ecosophy T." I do not agree with Callicott that metaphysical holism is part of Aldo Leopold's argument for his land ethic.

128. MacIntyre, *Dependent Rational Animals*, x.

129. U2, "One," from *The Joshua Tree* album.

130. We cannot, therefore, equate the rejection of social holism in favor of a metaphysics recognizing the existence of distinct individual persons with endorsement of a much more specific "liberal" version of individualism of the kind that Michael Sandel critiques as "disposed selves" or atoms in a social void; see *Liberalism and the Limits of Justice*, esp. 54–65. Even much weaker conceptions of the individuality of personal selves are sufficient to entail the falsehood of social holism.

131. Raymond Belliotti, *Happiness Is Overrated*, 87–88.

132. Ibid., 86.

133. Ibid., 85.

134. What about rejecting WET instead? As I suggest in sketching the existential core argument (chap. 4, sec. 1.2), WET probably oversimplifies the diversity of our prepurposive motives, but non-erosiac PPMs are unlikely to have the complexity or responsiveness to rational grounds that we find in purposive motives involved in virtues, friendship, the practices, and so on. Thus WET is an acceptable simplifying assumption for our task; it allows us to avoid surveying every type of prepurposive motive before looking at the primary candidates for projective motivation.

9. Divine and Human Creativity: From Plato to Levinas

1. Audi, *The Good in the Right*, 124.
2. Ibid.
3. Bradley, "Definition of Will," no. II, 149.
4. Ibid., 150.
5. Pink, *Psychology of Freedom*, 15.
6. See Goetz, "Libertarian Choice," 202.
7. Mele, *Autonomous Agents*, 37. The representational component of this definition may need refining, for it seems as though I could want *to eat* an apple simply by wanting the apple and believing that I could eat it (without, say, visualizing myself eating it). However, I still have to represent something as the object of desire.
8. In this, even if "choice" or *prohairesis* is limited to deliberation about means to ends already set, *boulēsis* is part of reason. But I would follow Eugene Garver's insightful argument that in *Topics* III, Aristotle gives us a way to think of deliberation as extending to all ends subordinate to happiness itself (see Garver, "Choosing the Good in Aristotle's *Topics*").
9. See my article, "The Essence of Eschatology."
10. A discussion of Plato's use of eschatological myths in the *Phaedo*, *Republic*, *Laws*, and elsewhere is beyond the scope of this book, but there is some evidence for a personalization of the Divine in the figure of Aphrodite in the *Seventh Letter* (335b). Plato seems to use this goddess symbol for the form of Beauty (see also *Phaedrus* 265b).
11. McPherran, "Socratic Piety in the *Euthyphro*," 296. McPherran paraphrases this argument from L. Versenji, *Socratic Piety in the Euthyphro* (University Press of America, 1982). He does not actually agree with it but protests that "Socrates clearly believes that the gods act and have given men good things" (296). I think McPherran is correct about this, but it only goes to show why Plato is forced to envision a different form of motivation for the Divine. As McPherran emphasizes, for Socrates in the *Euthyphro*, we cannot know what the chief *ergon* (function, work) of the gods is (298); but apparently by the *Timaeus*, Plato thought something could be said about this, as did Aristotle by the end of his *Metaphysics*.
12. *Republic* II, 381B. Paul Shorey's translation in *Plato: Collected Dialogues*, reads: "But God, surely, and everything that belongs to God, is in every way in the best possible state" (628).
13. *Republic* II, 381B–C.
14. This gloss explains why I am ignoring traditional objections that premise 2 is a false dilemma, since God could change in some value-neutral way that makes him neither better nor worse; see, e.g., Hasker, "Philosophical Perspective," 132. Although this objection has much force against my first reconstruction of the argument, it is less plausible for agent-caused change that is motivated in the way required by the erosiac model, as in my second reconstruction.
15. For the defender of a process conception of perfection can insist that even for God, there are goods that are not directly actualizable without going through states in which one is moving toward them but still lacking them. To lack such

goods is *not* to lack a good that one could *possibly* have now, instantly, without change. This should lead the process theologian to reject premise 7.

16. Nygren, *Agape and Eros*, 175.

17. Lovejoy, *The Great Chain of Being*, 49.

18. The motivational paradox I am emphasizing here is closely related to the metaphysical problem that Thomas Morris calls the "dilemma of created goodness." This dilemma says that either the created universe has no ontological value, in which case it was pointless to create it, or if it does have such value, then *"God plus the universe* is greater than *God alone";* see Morris, *Our Idea of God,* 142. Morris tries to resolve this problem by arguing that the Anselmian requires only that God is the greatest possible individual *being,* and this is consistent with the thesis that "the state of affairs consisting in God's sharing existence with our created universe is greater than the state of affairs consisting in God's existing in pristine isolation or solitude" (143). But while Leibniz would certainly accept both these theses, I doubt that either Plato or Anselm would have accepted the second, since *(pace* Morris) it probably entails that a perfectly good God would *have* to create whatever other beings would add value to the total state. Morris also adds that God and the world cannot constitute a single entity, which would then be greater in metaphysical perfection than God, because "it is just conceptually precluded by perfect being theology that God ever be considered a part of a larger and more valuable whole, an entity distinct from, but partially composed by God" (143). But either this directly begs the question or the Spinozist can say that the Divine must consist in the entire Chain of Being, and not just its highest member, because the totality of the Chain is the most valuable substance. So there is no evident escape for the Anselmian in either of these moves. It may help Morris's case if we believe Robert Adams's argument that since a morally perfect being can act on the motive of grace, then such a being need not create only the objectively best possible universe; see Robert M. Adams, "Must God Create the Best?" But then the motive of grace must by its nature be one kind of projective or essentially volitional motive in my sense.

19. This is the main reason for the defense of an "open" rather than "impassible" notion of divine perfection in Pinnock, Rice, Sanders, Hasker, and Basinger, *The Openness of God.* See, in particular, Richard Rice's discussion of divine agapē, and William Hasker's discussion of God as active in time.

20. To see that this is a valid inference, it can be symbolized as a syllogistic deduction: (1) Agē, (2) Ame, (3) Aēm̄ [contrapositive of 2]; (4) Agm̄ [by 1, 3, Barbara].

21. I am not, of course, attributing to Plato the notion of creation *ex nihilo.* The point also applies if the Demiurge's function is only to form a world out of undifferentiated stuff, *aperion plethos,* or prime matter. I agree with Levinas that properly understood, the very idea of creation *ex nihilo* requires giving being to things *radically other* than oneself (not mere extensions or reflections of one's mind or parts of one's substance), and this in turn requires projective motivation, which alone can aim at ends alterior to one's own being.

22. Robinson, *Plato's Psychology,* 117.

23. Ibid., 115.
24. Plato, *Philebus* 33b.
25. Ibid., 34e.
26. Ibid., 35a.
27. Ibid., 35b–b.
28. Ibid., 60c.
29. Ibid., 61a.
30. Nussbaum, *Therapy of Desire*, 256.
31. Lewis, *Problem of Pain*, chap. 3, 50–51.

32. And this ambiguity remains, we should note, in Plato's attempt to show that a perfect soul would necessarily have to will the existence of every form of value outside itself.

33. They are superfluous only in the sense that they are not erosiacally desired, not in the sense that they have no value at all. God could perhaps recognize forms of possible value that do not draw Him toward them *unless* He decides to make them the object of His purpose (and something like this may be what Lewis *meant*). This is the basic idea in projective motivation.

34. Zagzebski, *Divine Motivation Theory*, 214 (emphasis added), citing Kretzmann, "General Problem of Creation," and "Problem of Creation."

35. Ibid., 214–15.
36. Kierkegaard, *Philosophical Fragments*, 24 (IV 193).
37. Ibid., 24–25 (IV 193–94).
38. Rice, "Biblical Support for a New Perspective," 21–22.
39. Ibid., 39.
40. Nygren, *Agape and Eros*, 77, quoted from the selection in Soble, *Eros, Agape, and Philia*, 87.

41. I do not say that Nygren intends to affirm this implication of his terminology; rather, he would probably affirm something close to Lewis's own Thomistic view that the creature's very being involves its being loved by its creator (a formulation I owe to my colleague Astrid O'Brien). However, this creative love must be a form of divine agapē rather than eros if we are to avoid reintroducing the paradox of divine creativity.

42. Zagzebski, *Divine Motivation Theory*, 218. Zagzebski also suggests that creating something X for the sake of manifesting love for X, while possibly not self-interested, still treats X "as a means" in a morally objectionable way (219). As I will make clear in the next chapter, this is an overbroad notion of what constitutes treating something as a means. On this conception, the only way not to treat X as a means would be to intend X *for no reason at all*, which is not what Kant demands.

43. Ibid., 217.

44. My distinction between grounding and motivating reasons, which is employed throughout the book, is indebted to Bond, *Reason and Value*, chap. 2. In particular, I agree with Bond's thesis that "grounds for action are internally tied, not to desire, but to value or worth conceived quite independently of desire" (27). However, I disagree with the way he ultimately ties value to human welfare.

45. If, as I argue throughout subsequent chapters, projective motivation still requires some kind of ground or reason, then creation *ex nihilo* as a supreme expression of self-motivating resolve still requires a *Why*. I do not think it disrespectful

to imagine that God has a *purpose* in creating the universe (or universes). An existential theology might suggest (tentatively and with appropriate humility) that precisely because the divine being lacks nothing, it is the one and only being capable of creating alterity out of itself, generating something totally *other* than itself. That some of these beings will be capable of valuing their own existence and the existence of their universe may be reason enough to create them for a being of perfect love. It may also be that as a *by-product*, God gains something from the communion with his creatures, from the encounter with alterity that his own creative love makes possible. If we reject the Platonic conception of perfection in favor of the idea of a perfection as a process of enrichment, then it is possible for God to gain something from the alterity of creatures.

46. The same is true of every kind of life, not just moral agents, according to Paul Taylor in *Respect for Nature*, 75. Taylor says that any X has "inherent worth" if it is intrinsically better for X's good or flourishing to be realized than not, independently of any volitional being's attitudes toward X; he distinguishes X's inherent worth in this sense from any evaluation of X's merits according to criteria that some Xs meet better than others (76).

47. Soble, *Structure of Love*, 9.
48. Ibid., 5.
49. Ibid., 6.
50. Ibid., 9.
51. Ibid., 11.
52. Ibid., 13.
53. Niebuhr, *Human Nature*, 28.
54. Kahn, "Discovering the Will," 235.
55. Dihle, *Theory of Will in Classical Antiquity*.
56. Kahn, "Discovering the Will," 236–37.
57. Hauerwas, *Character and the Christian Life*, 15.
58. Buber, *I and Thou*, 60–61.
59. Tolkien, "On Fairy-Stories," in *The Monsters and the Critics and Other Essays*, 145.
60. Hofstadter, *Metamagical Themas*, 528, 530.
61. Ibid., 533, 535.
62. Larmore, *Morals of Modernity*, 84.
63. Solomon, "Virtues of a Passionate Life," 97. Solomon makes the simple error of assuming that only erosiac states of motivation have any kind of "energy" or "enthusiasm" or dynamism, and so on. Thus he fails to see that even for Nietzsche, the will isn't reducible to eros.
64. That Plato is the ultimate source of both traditions only goes to confirm Lovejoy's recognition of the tension in his views and to confirm the old maxim that Western philosophy is but a series of footnotes to Plato's dialogues.
65. Of course, the borderlines between these groups are somewhat unclear, since some of the phenomenological realists were influenced by Christian existentialists, and Levinas's ethics is in some respects simply a radicalization of Martin Buber's conception of human and divine agapē.

66. Arendt, *Life of the Mind*, pt. 2, "Willing."
67. Ibid., pt. 2, 13–14.
68. Ibid., 14.
69. Ibid., 15.
70. This is the absence that Bernard Williams, in *Shame and Necessity*, attributes to the creation of artificial expectations in modern moral philosophy.
71. Arendt, *Life of the Mind*, pt. 2, 16.
72. Ibid., 18.
73. Ibid., 19–20.
74. Ibid., 20 22.
75. And there would be much to say about this; see her discussions of Hobbes, Spinoza, Schopenhauer, Ryle, Wittgenstein, Kant, and Descartes, which I will not try to summarize here (ibid., 23–28). I find Arendt very convincing, especially regarding the motives for the continual *evasion* of the will.
76. Arendt, *Life of the Mind*, pt. 2, 29.
77. Ibid., 30.
78. Ibid., 31.
79. Ibid., 36.
80. Someone trying to rebuild a shattered life may project seemingly modest goals such as getting up the next morning on time, getting to work on time, eventually being able to buy a home, "settle down" (whatever that may mean to her), and live a halfway *normal life*—and she may have very good grounds for such projects. For her, this is courage. Similarly, someone joining a monastery might devote himself to attaining a series of little steps designed to build a lifestyle of peace. Someone else might be trying to fit in better with the alien culture in which they now live. But there are bad reasons for setting small goals as well: the agent could be trying to prove to himself that he is too inferior or worthless to attempt anything great.
81. One might compare these two aspects in her account to the objective and subjective points of view in Thomas Nagel's account in *The View from Nowhere*.
82. Arendt, *Life of the Mind*, pt. 2, 30.
83. Ibid., 31. She approvingly cites Duns Scotus as anticipating Bergson on this point.
84. Ibid., 34.
85. Ibid., 37–38.
86. Ibid., 37. Note Arendt's allusion to Heidegger's notion of "care" (*Sorge*) as the being of *Dasein*.
87. Ibid., 44.
88. Levinas, *Totality and Infinity*, 104–5.
89. See my article, "Levinas's Agapeistic Metaphysics of Morals."
90. See Sartre, *Being and Nothingness*, pt. 3, chap. I, sec. 4 ("The Look") and chap. 3 ("Concrete Relations with Others"), esp. 482 (the comparison to Hegel's Master-Slave dialectic).
91. Levinas, *Totality and Infinity*, 47.
92. Ibid., 49.

93. Lingis, *Deathbound Subjectivity*, 142.

94. This position developed in particular through Levinas's reaction to the account of our experience of the Other in Husserl's fifth *Cartesian Meditation* and its descendent in Sartre's discussion of "The Look" in *Being and Nothingness*.

95. Levinas, *Ethics and Infinity*, 96–97.

96. Ibid.

97. Compare this to Levinas's commentary on a Talmudic passage discussing how we can have any relation to God as the Infinite or unnamable *En-Sof*. We cannot say that we "think" the Absolute God, since:

> Does not this word conjure up, if not vision, then at least aim, which in its way posits another end or sets it as its target? The text we have just quoted suggests a beginning that does not move towards an end, but traces, as it were, a relation without correlate. (Levinas, *Beyond the Verse*, 165)

This is typical of his hyperbolic style; to emphasize how different this relation is from those of classical intentionality, Levinas suggests that it cannot be described as a relation to an end or content of intentionality *at all*. Whether this hyperbole makes literal sense is another question, though.

98. Levinas, *Difficult Freedom*, 10. Note again the similarity to Kant's notion of the primacy of a practical reason, the core of which is given in an absolute *faktum*.

99. Levinas, *In the Time of Nations*, 158.

100. Levinas, *Beyond the Verse*, 161.

101. Levinas, *Totality and Infinity*, 197.

102. Kant's emphasis on the moral law as the *faktum* of pure reason through which alone we know freedom and on the primacy of practical reason is passed along through Herman Cohen's philosophy to Martin Buber and thence to Levinas and Jean-Luc Nancy. Hence Levinas compares the transcendent "infinity" of the Face whose Otherness I cannot contain to the infinity of ideas in Kant's thought (*Totality and Infinity*, 196). Of course, Kant still insisted that our fundamental duty is autonomous or arises as an implicit commitment of our will that, although inescapable, can still be regarded as self-authored. Levinas departs from this view in describing our original duty as heteronomous, or absolutely external to us in origin. Yet insofar as Levinas agrees with Kant that this calling to justice and love is already presupposed by the exercise of any free agency at all, he should also accept that its authority for us is implicit in the very structure of our agency. What he adds to Kant's picture is the insight that plurality, or the presence of others, is already presupposed by the structure and exercise of free agency.

103. Westphal, "Levinas and the Immediacy of the Face," 494.

104. Levinas, *Totality and Infinity*, 218–19.

105. Jeffrey Kosky, "After the Death of God," 243. However, Kosky confuses matters by concluding that for Levinas, "Responsibility . . . is not what ordinary morality means when it uses this term: it is not an active engagement or commitment that an autonomous I undertakes at its own free initiative" (239). For, aside from Hobbesian contractualism, all theories that give objective significance to moral demands (including Kant's and Kierkegaard's) regard our basic responsibilities as prior to the choice of individual agents among alternative possibilities.

Kosky's phrasing also misleadingly suggests that Levinas recognizes no autonomy in the agent's *response* to the call of the Face.

106. Levinas, *Totality and Infinity*, 196. To signal the distinctive meaning of this concept, I usually capitalize "Desire" in this sense.

107. Ibid., 33.

108. See Levinas, *Totality and Infinity*, 254–66. On this point, I am indebted to Meredith Gunning's dissertation, "About Face."

109. Levinas, *Difficult Freedom*, 9: "The violent man does not move out of himself. He takes, he possesses. Possession denies independent existence."

110. Desmond, *Desire, Dialectic, and Otherness*, 19.

111. For example, in the same passage, Desmond suggests that a person sometimes "paradoxically purposes to be without purposes and makes it his aim to be aimless" (19). But he does not recognize that such an aesthetic will to wantonness must be projective, since it cannot be explained in erosiac terms (see chap. 12, sec. 7). He also suggests that despair wills "to annihilate desire totally" (19) but does not draw the conclusion that despair is therefore a movement of nonerosiac motivation.

112. Ibid., 20.

113. Ibid., 21.

114. Levinas, *Totality and Infinity*, 80. Levinas thinks that Plato's description of the Form of the Good as "beyond Being" suggests a transcendence that exceeds the structuring power of our cognition, that can never be *our* object.

115. Levinas here cites Plato's *Philebus* 50e ff and *Republic* 584b ff. Earlier in this chapter, I discussed the idea of pure pleasures in relation to divine motivation and found at least some warrant for Levinas's claim that the idea of "metaphysical desire" is found in the *Philebus*. However, the claim that it is found in the *Symposium*, *Phaedrus*, or *Republic* I find much more debatable. For instance, Levinas is too optimistic in suggesting that Eros as presented in the *Symposium* could be interpreted as a superabundant being, "as the desire not of what one has lost, but absolute Desire. . . . Has not Plato, in rejecting the myth of Aristophanes, caught sight of the nonnostalgic character of Desire and of philosophy?" (63). Unfortunately not: for Aristophanes' story is rejected only in favor of a more subtle erosiac analysis, and philosophy remains a longing for wisdom. Only the perfectly wise being would be at rest for Plato.

116. Levinas, "Meaning and Sense," 94.

117. Levinas, *Totality and Infinity*, 103. While I agree that Plato did catch sight of this idea in his later dialogues, I cannot see this in the notion of the Good as transcending all other essences in the *Republic*. However, if Plato meant the Good to be a form that even gods could intelligibly pursue for its own sake, then Levinas was right.

118. Levinas, "Philosophy and the Idea of Infinity," 56. Note that by "love" here Levinas is referring to *erosiac* love.

119. Levinas, *Totality and Infinity*, 63.

120. Sleszynski, *Exploring the Self in Action*, 109.

121. Vedder, "Heidegger on Desire," 357.

122. Ibid.
123. Ibid., 358–59.
124. Levinas, *Totality and Infinity*, 34.
125. Ibid.
126. See Davenport, "*Schindler's List.*" Kosky also notes that "For Levinas, infinity signifies in my unending and ever-increasing response to the face of the other" (249).
127. This is how Desmond's description of infinite desire sounds: after repletion of some particular desire, "The gnawing sense of my nothingness returns, with redoubled hunger of ever dissatisfied desire: lack again, only endless now" (*Desire, Dialectic, and Otherness*, 24). And he acknowledges that infinite desire in this sense correlates to the "absorbing god" of pantheism as the end to its suffering (29).
128. What I suspect makes Levinas hesitate to say this—and thus confuses his account—is that he recognizes that "metaphysical Desire" in his sense still shares *something* of the structure of ordinary appetites. I make clear both the similarity and difference in the direction-of-fit analysis in the last section of this chapter.
129. Levinas, *Totality and Infinity*, 50.
130. Compare this to Levinas's remark in his essay, "God and Philosophy," 163:

> But this desire is of another order than the desire involved in hedonist or eudaimonist affectivity and activity, where the desirable is invested, reached, and identified as an objective of need. . . . It is a desire that is beyond satisfaction, and, unlike a need, does not identify a term or an end. This endless desire for what is beyond being is dis-inter*estedness*, transcendence—desire for the Good.

131. Levinas, *Otherwise than Being or Beyond Essence*, 96.
132. Levinas, "God and Philosophy," 164–65.
133. Levinas, *Time and the Other*, 116.
134. Levinas, "Ethics as First Philosophy," 85; *In the Time of Nations*, 160.
135. Caputo, *Deconstruction in a Nutshell*, 140–50.
136. Levinas, *Totality and Infinity*, 77.
137. Levinas, "Ethics as First Philosophy," 85.
138. Levinas, *Totality and Infinity*, 34.
139. I am indebted to Merold Westphal for this important point.
140. Levinas, *Totality and Infinity*, 257.
141. Ibid., 63.
142. Ibid., 226–47.
143. Ibid., 237.
144. Ibid., 229.
145. Ibid., 230.
146. Ibid., 227–28.
147. Llewelyn, *Emmanuel Levinas*, 103.
148. Levinas, *Totality and Infinity*, 226.
149. Ibid., 239.
150. Levinas, *Totality and Infinity*, 88, 303.

151. Ibid., 218. He adds, in Kierkegaardian fashion and against Sartre, that:

If the subjectivity were but a deficient mode of being, the distinguishing between will and reason would indeed result in conceiving the will as arbitrary, as a pure and simple negation of an embryonic or virtual reason dormant in an I. . . . If on the contrary, the subjectivity is fixed as a separated being in relation with an other absolutely other, . . . then the will is distinguished fundamentally from the intelligible, which it must not comprehend, and into which it must not disappear, for the intelligibility of the intelligible resides precisely in ethical behavior, that is, in the responsibility to which it invites the will" (218).

152. Ibid., 166.
153. Ibid.
154. Ibid., 227. The closest that Levinas comes to Buber's insight about art is in recognizing that the will can respond to mortality by aiming at "the founding of institutions" that may endure beyond its own death (236). But this art is nonegoistic only because its motive is purely moral again; it is not an instance of projective and *nonmoral* motivation in Levinas's anthropology.
155. Ibid., 217.
156. Ibid., 65.
157. Ibid., 236.
158. Ibid., 79.
159. Ibid., 219.
160. Ibid., 240. This is in part because infinity is only fully experienced in the effort to respond positively to alterity: *"The infinity of responsibility"* is defined precisely as *"a responsibility increasing in the measure that it is assumed"* (244, emphasis in original). Passing beyond need by election, the will discovers that the resources of its interiority are "infinite—in the incessant overflowing of duty accomplished by ever broader responsibilities" (246). Note the metaphor of superabundance here again. This analysis agrees with Meredith Gunning's argument in her dissertation, "About Face," chaps. 2 and 3.
161. Clarke, "Is the Ethical Eudaimonism of St. Thomas Too Self-Centered?" 201. Father Clarke tries to articulate a way of expanding Aquinas's account of the will to accommodate the idea of taking direct "delight in the intrinsic goodness or fullness of the perfection present intrinsically in the beings known" (204). But this seems to require acknowledging that the will can be projective and thus rejecting the formal egoism implied in "the desire to share this good, [or] be united with it" (204).
162. Marcel, *Creative Fidelity*, 49.
163. Ibid., 53.
164. See Crosby, *Selfhood of the Human Person*.
165. In particular, Scheler's complex and often problematic discussion of "Eudaemonism" in his *Formalism in Ethics and Non-Formal Ethics of Values*, chap. 5, requires more space for response than I could afford here.
166. My inspiration for this term is Heideggerian: I use "projection" because it connotes throwing something out ahead of ourselves, or putting something in

the functional position of being our goal or end, instead of simply finding it in that position because of its inherent qualities. As noted in chapter 1, projection in my sense—as self-motivation through setting ends and supplementing one's given motivation to pursue ends already set—has nothing to do with projection in the Freudian or Feuerbachian sense of attributing one's own traits to others.

167. Bertocci, *Person and Primary Emotions*, 5.

168. Ibid., 7.

169. Pink, *Psychology of Freedom*, 19. Pink also notes that whereas "intention is always directed at agency," "I can want E without wanting E to be brought about by my agency" (18). So desires are not as closely related to agency as our intentions, which are both formed by and aim at *our* actions.

170. This might seem at odds with Thomas Nagel's argument that there are both "motivated and unmotivated desires," or appetites that "simply assail us" as well as desires motivated by other more basic desires and possibly other considerations (*The Possibility of Altruism*, 29). But in response, we could simply say that the motivation produced in projection is a *motivated desire* that is not formed on the basis of any unmotivated desires, and this would be perfectly compatible with Nagel's model.

171. McDowell, "Virtue and Reason," 335.

172. On this topic, see John Hick's work on the cognitive significance or factual claim-making functions of religious belief and in particular his work on "eschatological verification" in *The John Hick Reader*.

173. We need, but do not appear to possess, a term for individual or plural cognitive faith-states that would be analogous to "belief" and "beliefs" as referring not to the general types of state but rather to particular instances thereof. One cannot talk about "faiths" as one talks about "beliefs," and I have no better suggestion than "faith beliefs."

174. I defend this thesis in more detail in chapters 12 and 14.

175. I might also be motivated to pursue it, for example, by the *desire* for employment, but this would be an additional motive rather than an exclusive alternative. Projective motivation and orektic desire often overdetermine pursuit of a single goal, though their relation remains contingent, so they can come apart in different circumstances.

176. As for the other main premise 6, the weak erosiac thesis is obviously true if Plato or Aristotle have correctly analyzed our prepurposive motives (which is quite possible even if their eudaimonist claims about the erosiac nature of *all* motivation are false).

10. Radical Evil and Projective Strength of Will

1. Kent, *Virtues of the Will*, 204.

2. This model also implies inadequate conceptions of "weakness of will" and of autonomy, but these are not my focus in the present book.

3. Broadie, *Ethics with Aristotle*, 80.

4. Aristotle, *NE*, III.5, 1114b2–5 (Ross, 1759).

5. Broadie, *Ethics with Aristotle*, 78.

6. Ibid., 81. It would be better here to refer to "refraining" from action rather than simply "failing" to act. We might also think that Aristotle's view is too demanding, that it is not always the agent's fault if she is not in the emotional condition necessary for her to choose well.

7. Ibid., 82.

8. Ibid., 101.

9. Urmson, "Aristotle's Doctrine of the Mean," 160.

10. Ibid., 161.

11. Urmson, 162.

12. Although he is not quite this explicit, I take this to be the point of Urmson's analysis, 163–64.

13. Foot, "Virtues and Vices," 169.

14. Urmson, "Aristotle's Doctrine of the Mean," 164–65.

15. Foot, "Virtues and Vices," 169. Foot, however, does not as readily admit how deep a problem this is for Aristotle's theory.

16. Urmson, "Aristotle's Doctrine of the Mean," 166–67.

17. Cooper describes the state of moral virtue as the extension of rational control: "A person whose reasoned view about what is worth caring about, doing, and experiencing [the noble] was fully reflected in the way she experienced non-rational desires" is virtuous if her reason itself is practically wise or properly judges the noble (Cooper, "Reason, Moral Virtue," 83). Thus, as we see in chapter 7, moral virtue is the disposition to desire for its own sake whatever reason judges as noble.

18. Ibid., 158.

19. Kenny, *Aristotle's Theory of the Will*, 78, 80.

20. Reeve, *Practices of Reason*, 89. I include "fully" here to indicate a corrupt conception of the noble, because the term "vicious" by itself is ambiguous: the akratic's *action* can be vicious, although her bouletic wish is not, and akratic agents either do not act on their prohairetic choice (Reeve, 90) or act without any *prohairesis* (Kenny, 70, 74, 84).

21. Joseph Butler, Sermon II, "Upon Human Nature," in *Five Sermons*, 40.

22. See, e.g., Hick, "An Irenaen Theodicy." In his soul-making theodicy, Hick admits to "assuming that the essence of moral evil is selfishness, the sacrificing of others to one's own interests. It consists, in Kantian terminology, in treating others, not as ends in themselves, but as means to one's own ends" (95). The problem with this initial assumption is that there are ways of failing to respect persons as ends that are not motivated by a desire for one's own happiness or good.

23. Foot, "Virtues and Vices," 170.

24. These are the medieval equivalents for Aristotle's three forms of *orexis*: "volition, appetite, and temper," as Kenny says, citing *NE*, 1225b21–26 (*Aristotle's Theory of the Will*, 69).

25. Taylor, *Good and Evil*, 192.

26. In Kant's sense, "radical evil" is a freely chosen yet contingently universal version of original sin; no human being has a holy will. It is similar to Alvin

Plantinga's notion that all possible human persons might be such that their counterfactuals of freedom include some wrongdoing; like Kant, Plantinga exaggerates by calling such a person "transworld *depraved*" (*The Nature of Necessity*, 186). I agree with Richard Bernstein that Kant's theory explains nothing but "simply reiterates the fact that human beings who are conscious of the moral law sometimes (freely) deviate from it" (*Radical Evil*, 33; also see Arendt, *Life of the Mind*, "Willing," 118). However, Pablo Muchnik argues convincingly that Kant's notion of "diabolic evil" refers to "doing evil for evil's sake" rather than for the sake of happiness (Muchnik, "Radical Evil," 46).

27. Neiman, *Evil in Modern Thought*, xii.

28. Hannah Arendt, *Eichmann in Jerusalem*, Postscript, 287. Arendt's evidence for this claim is clear in the trial record, despite the severe personal attacks she suffered for it. However, I am less sympathetic with Arendt's implications that Eichmann was "perfectly incapable of telling right from wrong" (26). For his repeated horror on visiting death camps to my mind suggests a clear sense of the barbarity of the slaughter that he was facilitating. On this question, see Jacob Rogozinski's thoughtful response to Arendt in "Hell on Earth."

29. Ibid., 289.

30. Richard Bernstein, *Radical Evil*, 218. Most of what needs to be said about Arendt on evil has been clearly set out in Bernstein's masterful treatment, to which I am indebted.

31. Ibid., 208.

32. Ibid., 210. Compare Augustine's Neoplatonic view that "not a leaf on a tree is created without a purpose, and no human being of any kind could be superfluous" (*Free Choice of the Will*, Book III, Sec. 23, 116).

33. The term "radical evil" is often used for large-scale atrocities, "offenses against human dignity so widespread, persistent, and organized that normal moral assessment seems inappropriate" (Nino, *Radical Evil on Trial*, vii). This consequentialist sense of radicality differs markedly from my volitionalist sense.

34. In holding this to be possible, I am following the view that an action's *overall* moral worth is a function of *both* the intrinsic moral legitimacy (or broadly ethical value) of the intended act itself (including its intended consequences and the intended mode of bringing them about) and the moral value of the motive for choosing this intention. This view is shared by Kantians and Aristotelians (see Foot, *Natural Goodness*, 72–73). Thus an act that aims to bring about some minor harm might be fairly low in negative moral worth, even if its motive was utterly malicious (e.g., to harm a person just because she was morally good). However, such a perverse motive would certainly make the act *more* evil than if it aimed to bring about the same undeserved minor harm out of simple avarice or lust. The reason, according to the existential model, is that in the former case, the agent actively works up her motivation to pursue the harm rather than simply being attracted toward it by some prior inclination.

35. Taylor, *Good and Evil*, 208. This also suggests that it is difficult for any simple form of utilitarianism to account for the distinctively negative moral status of radically evil motives.

36. Feinberg, "Psychological Egoism," 550–51. However, the term "disinterested" is potentially misleading in this context, for although it correctly suggests the lack of material *self-interest* in the motive, its negative form suggests detachment or abstraction rather than the positive earnestness, projective pathos, or energetic commitment of self involved in volitional striving or caring.

37. For example, Jonathan Dancy argues that there are no people who are "attracted by evil for its own sake" (see *Moral Reasons*, 4). He suggests that those who pursue another person's suffering as a final end see it as a good and are therefore "no counter-example to the maxim that to desire something is always to desire it *sub specie boni*" (ibid., 6). But this maxim is a tautology when desire is conceived substantively as *orexis* or when it is conceived formally as any intentional purpose. Dancy ignores the crucial distinction between purposive and prepurposive motives; certainly the radically evil person sees the victim's suffering as a "good" *once* he wills it but not prior to that (i.e., he does not first apprehend it as a good that prepurposively attracts him).

38. Colin McGinn, *Ethics, Evil, and Fiction*, 83.

39. Usage is fluid here, and several of these labels might have been applied to any of these six categories. So my use of them is somewhat stipulative.

40. In this case, contra McGinn, we are talking about someone whose brute preference for witnessing or causing pain involves a "primitive fascination" with the "*quale* of pain" in others (*Ethics, Evil, and Fiction*, 81).

41. See Taylor's discussion of these cases in *Good and Evil*, 193. Feinberg seems to make a similar error in conflating "pure evil" with finding it "great fun" to see another person in agony (see Feinberg, "Evil," in *Problems at the Roots of Law*, 128).

42. Dostoevsky, *The Brothers Karamazov*, pt. 2, Book V, chap. 4, 286.

43. Ibid., 290.

44. This was presumably the case for most Roman spectators, anyway. We can also easily imagine a small minority who were activated by far more vicious motives in watching these brutalities. For example, the Emperor Commodus, as fictionally portrayed in the film *Gladiator* (dir. Ridley Scott, Universal Studios, 2000), is a person actively striving to spite his opponents, not merely a blood-sport addict.

45. Taylor, *Good and Evil*, 207.

46. Fromm, *Anatomy of Human Destructiveness*, chaps. 12, 13.

47. Arguably, such agents are distinguished not only by having such perverse desires but by being *willing to act* on them (and thus developing or even refining these tastes). They are certainly more culpable if the movement from motivation to intention is voluntary, but this does not distinguish radically evil motives.

48. Such existential emptiness seems to be the main problem with Ray, a patient with a violent personality disorder treated by Carl Goldberg (*Speaking with the Devil*, 130), though Goldberg tries to trace Ray's motives to shame caused by his mother keeping her fatal illness secret from him.

49. Kekes, "The Reflexivity of Evil," 218–19.

50. Ibid., 220. It is not so clear that such agents never had any alternative to their corrupt moral worldviews. But I am not concerned here with Kekes' main thesis that such nonautonomous agents can be held responsible for their actions

because they are not relevantly different from autonomous agents, since "ultimately no agents have control over the possession of the capacities and opportunities on which their autonomy depends" (221). His strong claim that autonomy ultimately depends on constitutive moral luck is one that existentialists must reject.

51. Katz, *Ordinary People and Extraordinary Evil*, 31–32.

52. Dostoevsky, *The Brothers Karamazov*, pt. 2, Book V, chap. 4, 286.

53. This kind of breakdown in normal moral and psychological barriers to violence and disregard for others is often thought to be crucial to explaining atrocities. For example, Adam Morton hypothesizes that there is an evolved "violence inhibiting mechanism" in normal human agents that makes us "reluctant to cause distress" to others. This "barrier" is reduced in individuals who have been "violentized" by past experience and it completely fails to operate in sociopaths, who feel no inhibition against harming others when it serves their interests (see Morton, *On Evil*, chap. 2, "The Barrier Theory of Evil," 34–50). Note that such a prepurposive inhibition could also be present to greater or lesser degrees in agents who project radically evil ends. However, Morton clearly assumes that the motives normally held in check by the relevant barriers are simply egoistic. For example, he says that violent people imagine they can get their way by inspiring fear: "the sociopath has difficulty understanding that many human acts are performed either for the sake of the interaction itself or in order to benefit others" (51); and the psychopath thinks that all moral norms limiting pursuit of one's own advantage are merely "conventional" (52). Given this analysis, it is not surprising that Morton regards traditional "virtues" as the antidote to evil because they strengthen the barrier (or conform our appetites to it), whereas "evil motivation is the failure to block action that ought not even to have been considered" (55–56). There is a category error here: the barrier failure that Morton describes may indeed be common in *decisions* to perform harmful, violent, or cruel actions (moving from motive to intention), but it does not give us a distinctive type of evil *motive*. What is missing becomes apparent when we ask how normal agents can muster the "willpower" to overcome inhibitions against causing distress (45), or what it means for agents to adopt a "strategy" to avoid being inhibited (57) rather than being *passively* desensitized to distress by extreme conditions or frequent violence in their surroundings (see the discussion in the next section).

54. Katz, *Ordinary People and Extraordinary Evil*, 65.

55. Ibid., 69.

56. Goldberg, *Speaking with the Devil*, 4 (citing Gustave Gilbert's interviews with Nazis on trial at Nuremberg).

57. Kekes, "The Reflexivity of Evil," 219.

58. Directed by Jean-Jacques Annaud (Cristaldifilm, 1986); based on the novel by Umberto Eco.

59. Katz describes how Hess strove persistently to bring his feelings into line with the grim necessity to obey, how he *willed* to become indifferent to sufferings or incapable of sympathy (*Ordinary People and Extraordinary Evil*, 69–71). Katz quotes Hess's memory of steeling himself to exterminate the Gypsies, as Hitler ordered: "Nothing surely is harder than to grit one's teeth and go through with such a thing, coldly, pitilessly, and without mercy" (70).

60. See Stump, "Sanctification, Hardening of the Heart, and Frankfurt's Concept of Free Will." However, I note that Stump does not analyze the agent's higher-order will to pitilessness, or volitional identification with anti-compassion, as a process of projective motivation. My argument that volitional identification should be understood as projective willing will be given in the sequel to this work, *Autonomy and Authenticity*.

61. Katz, *Ordinary People and Extraordinary Evil*, 13. Compare Goldberg, *Speaking with the Devil*, 13.

62. Ibid., 25–26.

63. They should really say that they "found the point of it all" along the way, but they do not wholeheartedly embrace this point right away.

64. For example, it may be easier to find meaning in the regime's ideology than in the martyrdom required by refusal, which seems so much more abstract or apparently tenuous. Or, for those who have already profited from injustice or participated in collective crimes, going forward with total abandon may seem easier to will than repentance, public remorse, and trying to make amends. For religious fanatics, it may be much easier to believe that dying to destroy the infidel will be a sure ticket into heaven than it is to face the task of trying to build a worthwhile life in this world under conditions of hardship, sorrow, and grievance due to loss, injustice, social chaos, and lack of opportunities to engage in the practices or build stable family relationships (as in Palestinian territories today). This is what is commonly meant by saying that people in such circumstances may seize on "simple answers."

65. *Macbeth*, Act 5, Scene 7, 29–31, in *Complete Works of William Shakespeare*, 1026.

66. I developed these ideas further in my comments on Gerard Bradley's "Retribution: The Forgotten End of Punishment," presented at the Natural Law Colloquium hosted by the Fordham University School of Law, April 29, 2003.

67. Henrich von Kleist, *The Marquise of O and Other Stories*, 66–67. The butchery begins when Rugera is killed by his own father, which shows how intense religious fanaticism can be.

68. See Elster, *Alchemies of the Mind*, 219, on the psychology of revenge in ancient Greece—a culture that did not clearly distinguish accidental from intentional harms. Without this distinction, of course, just redress of wrongs can never be distinguished from vengeance against anyone who has harmed us or our family—and so the pure retributive motive cannot be separated from the will to revenge. This is chief among the problems Plato finds in the timocratic honor code of archaic Greek society.

69. McGinn also recognizes this tendency of "stern and lofty judiciousness" to turn corrupt: "the person becomes obsessed with visiting sufferings on the original villains" (*Ethics, Evil, and Fiction*, 70). This is presumably also what Jean-Luc Marion has in mind when he argues that retributive justice only perpetuates evil: "our desire for justice" turns into "desire for *our* justice" (*Prolegomena to Charity*, 11). But Marion appears to deny that a pure motivation to just punishment is possible, which is an exaggeration.

70. Dickens, *Tale of Two Cities*, Book III, chap. 12, 335.

71. Ibid., Book III, chap. 14, 354.
72. Ibid., 356.
73. Ibid., 363.
74. Tolkien, *Lord of the Rings*, pt. I, "The Fellowship of the Ring," chap. 2.
75. See Rawls, *A Theory of Justice*, sec. 80, "The Problem of Envy," 530–34.
76. Properly speaking, irascible anger refers only to a sudden and strong D2 desire that is not tightly connected to judgments of injustice. Such rage can motivate terrible acts. For example, it appears that in at least two incidents, American servicemen in Iraq have gone "berserk" and slaughtered innocent civilians after friends were killed by roadside bombs. When suppressed anger and frustration explode under inhuman pressure in this way, the resulting act may be inexcusable but its culpability is mitigated in comparison to "premeditated" malice.
77. Marion, *Prolegomena to Charity*, 12.
78. Rawls, *A Theory of Justice*, 532. He notes that he is following Kant's definition in *The Metaphysics of Morals*, II, sec. 36.
79. Ibid., 533.
80. In principle, we could conceive of a third attitude that would aim at comparative *inferiority* rather than comparative superiority or equality. An agent motivated by such a desire for comparative inferiority would be willing to sacrifice first-order goods in order to widen the difference between his holdings and the holdings of his comparison target. The fact that this third attitude is rare seems to reflect the egoistic structure of interest in comparative differences in holdings; the envious or superior agents see their goal as a (complex) part of their own well-being, and this is not possible for comparative inferiority. When inferiority is willed, it is usually as a means to a more fundamental rejection of one's agency or personal value (see chap. 12, sec. 9).
81. Rousseau, "Second Discourse on Human Inequality," pt. II, in *Basic Political Writings*, 78. This reveals a similar ambiguity in the German word *Schadenfreude*, which is usually translated as malicious gloating over another's misfortune. For such gloating can be motivated by simple envy, desire for superiority, social envy-enjoyment, or volitional spite—four quite distinct motive states.
82. Ibid., 68.
83. Reid, *Essays on the Active Powers of the Human Mind*, Essay III, "Of the Principles of Action," pt. II, sec. 5, 162.
84. Ibid., 167. This tracks my distinction between irascible anger as a sudden D2 desire and moral indignation that grounds a will to retributive justice.
85. For Reid emphasizes that "the very idea of justice which enters into cool and deliberate resentment," as opposed to animal *thumos*, "tends to restrain its exercise" (ibid., 173).
86. Ibid., 162.
87. Ibid., 163.
88. Ibid., 164.
89. McGinn, *Ethics, Evil, and Fiction*, 79–80.
90. Shakespeare, *King Richard the Third*, Act I, Scene I, ll. 28–30 (*The Complete Works of William Shakespeare*, 701).

91. Ibid., Act 5, Scene 3, l. 183 (744).
92. Ibid., Act 4, Scene 2, ll. 65–66 (732).
93. *Cape Fear*, directed by Martin Scorsese (Universal Studios, 1991); based on the novel by John McDonald. Another interesting example of spite is found in the film *Star Trek II: The Wrath of Khan*, directed by Nicholas Meyer (Paramount, 1982). Khan wants to avenge what he sees as Captain Kirk's unfair punishment of him years before. But this becomes a spiteful obsession that blinds him to every other possible good that he might pursue. Eventually, out of total hatred for Kirk, Khan risks everything in his unyielding quest to destroy the *Enterprise*. When beaten, he resolves to destroy himself and the remainder of his crew as a final means to take Kirk down with him. Fittingly, he quotes Captain Ahab in Melville's *Moby Dick*: "To the last I will grapple with thee"; "From hell's heart, I stab at thee! For hate's sake, I spit my last breath at thee!"
94. *Amadeus*, directed by Milton Forman, screenplay Peter Shaffer (Republic Pictures, 1984). Based on the play by Shaffer.
95. Similarly, if we think of "meanness" as an emotional state (the inverse of affection) that is open to suffering and enjoys it but waits passively for opportunities to enjoy it rather than actively pursuing or creating them, then spite would be distinct from "meanness" as well.
96. In the discussion of Sherman's account in chapter 8, sec. 4, I suggested that something like this may also be true in noble friendship, in which not only the good of the other but also the activity of being a friend to the other (i.e., pursuing the other's good in a reciprocal relationship) is cultivated as an end-in-itself. Thus we will first and second order final ends in willing friendship.
97. See Foot, *Natural Goodness*, 78. In *Natural Law and Natural Rights*, Finnis notes that in the UN Universal Declaration of Human Rights, the right to be free from torture is included among a small number of such rights that are *unqualified* by limitations that apply to other rights in order to meet the "just requirements of morality, public order, and the general welfare in a democratic society" (Art. 29). Finnis thinks the UN Declaration is right on this point (212–13). The UN Convention Against Torture (adopted 1975, entered into force in 1987, and ratified by the United States just in 1999) also states that "No exceptional circumstances whatsoever, whether a state of war or a threat of war, internal political instability or any other public emergency, may be invoked as a justification of torture" (Art. 2, sec. 2). Yet our government seems to have violated this law several times during the Iraq war.
98. On this point, see Elster's discussion of the perverse illocutionary attitude of Stalin's regime, seen in commands that can only be followed unwillingly rather than obeyed for the sake of willing loyalty (*Sour Grapes*, 63).
99. See Hegel, *Phenomenology of Spirit*, "Lordship and Bondage," sec. 191.
100. A point that needs special emphasis in an age when new technologies for selection among or even alteration of reproductive cells will soon make selection of particular physical and mental attributes in our children increasingly feasible as time goes on.
101. This limit is perhaps explored most fully in Mary Shelley's classic dark Romance novel, *Frankenstein*, which addresses the human dream of "playing God" by *making* a being with genuine alterity.

102. Such a theology of making has radical implications that remain little explored; for instance, all human property rights are rendered merely provisional and temporary, and all artwork belongs ultimately to God, not only to the human artist, for our creative powers themselves are given by God. See the discussion of subcreation in Tolkien, "On Fairy Stories."

103. Sartre, *Being and Nothingness*, 724. The phrase is misleading, because Sartre follows Plato in assuming that motivation is erosiac (see the discussion of lack, 135) and in positing his own version of the Transcendent Principle, according to which all projects *really* aim at the unifying goal of the for-itself, whose original project "can only aim at its own being" (721). Thus our willing is always ultimately focused on our self, though not necessarily on our eudaimonia.

104. Ibid., pt. III, chap. 3. Yet one of the main ways in which human beings try to achieve this paradoxical combination is through their works, including artistic creations. This is the direction from which Tolkien takes up what is otherwise the same problem of the ultimate limit on the human projective will: it cannot rightfully project the creation of absolute alterity (or what Levinas calls creation *ex nihilo*).

105. Still, while Augustine recognizes our "perverse imitation of God" or aspiration to master all other beings, in the same chapter he argues that no human being can be so corrupted as not to desire any kind of peace (*City of God*, Book XIX, chap. 12, 868). Thus his recognition of radical evil is limited by his eudaimonist theory of human nature.

106. See Tolkien, *Lord of the Rings*, Appendix A.

107. See Augustine, *On Free Choice of the Will*, Book III, sec. 125, 122.

108. See Tolkien, *Silmarillion*, chap. 1: "Ainulindaë" or "The Music of the Ainur." Marion makes an interesting argument that suicide's deepest aim is demonic autonomy: "absolute independence that renders me master of myself and the universe" (*Prolegomena to Charity*, 15). But he conflates this will to absolute disposal over oneself with "egoism."

109. Bernstein, *Radical Evil*, 218, citing Arendt's letter in reply to Gershom Scholem's critique of *Eichmann in Jerusalem*. However, this is my interpretation of Jaspers's references to mythic greatness.

110. Ibid., 218, citing Jaspers's 1946 letter to Arendt (in *Hannah Arendt/Karl Jaspers: Correspondence 1929–69*).

111. Ibid., citing Arendt's reply to Jaspers.

112. Milton, *Paradise Lost*, Book IV, 110. Hence Kierkegaard's emphasis on the distinction between "*not being able* to understand and not *willing* to understand" (*Sickness Unto Death*, 95).

113. I mention this issue in "Towards an Existential Virtue Ethics," 302–3.

114. See MacIntyre, "Once More on Kierkegaard," 353–54, citing Aquinas, *Summa Theologica*, I–II, Qu. 78, Art. 1.

115. Compare Augustine's dogma from I Timothy 6:10: "the root of all evil is greed, that is, willing to have more than enough" (Augustine, *Free Choice of the Will*, Book III, sec. 16, 104). Foot points out that Aquinas believes one can act "as one thinks one should not," which she calls "a very radical form of badness in the

will." But for Aquinas, this occurs only in the form of *akrasia*, giving in to emotions or appetites that pull toward lower goods. He admits neither demonic autonomy nor the kind of spiritual self-destruction or "spitefulness to oneself that Dostoyevsky unforgettably described in the *Notes from the Underground*" (Foot, *Natural Goodness*, 74).

116. Steele, "Does Evil Have a Cause?" 266.
117. Ibid., 267.
118. Ibid., 269.
119. Ibid., 272.
120. Kierkegaard, *Sickness Unto Death*, 68.
121. Ibid., 69. Kierkegaard actually thinks there is one more type of radical evil beyond what I have called demonic autonomy, namely, religious despair. Taking the theological problem of evil as his ground, the agent rebels "against all existence" out of hatred of God for creating him and the world (73–74). I have left religious despair out of my catalog because the existential account in this book is (at least provisionally) independent of faith.
122. Ibid., 98. However, I think we can recognize this without appealing to revelation.
123. See my analysis in "Aquinas's Teleological Libertarianism."
124. See Williams, "Internal and External Reasons," 102.
125. Although these may be apparent only by grace or personal revelation in entering the religious stage and therefore be incommunicable directly to others.
126. As we'll see in chapter 11, this reflects Kant's idea that to act on a maxim is always to give motive force to some previously felt impulse or rational consideration.
127. See "Towards an Existential Virtue Ethics," 271–79.
128. Kierkegaard, *Sickness Unto Death*, preface, 5.
129. Ibid., pt. I, 13.
130. Kupperman, *Character*, 14.
131. Ibid., 13.
132. Ibid., 14.
133. There is still an asymmetry between evil and good on the existential account, since a radically evil will is weakened by an inability to be *entirely* wholehearted (see Davenport, "Kierkegaard, Anxiety, and the Will," 178–81).
134. Robert C. Roberts, "Will Power and the Virtues," 123.
135. Ibid., 124–25.
136. Ibid., 124. See the discussion of maintaining intrinsic motivation in chap. 12, sec. 3.
137. Ibid., 122.
138. Ibid., 124.
139. Ibid., 126.
140. Randell Helms, "Tolkien's World," 104.
141. This is the truth behind Luc Bovens's amusing argument that total self-control makes him numb, or, in Elster's words, kills one's sense of adventure (see "Two Faces of Akratics Anonymous," 232). Projective strength of will necessarily cultivates such a sense rather than destroying it.

142. Roberts, "Will Power and the Virtues," 126.

143. Here I agree with Margaret Holmgren's argument against George Harris that strength of will involves not only depth of caring but also not falling apart when disaster strikes, and the resilience to find some positive way to continue expressing or developing one's cares: "Ultimately an integral breakdown . . . is not caused by caring about others, but by self-absorption. True caring about others leads to a focus on others rather than on oneself" (Holmgren, "Strength of Character," 397). As my mother says, a strong person tries to "cope." However, this requires a sense of one's intrinsic value as a caring agent (see chap. 13, sec. 2). Also, sometimes profound and lasting grief is the only authentic response to the circumstances; being temporarily paralyzed by it need not imply giving up forever. Holmgren's compelling account is missing only a projective understanding of the virtuous motivation she describes as "steadfastness of purpose" (407), which is compatible with (and may even require) strong emotional responses. The projective conception would also clarify the important sense in which a strong will is *not* tranquil (406).

144. The closest Roberts comes to this idea is in his notion of virtues of willpower as "skills of self-management," which are more than Brandt's patterns of relative strength and weakness among desires (128). Anger management, for example, is certainly something more active than simply having other desires stronger than one's anger whose ends happen to be frustrated by feeling or expressing anger. Rather, self-management is something actively initiated by the agent, something *willed*. As Barrett said long ago, "will-strength" is distinct both from virtue and from the ability to control one's passions. It is an ability to persevere consistently and earnestly in one's tasks (*Strength of Will*, 19–20).

145. For example, Mark Pestana, "Second Order Desires."

11. Scotus and Kant: The Moral Will and Its Limits

1. Kent, *Virtues of the Will*, 200.
2. Ibid., 209. As I have suggested, this is partly because of Augustine's perception of the possibility of radical evil, which cannot be just a disorder of the sense appetite.
3. Augustine, *On Free Choice of the Will*, Book I, sec. 13, 22.
4. Ibid., 213.
5. Ibid., 202, n. 4.
6. Ibid., 215.
7. Ibid., 216.
8. Ibid., 219, referring to the *Summa Theologica*, I–II, Qu. 56, Art. 4.
9. Ibid., 219–20.
10. Ibid., 222.
11. Ibid., 223.
12. Ibid., 227.
13. Ibid., 230.
14. Ibid., 231.
15. On this idea, see Cooper, "Unity of Virtue," 265. See also Irwin's discussion of the "supremacy thesis" in his essay, "The Virtues," 40.

16. As Kent puts it, for Walter, "the virtues of the sense appetite can be said to depend on the virtues of the will" (*Virtues of the Will*, 229). And "Henry argues that the will moves itself to willing before it commands the sense appetite. The will accordingly acquires virtues before the sense appetite." (229–30).

17. Ibid., 230.

18. Ibid., 234.

19. Ibid., 234.

20. Ibid., 235–36 (emphasis added).

21. Aristotle, *Nicomachean Ethics*, III.8, 1117a1–2.

22. Plato, *Republic* IV. Also see *Meno*, 78c–e.

23. O'Connell, *Plato on the Human Paradox*, 20. O'Connell points to the passages in the *Apology* where Socrates argues that it would be wrong to cease practicing philosophy to avoid banishment or death. Similar deontological attitudes are found in the *Crito*.

24. Ibid., 19. O'Connell describes this as the thesis of "teleologism": "the (eudaemonistic) happiness we ineradicably long for will inevitably be attained by our fulfilling our (deontological) duty" (18). This is part of the broader thesis that I call "external eudaimonism" (EE; see chap. 8), and the same reply is appropriate: even if O'Connell's teleological reconciliation is accurate, this cannot function as part of the agent's motive in fulfilling her duty or acting on deontological obligation (or justice).

25. Kent, *Virtues of the Will*, 239–40.

26. Ibid., 240, referring to *Ordinatio* III, suppl. dist. 33 (Scotus, *Duns Scotus on the Will and Morality*, 330).

27. Scotus, *Oxford Commentary on the Four Books*, Book II, d.25, 35, "Principal Arguments." I discuss this point from the *De Anima* in chapter 5. Notice that a deterministic relation between prepurposive motives and intentions entails TP, but TP by itself does not entail such a deterministic relation.

28. Ibid., Reply to the First Position (a), 36.

29. Ibid., Reply to the First Position (c), 37. He adds that it explains nothing to say that the phantasm presented to the intellect has negative and positive aspects, either of which can move the will depending on which it focuses on, because if these two external motives are equal in force, the will is paralyzed, and if not, then it is determined to go one way rather than the other (Reply to the First Position (e)).

30. Ibid., Reply to the Second Position (b), 38. Compare Augustine, *On Free Choice of the Will*, Book I, sec. 12, 19–20: "For what is so much in the power of the will as the will itself?"

31. Ibid., "The Principal Arguments Are Resolved" (d), 39.

32. Wolter in Scotus, *Duns Scotus on the Will and Morality*, Introduction, 31; also see 39 on *Ordinatio* II, dist. 37, q.2.

33. See Bernardine Bonansea, "Duns Scotus's Voluntarism," 105–8. I am uncertain of the history here, since Wolter describes the origin of the text inserted in later editions of the *Oxford Commentary* somewhat differently from Bonansea. See Wolter in Scotus, *Duns Scotus on the Will and Morality*, Introduction, 38.

34. Bonansea, "Duns Scotus's Voluntarism," 109.

35. Ibid., 110–11. On practical knowledge as inclining the will, see Scotus, *Duns Scotus on the Will and Morality*, 33. This seems to bring Scotus's view closer to Randolph Clarke's theory of agent causation, in which reasons exercise a causal influence on intentions.

36. In the Wadding reprint of Scotus's *Opera omnia*, tome VII, this work is entitled *Quaestiones subtilissimae super libros Metaphysicae Aristotelis*.

37. Actually Scotus, being overly charitable, denies that Aristotle really intended any such principle.

38. Wolter in Scotus, *Duns Scotus on the Will and Morality*, Introduction, 36.

39. Ibid. On this topic, see my discussion of existential freedom in "Towards an Existential Virtue Ethics," 280–81.

40. Kent, "Happiness and the Willing Agent," 61.

41. Bonansea, "Duns Scotus's Voluntarism," 86. However, Kent denies that Scotus really understands the will as "rational appetite:" see Kent, "Happiness and the Willing Agent," 61.

42. Bonansea, "Duns Scotus's Voluntarism," 87.

43. Ibid., 89, referring to the *Ordinatio*, Book One of the *Opus Oxoniense*, I, d.1, nn.16–17; II, 10–11; and *Opus Oxoniense*, II, d.43, qu.2, n.2; XIII, 493b–94a. However, Bonansea also notes Scotus's doubts about radical evil; on this point, see Arendt, *Life of the Mind*, pt. 2, 131.

44. Arendt, *Life of the Mind*, pt. 2, 143. Arendt adds that the will can sustain its own inherent delight since it is not a "mere desire to possess," which must cease "once the object is possessed" (143).

45. Bonansea, "Duns Scotus's Voluntarism," 90.

46. Ibid., 90–91.

47. Ibid., 91. For the relevant text, see *Ordinatio* IV, suppl. d.49, qq.9–10, Art.2 (Scotus, *Duns Scotus on the Will and Morality*, 187–89). Scotus's arguments on these points seem conclusive to me.

48. Wolter in Scotus, *Duns Scotus on the Will and Morality*, Introduction, 39.

49. *Ordinatio* IV, suppl. d.49, qq.9–10, Art.2 (Scotus, *Duns Scotus on the Will and Morality*, 189).

50. Wolter in ibid., Introduction, 39–40.

51. Boler, "Transcending the Natural," 110.

52. *Ordinatio* III, suppl. d.26 (Scotus, *Duns Scotus on the Will and Morality*, 179).

53. *Ordinatio* IV, suppl. d.49, qq.9–10, Art.1 (Scotus, *Duns Scotus on the Will and Morality*, 185).

54. *Ordinatio* III, d.17 (Scotus, *Duns Scotus on the Will and Morality*, 183).

55. *Ordinatio* IV, suppl. d.49, qq.9–10 (Scotus, *Duns Scotus on the Will and Morality*, 183).

56. Boler, "Transcending the Natural," 112.

57. Ibid., 113.

58. Ibid., 117. Although Boler finds Scotus's sense of "reason" somewhat paradoxical, what Scotus has in mind is apparently a reason that can discern intrinsic values unrelated to its own being or to the realization of its nature. Reason is

neither the slave of the appetites nor just the guide to happiness but the capacity to reach beyond oneself to values with the kind of radical *alterity* that Frankl's will to meaning requires (see chap. 12, sec. 5).

59. Ibid., 116. This is a clearer expression of Arendt's point that for Scotus, a human person can transcend his given nature or "factuality" (Arendt, *Life of the Mind*, pt. 2, 129).

60. Arendt, *Life of the Mind*, pt. 2, 131.

61. Boler, "Transcending the Natural," 122. As Boler points out, for Scotus, the motive of justice means loving something in itself, or for its own intrinsic value (118–19, quoting from *Ordinatio* II, d.6, q.2, n.11 [Scotus, *Duns Scotus on the Will and Morality*, 472–77]). Although Scotus and Anselm may not conceive the criteria of "rightness" for such proper love in terms of any formal universalizability test, they do not conceive it in eudaimonist terms either.

62. Arendt, *Life of the Mind*, pt. 2, 136. In a related passage, Arendt recognizes that for Aquinas, free choice is merely prohairetic: "*liberum arbitrium*" is only "free to select the means to a pre-designed end." By contrast, Scotus holds that the will "freely designs ends that are chosen for their own sakes." (132). What Arendt means is that such projected goals are pure rather than selected to promote the agent's well-being, but her terminology does not sufficiently reflect the key distinction between the *purity* and *finality* of ends. For example, she says that Aquinas never considers that "there could be an *activity* that has its end in itself" (123), which seems false; but what she means is that an activity such as a process of loving devotion could have an *agent-transcending* value for which the agent wills it.

63. Boler, "Transcending the Natural," 120.

64. *Ordinatio* III, suppl. d.27, Art.1 (Scotus, *Duns Scotus on the Will and Morality*, 425).

65. Ibid., Art.3, 435.

66. Scotus does distinguish between "the will itself in a purely natural state," including its freedom and two basic inclinations, and "the same will as informed by gifts of grace": *Ordinatio* IV, suppl. d.49, qq.9–10 (Scotus, *Duns Scotus on the Will and Morality*, 183). But its natural inclination to justice enables the will to posit ends that would have required infused grace in Aquinas's account.

67. Wolter in ibid., Introduction, 40.

68. Ibid., 179.

69. Ibid., Art.2 (Scotus, *Duns Scotus on the Will and Morality*, 195). However, Scotus does not go so far as to say that we can will misery or evil per se. His position is subtle because he holds in this section *both* that one cannot positively will to be miserable or nill being happy (since the appetite for eudaimonia remains natural and inevitable in all human agents) *and yet* that this does not imply that in every action, one wills happiness or nills misery necessarily. This is possible because the will can take a neutral attitude instead: when the intellect shows the will the possibility of happiness, "I grant that in most cases it will have volition, but it does not necessarily have any act," since it "can suspend itself from eliciting any act in particular with regard to this or that" (195). Scotus is picking up here on Aquinas's idea that the will can actively refrain from inner action or from making

any definite decision, but he adds that the will can posit and seek ends that are contrary to happiness, knowing that they are destructive, but not specifically *because* they are evil (e.g., fornication, 197). Thus the thesis that we do not will misery for its own sake involves denying radically evil volition; yet Scotus undermines the analysis of evil as a mere privation of the good.

70. Ibid., Art.1, 427.

71. Ibid., Art.2, 429.

72. Ibid. He adds that "they speak most improperly who claim that God is the object of charity insofar as he is the beatific object," if by this they mean the object of an act motivated by desire for beatitude (431), which is the goal of "the affection for the advantageous" (Art.3, 435).

73. *Ordinatio* II, d.39 (Scotus, *Duns Scotus on the Will and Morality*, 201–3).

74. Ibid., Art.3, 437. Scotus describes our agapic regard for human neighbors as part of agapic love for God, because the latter must be nonjealous, willing that all other persons capable of it also love God in the agapic sense (suppl. d.28, Art. I, 449–51). I think this account is inadequate, for it seems to allow only for indirect neighbor love and it overemphasizes jealousy as the root of all radical evil.

75. Wolter in ibid., Introduction, 93.

76. Ibid., Introduction, 92.

77. Aquinas, *Summa Theologica*, I–II, Qu. III, Art. 4, Obj. 5 (Oesterle, 32).

78. See my discussion of Augustine's conception of the good higher-order will in "Liberty of the Higher-Order Will," 441. Arendt simply says that for Augustine, the last end and happiness of human beings is love. She correctly recognizes that Aquinas cannot accept this theory because "For him, a love without desire is unthinkable" (*Life of the Mind*, pt. 2, 122).

79. For Aquinas's reply to Objection 5 seems to miss the point; he acknowledges only that "a good will, inasmuch as it is an inclination of the will, is posited among the good things that make a man happy," not that we can form a will to such a good first-order will as an end-in-itself (Oesterle, 33).

80. Aquinas, *Summa Theologica*, I–II, Qu. III, Art. 4, Respondo (Oesterle, 32).

81. Augustine, *On Free Choice of the Will*, Book III, sec. 3. When Augustine says that "if we will, and yet the will remains absent, then we are not really willing at all" (77), he is best understood as arguing that decision is immediately self-implementing: to will in the sense of deciding *is* to form an intention; hence if no action-guiding purpose arises, then one has not decided.

82. Aquinas, *Summa Theologica*, I–II, Qu. II, Art. 8, Respondo (Oesterle, 25).

83. Ibid., Qu. II, Art. 6, Obj. 2 (Oesterle, 22). Here Aquinas is discussing the thesis that happiness consists in pleasure, which he rejects, but his statement about the nature of ends is perfectly general and not rejected in his response.

84. Ibid., Qu. III, Art. 4, Rep. 5 (Oesterle, 33).

85. Ibid., Qu. IV, Art. 4, Respondo (Oesterle, 45). Notice that this distinction also applies to Kierkegaard's similar thesis that purity of heart (which is another term for rectitude) consists in placing God above all temporal goods. See Kierkegaard, "On the Occasion of a Confession."

86. Kant, *Groundwork* I, 395 (Paton, 62).

87. Ibid., 396 (Paton, 64).
88. Ibid., 396 (Paton, 64).
89. Ibid., 396 (Paton, 63).
90. Ibid.
91. This qualifier is necessary because, given *any* account of our formal telos whatsoever, it is always possible to *define* some sense of "good for the agent" as "fulfilling her formal telos." For example, Spaemann simply defines a life "turning out well" as a life that realizes whatever it is that is common to all intentional action (*Happiness and Benevolence*, 8). But as I have argued, the eudaimonia thesis has more content than this; it is not an empty tautology. For a life to turn out well in the Franciscan or Kantian sense is for the agent to achieve volitional rectitude, which is not a possible variant of eudaimonia as a motivating end.
92. The thesis that individual happiness is not our formal telos is not unique to deontological thinkers, of course. It is also found in Mill's acceptance of Carlyle's point that nobility requires "*Entsagen*," or willingness to "do without happiness" (*Utilitarianism*, chap. 2, 12). Mill's own conception of moral motivation implies that "it is possible to do without happiness" in sacrificing oneself for the greater good of a larger community (ibid., 15). But although Mill stands in basic agreement with Kant against Aristotle on this point, he still defines our highest end in terms of joint *eudaimonia* or maximal shared happiness. Nor does he recognize that positing such an end requires projective motivation; like Hume and Rousseau, he thinks that this motive can be developed out of natural prepurposive sympathetic emotions, "the social feelings of mankind—the desire to be in unity with our fellow creatures" (ibid., chap. 3, 30).
93. *Groundwork* I, 398 (Paton, 66).
94. Ibid., 399 (Paton, 67).
95. Murphy, *Natural Law and Practical Rationality*, 169.
96. Korsgaard, Introduction to Kant's *Groundwork of the Metaphysics of Morals*, tr. Mary Gregor, xiv. The four examples are the prudent shopkeeper, the despairing man who rejects suicide on principle, the philanthropist (who comes in sympathetic and unsympathetic versions), and the gout sufferer who rejects indulgence on principle rather than prudence.
97. Kant, *Groundwork* I, 399–400 (Paton 67–68) (emphasis in original). The four examples are the prudent shopkeeper, the despairing man who rejects suicide on principle, the philanthropist (who comes in sympathetic and unsympathetic versions), and the gout sufferer who rejects indulgence on principle rather than prudence.
98. Ibid., 400 (Paton, 68). A somewhat less awkward translation of this passage is found in the newer Cambridge edition by Mary Gregor (13).
99. In Part II, in the note defining inclination and interest, Kant contrasts "taking an interest in something" with "acting from interest" in it: "The first expression signifies practical interest in the action; the second pathological interest in the object of the action" (*Groundwork* II, 414, note; Paton 81). Note that only the second, desiderative kind of "interest" focuses exclusively on the object of the intention or purpose, since moral motivation is presumed to evaluate both the end *and* the means we intend to use in pursuing it.

100. Kant develops this idea in the preface to the *Groundwork*, where he argues that:

> Every one must admit that a law has to carry with it absolute necessity if it is to be valid morally—valid, that is, as a ground of obligation; that the command, "Thou shalt not lie" could not hold merely for men, other rational beings having no obligation to abide by it—and similarly with all other genuine moral laws. (*Groundwork* I, 389, Paton 57)

101. While this principle remains controversial, it has been well defended by Haji, who also provides a useful interpretation of the "can" clause; see *Deontic Morality and Control*, chap. 3.

102. I discuss Korsgaard's defense of this thesis, which I call the Kantian principle of action, in chap. 3, sec. 3.3. Note how it contrasts with Aristotle's view, according to which something like a maxim is involved *only* in deliberative choice (*prohairesis*), following from *boulēsis* or D3 desire.

103. This, of course, is the third proposition at *Groundwork* I, 400 (Paton 68; italics omitted).

104. This helps resolve the problem discussed by Palmquist in his essay, "Is Duty Kant's 'Motive' for Moral Action?" 171.

105. See Vedder, "Heidegger on Desire," 355.

106. *Groundwork* I, 400 (Paton 68).

107. Kant's point obviously cannot apply to states of affairs that include relational properties mentioning an agent-causal genesis, such as the property of "being produced by the intentional action of Hegel." The product-value of our realized purposes is assumed to be separable from this kind of relation to an agent's will; it does not supervene on such agent-related properties.

108. *Groundwork* I, 401 (Paton, 69) (emphasis added).

109. Ameriks offers a valuable summary of the recent literature in his essay, "Kant on the Good Will." My reading corresponds to what Ameriks calls Paton's "particular intention view" (193): when Kant says that only the good will is "good without qualification," he means that natural goods, including nonmorally admirable character traits such as cleverness, can all be misused (a point that comes from Plato through the Stoics). Thus his thesis is that only the good will is a *morally* unqualified good. There are contexts in which a good will is combined with qualities that have a negative natural value, such as stupidity (195); but though the moral motivation of the stupid man is not an unqualified good *simpliciter*, it remains a morally unqualified good. So interpreted, Kant's thesis is not quite a tautology, because it still tells us something important about the status of the second-order will to justice or fairness (see note 127 below).

110. Ameriks, "Kant, Hume, and the Problem of Moral Motivation," 97. A German version of this essay has appeared as "Kant und das Problem der moralischen Motivation."

111. In "The Ongoing Relevance of the Franciscan Tradition," Kent argues that Scotus understands this motive more broadly than Kant as including forms of agapic love (65).

112. Kant, *Groundwork* I, 401 (Paton, 68).

113. Ibid., 401, n. ** (Paton, 69) (emphasis in original).
114. Ibid.
115. *Groundwork* II, 418 (Paton, 85). Happiness is presented here not only as a maximizing ideal for well-being but as a totality of the kind that leads to antinomies in the *Critique of Pure Reason*. In the practical realm, the antinomy of the eudaimonist ideal is such that no "determinate concept" of this blessed state can even be formed, let alone regulate the will. This is because "happiness is an Ideal, not of Reason, but of imagination—an Ideal resting on merely empirical grounds, of which it is vain to expect that they should determine an action by which we could attain the totality of a series of consequences which is in fact infinite" (418–19; Paton, 86). Kant's point is closely related to my claim that there may be no single best combination of the final ends worth pursuing but rather a plurality of incommensurable combinations with sufficient practical coherence (see chap. 7, sec. 8, and "Towards an Existential Virtue Ethics"). Yet Rawls and others have shown that a good number of things that are at least general in content and empirically universal in application can be said about both happiness and the sort of rational agent capable of forming a conception of its good. The transcendental-pragmatic study of happiness is still vital for normative ethics and theories of justice, even if it is not determinate enough to pick out a single best type of life.
116. See Korsgaard, *The Sources of Normativity*, Lecture 3.
117. Kant, *Groundwork* I, 402–3 (Paton, 69–70).
118. Ameriks, "Kant, Hume, and the Problem of Moral Motivation," 92. See Kant, *Critique of Practical Reason*, chap. I, Theorem II, Corollary.
119. Kant, *Critique of Practical Reason*, Theorem II, Remark I, Ak. 22–24, 21–22. Kant's claim seems to be that these more refined or "cultured" desires are still commensurable with lower "sensual" appetites and appetites for entertainment, which can often prevail over the former. But my analysis of practices in chapter 8 shows that in some of the cases Kant considers, projective motivation is more likely than refined but still formally egoistic desire.
120. Ibid., Theorem I, Ak. 21, 19–20.
121. Kent notes that Scotus's conception of the appetite for happiness is broader than Kant's, since it includes desires that are not hedonistic: see "Ongoing Relevance of the Franciscan Tradition," 64–65.
122. Ibid., Theorem III, Remark II, Ak. 27, 26.
123. Ibid., sec. 8, Theorem IV, Remark I, Ak. 35, 35 (italics omitted).
124. Ibid., "Dialectic of Pure Practical Reason," Ak. 109, 115.
125. Watson, *Tradition(s)*, 107.
126. Thus Watson is not quite right to infer from Kant's remark that happiness is necessarily the desire of every finite rational being that "Willing per se is necessarily involved with happiness" (*Tradition(s)*, 106). This conflates the ubiquity thesis with the eudaimonia thesis. Kant identifies volition with an executive agency that forms and enacts intentions and he holds that this agency can intend ends irrespective of their product-value for the agent's well-being (even when the agent believes that they have such value). Nor does the inevitable *reference* to ends in our intentions imply that all our ends are chosen because of their perceived relation to our own happiness, although it *does* imply that even decisions to form intentions

on moral grounds must have some discernible end or goal with reference to which we can define a *non-eudaimonistic* notion of the "Good" that is dependent on and limited by (though not reducible to) the prior ideal of the "Right."

127. This resistance is apparent in the opening claim of the *Groundwork* which, as Otfried Höffe argues, implies that "In contrast to traditional moral philosophy, absolute goodness does not consist in a supreme object of the will . . . such as Aristotle's happiness, but in the good will itself" (Höffe, *Immanuel Kant*, 142).

128. Ameriks, "Kant, Hume, and the Problem of Moral Motivation," 99.

129. Kant, *Critique of Practical Reason*, sec. 7, "The Fundamental Law of Pure Practical Reason," Ak. 32, 32. This is what I called the Kantian principle of action (chap. 3, sec. 3).

130. Korsgaard, *The Sources of Normativity*, Lecture 3, 94.

131. Kant, *Critique of Practical Reason*, "The Principles of Pure Practical Reason," Remark II, Ak. 36, 37.

132. Ibid., "The Concept of an Object of Pure Practical Reason," Ak. 60, 62.

133. Of course, some Kant scholars use "laws" rather than "rules" for relating ends and means in maxims. Thus Höffe says that for Kant, "The capacity to act according to representations of laws is also called the will, so practical reason is simply the capacity to will" (Höffe, *Immanuel Kant*, 139).

134. Allison, "Spontaneity and Autonomy in Kant's Conception of the Self," 11.

135. As Allison says, according to Kant's incorporation principle, which covers "actions motivated by inclination as well as purely moral considerations," "although a finite rational agent is still sensuously or 'pathologically' affected, that is to say, it finds itself with a set of given inclinations and desires, which provide possible motives or reasons to act, it is not causally necessitated to act on the basis of any of them" (ibid., 13).

136. See Allison's discussion of the incorporation thesis in *Kant's Theory of Freedom*, chap. 2, 29–53; and in "Spontaneity and Autonomy in Kant's Conception of the Self."

137. Guyer, Review of Herman, *The Practice of Moral Judgment*, 406.

138. This follows unless the conditions for motivation are different in lower animals, which might be a possible Kantian response. Then Kant's thesis would be that in any rational being, her practical freedom or power of spontaneously determining motives by the incorporation of reasons into maxims prevents unincorporated incentives that *would* count as motivating animals from motivating such a rational being. This position, which begins a line of thought leading all the way to Sartre, implies that we can never be *unfreely motivated*, or moved against our will; but this view runs up against difficult counterexamples in psychology. Such a view probably results from linking motivation very strongly with action, so that having a motive entails an attempt to act on it. If combined with the idea that a rational being cannot act on a motive without freely "consenting," it follows that a ground must have consent to become a motive. But it is more plausible to hold that we can acquire motives without consent, though action on them may always require some type of consent by the agent.

139. Herman, "On the Value of Acting from the Motive of Duty," 11–12 (emphasis in original).

140. C. Nussbaum, "Kant's Changing Conception of the Causality of the Will," 269. Nussbaum emphasizes that the problem of understanding how the will can be noumenally free and yet initiate causal sequences in a closed and determined physical order arises both for the empirical will and for the pure will on Kant's account.

141. Allison, "Kant on Freedom," 126. Allison's use here of the term "projection" is convenient and suggestive for my purposes.

142. Ibid. (emphasis in original).

143. Höffe, *Immanuel Kant*, 139.

144. Its projective structure entails that a motive is "weakly independent" in this sense, which Kant extends to *all* human motivation. It also entails that the motivation is "strongly independent" of *desire* or inclination in Kant's sense, and in this sense projective motivation is psychologically *autonomous*. But, pace Kant, it does not entail impartial moral concern, because the considerations that ground projections may be contingent to the person or not motivated by the universalizability of these reasons—even if she thinks that they are universalizable.

145. As Allison has argued, autonomy means "independence" not only in the sense represented by "the capacity of the will to determine itself to act on the basis of self-imposed principles (which would include heteronomous principles)" but also in the sense that the will "recogniz[es] sufficient reasons to act that do not stem (even indirectly) from its needs as a sensuous being," as do the reasons made sufficient in heteronomous maxims or intentions (see Allison, "Spontaneity and Autonomy," 18).

146. Rauscher, "Kant's Conflation of Pure Practical Reason and Will," 579. Rauscher here cites the first *Critique* A802/B831.

147. As Allison notes, "heteronomy" is frequently misunderstood as "as simple lack of agency, a complete subjection of the will to the 'causality of nature'" (Allison, "Spontaneity and Autonomy," 17). Ameriks also cites Allison's point that it seems to be logically possible that motivational independence from desires "could take a non-moral form" (Ameriks, "Kant and Hegel on Freedom," 227).

148. Korsgaard, *The Sources of Normativity*, Lecture 3, 98. Alternatively, Korsgaard may mean that the will is always autonomous in the sense that it is always *under* the moral law, although it does not always live up to this obligation or act according to the law of its own freedom. Korsgaard also risks reinforcing this misunderstanding when she writes that for Kant, "The free will must be entirely self-determining" (97). For this is true *only* in the sense that prepurposive desires cannot *by themselves* determine the will for Kant, any more than they can for Scotus. Still, in many cases, without such prepurposive desires, the will would have no natural inclinations to adopt or incorporate; so the will often depends on the experience of natural and learned inclinations for Kant.

149. Ameriks argues that Kant's strongest conception of autonomy actually combines both these two conditions: our intention incorporates a "formal" or pure moral content not derivable from the lower faculty of desire, and our willing is the

"ultimate" efficient cause of our intention (Ameriks, "'Pure Reason of Itself Alone,'" 252–53). On this view, an autonomous will is both projectively motivated and spontaneous in the sense of transcendental freedom. For the sake of clarity, I have separated these two aspects and use "autonomy" for the former, that is for projective willing that does not "borrow" its motive from prepurposive desires. This entails that an autonomous intention is efficiently caused by the will rather than by prior desires, but not that willing itself is an ultimate cause.

150. Allison, *Kant's Theory of Freedom*, 98.

151. On this topic, see my paper, "From Autonomy to Morality: A Gap in Kant's Deduction of the Categorical Imperative" (unpublished).

152. Kant, *Critique of Practical Reason*, sec. 6, Problem II, Ak. 30, 29.

153. For example, deontic projection may figure prominently in citizens' having a "sense of justice" in Rawls's sense. For citizens must project the end of building basic political institutions that fellow citizens should count as substantively equal and fair from an impartial perspective, if they are to be committed to "justice" in the deontological sense.

154. Korsgaard, *The Sources of Normativity*, Lecture 3, 101 and 120–21.

155. Ibid., 101.

156. Ibid., Reply to Critics, 240.

157. Ibid., 119.

158. Ibid., 120.

159. Ibid., 121.

160. Gowans, "Practical Identities and Autonomy," 550.

161. Ibid., 551.

162. Ibid., 554–55.

163. Ibid., 557.

164. Ibid., 561.

165. Throughout I use the term "libertarianism" here to include both source-incompatibilist conceptions according to which responsibility requires agent-causation, and leeway-incompatibilist positions according to which responsibility requires the power, starting from a single state of affairs, to bring about any one of a morally significant range of alternative possible intentions. Leeway-liberty implies that the person is an uncaused source of intentions (though not necessarily an agent-cause), but being a spontaneous source of intentions may not entail leeway (at least some source-incompatibilists do not think leeway is required for responsibility). However, Kant, like Aristotle, does not seem to distinguish these two types of incompatibilist freedom in the efficient causation of intention.

166. Pink, *Psychology of Freedom*, 15–16.

167. Ibid., 6.

168. Ibid., 29.

169. Ibid., 23. Keep in mind that Pink uses "desire" in a generic, formally open sense. He does not offer a theory of motivation distinguishing between "desire" in various substantive senses and other types of motivation. So for him, acting against your most rational "desire" can only be akratic. On my account, by contrast, projections come in both akratic and nonakratic varieties.

170. Ibid., 30–31.

171. Steiner, *The Philosophy of Spiritual Activity*, 42 (emphasis in original).

172. As Steiner's quote from Robert Hamerling indicates, this worry about arbitrariness has led philosophers who conceive volition as executive agency to reject libertarian freedom:

> Should freedom of the will consist in being able to will something without reason, without a motive? But what does it mean to will something, other than to *have a reason* to do or strive for this rather than that? To will something without a reason, without a motive, would mean to will something *without willing it*. The concept of will is inseparable from that of motive. Without a motive to determine it, the will is an empty ability. (see Steiner, 41, quoting Hamerling's *Atomistik des Willens* [Hamburg, 1891], 2 vols., 213) (emphasis in original).

173. Ameriks, "Kant and Hegel on Freedom," 221.

174. Rauscher, "Kant's Conflation of Pure Practical Reason and Will," 579.

175. Ameriks, "Kant and Hegel on Freedom," 220. Ameriks's skepticism here depends in part on his view that the approach Kant takes in the *Critique of Practical Reason* after his "great reversal" is "vulnerable to charges of dogmatism" since the epistemic possibility remains that the connection between moral motivation and liberty is illusory. See Ameriks, "Pure Reason of Itself Alone," 254.

176. Ameriks, "Kant and Hegel on Freedom," 224. The citation within the extract is to Kant's *Critique of Pure Reason* (emphasis in original).

177. Ibid., 40.

178. This need not imply, however, that the agent *identifies* with these reasons or the motives they sanction in the stronger Frankfurtian sense of a wholehearted commitment to them. But it does force us to reconceive "wanton" personal agents (or wantons who can be held responsible) as still acting on maxims, rather than moved *brutum*.

179. Rauscher, "Kant's Conflation of Pure Practical Reason and Will," 583.

180. Allison, "Spontaneity and Autonomy," 16.

181. Allison, "Kant on Freedom," 127.

182. Ibid., 126.

183. Ibid., 127.

184. Ameriks, "Kant and Hegel on Freedom," 226. In particular, Ameriks thinks Kant fails to respond adequately to the Leibnizian, Wolffian, and Spinozistic compatibilisms of his day.

185. A simple symbolic reconstruction of this argument may be helpful. Where S = our seeing ourselves as moral agents (the standpoint of agency); D = "we can see ourselves as projecting ends for deontic reasons"; M = "the concept of moral necessity is intelligible to us"; C = "we can understand the concept of possible but nonactual actions, decisions, intentions, and motives of ours"; and L = "we enjoy leeway-libertarian freedom," the argument is:

1. $S \to D$
2. $D \to M$

3. M → C
4. ¬L → ¬C
5. C → L [4, MT]
6. S → L [1, 2, 3, 5, HS]

186. Note that the argument does not require that agents who see themselves as responsible must have a *reflective articulation* of the relevant modal concepts; a person may employ these concepts without naming them or having any theory of them. Also note that a stronger conclusion would follow if we could defend premise 4 as a thesis about the intelligibility of modal concepts *in general*. Premise 4 would then say that we possess the concept of nonactual possibilities only because of our leeway-libertarian freedom. This is not to suggest that we learn that things could be otherwise than they actually are from the experience of making choices (for, obviously, we never *experience* choosing otherwise than we actually do). Rather, the idea is that the concept of nonactual possibilities is innate in our repertoire (and brought to the interpretation of experience) precisely because it is required for our exercise of leeway-libertarian power. This strong version of premise 4 claims that the libertarian hypothesis is the best explanation of why we have modal beliefs and knowledge. It could be defended on the grounds that empirical explanations of our modal concepts fail and other *a priori* explanations remain ad hoc, whereas the power to bring about alternative decisions (starting from the same initial state) would clearly have to involve the ability to think of these options as *possibilities that might not be actualized*. Thus having such a power would explain why we have to have the basic concept of nonactual but possible states of affairs from which all other modal concepts are built. However, this stronger argument would probably not be compatible with Kant's epistemology (see Ameriks, "Pure Reason of Itself Alone," 259).

187. I still consider this a transcendental deduction, though it starts from *moral* experience rather than just experience. But its experiential premises do not include the "efficient" causal spontaneity of the agent. Contrast Ameriks, "Pure Reason of Itself Alone," 257.

188. Ibid., 222.

189. Ibid., 222. Allison also uses the term "two-aspect view" for his interpretation, but he means by this only that there are two epistemic perspectives, "two 'points of view' or 'ways of considering'" things (Allison, "Kant on Freedom," 128), rather than two real aspects in the metaphysical sense (which is still distinct, as Ameriks insists, from a full *two-worlds* or double-entity metaphysics).

190. Ameriks, "Reinhold's Challenge: Systematic Philosophy for the Public," msp. 22 (emphasis in original). It is difficult to say exactly how Kant thought agent-causation at the noumenal level and deterministic physical causation at the phenomenal level would mesh. I suggest that his proposal is an overdetermination model in which free decisions agent-cause physical events (D events) that also have natural event-causes. It is then nomologically possible for a given D event to happen with only its natural cause, since the agent-cause can be absent.

191. This may be where several post-Kantian German idealists depart radically from Kant. They are followed in recent Continental philosophy by a line of thinkers from Buber and Levinas to Nancy and Derrida who accept our liberty as justified by its necessary connection to our "conception of ourselves as moral agents"

(Ameriks, "Kant and Hegel on Freedom," 221). Unlike both Allison and Ameriks, these thinkers avoid the problem of a noumenal basis for libertarian freedom by taking the *practical perspective* opened by the *"faktum"* of moral responsibility to the Other as the *sole* ultimate perspective for our reason—the basis of a new, purely practical "metaphysics" in which interhuman relations and the moral unsubsumability of individual difference *replace* all theoretical judgments and ego-based apprehensions as the root of "knowledge." This move radicalizes Kant's notion of the primacy of the practical; for these writers, the *"faktum"* of the Other and our responsibility for her functions like an "intellectual intuition," but it is not a theoretical intuition of the ego at all (instead, this egological model of knowledge as cognitive appropriation in which our noetic acts construct our noemata is transcended). Ameriks follows Kant in rejecting such an *absolute* primacy of the practical, but this issue remains open and disputable.

192. This in turn requires either that we reject the closed, deterministic picture of physical nature or that we accept a dual-aspect view in which a nonphysical and potentially nondetermined aspect underlies the physical aspect of persons.

193. It is interesting to compare Kant's view with that of John Fischer and Mark Ravizza, who argue that "our status as morally responsible agents" should not be vulnerable to possible future scientific discovery that causal determinism is true (*Responsibility and Control*, 254). They think that libertarians cannot avoid this problem, whereas Kant thinks we can. I deny that a viable libertarian conception of moral freedom has to be insulated from potential empirical disconfirmation; rather, in his own time, Kant should have inferred from his *faktum* of obligation that Newtonian mechanics must be mistaken.

194. At least, Ameriks's argument here seems to obscure the difference between these two issues.

195. Ameriks, "Kant and Hegel on Freedom," 225–26, quoting Allison, *Kant's Theory of Freedom*, 51 (emphasis in original). In addition to the non sequitur described here, Ameriks thinks that Kant's mature position also suffers from assuming too uncritically that the conditions of moral responsibility require alternate possibilities of action. See Ameriks, "Reinhold's Challenge," 23–24.

196. Ameriks, "Kant and Hegel on Freedom," 226.

197. Ibid., 227.

198. Hence while Ameriks reads Kant's distinction between ends and grounds of an action to mean that "whatever the ends are which make up the overt content of our intentions, our actions can also have hidden grounds of a different form" (228), I instead read this distinction in terms of the two orders of agency and intention. The *end*, as Kant uses the term, concerns the intended goal of a first-order action, whereas the *ground* refers to the goal intended in the second-order intention on which the agent acts in deciding to form the first-order intention and adopt its first-order maxim.

199. As Ameriks notes, Kant would say that if acts with moral content arise because "our minds are made to operate as they do by something outside of (and unknown to) them, then in doing them we do not have a moral character at all" ("Pure Reason of Itself Alone," 253).

200. See the novel argument for such a libertarian alternative to agent causation in Goetz's "Libertarian Choice." Goetz defends the thesis that "choice is essentially an uncaused mental action done for a reason, purpose, or telos" (195). He relies in part on Frankfurt's point in a famous critique of causal models of action that "It is an epistemological feature of an agent who knows that he is making a choice that he knows this *while* he is choosing"; yet on causal accounts, he "cannot possess this knowledge in virtue of his awareness of the choice itself," but only by virtue of his awareness of its causes could he tell that it is a choice rather than another kind of event (these being distinguished only causally on such accounts) (198; emphasis in original). Goetz also incisively defends the idea that choices can be actions with reasons that *underdetermine* rather than cause them, without this making choices "random" in any relevant sense (199–200).

201. The problem with this is that the "self" of the agent who motivates herself in projecting ends is *being formed* precisely by these volitional efforts. Accounts of agent causation in contemporary debates about moral freedom tend to avoid dealing with this feedback loop by sticking with a thin notion of the agent rather than equating the agent who agent-causes her decisions with a psychologically thick character-self. An existential version of agent-causation would not equate the agent with a pure substance but rather with a self-forming practical identity.

202. Allison, "Kant on Freedom," 127 (emphasis added).

203. However, for a sketch, see my essay, "Liberty of the Higher-Order Will."

204. Ameriks mentions the argument from "the claim that moral demands have an unconditional form which cannot be grounded in any feature of our contingent 'natural constitution,'" and he objects that this argument does not show that acting on such an autonomous principle requires "*efficiently* and freely determining" one's intention in the libertarian sense ("Kant and Hegel on Freedom," 227). But I portray this argument only as establishing that projective motivation is essential to the standpoint of moral agency, not that this in turn entails libertarian freedom.

205. Ameriks, "Kant and Hegel on Freedom," 225 (emphasis added). In another essay, Ameriks briefly considers this "kind of phenomenological approach" to freedom implicit in the fact of pure reason (see "Pure Reason of Itself Alone," 254–55).

12. Existential Psychology and Intrinsic Motivation: Deci, Maslow, and Frankl

1. Deci, *Intrinsic Motivation*, 7.
2. Ibid., 5–18.
3. Ibid., 14.
4. Ibid., 12.
5. Mook, *Motivation: The Organization of Action*, chaps. 3–10.
6. Ibid., chaps. 12–14.
7. Kupperman, *Character*, 160–62.
8. Frederick and McNeal, *Inner Strengths*, 136.

9. Ibid., 140.
10. Ibid., 141.
11. Ibid., 142, ellipses in original. I worry in particular about the suggestion that inner strength all by itself should be sufficient to take the agent to her goals; this idea may produce undue self-recrimination if failure occurs. It would be better if the authors were clearer about what we can do by our willpower and what we require additional resources to accomplish. Nevertheless, this and similar recent work on "ego-strengthening" raise interesting questions about how in practice people can be encouraged to recognize and exercise their power of projective motivation and change their volitional habits. In this regard, I put more faith in the logotherapeutic methods described by Frankl's school (discussed below).
12. The same goes for popular works such as Parinello, *The Power of Will*. He starts with clear examples of setting "your sights on the goal" and following through with tenacity (1–2) that illustrate projective motivation. He also associates volitional strength with wholeheartedness or motivational unity (4); he uses Deci's language of "self-determination" to refer to being "filled with purpose, resolve, intention" (22); and he recognizes that materialistic values can block awareness of goals to which we can authentically devote ourselves (30–32). But much of his book emphasizes learning about our own cognitive styles and finding our heart's desires, which is likely to produce obsessive self-monitoring and an inward focus. Parinello also emphasizes ways to alter our beliefs for empowerment, which obscures the fundamental relation between projective motivation and its rational grounds; while it is crucial to believe in potential, it is also important that our goals not be set on the basis of manipulated beliefs: conviction about values is not a *means* to volitional strength.
13. Deci, *Intrinsic Motivation*, 26–27.
14. Ibid., 29, citing White (1959).
15. Ibid.
16. Ibid., 33.
17. Wallach and Wallach, *Psychology's Sanction for Selfishness*, 61.
18. Ibid., 62. On Allport's idea that an activity initiated because of an extrinsic motive "can become intrinsically interesting," see also Deci, *Intrinsic Motivation*, 25, and Cavalier, *Personal Motivation*, chap. 1.
19. Wallach and Wallach, *Psychology's Sanction for Selfishness*, 64.
20. Ibid., 66.
21. Kierkegaard, *Either/Or*, vol. I, "The Rotation of Crops," 285.
22. As noted earlier, the goals internal to playing certain games or sports may lack this extra value feature because they are set by the arbitrary conventions of the game. This explains why games or sport-like practices are closer to the infant's play, and much of their value lies in *preparing* us to engage in practices and relationships whose defining ends have non-arbitrary values set by nature rather than convention.
23. Gilbert, *Democratic Individuality*, 273.
24. Ibid., 275.
25. Wallach and Wallach, *Psychology's Sanction for Selfishness*, 69–75.

26. Ibid., 72.

27. Mook, *Motivation*, 574–75. Note that here, Mook also conflates second-order pleasure as a side effect of intrinsic interest in the car with the agent's motivating goal, which in this case has to be something like the car's beauty, its place in history, the excellent functioning of its parts, and so on (not his own pleasure). Mook also seems to take it for granted that "jobs" are always motivated solely as a means to external goods such as money.

28. Deci, *Intrinsic Motivation*, 23.

29. Ibid., 83.

30. Ryan and Deci, "Self-Determination Theory and the Facilitation of Intrinsic Motivation, Social Development, and Well-Being," 68, col. 1.

31. Ibid., 73, col. 2.

32. Ibid., 74, col. 1.

33. Ibid., 69, col. 2.

34. Ibid., 74, col. 1.

35. Ibid., 70, col. 2.

36. Ibid., 69, col. 2.

37. Ibid., 71, col. 2, where intrinsic motivation is defined as "doing an activity for the inherent satisfaction of the activity itself" rather than for some separate result.

38. Ibid., 70, col. 1.

39. Deci, *Intrinsic Motivation*, 23.

40. Ibid., 30–54.

41. Ibid., 77–89. See Salvatore Maddi, "Existential Psychotherapy." Also see Maddi's more recent work on existential courage and hardiness.

42. Ibid., 55. See Robert White, "Motivation Reconsidered: The Concept of Competence." *Psychological Review*, 66.5 (1959): 297–331.

43. Ibid., 56. See Jerome Kagan, "Motives and Development." *Journal of Personality and Social Psychology* 22 (1972): 51–66.

44. Ibid., 57.

45. Ryan and Deci, "Self-Determination Theory," 68, col. 2.

46. Ibid., 74, col. 2, 75, col. 1.

47. Deci, *Intrinsic Motivation*, 101.

48. Deci and Ryan, "The 'What' and the 'Why' of Goal Pursuits," 229, col. 2.

49. Ibid., 229, col. 1.

50. Deci, *Intrinsic Motivation*, 61 (emphasis added). Another version of the same formula is: "Intrinsically motivated behavior is behavior which is *motivated by* a person's need for feeling competent and self-determining in dealing with his environment" (100; emphasis added). In both versions, the agent's own psychic development, integration, and fulfillment are explicitly made the *aim* (though the agent might not be conscious of intending such goals).

51. Deci and Ryan, "The 'What' and the 'Why' of Goal Pursuits," 230, cols. 1–2.

52. Ibid., 230, col. 1.

53. Badhwar, "Friends as Ends in Themselves," 168. In fact, she wants to make the stronger claim that self-benefit is "an essential element" in end-love and *not* merely an unintended result (ibid.).

54. Ibid., 173.

55. Korsgaard, "Two Distinctions in Goodness," 172.

56. Badhwar says, "Hence pleasure or delight is intrinsic to perceiving and responding to someone as loveable by her very nature—to contemplating the person loved. Happiness is related to end-love not as goal to means, but rather, as element to complex whole" (174).

57. Bandura and Schunk, "Cultivating Competence," 586, col. 2.

58. Ibid., 587, col. 2. Bandura and Shunk argue in detail that setting smaller and more attainable subgoals is an effective way of helping agents to develop intrinsic motivation to pursue larger or more distant ends. Among a group of elementary school students with poor performance and low interest in math, they found that mastery of some simple skills built a sense of "self-efficacy" that reinforced the students' motivation. "Children who set themselves attainable subgoals progressed rapidly in self-directed learning" (595, col. 1). This seems to confirm Barrett's old hypothesis that "one of the best exercises for the will is to put before itself a clear, well-defined task which is not too difficult and to set itself in all earnestness to accomplish it" (*Strength of Will*, 27).

59. Deci and Ryan, 227, col. 2 (emphasis added).

60. Ibid., 228, col. 1.

61. Deci, *Intrinsic Motivation*, 55.

62. Ibid. The distinction between satiable inclinations and constant drives itself is plausible enough and has a long pedigree. Thomas Reid recognizes it in distinguishing between "appetites" that involve an "uneasy sensation" that can be "sated by their objects for a time," and "desires" that are constant, among which he includes "the desire of power, the desire of esteem, and the desire of knowledge" (*Essays on the Active Powers of the Human Mind*, Essay III: The Principles of Action, chap. 2, 128). The similarity to Deci's drive for competence is intriguing.

63. Deci and Ryan, "The 'What' and the 'Why' of Goal Pursuits," 230, col. 1.

64. Deci, *Intrinsic Motivation*, 84.

65. Maslow has influenced a whole generation of humanistic psychotherapists, some of whom adopt an Eastern interpretation of "self-actualization" as a religious ascent beyond individual selfhood. A good example is Dr. Roberto Assagioli, who takes Maslow's "Theory Z" to imply that the highest type of self-actualization involves "Transpersonal Will" or mystical transport outside one's individual identity (*The Act of Will*, 119 [22]). Assagioli infers that humanitarian motives must have this character because he follows the paradigmatically Eastern assumption that "personal will" is egoistic and exhibits "the drive to personal self-assertion" (117). His book illustrates the tendency in humanistic psychotherapy to recognize many salient functions of the striving will (he lists "intensity," "concentration," "determination," "resoluteness," "persistence," "initiative," and "integration" among other aspects (19) without any rigorous philosophical framework for their explanation.

66. I paraphrase this list from Mook, *Motivation*, 559–61. See also Deci, *Intrinsic Motivation*, 83. The original source is Abraham Maslow, *Motivation and Personality*, 2nd. ed. (Harper & Row, 1970).

67. Mook rightly criticizes this idea that lower ends are lexically prior to higher ends on the scale and must be fully satisfied as a precondition to devoting *any*

attention to the latter. For "People have starved themselves to make a political point. . . . [and] Young men and women may literally risk their lives to avoid or avenge being 'dissed' . . . they are putting esteem before safety needs—a clear inversion of Maslow's order" (Mook, *Motivation*, 571–72).

68. Mook, *Motivation*, 572. Mook also raises important questions about autonomy and independence from others as criteria for self-actualized persons: Are these criteria objectively grounded or do they just reflect Maslow's personal biases in determining who counts as paradigm cases of "self-actualized" persons? Could they also reflect cultural biases of Western individualism? (572–73).

69. On the Frankfurtian reading of Kierkegaardian aestheticism, see my essay "The Meaning of Kierkegaard's Choice between the Aesthetic and the Ethical," reprinted in *Kierkegaard After MacIntyre*, chap. 4.

70. Consider Ivan Goncharov's character Oblomov, who Gabrielle Taylor describes as being opposed to making any kind of effort since this "interferes with enjoyment" of his riches ("Deadly Vices?" 162).

71. Ryan and Deci, "Self-Determination Theory," 71, col. 1.

72. Mook, *Motivation*, 569.

73. Ibid., 574. On this point, Ryan and Deci summarize the empirical research by saying, "all expected tangible rewards made contingent on task performance do reliably undermine intrinsic motivation" for the task; see Ryan and Deci, "Self-Determination Theory," 70, col. 2.

74. Cavalier, *Personal Motivation*, 8.

75. Mook, 583. The original sources are David McClelland, *The Achieving Society* (Van Nostrand, 1961) and *The Roots of Consciousness* (Van Nostrand, 1964). It could be asked whether the high value placed on achievement is a cause of such economic development or, rather, its cultural effect (if a higher standard of living encourages achievement motives). But this correlation does agree with the positive appreciation of the striving will in paradigmatically Western cultural values (though not always in actual Western philosophy), as I argue in chapter 2.

76. Mook notes that McClelland really focuses on "a particular kind of achievement orientation" (*Motivation*, 543) in which the agent "tends to set moderate goals" and "wants concrete, rapid knowledge of how well she is doing" (ibid., 544). Note that an agent projectively willing his goals might appear instead as achievement-driven if he simply had a low tolerance for lack of agent-related by-product benefits, such as pride or recognition from others.

77. See Greene, *The Elegant Universe*, 185–87.

78. Ibid., 197–98.

79. Thus Robert Cavalier says that true artists and scholars "do not live their lives for approbation or applause," but live in the "flow" of their activity (*Personal Motivation*, 8).

80. Frankl, *From Death Camp to Existentialism*.

81. Frankl, *Man's Search for Meaning*.

82. See Frankl, *Unheard Cry for Meaning*, 29.

83. Frankl, *Man's Search for Meaning*, 79.

84. Ibid., 107.

85. Ibid., 111.

86. Ibid., 113–14.
87. Ibid., 118–20.
88. See Mook, *Motivation*, 556–61. For more detail, see Seligman and Abramson, "Learned Helplessness in Humans."
89. Frankl, *Man's Search for Meaning*, 121. Of course, the agent may need to see some real prospect of pursuing a worthwhile goal in order to avoid the sense of helplessness.
90. Ibid., 122.
91. Ibid., 164.
92. Ibid., 164.
93. Ibid., 164.
94. Senator John McCain frequently used this refrain in stump speeches during his presidential campaign in 2000.
95. Frankl, *The Will to Meaning*, 31.
96. Ibid., 32, quoting Allport, *Becoming* (Yale University Press, 1955).
97. Frankl, *Man's Search for Meaning*, 166. The last sentence in this key passage, it should be noted, corresponds almost exactly to Martin Buber's description of creative activity and meaningful work as an I-Thou experience; see Buber, *I and Thou*, 91.
98. Ibid., 179. Frankl's existentialism is surely informed on this point by Dostoyevsky's.
99. Ibid., 180–81.
100. Frankl, *The Will to Meaning*, 41. Yet Frankl agrees with Bassis in finding the will to meaning operative even in the creative explorations of the infant (42, n. 19), just as Buber finds the infant reaching out for encounter with alterity in his theory of an innate "drive to pan-relation" (Buber, *I and Thou*, 78).
101. Ibid., 52.
102. Lewis, *Screwtape Letters*, Letter 19, 83.
103. Frankl, *Man's Search for Meaning*, 156.
104. Frankl, *Unheard Cry for Meaning*, 33.
105. Frankl, *Man's Search for Meaning*, 175.
106. Frankl, *The Will to Meaning*, 38. Likewise, Frankl says that "the pleasure principle is self-defeating" because the most significant pleasures are by-products (33), and that Adler's "status drive . . . also proves to be self-defeating, insofar as a person who displays and exhibits his status drive will sooner or later be dismissed as a status-seeker" (34).
107. Ibid., 38, quoting Maslow's *Eupsychian Management*, 136.
108. Frankl, *Unheard Cry for Meaning*, 35–36 (emphasis added). Note the similarity to Marcel's description of "self-donation." A similar paradox is encountered in religious faith, as I argue in a recent article on "Eschatological Ultimacy and the Best Possible Hereafter," 36–67. I describe this paradox as part of the complex relationship between ethical and eschatological meaning: the hope for a final or ultimate validation of ethical endeavor cannot be the motivating purpose of religious faith or fidelity to God, or it becomes egoistic and thus fails as ethical endeavor (37–42). Since eschatological hope is closely related to the problem of

existential meaningfulness in a human life, the similarity between these paradoxes is not accidental. However, although I follow Kierkegaard in the belief that the religious dimension is essential to a *fully* meaningful life achieving its *existential telos*, I do not explore that ultimate level of existential meaning in this book.

109. Frankl, *Man's Search for Meaning*, 153.

110. Frankfurt, "The Importance of What We Care About," in *The Importance of What We Care About*, 89.

111. Frankl, *Man's Search for Meaning*, 156.

112. Ibid., 157. Frankl says here that values "pull" us, but he does not mean that they appeal to us only via erosiac desire. Rather, he means to contrast projective motivation with psychodynamic drives that "push" us by way of instinctive inclinations. For example, he says that moral and religious motivation are not "drives" but are, rather, freely created in response to the appearance of moral and religious values outside us: "Man is never driven to moral behavior; in each case he decides to behave morally . . . he does so for the sake of a cause to which he commits himself, or for a person whom he loves, or for the sake of his God." (158). He also distinguishes these pure moral motives from the by-product result of moral sainthood to which they can lead: "I think that even the saints did not care for anything other than simply to serve God, and I doubt that they ever had it in mind to become saints. If that were the case, they would have become only perfectionists rather than saints" (158). We find the same distinction between "being driven to something on the one hand and striving for something on the other" in *The Will to Meaning*, 43.

113. Frankl, *The Will to Meaning*, 44.

114. Ibid., 52.

115. Ibid., 8.

116. Noddings, *Caring*, 14.

117. Ibid., 12.

118. Ibid., 14.

119. Ibid., 16.

120. Frankfurt, "The Importance of What We Care About," 89.

121. Noddings, *Caring*, 17.

122. Frankl, *Man's Search for Meaning*, 175.

123. As we will see when this concept is applied to the theory of autonomy, it is also possible in special cases to project ends or goals that involve or mention oneself and even one's own psychic states. For example, I can will not to be moved by envy, or will to become a more sympathetic person, etc. In accordance with the requirement of formal non-narcissism, this will be because these psychic states toward which we can projectively direct ourselves in different ways have in themselves (or in their raw form) a certain fundamental alienness from the self that forms and defines itself through projective willing. This is why we can volitionally identify ourselves with them or volitionally alienate ourselves from them through projective commitment to them or to their opposites, respectively.

124. Frankl, *The Will to Meaning*, 55.

125. At least not, so existential theology would add, without the miraculous aid of divine grace or a miracle in which God supplies the missing color of alterity. For example, this is what the blue fairy provides in the tale of Pinocchio.

126. On this point, see my paper on "Eschatological Ultimacy and the Best Possible Hereafter," 63–64.

127. Levinas, *Totality and Infinity*, 63 (emphasis added).

128. Noddings, *Caring*, 23.

129. Blustein, *Care and Commitment*, 29.

130. Frankl himself does not emphasize this point and he seems to assume that authentic commitment to self-transcending ends will generally be aimed at *positive* values rather than at harm and destruction. For example, he suggests at one point that logotherapy "would define good and bad in terms of what promotes, or blocks, the fulfillment of meaning, irrespective of whether it is one's own meaning or that of someone else" (Frankl, *The Will to Meaning*, 68). But this would imply either that no evil project could be fulfilling or meaningful to the agent (which is false), or that radically evil projects are really good (which Frankl does not mean to assert). Kierkegaard avoided this error of moralizing volitional authenticity, and I follow him on this point.

131. Blustein, *Care and Commitment*, 62.

132. Noddings, *Caring*, 7 (italics omitted).

133. Ibid., 6.

134. Ibid., 19.

135. Ibid., 27.

136. Ibid., 5.

137. Frankfurt, "On the Usefulness of Final Ends."

138. Frankfurt, *The Reasons of Love*. This book is a much-developed version of Frankfurt's earlier essay "On Caring," with about twice as much text as that essay. Some passages are largely repeated from the earlier essay, but there are important changes and much new material.

139. Ibid., 7.

140. Ibid., 7. Moreover, neither Frankfurt nor I contend that it is *only* in virtue of projects and purposes that an agent's life acquires a first-personal sense of meaning. I take up this point in the concluding chapter.

141. Ibid., 8.

142. Frankfurt, *Reasons of Love*, 58.

143. Frankfurt, "On the Usefulness of Final Ends," 4.

144. Ibid., 5.

145. Ibid., 6.

146. Ibid., 8–9 (emphasis in original).

147. Ibid., 9. Frankfurt offers as an example that the highly noble end happens to require only pressing a button. Here is a variation: imagine someone who has inherited (or found or won) an enormous fortune, who could do great good with it by simply donating most of it to well-established charities but who decides instead to reserve some of it for more complex forms of philanthropy or for starting new businesses. This agent finds more meaning in the challenge of making something unique out of this opportunity, applying their creative powers to these resources. Someone else whose life was already full of projects she did not want to put aside for new ventures using this fortune might choose the donation option.

148. Like "existential meaningfulness," the terminology of "existential value" is also mine rather than Frankfurt's.

149. Ibid., 14.

150. Frankfurt, *Reasons of Love*, 59.

151. Ibid., 60.

152. Ibid., 61 (emphasis added).

153. The same goes for the construal of indirect "self-love" in Frankfurt's third lecture in *Reasons of Love*.

154. Frankfurt, "On the Usefulness of Final Ends," 13.

155. Ibid., 14.

156. Frankfurt, *Reasons of Love*, 58.

157. See Rawls, *A Theory of Justice*, sec. 61, 400. See also sec. 67.

158. Honneth, *Struggle for Recognition*, Introduction by Joel Anderson, xi.

159. Ibid., xvi.

160. This is the kind of self-respect that Thomas Hill, Jr., defends in explaining Kant's view that "the avoidance of servility is a duty to oneself" ("Servility and Self-Respect," 16).

161. This is the attitude that Honneth describes as basic self-confidence, which begins with security and attentive nurturing in early childhood (*Struggle for Recognition*, xiii).

162. This is the kind of distinctiveness that G. H. Mead emphasized in his analysis of specialization in the division of labor in *Mind, Self, and Society* (ibid., xvi).

163. Erica Goode, "Deflating Self-Esteem's Role in Society's Ills," *New York Times*, October 1, 2002, F5–6. It is apparent from this article, however, that psychologists studying self-esteem do not make clear distinctions between the four kinds of positive self-regarding attitudes that I distinguish here. Compare Goode's results to Jean Twenge's argument in *Generation Me* that obsession with self-esteem is making teens unhappy.

164. Rawls, *A Theory of Justice*, sec. 67, 440 (emphasis added).

165. Ibid. Note that while confidence in our potential can be directly encouraged to an extent by significant others (and this is obviously crucial for young children), its full development also depends on experiencing some level of success in intrinsically worthwhile and challenging endeavors. As we have seen, this is how by-product satisfaction can play a role as a necessary condition for sustaining devotion to an endeavor. It follows that neither component of Rawlsian self-esteem can be fully guaranteed by the political or educational system.

166. Ibid., 441–42.

167. Hill, "Self-Respect Reconsidered," 21.

168. Ibid., 22.

169. Ibid., 21 n. 5; 23. Hill does not enumerate these ways of failing to achieve this kind of self-respect, but the distinctions are suggested in his discussion. In particular, his examples of the artist who sells out, the actress turned prostitute, and the teacher in *The Blue Angel* all fail in the second way by violating their own ideals (23), whereas his neighbor who has no "personal standards" or "high ideals of self-improvement" is *worse*, since he is ethically wanton (19). Thus Hill is mistaken in suggesting that their problem is not weakness of will because they made

deliberate changes in their life plans (20). They may not have been overcome by violent pathos, but they still failed to will their higher ends with sufficient resolve or to commit themselves strongly enough to their values and ideals; their adaptive preferences are the result of their volitional weakness.

170. Gordon, "Book of Days."
171. Ibid., 19.
172. Bratman, "Responsibility and Planning," 166, 170.
173. Gordon, "Book of Days," 20.
174. Ibid., 21.
175. Ibid., 22. The story of defacing Marcy's calendar is so poignantly written that it would be difficult to doubt its authenticity as a public confession, and I even suspect Gordon of what Kierkegaard called "indirect communication," that is, sending a private message of serious apology, concealed in this public document, to Marcy. But since this essay is also reflective and self-deprecating in a sense, it is hard to be *sure* of its authenticity. It would be worthwhile trying to identify marks that distinguish authentic apology from merely aesthetic self-deprecation (with morose pleasure in one's lowness). I think a sense of poignance is one of these marks, and Gordon's analysis of why she defaced Marcy's calendar is strikingly poignant. The trouble is that almost any emotion can be faked, even to oneself.
176. Ibid., 23.
177. Ibid., 22.
178. Ibid., 30.
179. Which shows that writing about the self-defeating nature of self-obsession is no sure antidote to the problem. Indeed, it may only take speculative detachment from oneself to an even higher order.
180. Ibid., 31.
181. Ibid., 31. There is an interesting connection between this and Michael Stocker's dictum that "the unfelt life" is not worth living ("How Emotions Reveal Value," 182). See my discussion of noninstrumental emotional expression (which volitional engagement supports) in "The Binding Value of Earnest Emotional Valuation."
182. This sort of move is not unknown in literary history. Kierkegaard found himself unable authentically to "engage" his beloved Regine because he was ultimately more interested in *reflecting on* being engaged than in Regine. He did at least get off the fence by rescinding the engagement to spare her the trouble of living with his self-absorption and family curse. But then he spent the rest of his life reflecting on what had gone wrong and recommending projective investment in life as the way to avoid his mistake—something he himself managed only by passionate engagement in *writing* about the virtues of existential willing. Perhaps the reason things did not work out was that Regine was too much like Marcy. If she had been more like Emily Gordon, Kierkegaard might have found his kindred spirit.
183. Of course, I do not say this to imply that Gordon really remains narcissistic or self-absorbed, despite her regrets. Rather, I want only to warn us away from the misconception that regret—and its literary expression—is sufficient to reveal devotions of the striving will. Unlike remorse, which is a volitional state involving

a commitment to reject the wrong done, regret is a sub-volitional emotion that may not motivate any action.

184. Sartre, *Being and Nothingness*, pt. IV, chap. I, 607.

185. Ibid., 607–8 (emphasis in original). Sartre might very well be thinking of the underground man's insistence that even a toothache can be used for spite, since a person can "find pleasure in the consciousness of his own degradation" (*Notes from Underground*, 25).

186. Izenberg, *The Existentialist Critique of Freud*, 8. In Sartre, the (futile) will not to be free, or to be a thing, is the more general concept, and the will to inferiority is only one species of it.

187. In this thought, I believe we find the beginning of a neo-Kantian ground not only for an ethics of duties to persons but also for an *agapē ethics*. For what such an ethics principally requires (if it is to have any rational foundation outside of arbitrary divine command) is that the existential will is *eo ipso* or "always-already" committed to the absolute intrinsic value of any person or any agent-self capable of such willing as something it is always *more important* to care about than anything else. The idea is to show that if anything can be worth caring about it, then individual persons whose essence consists in a will capable of forming cares must themselves be of overriding importance or more deserving of care than anything else. The paradox is that this yields a universal requirement to devote essentially particularistic care to *each* person, and the apparent impossibility of this demand must somehow be resolved.

13. Caring, Aretaic Commitment, and Existential Resolve

1. I believe this is true whether happiness is understood as involving a subjective element (a sense of overall contentment or feeling that everything is as it should be, that one's life is on course) or as an objective flourishing that applies to any human being who has all she needs and has fully developed her natural potential. I have argued for this distinction between the happiness and meaningfulness of a life in "Towards an Existential Virtue Ethics."

2. Frankfurt, "The Importance of What We Care About," 82.

3. Ibid., 83.

4. Williams, "Persons, Character, and Morality," in *Moral Luck*, 11. One potential problem with this characterization of ground projects is that it implies that a person who finds his ground projects frustrated or unpursuable, given contingencies of fortune (e.g., the people he loves die), would have no strong motive to go on living. Williams says that hope for other things may keep him going and he may have more than one ground project (13). But a person who finds his entire "nexus" of projects void might try to discover or form *new* ground projects—a process that makes sense on the existential account of the striving will but not on Williams's own moral psychology.

5. Ibid., 13. A similar answer to Parfit's arguments that identity between earlier and later selves is a matter of degree is given by MacIntyre in *After Virtue*, 2nd ed., chap. 15: "The self inhabits a character whose unity is given as the unity of a

character" (217). The difference is that MacIntyre is clearer than Williams or Frankfurt that the self's experience of its practical unity in memory, present action, and future prospects has a *narrative* structure with interpersonal conditions such as a shared language game. But then, in MacIntyre's analysis, the role of cares and ground projects is played by the less helpful notion of "longer and longest-term intentions" (208). One needs to put insights from Frankfurt, Williams, and MacIntyre together to get a complete picture.

6. Frankfurt, "The Importance of What We Care About," 83–84.
7. Noddings, *Caring*, 16.
8. Ibid., 10.
9. Ibid., 5.
10. Frankfurt, "On Caring," 156.
11. Ibid., 157. However, I doubt the close link between happiness and caring that Frankfurt suggests here. In my view, which is closer to Kant's, a person who cares about something and achieves the goals this requires will experience his life as valuable and worthwhile as well as meaningful, but not necessarily as happier in the eudaimonistic sense of lacking nothing. And even where happiness does follow from successfully pursuing that which we care about, it is at first primarily a byproduct and not the motive of the caring agent, though the resulting sense of effectiveness can help sustain the agent's commitment over the long term (see chap. 12).
12. Ibid., 158.
13. Ibid., 160.
14. Ibid., 160–61.
15. Frankfurt, "The Importance of What We Care About," 83.
16. Ibid., 87. Note that in referring to motives that are "not merely his own" Frankfurt must mean "not merely consciously experienced by him." This fits with his view that the experience of some psychic state by the agent *as conscious subject* does not necessarily make that psychic state autonomous or entail that it belongs to his deeper volitional self, which is narrower than his field of consciousness.
17. Frankfurt, "Identification and Wholeheartedness," 166–72.
18. Frankfurt, "The Faintest Passion."
19. Frankfurt, "Reply to Gary Watson," 161.
20. I disagree with this conclusion and the model from which it follows since, unlike Frankfurt, I hold that identification involves as a necessary (but not sufficient) condition a kind evaluation of desires that is always linked to caring about some final end, so I hold that identification is always rooted in caring. However, the analysis of volitional identification as part of the theory of personal autonomy is the task of the sequel to the present book.
21. Ibid., 161.
22. Frankfurt, *The Reasons of Love*, 16 (emphasis added).
23. Frankfurt, "On Caring," 161–62.
24. Frankfurt, "The Importance of What We Care About," 85.
25. Ibid., 88.
26. This was the Hobbesian definition of the will, or of what Kane would call appetitive willing, that Frankfurt offered in his essay, "Freedom of the Will and

the Concept of the Person," 14. But Frankfurt's later essays clearly move away from this conception of willing toward distinctively volitional states in the higher-order will.

27. This is the sense of "decision" that Frankfurt discusses in analyzing Descartes's argument that our will's power is unlimited in its own nature; see Frankfurt, "Concerning the Freedom and Limits of the Will," 78–79. Will as the capacity for decision in this sense is similar to the notion of second-order executive agency discussed in chapter 3.

28. Frankfurt, "The Importance of What We Care About," 84.

29. Ibid., 85.

30. On this point, see Blustein's useful discussion in *Caring and Commitment*, 62–65 and 79.

31. Frankfurt, "The Importance of What We Care About," 84 (first emphasis added). I would add that when these remarks about decision are taken in the context of Frankfurt's other essays, "Identification and Externality" and "Identification and Wholeheartedness," the implied relationship between caring and decision seems to me rather more complex than Frankfurt suggests in "The Importance of What We Care About."

32. Ibid., 87 (emphasis added).

33. Ibid., 90.

34. Frankfurt, "On the Usefulness of Final Ends," 10.

35. And this is doubtless why Robert Kane describes the striving will as operative in making decisions involving libertarian freedom or "self-formed willings."

36. *Tombstone*, directed by George Cosmatos (Walt Disney, 1993).

37. Frankfurt, *The Reasons of Love*, 10:

> This notion is rampantly ubiquitous. It is also heavily overburdened and a bit limp. People routinely deploy it in a number of different roles, to refer to a disparate and unruly assortment of psychic conditions and events. Moreover, its various meanings are rarely distinguished; nor is there much effort to clarify how they are related.

I strongly agree with this complaint about contemporary analytic moral psychology: we need to work with distinct substantive senses of "desire."

38. Frankfurt, "The Importance of What We Care About," 85.

39. Frankfurt, "Autonomy, Necessity, and Love," 443–44.

40. Ibid., 434.

41. Ibid., 436. See Kant's *Groundwork*, Ak. 432–33, 99–100.

42. In the *Groundwork*, Kant says that an autonomous will must be "a law unto itself (independently of every property belonging to the objects of volitions)" (Ak. 440, 108). But not all these properties are objects of erosiac desire; some of them ground the formation of projects that define individual identities. Such practical identities need not be universal requirements for all responsible beings. So Frankfurt is correct in his reply to Kant, but existentialists will not concede that an individual has an innate "personal essence" of the kind that Frankfurt imagines as defining the true self.

43. Frankfurt, "Autonomy, Necessity, and Love," 437.

44. Ibid., 437.
45. Ibid., 438.
46. Ibid., 439. This is Frankfurt's phrasing for a goal that is distinct from the agent's simple being (her embodied mind before extension by volitional projection).
47. Frankfurt, "On Caring," 167.
48. Although the striving will has no essential relationship to the emotions of anger or brave habits of action, it was associated with these dispositions in classical Greece because it was primarily in these contexts that striving will was most clearly recognized by that culture. This is similar to the sense of personal "passion" that Kierkegaard employs in connection with the will in his pseudonymous works, which I discuss in *Kierkegaard After MacIntyre*.
49. Frankfurt, "On Caring," 168.
50. This help explains the sense in which Kant held that proper self-love could be a duty and the sense in which at least some theologians have held that self-directed agapē is required by the love commandments.
51. Frankfurt, "Autonomy, Necessity, and Love," 442 (emphasis added). I note that Frankfurt's phrasing in this section suggests what I have called "liberty of the higher-order will" with respect to these inherently neutral raw materials of the psyche: "Whether a person identifies himself with these passions, or whether they occur as alien forces that remain outside the boundaries of his volitional authority, depends upon what he himself want his will to be." This seems to imply that the agent has the power to bring about either higher-order attitude toward a given passion.
52. Ibid., 443.
53. Ibid., 440.
54. Frankfurt provides this argument in other papers, such as "Rationality and the Unthinkable" and "The Necessity of Ideals." I hope to address it more fully in my later book on an existential theory of autonomy.
55. Frankfurt, "Freedom of the Will and the Concept of a Person," 12.
56. Ross, *The Right and the Good*, chap. 2, 37.
57. Hence, in my existential account, commitment is the more fundamental notion in terms of which promising should be defined, and making a promise is only one kind of commitment. Contracts as legally or conventionally defined are commitments only in a derivative sense, not in the most fundamental volitional sense.
58. Frankfurt, *The Reasons of Love*, 53.
59. By a first-order state of affairs, I simply mean one that includes no mention of any motivational state of persons. I use the term "consequence-transcending" to indicate that although the value *includes* the goodness of certain kinds of first-order states of affairs, it has further content that cannot be reduced to the value of states of affairs (as opposed to the intrinsic value of certain types of action).
60. MacIntyre, *After Virtue*, 198.
61. Williams, "A Critique of Utilitarianism," 116.
62. Ibid., 113–114.

63. Kierkegaard, *Stages on Life's Way*, 410. See my essay, "The Ethical and Religious Significance."
64. Williams, "A Critique of Utilitarianism," 115.
65. Ibid., 116.
66. Ibid., 116.
67. Such an agent, whose ground projects are completely unresponsive to reasons (including considerations about consequences), would be a fanatic in one serious sense of that term. Fanatics are a proper subset of those who display infinite passion in Kierkegaard's sense, but it is possible to display such passion without being fanatical as well (displaying such passion does not entail fanaticism). On this issue, see Annette Baier, "Caring about Caring: A Reply to Frankfurt."
68. On the contrary, ground projects and other existentially less central cares or commitments almost always guide action *in part* through determining the relevance and importance that different kinds of consequences should have in our considerations or through guiding our sense of how to make this determination. And as Williams points out, principles can be nonconsequentialist without requiring us to do certain things or pursue certain causes "whatever the consequences," *however extreme*; instead, such principles can be limited in scope such that they do not apply in highly bizarre situations where the consequences of following the principles would be too extreme (Williams, "A Critique of Utilitarianism," 90–91).
69. Ibid., 89.
70. Flanagan, *Varieties of Moral Personality*, 70.
71. Ibid., 76.
72. Ibid., 77.
73. This point is analogous to the inherent importance of responding emotionally to how things really stand in one's view, whether or not this maximizes the satisfaction of our own desires or collective utility. On this idea, see Davenport, "Binding Value of Earnest Emotional Valuation."
74. Kierkegaard, *Stages on Life's Way*, 411.
75. It so happens that Abraham Lincoln fits Kierkegaard's description of a politician who foresees the social costs of his early death. Imagine that Lincoln had been unwilling to risk assassination by issuing the Emancipation Proclamation because he could foresee that his absence might let extremists prevent a lasting peace. Or imagine that Nelson Mandela had been unwilling to risk ending his life in obscurity in a forgotten prison because he feared that then no one else would be able to lead the resistance to apartheid. This kind of calculation is the perversion of every pure motive. We cannot remain true to our commitments if we try to factor in accommodations for every possible turn of chance. This does not mean that we should be careless with our lives, fear nothing, or throw them away needlessly (as Alexander Hamilton did in his duel). But to be willing *to die for something* means being willing, past a point, not to consider some of the possible consequences of dying for it; in other words, it means principled restrictions on probable consequences to which we will be sensitive in deciding how to act.
76. Elizabeth Anderson, "Reasons, Attitudes, and Values," 541.

77. Ibid., 542.
78. Ibid., 544. For this point, Anderson cites Scheffler, "Agent-Centered Restrictions, Rationality, and the Virtues."
79. Ibid., 544.
80. Ibid., 543. This principle was suggested by Nicholas Sturgeon as an alternative formulation of Anderson's own neo-Kantian principle of respect for persons.
81. Ibid., 545.
82. Blustein, *Care and Commitment*, 35.
83. Compare this to Kierkegaard's young lad in *Fear and Trembling*, who has to give up pursuing his princess even though he remains infinitely devoted to her. See my discussion of infinite resignation in "Faith as Eschatological Trust in *Fear and Trembling*."
84. Frankfurt, *The Reasons of Love*, 59. This interpretation helps align Frankfurt's view with the conclusions reached in chap. 12, sec. 6: the agent-related by-product benefits must not initially motivate the kind of care or love that can generate these benefits. As a result, at least up to some point, caring devotion can continue and be expressed in ways that do not happen to generate these benefits to the agent.
85. Blustein, *Care and Commitment*, 27.
86. Ibid., 28.
87. Ibid.
88. Ibid., 30.
89. Ibid., 31.
90. Ibid. One problem with this terminology is that "disinterested" care can suggest aloofness or emotional detachment, but the kind of caring Blustein has in mind can be energetically focused in its concern for the target and is also compatible with caring *for* the target and other types of emotional bond with the target.
91. Ibid., 38.
92. Ibid., 39. But the example that Blustein gives here is a self-interested caring about becoming slim.
93. Ibid., 46.
94. Ibid., 46–47.
95. If what is usually a hobby—e.g., building Lego models or collecting rare coins—becomes a deep commitment central to one's life-narrative, or even a ground project, then it is no longer properly called a hobby. One now builds Lego structures as fine art or makes a profession of coin collecting, etc.
96. Ibid., 49–50.
97. Blustein explores the notions of integration, coherence, and stability at 58–59.
98. Ibid., 70.
99. Ibid., 71.
100. As Blustein recognizes on 77.
101. For example, in her "Two Distinctions in Goodness," Korsgaard limits "intrinsic" value to value that something has in all possible circumstances (170) and holds that some "extrinsic" or context-dependent value is final or valued "as

an end" (172). I have been concerned primarily with the difference between final and instrumental value but without conceiving all final value as targetable or as a potential "end" of intention.

102. Blustein, *Care and Commitment*, 94.
103. Ibid., 98.
104. See also ibid., 88.
105. See ibid., 96.
106. See ibid., 102–3.
107. Ibid., 103.

14. An Existential Objectivist Account of What Is Worth Caring About

1. Ordinarily, the cognitive and projective sides may form a whole experience and seem inseparable, although they can be distinguished in philosophical abstraction.

2. There is much discussion of list theories these days. For example, see Derek Parfit, *Reasons and Persons*, 4; Shelly Kagan, "Limits of Well-Being," 170; Nicholas Rescher, *Objectivity*, chap. 11.

3. Sartre, *Being and Nothingness*, pt. I, chap. I, sec. 5, 77.

4. Of course, in his famous essay on "Existentialism and Humanism," Sartre ends up in what is really an unstable position intermediate between objectivism and subjectivism: like Kant, he affirms that we make some kind of universal validity claim in choosing any value as a basis for our decision; but he denies that such an evaluative validity claim has any objective truth-makers. It is no wonder, then, that this essay confuses the brightest undergraduates.

5. Blustein, *Care and Commitment*, 33.
6. Ibid., 40–41.
7. Ibid., 40.
8. Ibid., 24.
9. Ibid., 64–65.
10. See Williams, *Ethics and the Limits of Philosophy*, chap. 10.
11. See Anscombe, "Modern Moral Philosophy."
12. As Alex Voorhoeve calls it in his interview with Harry Frankfurt, "Harry Frankfurt on the Necessity of Love," http://www.ucl.ac.uk/~uctyaev/frankfurt1.pdf.
13. Habermas, "Are There Postmetaphysical Answers to the Question: What Is the 'Correct Life?'" Habermas moderates his phasing somewhat in the published version of the essay included in his book, *The Future of Human Nature*.
14. As a brief sample of such works, consider John Drummond's "Moral Encounters" and "Moral Objectivity: Husserl's Sentiments of the Understanding."
15. Kupperman, *Character*, 117.
16. Frankfurt, "The Importance of What We Care About," 91.
17. Frankfurt, "Comments on MacIntyre," 321. Note that this response was published in the same volume as Frankfurt's essay, "The Importance of What We Care About" and serves as a kind of addendum to that essay.

18. Frankfurt still appears to accept that a person's character can fairly be judged on the basis of what they care about. For he says in *The Reasons of Love* that "What a person loves, or what he does not love, may be counted to his credit. Or it may discredit him: it may be taken to show that he has a bad moral character" (67). Other non-moral forms of praise and blame may surely also apply (as Thomas Hill argues; see chap. 11). Yet Frankfurt seems to think this is compatible with holding that "love need not be grounded in any judgment or perception concerning the value of its object" (67). There is a *prima facie* contradiction here.

19. *Saving Private Ryan*, directed by Steven Spielberg, written by Robert Rodat (Dreamworks, 1998).

20. I have addressed historical conditioning of our duties in four unpublished talks on agapē, "Time and Responsibility."

21. Frankfurt, "The Importance of What We Care About," 91.

22. Ibid., 93.

23. Frankfurt, "Rationality and the Unthinkable," 185.

24. Ibid., 186.

25. C. Taylor, *The Ethics of Authenticity*, 33.

26. Ibid.

27. Ibid., 34.

28. Ibid., 35.

29. J. Anderson, "A Social Conception of Personal Autonomy: Volitional Identity, Strong Evaluation, and Intersubjective Accountability," sec. 4.4, 89. Anderson's dissertation discusses in detail the prospects for an intersubjective approach to norms governing cares and life plans and defends an extension of Habermasian discourse theory to "ethical-existential" evaluation. I regard this project as a close cousin of existential objectivism.

30. Ibid., 91. See also J. Anderson, "The Personal Lives of Strong Evaluators: Identity, Pluralism, and Ontology in Charles Taylor's Value Theory."

31. Taylor, *Sources of the Self*, 14.

32. J. Anderson rightly notes, against Flanagan, that Taylor recognizes some broadly aesthetic or non-moral evaluative judgments as strongly evaluative (ibid., 95). Yet strong evaluation is fundamentally anticonsequentialist, since it invokes contrasts between items that are *ordinally* higher or lower and hence not subject to balancing against one another or to trade-off. In that sense, a broadly ethical affirmation of values that cannot be treated in consequentialist fashion is built into the idea of strong evaluation, which is therefore closely tied to what I call aretaic commitment.

33. Taylor, *Sources of the Self*, 15.

34. Ibid., 23.

35. Except in the case of sport practices, in which the end is conventional, but its pursuit is challenging in beneficial ways, affording opportunities for the development of excellences.

36. From the song "Climb Every Mountain," by Rodgers and Hammerstein, in *The Sound of Music*, directed by Robert Wise (Twentieth Century Fox, 1965). Of course, in using this example I do not mean to endorse the sexism in this movie.

37. As Taylor says, one criterion for the worth of my life concerns "what kind of life would fulfill the promise implicit in my particular talents, or the demands incumbent on someone with my endowment" (*Sources of the Self*, 14). The criticism that someone has "wasted" his talents or "missed" his calling is usually made in the illocutionary mode of a validity claim about relevant grounds for caring. See the further discussion of "personal fit" in sec. 4.3.

38. Tate and Harris, "Persons, Free Will, and the Problem of Evil," conference manuscript, 12–13.

39. Ibid., 14.

40. Emphasis added. As fate would have it, I wrote this example on October 10, 2004, before learning that Reeve had died that very day.

41. Frankfurt, "The Importance of What We Care About," 92.

42. Blustein, *Care and Commitment*, 43.

43. Ibid.; we "derive personal value from the impersonal pursuit." This is also the view that Blustein finds in Loren Lomasky's work (45).

44. Frankfurt, "The Importance of What We Care About," 93.

45. Ibid., 93.

46. Note that this disjunctive pair of diagnoses leaps to mind for a case such as the person obsessed with not stepping on cracks in the pavement. He is either in the grip of some delusion about the effects or symbolic importance of stepping on a crack or recognizes the unimportance of his goal yet finds himself unable to break the habit.

47. Blustein, *Care and Commitment*, 47, citing Lomasky, 241.

48. Ibid., 47.

49. Ibid., 61. One explanation for this may be that the agent's doubts about his judgments or sensitivities to values worth caring about undermine his trust in any apparent reasons to project new ends. Precisely because earnest conviction about objective grounds for caring is necessary for volitional commitment, self-doubt and value-skepticism sap the will's strength.

50. Frankfurt, "The Importance of What We Care About," 91.

51. See my "The Meaning of Kierkegaard's Choice."

52. Frankfurt, "The Importance of What We Care About," 92–93.

53. Ibid., 93.

54. In his latest book, *The Reasons of Love*, Frankfurt seems to drop the caveat from this claim and assert the stronger thesis that for all genuine cares, the only valid justification is ultimately this process-focused agent-relative existential value of caring itself (23–26).

55. Frankfurt, "On Caring," 162.

56. Frankfurt, "Autonomy, Necessity, and Love," 438. This passage is immediately followed by the analysis of active love as pure of ulterior motives, including even enjoyment of activities involved in loving (see chap. 13, sec. 2.4).

57. Frankfurt, "The Importance of What We Care About," 94, see n. 4. If anyone imagines that this reference to reasonless divine creativity was meant light-heartedly, they should consult Frankfurt's essay "On God's Creation." In this innovative reading of *Genesis*, Frankfurt argues that in His original speech-acts, God

forms Himself by first defining His own volitions without any prior reason for causing order to arise in chaos (136).

58. Frankfurt, *The Reasons of Love*, 63.
59. Ibid., 38.
60. Frankfurt, "Reply to Gary Watson," 161.
61. Blustein, *Care and Commitment*, 44.
62. Ibid., 65.
63. Wolf, "The True, the Good, and the Loveable," 229.
64. Ibid.
65. Ibid., 230. This rejection is obviously linked to Wolf's well-known critique of "moral saints" (which unfortunately caricatures sainthood as involving moral monomania and inflexibility).
66. Ibid., 231. Indeed, everyone is familiar with parents who make this error, often with disastrous results.
67. Frankfurt, *The Reasons of Love*, 39.
68. Ibid., 43. He actually refers here to the love of infants and small children whose personal qualities cannot yet be a very significant criterion.
69. MacIntyre, *Dependent Rational Animals*, 90–91 (emphasis added).
70. Wolf, "The True, the Good, and the Loveable," 231.
71. Thus Wolf's version is more reasonable than Madonna's more assertive conception of self-respect: "Don't go for second-best, baby; put yourself to the test!" from the song "Express Yourself," by Madonna and Stephen Bray, on the album *Like A Prayer* (Sire Records, 1989).
72. Wolf, "The True, the Good, and the Loveable," 232. This is not to be equated with Nietzsche's claim that what makes something worthy of care is the potential for caring about it to give us distinction, greatness in comparison with peers, or ascendance over the puerile masses of the world. There are perhaps contexts in which distinctiveness can be a valid ground for forming some project, but this cannot be generalized. Nietzsche's conception of the proper grounds for caring replaces ethics with the imperatives of the *conatus ascendi*, which limits the will to a complex kind of egoism, reducing projective motivation to *libido dominandi*.
73. Ibid. This way of construing Augustine's doctrine of *ordo amoris* saves it from being read as requiring strict proportionality between the value of final ends and the care we devote to them.
74. Ibid., 233.
75. *Bend It Like Beckham*, directed by Gurinder Chadha (Twentieth Century Fox, 2002).
76. Frankfurt, *The Reasons of Love*, 12. The same point is made in each of Frankfurt's other essays on caring.
77. Frankfurt, "On Caring," 158.
78. Frankfurt, *The Reasons of Love*, 21.
79. Frankfurt, "The Importance of What We Care About," 90.
80. Frankfurt, *The Reasons of Love*, 56.
81. Frankfurt, "On Caring," 164.
82. Frankfurt, *The Reasons of Love*, 13, my emphasis.

83. Blustein, *Care and Commitment*, 51.
84. Tracey Ullmann, "They Don't Know," on the album *You Broke My Heart in Seventeen Places* (Stiff Records, 1983).
85. I recognize that personal appropriation of some values by the will, taking them as initial grounds for projective motivation, often results in clearer or more nuanced understanding of these values themselves (this effect is especially clear when loving particular persons results in "getting to know them" better). In other words, although an evaluative attitude of some kind precedes and grounds every project, cognitive changes follow from the projective motivation. On this idea, see my essay, "Towards an Existential Virtue Ethics," 304–9. What I say there about moral sensitivity I would now say about sensitivity to all the values that can rationally ground volitional caring of all kinds.
86. Unless the question is one of *faith*, but that is a different question from love.
87. Stocker, "The Schizophrenia of Modern Ethical Theories," reprinted in *Virtue Ethics*.
88. Noddings, *Caring*, 5.
89. Ibid., 25.
90. Ibid., 18.
91. Frankfurt, *The Reasons of Love*, 38.
92. Ibid., 43.
93. Ibid., 44.
94. Blustein believes it is possible to care universally about all persons, but he also contrasts agapē with essentially particularistic care: "such love is not concerned with others as particular and unique persons" (*Care and Commitment*, 37). By contrast, I think that true agapic regard is distinguished from universal benevolence precisely by taking the uniqueness that makes essentially particularistic care possible as the ultimate ground for loving persons *qua* their individuality as persons.
95. Herman, "Bootstrapping," 261.
96. Ibid., 257.
97. Ibid., 256.
98. See Raz, *Value, Respect, and Attachment*. Closely related themes are found in Raz's earlier book, *Engaging Reason: On the Theory of Value and Action*.
99. Raz, *Value, Respect, and Attachment*, 3.
100. Ibid., 8.
101. Ibid., 16.
102. Ibid., 17, n. 5.
103. Ibid., 18.
104. Ibid., 19.
105. Ibid., 20–21. Clearly, here Raz regards "attachment" as actively generated by the agent. He also distinguishes "meaning" from eudaimonia, as the existential approach requires, for "There is value in sadness and disappointment. They have value because they too can be meaningful elements of one's life" (15). This insight is overlooked by Frankfurt when he argues that we have to be careful never to be frustrated by our cares.

106. Ibid., 20.

107. A striking parallel is found in Blustein, who also affirms both these components as necessary for existential meaning:

> The values that govern our lives can endow our lives with meaning only if they are personal ones. Impersonal value alone cannot give my life meaning. . . . On the other hand, if something that has value for me does not point beyond itself to self-transcendent value, if something that I care about is not believed by me to *warrant* my care because it has genuine worth and importance, then it cannot give meaning to my life. (*Care and Commitment*, 48)

108. In *Saving Private Ryan*, for example, Private Ryan is partially individuated as an appropriate object of special attention for Chief of Staff George Marshall because his brothers have already all died in combat. Though logically this scenario could be repeated, it was (what Raz calls) "de facto" unique. It is also among General Marshall's grounds for devoting extraordinary effort and cost to saving Ryan that President Lincoln recorded such profound grief and collective indebtedness of all future Americans to the mother of five brothers, *all* of whom were killed serving the Union army in the Civil War. Marshall's projection of the goal "that James Ryan be saved" is partially due to conceiving that goal as including the historically singularizing specification, "so that what happened to this mother during the Civil War shall not be repeated." And that in turn reflects his own sense of indebtedness, on behalf of all Americans, to that particular mother who "laid so costly a sacrifice upon the altar of freedom." Thus collective indebtedness can also single out new ends as uniquely significant as history unfolds, and one strand of the web of responsibility is woven to others in ways that we could never completely unravel.

109. Raz, *Value, Respect, and Attachment*, 14–15.

110. Ibid., 23.

111. Ibid., 20.

112. I also make reference to this dynamic, for example, in explaining how certain types of radically evil will can be seen by their agents as grounded in agent-relative reasons (see chap. 10, sec. 2.2).

113. Ibid., 24.

114. Ibid., 26.

115. Ibid., 33.

116. Cindy Lauper, "True Colors," from the album *True Colors* (Sony Records, 1990).

117. Raz, *Value, Respect, and Attachment*, 31.

118. Most of the rest of Raz's analysis in *Value, Respect, and Attachment* focuses on how to understand the universality of values that is a key aspect of their intelligibility, the social dependence of many values, and the status of moral values demanding respect for persons.

119. In her recent Presidential Address to the Central Division of the APA (March 2006), Eleonore Stump offered a Thomistic solution to this problem that involves two conditions for love: (1) desiring the good of the other, which does not depend on their intrinsic or relational properties; and (2) desiring some kind of

union with the other, which is sensitive to their intrinsic and relational properties. Although this is an interesting way of trying to avoid both extremes, the problem is that condition 2 presupposes a eudaimonist conception of motivation, whereas condition 1 requires projective motivation. The existential model of striving will thus provide a more adequate basis for analyzing different forms of love, including not only agapē (as I argue in chap. 9) but also romantic love, in which a kind of emotional union is intended. However, an existential account of romantic love must await a full existential theory of emotions that builds on the conception of striving will developed in this book.

120. J. Anderson, "Personal Lives of Strong Evaluators," 18. As Anderson notes, the problem with Taylor's account lies in his tight link "between *endorsing* a good and being *moved* by it" (33); his eudaimonist model of motivation leaves no room for projective motivation to take general value grounds and particularize them in personal projects.

121. Raz's model also comes closer to what Anderson calls a "realist approach based on properties of situations," which can include individuating histories of agents and their self-interpretations (ibid., 34).

122. Wolf, "The True, the Good, and the Loveable," 234.

123. Ibid., 236.

124. See Nozick, *Anarchy, State, and Utopia*, 42–43.

125. See Frankfurt, *On Bullshit*.

126. Frankfurt, "On the Necessity of Ideals," 25.

127. Ibid., 26.

128. Ibid.

129. Frankfurt, *Reasons of Love*, 24.

130. Ibid.

131. Frankfurt, "The Importance of What We Care About," 93 (emphasis added).

132. Nozick, *Philosophical Explanations*, 595. Nozick may have learned this from Viktor Frankl (see 579–80).

133. Frankfurt, "On the Necessity of Ideals," 25. However, he footnotes papers by Blasi, Rorty, Tugendhat, Wren, Haste, and Nunner-Winkler in *The Moral Self* as fruitfully addressing these questions.

134. Frankfurt, *Reasons of Love*, 23.

135. See O'Connor's critique of the demand for uniquely rational options in *Persons and Causes*, 90–93.

136. Frankfurt, *Reasons of Love*, 40, n. 4.

137. Ibid., 25.

138. Leopold, *A Sand County Almanac and Sketches Here and There*, "Wisconsin," 96.

139. For this reason, I am not convinced by Frankfurt's argument that because our confident love of our children is not based on rational arguments, it must not be grounded in objective values (*Reasons of Love*, 29). The intrinsic value of the child, his or her potential, and his or her historical relation to us are all good reasons for our love, although these values are not first revealed to us by reasoning

about the implicit commitments of agency; the existential objectivist position is not a kind of Kantian rationalism extended to nonmoral values. In addition to the rationalist, subjectivist, and existential accounts I have mentioned, a fourth approach inspired by Aquinas is offered by Eleonore Stump in her recent Presidential Address to the Central Division meeting of the APA (Chicago, April 2006).

140. Frankfurt, *Reasons of Love*, 26.

141. Of course, volitional devotion to such an end makes an art form of it, which is something quite distinct from ordinary appetites for various first-order pleasures (sensual, entertaining, etc.).

142. The qualifier "almost" is important here, given my suspicion of volitional necessity.

143. Wolf, "The True, the Good, and the Loveable," 236.

144. I believe this also to be an implication of Heidegger's analysis of *Dasein* in *Being and Time*.

145. Larmore, *The Morals of Modernity*, 87.

146. See Adams, *Finite and Infinite Goods*, esp. chaps. 3–7; Audi, *The Good in the Right*; Dancy, *Practical Reality*; Kupperman, *Values . . . and What Follows*; Gewirth, *Self-Fulfillment*; Grünberg, *The Mystery of Values*; von Wright, *The Varieties of Goodness*; Harman and Thomson, *Moral Relativism and Moral Objectivity*; Lemos, *Intrinsic Value*; the essays from *Social Philosophy and Policy* reprinted in Paul, Miller, and Paul, *The Good Life and the Human Good*; Ryn, *Will, Imagination, and Reason*; Rescher, *Human Interests*, esp. chaps. 13, 14, and 16; Scanlon, *What We Owe to Each Other*; Tiberius, *Deliberation about the Good*, esp. chap. 7. Of course expressive antinaturalist theories still abound in contemporary metaethics, especially concerning moral norms; see, e.g., Blackburn, "Supervenience Revisited"; Brandt, *Facts, Values, and Morality*; Gibbard, *Wise Choices, Apt Feelings*; and Railton, "Nonfactualism about Normative Discourse." However, many others now argue that emotions themselves involve a kind of axiological evaluation of objects in the world in terms of which they can be judged adequate or not; see, e.g., de Sousa, *The Rationality of Emotion*, chap. 12 (although de Sousa eventually denies the contrast between subjective appropriation and objective apprehension of values, 319). Partially cognitive conceptions of emotion fit well with the Aristotelian idea that emotional tendencies to some extent reflect one's value-judgmental dispositions.

147. Liberman, *Commitment, Values, and Moral Realism*, 1–2.

148. See Chulef, Read, and Walsh, "A Hierarchical Taxonomy of Human Goals."

149. I emphasize that my list includes most of the goods one finds in recent natural-law theories, such as the list of goods basic to well-being in Murphy, *Natural Law and Practical Rationality*; but my list includes goods that range outside human well-being altogether, such as environmental goods and abstract values. In that respect, my list is more like the ones found in the "phenomenological realist" school of Dietrich von Hildebrande.

150. Since I have said little about this kind of reason until now, an example is in order. In *All Creatures Great and Small*, James Herriot does not start out with the intention of working as a vet in Yorkshire, but he seizes a lucky opportunity and

becomes ever more deeply engaged in Farnon's lively practice, the troubles and joys of the Yorkshire folk, and the beauty of this land. This whole gestalt of values worth caring about is crystallized or held together for this one individual by the initial prospect or opportunity, which is a historically unique prospective consideration.

151. I include this kind of individual ground to accommodate Frankfurt's idea of volitional necessities, although I do not endorse this idea.

152. Bugbee, *The Inward Morning*, October 8 entry, 69.

153. Blustein, *Care and Commitment*, 24.

154. See Festinger, *A Theory of Cognitive Dissonance*.

155. See Seligman and Abramson, "Learned Helplessness in Humans"; and Peterson and Seligman, "Causal Explanations and Depression."

156. Blustein, *Care and Commitment*, 25.

157. Kekes, *The Morality of Pluralism*, 11; see also Kekes, *Moral Wisdom and Good Lives*.

158. Ibid., 14.

159. Ibid., 15.

160. Ibid., 19.

161. See Flanagan's responses to Bernard Williams's contention that personal projects can trump impartial moral requirements; *The Varieties of Moral Personality*, chaps. 3 and 4.

Conclusion: The Danger of Willfulness Revisited

1. Here I want to acknowledge serious questions recently raised by John Lippitt about what work the notion of narrative unity can do in an existential account of virtue and whether it might not overvalorize planning relative to surprise or openness to being changed through encounters and unanticipatable events. See Lippitt's review of *Kierkegaard after MacIntyre* in *Faith and Philosophy* and his essay on this topic forthcoming in *Inquiry*.

2. Schalow, "Beyond Decisionism and Anarchy," 360.

3. Ibid.

4. Ibid., 363. This is why, in his debate with an adversary bent on immortality, Captain Picard says that "our mortality defines us." See *Star Trek Generations*, directed by David Carson, written by Rick Berman (Paramount Pictures, 1994).

5. Ibid., 364. Unfortunately, though, Schalow seems to infer from this that we should move beyond the idea of "a will" as "the centralization of [freedom's] power" (ibid., 366). I hope to have shown instead that the idea of willing itself need not be rejected to overcome the dangers of pure voluntarism.

6. Noddings, *Caring*, 24.

7. Ehman, *The Authentic Self*, 12–13.

8. Ibid., 13.

9. Gabrielle Taylor, "Deadly Vices?" 168.

10. Ehman, *The Authentic Self*, 14.

11. Ibid., 14–15.

12. Ibid., 15.
13. Ibid., 16.
14. Ibid., 17.
15. Ibid., 18.
16. Ibid., 21–23.
17. Ibid., 31.
18. Ibid., 32.
19. Ibid., 33.
20. Ibid., 34.

21. This is also true for Kant on my reading of his theory of the foundation of moral norms. For I understand Kant as saying that in willing anything, we are in part *responding* to and thus *implicitly affirming* our own infinite noninstrumental value as agents capable of liberty and projective motivation (and in particular, the motive of duty). This value is not itself something *created* by the will; rather, the will is always already implicitly committed to it and, willy-nilly, expresses it, whatever it wills. Hence the pragmatic contradiction in maxims that deny this value.

22. Ibid., 38.
23. Ibid., 44.
24. Ibid., 61.

25. Heidegger, "Question Concerning Technology," in *Question Concerning Technology and Other Essays*, 32.

26. Oliver, "Yes! No!" in *Owls and Other Fantasies*, 27.

27. Edward Mooney, *Selves in Discord and Resolve*, 19. Mooney's analysis also raises questions about the role of leeway-libertarian freedom in identity-formation that must be postponed for future work on autonomy.

28. Ibid., 39–40. Mooney makes this point in his unsurpassed commentary on Kierkegaard's discussion of Job in *Repetition*.

29. For this objection, I am indebted to Steve Watson; see also his *Traditions(s)*, 141. Heidegger's notion of the "will to will" is found in "Word of Nietzsche" in *Question Concerning Technology and Other Essays*.

30. This idea of a balance between "self-choice" and "self-reception" comes from Mooney, *Selves in Discord and Resolve*, chap. 2.

Glossary of Definitions, Technical Terms, and Abbreviations

Agent-transcending product-goods definitive of a practice: those goods that a practice distinctively produces for the community, which an agent must value intrinsically and take as (among) her final ends in order to count as authentically engaged in the practice.

Agent-relative process-goods internal to a practice: goods that arise for the agent as by-products of his engaging in the practice, or from his pursuing and/or realizing the goods definitive of the practice for their own sake.

Aristotelian principle (AP): John Rawls's hypothesis that human agents naturally tend to enjoy the development and exercise of their talents and capacities, and this enjoyment increases as the challenges become more complex and draw on a more diverse array of abilities.

Complexity caveat: this concerns the relation between formed cares and rational grounds for caring; some objective grounds for caring about a given goal may be relevant to an agent or rational for him to consider only if he has, or has not, already formed other cares and purposes of particular kinds.

Egoism:

    Abstract egoism: the self-defeating doctrine that we ought to aim only at second-order (or by-product) fulfillment as our sole final end.

    Formal egoism (FE):
    1. *Thin definition*: every end that an agent pursues she chooses as part of her self-realization or self-perfection; or
    2. *Thick definition*: every motive on which an agent acts aims at some end apprehended as part of his self-realization because it is something the lack of which

has become salient to him by brute attraction or evaluative judgment. Thus every final end is agent-relative in the sense that it is pursued *for appropriation or experience* by the agent.

Material psychological egoism (MPE) or "simple material egoism": all our actions are ultimately motivated by desires for self-interested first-order intrinsic goods. All our actions are conceived either as constituting such goods or as instrumental to them.

Complex material egoism: expands the list of psychologically possible goals to include higher-order self-interested goods (such as comparative advantages or changes in interpersonal differences).

Moral egoism (short for "material moral egoism" or MME): this is one type of the **Self-interest conception of practical reason** that Parfit calls "S." It holds that we *ought* to do only what we think will maximize our material advantages (simple or complex).

Ends: goals intentionally pursued by human agents; purposes that explain human action as voluntary; objects of desire (goods) when pursued in action.

Comprehensive end/good: the one second-order fully final end that holistically includes all objectively desirable first-order final ends as its proper parts, such that its intrinsic value *embraces* theirs; the ideal relationship among first-order goods, whose full intrinsic value is realized only within the ordered whole that is the comprehensive good.

Dominant end/good: the uniquely highest end/good among a list of fully final ends, which does *not* include all other objectively valuable goods (holistically *or* nonholistically): there are other final ends that are not desired for the sake of this highest end (i.e., not desired as means to or as parts of this highest good). Yet it is the most important or valuable of all fully final ends.

Final ends/intrinsic goods: goals pursued for their own sake, or goods desired for their terminal value (whether or not they are also valued as means to other distinct ends). Finality equals "completeness" in the simplest Aristotelian sense of this term. (Note: this definition does not try to capture Korsgaard's further distinction between relational and nonrelational types of terminal value).

Fully final ends/unconditionally complete goods: final ends that are not desired as means to any other ends; goods desired *only* for their terminal value, not for their instrumental value in producing other distinct goods.

Highest end/highest good: a fully final end or unconditionally complete good (willed only for its own sake) that, given our nature, we should recognize as having the greatest possible level of intrinsic value or importance for human life. (A highest end is not *ultimate* if there is more than one good of this highest order; and even a uniquely highest end might not be comprehensive but only dominant.)

Sufficient end: a fully final goal whose attainment is sufficient to make our life lack nothing objectively desirable, or sufficient to satisfy all *orektic* desire.

Ultimate end/ultimate good: the end that is uniquely highest because it is comprehensive and thus sufficient. A-eudaimonism adds further conditions to this definition to supply *a priori* reasons for thinking that there must be such an ultimate end.

Erosiac desire: motives having the structure of "lack seeking satisfaction," in which the agent is passively pulled or attracted toward an intentional content that promises to get her closer to completeness, which is a state unperturbed by any prepurposively felt absence of goods. Thus the intentional object of an erosiac desire by definition includes the agent experiencing, appropriating, possessing, or enjoying some good; it aims at the agent's well-being through this pictured relationship. Sexual appetite for bodily contact ("erotic" desire in the narrow sense) is only one paradigm species of the general class of erosiac desire. (See **Egoism: formal egoism**; contrasts with **Projective motivation**).

Erosiac theses:

Strong erosiac thesis (SET): all motives on which we act are erosiac in form.

Weak erosiac thesis (WET): all *prepurposive* human motives (PPMs) are erosiac in form.

Eudaimonia thesis: a human agent's formal telos F is *eudaimonia* (the agent's happiness in its maximally holistic sense), and thus her embracing motive (which is the jointure of all her other motives) is *orektic* desire for *eudaimonia*.

Eudaimonia: happiness in the holistic sense; a life lacking no good that could make it better, more valuable, or more worth living; flourishing in a sense that includes the agent's settled *recognition* of his blessed state (a substantive psychological condition beyond the formal requirement of performing one's natural function).

Eudaimonism

External eudaimonism (EEu): the conjunction of REu with the denial of PE: our eudaimonia as a by-product can *rationally justify* a set of dispositions and activities, yet our desire for eudaimonia will not enter into all those dispositions or motivate all those activities.

Indirect eudaimonism (IEu): a consequentialist version of EEu that tells us to do whatever will maximize our eudaimonia, including cultivating whatever motives, beliefs, actions, and practices of ethical judgment are most likely to allow us to flourish and to appreciate this flourishing.

Psychological eudaimonism (PE): the thesis that all our motives, including moral motives, are unified in the desire for eudaimonia as the holistic end that embraces all other final ends as its proper parts (PE equals the conjunction of the **Jointure** and **Eudaimonia** theses; implies **Egoism: formal egoism**).

Glossary

A-eudaimonism: an idealized reconstruction of the versions of PE attributable to Aristotle and Aquinas.

Rational eudaimonism (REu): the thesis that an agent's practical reasons for action are all unified (in the justificatory sense) in considerations concerning the agent's flourishing and its necessary conditions. Thus motives and dispositions contributing to the agent's eudaimonia as a by-product are rationally justified according to REu.

Existential objectivism (EO): the goal-setting and goal-pursuing activity of the striving will is always performed *in light of* values or goods that (appear to the agent to) *ground* or provide objective reasons for this volitional activity. Projective motivation thus includes an implicit claim of intersubjective validity for the reasons that ground ways of life, modes of caring, or different types of personal ethos. See also **Grounding thesis** and **Complexity caveat**.

Existential subjectivism (ES): the denial of EO. ES holds that cares and volitional commitments in general are inscrutably personal in origin or even essential to the agent's subjective motivational set and make no validity-claim upon others that could be rationally criticizable on the basis of independent criteria.

Grounding thesis: any end E that is willed in the projective sense is set on the basis of grounds for valuing E or reasons for valuing the *process* of pursuing E (or both), where these considerations are neither (1) chosen by the agent, nor (2) constituted simply by desires for E in the erosiac sense. In other words, in order to project E, the agent must see some kind of *agent-transcending* value either in the realization of E or in the process or activity of her pursuing E (or both). See also **Existential objectivism**.

Inclusion in a goal:

    Holistic inclusion: state of affairs A is included holistically in goal B if, whenever A is pursued as final, it is pursued *as* a constituent part of B (where the part-whole relation is non-mereological). A's finality is an aspect of the finality of B; A is pursued as an expression of B or way of participating in B, and in such a way that it fits with the other parts of B.

    Nonholistic inclusion: state of affairs A is included nonholistically in goal B if A is always pursued partly or wholly as a *means* to B (nonholistic inclusion is mereological in the sense that A is simply added to a list of other means to B, without necessarily having any intrinsic relation to these other means).

Independence relation between motives of different orders: M_1 and M_2 are *motivationally independent* if and only if M_2 does not psychologically explain the existence of M_1 by motivating the agent to acquire, develop, or foster M_1 as a means to satisfying M_2 or as part of M_2.

Insufficiency principle (IP): (1) factual and evaluative judgments by themselves do not necessarily generate a corresponding motivation to pursue the relevant good or avoid the relevant harm; the agent can make such judgments seriously without necessarily being moved to act on them; (2) even when they do motivate, such judgments are always insufficient to cause a corresponding intention to act as the judgment indicates, until they are taken up in decision.

Joint goods: values that can be realized only by the joint action of more than one human agent, in which each intends his or her act partly or wholly because others are willing to do likewise on the same understanding that this will be a joint action. Such goods can be produced or enjoyed only together as common goods.

Jointure thesis: there is exactly one unified *formal* telos F such that our motivation to pursue F embraces all our motives, in the sense that they are parts of, or expressions or instantiations of, the motivation to pursue F.

Kantian principle of action (KPA): any voluntary action A involves the agent's implicit endorsement of some *practical reason* for A-ing in such circumstances, which he must then regard as a consideration with *normative* force in favor of A-ing in any similar circumstance.

Naturalistic thesis: human flourishing will be realized by whatever activities and states completely develop, exploit, and express the full potential of our *natural kind* or are required as necessary conditions of this complete expression of the full potential defined by our natural kind.

Nontransferability of desire to by-product satisfaction: if the desire for and pursuit of some end X produces some by-product satisfaction S, the same desire for X cannot transfer to S or include S among its objects.

Normative worth (NW): the intersubjectively accessible, rationally evaluable value in some potential object of care or process of caring that makes it objectively worth caring about (contrasts with **Personal importance**).

Nygren's fallacy (as a false conditional): If agent S loves X because of X's objective value V, then S's love must be an erosiac appetite for V; (as a false dichotomy): all love is either groundless or erosiac.

Orexis: Aristotle's general term for all forms of erosiac desire, including lower appetites (*epithumia*), passions such as sudden anger (*thumos*); and rational wishes (*boulēsis*). Orexis originally signified reaching out one's hand for something.

Paradox of material egoism: a type of *pragmatic self-defeat* in motivation. Following material egoism as a normative doctrine, an agent fails to pursue any agent-transcending first-order goods for their own sake and thereby makes his life worse or lowers his overall well-being, thus frustrating his primary self-regarding aim.

Paradox of eudaimonism: the pure motive of virtue conflicts with the formal egoism involved in the **Eudaimonia thesis**. Since virtuous acts aim at "the noble" rather than at the agent's eudaimonia, the latter can be at most an unintended by-product of virtuous motivation and action.

Paradox of utilitarianism: the collective happiness of all relevant agents may be maximized only if some (or most) of these agents act on nonutilitarian motives or subscribe to practical principles that conflict with the direct application of the greatest happiness principle.

Personal importance (PI): the kind of agent-relative importance or value-to-an-agent that something or someone *derives from* the agent's caring about it or them, rather than operating as a prior agent-neutral ground for his caring. Personal importance is thus agent-relative and not universalizable (contrasts with **Normative worth**).

Platonic principle (positive formulation): in every action, we intend an end perceived as an apparent good for us or for our group; we choose this end as adding materially to our well-being or to the well-being of our community in some way. (Negative formulation): we never act with harm to ourselves or our community as our final end, since that would be to create some lack or want in ourselves for its own sake.

Projective motivation: an *essentially volitional* type of purposive motivation that does not derive from prepurposive motives but is generated by the agent in the process of setting new goals, forming new projects, or supplementing existing motives for carrying out already formed purposes. The intentional content of a projective motive is actively established rather than drawing the mind toward it, and therefore this content can be pure of perceived relation to the agent's well-being (contrasts with **Erosaic desire**.) (This volitional sense of "projective" is unrelated to "projection" in the psychoanalytic sense of mistaking subjective qualities of one's own thought for real properties of objects outside one's mind.)

Prepurposive motives (PPMs): conative psychic states, such as desires and some emotions, that motivate or incline us to act without necessarily entailing an intention to act on them or a formed purpose (contrasts with **Purposive motivation**).

Proportionalism: a version of objectivism about values that holds that an ethical will must care about each thing strictly in proportion to its objective importance in a rigid hierarchy of normative worth. (This usage is unrelated to "proportionalism" as a normative doctrine concerning when negative side effects of a contemplated action are acceptable).

Purposive motivation: the motivation to act that guides or directs a standing intention, purpose, or plan of action; the motivation guiding or directing the agent when she acts on purpose (contrasts with **Prepurposive motivation**).

Self-interest conception of practical reason (S): Derek Parfit's maximally generalized formulation of moral egoism as the doctrine that we should cultivate whatever habits, motives, beliefs, and practices of ethical judgment are most likely to maximize our individual welfare.

Pure aretaic naturalism: a human life regulated by virtuous dispositions of character will tend to be a flourishing life, where this consists of objective goods by which we realize *the good of our natural kind*, whether or not this involves subjective recognition of happiness. As with external eudaimonism, on this model, the virtuous agent may not be motivated by a desire for the flourishing that virtue tends to produce.

Pure motives: motives involving *no self-interest*; motives that are pure of both formal and material egoism because they aim at some agent-transcending goal (not formally or materially connected to the agent's well-being) as a final end.

Subsumption of motives:

General principle of subsumption (GPS): (1) subsumption of a first-order motive M_1 under a second-order motive M_2 entails the motivational independence of the M_1 from M_2; (2) and entails the metaphysical dependence of M_2 on M_1.

Special principle of subsumption (SPS): if first-order motive M_1 is pure, and M_2 is the second-order desire for eudaimonia as a whole, then if M_1 is subsumed under M_2, it follows necessarily that M_1 is motivationally independent of M_2.

Subsumption relation between motives: a first-order motive M_1 (for end X, which is not a motive-state of the agent) is *subsumed* by a second-order motive M_2 (for end Y) when Y is either: (1) the mere *existence* of M_1, or (2) the satisfaction of M_1 by the *realization* of X.

Telos, erosiac:

Formal telos (F): F holistically embraces all the goods that we can rationally pursue, and desire for F thus underlies all our other motives, such that whatever we are motivated to pursue, we pursue either as a means to, as part of, or under the aspect of F (whether reflectively or only tacitly).

Material telos (M): that in which our formal telos F actually consists or that which constitutes or causes F to be realized for us. The content of M may not be apparent to us even if we understand our desires as pointing to some embracing good (F) that would be completely fulfilling. M is thus ontologically constitutive of F but epistemically distinct from F.

Telos, existential

Natural telos: a normative concept of our natural design or function, including the types of motives we are meant to develop, or volitional activities we are meant to engage in. The agent's realizing her natural telos or performing well this natural function is not equivalent to her *flourishing* (in prior, substantive senses of that concept) or to her experiencing her life as *eudaimon*, or filled with well-being. Eudaimonia and flourishing may be contingent *by-products* of fulfilling our natural function.

Motivational telos: the set of ends E that it is our function to care about for their own sake or that we care about when we are fulfilling our design plan or performing our natural function. "Living according to our nature" and "realizing our natural telos" are *not* included in E. Rather, these results *follow* from willing the ends included in our motivational telos.

Material existential telos: a substantive conception or list of ends included in our motivational telos, which may also specify the relationships among these ends, higher-order regulative goals, and the kinds of value-insight or practical reasons that are required to will these ends for their own sake.

Transcendent principle (Trans):

   Strong Transcendent principle (Plato): if an end e is pursued for its own sake (or as final), then it is pursued as comprehensive (Fe → Ce). We may think of this as a conjunction of two simpler theses: if e is final, then it is complete/fully final; and if e is fully final, then it is comprehensive [(Fe → FFe) & (FFe → Ce)]. If we combine this with the plausible premise that finite, earthly goods are not comprehensively good, it follows that they are not truly pursued as final: we really desire the goods of this life for their resemblance to or participation in a transcendent good that is comprehensive; through them, we hope to get to this all-embracing transcendent good.

   Weak Transcendent principle (Aristotle): if end e is fully final, then it is comprehensive (FFe → Ce). Only the comprehensive good is pursued solely for its own sake; all noncomprehensive final ends are either (a) also pursued as a means to other ends or (b) pursued *as* constitutive components of the comprehensive good.

Transmission principle (TP): All the motivation present in the formation of intentions and the carrying out of intentions derives both its (1) *all* its strength and (2) *all* its intentional direction and content immediately from prior prepurposive psychological states (PPMs) that are either (a) already motivating in their own right (such as desires) or (b) motivating when combined with these (such as beliefs).

Tutelage thesis: no one can ever *voluntarily* enter into a practice (or similarly complex activity) in such a way as to realize its internal agent-related goods; to realize these internal process-goods always requires that the agent be induced by external influence and persuasion appealing to prior motives to engage in the relevant activity and then switch to the requisite pure motives later on.

Ubiquity thesis (UT): Every morally responsible agent desires his or her own happiness, flourishing, or self-realization (in addition to whatever other motives she may have).

Bibliography

1. Generally, if more than one chapter in an edited book or one essay in a collection of essays is cited, then the edited volume or collection has its own separate entry here, and each of the chapters or essays cited has its own entry with abbreviated information on the book in which it is found.
2. When only one chapter or essay from an edited volume is referenced, the entry for the chapter or essay usually includes full information on the book in which it is found.
3. The entries for most articles reprinted in such collections include only the information on the reprinted version; a few include information on the original publication of the article, followed by the book in which the article is reprinted.
4. Unless otherwise noted in the entry for a given work, chapter notes always refer to the latest version or reprint of an article in the bibliography entry.
5. I generally refer to the primary name of the publisher for each work listed here rather than to different imprints (Clarendon, Belknap, etc.), except where the imprint helps identify the edition cited. Unless the publisher is obscure, I also generally omit the place of publication, since most publishers now publish in many cities.
6. Every scholarly or literary source referenced in the chapter notes should have a full entry here, excluding a few Web sites, popular movies, musical records, newspapers, popular periodicals, and references to another work within a primary citation.
7. A few sources used as general background but not explicitly cited in any note are also included here for convenience.

Ackrill, J. L. "Aristotle on Eudaimonia." *Proceedings of the British Academy* 60 (1974):339–59. Reprinted in Rorty, *Essays on Aristotle's Ethics*, 15–33; and in Sherman, *Aristotle: Critical Essays*, 57–78.

Bibliography

Adams, Robert M. *Finite and Infinite Goods*. Oxford University Press, 1999.
———. "Must God Create the Best?" In *The Concept of God*, edited by Thomas V. Morris, 91–106. Oxford University Press, 1987.
Allison, Henry. *Idealism and Freedom: Essays on Kant's Theoretical and Practical Philosophy*. Cambridge University Press, 1996.
———. "Kant on Freedom: A Reply to My Critics." *Inquiry* 36 (1993). Reprinted in Allison, *Idealism and Freedom*.
———. *Kant's Theory of Freedom*. Cambridge University Press, 1990.
———. "Spontaneity and Autonomy in Kant's Conception of the Self." In Ameriks and Sturma, *The Modern Subject*, 11–30. Reprinted in Allison, *Idealism and Freedom*. The original version of this paper was presented at the Conference on German Idealism, University of Notre Dame, April 8, 1994.
American Heritage Dictionary. 2nd ed. Houghton Mifflin, 1982.
Ameriks, Karl. "From Kant to Frank: The Ineliminable Subject." In Ameriks and Sturma, *The Modern Subject*, 217–30.
———. *Interpreting Kant's Critiques*. Oxford University Press, 2003.
———. "Kant and Hegel on Freedom: Two New Interpretations." *Inquiry* 35.2 (June 1992):219–32. Reprinted in Ameriks, *Interpreting Kant's Critiques*, 212–25. Citations are to the original version.
———. *Kant and the Historical Turn: Philosophy as Critical Interpretation*. Oxford University Press, 2006.
———. "Kant and Motivational Externalism." In *Moralische Motivation. Kant und die Alternativen*, edited by H. Klemme, M. Kühn, and D. Schönecker. Hamburg: Meiner Verlag, 2006. Reprinted as "Kant, Hume, and the Problem of Moral Motivation" in Ameriks, *Kant and the Historical Turn*.
———. "Kant on the Good Will." In *Grundlegung der Metaphysik der Sitten*, edited by Otfried Höffe. Klostermann, 1998. Reprinted in Ameriks, *Interpreting Kant's Critiques*, 193–211.
———. *Kant's Concept of Mind*. Oxford University Press, 1982; new ed. 2000.
———. "Kant und das Problem der moralischen Motivation." In *Kants Ethik*, edited by K. Ameriks and D. Sturma, 97–116. Paderborn: Mentis, 2004.
———. "Reinhold's Challenge: Systematic Philosophy for the Public." In *Die Philosophie Karl Leonhard Reinholds. Fichte-Studien*. Supplementa 16, edited by M. Bondeli and A. Lazzari, 77–103. Rodopi, 2002.
Ameriks, Karl, and Dieter Sturma, eds. *The Modern Subject: Conceptions of the Self in Classical German Philosophy*. SUNY Press, 1995.
Anderson, Elizabeth. "Reasons, Attitudes, and Values: Replies to Sturgeon and Piper." *Ethics* 106.3 (April, 1996):538–54.
———. *Value in Ethics and Economics*. Harvard University Press, 1993.
Anderson, Joel. "Autonomy and the Authority of Personal Commitments: From Internal Coherence to Social Normativity." *Philosophical Explorations* 6 (2003):90–108.
———. "Disputing Autonomy: Structural Hierarchicalism, Procedural Hierarchicalism, and the Grounds for Ascription." Paper presented at the Central Division Meeting of the American Philosophical Association, Chicago, April 1995.

———. "The Personal Lives of Strong Evaluators: Identity, Pluralism, and Ontology in Charles Taylor's Value Theory." *Constellations* 3 (1996):17–38. Reprinted in *The Problematic Reality of Values*, edited by J. Bransen and M. Slors, 97–115. Assen: Van Gorcem, 1996.

———. "A Social Conception of Personal Autonomy: Volitional Identity, Strong Evaluation, and Intersubjective Accountability." Ph.D. diss., Northwestern University, 1996.

Anns, Julia. *The Morality of Happiness*. Oxford University Press, 1993.

———. "Self-Love in Aristotle," *Southern Journal of Philosophy*, edited by Timothy Roche. 27 (1988, suppl.):1–18.

Anscombe, Elizabeth (G. E. M.). *Intention*. Oxford University Press, 1957.

———. "Modern Moral Philosophy." *Philosophy* 33 (1958). Reprinted in Crisp and Slote, *Virtue Ethics*, 26–44. Also in Anscombe, *Ethics, Religion, and Politics*. University of Minnesota Press, 1981.

Anselm, *De libertate arbitrii*. Vol. 2 of *Anselm of Canterbury*. Edited and translated by Jasper Hopkins and Herbert Richardson. Edwin Mellen Press, 1976.

Aquinas, Thomas. *Creation*. Vol. 2 of *Summa Contra Gentiles*. Translated by James F. Anderson. University of Notre Dame Press, 1975.

———. *Salvation*. Vol. 4 of *Summa Contra Gentiles*. Translated by Charles O'Neil. University of Notre Dame Press, 1975.

———. *Summa Theologica*. Translated by the Fathers of the English Dominican Province. London: Burns Oates & Washbourne, 1923. All references to the *Summa Theologica* are to this translation unless otherwise specified.

———. *Treatise on Happiness* [Questions I–XXI of the *Summa Theologica*, IIa]. Translated by John Oesterle. Reprinted by University of Notre Dame Press, 1983. References to this translation include "Oesterle" in parentheses.

Arendt, Hannah. *Essays in Understanding: 1930–1954*. Edited by Jerome Kohn. Harcourt Brace, 1994.

———. *The Life of the Mind*. Edited by Mary McCarthy. Harcourt Brace Jovanovich, 1971. Includes *Thinking* (Part 1) and *Willing* (Part 2).

Aristotle. *De anima*. Translated by J. A. Smith. In *The Basic Works of Aristotle*, edited by Richard McKeon. Random House, 1941.

———. *Metaphysics*. Translated by W. D. Ross. Vol. 2 of *The Complete Works of Aristotle: The Revised Oxford Translation*, edited by Jonathan Barnes. Bollingen Series, vol. 71.2. Princeton University Press/Bollingen Foundation, 1984.

———. *Nicomachean Ethics*. Translated by W. D. Ross. Vol. 2 of *The Complete Works of Aristotle: The Revised Oxford Translation*.

———. *Nicomachean Ethics*. 2nd ed. Translated with an introduction by Terence Irwin. Hackett, 1999. Unless otherwise noted, citations to the *Ethics* are from this translation.

Auden, W. H. "The Quest Hero." Reprinted in *Tolkien and the Critics*, edited by Neil Isaacs and Rose Zimbardo. University of Notre Dame Press, 1976.

Audi, Robert. *Action, Intention, and Reason*. Cornell University Press, 1993.

———. *Moral Knowledge and Ethical Character*. Oxford University Press, 1997.

———. *The Good in the Right*. Princeton University Press, 2004.

Augustine. *The City of God*. Translated by Henry Bettenson. Penguin, 1984.
———. *On Free Choice of the Will*. Edited and translated by Thomas Williams. Hackett, 1993.
Bacon, Francis. *The Advancement of Learning*. Edited by G. W. Kitchin, introduction by Arthur Johnston. Dent/Everyman's Library, 1973.
———. *The New Organon* [*Novum Organon*, 1620]. Edited by Lisa Jardine and Michael Silverthorne. Cambridge University Press, 2000.
Badhwar, Neera Kapur. "Friends as Ends in Themselves." In Soble, *Eros, Agape, and Philia*, 165–87.
Baier, Annette C. "Caring about Caring: A Reply to Frankfurt." *Synthese* 53, no. 2 (November 1982):273–90.
Baille, James. *Problems in Personal Identity*. Paragon House, 1993.
Bandura, Albert, and Dale Schunk. "Cultivating Competence, Self-Efficacy, and Intrinsic Interest Through Proximal Self-Motivation." *Journal of Personality and Social Psychology* 41.3 (1981):586–98.
Barrett, E. Boyd, S.J. *Strength of Will*. New York: P. J. Kennedy & Sons, 1915, 1917 impression.
Batson, C. D. *The Altruism Question*. Erlbaum, 1991.
Baur, Michael. "Heidegger and Aquinas on the Self as Substance." *American Catholic Philosophical Quarterly* 70.3 (1996):317–37.
Benhabib, Seyla. *Situating the Self: Gender, Community, and Postmodernism in Contemporary Ethics*. Routledge, 1992.
Benson, Paul. "Free Agency and Self-Worth." *Journal of Philosophy* 91.12 (December 1994):650–68.
Bernstein, Richard J. *Radical Evil: A Philosophical Investigation*. Polity Press, 2002.
Bertocci, Peter. *The Person and Primary Emotions*. Springer-Verlag, 1988.
The Bhagavad Gita. Translated by Juan Mascaró. Penguin, 1962.
Blackburn, Simon. *Ruling Passions*. Oxford University Press, 1998.
———. "Supervenience Revisited." In *Essays on Moral Realism*, edited by Geoffrey Sayre-McCord. Cornell University Press, 1988.
Blustein, Jeffrey. *Care and Commitment*. Oxford University Press, 1991.
Boler, John. "Transcending the Natural: Duns Scotus on the Two Affections of the Will." In *Duns Scotus*, edited by Alan Wolter, *American Catholic Philosophical Quarterly* 67.1 (Winter 1993):109–26.
Bonansea, Bernardine. "Duns Scotus's Voluntarism." In *John Duns Scotus, 1265–1965*, edited by John Ryan and Bernardine Bonansea, 83–121. Catholic University of America Press, 1965.
Bond, E. J. *Reason and Value*. Cambridge University Press, 1983.
Bostock, David. *Aristotle's Ethics*. Oxford University Press, 2000.
Bovens, Luc. "Two Faces of Akratics Anonymous." *Analysis* 59.4 (October 1999):230–36.
Bradley, F. H. "The Definition of Will," No. II. *Mind* 46 (April 1903):145–76.
Brandt, Richard. *Facts, Values, and Morality*. Cambridge University Press, 1996.
Bratman, Michael. "Responsibility and Planning." *Journal of Ethics* 1 (1997):27–43. Reprinted in Bratman, *Faces of Intention*, 165–84. Cambridge University Press, 1999.

Breazeale, Daniel. "Check or Checkmate? On the Finitude of the Fichtean Self." In Ameriks and Sturma, *The Modern Subject*, 87–114.

Bremmer, Jan. *The Early Greek Concept of the Soul*. Princeton University Press, 1983.

Bretlinger, John. "The Nature of Love." In *The Symposium of Plato*, edited by Bretlinger, translated Suzy Gronden, 113–29. University of Massachusetts Press, 1970. Reprinted in Soble, *Eros, Agape, and Philia*, 136–48.

Brink, David O. "Rational Egoism, Self, and Others." In Flanagan and Rorty, *Identity, Character, and Morality*, 339–78.

Broadie, Sarah. *Ethics with Aristotle*. Oxford University Press, 1991.

Brower, Bruce. "Virtue Concepts and Ethical Realism." *Journal of Philosophy* 85 (December 1988):675–93.

Buber, Martin. *Between Man and Man*. Translated by Ronald Gregor Smith, introduction by Maurice Friedman. Macmillan, 1965.

———. *I and Thou*. Translated by Walter Kaufmann. Scribner's, 1970.

———. *The Way of Man According to the Teachings of Hasidism*. Citadel Press, 1966.

Bugbee, Henry. *The Inward Morning: A Philosophical Exploration in Journal Form*. Introduction by Edward Mooney. University of Georgia Press, 1999.

Buss, Sarah. "Autonomy Reconsidered." *Midwest Studies in Philosophy* 19 (1994):95–121.

Buss, Sarah, and Lee Overton, eds. *Contours of Agency: Essays on Themes from Harry Frankfurt*. MIT Press, 2002.

Butler, Joseph. *Five Sermons Preached at Rolls Chapel and a Dissertation Upon the Nature of Virtue*. Edited and introduction by Stephen Darwall. Hackett, 1983.

Cadava, Eduardo, Peter Connor, and Jean-Luc Nancy, eds. *Who Comes after the Subject?* Routledge, 1991.

Calhoun, Cheshire. "Standing for Something." *Journal of Philosophy* 92.5 (May 1995):235–60.

Callicott, J. Baird. "The Conceptual Foundations of the Land Ethic." In *Environmental Ethics*, edited by Louis Pojman, 3rd ed., 126–35. Wadsworth, 1998.

Caputo, John, and Jacques Derrida. *Deconstruction in a Nutshell: A Conversation with Jacques Derrida*. Fordham University Press, 1997.

Carr, David. "The Cardinal Virtues and Plato's Moral Psychology." *Philosophical Quarterly* 38.151 (1988):186–200.

Casey, John. *Pagan Virtue: An Essay in Ethics*. Oxford University Press, 1990.

Cassam, Quassim, ed. *Self-Knowledge*. Oxford University Press, 1994.

Cavalier, Robert. *Personal Motivation: A Model for Decision-Making*. Praeger Publishers, 2000.

Chisholm, Roderick. *Brentano and Intrinsic Value*. Cambridge University Press, 1986.

Christman, John, ed. *The Inner Citadel: Essays on Individual Autonomy*. Oxford University Press, 1989.

Christman, John and Joel Anderson, eds. *Autonomy and the Challenges to Liberalism*. Cambridge University Press, 2005.

Chulef, Ada, Stephen Read, and David Walsh. "A Hierarchical Taxonomy of Human Goals." *Motivation and Emotion* 25.3 (September 2001):191–232.

Cicero. *On Moral Ends [De finibus]*. Edited by Julia Annas, translated by Raphael Woolf. Cambridge University Press, 2001.

Clark, Mary T. *Augustine: Philosopher of Freedom*. Desclée, 1954.

Clarke, W. Norris. "Is the Ethical Eudaimonism of St. Thomas Too Self-Centered?" In *Commentaries on Moral Philosophy*, edited by Raimer Ibana and Angelli Tugado. Philippine Commission on Higher Education, 1998.

Cooper, John M. *Reason and Emotion: Essays on Ancient Moral Psychology and Ethical Theory*. Princeton University Press, 1999.

———. *Reason and the Human Good in Aristotle*. Harvard University Press, 1975. Reprinted as paperback by Hackett Publishing, 1986. Citations are to the Hackett paperback.

———. "Reason, Moral Virtue, and Moral Value." In *Rationality in Greek Thought*, edited by M. Frede and G. Striker, 81–114. Oxford University Press, 1996.

———. "The Unity of Virtue." In *Virtue and Vice*, edited by Ellen Paul, Fred Miller, and Jeffrey Paul, 233–74. Cambridge University Press, 1998.

Copjec, Joan, ed. *Radical Evil*. Verso, 1996.

Copleston, Frederick. *Medieval Philosophy*. Vol. 2 of *A History of Philosophy*. Newman Press, 1962. Reprinted by Image Books/Bantam Doubleday Dell, 1993.

Crisp, Roger, ed. *How Should One Live? Essays on the Virtues*. Oxford University Press, 1996.

Crisp, Roger, and Michael Slote, eds. *Virtue Ethics*. Oxford University Press, 1997.

Crosby, John. *The Selfhood of the Human Person*. Catholic University of America Press, 1997.

Cudworth, Ralph. *A Treatise Concerning Eternal and Immutable Morality* and *A Treatise of Freewill* [London, 1731]. Edited by Sarah Hutton. Cambridge University Press, 1996.

Dancy, Jonathan. *Moral Reasons*. Blackwell Publishers, 1993. Reprinted 1994.

———. *Practical Reality*. Oxford University Press, 2000.

Davenport, John. "Aquinas's Teleological Libertarianism." In *Analytical Thomism: Traditions in Dialogue*, edited by Matthew Pugh, 119–46. Ashgate Press, 2006.

———. "The Binding Value of Earnest Emotional Valuation." *International Journal of Decision Ethics* 2.1 (Fall 2005):107–24.

———. "Entangled Freedom: Ethical Authority, Original Sin, and Choice in Kierkegaard's *Concept of Anxiety*." *Kierkegaardiana* 21 (2001):131–51.

———. "Eschatological Ultimacy and the Best Possible Hereafter." *Ultimate Reality and Meaning* 25.1 (March 2002):36–67.

———. "The Essence of Eschatology: A Modal Interpretation." *Ultimate Reality and Meaning* 19.3 (September, 1996):206–39.

———. "The Ethical and Religious Significance of Taciturnus's Letter in Kierkegaard's *Stages on Life's Way*." In *Stages on Life's Way*, vol. 11 of *The International Kierkegaard Commentary*, edited by Robert Perkins, 213–44. Mercer University Press, 2000.

———. "Faith as Eschatological Trust in *Fear and Trembling*." Forthcoming in *Ethics, Love, and Faith in Kierkegaard: A Philosophical Engagement*, edited by Edward Mooney. Indiana University Press, 2008 (forthcoming).

———. "Fischer and Ravizza on Moral Sanity and Weakness of Will." *Journal of Ethics* 6 (2002):235–59.

———. "Happy Endings and Religious Hope: The *Lord of the Rings* as an Epic Fairy Tale." In *The Lord of the Rings and Philosophy*, edited by Gregory Bassham and Eric Bronson, 204–18. Open Court, 2003.

———. "Kierkegaard, Anxiety, and the Will." In *Kierkegaard Studies Yearbook*, vol. 6, edited by Niels Jørgen Cappelørn, Hermann Deuser, and Jon Stewart, 158–81. Walter de Gruyter, 2001.

———. "Levinas's Agapeistic Metaphysics of Morals." *Journal of Religious Ethics* 26.2 (Fall 1998):331–66.

———. "Liberty of the Higher-Order Will: Frankfurt and Augustine." *Faith and Philosophy* 19.4 (October 2002):437–61.

———. "The Meaning of Kierkegaard's Choice between the Aesthetic and the Ethical: A Response to MacIntyre." *Southwest Philosophy Review* 11.2 (August, 1995):73–108. Revised and reprinted in Davenport and Rudd, *Kierkegaard After MacIntyre*, 75–112.

———. "A Phenomenology of the Profane: Heidegger, Blumenberg, and the Structure of the 'Chthonic.'" *JBSP: Journal of the British Society of Phenomenology* 30.2 (May, 1999):183–207.

———. "Review of Murphy: *Natural Law and Practical Rationality*." *International Philosophical Quarterly* 43.2 (June 2003):229–40.

———. "*Schindler's List*: A Personal Kierkegaardian Reflection." *Religious Humanism* 34.3/4 (Summer/Fall 2000):13–23.

———. "Time and Responsibility: Neighbor-Love and History." Four talks given at All Souls Unitarian Universalist Church, New York, N.Y., January 2002.

———. "Towards an Existential Virtue Ethics: Kierkegaard and MacIntyre." In Davenport and Rudd, *Kierkegaard after MacIntyre*, 265–324.

Davenport, John, and Anthony Rudd, eds. *Kierkegaard After MacIntyre*. Open Court, 2001.

Davidson, Donald. *Essays on Actions and Events*. Oxford University Press, 1980.

Davis, Wayne A. "The Two Senses of Desire." In *The Ways of Desire*, edited by Joel Marks, 63–82. Chicago: Precedent Publishing, 1986.

Deci, Edward L. *Intrinsic Motivation*. Vol. 1 of *Perspectives in Social Psychology*. Plenum, 1976.

Deci, Edward L., and Richard M. Ryan. *Intrinsic Motivation and Self-Determination in Human Behavior*. Vol. 8 of *Perspectives in Social Psychology*. Plenum, 1985. Reprinted 1990.

———. "The 'What' and the 'Why' of Goal Pursuits: Human Needs and the Self-Determination of Behavior." *Psychological Inquiry* 11.4 (2000):227–68.

Delancey, Craig. *Passionate Engines: What Emotions Reveal about Mind and Artificial Intelligence*. Oxford University Press, 2002.

Dennett, Daniel. "Conditions of Personhood." In *Brainstorms: Philosophical Essays on Mind and Psychology*, chap. 14. Bradford Books, 1978.

———. *Content and Consciousness and Content*. Routledge & Kegan Paul, 1969. Reprinted 1993.

———. *Elbow Room: The Varieties of Free Will Worth Wanting*. MIT Press, 1984. Reprinted 1993.

———. *Consciousness Explained*. Little, Brown/Back Bay Books, 1991.
———. *The Intentional Stance*. MIT Press, 1987.
———. "Mechanism and Responsibility." In *Essays on Freedom of Action*, edited by Ted Honderich. Routledge & Kegan Paul, 1973. Reprinted in Watson, *Free Will*, 150–73. 1982.
Descartes, René. *Meditations on First Philosophy*. 2nd ed., translated by Donald A. Cress. Hackett, 1989.
Desmond, William. *Desire, Dialectic, and Otherness: An Essay on Origins*. Yale University Press, 1987.
De Sousa, Ronald. *The Rationality of Emotion*. MIT Press, 1987.
Dewey, John. *Human Nature and Conduct*. George Allen & Unwin, 1922.
The Dhammapada: The Path of Perfection. Translated by Juan Mascaró. Penguin, 1973.
Dickens, Charles. *A Tale of Two Cities*. Dent/Everyman's Library, 1979.
Dihle, Albrecht. *The Theory of Will in Classical Antiquity*. University of California Press, 1982.
Donaldson, Stephen. *Chaos and Order*. Bantam Doubleday, 1994.
———. *A Dark and Hungry God Arises*. Bantam Doubleday, 1994.
———. *The Power That Preserves*. Del Rey, 1979; reissued 1987.
Dostoyevsky, Fyodor. *Notes from Underground; The Double*. Translated by J. Coulson. Penguin Books, 1972. Reprinted 1982.
———. *The Brothers Karamazov*. Translated by Andrew MacAndrew. Bantam Classics, 1981.
Drummond, John J. "Agency, Agents, and (Sometimes) Patients." In *The Truthful and the Good: Essays in Honor of Robert Sokolowski*, 145–58. Kluwer, 1996.
———. "Moral Encounters." *Recherches Husserliennes* 16 (2001):39–60.
———. "Moral Objectivity: Husserl's Sentiments of the Understanding." *Husserl Studies* 12 (1995):165–83.
Dunn, Robert. *The Possibility of Weakness of Will*. Hackett, 1987.
Ehman, Robert. *The Authentic Self*. Prometheus, 1994.
Elster, Jon. *Alchemies of the Mind*. Cambridge University Press, 1999.
———. *Sour Grapes: Studies in the Subversion of Rationality*. Cambridge University Press, 1983.
———. *Strong Feelings: Emotions, Addiction, and Human Behavior*. MIT Press, 1999.
———. *Ulysses and the Sirens: Studies in Rationality and Irrationality*. Cambridge University Press, 1979.
———, ed. *The Multiple Self*. Cambridge University Press, 1985.
Engberg-Pedersen, Troels. *Aristotle's Theory of Moral Insight*. Oxford University Press, 1983.
Engel, David. "Plato's Denial of Willful Wrongdoing." Paper delivered at the Pacific Division meeting of the American Philosophical Association Meeting, Seattle, Washington, March 1996.
Erasmus and Luther, *Discourse on Free Will*. Translated by Ernst F. Winter. Ungar Publishing, 1961.
Eysenck, Hans J., and Michael W. Eysenck. *Personality and Individual Differences: A Natural Science Approach*. Plenum, 1985.

Farber, Leslie. *Ways of the Will.* Expanded ed. Basic Books, 2000.
Feinberg, Joel. "Psychological Egoism." In *Reason and Responsibility*, 4th ed., 547–59. Wadsworth, 1978. Reprinted in *Ethics*, edited by Cahn and Markie, 557–65. Oxford University Press, 1998.
Ferrari, Giovanni R. F. "Platonic Love." In *The Cambridge Companion to Plato*, edited by Richard Kraut, 248–76. Cambridge University Press, 1992.
Festinger, Leon. *A Theory of Cognitive Dissonance.* Stanford University Press, 1957.
Fichte, J. G. *Foundations of Transcendental Philosophy: (Wissenschaftslehre) Novo Methodo (1796/99).* Translated and edited by Daniel Breazeale. Cornell University Press, 1992.
Finnis, John. *Natural Law and Natural Rights.* Oxford University Press, 1980.
Fischer, John M. "Responsibility and Control." *Journal of Philosophy* 89 (January 1982):24–40. Reprinted in Fischer, *Moral Responsibility*, 174–90.
———, ed. *Moral Responsibility.* Cornell University Press, 1986.
Fischer, John, and Mark Ravizza, eds. *Perspectives on Moral Responsibility.* Cornell University Press, 1993.
———. *Responsibility and Control.* Cambridge University Press, 1998.
Flanagan, Owen. *Consciousness Reconsidered.* MIT Press, 1992.
———. *Varieties of Moral Personality: Ethics and Psychological Realism.* Harvard University Press, 1991.
Flanagan Owen, and Amélie O. Rorty, eds. *Identity, Character, and Morality: Essays in Moral Psychology.* MIT Press, 1990.
Flynn, Thomas R. *Sartre and Marxist Existentialism.* Chicago University Press, 1984.
Foot, Philippa. *Natural Goodness.* Oxford University Press, 2001.
———. "Virtues and Vices." In Crisp and Slote, *Virtue Ethics*, 163–77.
———. *Virtues and Vices and Other Essays in Moral Philosophy.* University of California Press, 1978.
Fortenbaugh, W. W. *Aristotle on Emotions.* Harper and Row, 1975.
Frank, Manfred. "Is Self-Consciousness a Case of *présence à soi*? Towards a Meta-Critique of the Recent French Critique of Metaphysics." In *Derrida: A Critical Reader*, edited by David Wood, 218–34. Blackwell, 1992.
———. "Is Subjectivity a Non-Thing, and Absurdity [Unding]? On Some Difficulties in Naturalistic Reductions of Self-Consciousness." In Ameriks and Sturma, *The Modern Subject*, 177–98.
———. "Mental Familiarity and Epistemic Self-Ascription." Paper presented at the Ernan McMullin Perspectives in Philosophy Lecture Series: "The Philosophy of Manfred Frank." University of Notre Dame, Indiana, March 26, 1996.
Frankfurt, Harry. "Autonomy, Necessity, and Love." In *Vernunftbegriffe in der Moderne: Stuttgarter Hegel Kongress, 1993*, edited by Hans Friedrich Fulda and Rolf-Peter Horstmann, 433–47. Klett-Cotta, 1994. Reprinted in Frankfurt, *Necessity, Volition, and Love*. Citations are to the original version of this essay.
———. "Comments on MacIntyre." *Synthese* 53.2 (1982):319–21.
———. "Concerning the Freedom and the Limits of the Will." *Philosophical Topics* 17.1 (Spring, 1989):119–30. Reprinted in Frankfurt, *Necessity, Volition, and Love*. Citations are to the original article.

———. "The Faintest Passion." Presidential Address of the Eastern Division of the APA, *Proceedings and Addresses of the APA* 66 (1992):5–16. Reprinted in Frankfurt, *Necessity, Volition, and Love.* Citations are to the original article.

———. "Freedom of the Will and the Concept of a Person." *Journal of Philosophy* 68.1 (January, 1971). Reprinted in Frankfurt, *The Importance of What We Care About,* 11–25.

———. "Identification and Wholeheartedness." In *Responsibility, Character, and the Emotions: New Essays in Moral Psychology,* edited by Ferdinand David Schoeman. Cambridge University Press, 1987. Reprinted in Frankfurt, *The Importance of What We Care About,* 159–76.

———. "The Importance of What We Care About." *Synthese* 53.2 (1982). Reprinted in Frankfurt, *The Importance of What We Care About,* 80–94.

———. *The Importance of What We Care About.* Cambridge University Press, 1988. All essays appearing in this book are cited by page numbers in this volume, not the pages of the original articles.

———. *Necessity, Volition, and Love.* Cambridge University Press, 1999.

———. "On Bullshit," *Raritan* 6.2 (1986). Reprinted in Frankfurt, *The Importance of What We Care About.* Reprinted as Frankfurt, *On Bullshit.* Princeton University Press, 2005.

———. "On Caring." In Frankfurt, *Necessity, Volition, and Love,* 155–80.

———. "On God's Creation." In *Reasoned Faith,* edited by Eleonore Stump. Cornell University Press, 1993. Reprinted in Frankfurt, *Necessity, Volition, and Love.* Citations are to the original article.

———. "On the Necessity of Ideals." In *The Moral Self,* edited by Gil Noam and Thomas Wren, 16–27. MIT Press, 1993. Reprinted in Frankfurt, *Necessity, Volition, and Love.* Citations are to the original article.

———. "On the Usefulness of Final Ends." *Iyyun: Jerusalem Philosophical Quarterly* 41 (January, 1992):3–19. Reprinted in Frankfurt, *Necessity, Volition, and Love.* Citations are to the original article.

———. "The Problem of Action." *American Philosophical Quarterly* 15 (1978). Reprinted in Frankfurt, *The Importance of What We Care About,* 69–79.

———. "Rationality and the Unthinkable." In Frankfurt, *The Importance of What We Care About,* 177–90.

———. *The Reasons of Love.* Princeton University Press, 2004.

———. "Reply to Gary Watson." In *Contours of Agency,* edited by Buss and Overton, 160–64. 2002.

Frankl, Viktor. *From Death Camp to Existentialism: A Psychiatrist's Path to a New Therapy.* Beacon Press, 1959.

———. *Man's Search for Meaning: An Introduction to Logotherapy.* Translated by Ilse Lasch. Pocket Books/Simon and Schuster, 1963. 3rd ed. Simon and Schuster, 1984. Citations are to the 1963 edition except where otherwise noted.

———. *Man's Search for Ultimate Meaning.* Barnes and Noble/MJF, 2000.

———. *The Unheard Cry for Meaning.* Touchstone/Simon and Schuster, 1978.

———. *The Will to Meaning.* Expanded ed. Meridian/Penguin, 1988.

Fraser, J. T. *Of Time, Passion, and Knowledge.* 2nd. ed. Princeton University Press, 1990.

Frederick, Claire, and Shirley McNeal. *Inner Strengths: Contemporary Psychotherapy and Hypnosis for Inner Strengthening.* Erlbaum, 1999.

Fromm, Erich. *The Anatomy of Human Destructiveness.* Henry Holt, 1973. Reprinted 1992.

———. *Marx's Concept of Man.* Translated by T. B. Bottomore. Frederick Ungar, 1961. Reprinted 1980.

Gadamer, Hans-Georg, *The Idea of the Good in Platonic-Aristotelian Philosophy.* Translated by P. C. Smith. Yale University Press, 1986.

Garver, Eugene, "Choosing the Good in Aristotle's *Topics.*" In *From Puzzles to Principles? Essays on Aristotle's Dialectic,* edited by May Sim, 107–24. Lexington Books, 1999.

Gert, Bernard, and Timothy J. Duggan, "Free Will as the Ability to Will." In Fischer, *Moral Responsibility,* 205–24.

Gewirth, Alan. *Self-Fulfillment:* Princeton University Press, 1998.

Gibbard, Alan. *Wise Choices, Apt Feelings.* Harvard University Press, 1990.

Gilbert, Alan. *Democratic Individuality.* Cambridge University Press, 1990.

Ginet, Carl. *On Action.* Cambridge University Press, 1990.

———. "Voluntary Exertion of the Body: A Volitional Account." *Theory and Decision* 20 (May, 1986):223–45.

Goetz, Stewart. "Libertarian Choice." *Faith and Philosophy* 14.2 (April 1997):195–221.

Gordon, Emily Fox. "Book of Days." *American Scholar* 72.1 (Winter 2003):17–31.

———. *The Mockingbird Years.* HarperCollins, 2001.

Gottlieb, Paula. "Aristotle's Ethical Egoism." *Pacific Philosophical Quarterly* 77 (1996):1–18.

Gosling, Justin. *Weakness of the Will.* Routledge, 1990.

Gould, Thomas. *The Ancient Quarrel between Poetry and Philosophy.* Princeton University Press, 1990.

Gowans, Christopher W. *Philosophy of the Buddha.* Routledge, 2003.

———. "Practical Identities and Autonomy: Korsgaard's Reformation of Kant's Moral Philosophy." *Philosophy and Phenomenological Research* 64.3 (May 2002):546–70.

Grant, Alexander. *The Ethics of Aristotle: Essays and Notes.* 4th ed., revised. Longmans, 1885.

Green, Arnold. *Hobbes and Human Nature.* Transactions Publishers, 1993.

Greene, Brian. *The Elegant Universe.* Random House/Vintage, 2000.

Grünberg, Ludwig. *The Mystery of Values.* Rodopia, 2000.

Gunning, Meredith. "About Face: Altered States of Subjectivity in Levinas." Ph.D. diss., Fordham University, 2006.

Guyer, Paul. Review of Herman, *The Practice of Moral Judgment. Ethics* 106.2 (January 1996):404–23.

Habermas, Jürgen. "Are There Postmetaphysical Answers to the Question: What Is the 'Correct Life'?" Translated William Rehg. Paper presented at the New School of Social Research, New York, N.Y., October 5, 2001. Published in modified form in Habermas, *The Future of Human Nature.* Polity Press, 2003.

———. *Discourse Ethics: Notes on a Program of Philosophical Justification*. In *Moral Consciousness and Communicative Action*, translated by Christian Lenhardt and Shierry Weber Nicholsen. MIT Press, 1990.

———. *The Philosophical Discourse of Modernity: Twelve Lectures*. Translated by Frederick G. Lawrence. MIT Press, 1987.

———. *Reason and the Rationalization of Society*. Vol. I of *The Theory of Communicative Action*, translated Thomas McCarthy. Beacon Press, 1984.

Haeffner, Gerd. *The Human Situation: A Philosophical Anthropology*. Translated by Eric Watkins. University of Notre Dame Press, 1989.

Hammarskjöld, Dag. *Markings*. Translated by W. H. Auden and Leif Sjöberg. Faber and Faber, 1964.

Hampshire, Stuart. *Freedom of the Individual*. Expanded ed. Princeton University Press, 1975.

Hampton, Cynthia. *Pleasure, Knowledge, and Being: An Analysis of Plato's Philebus*. SUNY Press, 1990.

Hardie, W. F. R. *Aristotle's Ethical Theory*. Oxford University Press, 1968.

———. "The Final Good in Aristotle's Ethics." *Philosophy* 40 (1965):277–95.

Harkavy, Allan. *Human Will: The Search for Its Physical Basis*. Peter Lang, 1995.

Harman, Gilbert, and Judith Jarvis Thomson. *Moral Relativism and Moral Objectivity*. Blackwell, 1996.

Hasker, William. "A Philosophical Perspective." In Pinnock, Rice, Sanders, Hasker, and Basinger, *The Openness of God*, 126–54.

Hauerwas, Stanley. *Character and the Christian Life*. 2nd ed. University of Notre Dame Press, 1984.

Hegel, G. W. F. *Phenomenology of Spirit*. Translated by A. V. Miller, introduction by J. N. Findlay. Oxford University Press, 1977.

Heidegger, Martin. *Being and Time*. 7th ed., translated by John Macquarrie and Edward Robinson. Harper & Row, 1962.

———. *Poetry, Language, Thought*. Translated by Albert Hofstadter. Harper & Row, 1971.

———. *The Question Concerning Technology and Other Essays*. Translated by William Lovitt. Harper and Row, 1977.

Hekman, Susan J. *Moral Voices/Moral Selves*. Penn State University Press, 1995.

Helms, Randall. *Tolkien's World*. Houghton Mifflin Company, 1974.

Henrich, Dieter. "Fichte's Original Insight." Translated David Lachterman. In *Contemporary German Philosophy*, vol. 1, 15–54. Penn State University Press, 1982.

———. "Self-Consciousness, A Critical Introduction to a Theory." *Man and World* 4.1 (February 1971):3–28.

———. *The Unity of Reason: Essays on Kant's Philosophy*. Edited by Richard Velkley. Harvard University Press, 1994.

Herman, Barbara. "Bootstrapping." In Buss and Overton, *Contours of Agency*, 253–73.

———. "On the Value of Acting from the Motive of Duty." In *The Practice of Moral Judgment*. Harvard University Press, 1993.

Herriot, James. *All Creatures Great and Small*. St. Martin's Press, 1972.

Hick, John. "An Irenaen Theodicy." In *A John Hick Reader*, edited by Paul Badham, 88–105. Trinity Press International, 1990.
Hill, Susanne. "Two Perspectives on the Ultimate End." In *The Crossroads of Norm and Nature*, edited by May Sim, 99–114. Roman and Littlefield, 1995.
Hill, Thomas Jr. *Autonomy and Self-Respect*. Cambridge University Press, 1991.
———. "Self-Respect Reconsidered." In Hill, *Autonomy and Self-Respect*, 19–24.
———. "Servility and Self-Respect." In Hill, *Autonomy and Self-Respect*, 4–18.
Hobbes, Thomas. *Leviathan*. Edited by C. B. Macpherson. Penguin Classics, 1985.
———. *Man and Citizen*. Edited by Bernard Gert, translated C. Wood, T. S. K. Scott-Craig, and B. Gert. Hackett, 1991.
Hobbs, Angela. *Plato and the Hero*. Cambridge University Press, 2000.
Höffe, Otfried. *Immanuel Kant*. Translated by Marshall Farrier. SUNY Press, 1994.
Hofstadter, Douglas. *Metamagical Themas*. Bantam Books, 1996.
Hollis, Martin, and Robert Sugden, "Rationality in Action." *Mind* 102 (January 1993):1–35.
Holmgren, Margaret. "Strength of Character." *Journal of Value Inquiry* 38 (2004):393–409.
Honneth, Alex. *The Struggle for Recognition*. Translated by Joel Anderson. MIT Press, 1996.
Hume, David. *A Treatise of Human Nature*. 2nd ed., edited by David Selbe-Bigge and Paul Nidditch. Oxford University Press, 1978.
Hurka, Thomas. *Perfectionism*. Oxford University Press, 1993.
Husserl, Edmund. *Ideas Pertaining to a Pure Phenomenology and Phenomenological Philosophy: General Introduction to Pure Phenomenology*. Translated by W. R. Boyce-Gibson. Collier Books, 1962.
Huxley, Aldous. *The Perennial Philosophy*. London: Chatto & Windus; Toronto: Oxford University Press, 1946.
I Ching. Translated by Richard Wilhelm and Cary Baynes. Bollingen Series, vol. 19, 3rd ed. Princeton University Press, 1977; Bollingen Foundation, 1950.
Irwin, Terence. *Plato's Ethics*. Oxford University Press, 1995.
———. "The Virtues: Theory and Common Sense in Greek Philosophy." In Crisp, *How Should One Live?* 37–55.
James, William. *The Principles of Psychology*. Vol. 2. Dover, 1950.
Jaspers, Karl. *Basic Philosophical Writings*. Translated by E. Ehrlich, L. Ehrlich, and G. Pepper. Ohio University Press, 1986.
———. *Way to Wisdom*. Translated by Ralph Manheim. Yale University Press, 1954.
Jensen, Henning. *Motivation and the Moral Sense in Francis Hutcheson's Ethical Theory*. Martinus Nijhoff, 1971.
Jones, William. *Morality and Freedom in the Philosophy of Immanuel Kant*. Oxford University Press, 1940.
Kagan, Shelly. "The Limits of Well-Being." *Social Philosophy & Policy* 9.2 (1992):169–89.
Kahn, Charles H. "Discovering the Will: From Aristotle to Augustine." In *The Question of "Eclecticism": Studies in Later Greek Philosophy*, edited by J. M. Dillon and A. A. Long. University of California Press, 1988.

Kamler, Howard. *Identification and Character: A Book on Psychological Development.* SUNY Press, 1994.
Kane, Robert. *The Significance of Free Will.* Oxford University Press, 1998.
Kant, Immanuel. *Critique of Judgement.* Translated by J. H. Bernard. Hafner Press/Macmillan, 1951.
———. *Critique of Practical Reason.* 3rd. ed. Edited and translated by Lewis White Beck. Macmillan, 1993. In citations to this text, the standard Academy edition page numbers are labeled "Ak" and precede the translation page numbers.
———. *Groundwork of the Metaphysics of Morals.* 3rd. ed. Translated by H. J. Paton. Harper & Row, 1956. In citations to this text, the standard Academy edition page numbers are labeled "Ak" and precede the translation page numbers.
———. *Groundwork of the Metaphysics of Morals.* Translated by Mary Gregor, Introduction by Christine Korsgaard. Cambridge University Press, 1998.
Katz, Fred. *Ordinary People and Extraordinary Evil.* SUNY Press, 1993.
Kekes, John. *Facing Evil.* Princeton University Press, 1990.
———. *The Morality of Pluralism.* Princeton University Press, 1993.
———. *Moral Wisdom and Good Lives.* Cornell University Press, 1995.
———. "The Reflexivity of Evil." In *Virtue and Vice,* edited by Ellen Paul, Fred Miller, and Jeffrey Paul, 216–32. Cambridge University Press, 1998.
Kenny, Anthony. *Aristotle's Theory of the Will.* Duckworth/Yale University Press, 1979.
Kent, Bonnie. "Happiness and the Willing Agent: The Ongoing Relevance of the Franciscan Tradition." *Proceedings of the American Catholic Philosophical Association* 78 (2004):59–70.
———. *Virtues of the Will: The Transformation of Ethics in the Late Thirteenth Century.* Catholic University of America Press, 1995.
Kierkegaard, Søren. *Concluding Unscientific Postscript.* Translated by David F. Swenson and Walter Lowrie. Princeton University Press, 1941.
———. *Either/Or.* Vol. 1. Translated by Howard V. Hong and Edna H. Hong. Princeton University Press, 1987.
———. *Either/Or.* Vol. 2. Translated by Walter Lowrie. Princeton University Press, 1944.
———. *Fear and Trembling.* Translated by Howard V. Hong and Edna H. Hong. Princeton University Press, 1984.
———. "On the Occasion of a Confession: Purity of Heart Is to Will One Thing." In *Upbuilding Discourses in Various Spirits,* translated by Howard V. Hong and Edna H. Hong. Princeton University Press, 1993.
———. *Sickness unto Death: A Christian Psychological Exposition for Upbuilding and Awakening.* Translated by Howard V. Hong and Edna H. Hong. Princeton University Press, 1980.
———. *Stages on Life's Way.* Translated by Howard V. Hong and Edna H. Hong. Princeton University Press, 1988.
Kleist, Heinrich von. *The Marquise of O and Other Stories.* Translated and Introduced by D. Luke and N. Reeves. Penguin Classics, 1978. Reprinted 1985.
Korsgaard, Christine M. *Creating the Kingdom of Ends.* Cambridge University Press, 1996.

———. "Kant's Analysis of Obligation: The Argument of *Foundations I*." *Monist* 72.3 (July 1989). Reprinted in Korsgaard, *Creating the Kingdom of Ends*, 43–76.
———. *The Myth of Egoism* (Lindley Lecture). University of Kansas Press 1999.
———. *The Sources of Normativity*. Cambridge University Press, 1996.
———. "Two Distinctions in Goodness." *Philosophical Review* 92.2 (April 1983):169–95.
Kosky, Jeffrey. "After the Death of God: Emmanuel Levinas and the Ethical Possibility of God." *Journal of Religious Ethics* 24.2 (Fall 1996):235–60.
Kraut, Richard. *Aristotle on the Human Good*. Princeton University Press, 1989.
———. "Aristotle on the Human Good: An Overview." In Sherman, *Aristotle: Critical Essays*, 79–104.
———. "Comments on Julia Annas's 'Self-Love in Aristotle.'" Edited by Timothy Roche. *Southern Journal of Philosophy* 27 (1988, Suppl.):19–23.
———. "Two Conceptions of Happiness." *Philosophical Review* 88.2 (April 1979):167–97. Parts of this paper are reprinted in Kraut, *Aristotle on the Human Good*.
Kupperman, Joel. *Character*. Oxford University Press, 1991.
———. *Value . . . and What Follows*. Oxford University Press, 1999.
Larmore, Charles. *The Morals of Modernity*. Cambridge University Press, 1996.
Lear, Jonathan. *Aristotle: The Desire to Understand*. Cambridge University Press, 1988.
Le Guin, Ursula. *The Wizard of Earthsea*. Parnassus Press, 1968. Reprinted in *Earthsea Trilogy*. Penguin, 1979, 1987.
Lemos, Noah. *Intrinsic Value*. Cambridge University Press, 1994.
Leopold, Aldo. *A Sand County Almanac and Sketches Here and There*. 2nd ed. Oxford University Press, 2000.
Levinas, Emmanuel. *Beyond the Verse: Talmudic Readings and Lectures*. Translated by Gary Mole. Indiana University Press, 1994.
———. *Collected Philosophical Papers*. Translated by Alphonso Lingis. Martinus Nijhoff/Kluwer, 1987.
———. *Difficult Freedom: Essays on Judaism*. Translated by Séan Hand. The Johns Hopkins University Press, 1990.
———. *Ethics and Infinity: A Conversation with Phillipe Nemo*. Translated by Richard Cohen. Pittsburgh University Press, 1985.
———. "Ethics as First Philosophy." Translated by Séan Hand and Michael Temple. In *The Levinas Reader*, edited by Séan Hand, 75–86. Basil Blackwell, 1989.
———. "God and Philosophy." In *Collected Philosophical Papers*, 1987, 153–74.
———. *In the Time of Nations*. Translated by Michael Smith. Indiana University Press, 1994.
———. "Meaning and Sense." In *Collected Philosophical Papers*, 1987, 75–108.
———. *Otherwise than Being or Beyond Essence*. Translated by Alphonso Lingis. Martinus Nijhoff, 1981.
———. *Outside the Subject*. Translated by Michael B. Smith. Stanford University Press, 1993.
———. "Philosophy and the Idea of Infinity." In *Collected Philosophical Papers*, 1987, 47–60.

———. *Time and the Other*. Translated by Richard Cohen. Duquesne University Press, 1987.
———. *Totality and Infinity*. Translated by Alphonso Lingis. Duquesne University Press, 1969.
Lewis, C. S. *The Abolition of Man: How Education Develops Man's Sense of Morality*. Collier Books/Macmillan, 1955.
———. *The Problem of Pain*. Macmillan Publishing, 1962.
———. *The Screwtape Letters*. Illustrated ed. William Collins, 1985.
———. "The Weight of Glory." In *The Weight of Glory and Other Addresses*, edited by Walter Hooper. Touchstone/Simon and Schuster, 1996. This essay is also found in C. S. Lewis, *Screwtape Proposes a Toast*. Macmillan, 1949.
Lewis, David. "Desire as Belief II." *Mind* 105 (April 1996):303–13.
Liberman, Marcel. *Commitment, Values, and Moral Realism*. Cambridge University Press, 1998.
Lieberman, E. James. *Acts of Will: The Life and Work of Otto Rank*. Free Press / Macmillan, 1985.
Lingis, Alphonso. *Deathbound Subjectivity*. Indiana University Press, 1989.
Lippitt, John. Review of *Kierkegaard After MacIntyre*, edited by J. Davenport and A. Rudd. *Faith and Philosophy* 22.4 (October 2005):496–502.
Llewelyn, John. *Emmanuel Levinas: The Genealogy of Ethics*. Routledge, 1995.
Locke, Don. "Three Concepts of Free Action: I." *Proceedings of the Aristotelian Society* 49 (1975, Suppl.):95–112.
Locke, John. *An Essay Concerning Human Understanding*. Edited by Peter H. Nidditch. Oxford University Press, 1975.
Lomasky, Loren. *Persons, Rights, and the Moral Community*. Oxford University Press, 1987.
Lovejoy, Arthur O. *The Great Chain of Being*. Harvard University Press, 1936. Reprinted 1964.
Luther, Martin. *Bondage of the Will [De servo arbitrio]*. Excerpted in *Erasmus-Luther: Discourse on Free Will*, edited and translated by Ernst F. Winter. Ungar, 1961.
MacIntyre, Alasdair. *After Virtue*. 2nd ed. University of Notre Dame Press, 1984.
———. *Dependent Rational Animals*. Open Court, 1999.
———. "How Moral Agents Became Ghosts, or Why the History of Ethics Diverged from that of the Philosophy of Mind." *Synthese* 53 (1982):295–312.
———. "Once More on Kierkegaard." In Davenport and Rudd, *Kierkegaard After MacIntyre*, 339–56.
———. "Virtue Ethics." In *Encyclopedia of Ethics*, 1276–82. Garland, 1992.
Macquarrie, John. *Studies in Christian Existentialism*. McGill University Press, 1965. Reprinted by SCM Press, 1966.
Maddi, Salvatore. "Existential Psychotherapy." In *Contemporary Psychotherapy*, edited by J. Garske and S. Lynn. Merrill Publishers, 1966.
Marion, Jean-Luc. *Prolegomena to Charity*. Translated by Stephen Lewis. Fordham University Press, 2002.
Maritain, Jacques. *Man and the State*. University of Chicago Press/Phoenix Books, 1951.

———. *The Person and the Common Good.* Translated by John J. Fitzgerald. University of Notre Dame Press, 1966. Reprinted 1985.
Maslow, Abraham. *Eupsychian Management.* Homewood, IL: Irwin, 1965.
May, Rollo. *Love and Will.* Norton, 1969.
McCall, Catherine. *Concepts of Person: An Analysis of Person, Self, and Human Being.* Avebury Press, 1990.
McDowell, John. "Virtue and Reason." *Monist* 62 (July 1979):331–50.
McGinn, Colin. *The Character of Mind.* Oxford University Press, 1982.
———. *Ethics, Evil, and Fiction.* Oxford University Press, 1997.
McInerny, Ralph. *St. Thomas Aquinas.* University of Notre Dame Press, 1982.
McIntosh, Donald. *Self, Person, World: The Interplay of Conscious and Unconscious in Human Life.* Northwestern University Press, 1995.
McPherran, Mark. "Socratic Piety in the *Euthyphro.*" *Journal of the History of Philosophy* 23.3 (July 1985):283–309.
Mead, George Herbert. *Mind, Self, and Society from the Standpoint of a Social Behaviorist,* edited by C. Morris. University of Chicago Press, 1934. Reprinted 1969.
Mele, Alfred. *Autonomous Agents.* Oxford University Press, 2001.
———. "Moral Cognitivism and Listlessness." *Ethics* 106.4 (July 1996):727–53.
Menand, Louis. *The Metaphysical Club: A Story of Ideas in America.* Farrar, Straus, and Giroux, 2001.
Meyer, Susan Sauvé. "*Thumos*, Endurance, and Emotion in Plato's *Republic.*" Paper presented at the Eastern Division meeting of the American Philosophical Association, New York, N.Y., December 30, 1996.
Meyerson, Denise. "When Are My Actions due to Me?" *Analysis* 54.3 (July 1994):171–74.
Mill, John Stuart. *Utilitarianism.* Edited by George Sher. Hackett, 1979.
Miller, Jonathan. *The Body Question.* Vintage, 1978.
Miller, Laurence. *Inner Natures: Brain, Self, and Personality.* St. Martin's Press, 1990.
Milton. *Paradise Lost.* In *Norton Anthology of English Literature*, edited by M. H. Abrams. 4th ed., vol. 1. Norton, 1979.
Mook, Douglas. *Motivation: The Organization of Action.* 2nd ed. Norton, 1996.
Mooney, Edward. *Selves in Discord and Resolve.* Routledge, 1996.
Moore, G. E. *Principia Ethica.* Prometheus, 1988.
Morgenbesser, Sidney, and James Walsh, eds., *Free Will.* Prentice Hall, 1962.
Morillo, Carolyn. "The Reward Event and Motivation." *Journal of Philosophy* 87.4 (April 1990):169–86.
Morton, Adam. *On Evil.* Routledge, 2004.
Morris, Thomas. *Our Idea of God.* University of Notre Dame Press, 1991.
Moya, Carlos. *The Philosophy of Action.* Polity, 1990.
Muchnik, Pablo. "Radical Evil: Between the Trivial and the Diabolic." *Contemporary Philosophy* 23.3–4 (2001):43–47.
Murdoch, Iris. *Metaphysics as Guide to Morals.* Penguin, 1992.
———. *The Sovereignty of the Good.* Routledge, 1989.
Murphy, Mark C. *Natural Law and Practical Rationality.* Cambridge University Press, 2002.

Murray, Patrick T. *Hegel's Philosophy of Will and Mind*. Edwin Mellen, 1991.
Naess, Arne. "Ecosophy T: Deep vs Shallow Ecology." In *Environmental Ethics*, edited by Louis Pojman, 150–56. 3rd ed. Wadsworth, 1998.
Nagel, Thomas. *The Possibility of Altruism*. Princeton University Press, 1970.
———. "Subjective and Objective." In Nagel, *Mortal Questions*. Cambridge University Press, 1979.
———. *The View from Nowhere*. Oxford University Press, 1986.
Nancy, Jean-Luc. *The Experience of Freedom*. Translated by Bridget McDonald. Stanford University Press, 1993.
Nathan, N. M. L. "Self and Will." *International Journal of Philosophical Studies* 5.1 (March 1997):81–94.
———. *Will and World*. Oxford University Press, 1992.
Neiman, Susan. *Evil in Modern Thought: An Alternative History of Philosophy*. Princeton University Press, 2002. Reprinted with new preface 2004.
Niebuhr, Reinhold. *Human Nature*. Vol. I of *The Nature and Destiny of Man* (Gifford Lectures). Scribner's, 1964.
Nietzsche, Friedrich. *Beyond Good and Evil*. Translated by Walter Kaufmann. Vintage, 1989.
Nino, Carlos. *Radical Evil on Trial*. Yale University Press, 1996.
Noam, Gil, and Thomas Wren, eds. *The Moral Self*. MIT Press, 1993.
Noddings, Nel. *Caring: A Feminine Approach to Ethics and Moral Education*. University of California Press, 1984.
Nozick, Robert. *Anarchy, State, and Utopia*. Basic Books/Harper Collins, 1974.
———. *The Nature of Rationality*. Princeton University Press, 1993.
———. *Philosophical Explanations*. Harvard University Press, 1981.
Nussbaum, Charles. "Kant's Changing Conception of the Causality of the Will." *International Philosophical Quarterly* 36.3 (September 1996):265–85.
Nussbaum, Martha. *The Fragility of Goodness: Luck and Ethics in Greek Tragedy and Philosophy*. Cambridge University Press, 1986.
———. *The Therapy of Desire*. Princeton University Press, 1994.
Nygren, Anders. *Agape and Eros*. Translated by Philip Watson. Westminster Press, 1953.
Oberdiek, Hans. "The Will." In *The Handbook of Western Philosophy*, edited by G. H. R. Parkinson, 463–88. Macmillan/Routledge, 1988.
O'Connell, Robert J., S.J. *Plato on the Human Paradox*. Fordham University Press, 1997.
O'Connor, Timothy. *Persons and Causes*. Oxford University Press, 2000.
Olafson, Frederick. *Principles and Persons: An Ethical Interpretation of Existentialism*. Johns Hopkins Press, 1967.
———. *What Is a Human Being? A Heideggerian View*. Cambridge University Press, 1995.
Oliver, Mary. *Owls and Other Fantasies: Poems and Essays*. Beacon, 2003.
O'Neill, Onora. *Constructions of Reason: Explorations of Kant's Practical Philosophy*. Cambridge University Press, 1989.
O'Shaughnessy, Brian. "Trying (as the Mental 'Pineal Gland')." *Journal of Philosophy* 70 (1973):365–86.

———. *The Will*. Vols. 1, 2. Cambridge University Press, 1980.
Palmquist, Stephen. "Is Duty Kant's 'Motive' for Moral Action?" *Ratio* 28.2 (December 1986):168–74.
Parfit, Derek. *Reasons and Persons*. Oxford University Press, 1987.
Parinello, Anthony. *The Power of Will*. Chandler House, 1998.
Pascal, Blaise. *Pensée*. Translated by A. J. Krailsheimer. Penguin, 1966. Reprinted 1988.
Ellen Paul, Fred Miller, and Jeffrey Paul, eds. *The Good Life and the Human Good*. Cambridge University Press, 1992.
Payne, Andrew. "Practical Reason and the Comparison of Lives in the Speech of Diotima," Paper presented at the University of Notre Dame Philosophy Colloquium, Notre Dame, Indiana, February 13, 1998.
———. "The Refutation of Agathon: *Symposium* 199c–201c." *Ancient Philosophy* 19 (1999):235–53.
Peacocke, Arthur, and Grant Gillett, eds. *Persons and Personality*. Blackwell, 1987.
Pestana, Mark. "Second Order Desires and Strength of Will." *Modern Schoolman* 73 (January 1996):173–82.
Peterson, Christopher and Martin Seligman. "Causal Explanations and Depression." *Psychological Review* 91 (1984):347–72.
Pfänder, Alexander. *Phenomenology of Willing and Motivation*. Translated by Herbert Spiegelberg. Northwestern University Press, 1967.
Pincoffs, Edmund. *Quandaries and Virtues*. University of Kansas Press, 1986.
Pink, Thomas. *The Psychology of Freedom*. Cambridge University Press, 1996.
Pink, Thomas, and M. W. F. Stone, eds. *The Will and Human Action: From Antiquity to the Present Day*. Routledge, 2004. This book came to my attention too late to receive attention in the present work, but its topics are closely related to mine.
Pinnock, C., R. Rice, J. Sanders, W. Hasker, and D. Basinger. *The Openness of God*. InterVarsity, 1994.
Pippin, Robert. *Hegel's Idealism: The Satisfactions of Self-Consciousness*. Cambridge University Press, 1989.
———. "Review article: Horstmann, Siep, and German Idealism." *European Journal of Philosophy* 2.1 (1994):85–95.
Plantinga, Alvin. *The Nature of Necessity*. Oxford University Press, 1974. Reprinted 1992.
Plato, *Collected Dialogues*. Edited by Edith Hamilton and Huntington Cairns. Bollingen Series, vol. 71. Princeton University Press, 1963. All citations of Plato refer to translations in this volume unless otherwise noted.
———. *Great Dialogues of Plato*. Edited by W. H. D. Rouse, Eric Warmington, and Philip Rouse. Mentor/Penguin, 1984.
———. *Gorgias*. Translated by Donald Zeyl. Hackett, 1987.
Pojman, Louis P. *The Logic of Subjectivity: Kierkegaard's Philosophy of Religion*. University of Alabama Press, 1984.
Politis, Vasilis. "The Primacy of Self-Love in the *Nicomachean Ethics*." In *Oxford Studies in Ancient Philosophy*. Vol. 11, 153–74. Oxford University Press, 1993.
Poteat, William H. "Persons and Places: Paradigms in Communication." In Poteat, *The Primacy of Persons and the Language of Culture*, edited by James Nickell and James Stines. University of Missouri Press, 1993.

Price, A. W. *Love and Friendship in Plato and Aristotle*. Oxford University Press, 1989.
Purinton, Jeffrey S. "Aristotle's Definition of Happiness (*NE* I.7, 1098a16–18)." *Oxford Studies in Ancient Philosophy* 16 (1998):259–97.
Railton, Peter. "Nonfactualism about Normative Discourse." *Philosophy and Phenomenological Research* 52.4 (December 1992):961–68.
Rank, Otto. *Truth and Reality*. Translated and with an introduction by Jessie Taft. Knopf, 1936. Reprinted by Norton, 1978.
———. *Will Therapy*. Translated by Jessie Taft. Knopf, 1936. Reprinted by Norton, 1978.
Rauscher, Frederick. "Kant's Conflation of Pure Practical Reason and Will." *Proceedings of the Eighth International Kant Congress*. Vol. 2. Marquette University Press, 1995.
Rawls, John. *Political Liberalism*. Columbia University Press, 1993.
———. *A Theory of Justice*. 1st ed. Harvard University Press, 1971.
Raz, Joseph. *Engaging Reason: On the Theory of Value and Action*. Oxford University Press, 1999.
———. *Value, Respect, and Attachment*. Cambridge University Press, 2001.
Reeve, C. D. C. *Practices of Reason: Aristotle's Nicomachean Ethics*. Oxford University Press, 1992.
Reid, Thomas. *Essays on the Active Powers of the Human Mind*. Vols. 3 and 4 of *The Works of Thomas Reid*. Charlestown, Mass.: Samuel Ethridge, 1815. Introduction by Baruch Brody. MIT Press, 1969.
Reps, Paul, ed. *Zen Flesh, Zen Bones*. Penguin, 1986.
Rescher, Nicholas. *Human Interests: Reflections on Philosophical Anthropology*. Stanford University Press, 1990.
———. *Objectivity: The Obligations of Impersonal Reason*. University of Notre Dame Press, 1997.
Rice, Richard. "Biblical Support for a New Perspective." In Pinnock, Rice, Sanders, Hasker, and Basinger, *The Openness of God*, 11–59. 1994.
Richardson, Henry S. "Desire and the Good in *De anima*." In *Essays on Aristotle's De anima*, edited by Martha C. Nussbaum and Amélie O. Rorty, 381–400. Oxford University Press, 1992.
Ricoeur, Paul. *The Conflict of Interpretations: Essays in Hermeneutics*. Edited by Don Ihde. Northwestern University Press, 1974.
———. *Oneself as Another*. Translated by Kathleen Blamey. University of Chicago Press, 1992.
Rist, John M. *The Mind of Aristotle: A Study in Philosophical Growth*. University of Toronto Press, 1989.
Roberts, Robert C. "Will Power and the Virtues." *Philosophical Review* 93 (1984). Reprinted in *The Virtues*, edited by Robert Kruschwitz and Robert Roberts. Wadsworth Publishing, 1987. Citations are to the original article.
Robinson, T. M. *Plato's Psychology*. University of Toronto Press, 1995.
Rogozinski, Jacob. "Hell on Earth: Hannah Arendt in the Face of Hitler." Translated by Peter Dews. *Philosophy Today* 37.2 (Fall 1993):257–74.
Rorty, Amélie O., ed. *Essays on Aristotle's Ethics*. University of California Press, 1980.

———. *Explaining Emotions*. University of California Press, 1980.
———. *The Identities of Persons*. University of California Press, 1976.
Ross, W. D. *The Right and the Good*. Hackett, 1988.
Rouner, Leroy, ed. *Selves, People, and Persons: What Does It Mean to Be a Self?* University of Notre Dame Press, 1992.
Rousseau, Jean-Jacques. *Discourse Concerning the Origins of Human Inequality*. In Rousseau, *The Basic Political Writings*, translated by Donald Cress. Hackett, 1987.
Ryan, Richard M., and Edward L. Deci. "Self-Determination Theory and the Facilitation of Intrinsic Motivation, Social Development, and Well-Being." *American Psychologist* (January 2000):68–78.
Ryle, Gilbert. *The Concept of Mind*. University of Chicago Press, 1949.
Ryn, Claes. *Will, Imagination, and Reason: Irving Babbitt and the Problem of Reality*. Regnery, 1986.
Sandel, Michael. *Liberalism and the Limits of Justice*. 2nd. ed. Cambridge University Press, 1982, 1998.
Sartre, Jean-Paul. *Being and Nothingness*. Translated by Hazel E. Barnes. Washington Square Press, 1956.
———. *Existentialism and Humanism*. Translated by Philip Mariet. Methuen, 1948.
———. *L'Existentialisme est un humanisme*. Les Editions Nagel, 1946.
Scanlon, Thomas. *What We Owe to Each Other*. Harvard University Press, 1998.
Schalow, Frank. "Beyond Decisionism and Anarchy: The Task of Rethinking Resolve." *Man and World* 28 (1995):359–76.
———. *Imagination and Existence: Heidegger's Retrieval of the Kantian Ethic*. University Press of America, 1986.
Scheffler, Samuel. "Agent-Centered Restrictions, Rationality, and the Virtues." *Mind* 94 (1985):409–19.
———. *The Rejection of Consequentialism*. Rev. ed. Oxford University Press, 1994.
Scheler, Max. *Formalism in Ethics and Non-Formal Ethics of Values: A New Attempt toward the Foundation of an Ethical Personalism*. Translated by Manfred S. Frings and Roger L. Funk. Northwestern University Press, 1973.
Schopenhauer, Arthur. *On the Freedom of the Will*. Translated by Konstantin Kolenda. Blackwell, 1985.
Scott, Michael. "Wittgenstein's Theory of Action." *Philosophical Quarterly* 46.184 (July 1996):347–63.
Scotus, Duns. *Duns Scotus on the Will and Morality*. Edited and translated by Alan B. Wolter. Catholic University of America Press, 1986. The pagination of the 1997 paperback reprint differs from this edition from page 127 onward because the Latin facing pages are omitted.
———. *The Oxford Commentary on the Four Books of the Master of Sentences*. Translated by James Walsh. Book II, d.25, "The Single Question," excerpted in *Free Will*, edited by Sidney Morgenbesser and James Walsh, 35–39. Prentice-Hall, 1962.
Searle, John R. *The Rediscovery of Mind*. MIT Press, 1992.
Seligman, Martin, E. P. Abramson, and M. Teasdale. "Learned Helplessness in Humans: Critique and Reformulation." *Journal of Abnormal Psychology* 87 (1978):49–78.

Shakespeare, William. *The Complete Works of William Shakespeare.* Edited by Peter Alexander. Collins, 1951. Reprinted 1983.
Sherman, Nancy. *The Fabric of Character.* Oxford University Press, 1989.
———, ed. *Aristotle: Critical Essays.* Rowman & Littlefield, 1999.
Sidgwick, Henry. *The Methods of Ethics.* 7th ed. Macmillan, 1907. Reprinted by Hackett, 1981.
Sim, Mary, ed. *The Crossroads of Norm and Nature: Essays on Aristotle's Ethics and Metaphysics.* Rowman & Littlefield, 1995.
Sleszynski, Darius. *Exploring the Self in Action.* Trans Humana Press, 1997.
Slote, Michael. "Agent-Based Virtue Ethics." In Crisp and Slote, *Virtue Ethics,* 239–62.
Smith, John E. *Jonathan Edwards: Puritan, Preacher, Philosopher.* University of Notre Dame Press, 1992.
Sober, Elliott, and David S. Wilson. *Unto Others: The Evolution and Psychology of Unselfish Behavior.* Harvard University Press, 1998.
Soble, Alan. *The Structure of Love.* Yale University Press, 1990.
———, ed. *Eros, Agape, and Philia.* Paragon, 1989.
Solomon, Robert C. "The Virtues of a Passionate Life: Erosiac Love and the 'Will to Power.'" *Social Philosophy and Policy* 15.1 (Winter 1998):91–118.
Spaemann, Robert. *Happiness and Benevolence.* Translated by Jeremiah Alberg, S.J. University of Notre Dame Press, 2000.
Stampe, Dennis, and Martha Gibson. "Of One's Own Free Will." *Philosophy and Phenomenological Research* 52.3 (September 1992):529–50.
Staten, Henry. "Radical Evil Revived: Hitler, Kant, Luther, Neo-Lacanianism." *Radical Philosophy* 98 (November/December, 1999):6–15.
Steedman, Ian, and Ulrich Krause. "Goethe's Faust, Arrow's Possibility Theorem and the Individual Decision-Taker." In *The Multiple Self,* edited by Jon Elster, 197–232. Cambridge University Press, 1985.
Steele, Carlos. "Does Evil Have a Cause? Augustine's Perplexity and Thomas's Answer." *Review of Metaphysics* 48.2 (December 1994):251–74.
Steiner, Rudolph. *The Philosophy of Spiritual Activity.* Steiner Publications, 1963.
Stocker, Michael. "The Schizophrenia of Modern Ethical Theories." *Journal of Philosophy* 73 (1976):453–66. Reprinted in Crisp and Slote, *Virtue Ethics,* 66–78.
———. "How Emotions Reveal Value and Help Cure the Schizophrenia of Modern Ethical Theories. In Crisp, *How Should One Live?* 173–90.
Strawson, Galen. *Freedom and Belief.* Oxford University Press, 1986.
Strawson, Peter. *The Bounds of Sense.* Methuen, 1966. Reprinted by Routledge, 1989.
Stump, Eleonore. "Sanctification, Hardening of the Heart, and Frankfurt's Concept of Free Will." In Fischer and Ravizza, *Perspectives on Moral Responsibility,* 211–34.
———. "Intellect, Will, and the Principle of Alternate Possibilities." in *Christian Theism and the Problems of Philosophy,* edited by Michael Beaty. University of Notre Dame Press, 1990. Reprinted in Fischer and Ravizza, *Perspectives on Moral Responsibility,* 237–62.
Sturma, Dieter. *Kant über Selbstbewusstein.* Hildesheim, 1986.

———. "Self-Consciousness and the Philosophy of Mind. A Kantian Reconsideration." In *Proceedings of the Eighth International Kant Congress*, vol. I.2, edited by H. Robinson et al. Marquette University Press, 1995.

Sturma, Dieter, and Karl Ameriks, eds. *The Modern Subject: Conceptions of the Self in Classical German Philosophy*. SUNY Press, 1995.

Sverdlik, Steven. "Motive and Rightness." *Ethics* 106 no. 2 (January 1996): 327–49.

Swantson, Christine. *Virtue Ethics: A Pluralistic View*. New ed. Oxford University Press, 2005.

Tate, Margaret Watkins, and James Harris. "Persons, Free Will, and the Problem of Evil." Paper presented at the Philosophy of Religion conference, San Antonio, Texas, 1997.

Taylor, Charles. *The Ethics of Authenticity*. Harvard University Press, 1991.

———. "Responsibility for Self." In G. Watson, *Free Will*, 111–26.

———. *Sources of the Self*. Harvard University Press, 1989.

Taylor, Paul. *Respect for Nature*. Princeton University Press, 1986.

Taylor, Richard. *Action and Purpose*. Prentice-Hall, 1966.

———. *Good and Evil*. Macmillan/Collier, 1971.

The Ten Principal Upanishads. Translated by S. P. Swami and W. B. Yeats. Faber and Faber, 1937.

Thomas, Kenneth W. *Intrinsic Motivation at Work: Building Energy and Commitment*. Berrett-Koehler Publishers, 2000. Reprinted 2002.

Tiberius, Valerie. *Deliberation about the Good*. Garland Publishing, 2000.

Tillich, Paul. *Love, Power, and Justice*. Oxford University Press, 1954.

Timmons, Mark. "Kant and the Possibility of Moral Motivation." *Southern Journal of Philosophy* 23.3 (1985):377–98.

Tolkien, J. R. R. "*Beowulf*: The Monsters and the Critics." In *The Monsters and the Critics and Other Essays*.

———. "The Homecoming of Beorhtnoth Beorhthelm's Son." In *Tree and Leaf*. George Allen & Unwin, 1975.

———. *The Letters of J. R. R. Tolkien*. Edited by Humphrey Carpenter and Christopher Tolkien. George Allen & Unwin, 1981.

———. *The Lord of the Rings*. Collectors, ed. Houghton Mifflin, 1965.

———. *The Monsters and the Critics and Other Essays*. Edited by Christopher Tolkien. HarperCollins, 1997.

———. "On Fairy-Stories." In *The Monsters and the Critics and Other Essays*. Allen and Unwin, 1983. Also in *Tree and Leaf*. Allen and Unwin, 1966. Reprinted in *The Tolkien Reader*. Ballantine, 1966.

———. *The Silmarillion*. Edited by Christopher Tolkien. 2nd ed. Houghton Mifflin, 2001.

Twenge, Jean M. *Generation Me: Why Young Americans Are More Confident, Assertive, Entitled—and More Miserable Than Ever*. Free Press, 2006.

Tugendhat, Ernst. *Self-Consciousness and Self-Determination*. Translated and with an introduction by Paul Stern. MIT Press, 1986.

Tzu, Lao. *Tao Te Chin*. Translated by Victor Mair. Bantam Books, 1990.

Urmson, J. O. "Aristotle's Doctrine of the Mean." In Rorty, *Essays on Aristotle's Ethics*, 157–70.
Vander Waerdt, P. A. "The Peripatetic Interpretation of Plato's Tripartite Psychology." *Greek, Roman, and Byzantine Studies* 26.3 (Autumn 1985):283–302.
Van Inwagen, Peter. *An Essay on Free Will*. Oxford University Press, 1983.
Vedder, Ben. "Heidegger on Desire." *Continental Philosophy Review* 31 (1998):353–68.
Velkley, Richard. *Freedom and the End of Reason: On the Moral Foundations of Kant's Critical Philosophy*. University of Chicago Press, 1989.
Velleman, J. David. "The Possibility of Practical Reason." *Ethics* 106.4 (July 1996):694–726.
———. *Practical Reflection*. Princeton University Press, 1989.
———. "What Happens When Someone Acts?" *Mind* 101 (1992):461–81. Reprinted in Fischer and Ravizza, *Perspectives on Moral Responsibility*, 188–210.
Versenji, Laszlo. *Holiness and Justice: An Interpretation of Plato's Euthyphro*. Rowman and Littlefield, 1982.
Vlastos, Gregory. "The Individual as an Object of Love in Plato." In *Platonic Studies*, edited by Vlastos, 3–42. Princeton University Press, 1973. Reprinted in Soble, *Eros, Agape, and Philia*, 96–135.
Von Wright, George Henrik. *The Varieties of Goodness*. Routledge & Kegan Paul, 1963. Reprinted by Thoemmes Press, 1997.
Wallach, Michael, and Lise Wallach. *Psychology's Sanction for Selfishness*. W. H. Freeman, 1983.
Watson, Gary. "Free Action and Free Will." *Mind* 96.382 (April 1987):145–171.
———. "Free Agency." *Journal of Philosophy* 72.8 (April, 1975). Reprinted in G. Watson, *Free Will*, 96–110.
———. "On the Primacy of Character." In Flanagan and Rorty, *Identity, Character, and Morality*, chap. 19.
———, ed. *Free Will*. 1st ed. Oxford University Press, 1982.
Watson, Stephen H. *Tradition(s): On Community, Remembrance, and Virtue in Classical German Thought*. Indiana University Press, 1997.
———. *Tradition(s) II: Hermeneutics, Ethics, and the Dispensation of the Good*. Indiana University Press, 2001.
Westphal, Merold. "Levinas and the Immediacy of the Face." *Faith and Philosophy* 10.4 (October 1993):486–502.
———. *Overcoming Onto-Theology*. Fordham University Press, 2001.
White, Alan. *Schelling: An Introduction to the System of Freedom*. Yale University Press, 1983.
White, Morton. "Desire and Desirability: A Rejoinder to a Posthumous Reply by John Dewey." *Journal of Philosophy* 93.5 (May 1996):229–42.
White, Stephen. *Sovereign Virtue: Aristotle on the Relation between Happiness and Prosperity*. Stanford University Press, 1992.
Williams, Bernard. "A Critique of Utilitarianism." In J. J. C. Smart and Bernard Williams, *Utilitarianism: For and Against*. Cambridge University Press, 1973.
———. *Ethics and the Limits of Philosophy*. Harvard University Press, 1985.

———. "Internal and External Reasons." In *Rational Action*, edited by Ross Harrison. Cambridge University Press, 1980. Reprinted in Williams, *Moral Luck*, 101–23.

———. *Making Sense of Humanity and Other Philosophical Papers (1982–1993)*. Cambridge University Press, 1995.

———. *Morality: An Introduction to Ethics*. Harper Torchbooks, 1972.

———. *Moral Luck: Philosophical Papers, 1973–1980*. Cambridge University Press, 1981.

———. "Persons, Character, and Morality." In Rorty, *The Identities of Persons*. Reprinted in Williams, *Moral Luck*, 1–19.

———. *Problems of the Self: Philosophical Papers, 1956–1972*. Cambridge University Press, 1973.

———. "The Self and the Future." *Philosophical Review* 79 (April 1970):161–80. Reprinted in Williams, *Problems of the Self*.

———. *Shame and Necessity*. University of California Press, 1993.

Williams, Clifford. *Free Will and Determinism: A Dialogue*. Hackett, 1980.

Wilson, George B. "Goals—Or Ideals?" *Human Development* 3 (Fall 2003):33–35.

Winch, Peter. "Wittgenstein's Treatment of the Will." *Ratio* 10 (1968):38–53.

Wittgenstein, Ludwig. *The Blue and Brown Books*. 2nd ed. Harper Torchbooks/Blackwell, 1960.

———. *Philosophical Investigations*. 3rd ed. Translated by G. E. M. Anscombe. Macmillan/Blackwell, 1958.

———. *Remarks on the Philosophy of Psychology*. Vol. I. Edited by G. E. M. Anscombe and G. H. von Wright. University of Chicago Press/Blackwell, 1980.

Wolf, Susan. *Freedom within Reason*. Oxford University Press, 1990.

———. "The True, the Good, and the Loveable: Frankfurt's Avoidance of Objectivity." In Buss and Overton, *Contours of Agency*, 227–44.

Wollheim, Richard. *On the Emotions*. Yale University Press, 1999.

———. "On Persons and Their Lives." In Rorty, *Explaining Emotions*, 299–322.

Wood, Allen. "The Emptiness of the Moral Will." *The Monist* 72.3 (July 1989):454–83.

Wright, David, ed. and trans. *Beowulf: A Prose Translation*. Penguin, 1957.

Yalom, Irwin. *Existential Psychotherapy*. HarperCollins/Basic Books, 1980.

Yovel, Yirmiyahu. "Kant and the History of the Will." In *Kant's Legacy: Essays in Honor of Lewis White Beck*. edited by Predrag Cicovacki. University of Rochester Press, 2001.

Zagzebski, Linda. *Divine Motivation Theory*. Cambridge University Press, 2004.

Index

Readers may also want to consult the glossary for abbreviations and definitions of technical terms, and the table of contents for a detailed listing of subsections.

Ackrill, J. L., 183, 192–94
action theory, vii, 26, 6, 8, 11–12, 21, 26, 46–85, 86–88, 118, 149, 287, 320–21, 419, 552, 569n140
Adams, Robert, 599
aesthete/aestheticism, 369, 423, 433, 453, 455, 523, 595n99, 604n111, 635n69
aesthetics, 110, 129, 249–50, 318, 457, 524–25, 529, 648n32
affectio justitiae, 380–82, 395
agapē, 16–19, 25–26, 43, 95, 107, 284, 296, 298–300, 302, 310–15, 318–19, 324, 354, 382–83, 503–5, 515, 528, 540–41, 546, 562n34, 576n83, 596n111, 601n65, 621n74. *See also* charity; divine motivation; just generosity; neighbor-love
agapic ethics, xxii, 17, 289, 298, 307–9, 384, 405, 458, 641n187, 644n50
agency, 3, 6, 7, 16, 21, 49, 51, 53–56, 62, 68–78, 81–82, 84, 87, 118, 165, 287, 308, 317, 319, 352, 358, 368–69, 381, 398–400, 404, 406–8, 410–16, 425, 430, 438, 452, 453, 455, 460, 468, 478, 484, 490, 505–6, 536, 540, 561n185, 569n151, 603n102, 607n169
  first-order, 56, 62, 65–66, 69
  second-order, 49, 51, 54, 69–70, 72–73, 76, 78–79, 86, 113, 116–17, 322, 377, 392–93, 406–8, 410, 459, 467, 558n138, 559n152, 560n160, 624n125, 628n172, 643n27
agent-causation, 79, 83, 291, 407–8, 413, 415, 491, 598n14, 623n107, 627n165, 629n190, 631n201
akrasia, 17, 75, 84, 97, 112, 114, 327, 330–31, 366, 486, 507, 569n139, 569n140, 607n2, 616n115, 639n169. *See also* leeway-liberty
Allison, Henry, 398–99, 401, 409–11, 422, 413–14, 416, 625n135, 626n145, 630n191
alterity, ix, 16–17, 20, 24, 26, 42–43, 152, 167, 284, 287, 289, 302, 307–18, 336, 357, 360–61, 384, 440–42, 458, 527, 534–35, 541–45, 547, 563, 601n145, 603, 604n105, 605n126.
  creating alterity, 360–61.
  See also face, the; Levinas; values, alterity of
Ameriks, Karl, xv, 393, 397, 409–11, 413–16, 623n109, 626n149, 630n191, 631n201
Anderson, Elizabeth, 478–81
Anderson, Joel, 449, 497, 519, 648n29–n32
anger, malicious, 336, 346, 350, 352, 355
Annas, Julia, 15, 147–48, 206–18, 223, 230, 240, 242, 259, 263, 588n33
Anscombe, Elizabeth, 56, 61, 74, 126, 491, 556n87

Anselm, 379–81, 384, 387, 395, 599n18
Aquinas, Thomas, 14–16, 20, 25, 51, 58, 65, 70, 77–78, 80–81, 102, 106–13, 121, 154, 171, 176, 183
Arendt, Hannah, 3, 16–17, 26, 287, 289, 303–6, 315–16, 333, 357, 363, 378, 381–82, 620n62, 621n78
aretaic commitment: see commitment
arête: see virtue
Aristotelian Principle (from Rawls), 261, 657
Aristotle, 3, 8, 13–15, 23–27, 33–34, 58, 62, 64–65, 70, 82, 84, 86, 91, 93, 95, 104, 111–14, 118–26, 129–31, 134–43, 147, 153–54, 171–75, 230–37, 240–44, 247–48, 251, 257, 260, 265, 269, 272–73, 281–82, 288, 296, 303, 319, 321, 326–32, 365–66, 369, 371–77, 387, 424–28, 436, 445–47, 458, 506
  as committed to the erosaic thesis and thus formal egoism, 142
  as allowing for good passion, 33–34
  bipartitism, 118–19, 138, 570n157, 570n169
  criteria for the ultimate end, 185–86
  doctrine of the mean, 326–29
  function argument, 186, 189–94, 199–200, 233, 566n102, 585n64, 585n71
  maximal inclusivism, 187, 189–91, 194–95, 198, 236, 273
  on hierarchy of ends (in *Nicomachean Ethics* I), 172–87
  on friendship (key passages), 206–7, 211–14, 221, 241–42, 281
  on relation of crafts and ends, 173–75
  on parts of the soul, 118–21, 137–39
  on security against misfortune, 176–77, 186, 190, 207, 218–19
  on theoria/contemplation, 187–89, 191, 193, 242
  on virtuous motivation, 202–4, 236–37
  on voluntariness, 64–65
  regress argument for final ends, 171–73, 178–80, 580n5
  priority thesis, 221
  De anima, 112, 122–25, 135, 138, 147, 174, 187, 225, 376.
  See also A-eudaimonism; desires, D2, D3; ends; friendship; magnanimity; *orexis*; *prohairesis*

art, 35, 41, 110, 152, 158, 160, 173–74, 185, 253–56, 259, 302–4
  See also aesthetics; creativity; practices.
Auden, W. H., 5, 99
Audi, Robert, 63–64, 67, 287, 554n42, 557n103, 492, 498, 525, 529
Augustine, 28, 35–37, 70, 73, 115, 301, 303, 306, 327, 361–62, 364, 372, 376, 380, 382, 384–87, 394, 615n105, 621n78, 650n73
authenticity, xx–xxi, 20–21, 44, 64–65, 190, 232, 256–61, 341, 425, 454, 481, 501, 508, 534, 540, 542–46, 638n130, 640n175
autonomy, xvi–xxii, 9, 20–21, 27, 41, 60, 63, 66, 69, 72–73, 78, 83, 99, 140, 164–65, 363, 372, 393, 401–2, 410, 414, 425–27, 430–34, 449, 542, 552, 569n143, 627n149, 637n123
  as dependent on agent-transcending goods, 18, 20–22, 489, 505, 516, 527
  as explained by projective caring/love, xxi, 20–22, 60, 459, 465–68, 472, 489, 515, 612n60
  as a goal of intrinsic motivation, 425–27, 430–31, 434
  as moral motivation, 393, 401–2, 410, 414, 626n145
  as part of action theory, 63–73, 99, 112
  as reflexive and targetable, 164–65, 542
  demonic, 336, 356, 362, 364, 370, 378, 615n108, 616n115.
  See also values, alterity of.
aversion, 48–51, 54, 104, 124, 134, 136, 268, 331, 335, 356, 374, 387, 395, 423, 446

Bacon, Francis, 37–8, 41–42
bad faith, xxi, 164, 304, 341
Badhwar, Neera Kapur, 428, 432, 443
Bernstein, Richard, 353, 363, 609n26
Blustein, Jeffrey, 19, 32, 442–43, 458, 474, 479, 482–84, 486, 489, 500, 502, 506, 512, 527, 536, 646n90, 646n97, 651n94, 652n10
Boler, John, 380–82
Bonansea, Bernardine, 379, 382, 618n33
boredom, 30, 337–38, 423, 440, 446

Bostock, David, 178–79, 183–84, 581n13, 582n70, 583n38
boulēsis, 58, 70, 98, 100, 102, 121, 123, 131, 135, 137–39, 240, 243, 320, 327–31, 365, 372, 374, 623n102, 661
Bratman, Michael, 59, 76, 453
Broadie, Sarah, 119, 121, 204–6, 220, 328
Buber, Martin, 17, 302, 315–16, 384, 440–41, 443, 491, 519, 541, 545, 629n191, 636n9
Buddhism, 28–29, 30–35, 280, 477
Butler, Joseph, 51–52, 144, 162, 315, 331–34, 352, 428
by-product goods: *see* goods,
by-product satisfaction: *see* satisfaction.

Callicott, J. Baird, 280, 597n127
Cambridge Platonists, 49–51, 553n20, 553n26
Caputo, John, 153–54, 578n114
Carr, David, 114, 569n140
care/caring, xxi–xxii, 8, 15, 19–24, 27, 30, 32, 34, 43–47, 53, 73, 77, 128, 151, 155, 159–62, 165, 186, 192, 194, 213, 215–16, 219, 223, 229, 232, 237, 241, 249–50, 253, 264–65, 271–72, 276–80, 284, 289, 294–95, 298–302, 312, 314, 325, 328, 332, 342, 348, 351–54, 367, 369–71, 405, 417, 424, 429, 433, 437, 440–53, 458–533, 535–44, 595n95, 608n17, 610n36, 617n143, 642n20, 646n84, 649n37, 655n150
  and volitional love, 468–72
  as self-sustaining over time, 349, 431, 473–77, 485, 513
  structure of, 473.
  See also commitment; devotion; goods worth caring about
character, xvii, xix–xxi, 4–8, 10, 12, 21–22, 38, 40, 46, 58, 64, 75, 79, 81, 83, 109, 112, 116–17, 177, 186, 202, 206, 215, 217–20, 231–34, 241, 258, 261, 265, 269, 273, 318, 327, 335–38, 348, 350, 353, 365–74, 384, 406–8, 416–17, 421, 448–54, 457, 459, 465, 469, 472–75, 488–92, 494–97, 503, 505, 519, 528–33, 542

dispositions of, 177, 202, 207, 329–31, 367, 434;
  personal ethos of, xx, 11–12, 79, 343, 408, 417, 420, 459, 460, 472–77, 483, 488, 503, 521, 540–43
  volitional, 648n18
charity, 371, 383–84, 563n37, 596n111.
  See also agapē, just generosity, neighbor-love
children, 114–15, 141, 252, 264–67, 337, 360, 375, 422–24, 433, 438, 449–50, 470, 477, 506–8, 513–14, 518–21, 523, 526, 559n143, 570n161, 570n165, 634n58, 639n165, 653n139.
  See also infants
Cicero, 34–35, 195, 547n4
Clarke, W. Norris, 318, 606n161
coherence
  existential, 183, 185, 232, 454, 528, 535, 544
  practical, 232, 442, 533, 535, 540, 543, 624n115, 642n5.
  See also integrity; narrative unity
commitment, xxii, 4–7, 17, 19–23, 31, 33, 44, 45, 59, 64, 68, 74–77
  aretaic, 19, 22, 325, 474, 478, 481, 484, 485, 488, 523, 525, 540, 545, 648n32
  defininition of aretaic, 484–85
  identity-defining, 5, 73
  implicit, 307, 362, 402, 469
  personal, 18, 59, 60, 63
  self-defining, 11, 19.
  See also devotion
complexity caveat (concerning existential objectivism), 513, 517
conation/conative, 10, 70, 89–90, 135, 310, 319–23, 559n145, 662
conatus ascendi, 12, 34, 38, 40, 105, 125, 310, 316, 384, 650n72
Cooper, John M., 121–22, 129, 135, 235–40, 251, 253, 568, 571n171, 574n43, 591n14, 608n17
courage, 5, 8, 31, 35, 37, 112–15, 164, 300, 316, 327, 340, 346, 366–68, 372–73, 375, 475, 579, 568n129, 569n140, 587n23, 589n62, 602n80, 633n41

694 Index

creativity, human, 16, 38, 282, 302–3, 308, 315, 318, 340, 425, 520, 615n102
creativity, divine, 16–19, 84, 113, 289, 295, 319, 441, 599n18, 600n41, 649n57
Crosby, John, 318
Cudworth, Ralph, 50–51, 553

Dancy, Jonathan, 13, 610n37, 654n146
Davenport, John, xx, 548n5, 550n47, 555n74, 576n106, 594n80
Davidson, Donald, 56, 61–62, 65, 74–76, 89, 399, 468, 556n95
Deci, Edward L, 418–19, 424–28, 430–33, 451, 548n24
demonic, *see* autonomy, demonic
Dennett, Daniel, xviii, 49, 61–62, 556n87
deontic obligation, 16, 18, 85, 92, 244, 273, 289, 400–6, 411, 451, 457, 459, 528, 536
deontology, 269, 375, 405, 492, 514, 537, 618n24
  See also Kant; moral law
Descartes, René, 49, 65, 559n152, 643n27
desire
  erosiac, 13, 27, 107, 112, 122, 146, 181, 198, 199, 214, 238, 283, 287, 297, 320, 322, 323, 356, 359, 368, 369, 378, 406, 422, 643n42
  evaluative, 98, 100, 128, 130, 134, 140, 143, 172, 328, 565
  first-order, 144, 145, 151, 222, 223, 224
  metaphysical, xvi, xxii, 26, 310–18, 604n115, 605n128. *See also* Levinas.
  non-erosiac, 92, 562n15
  nontransferability of to by-products, 240
  orektic: *see* orexis
  second-order, 27, 145, 157, 222, 223, 224, 225, 227, 229, 351, 456
  type $D1$, 91, 98–100, 104, 123–27, 130–31, 135–36, 139, 142–45, 152, 172, 203, 206, 223, 259, 265, 267, 294, 311, 324, 327, 335, 342–43, 387, 388, 394, 400, 433, 437, 460, 565n81, 568n134, 572n15
  type $D2$, 98, 100, 104, 113, 125–45, 148, 152, 172, 186, 203, 206, 215, 255, 259, 261, 262, 268, 288, 294, 327, 332, 335, 337–39, 345, 351, 356, 367, 381, 387, 394, 400, 433, 437, 460, 469, 470, 486, 493, 505, 508, 565n81, 568n134, 572n20, 574n49, 579n140, 613n76
  type $D3$, 91, 98–101, 104, 108–10, 113–14, 126–28, 130–48, 152, 172–73, 186–87, 202, 206, 212, 223, 226–29, 249, 259, 262, 265–69, 279, 288, 294, 319, 320, 323–24, 327–28, 331–32, 342–43, 346–47, 365, 367, 376, 381, 388, 394, 400, 433, 435, 437, 440–43, 458, 462, 469–70, 565n81, 572n15, 574n39.
  See also motivation.
Desmond, William, 125, 311, 604n111, 605n127
devotion, volitional, 18, 268, 431, 443, 462, 478, 484, 508, 509, 535, 541, 543
Dewey, John, 205, 573n39
Dickens, Charles, 347–48
Diotima, 101, 103–11, 176, 526, 566n85, 584n51, 567n107
direction of fit, 90–91, 320–24
  world to content, 320–23
  world to mind, 288
  agent to content, 321–22, 406
domination, 27, 35, 38, 40, 42, 333, 336, 352, 357, 359, 551n58. *See also* evil, radical
dominant end: see *ends*
Donaldson, Stephen, xvi, 549n11, 559n160
Dostoyevsky, Fyodor, 337, 340, 452, 616n115
Drummond, John, 279, 647n14
duty, 26–27, 80, 273–84, 308, 310, 313, 316–18, 375, 383–84, 387–90, 393–95, 401–3, 416, 457, 469–70, 473, 490, 531, 603n102.
  motive of, 18, 26, 27, 243, 347, 371, 388–98, 402, 406, 458, 469, 479, 481, 591n17, 592n29, 618n24, 656n21
  to self, 639n160, 644n50.
  See also motivation, moral

earnestness, 366–69, 544, 610n36, 640n181, 645n73, 649n49. *See also* sincerity

Eastern attitude, 11, 29, 32, 38, 42, 551, 569n143. *See also* Western attitude
egoism, 27
  abstract, 163, 167, 168, 200, 332
  complex material, 157
  formal, 13, 15, 84, 106–8, 142–49, 152–54, 162–63, 167–68, 184, 196, 201–2, 208, 211, 214–17, 221, 231, 242, 260, 273, 280, 311, 379, 387, 428, 439–42, 470, 506, 567n107, 575n80, 584n50, 606n161
  material psychological, 33, 84, 96, 106–7, 143, 148, 154, 156–59, 161–63, 167, 172, 207, 213, 243, 260, 579n140
  moral, 142, 148–49, 152, 576n95, 576n98, 577n111
  rational, 150, 245, 280, 557n107, 576n84, 577n111
  psychological, 577n111
Eichmann, Adolf, 333, 609n28
Ehman, Robert, 541–43
Elster, Jon, 27, 163–66, 211, 240, 253, 257, 439, 453–54, 574n54, 580n146–151, 614
emotion, xxi, 7, 9, 22–23, 33–34, 54, 64, 69, 73, 77, 81–82, 87–89, 94, 113–16, 121, 135, 157, 164–65, 228, 248, 268, 301, 328–31, 338, 342, 346, 351, 353, 367–70, 373–75, 384, 388, 394–95, 400, 420, 455, 462, 471, 473, 485, 508, 526, 528, 542, 562n9, 572n15, 614n95, 640n181, 645n73, 653n119, 654n146. *See also* envy; love
ends
  comprehensive, 192, 236
  dominant, 187
  final, 6, 9, 105, 108, 111, 114, 147–48, 153, 155, 157, 160–62, 172–89, 193, 196, 207, 210, 212, 215–16, 225, 229, 231, 236–42, 244, 258, 271, 275, 279, 500
  fully final, 180, 184, 185, 189
  highest, 4, 174, 201, 236, 388, 403, 432, 476, 490, 541, 580, 582, 622
  holistic inclusion, 15, 180–83, 185, 192–93, 217, 237, 365, 581n13
  inclusive, 178–79, 187, 193, 214, 236
  non-holistic inclusion, 175, 177–80, 183, 185, 188–91, 580n5, 581n13, 581n17, 582n20, 583n35, 584n44
  sufficient, 196
  ultimate/uniquely highest, 6–7, 106, 140, 146, 148, 162, 167, 172, 174–78, 180–90, 236–37, 243–44, 374, 378, 379, 383, 385, 421, 580, 584; criteria for 185–86
  unconditionally complete, 178–79, 184–85, 189, 196.
  See also goals; Aristotle, regress argument.
Enkrateia, 17–18, 65, 112, 114, 327, 329–32, 366–70, 374, 454, 486
  See also self-control
envy, 157, 249, 330, 350–55, 562n9, 613n81
Epicureans, 33–35, 94
epithumia, 93, 102–4, 123–26, 131, 135–39, 328, 565n81, 572n13
eros, 94–95, 101–13, 107, 109, 284, 300, 309, 311–14, 470, 604n115
erosiac motivation (definition of), 26, 95, 111, 120–21, 141, 335, 437, 504, 562n15, 570n168; versus "erosic," 563n33
  See also desire, erosiac; *orexis*
erosiac theses
  strong erosiac thesis (SET), 91, 98, 101, 106–8, 121, 147, 187, 191, 197, 198, 202, 294–95, 299, 405, 438, 585n69, 588n43
  weak erosiac thesis (WET), 91, 122, 142, 198, 201, 283, 562n15, 597n134, 607n176
erotic, 95, 146, 500, 526
  See also eros.
eschatology, 607n172, 636n108
essentially particularistic regard, 347, 514–15, 518, 530, 542, 567n107, 588n44, 641n187, 651n94. *See also* care; love; spite
esteem: *see* self-esteem
ethics/ethical
  ethical life, 142, 232, 449, 540
  ethical norms, 167, 405, 495, 588n37
  ethical theory, 177, 458, 486
  metaethics, 45, 489, 505, 527, 654n146
  normative, xxi–xxii, 21, 44, 192, 199, 273, 282, 489, 491, 624n115

virtue ethics, 12, 15–16, 25, 84, 200–1, 214–15, 231–35, 248, 256, 269–73, 282, 284, 331, 405, 488, 490, 588n37, 595n99, 595n102. *See also* morality; virtues

ethos of a person, xx, 11–12, 79, 343, 408, 417, 420, 459, 460, 472–77, 483, 488, 503, 521, 540–43, 660. *See also* character.

eudaimonia thesis, 197–98, 216, 219, 225, 231, 235, 242–43, 273, 275, 280, 283, 442, 585n68, 622n91, 624n126

eudaimonism, 8, 11, 15–16, 19, 21, 26, 84, 86, 106, 121, 142–43, 171, 187, 192, 194–99, 201–2, 211, 213, 215, 219–24, 227, 231, 233, 235, 238, 240–44, 247–50, 263, 273, 275, 279–83, 326, 370–71, 380, 384, 405, 439, 446–47, 537, 548, 582n20, 584n62, 588n37, 588n43, 595n102, 615n103, 653n119

A-eudaimonism, 15, 20, 27, 171, 195–202, 214, 221, 231, 233, 242–44, 247, 263, 269, 272, 365, 379, 382, 439, 536, 548

A-eudaimonist core argument, 27, 198–200, 283, 327

external eudaimonism, 16, 216, 245, 263, 271, 595n99, 618n24

indirect eudaimonism, 16, 235, 245–48, 263, 592n30

psychological eudaimonism, 11, 14, 16, 17, 19, 92, 97, 121, 171, 216, 263, 548n27, 587n19

rational eudaimonism, 14–15, 216, 247–48, 263, 562n13.

See also paradox of eudaimonism

evaluative desires: *see* desires, D3

evil, xx, 5, 32, 35, 37, 43, 51, 96, 107, 211, 326, 330–47, 351–52, 359–67, 375, 378, 393, 442, 444, 534, 535, 539–40

demonic autonomy, 361, 362, 364, 378, 615n108, 616n115, 616n121

fanatical cruelty, 336, 339

malice, 326, 332–33, 335–37, 346–48, 363–64

radical evil, 11, 17–18, 25, 84, 157, 289, 325–39, 348, 357, 363–64, 371, 405, 456–58, 540, 608n26, 609n33,
615n105, 616n121, 617n2, 619n43, 621n71

religious despair, 616n121

transworld depravity, 609n26. *See also* spite; vengeance

excellence: *see* virtue

existentialism

and problem of isolation, xviii

as a tradition, xviii–xxii, 4, 25, 233, 367, 440, 454, 546, 636

existential core argument, 90–92, 325, 597n134

existential objectivism, 12, 405, 488–90, 496, 498, 500–1, 505–6, 509–13, 516, 519, 527, 535–36, 543, 648n29

existential nobility, 478

existential subjectivism, 490, 507

existential theology, 84, 601n45, 637n125

new existentialism, xxii, 8, 83, 326, 539, 540, 543.

See also meaning, existential; telos, existential

Face, the, 16–17, 20, 24, 26, 42–43, 152, 167, 284, 287, 289, 302, 307–18, 336, 357, 360–61, 384, 440–42, 458, 527, 534–35, 541–45, 547, 563, 601n145, 603, 604n105, 605n126. *See also* alterity; Levinas.

Farber, Leslie, 3, 453

Feinberg, Joel, 44, 122, 149, 150, 153, 157–62, 167, 211, 262, 331, 334, 439, 475, 528n115, 610n36

Ferrari, Giovanni, 105–6, 109–10

Fichte, J. G., xviii, 7, 43, 308, 556n84

Flanagan, Owen, xviii, 477, 491, 552n84

flourishing, 132, 134, 140–42, 148, 187, 206, 225–26, 233, 236–37, 239, 248, 250, 254, 259, 263–64, 269–74, 277, 279, 327, 349, 380, 382, 432–33, 473–75, 481–82, 489, 498, 509, 528, 530–31, 540, 573n37, 601n46, 641n1. *See also* eudaimonism

Foot, Philippa, 329–32

Frankfurt, Harry, xv, xvii, xxi, 7, 17, 19, 21, 24, 27, 32, 45–46, 69, 73, 112, 161–62, 234, 248, 418, 438, 443–49, 458–60, 475, 480, 482, 487–90, 494–523, 535, 541, 559n152,

590n140, 628n178, 631n200,
638n140, 641n5, 642n11, 642n16,
642n20, 643n31, 643n42, 644n51,
646n84, 648n18, 649n56–57,
651n105, 653n139
Frankl, Viktor, 7, 19, 25, 332, 335, 418,
436–43, 449, 451–54, 475, 489,
527, 636n100, 637n112, 638n130
freedom of the will, xxi, 50, 57, 407, 409,
417, 628n172, 642n26
  leeway-liberty, xi, xiv, 6, 18, 57–58, 60–
    63, 70, 78, 83, 142, 197, 234, 273,
    371–72, 376–82, 409, 411–12, 416,
    472, 627n165, 628n185, 629n186,
    642n26, 656n27
  libertarian freedom, xvii, xx, 6, 18, 58,
    60–63, 70, 78, 83, 142, 197, 234,
    273, 371–72, 376–82, 409, 411–12,
    416, 627n165, 630n191, 631n204,
    642n26, 643n35, 644n51, 656n27.
  See also agent-causation
Freud, 43, 48, 80, 327, 419–24, 437–39,
552n81
friendship, 11, 16, 72–73, 95–96, 188,
194, 201, 206–8, 211–12, 217–22,
234–35, 237, 248–51, 258, 260,
263–64, 271, 277, 324, 355, 359,
366, 383, 404, 424, 428, 434, 457,
489, 506, 512–14, 518, 524, 535,
542, 563n35, 563n37, 566n87,
587n23, 588n49, 593n53, 614n96
  general structure of, 258
Fromm, Erich, 259–60, 302, 338,
658n134
fulfillment, by-product, 264, 428. *See also*
  satisfaction; pleasure

Gilbert, Alan, 259, 423
glory, 30, 34, 151–52, 156, 167, 176, 208,
345, 372, 380, 450, 520. *See also*
honor
God/divine, xx, 5, 9, 16–19, 35–37, 59,
106–10, 176, 197, 265, 287–302,
304, 307, 309, 316, 319, 324, 340,
355, 360–62, 367–77, 378–86, 416,
441–42, 503–5, 530, 598n11,
598n15, 599n18, 599n19, 600n33,
601n45, 603n97, 615n102, 636n108.
See also creativity, divine.

goals
  directly targetable, 13, 111, 163, 277,
    445, 449, 647n101
  goal-setting, 7, 28, 44, 319, 332, 415,
    421, 423, 432, 488, 502
  indirectly targetable 266, 442–43, 542
  mutually targetable, 278–79
  nontargetable, 13, 110–11, 163–65,
    257–58, 265–66, 277, 448.
  See also ends; life goals.
goods
  agent-relative, 98, 102, 146, 152, 156,
    167–68, 206, 226, 241, 257, 264–
    67, 274, 396, 426, 431, 442, 448,
    462, 500, 502, 503, 508, 516, 517,
    518, 520, 521, 523, 533, 535,
    576n84, 649n54
  agent-transcending, 153, 156, 159–62,
    168, 225–27, 253, 255–58, 264–67,
    274–75, 278, 280, 315, 318, 332,
    339, 341–42, 347, 403, 424, 429–
    35, 439, 445, 470, 479, 516, 521,
    533, 534, 540, 579n140, 620n62
  basic, 488, 528–33, 537
  by-product goods, 201, 212, 259, 262,
    418, 429, 430, 443, 521
  common, 173, 253, 274–80, 529,
    596n115
  definitive of a practice, good life, 16–19,
    27, 33, 36, 84, 101, 106, 113, 197,
    265, 287–90, 294–304, 307, 309,
    319, 324, 340, 360, 384, 405, 416,
    441, 442, 487, 489–90, 503–6, 530
  joint, 14, 274–78, 596n114, 596n118
  list of goods worth caring about, 528–33
  process-goods, 17, 20, 528, 532–33
  product-goods/values, 4, 17, 19, 108,
    111, 163, 388, 393, 444–48, 478,
    483, 488, 503, 623n107
  religious, 530.
  See also values
Gordon, Emily Fox, 452–55
Gottlieb, Paula, 213, 216, 235, 240–45
Gowans, Christopher, 31, 404–5
ground projects: *see* projects.
grounding thesis, 318, 488
grounds for caring, xx, 19, 46, 445, 487–
  89, 501–3, 507–13, 518–21, 524,
  530, 534–35, 649n37, 649n49,
  650n72, 653n139

698   Index

consequence-transcending, 19, 483, 644n59
backward-looking, 342, 347, 402, 473, 479, 481, 485, 517, 519.
See also goods; values

Habermas, Jürgen, xvii, 68, 131, 405, 492–93, 558n129, 647n13, 648n29
Hardie, W. F. R, 192–93, 580n2, 583n38
Hauerwas, Stanley, 5, 8, 81–82, 123, 301, 561n194
hedonism, 30, 33, 145, 150, 157–62, 167, 213, 337, 403, 577n110, 578n115, 579n141. *See also* paradox of hedonism
Hegel, G. W. F., 305, 307–8, 311, 359–60, 408, 423, 449–50, 497, 563, 623n107
Heidegger, Martin, 183, 303, 304, 307, 312–13, 391, 461, 518, 540–44, 656n29
Herman, Barbara, 398–99, 515
Hill, Thomas Jr., 451, 639n160, 648n18
Hobbes, Thomas, xvi, 40–41, 48–54, 64, 67, 97, 106, 151–52, 156, 167, 274, 278, 312, 315, 351, 396, 399, 422, 424, 437, 450, 462, 555n57, 565n42, 577n105, 602–3, 642n26
hobbies, 424, 483, 499, 507, 512, 518, 524, 525, 531, 646n95
Holmgren, Margaret, 617n143
Honneth, Axel, 449, 451
honor, 34–35, 96, 105, 115–19, 151, 172, 176, 182, 188, 190, 218, 243, 330, 340, 364, 450–51, 585n2
honor code, 5, 34, 37, 113, 549n24, 612n68.
See also self-esteem; timocracy
Hume, David, xix, 9, 49–51, 54, 87, 99, 126, 133–34, 288, 393, 398, 405–6, 496, 553n11, 573n36
Husserl, Edmund, xviii–xxi, 279, 308–9, 603n94
Huxley, Aldous, 30, 33

identification: volitional, xxi, 23, 60, 73, 342, 463–65, 472, 612n60, 642n20, 643n31. *See also* autonomy; Frankfurt
impassibility, 290, 294, 198. *See also* creativity, divine; superabundancy

impulses, 18, 26, 93–94, 98, 100, 112, 123–27, 135–36, 149, 172, 264, 295, 328–29, 400–1, 403, 410. *See also* desire, type D1
inclusion in a goal: *see* ends
infants, 125, 422, 423, 570n161, 636n100, 650n68. *See also* children
integrity, 5, 30, 44, 107, 358, 368, 427, 484, 486, 495, 512, 545. *See also* caring; sincerity.
intellectual appetite, 13, 112, 118–22, 139, 327, 372, 384–85. *See also* rational appetite.
intentions, 6, 10–12, 31, 47, 56–83, 87–90, 121, 128, 205, 268, 287, 288, 319–22, 377, 381, 385, 387, 389, 391, 395, 397, 399–402, 406–8, 410, 412, 414–16, 451, 460, 466–69, 486, 491. *See also* action theory
intention-formation, 78–79, 82–83, 87, 389, 400–1, 408, 467, 556n92, 571n171. *See also* decision
intentionality, xii, 43, 68, 75, 101, 300, 308, 311, 419, 603n97
internalism about motivation, 45, 134
intrinsic value: *see* value.
Irwin, Terence, 97, 100, 175, 179, 182–83, 194, 569n139, 581n14, 588n49

James, William, 52–55, 292, 420, 554, 598n8
Jaspers, Karl, 363, 439, 615n109
jealousy, 355, 621n74. *See also* envy
joint goods: *see* goods, joint
jointure thesis, 197–99, 227, 232, 283, 585n68, 661
just generosity, 596n111. *See also* agapē; neighbor-love.
justice, 18, 20, 23, 35, 46, 116, 148, 149, 152, 177, 192, 212–14, 244, 277, 279, 318, 326, 329–32, 341, 345–49, 362–63, 368–75, 379–83, 386–88, 391, 394, 396, 402–3, 449, 457, 459, 466, 475, 490–93, 521–22, 528–29, 536, 540, 596n119, 612n69, 613n76, 620n61, 627n153. *See also* morality; will to justice.

Kahn, Charles, 70, 301
kalon, 40, 115, 172, 202, 203, 283, 586n17, 589n62. *See also* noble.

Kane, Robert, 56–60, 63–64, 73–80, 87, 114, 557*n*105, 642*n*26, 643*n*35
Kant, Immanuel, xviii, 3–4, 16, 18–20, 24–27, 31, 46, 52, 76, 81, 84, 92, 117, 148, 177, 233, 246–47, 279, 281, 289, 302, 310, 315, 317, 332–33, 371, 384–406, 409–16, 432, 456, 458, 466, 469–70, 472, 478–81, 489, 492, 546, 580*n*146, 603*n*102, 609*n*26, 622*n*99–99, 623*n*100, 620*n*107, 623*n*109, 624*n*115, 624*n*119, 624*n*126, 625*n*126–138, 626*n*144–149, 627*n*165, 628*n*175, 629*n*186–191, 630*n*191–193, 630*n*198–199, 631*n*204, 643*n*42, 656*n*21. *See also* duty, motive of
Kantian principle of action (KPA), 77, 390, 623*n*107
Kekes, John, 339, 341, 536, 610*n*50
Kenny, Anthony, 330, 582*n*70
Kent, Bonnie, 327, 372–75, 378, 618*n*16, 624*n*121
Kierkegaard, Søren, xix–xx, 4–5, 17, 20, 183, 298–99, 326, 376, 423, 433, 440, 453, 474, 476, 478, 502, 516, 523, 545, 547*n*4, 595*n*99, 621*n*85, 637*n*108, 638*n*130, 640*n*182
  on radical evil, 363–69, 616*n*21
Korsgaard, Christine M, 18, 15, 76–77, 140–41, 149–50, 162, 389, 395, 397, 401–5, 428, 469, 622*n*96, 623*n*102, 626*n*148, 658
Kosky, Jeffrey, 310, 603–5
Kraut, Richard, 15, 87–92, 94, 206, 208–9, 213, 216, 218, 221–24, 247, 577*n*110, 581*n*15, 584, 589*n*58
Kupperman, Joel, 30, 367, 421, 491, 493

Lao Tze, 30
Larmore, Charles, 302, 527
Lear, Jonathan, 186, 237
learned helplessness, 436
Leopold, Aldo, 522–23, 597*n*127
Levinas, Emmanuel, 16–17, 20–24, 26, 42–43, 287, 289, 300, 303, 307–18, 384, 441, 442, 491, 534, 543, 545, 563*n*35, 572*n*20, 599*n*21, 603*n*97, 603*n*102, 604*n*114–115, 605*n*128, 605*n*130, 606*n*154, 615*n*104

Lewis, C. S., 296–97, 438, 570*n*168, 600*n*41
liberalism, political, 19, 490–94
libertarian freedom: *see* freedom of the will
libido dominandi,12, 35, 38, 40, 650*n*72
life goals, 44, 64, 280, 286, 333, 337, 368, 384, 415, 449, 451, 476, 488, 491–92, 497, 532
  See also ground projects
life-meaning, 8, 19, 37, 443, 446, 652*n*107. *See also* meaning, personal
life-narrative, 83, 477, 546. *See also* narrative unity
life plan, 19, 261, 449, 493, 536
Lincoln, Abraham, 645*n*75, 652*n*108
Lippitt, John, 655*n*1
Locke, John, 49–51, 67, 145, 559*n*145
Logotherapy, 19, 418, 437, 439, 638*n*130
love
  romantic, 164, 166, 356, 469, 530, 653*n*119
  parental, 470, 477, 506–7, 530
  property-based, 95, 300
  volitional, 19, 469–72, 480, 486, 488, 514.
  See also agapē; care; eros; essentially particularistic regard; friendship
Lovejoy, Arthur O., 292–95, 297, 601*n*64
Luther, Martin, 36–40, 317

MacIntyre, Alasdair, ix, 16, 18, 25, 69, 99, 126, 131, 140–42, 213, 237, 241, 251–52, 255–57, 259–62, 265–66, 274, 276–80, 303, 341, 363–64, 425, 452, 474, 506, 517, 552*n*1, 564*n*61, 575*n*69, 587*n*30, 593*n*56, 594*n*84, 596*n*111, 596*n*114, 596*n*118, 641*n*5
magnanimity, 177, 218–21, 230, 248, 327, 450, 591*n*21. *See also* self-esteem
malevolence, 153, 336, 352, 357–59, 361–62, 364
Marion, Jean-Luc, 350, 612*n*69, 615*n*108
Maslow, Abraham, 19, 419, 425, 432–33, 435–37, 439, 634*n*65,
Marshall, General George, 652*n*108
McDowell, John, 135, 320, 595*n*99
McPherran, Mark, 290, 598*n*11
meaning
  existential meaning (as distinct from happiness), 440–45, 449, 516, 532, 637*n*108, 638*n*147, 652*n*107

personal, 19, 230, 440, 444–45, 475, 476, 492, 516, 527, 545–46, 589n65
will to meaning, 325, 436, 438–39, 620n58.
See also life-meaning; narrative unity; ethos of a person
Mele, Alfred, 74, 98, 112, 134, 288, 560n164, 573n21
middle part of the soul, 112–13, 316, 569n142, 570n169. *See also* thumos.
Mill, John Stuart, 37, 63, 159–60, 553n16, 57–79, 592n34
Milton, John: *Paradise Lost*, 35, 362–63
Molinism, xvii, 83, 590n76
morality, 32, 149, 237, 242, 246, 341, 362, 373, 380, 382, 391, 403, 466, 469, 489–90, 502, 520, 530, 588n33
  moral law, 18, 382, 388, 389, 391, 394, 395, 397, 401, 410, 469, 603n102, 626n148
  moral norms, 272, 346, 362, 459, 537, 611n53, 654n146, 656n21
  moral theory, xxi, 8, 44–46, 64, 200–1, 269, 272–73, 326, 375, 449, 459, 490, 506, 514.
See also ethics; motivation, moral
motive switches, 339, 344, 347, 356
Mook, Douglas, 420, 424, 433–35
Mooney, Edward, ix, 545
Moore, G. E., 19, 133, 150, 576n84, 581, 591
Morillo, Carolyn, 155, 156–59
motivation/motives,
  effectance, 426
  erosiac: *see* erosiac model; desire
  formal/thin senses of, 13, 287–89, 468
  intrinsic, 9, 19, 21, 418, 424–34, 535, 633n37, 633n50, 634n58, 635n73
  moral, 11, 16, 18–19, 84, 89, 118, 201–2, 231, 246, 289, 311, 318, 325, 370–71, 392, 397–98, 401–2, 406, 410, 534, 622n91
motives in general
  non-erosiac, 92
  orektic: *see* orexis
  prepurposive, 77, 87, 90–92, 122, 198, 262, 324, 338, 376, 398–99, 418, 420, 435, 471, 474, 481, 487, 504, 562n15, 597n134, 607n176, 610n37, 626n148

projective, xv–xvi, xxi, 7–23, 26–27, 42, 82–86, 90–92, 168, 200, 202, 229–30, 232–35, 259, 260–61, 267, 275, 279–80, 287–89, 295–99, 303, 305, 313, 315–25, 332, 334–35, 338, 340–41, 344, 363, 366, 371, 376, 383–84, 387, 391, 393, 396, 400–11, 414–18, 421, 423, 426, 436, 438, 440–42, 458–59, 467, 472, 488–89, 498, 502, 504–5, 516–19, 524, 531, 535, 539, 543, 600n45, 626n144, 637n112; as essentially volitional motivation, 80–83; definition of, 9–10, 606n166; general structure of, 322.
See also will; striving
pure, 153, 214, 219, 220, 225–27, 229–31, 236, 245–48, 256–59, 263–65, 267, 274, 282, 387, 393, 396–97, 480, 506, 579n140, 586n6, 612n69, 620n62, 637n112, 645n73, 645n75
purposive, 90–91, 128, 275, 283, 320, 322, 380, 398, 400, 479, 508, 597n134
self-motivation, xvi, xix, xxi, 8–9, 12, 18, 28, 46, 52, 73, 80, 283, 295, 297, 301, 320, 369, 388, 406, 410, 425, 471, 486, 535, 547n3, 607n166
theories of, 10, 21
See also desire; eudaimonism
Moya, Carlos, 59, 62, 67–68, 74–78
Murdoch, Iris, xii, 80, 94, 256
Murphy, Mark C., 130, 388, 585–86
Myers-Briggs type inventory, 21, 47, 408, 552n2. *See also* personality type

Nagel, Thomas, 77, 268, 506, 607n170
Nancy, Jean-Luc, 26, 43, 551n76
narrative, 5, 12, 68–69, 75, 77, 99, 183, 185, 459, 476–79, 484, 492, 503, 513, 523, 525, 536, 642n5. *See also* life-narrative
narrative unity, xix, 183, 185, 459, 479, 484, 655n1. *See also* coherence, practical
Natural law theory, 19, 348, 488, 519, 537
Naturalistic thesis, 200, 661
neighbor-love, 43, 300, 310, 314, 318, 563n37, 596n111. *See also* agapē.

neo-Aristotelianism, xii, xvi, 15–16, 25, 122, 202, 234–35, 259, 280, 405, 537
Nietzsche, Friedrich, 20, 26, 28, 40–43, 117, 273, 302–4, 348, 438, 450, 455, 459, 527, 549n7, 550n55, 551. *See also* will to power.
noble, the, 15, 34, 105, 114–15, 191, 202–4, 207–8, 211–14, 216, 218–20, 229, 232, 236–37, 241–43, 247–48, 283, 328–32, 387, 528, 587n23. *See also kalon.*
nobility, 14, 40, 115, 172, 203, 207, 210, 218–10, 236, 239–40, 243–44, 346, 481, 564n42, 622n92
Noddings, Nel, 440–43, 459, 461, 489, 514, 541
non-targetable goals: *see* goals.
normative worth, 496–97, 500–2, 521–22, 525, 535. *See also* values.
Nozick, Robert, 519, 521, 527
Nussbaum, Martha, 33–34, 93–94, 124–47, 248, 296, 563, 572n15, 581n11
Nygren, Anders, 17, 24, 107, 292, 298–300, 309, 314, 428, 563n34, 567n107, 608n41
Nygren's fallacy, 313, 503–5

Oberdiek, Hans, 49–50, 54, 65–66, 113, 119
O'Connell, Robert J., S.J, 375, 618n24
Oliver, Mary, 544–45
optionality of ends, 509–10, 515–16, 536
orexis, 92–95, 102–3, 122–24, 137–39, 144, 147–48, 168, 191, 206, 319, 321, 406, 563n32, 572n13, 608n24. *See also* desire, erosiac; egoism, formal; motivation
O'Shaughnessy, Brian, 58, 63, 67, 71, 554n46, 555–56

Palmquist, Stephen, 624n104
paradoxes
 of abstract egoism, 162–63, 167, 200
 of eudaimonism, 15, 201–2, 213, 219–22, 224, 227, 231–35, 238–43, 247–48, 250, 263, 273, 275, 279–83, 446, 587n30, 590n1
 of hedonism, 160–62, 167, 578n115
 of formal egoism, 162–63
 of material egoism, 161–63, 167, 200
 of utilitarianism, 244
Parfit, Derek, 44, 160, 161, 243, 244–47, 557n100, 579n140, 588n34, 592n31, 592n36
passion, 31, 33, 38, 50, 115–16, 119, 123, 137, 232, 248, 296, 301, 315, 319, 329–30, 345, 367, 369, 471, 476, 478, 549; infinite: 4, 476, 645n67
pathos, 93, 94, 137
Payne, Andrew, 102–3, 565n77, 565n81, 566n102
personal affinity, 508–9, 511, 516–18, 522, 526, 533. *See also* grounds for caring
personal appropriation of values, 485, 500–3, 516, 519, 651n85. *See also* meaning, personal
personal importance, 483, 500–2
personality type theory, 21, 47, 408, 552
personhood, xvii–xxi, 28, 233, 273, 408, 417, 460, 469, 472, 486, 490, 519, 537, 543, 558n138
phenomena/phenomenal quality, xxii–xxiv, 17, 80, 90, 132, 414, 571n10, 629n190
phenomenological realists, 289, 302, 318, 336, 601n65, 654n149
phenomenological method, xxii–xxiv, 23
phenomenology, xxii, 10, 13, 45, 78, 79, 222, 287, 307–9, 405, 411, 417, 493
Piaget, Jean, 422
Pincoffs, Edmund, 205, 586n14
Pink, Thomas, 49, 56, 65, 69–78, 82–83, 86, 117, 287–88, 319, 322, 377, 406, 407, 555n65, 558n140, 559n145, 559n146, 559n152, 561n196, 561n198, 569n151, 607n169, 627n169. *See also* second-order agency.
Pinnock, Charles, 599n19
Pippin, Robert, 548
Plantinga, Alvin, 609n26
Plato, 182, 190, 330, 359, 374, 571n6
 and crafts, 220, 253, 258, 564n61, 582n23
 and erosiac desire, 8, 10, 13, 84, 91–94, 97, 100–5, 112, 122, 139, 146, 173, 306, 310, 21, 437, 567n107, 568n134, 615n102

702   Index

and eudaimonism, 97–99, 101, 142, 142, 176, 270, 375
and motivational internalism, 100
Diotima's ascent, 110
eschatological myths, 598n10
Form of the Good, 172, 604n114, 604n117
late Plato and divine motivation, 16–17, 290–96, 311–12, 598n11, 601n45, 604n115, 604n117
on friendship, 95–96, 212, 220
on politics, 371–72
on thumos, 111–16, 119–20, 569n140, 569n143, 570n159
on types of desire, 97–101, 125, 131–32, 173, 321, 371, 437, 564n54, 565n81, 568n131
tripartite soul, 118–19, 137, 568n130, 569n164, 570n157
versus Homer, 31, 34, 612n68
Apology, 218, 564n48, 618n23
Cratylus, 93–94,
Euthyphro, 598n11
Gorgias, 30, 97, 223, 564n42, 571n141
Lysis, 95–97, 104, 220, 290, 566n87
Meno, 96, 99–100, 132, 290
Phaedrus, 295, 547n4, 562n20, 563n26, 565n69, 566n88
Philebus, 582n20, 604n115
Republic, 97–100, 103–4, 110, 114, 173, 212, 220, 253, 289–92, 564n54, 568n130, 569n164, 604n115, 604n117
Symposium, 13, 26, 100–6, 142, 163, 166, 176, 437, 523, 565n81, 566n102
See also Transcendent principle
Platonic love, 107, 290, 563n38, 567n107
Platonic Principle of motivation, 96, 99–100, 106, 132, 139, 292, 331
play, 228, 261, 423
pleasure
and pain, 50, 123, 135–37, 400
brutal/cruel, 337
deviant, 340
derivative/by-product, 144, 155–56, 160, 213, 378, 578n130, 633n27, 636n106
entertainment, 126, 145, 151, 154, 162, 175, 261, 262, 266, 327, 334–38, 404, 425
first-order and second-order, 154–55, 202, 205, 359, 578n115
higher and lower, 579n141
of domination, 352
physical, 136, 190, 295, 578n125, 579n141
pleasure principle, 438, 636n106
sensual, 113, 151, 162, 187, 190, 209, 243, 327, 330, 338, 344, 364, 568n131
tranquility, 33, 162, 306, 579n130, 617n143
vindictive, 345, 378
political philosophy, xx, xxii, 39, 490–91. *See also* justice; MacIntyre; Rawls; Sandel
Politis, Vasilis, 221, 222, 588, 589
practices, 11, 16, 140, 228, 248, 251–68, 275, 279, 316, 324, 340–41, 344–45, 349, 352, 367, 422–24, 434, 439, 452, 457, 474–77, 498–500, 508, 517, 529, 540, 544, 564n61, 593n56, 593n59, 593n60, 632n22, 648n35
general structure of, 257
preferences, 58, 73, 98, 99, 130–37, 156, 172, 186, 261, 268, 324, 351, 449, 494, 505; brute, 126–31, 137, 140, 305, 490, 513, 568n134, 610n40
second-order, 464.
See also desires, type D2
prepurposive motives: *see* motives
process-values: *see* goods
product-values: *see* goods
prohairesis, 70, 98, 119–22, 138–39, 142, 205, 241, 328–31, 382, 571n171, 574n43, 575n61, 598n8, 608n20, 623n102
projects
ground projects, 19, 45, 459–60, 472, 476–77, 481, 488, 521, 523, 525, 528, 534–35, 641n4, 645n68. *See also* motivation, projective.
projection, psychological, 9
projective motivation: *see* motivation
proportionalism (as a doctrine concerning caring), 505–7, 512–13, 650n73
psychology
behaviorism, 47, 419–20, 424
contemporary theories, 232, 418–21

empirical, xix, 21, 45, 78, 158–59, 162, 418–19, 422, 426, 434, 528, 552n84, 556n92
existential, 80, 458
humanistic, 419–21, 426, 432, 634n65.
See also motivation, intrinsic.
psychoanalysis, 16, 19, 289, 312, 405, 417–23, 437, 439
pure aretaic naturalism, 269–73
pure motives: see motivation; agent-transcending goods.
Purinton, Jeffrey S., 191–95, 584n62
purposive motivation: see motivation.

radical evil: see evil
Railton, Peter, 44, 654n146
Rank, Otto, 43–44, 80, 552n81, 561n189
rational appetite, 33, 58, 84, 120, 284, 320, 365, 374, 378, 570n161, 619n40. See also intellectual appetite.
Rauscher, Frederick, 401, 409–10
Rawls, John, 39, 148, 149, 161, 177, 244, 261–62, 269–70, 277, 350, 351, 405, 418, 449–52, 490–92, 522, 624n115, 627n153
Raz, Joseph, 20, 513, 515–19, 527, 651n98, 652n108, 652n118, 653n121
rectitude, 375, 381, 384–85, 387, 395, 402, 621n85, 622n91.
See also reverence; will to justice
Reeve, C. D. C., 331, 608n20
Reeve, Christopher, 499, 649n40
regress argument against decisions-as-agency, 55–56, 71, 548n17.
See also decisions; volitionalism
Reid, Thomas, 51–52, 352, 613n85, 634n62
religion: see God
Rescher, Nicholas, 647n2, 654n146
resoluteness, 6–7, 76, 435, 541, 634n65
resolve, xxiii, 4, 7, 9, 12, 17, 22, 35, 45–46, 54, 64, 73, 80–82, 95, 120, 235, 262, 280, 283, 298, 301–2, 314–15, 320, 346, 364, 368, 370, 384, 400, 415, 421, 440, 455, 461, 465–67, 472, 474, 484, 486, 488, 501, 516, 535, 540, 600n40, 632n12, 640n169
respect, moral, 18, 107, 215, 315, 342, 388, 391, 394, 451, 479, 540, 543, 608n22, 652n118. See also self-respect

reverence, 391–95. See also rectitude; respect; moral values, unconditional respect for
revenge: see vengeance
reward-event theory, 157–59
Rice, Richard, 298–99, 599n19
Ricoeur, Paul, 491
Rist, John, 112,
Roberts, Robert C., 368–70, 572n15, 615n144
Robinson, T. M., 295, 568n130
Rogozinski, Jacob, 609n28
Ross, W. D., 19, 237, 473
Rousseau, Jean-Jacques, 157, 351–52, 613n81
Ryan, Richard, 425–33, 548n24, 635n73
Ryle, Gilbert, 6–7, 47, 49, 54, 56, 62, 65, 548n17, 552n1

sadistic cruelty, 337–42, 359, 589n63. See also radical evil.
Sandel, Michael, xviii, 404, 490, 597n130
Sartre, Jean-Paul, xviii–xix, 43, 316, 360, 440, 441, 455–56, 465–66, 488, 489, 491, 542, 556n84, 586n15, 590n76, 603n94, 615n103, 625n138, 641n185, 647n4
satisfaction
  by-product satisfaction, 144–46, 154–61, 240, 368, 639n165
  second-order, 155, 161–63, 166–67, 259, 266, 270, 275, 339, 456, 578n115.
  See also fulfillment
Saving Private Ryan, 495, 517, 519, 652n108
Scanlon, Thomas, 596n119, 654n146
Schalow, Frank, 540, 655n5
Scheler, Max, 289, 318, 606n165
Schopenhauer, Arthur, 43, 52, 554n34, 602n75
Scott, Michael, 554n60, 558n128
Scotus, Duns, 16, 18–19, 25, 81, 84, 92, 192, 301–3, 318, 371–87, 391–96, 403–6, 432, 578n114, 618n29, 619n35, 619n43, 619n58, 620n62, 620n66, 620n69, 621n74, 623n111, 624n121
second-order desire: see desire
self-actualization, 418, 425, 426, 432–36, 439, 441, 634n65, 635n68. See also Maslow

self-control, 17–18, 65, 112, 119, 219, 327–30, 332, 366–70, 374, 454, 486, 569n140. *See also enkrateia*
self-determination: *see* autonomy.
self-determination theory, 425–31, 548n24, 632n12. *See also* motivation, intrinsic
self-esteem, 39, 220, 449–51, 498, 639n163
self-motivation: *see* motivation
self-realization, 41, 146–47, 168, 260–61, 264, 314–15, 380, 382, 384, 422
self-relations: intrasubjective, 465, 473
self-respect, 387, 449–52, 478, 639n160, 639n163, 639n165
self-sufficiency, 34, 93–94, 97, 180–81, 186–87, 194, 217, 220, 248, 249
Seligman, Martin, 436
Shakespeare, William
  Hamlet, 452
  Macbeth, 346
  Richard III, 354
Sherman, Nancy, 221, 235, 248–51, 342, 593n51, 614n96
Sidgwick, Henry, 146–48, 577n110
simple weighing, 114, 127, 131
sincerity, 385, 481, 485, 526. *See also* authenticity; earnestness
Slote, Michael, 271, 273, 595n99–101
Smith, Adam, 50
Sober, Elliott, 136–37, 156, 579n129
Soble, Alan, 91, 95, 300. *See also* motivation, erosiac
Solomon, Robert C., 40, 563n33, 601n33
Sound of Music, 498–500, 508–9, 648n36
Spaemann, Robert, 622n91
Spinoza, 40, 280–81, 292–94, 318, 551n57, 559n18
spite, 36, 330, 350, 353–57, 363–64, 456, 610n44, 613n81, 614n93–95, 616n115, 641n85. *See also* radical evil
stability against fortune, 33, 176–77
Stampe, Dennis, 72–73, 78, 559n158
Steele, Carlos, 364
Steiner, Rudolph, 408, 628n172
Stocker, Michael, 44, 459, 514, 515, 517, 518, 588n44, 640n181
Stoics, 33–35, 70, 121, 195, 372–74, 385–86, 571n171

Stump, Eleonore, 342, 612n60, 652n119, 654n139
subsumption of motives, 224–27
  general principle of, 224
  special principle of, 227
  relation between motives, 224
superabundancy, 293, 295–98, 302, 307, 309, 315, 318, 377, 381, 604. *See also* divine motivation
supremacy thesis about virtue, 221, 617n15
Sverdlik, Steven, 88–89, 562n9
Swanton, Christine, 596n105

targetable goals: *see* goals.
Tate, Margaret Watkins, 499,
Taylor, Charles, 37–38, 114, 127, 131, 497, 519, 648n32
Taylor, Gabrielle, 541, 635n70, 649n37, 653n120
Taylor, Paul, 601n46
Taylor, Richard, 81, 332, 334, 337–39, 609n35
telos, 16, 20, 37, 99, 104, 107, 147, 194–99, 212, 233, 252, 259, 304, 313, 321, 386, 387, 420, 427, 431, 432, 520, 544
  erosiac, formal, 195–200, 233, 242, 312, 374, 386–87, 427, 431–32, 622n92
  erosiac, material, 188–92, 194, 196–97, 199–200, 216, 242, 247, 374, 384
  existential/non-erosiac, 312, 360, 386–87, 428, 431–32, 439, 503, 540, 622n92, 637n108
  material conceptions of, 432
  motivational, 431–32
  natural/functional, 140, 381, 427, 431–32, 503, 524, 544
thumos, 13, 33, 93, 113–20, 123, 131, 384, 568n131, 570n159, 613n85. *See also* middle part of the soul
Tiberius, Valerie, 654n146
Tillich, Paul, 145, 576n83
timocracy, 31, 34–35, 115, 218, 372, 549n24, 587n23, 612n68. *See also* honor; Plato
Tolkien, J. R. R., xvi, 5, 302, 315, 360, 361, 362, 544, 551n58 615n102, 615n104, 615n108

torture, 313, 349, 357, 358, 359, 361, 592*n*34, 614*n*97
traditions, xv, 16, 28–29, 32, 147, 280, 281, 300, 490, 518, 534, 546, 568*n*129
  "Eastern," 12, 31–33, 38, 307, 317, 327, 551*n*57, 589*n*57, 634*n*65
  "Western," 12, 39–42, 282, 635*n*75
Transcendent principle, 111, 184, 615*n*103
  strong, 583*n*35
  weak, 184–86, 202, 210, 583*n*35
Transmission principle, 87–89, 91, 120, 198, 201, 282–83, 287, 405, 562*n*13, 618*n*27
Tutelage thesis, 266–67

Ubiquity thesis, 148, 624*n*126
Urmson, J. O., 329, 330, 331, 373
utilitarianism, 50, 116, 160–62, 241–44, 269, 273, 405, 459, 473, 476–77, 484, 514, 515, 541, 645*n*68
  government house, 244
  indirect, 244, 592*n*34
  paradox of, 244

values
  alterity of, 20, 152, 167, 315, 318, 440–41, 455, 457, 485, 527, 535, 561*n*189
  consequence-transcending, 474–75, 483, 644*n*59
  expression of, 474–78, 481, 483–85
  extrinsic, 424–26, 434, 646*n*101
  intrinsic, 19–20, 23, 40, 175, 226, 238–40, 244, 267, 278, 287, 291, 299, 302, 350–51, 356, 387, 392–93, 428–29, 437, 443, 458–59, 473–75, 478, 481, 484–85, 509–12, 523, 528, 542, 581*n*7, 619*n*59, 641*n*187, 646*n*101, 653*n*139
  instrumental, 132, 324, 364, 392, 445–48, 475, 478, 591*n*15
  metaphysical status of, 9, 23, 323, 487
  moderate realism about, 9, 23, 505
  objective, 19, 489, 502–5, 521, 523–27, 545
  theory of, 23–24, 489, 527
  unconditional respect for, 474–78, 481, 483–86, 516
Van Inwagen, Peter, 60

Vedder, Ben, 93, 312
Velkley, Richard
Velleman, J. David
vengeance, 347–49, 355, 612n68
vice, 17–18, 271, 326–33, 339, 352, 366, 372–73, 507, 595*n*99. *See also* envy; evil; jealousy; spite
virtue, 5, 8, 23, 33–35, 84, 97, 110, 113–14, 134, 164, 172, 176–79, 182, 187–95, 201–22, 230–37, 242, 246–48, 263–64, 269–76, 279–84, 326–32, 362, 368–69, 371–75, 383–84, 475, 540–42, 564*n*61, 584*n*44, 585*n*3, 588*n*37, 594–5*n*95, 595*n*99, 595*n*102, 617*n*144
  excellence, 181, 190, 194, 202–3, 217, 237, 251–58, 269, 282, 292, 324, 239, 352, 415, 429, 450, 474–75, 493, 498, 507, 517, 529, 590*n*70, 593*n*59
  existential virtue ethics, 273, 284, 488, 588*n*37.
  See also charity; courage; friendship; justice; magnanimity; wisdom
virtue-inclusivism, 191
Vlastos, Gregory 107, 567*n*106
volition: *see* agency; decision; freedom of the will; will.
volitionalism, 55, 58, 63–68, 78–79, 554*n*42
volitional agency, 53, 62, 287, 478
volitional commitment, 20, 343, 464–66, 488, 534, 649*n*49. *See also* commitment
volitional resolve 7, 22, 298, 370, 415, 440, 472, 516, 523
volitional stability, 461, 535
volitionally necessary caring, 463
voluntarism, xix, 43, 50, 60, 301, 366
Von Hildebrande, Dietrich, 318, 654*n*149
Von Wright, G. H., 204

Wallach, Michael, 422, 424
wantonness, 165, 367, 433, 451–55, 464, 512, 523, 541, 580*n*151, 628*n*171, 639*n*169
  and aestheticism, 604*n*11
  and bullshit, 519
Watson, Gary, 16, 99–100, 112, 130–31, 136, 269–73, 462–64, 595*n*102

Watson, Stephen, xv, 563n35, 624n126, 656n29
welfare, 130, 152, 205, 208–9, 331, 388, 424, 519, 521, 530, 577n111, 595n102
well-being, 14, 23, 37, 73, 96, 104–8, 118, 130–32, 140–43, 146–52, 156–57, 160–63, 181, 191, 202, 206–9, 223, 225, 229–30, 239, 243–44, 249, 252, 267, 270–71, 277–78, 282–83, 305, 312–13, 319–20, 324, 350, 352, 356, 359, 364, 378–80, 427–28, 435, 471, 473–75, 482, 528–31, 577n107, 579n140, 594–95n95
Western attitude, 37–40, 44, 539–40, 579n130. *See also* Eastern attitude
Westphal, Merold, 310
White, Morton, 573n39
White, Stephen, 174, 580n3, 581n16, 582n25
willing
  heroic, 4–6, 8, 12, 28–46, 116–18, 536, 589n57
  strength of will, 4–5, 16–17, 94, 113–14, 120, 326–70, 466, 486, 540, 543–44, 617n143
  striving will, 4–5, 7–8, 11–13, 16, 28–29, 31, 38–42, 58, 64, 79–80, 82–85, 90, 112–13, 118, 202, 216, 232–33, 260–61, 265, 275, 281–84, 287, 289, 300–1, 318–20, 322, 325, 327, 330, 334, 345–46, 350, 359, 362, 370, 376, 384, 393, 406–7, 429–30, 436–37, 451, 458–59, 464–68, 471–72, 484, 488, 502, 505, 526–27, 539–45, 588n43, 634n65, 635n75, 644n48, 653n119

weakness of will, 16–17, 75, 322, 327, 339, 365–70, 539, 639n169. *See also akrasia*
willfulness, 12, 29, 35–36, 39–40, 43, 115, 317
willpower, 18, 38–39, 42, 302, 319, 347, 361, 363, 368–369, 421, 472, 503, 611n53, 617n143, 632n11
will to justice, 18, 84, 318, 346–47, 373, 381, 383, 393–96, 457, 540, 620n61, 620n66, 623n109. *See also* rectitude; Scotus
will to power, 20, 39–40, 43, 273, 302, 336, 357, 361, 439, 455, 550n55. *See also* decision; agency; volition.
Williams, Bernard, 45, 49, 87, 116–18, 142–43, 160–62, 200, 204, 217, 232–34, 365, 460, 475–77, 481, 514, 561n3, 641n4, 645n68
Wilson, David, 137, 156, 579n129
Wilson, George, 7
Winch, Peter, 555n64
wisdom, 31, 35, 97, 103–5, 110, 114–15, 142, 182, 192, 197, 203, 301, 329, 386, 494, 526
Wittgenstein, Ludwig, 54–56, 68, 71, 555n65, 555n67, 558n128
Wolf, Susan, 505–8, 511, 513, 519, 527, 650n71
Wollheim, Richard, 562n9
Wood, Allen, 409
worth, inherent, 601n46
worth, intrinsic, 256, 379. *See also* value, intrinsic.

Yalom, Irwin, 3, 7, 48
Yovel, Yirmiyahu, 41–42

Zagzebski, Linda, 297–99, 600n42